Bonus Material!

Thank you for purchasing a new copy of *Web Development and Design Foundations with XHTML*, **Fourth Edition!** Your textbook includes six months of prepaid access to the book's Companion Website. This prepaid subscription provides you with full access to all student support areas, including these resources and tutorials that you'll find useful as you take your course:

- Tutorial: Using FTP to Publish on the Web.
- Tutorial: Macromedia® Dreamweaver®.
- Student Starter Files.
- Hands-On Practice solutions.
- Bonus Chapter: XHTML Frames.

To activate your prepaid subscription:

You will need to register online using a computer with an Internet connection and a Web browser. You will also need a valid email address and the student access code that is printed beneath the scratch-off coating. Registration takes just a couple of minutes and only needs to be completed once.

1. Go to **http://www.aw.com/felke**.

2. Click on **Student Resources**.

3. Click the **Register** button.

4. Use a coin to scratch off the gray coating below and reveal your student access code.*
   Do not use a knife or other sharp object, which can damage the code.

5. Enter your student access code on the registration page. Do not type the dashes. You can use lowercase or uppercase letters.

6. Follow the on-screen instructions. If you need help at any time during the online registration process, simply click the "**Need Help?**" icon.

7. Once your personal Login Name and Password are confirmed, you can begin using the *Web Development and Design Foundations with XHTML*, Fourth Edition, Companion Website!

To log in after you have registered:

You only need to register for this Companion Website once. After that, you can access the site by going to **http://www.aw.com/felke**, clicking **Student Resources**, and providing your Login Name and Password when prompted.

*__IMPORTANT:__ The access code on this page can only be used once to establish a subscription to the *Web Development and Design Foundations with XHTML*, Fourth Edition, Companion Website. This subscription is valid for six months upon activation and is not transferable. If this access code has already been scratched off, it may no longer be valid. If this is the case, you can purchase a subscription online. Go to http://www.aw.com/felke, click on "Student Resources," and follow the steps to purchase access.

Web Development
& Design Foundations

EDITION
4

with XHTML

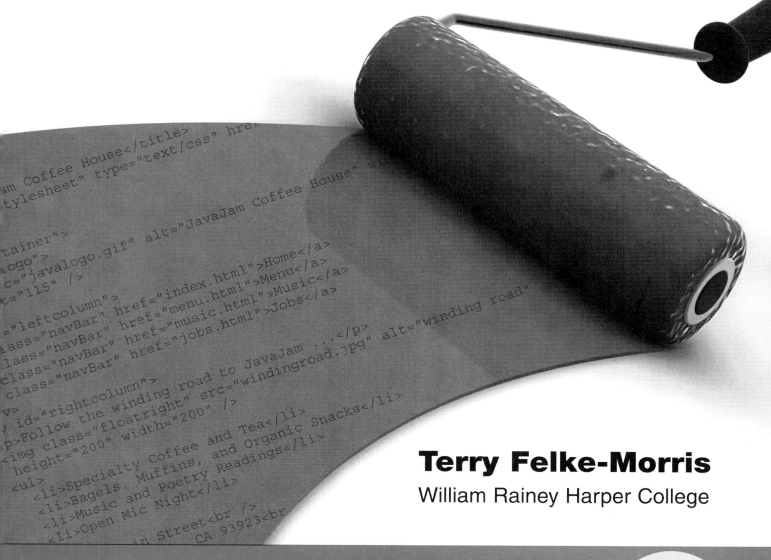

Terry Felke-Morris

William Rainey Harper College

Web Development & Design Foundations

EDITION **4**

with XHTML

PEARSON

Addison
Wesley

Boston San Francisco New York
London Toronto Sydney Tokyo Singapore Madrid
Mexico City Munich Paris Cape Town Hong Kong Montreal

Executive Editor	*Michael Hirsch*
Associate Editor	*Lindsey Triebel*
Editorial Assistant	*Stephanie Sellinger*
Associate Managing Editor	*Jeffrey Holcomb*
Cover Designer	*Joyce Cosentino Wells*
Digital Assets Manager	*Marianne Groth*
Senior Media Producer	*Bethany Tidd*
Marketing Manager	*Erin Davis*
Senior Manufacturing Buyer	*Carol Melville*
Production Coordination, Text Design, and Composition	*Gillian Hall, The Aardvark Group*
Copyeditor	*Kathleen Cantwell, C4 Technologies*
Proofreader	*Holly McLean-Aldis*
Cover Image	*© Shutterstock/Bet Noire*

Many of the designations used by manufacturers and sellers to distinguish their products are claimed as trademarks. Where those designations appear in this book, and Addison-Wesley was aware of a trademark claim, the designations have been printed in initial caps or all caps.

Photographs on pages 131–132 are copyrighted by Karen Felke and used by special permission. All other photographs are copyrighted by Terry Ann Morris. The Web Design Best Practices Checklist (Table 5.1) on pages 200–201 is copyrighted by Terry Ann Morris (http://www.terrymorris.net).

The interior of this book was composed using QuarkXpress 6.5 with ETM v2. The basal text is set in Sabon.

Library of Congress Cataloging-in-Publication Data available upon request.

ISBN-13: 978-0-321-53019-6
ISBN-10: 0-321-53019-5

1 2 3 4 5 6 7 8 9 10—EB—12 11 10 09 08

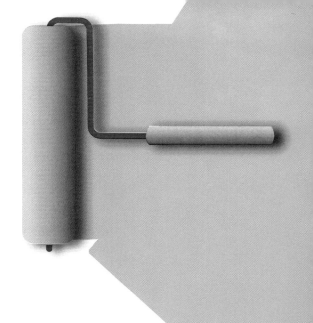

Preface

Web Development and Design Foundations with XHTML is intended for use in a beginning Web development course. Since CSS has become a standard for Web design, this edition now introduces CSS early on and integrates this topic throughout the text, including CSS-based page layouts. The text covers the basics that Web developers need to develop their skills:

- Internet concepts
- Creating Web pages with XHTML
- Configuring text, color, and page layout with CSS
- Web design best practices
- Accessibility standards
- The Web development process
- Using media and interactivity on Web pages
- Web site promotion
- E-commerce and the Web
- JavaScript™

A special feature of this text is the *Web Developer's Handbook*, which is a collection of appendixes providing resources such as an XHTML reference, a comparison of HTML and XHTML, a CSS reference, and Section 508 Standards reference.

Student files are available for download from the Companion Website for this book at http://www.aw.com/felke. These files include solutions to the Hands-On Practice exercises, Web Site Case Study starter files, an introduction to FTP, and three Adobe® Dreamweaver® tutorials. See the access card in the front of this book for further instructions.

Organization of the Text

The textbook is designed to be used in a flexible manner, and it can adapt easily to suit a variety of course and student needs. Chapter 1 provides introductory material, which may be skipped or covered depending on the background of students. Chapters 2 through 4 introduce XHTML and CSS coding. Chapter 5 discusses Web design best practices and can be covered anytime after Chapter 2 (or even along with Chapter 2). Chapters 6 through 9 continue with XHTML and CSS topics.

Any of the following chapters may be skipped or assigned as independent study, depending on time constraints and student needs: Chapter 10 (Web Site Development), Chapter 11 (Web Multimedia and Interactivity), Chapter 12 (E-Commerce Overview), Chapter 13 (Web Promotion), and Chapter 14 (A Brief Look at JavaScript). Students usually enjoy the three Dreamweaver tutorials, which are available for download from the Companion Website for this book at http://www.aw.com/felke. The Companion Website also provides an FTP tutorial and a bonus chapter on frames. A chapter dependency chart is shown in Figure P.1.

Figure P.1
The textbook is flexible and can be adapted to individual needs

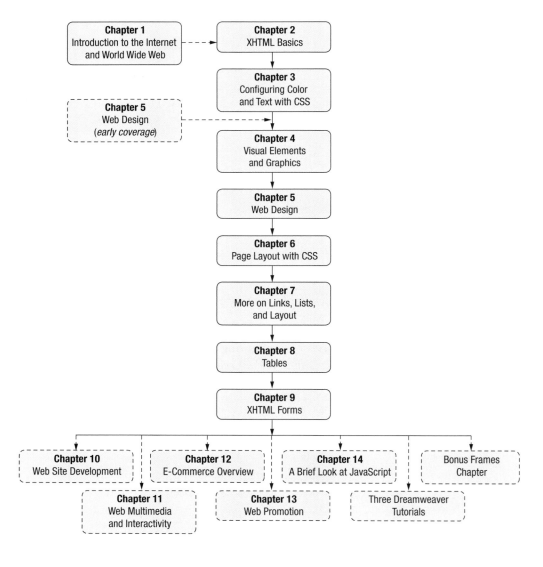

Brief Overview of Each Chapter

Chapter 1: Introduction to the Internet and the World Wide Web. This brief introduction covers the terms and concepts related to the Internet and the Web with which Web developers need to be familiar. For many students, some of this will be a review. Chapter 1 provides the base of knowledge on which the rest of the book is built.

Chapter 2: XHTML Basics. As HTML and XHTML are introduced, examples and exercises encourage students to create sample pages and gain useful experience. Solution pages for the Hands-On Practice are available in the student files.

Chapter 3: Configuring Color and Text with CSS. The technique of using Cascading Style Sheets to configure the color and text on Web pages is introduced. Students are encouraged to create sample pages as they read through the text. Sample pages for the Hands-On Practice are available in the student files.

Chapter 4: Visual Elements and Graphics. This chapter discusses the use of color and graphics on Web pages. Students are encouraged to create pages as they read through the text. Sample pages for the Hands-On Practice are available in the student files.

Chapter 5: Web Design. This chapter focuses on recommended Web site design practices and accessibility. Some of this is reinforcement because hints about recommended Web site design practices is incorporated into the XHTML chapters.

Chapter 6: Page Layout with CSS. This chapter continues the study of CSS begun earlier and introduces techniques for positioning and floating Web page elements, including a two-column CSS page layout. Sample pages for the Hands-On Practice are available in the student files.

Chapter 7: More on Links, Lists, and Layout. This chapter revisits earlier topics and introduces more advanced techniques related to hyperlinks, configuring navigation links in an unordered list, and a three-column CSS page layout. Students are encouraged to create pages as they read through the text. Sample pages for the Hands-On Practice are available in the student files.

Chapter 8: Tables. This chapter focuses on the XHTML elements used to create tables. Methods of configuring the table with CSS are introduced. Students are encouraged to create pages as they read through the text. Sample pages for the Hands-On Practice are available in the student files.

Chapter 9: XHTML Forms. This chapter focuses on the XHTML elements used to create forms. Methods of configuring the form with CSS are introduced. Students are encouraged to create sample pages as they read through the text. Sample pages for the Hands-On Practice are available in the student files.

Chapter 10: Web Site Development. A focus on the process of Web site development includes the job roles needed for a large-scale project, the Web development process, and Web hosting. A Web host checklist is included in this chapter.

Chapter 11: Web Multimedia and Interactivity. This chapter offers an overview of topics related to adding media and interactivity to Web pages. These topics include video, audio, Flash®, Java™ applets, JavaScript, DHTML, and Ajax. Students are encouraged to create pages as the topics are discussed. Sample pages for the Hands-On Practice are available in the student files.

Chapter 12: E-Commerce Overview. This chapter introduces e-commerce, security, and order processing on the Web.

Chapter 13: Web Promotion. This chapter discusses site promotion, from the Web developer's point of view, focusing on search engines and indexes.

Chapter 14: A Brief Look at JavaScript. This chapter provides an introduction to client-side scripting using JavaScript. Sample pages for the Hands-On Practice are available in the student files.

***Web Developer's Handbook* Appendixes:** The *Handbook* contains appendixes that include resources and tutorials useful to students, such as an XHTML reference, a list of special characters, a CSS property reference, a comparison of HTML and XHTML, and a Section 508 Standards reference.

Features of the Text

Well-Rounded Selection of Topics. This text includes both "hard" skills such as XHTML, CSS and JavaScript (Chapters 2, 3, 4, 6, 7, 8, 9, and 14) and "soft" skills such as Web design (Chapter 5), Web site promotion (Chapter 13), and e-commerce (Chapter 12). Two methods of publishing pages to the Web (using an FTP application and Dreamweaver) are demonstrated in the student files. This well-rounded foundation will help students as they pursue careers in Web development. Students and instructors will find classes more interesting because they can discuss, integrate, and apply both hard and soft skills as students create Web pages and Web sites.

Hands-On Practice. Web development is a skill and skills are best learned by hands-on practice. This text emphasizes hands-on practice through practice exercises within the chapters, end-of-chapter exercises, and the development of Web sites through ongoing real-world case studies. The variety of exercises provides instructors with a choice of assignments for a particular course or semester.

Web Site Case Studies. There are four case studies that continue throughout most of the text (beginning at Chapter 2). An additional case study begins in Chapter 5. The case studies serve to reinforce skills discussed in each chapter. Instructors can cycle assignments from semester to semester or allow students to choose the case study that most interests them. Sample solutions to the case studies are available on the Instructor Resource Center at http://www.aw.com/irc.

Web Research. Each chapter offers Web research activities that encourage students to study topics introduced in the chapter.

Focus on Web Design. Most chapters offer additional activities that explore Web design topics related to the chapter. These activities can be used to reinforce, extend, and enhance the course topics.

FAQs. In her Web development courses, the author is frequently asked similar questions by students. They are included in the book and are marked with the identifying FAQ logo.

Checkpoints. Each chapter contains two or three Checkpoints—groups of questions intended for students to self-assess their understanding of the material. A special Checkpoint icon appears with each group of questions.

Focus on Accessibility

Focus on Accessibility. Developing accessible Web sites is more important than ever, and this text is infused with accessibility techniques throughout. The special icon shown here makes accessibility information easy to find.

Focus on Ethics

Focus on Ethics. Ethics issues as related to Web development are highlighted throughout the text with the special ethics icon shown here.

See the center color insert

Color Insert. Some figures also appear in the 12-page full-color insert. These figures are identified with the tag shown here.

Reference Materials. *Web Developer's Handbook* Appendixes offer reference material, including an XHTML reference, a list of special characters, a CSS property reference, a comparison of HTML and XHTML, and a Section 508 Standards reference.

Supplemental Materials

Student Resources. The following resources are available to all readers of this book at http://www.aw.com/felke:

- Student files for Web page exercises and Web Site Case Study assignments
- Adobe Dreamweaver tutorials
- FTP tutorial
- Bonus frames chapter
- A complimentary access code for this resource is available with a new copy of this book. Subscriptions may also be purchased online.

Instructor Resources. The following supplements are available to qualified instructors only. Visit the Addison-Wesley Instructor Resource Center (http://www.aw.com/irc) or send an e-mail to computing@aw.com for information on how to access them:

- Solutions to the end-of-chapter exercises
- Solutions for the case study assignments
- Test questions
- PowerPoint® presentations
- Sample syllabi

Author's Web Site. In addition to the publisher's Companion Website for this book, the author maintains a Web site at http://www.webdevfoundations.net. This Web site contains additional resources including a color chart, Flash learning/review games, Adobe Flash Tutorial, Adobe Fireworks® Tutorial, Adobe Photoshop® Tutorial, and a page for each chapter with examples, links, and updates. This Web site is not supported by the publisher.

World Organization of Webmasters (WOW). The World Organization of Webmasters designated this book as a recommended learning resource (http://www.webprofessionals.org/education/resources/self_study/s2.html) for the WOW Certified Web Designer Associate (CWDSA) certification exam.

Acknowledgments

Very special thanks go to the people at Addison-Wesley: Michael Hirsch, Lindsey Triebel, Michelle Brown, Joyce Wells, Bethany Tidd, Jeffrey Holcomb, and Erin Davis. Thank you also to Gillian Hall at The Aardvark Group and Kathleen Cantwell at C4 Technologies for their timely assistance and suggestions.

Thank you to the following people for their reviews, comments, and suggestions for this fourth edition:

Ross Beveridge—*Colorado State University*
James Bell—*Central Virginia Community College*
Elizabeth Drake—*Santa Fe Community College*
Mark DuBois—*Illinois Central College;*
              Director of Education, World Organization of Webmasters
Sharon Gray—*Augustana College*
Jean Kent—*Seattle Community College*
Nancy Lee—*College of Southern Nevada*
Les Lusk—*Seminole Community College*
Anita Philipp—*Oklahoma City Community College*
Karen Kowal Wiggins—*Wisconsin Indianhead Technical College*

Thank you to those who provided reviews and comments for the third edition:

Carolyn Andres—*Richland College*
Karmen Blake—*Spokane Community College*
Dan Dao—*Richland College*
Joyce M. Dick—*Northeast Iowa Community College*
Elizabeth Drake—*Santa Fe Community College*
Genny Espinoza—*Richland College*
Lisa Hopkins—*Tulsa Community College*
Barbara James—*Richland Community College*
Nilofar Kadivi—*Richland Community College*
Jean Kent—*Seattle Community College*
Manasseh Lee—*Richland Community College*
Kyle Loewenhagen—*Chippewa Valley Technical College*
Michael J. Losacco—*College of DuPage*
Cindy Mortensen—*Truckee Meadows Community College*
John Nadzam—*Community College of Allegheny County*
Brita E. Penttila—*Wake Technical Community College*
Anita Philipp—*Oklahoma City Community College*
Jerry Ross—*Lane Community College*
Noah Singer—*Tulsa Community College*
Alan Strozer—*Canyons College*
Tebring Wrigley—*Community College of Allegheny County*
Michelle Youngblood-Petty—*Richland College*

Thank you to Mark DuBois, Professor at Illinois Central College and WOW (World Organization of Webmasters) Director of Education, for his most careful review and many constructive suggestions for improving this book. A special thank you also goes to Jean Kent, North Seattle Community College, for taking time to provide additional feedback and sharing student comments about the book.

Thanks are in order to colleagues at William Rainey Harper College for their support and encouragement, especially Sue Bajt, Ken Perkins, Geetha Rao, Sarah Stark, Enrique D'Amico, and David Braunschweig.

Most of all, I would like to thank my family for their patience and encouragement. My wonderful husband, Greg Morris, has been a constant source of love, understanding, support, and encouragement. Thank you, Greg! A big shout-out to my children, James and Karen Felke, who grew up thinking that everyone's mom had their own Web page. Thank you both for your understanding, patience, and timely suggestions! Of course, this wouldn't be complete without mentioning my dog, Sparky, whose playful antics and quirky personality helped to brighten long hours spent at the computer.

About the Author

Terry Felke-Morris is an Associate Professor at William Rainey Harper College in Palatine, Illinois. She holds a Master of Science degree in information systems and numerous certifications, including Adobe Certified Dreamweaver 8 Developer, WOW Certified Associate Webmaster, Microsoft Certified Professional, Master CIW Designer, and CIW Certified Instructor.

Ms. Felke-Morris has been honored with Harper College's Glenn A. Reich Memorial Award for Instructional Technology in recognition of her work in designing the college's CIS Web development program and courses. In 2006, she received the Blackboard Greenhouse Exemplary Online Course Award for use of Internet technology in the academic environment.

Ms. Felke-Morris has over 20 years of information technology experience in business and industry. She published her first Web site in 1996 and has been working with the Web ever since. Ms. Felke-Morris helped to develop the Web Development certificate and degree programs at William Rainey Harper College and currently is the lead faculty member in that area. For more information about Ms. Felke-Morris, visit http://terrymorris.net.

Contents

CHAPTER **3**

Configuring Color and Text with CSS   75

CHAPTER **4**

Visual Elements and Graphics   121

Introduction to the Internet and World Wide Web

Chapter Objectives In this chapter, you will learn about ...

- The evolution of the Internet, Internet standards organizations, and the difference between the Internet, intranets, and extranets

- The beginning of the World Wide Web, ethical use of information on the Web, Web accessibility, and future Internet trends

- The client/server model, Internet protocols, networks, URLs and domain names, and markup languages

The Internet and the Web are parts of our daily lives.
How did they begin? What networking protocols and programming languages work behind the scenes to display a Web page? This chapter provides an introduction to some of these topics and is a foundation for the information that Web developers need to know. Some material in this chapter may be a review from your life experience or earlier studies.

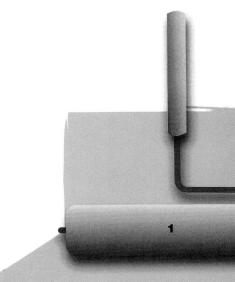

1.1 Evolution of the Internet

The **Internet,** the interconnected network of computer networks, seems to be everywhere today. It has become part of our lives. You can't watch television or listen to the radio without being urged to visit a Web site. Even newspapers have their place on the Net.

The Internet began as a network to connect computers at research facilities and universities. Messages in this network would travel to their destination by multiple routes or paths. This would allow the network to function even if parts of it were broken or destroyed. The message would be rerouted through a functioning portion of the network while traveling to its destination. This network was proposed to the Advanced Research Projects Agency (ARPA)—and the ARPAnet was born. Four computers (located at UCLA, Stanford Research Institute, University of California Santa Barbara, and the University of Utah) were connected by the end of 1969.

As time went on, other networks, such as the National Science Foundation's NSFnet, were created and connected with the ARPAnet. Use of this interconnected network, or Internet, was originally limited to government, research, and educational purposes. Even with this restriction, by 1989 there were over 100,000 hosts on the Internet. The ban on commercial use was lifted in 1991, and by the end of 1992 there were over 1 million hosts connected. Hobbes' Internet Timeline reports that as of 2006, there were over 439 million host computers on the Internet. The communications protocol that enabled all this to happen is the Transmission Control Protocol/Internet Protocol (TCP/IP), proposed by Vinton Cerf and Robert Kahn.

If you are interested in the history of the Internet, visit either of the following links for more information.

- A brief history of the Internet written by the people who created it can be found at http://www.isoc.org/internet/history/brief.shtml.
- For a classic treatment of the Internet's history, visit Hobbes' Internet Timeline at http://www.zakon.org/robert/internet/timeline/.

 How can I tell whether a Web page is a reliable source of information?

There are many Web sites—but which ones are reliable sources of information? When visiting Web sites to find information it is important not to take everything at face value.

First, evaluate the credibility of the Web site itself. Does it have its own domain name, such as http://mywebsite.com, or is it a free Web site consisting of just a folder of files hosted on a free Web server? The URL of a site hosted on a free Web server usually includes part of the free Web server's name and might begin with something such as http://mysite.tripod.com or http://www.angelfire.com/foldername/mysite. Information obtained from a Web site that has its own domain name will usually (but not always) be more reliable than information obtained from a free Web site.

Evaluate the type of domain name—is it a nonprofit organization (.org), a business (.com or .biz), an educational institution (.edu)? Businesses may provide information in a way that gives them an advantage, so be careful. Nonprofit organizations or schools will sometimes treat a subject more objectively.

Another item to look at is the date the Web page was created or last updated. Although some information is timeless, very often a Web page that has not been updated for several years is outdated and not the best source of information.

1.2 Internet, Intranets, and Extranets

The Internet is an interconnected network of computer networks that is globally accessible. When an organization needs the communication capabilities of the Internet but doesn't want its information to be accessible to everyone, either an intranet or extranet is appropriate.

An **intranet** is a private network that is contained within an organization or business. Its purpose is to share organizational information and resources among coworkers. When an intranet connects to the outside Internet, usually a gateway or firewall protects the intranet from unauthorized access.

An **extranet** is a private network that securely shares part of an organization's information or operations with external partners such as suppliers, vendors, and customers. Extranets can be used to exchange data, share information exclusively with business partners, and collaborate with other organizations. Privacy and security are important issues in extranet use. Digital certificates, encryption of messages, and virtual private networks (VPNs) are some technologies used to provide privacy and security for an extranet. Digital certificates and encryption used in e-commerce are discussed in Chapter 12.

The Evolution of the World Wide Web

Recall that the original Internet—the ARPAnet—began with four hosts. The number of host computers connected to the Internet grew each year. However, the communication was text-based and the information stored on computers connected to the Internet was not easy to obtain. Initially, the use of the Internet was limited to academics, researchers, students, and government employees. Even with these restrictions there were over 300,000 hosts in 1990.

Why did the Internet grow from 300,000 hosts in 1990 to over 109 million in just over a decade? In the early 1990s, the convergence of three events occurred to cause explosive growth of the Internet.

In 1991, the NSFnet removed the restriction on commercial use of the Internet, setting the stage for future electronic commerce. Businesses were now welcome on the Internet. However, while businesses were no longer banned, the Internet was still text-based and not easy to use. The next developments solved this issue.

While working at CERN, a research facility in Switzerland, Tim Berners-Lee envisioned a means of communication for scientists where they could easily "hyperlink" to another research paper or article and immediately view it. Berners-Lee created the **World Wide Web** to fulfill this need and in 1991 he posted the code in a newsgroup. This version of the World Wide Web used **Hypertext Transfer Protocol (HTTP)** to communicate between the client computer and the Web server, used **Hypertext Markup Language (HTML)** to format the documents, and was text-based.

In 1993, the first graphics-based Web browser, Mosaic, became available. Marc Andreessen and graduate students working at the National Center for Supercomputing Applications (NCSA) at the University of Illinois Urbana-Champaign developed Mosaic. Some individuals in this group later created another well-known Web browser— Netscape Navigator.

The combination of commercial use, HTTP, and a graphical user interface made the information on the Internet much easier to access. The World Wide Web—the graphical user interface to the information stored on computers connected to the Internet—had arrived!

1.3 Standards and Coordination

You are probably aware that no single person or group runs the entire Internet. Each separate network is managed individually. However, there are a number of groups that develop standards and guidelines. These groups are a driving force in the growth and evolution of the Internet.

The **Internet Society**, http://www.isoc.org, is a professional organization that provides leadership in issues related to the future of the Internet. The Internet Society is the organizational home for the groups responsible for Internet infrastructure standards, including the **Internet Engineering Task Force (IETF)** and the **Internet Architecture Board (IAB)**.

You can think of the IETF as the protocol engineering and development arm of the Internet. It is the principal body engaged in the development of new Internet standard specifications. The IETF is an open international community of network designers, operators, vendors, and researchers concerned with the evolution of Internet architecture and the smooth operation of the Internet. The actual technical work of the IETF is completed in its working groups. These working groups are organized into areas by topic, such as security and routing.

The IAB is responsible for defining the overall architecture of the Internet, by providing guidance and broad direction to the IETF. As a function of this purpose, the IAB is responsible for the publication of the **Request for Comments (RFC)** document series.

An RFC is a formal document from the IETF that is drafted by a committee and subsequently reviewed by interested parties. RFCs are available for online review at http://www.ietf.org/rfc.html. Some RFCs are informational in nature, while others are meant to become Internet standards. In the latter case, the final version of the RFC becomes a new standard. Future changes to the standard must be made through subsequent RFCs.

The **Internet Corporation for Assigned Numbers and Names (ICANN)**, http://www.icann.org, was created in 1998 and is a nonprofit organization. Its main function is to coordinate the assignment of Internet domain names, IP address numbers, protocol parameters, and protocol port numbers. Prior to 1998, the **Internet Assigned Numbers Authority (IANA)** coordinated these functions. IANA still performs certain functions under the guidance of ICANN and maintains a Web site at http://www.iana.org.

1.4 Standards and the World Wide Web Consortium

As with the Internet in general, no one person or group runs the World Wide Web. However, the **World Wide Web Consortium (W3C)**, http://www.w3.org, takes a proactive role in developing recommendations and prototype technologies related to the Web. Four major areas that the W3C addresses are Web architecture, user interface, technology and society, and the **Web Accessibility Initiative (WAI)**. In an effort to standardize Web technologies, the W3C produces specifications called recommendations.

The W3C Recommendations are created in working groups with input from many major corporations involved in building Web technologies. These recommendations are not rules; they are guidelines. Major software companies that build Web browsers, such as Microsoft and Netscape, do not always follow the W3C Recommendations. This makes life difficult for Web developers because not all browsers will display a Web page in exactly the same way.

The good news is that there is a convergence toward the W3C Recommendations in new versions of major browsers. There are even organized groups such as The Web Standards Project, http://webstandards.org, whose mission is to promote W3C Recommendations (often called Web standards) not only to the creators of browsers but also to Web developers and designers.

Accessibility and the Web

Focus on Accessibility

The Web Accessibility Initiative (WAI), http://www.w3.org/WAI/, is a major area of work by the W3C. Since the Web has become an integral part of daily life, there is a need for all individuals to be able to access it. According to Tim Berners-Lee at http://www.w3.org/WAI/, "The power of the Web is in its universality. Access by everyone regardless of disability is an essential aspect."

The Web can present barriers to individuals with visual, auditory, physical, and neurological disabilities. The WAI has developed recommendations for Web content developers, Web authoring tool developers, Web browser developers, and developers of other user agents to facilitate use of the Web by those with special needs. See the WAI's Web Content Accessibility Guidelines (WCAG) at http://www.w3.org/WAI/WCAG20/quickref/ for a list of these recommendations.

The Americans with Disabilities Act (ADA) of 1990 is a Federal civil rights law that prohibits discrimination against people with disabilities. The ADA requires that business, federal, and state services are accessible to individuals with disabilities. A 1996 Department of Justice ruling, http://www.usdoj.gov/crt/foia/cltr204.txt, indicated that ADA accessibility requirements apply to Internet resources.

Section 508 of the Federal Rehabilitation Act was amended in 1998 to require that U.S. government agencies give individuals with disabilities access to information technology that is comparable to the access available to others. This law requires developers creating information technology (including Web pages) for use by the federal government to provide for **accessibility**. The Federal IT Accessibility Initiative, http://www.section508.gov, provides accessibility requirement resources for information technology developers. In recent years, state governments have also begun to encourage and promote Web accessibility. The Illinois Web Accessibility Standards, http://www100.state.il.us/ito/iwas1_2.cfm, are an example of this trend.

Forward-thinking Web developers design with accessibility in mind. Providing access for visitors with visual, auditory, and other challenges should be an integral part of Web design rather than an afterthought.

A person with visual difficulties may not be able to use graphical navigation buttons and may use a screen reader device to provide an audible description of the Web page. By making a few simple changes, such as providing text descriptions for the images and perhaps providing a text navigation area at the bottom of the page, Web developers can make the page accessible. Often, providing for accessibility increases the usability of the Web site for all visitors. For example, text in high contrast to the background is easier for everyone to read. As this text introduces Web development and design techniques, corresponding Web accessibility and usability issues are discussed.

Ethical Use of Information on the Web

Focus on Ethics

This wonderful technology called the World Wide Web provides us with information, graphics, and music—all virtually free (after you pay your Internet service provider, of course). Let's consider the following issues relating to the ethical use of this information:

- Is it acceptable to copy someone's graphic to use on your own Web site?
- Is it acceptable to copy someone's Web site design to use on your own site or on a client's site?
- Is it acceptable to copy an essay that appears on a Web page and use it or parts of it as your own writing?
- Is it acceptable to insult someone on your Web site or link to their site in a derogatory manner?

The answer to all these questions is no. Using someone's graphic without permission is the same as stealing it. In fact, if you link to it you are actually using up some of their bandwidth and may be costing them money. Copying the Web site design of another person or company is also a form of stealing. The Web site http://pirated-sites.com presents a somewhat quirky look at this issue. Any text or graphic on a Web site is automatically copyrighted in the United States whether or not a copyright symbol appears on the site. Insulting a person or company on your Web site or linking to them in a derogatory manner could be considered a form of defamation.

Issues like these, related to intellectual property, copyright, and freedom of speech are regularly discussed and decided in courts of law. Good Web etiquette requires that you ask permission before using others' work, give credit for what you use ("fair use" in the U.S. copyright law), and exercise your freedom of speech in a manner that is not harmful to others. The **World Intellectual Property Organization (WIPO)**, http://wipo.int, is dedicated to protecting intellectual property rights internationally.

What if you'd like to retain ownership but make it easy for others to use or adapt your work? Creative Commons, http://creativecommons.org, is a nonprofit organization that provides free services that allow authors and artists to register a type of a copyright license called a Creative Commons license. There are several licenses to choose from—depending on the rights you wish to grant. The Creative Commons license informs others exactly what they can and cannot do with your creative work. See http://meyerweb.com/eric/tools/color-blend for a Web page licensed under a Creative Commons Attribution-ShareAlike 1.0 License with "Some Rights Reserved."

CHECKPOINT 1.1

1. Describe the difference between the Internet and an intranet.
2. Explain three events that contributed to the commercialization and exponential growth of the Internet.
3. Describe the difference between the Internet and the Web.

1.5 Network Overview

A **network** consists of two or more computers connected for the purpose of communicating and sharing resources. Common components of a network are shown in Figure 1.1 and include the following:

- Server computer(s)
- Client workstation computer(s)
- Shared devices such as printers
- Networking devices (hub) and the media that connect them

Figure 1.1
Common components of a network

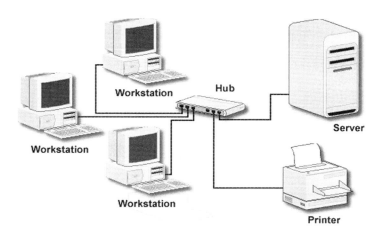

The **clients** are the computers used by individuals, such as a PC on a desk. The **server** receives requests from client computers for resources such as files. Computers used as servers are usually kept in a protected, secure area and are only accessed by network administrators. Networking devices such as hubs and switches provide network connections for computers, and routers direct information from one network to another. The **media** connecting the clients, servers, peripherals, and networking devices may consist of copper cables, fiber optic cables, or wireless technologies.

Networks vary in scale. A **Local Area Network (LAN)** is usually confined to a single building or group of connected buildings. Your school computer lab may use a LAN. If you work in an office, you probably use a computer connected to a LAN. Recently, many people have begun to set up LANs in their homes to share resources among computers. A **Metropolitan Area Network (MAN)** connects users with computer resources in a geographical area. It also can be used to connect two or more LANs. A **Wide Area Network (WAN)** is geographically dispersed and usually uses some form of public or commercial communications network. For example, an organization with offices on both the East and West Coasts of the United States probably uses a WAN to provide a link between the LANs at each of the offices. See Figure 1.2 for a diagram of this connectivity.

Figure 1.2
WAN connecting
two LANs

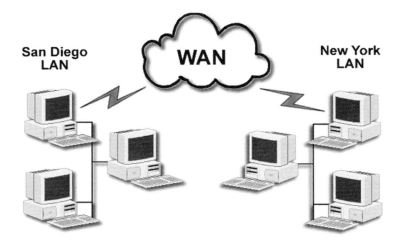

A **backbone** is a high-capacity communication link that carries data gathered from smaller links that interconnect with it. On the Internet, a backbone is a set of paths that local or regional networks (MANs) connect to for long-distance interconnection. The Internet is a group of interconnected networks with very high-speed connectivity provided by the Internet backbones. Figure 1.3 shows a commercial backbone network map generated by http://www.caida.org/tools/visualization/mapnet/Backbones.

Figure 1.3
A commercial
backbone network

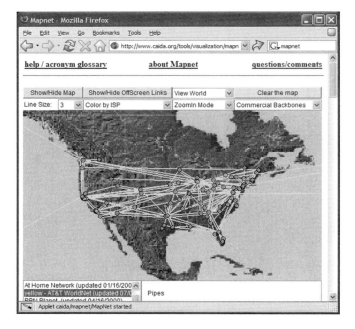

Access points or junctions to the Internet backbone in major cities are called **Network Access Points (NAPs)**. Chicago, New York, and San Francisco are three key NAPs in the United States.

1.6 The Client/Server Model

The term **client/server** dates from the last millennium (the 1980s) and refers to personal computers joined by a network. Client/server can also describe a relationship between two computer programs—the client and the server. The client requests some type of service (such as a file or database access) from the server. The server fulfills the request and transmits the results to the client over a network. While both the client and the server programs can reside on the same computer, typically they run on different computers. It is common for a server to handle requests from multiple clients.

The Internet is a great example of client/server architecture at work. Consider the following scenario: An individual is at a computer using a Web browser client to access the Internet. The individual uses the Web browser to visit a Web site, let's say http://www.yahoo.com. The server is the Web server program running on the computer with an IP address that corresponds to yahoo.com. It is contacted, locates the Web page and related resources that were requested, and responds by sending them to the individual.

In short, here's how to distinguish between Web clients and Web servers:

Web Client

- Connected to the Internet when needed
- Usually runs Web browser (client) software such as Internet Explorer or Netscape
- Uses HTTP
- Requests Web pages from a server
- Receives Web pages and files from a server

Web Server

- Continually connected to the Internet
- Runs Web server software (such as Apache or Internet Information Server)
- Uses HTTP
- Receives a request for the Web page
- Responds to the request and transmits the status code, Web page, and associated files

When clients and servers exchange files, they often need to indicate the type of file that is being transferred; this is done through the use of a MIME type. **Multi-Purpose Internet Mail Extensions (MIME)** are rules that allow multimedia documents to be exchanged among many different computer systems. MIME was initially intended to extend the original Internet e-mail protocol, but it is also used by HTTP. MIME provides for the exchange of seven different media types on the Internet: audio, video, image, application, message, multipart, and text. MIME also uses subtypes to further describe the data. The MIME type of a Web page is text/html. MIME types of gif and jpeg images are image/gif and image/jpeg respectively.

A Web server determines the MIME type of a file before it is transmitted to the Web browser. The MIME type is sent along with the document. The Web browser uses the MIME type to determine how to display the document.

How does information get transferred from the Web server to the Web browser? Clients (such as Web browsers) and servers (such as a Web server) exchange information through the use of communication protocols such as HTTP, **TCP**, and **IP**.

1.7 Internet Protocols

Protocols are rules that describe how clients and servers communicate with each other over a network. There is no single protocol that makes the Internet and Web work—a number of protocols with specific functions are needed.

File Transfer Protocol (FTP)

File Transfer Protocol (FTP) is a set of rules that allow files to be exchanged between computers on the Internet. Unlike HTTP, which is used by Web browsers to request Web pages and their associated files in order to display a Web page, FTP is used simply to move files from one computer to another. Web developers commonly use FTP to transfer Web page files from their computers to Web servers. FTP is also commonly used to download programs and files from other servers to individual computers.

E-mail Protocols

Most of us take e-mail for granted, but there are two servers involved in its smooth functioning—an incoming mail server and an outgoing mail server. When you send e-mail to others, **Simple Mail Transfer Protocol (SMTP)** is used. When you receive e-mail, **Post Office Protocol** (POP; currently **POP3**) and **Internet Message Access Protocol (IMAP)** can be used.

Hypertext Transfer Protocol (HTTP)

HTTP is a set of rules for exchanging files such as text, graphic images, sound, video, and other multimedia files on the Web. Web browsers and Web servers usually use this protocol. When the user of a Web browser requests a file by typing a Web site address or clicking a hyperlink, the browser builds an HTTP request and sends it to the server. The Web server in the destination machine receives the request, does any necessary processing, and responds with the requested file and any associated media files.

Transmission Control Protocol/Internet Protocol (TCP/IP)

Transmission Control Protocol/Internet Protocol (TCP/IP) has been adopted as the official communication protocol of the Internet. TCP and IP have different functions that work together to ensure reliable communication over the Internet.

TCP. The purpose of TCP is to ensure the integrity of network communication. TCP starts by breaking files and messages into individual units called **packets**. These packets (see Figure 1.4) contain information such as the destination, source, sequence number, and checksum values used to verify the integrity of the data.

Figure 1.4
TCP packet

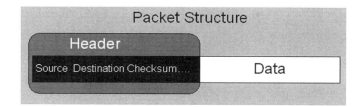

TCP is used together with IP to transmit files efficiently over the Internet. IP takes over after TCP creates the packets, using IP addressing to send each packet over the Internet using the best path at the particular time. When the destination address is reached, TCP verifies the integrity of each packet using the checksum, requests a resend if a packet is damaged, and reassembles the file or message from the multiple packets.

IP. Working in harmony with TCP, IP is a set of rules that controls how data is sent between computers on the Internet. IP routes a packet to the correct destination address. Once sent, the packet gets successively forwarded to the next closest router (a hardware device designed to move network traffic) until it reaches its destination.

Each device connected to the Internet has a unique numeric **IP address**. These addresses consist of a set of four groups of numbers, called octets. The current version of IP, IPv4, uses 32-bit (binary digit) addressing. This results in a decimal number in the format of xxx.xxx.xxx.xxx, where each xxx is a value from 0 to 255. The IP address may correspond to a domain name. The **Domain Name System (DNS)** associates these IP addresses with the text-based URLs and domain names you type into a Web browser address box (more on this later). For example, at the time this was written the IP address of Google was 64.233.187.99.

You can enter this number in the address text box in a Web browser (as shown in Figure 1.5), press (Enter), and the Google home page will display. Of course, it's much

Figure 1.5
Entering an IP address in a Web browser

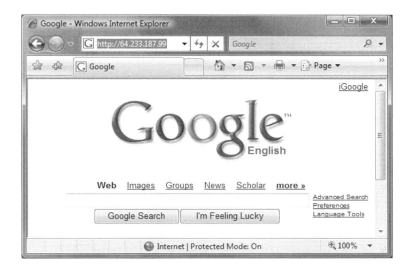

easier to type "google.com," which is why domain names such as google.com were created in the first place!

Since long strings of numbers are difficult for humans to remember, the Domain Name System was introduced as a way to associate text-based names with numeric IP addresses.

1.8 URLs and Domain Names

URLs

The **Uniform Resource Locator** (**URL**) represents the address of a resource that is available on the Internet. This resource could be for example, a Web page, a graphic file, or a Java applet. The URL consists of the protocol, the domain name, and the hierarchical location of the file on the Web server.

The URL http://www.webdevfoundations.net, shown in Figure 1.6, denotes the use of HTTP protocol and the Web server named www at the domain name of webdevfoundations.net. In this case, the root file (usually index.html or index.htm) will be displayed.

Figure 1.6
Parts of a URL

If the URL was of the form http://www.webdevfoundations.net/chapter1/links.html, as shown in Figure 1.7, it would denote the use of HTTP protocol and a Web server named www at the domain name of webdevfoundations.net. The resource to be displayed is the Web page named links.html in the chapter1 folder.

Figure 1.7
URL describing a file within a folder

What is a Universal Resource Locator?

Officially, URL stands for Uniform Resource Locator; but originally, Tim Berners-Lee (the inventor of the Web) envisioned a Universal Resource Locator. That is why some texts or Web pages refer to the URL in that manner. Read Tim Berners-Lee's book *Weaving the Web* for an interesting view of the creation of the Web.

Figure 1.8 shows a URL used to display files available for FTP download in the format of ftp://ftp.microsoft.com. This denotes the use of the FTP protocol, the server named ftp, and the domain name of microsoft.com.

Figure 1.8
URL using FTP

Domain Names

A **domain name** locates an organization or other entity on the Internet. The purpose of the Domain Name System (DNS) is to divide the Internet into logical groups and understandable names by identifying the exact address and type of the organization. The DNS associates the text-based domain names with the unique numeric IP address assigned to a device.

Let's consider the domain name www.yahoo.com. The .com is the top-level domain name. The portion yahoo.com is the domain name that is registered to Yahoo! and is considered a second-level domain name. The www is the name of the Web server (sometimes called **Web host server**) at the yahoo.com domain. Taken all together, www.yahoo.com is considered to be a **Fully-Qualified Domain Name (FQDN)**.

Top-Level Domain Names (TLDs). A top-level domain (TLD) identifies the rightmost part of the domain name. A TLD is either a generic top-level domain, such as com for commercial, or a country code top-level domain, such as fr for France. ICANN administers the generic top-level domains shown in Table 1.1.

Table 1.1 Top-level domains

Generic TLD	Used By
.aero	Air-transport industry
.asia	Pan-Asia and Asia Pacific community
.biz	Businesses
.cat	Catalan linguistic and cultural community
.com	Commercial entities
.coop	Cooperative
.edu	Restricted to accredited degree-granting institutions of higher education
.gov	Restricted to government use
.info	Unrestricted use
.int	International organization (rarely used)
.jobs	Human resource management community
.mil	Restricted to military use
.mobi	Corresponds to a .com Web site—the .mobi site is designed for easy access by mobile devices
.museum	Museums
.name	Individuals
.net	Entities associated with network support of the Internet, usually Internet service providers or telecommunication companies
.org	Nonprofit entities
.pro	Accountants, physicians, and lawyers
.tel	Contact information for individuals and businesses
.travel	Travel industry

The .com, .org, and .net TLD designations are currently used on the honor system, which means that an individual who owns a shoe store (not related to networking) can register shoes.net.

Country Code Top-Level Domain Names. Two-character country codes have also been assigned as top-level domain names. These were originally intended to be meaningful and relate the domain name country code to the geographical location of the individual or organization that registered the name. In practice, it is fairly easy to obtain a domain name with a country code TLD that is not local to the registrant. See http://register.com and many other domain name registration companies for examples. Table 1.2 lists some popular country codes used on the Web.

Table 1.2 Country codes

Country Code TLD	Country
.au	Australia
.de	Germany
.in	India
.jp	Japan
.nl	The Netherlands
.us	United States
.eu	European Union (a group of countries rather than a single country)

The IANA Web site at http://www.iana.org/cctld/cctld-whois.htm has a complete list. Domain names with country codes are often used for municipalities, schools, and community colleges in the United States. The domain name www.harper.cc.il.us denotes the United States, Illinois, community college, Harper, and the Web server named www as the site for William Rainey Harper College in Illinois.

The DNS associates domain names with IP addresses. The following happens each time a new URL is typed into a Web browser:

1. The DNS is accessed.
2. The corresponding IP address is obtained and returned to the Web browser.
3. The Web browser sends an HTTP request to the destination computer with the corresponding IP address.
4. The HTTP request is received by the Web server.
5. The necessary files are located and sent by HTTP responses to the Web browser.
6. The Web browser renders and displays the Web page and associated files.

The next time you wonder why it's taking so long to display a Web page, think about all of the processing that goes on behind the scenes.

1.9 Markup Languages

Markup languages consist of sets of directions that tell the browser software (and other user agents such as mobile phones) how to display and manage a Web document. These directions are usually called tags and perform functions such as displaying graphics, formatting text, and referencing hyperlinks.

Standard Generalized Markup Language (SGML)

Standard Generalized Markup Language (SGML) is a standard for specifying a markup language or tag set. SGML in itself is not a document language, but a description of how to specify one and create a document type definition (DTD). When Tim Berners-Lee created HTML, he used SGML to create the specification.

Hypertext Markup Language (HTML)

HTML is the set of markup symbols or codes placed in a file intended for display on a Web browser. The Web browser renders the code in the HTML file and displays the Web page document and associated files. The W3C (http://www.w3.org) sets the standards for HTML. Although the most recent version of HTML is called **XHTML 1.1**, this text uses XHTML 1.0 because it is less strict and is well-supported by popular browsers.

Extensible Markup Language (XML)

XML was developed by the W3C as a flexible method to create common information formats and share the format and the information on the Web. It is a text-based syntax designed to describe, deliver, and exchange structured information. It is not intended to replace HTML, but to extend the power of HTML by separating data from presentation. Using XML, developers can create whatever tags they need to describe their information.

Extensible Hypertext Markup Language (XHTML)

XHTML was developed by the W3C to reformulate HTML 4.01 as an application of XML. It combines the formatting strengths of HTML 4.01 *and* the data structure and extensibility strengths of XML.

The primary advantages of XHTML include the ability to extend the language by creating new tags and the promise of increased platform interoperability as mobile devices are used more frequently to access the Web.

The Next Version of (X)HTML

As this was written, the W3C's HTML Working Group (HTML WG) was busy creating a draft recommendation for HTML 5—which is intended to be the next version of HTML 4 and XHTML 1. Check the blog on the textbook's Web site, http://webdevfoundations.net, for new developments.

CHECKPOINT 1.2

1. Describe the components of the client/server model as applied to the Internet.

2. Identify two protocols used on the Internet to convey information that use the Internet but do not use the Web.

3. Explain the similarities and differences between a URL and a domain name.

1.10 Internet and Web Trends

E-commerce, the buying and selling of goods on the Internet, is already an important part of the Web. According to a recent study by Jupiter Research (http://www.jupitermedia.com/corporate/releases/06.02.06-newjupresearch.html), revenue generated by e-commerce will continue to grow. By 2010, $144 million in online retail sales are projected. With 694 million people online worldwide (http://www.comscore.com/press/release.asp?press=849), that's quite a few potential shoppers!

As wireless Web access becomes more commonplace, e-commerce and Internet access not only will be regularly done from stationary computers but also from mobile devices—Palm Pilots, Pocket PCs, personal digital assistants (PDAs), cell phones, and Internet appliances we haven't even imagined yet.

As wireless access grows, so will the need for skilled technical workers. Expect to see a demand for network engineers familiar with wireless network technologies, such as Wireless Access Protocol (WAP), Bluetooth, and WiMAX. Web developers who are knowledgeable about markup languages such as Wireless Markup Language (WML), XML, and XHTML Basic will be sought as employees and consultants.

What is an Internet appliance?

An Internet appliance is a device that is designed to access the Internet. It is different from PCs and Palm Pilots in that they are multipurpose devices, while an Internet appliance is a single-purpose device. As you read this, companies are working to develop new Internet-ready devices, ranging from digital cameras that instantly post photos on the Web, to Internet-connected wearable computers, Internet-enabled printers, and Internet-enabled point-of-sale (POS) terminals.

How do we keep track of all the devices (wireless and otherwise) that are connected to the Internet? You are already aware that each device on the Internet is assigned a unique number called an IP address. Currently, IPv4 is being used. Theoretically, this allows for at most 4 billion possible IP addresses (although many potential addresses are reserved for special uses). With the proliferation of mobile devices, even this many addresses may not be enough. **IP Version 6 (IPv6)** will provide a huge increase in the number of possible addresses and many technological advances.

What is IPv6?

IPv6, Internet Protocol Version 6, is the most recent version of the Internet Protocol. IPv6 was designed as an evolutionary set of improvements to the current IPv4 and is backwardly compatible with it. Service providers and Internet users can update to IPv6 independently without having to coordinate with each other.

IPv6 provides for more Internet addresses because the IP address is lengthened from 32 bits to 128 bits. This means that there are potentially 2,128 unique IP addresses possible, or 340,282,366,920,938,463,463,347,607,431,768,211,456. (Now there will be enough IP addresses for everyone's PC, notebook, cell phone, pager, PDA, automobile, toaster, and so on!)

The development of the Internet2 is another effort in advancing Internet technology. The Internet2 consortium comprises more than one hundred U.S. universities in partnership with industry and government. Their mission is to develop and deploy advanced network applications and technologies, focusing on applications related to learning and research such as telemedicine, digital libraries, and virtual laboratories. Visit the Internet2 Web site at http://www.internet2.edu for information on this initiative.

Another area to watch is Web services. A **Web service** is a self-describing, self-contained application that provides some business functionality through an Internet connection. For example, an organization could create a Web service to facilitate information exchange with its partners or vendors. The Universal Discovery, Description, and Integration (UDDI) standard, http://uddi.xml.org, is backed by a number of technology companies, including IBM, Microsoft, and Sun Microsystems. Essentially, UDDI provides a method of describing a service, invoking a service, and locating available services. Microsoft's .NET platform supports Web services. Microsoft and IBM jointly developed Web Services Description Language (WSDL) to facilitate the use of Web services.

While the Web service initiative is driven by large corporations, the trend of keeping a Web log, or blog, has been driven by individuals as a forum for personal expression. A **blog** is a journal that is available on the Web—it's a frequently updated page with a chronological list of ideas and links. Blog topics range from political journals to technical information to personal diaries. Blogs can focus on one subject or range across a diverse group of topics—it's up to the person, called a blogger, who creates and maintains the blog. Bloggers usually update their blogs daily with easy-to-use software designed to allow people with little or no technical background to update and maintain the blog. The PEW Internet & American Life Project (http://www.pewinternet.org) reports that 39 percent of American adults read blogs daily and about 8 percent of American adults keep a blog. Many blogs are hosted at blog communities such as http://blogspot.com, http://www.diaryland.com, or http://www.xanga.com. Others are hosted at individual Web sites, such as the blog kept by the CSS expert Eric Meyer at http://meyerweb.com. Businesses have noted the value of blogs as communication and customer relationship tools. Companies such as IBM, http://www.ibm.com/developerworks/blogs/, and Adobe, http://weblogs.macromedia.com/mxna/, utilize blogs in this manner.

Really Simple Syndication or Rich Site Summary (RSS) is commonly used to create newsfeeds from blog postings and other Web sites. The RSS feeds contain a summary of new items posted to the site. The URL to the RSS feed is usually indicated by the letters XML or RSS in white text within an orange rectangle. A **newsreader** is needed to access the information. Some browsers, such as Firefox, Safari, and Internet Explorer 7 can display RSS feeds. Commercial and shareware newsreader applications are also available. The newsreader will poll the feed URL at intervals and display the new headlines when requested. RSS provides Web site developers with a method to push new content to interested parties and (hopefully) generate return visits to the site.

Podcasts are audio files on the Web—they may take the format of an audio blog, radio show, or interview. Podcasts are typically delivered by an RSS feed but can also be made available by recording an MP3 file and providing a link on a Web page. These files can be saved to your computer or to an MP3 player (such as an iPod) for later listening. Forrester Research (http://forrester.com/Research/Document/Excerpt/0,7211,36428,00.html) predicts that by 2010 more than 12.3 million households will use **podcasting**.

A **wiki** is a Web site that can be updated immediately at any time by visitors using a simple form on a Web page. Some wikis are intended for a small group of people, such as the members of an organization. The most powerful wiki is Wikipedia, http://wikipedia.org, an online encyclopedia, which can be updated by anyone at anytime. This is a form of social software in action—visitors sharing their collective knowledge to create a resource freely used by all. While there have been isolated incidents of practical jokes and occasionally inaccurate information posted at Wikipedia, the information and resource links are a good starting point when exploring a topic.

Blogs and wikis have provided Web visitors new methods to utilize and interact with Web sites and other people—referred to as **social computing** or social networking. Flickr (http://www.flickr.com/) and del.icio.us (http://del.icio.us/) are two social software sites that provide information-sharing opportunities. Flickr, a photo sharing site, calls itself the "best way to store, search, sort, and share your photos." Recently acquired by Yahoo!, del.icio.us is a collection of favorite sites—allowing registered users to post lists of favorites, share their favorites with others, and discover new sites. Wikipedia, Flickr, and del.icio.us are examples of what is called **Web 2.0**. While a consensus on the definition of Web 2.0 still needs to be reached, think of it as the next step in the transition of the Web from isolated static Web sites to a platform that utilizes technology to provide rich interfaces and social networking opportunities. Read Tim O'Reilly's informative Web 2.0 essay at http://oreillynet.com/pub/a/oreilly/tim/news/2005/09/30/what-is-web-20.html for more information on this developing topic.

The single future trend that you can expect to remain the same is the trend of constant change. Internet- and Web-related technologies are in a constant state of development and improvement. If constant change and the need to learn something new excites you, Web development is a fascinating field. The skills and knowledge you gain in this book should provide a solid foundation for your future learning.

What is the next big thing on the Web?

The Web is changing by the minute. Check the textbook's companion Web site at http://webdevfoundations.net for a blog that will help you stay current about Web trends.

CHAPTER SUMMARY

This chapter provided a brief overview of Internet, Web, and introductory networking concepts. Much of this information may be familiar to you. Visit the textbook Web site at http://www.webdevfoundations.net for the links listed in this chapter and for updated information.

Key Terms

accessibility
backbone
blog
client/server
clients
domain name
Domain Name System (DNS)
extranet
File Transfer Protocol (FTP)
Fully-Qualified Domain Name (FQDN)
Hypertext Markup Language (HTML)
Hypertext Transfer Protocol (HTTP)
Internet
Internet Architecture Board (IAB)
Internet Assigned Numbers Authority (IANA)
Internet Corporation for Assigned Numbers and Names (ICANN)
Internet Engineering Task Force (IETF)
Internet Message Access Protocol (IMAP)

Internet Society
intranet
IP
IP address
IP Version 6 (IPv6)
Local Area Network (LAN)
markup languages
media
Metropolitan Area Network (MAN)
Multi-Purpose Internet Mail Extensions (MIME)
network
Network Access Points (NAPs)
newsreader
packets
podcasting
Post Office Protocol (POP3)
protocols
Really Simple Syndication or Rich Site Summary (RSS)
Request for Comments (RFC)
server
Simple Mail Transfer Protocol (SMTP)

social computing
Standard Generalized Markup Language (SGML)
TCP
Top-level domain (TLD)
Transmission Control Protocol/Internet Protocol (TCP/IP)
Uniform Resource Locator (URL)
Web 2.0
Web Accessibility Initiative (WAI)
Web host server
Web service
Wide Area Network (WAN)
wiki
World Intellectual Property Organization (WIPO)
World Wide Web
World Wide Web Consortium (W3C)
XHTML
XML

Review Questions

Multiple Choice

1. Of the following organizations, which one studies technical problems of the Internet and proposes solutions?
   a. Assigned Numbers Authority (IANA)
   b. Engineering Task Force (IETF)
   c. Corporation for Assigned Numbers and Names (ICANN)
   d. World Wide Web Consortium (W3C)

2. Which of the following is a network that covers a small area, such as a group of buildings or campus?
   a. LAN
   b. WAN
   c. Internet
   d. WWW

3. At which of the following organizations did individuals develop the World Wide Web?

   a. CERN
   b. NCSA
   c. NSF
   d. ARPA

4. What is a unique text-based Internet address corresponding to a computer's unique numeric IP address called?

   a. IP address
   b. domain name
   c. URL
   d. user name

5. New Top-Level Domains (TLDs) are coordinated by which of the following?

   a. ICANN
   b. no one, because anyone can add a TLD to the DNS
   c. W3C
   d. TCP

True or False

6. _____ Markup languages contain sets of directions that tell the browser software (and other user-agents such as cell phones) how to display and manage a Web document.

7. _____ The World Wide Web was developed to allow companies to advertise over the Internet.

8. _____ A numerical Internet address used to identify computers is called an IP address.

9. _____ A domain name that ends in .com indicates that it is a computer company.

Fill in the Blank

10. _____ combines the formatting strengths of HTML 4.0 and the data structure and extensibility strengths of XML.

11. A standard language used for specifying a markup language or tag set is _____.

12. _____ is the set of markup symbols or codes placed in a file intended for display on a Web browser.

13. A language using a text-based syntax intended to extend the power of HTML by separating data from presentation is called _____.

14. Access points or junctions to the Internet backbone are called _____.

15. The purpose of _____ is to ensure the integrity of the communication.

Hands-On Exercise

1. Create a blog to document your learning experiences as you study Web development. Visit one of the many sites that offer free blogs, such as http://blogspot.com, http://www.diaryland.com, or http://www.xanga.com. Follow their instructions to establish your own blog. Your blog could be a place to note Web sites that you find useful or interesting. You might report on sites that contain useful Web design resources. You might describe sites that have interesting features, such as compelling graphics or easy to use navigation. Write a few sentences about the site that you find intriguing. After you begin to develop your own sites, you could include the URLs and reasons for your design decisions. Share this blog with your fellow students and friends. Display your page in a browser and print the page. Hand in the printout to your instructor.

Web Research

1. The World Wide Web Consortium creates standards for the Web. Visit its site at http://www.w3c.org and then answer the following questions:

   a. How did the W3C get started?

   b. Who can join the W3C? What does it cost to join?

   c. The W3C home page lists a number of technologies. Choose one that interests you, click its link, and read the associated pages. List three facts or issues you discover.

2. The Internet Society takes an active leadership role in issues related to the Internet. Visit its site at http://www.isoc.org and answer the following questions:

   a. Why was the Internet Society created?

   b. Determine the local chapter closest to you. Visit its Web site. List the Web site URL and an activity or service that the chapter provides.

   c. How can you join the Internet Society? What does it cost to join? Would you recommend that a beginning Web developer join the Internet Society? Why or why not?

3. The World Organization of Webmasters (WOW) is a professional association dedicated to the support of individuals and organizations that create and manage Web sites. Visit its site at http://www.joinwow.org and answer the following questions:

   a. How can you join WOW? What does it cost to join?

   b. List one of the events that WOW participates in. Would you like to attend this event? Why or why not?

   c. List three ways that WOW can help you in your future career as a Web developer.

Focus on Web Design

1. Visit a Web site referenced in this chapter that interests you. Print the home page or one other pertinent page from the site. Write a one-page summary and your reaction to the site. Address the following topics:

   a. What is the purpose of the site?

   b. Who is the intended audience?

   c. Do you think that the site reaches its intended audience? Why or why not?

   d. Is the site useful to you? Why or why not?

   e. List one interesting fact or issue that this site addresses.

   f. Would you encourage others to visit this site?

   g. How could this site be improved?

XHTML Basics

Chapter Objectives   In this chapter, you will learn about ...

- The development of HTML
- The transition from HTML to XHTML
- XHTML syntax, elements, and document type definitions
- The anatomy of a Web page
- Formatting the body of a Web page

- Formatting the text on a Web page
- Physical and logical style elements
- Special characters
- Using the anchor element to link from page to page
- Creating absolute, relative, and e-mail links

This chapter introduces Hypertext Markup Language (HTML), the language used to create Web pages, and eXtensible Hypertext Markup Language (XHTML), the latest version of HTML. The chapter begins with an introduction to the syntax of XHTML, continues with the anatomy of a Web page, and introduces block-level and inline formatting and demonstrates hyperlinks as sample pages are created. You will learn more if you work along with the sample pages in the text. Coding XHTML is a skill and every skill improves with practice.

2.1 What Is HTML?

The World Wide Web is composed of files containing **Hypertext Markup Language (HTML)** and other markup languages that describe Web pages. HTML was developed using Standard Generalized Markup Language (SGML). SGML prescribes a standard format for embedding descriptive markup within a document and for describing the structure of a document. SGML is not in itself a document language, but rather a description of how to specify one and create a **document type definition (DTD)**.

The W3C, http://w3c.org, sets the standards for HTML and its related languages. HTML (like the Web itself) is in a constant state of change.

HTML is the set of markup symbols or codes placed in a file intended for display on a Web browser page. These markup symbols and codes identify structural elements such as paragraphs, headings, and lists. HTML can also be used to place media (such as graphics, video, and audio) on a Web page and describe fill-in forms. The browser interprets the markup code and renders the page. HTML permits the platform-independent display of information across a network. That is, no matter what type of computer a Web page was created on, any browser running on any operating system can display the page.

Each individual markup code is referred to as an **element** or **tag**. Each tag has a purpose. Tags are enclosed in angle brackets, the < and > symbols. Most tags come in pairs: an opening tag and a closing tag. These tags act as containers and are sometimes referred to as container tags. For example, the text that is between the **`<title>`** and **`</title>`** tags on a Web page would display in the title bar on the browser window.

Some tags are used alone and are not part of a pair. For example, a tag that displays a horizontal line on a Web page, `<hr />`, is a stand-alone or self-contained tag and does not have a closing tag. You will become familiar with these as you use them. Most tags can be modified with **attributes** that further describe their purpose.

2.2 Why XHTML and Not HTML?

The newest version of HTML used today is actually **eXtensible HyperText Markup Language (XHTML)**. XHTML uses the tags and attributes of HTML along with the syntax of XML. While many Web pages and Web authoring tools still use HTML, as a Web developer you must learn about XHTML because you will be seeing a lot of it in the future.

Why was a new version needed? HTML was originally developed to provide access to electronic documents via a Web browser. Web browsers that evolved along with HTML were written to forgive coding errors, ignore syntax errors, and allow "sloppy" HTML code. Web browsers contain many program instructions that are designed to ignore mistakes such as missing ending tags and to guess how the developer meant the page to display. This is not a problem for a personal computer, which has relatively large processing power. However, this could be an issue for electronic devices with fewer resources, such as a personal digital assistant (PDA) or mobile phone.

Also, as new versions of Web browsers were developed and competed for market share, they often created their own proprietary extensions to HTML—tags that were not part of the standard and supported by one browser only. This created a lot of nonstandard HTML pages, and browsers are coded to accept this and ignore tags they don't recognize. However, this extra processing is not efficient, especially for devices with limited resources.

Finally, HTML is a structural language—it was originally intended to mark up printed documents for online viewing. It describes the structure of the document instead of the contents or information contained in the document. The Web has changed from a medium used to display electronic versions of paper documents to a medium that provides diverse information for a variety of devices. HTML does not fit this need. How will a table 600 pixels wide be displayed on a mobile phone? With the expansion of the Web to include devices other than personal computers, the need for a descriptive rather than structural language became evident and XHTML was created.

The purpose of XHTML was to provide a foundation for device-independent Web access. XHTML was developed by the W3C to be the reformulation of HTML as an application of XML. Tim Berners-Lee, the W3C director and inventor of the Web, stated in a press release (http://www.w3.org/2000/01/xhtml-pressrelease), "XHTML 1.0 connects the present Web to the future Web. It provides the bridge to page and site authors for entering the structured data, XML world, while still being able to maintain operability with user agents that support HTML 4." XHTML combines the formatting strengths of HTML and the data structure and extensibility strengths of XML. Since XHTML was designed using XML, let's take a quick look at XML.

XML (eXtensible Markup Language) is the W3C standard method for creating new markup languages that will support the display of nontraditional content such as mathematical notation, as well as support newer display devices such as PDAs and mobile phones. XML can fulfill these diverse needs because it is an extensible language—it is designed to allow the definition of new tags or markup. The syntax of XML is very exacting because the portable devices will not have to waste processing power guessing how the document should display, but will be able to display information efficiently. XHTML, which combines the language of HTML with the syntax of XML, is a markup language that should adapt to future needs.

An XML document must be well formed. A **well-formed document** is a document that adheres to the syntax rules of the language. The XHTML examples in the text will guide you in creating well-formed Web pages using XHTML. As a starting point, it is recommended that XML documents begin with an XML declaration. The basic form of this declaration is as follows:

```
<?xml version="1.0" encoding="UTF-8"?>
```

This XML declaration indicates that the document is based on the XML 1.0 standard. It also indicates the character encoding (the internal representation of letters, numbers, and symbols) in this document is UTF-8, a form of Unicode. This XML declaration will be the first line in each Web page that you write. See Appendix D, Comparison of HTML and XHTML, for a list of the key syntax rules of XML.

2.3 Document Type Definition

Because multiple versions and types of HTML and XHTML exist, the W3C recommends identifying the type of markup language used in a Web page document. Recall from Chapter 1 that XHTML 1.1 is the most recent version of HTML. However, XHTML 1.1 is not yet well supported by popular browsers. For this reason, we will follow the W3C XHTML 1.0 Recommendation. The three types of XHTML 1.0, **XHTML 1.0 Transitional**, **XHTML 1.0 Strict**, and **XHTML 1.0 Frameset**, are defined in Table 2.1.

Table 2.1 XHTML document types

Document Type Definition	Description
XHTML 1.0 Transitional	The least strict specification for XHTML 1.0; allows the use of Cascading Style Sheets and traditional formatting instructions such as fonts; used for most of the coding in this book
XHTML 1.0 Strict	Requires the exclusive use of Cascading Style Sheets; not used in this book
XHTML 1.0 Frameset	Required for pages using XHTML framesets; not used in this book

The version and type of XHTML is listed in the Document Type Definition (DTD) tag (commonly called the **DOCTYPE**). The DTD identifies the version and type of XHTML contained in your document. Browsers and HTML code validators can use the information in the DTD when processing the Web page. The DTD tag is placed at the top of a Web page document, even before the `<html>` tag. The DTD for XHTML 1.0 Transitional is as follows:

```
<!DOCTYPE html PUBLIC "-//W3C//DTD XHTML 1.0 Transitional//EN"
   "http://www.w3.org/TR/xhtml1/DTD/xhtml1-transitional.dtd">
```

You will place the DTD as the second line in each Web page document you create. Are you ready to create your first Web page?

2.4 Your First Web Page

After the XML declaration and the DTD, each Web page begins with an opening `<html>` tag and ends with a closing `</html>` tag. These tags indicate that the text between them is HTML formatted. It tells the browser how to interpret the document.

```
<?xml version="1.0" encoding="UTF-8"?>
<!DOCTYPE html PUBLIC "-//W3C//DTD XHTML 1.0 Transitional//EN"
   "http://www.w3.org/TR/xhtml1/DTD/xhtml1-transitional.dtd">
<html> an opening tag
... page information goes here
</html> a closing tag
```

There are two sections on a Web page: the **head** and the **body**. The head section, sometimes called the **header**, contains information that describes the Web page document.

Tags that are located in the head section include the title of the Web page, keywords that can be used by search engines, and references to scripts and styles. Many of these do not show directly on the Web page. The head section begins with the **<head>** tag and ends with the </head> tag.

The body section contains text and elements that do show directly on the Web page. The purpose of the body section is to describe the contents of the Web page. You will spend most of your time coding XHTML in the body of a Web page. If you type text in the body section, it will appear directly on the page.

The body section begins with the **<body>** tag and ends with the </body> tag.

The following code sample describes the anatomy of a Web page: a header section followed by a body section.

```
<?xml version="1.0" encoding="UTF-8"?>
<!DOCTYPE html PUBLIC "-//W3C//DTD XHTML 1.0 Transitional//EN"
  "http://www.w3.org/TR/xhtml1/DTD/xhtml1-transitional.dtd">
<html>
<head>
... header information goes here
</head>
<body>
... body information goes here
</body>
</html>
```

Notice that the XHTML tags are lowercase. This conforms to XML syntax. Notice also that the DTD statement does not follow this syntax. The DTD statement indicates the markup language being used and has its own formatting—mixed case.

In XHTML, the <html> tag also needs to describe the **XML namespace (xmlns)**, which is the location of the documentation for the elements being used. This additional information is added to the <html> tag in the form of an attribute. The xmlns attribute points to the URL of the XHTML namespace used in the document, the standard http://www.w3.org/1999/xhtml. The optional lang and xml:lang attributes (described in Appendix A, XHTML Reference) specify the spoken language of the document. Search engines and screen readers may access these attributes.

FAQ

What are Web page editors?

No special software is needed to create an XHTML document—all you need is a text editor. Notepad is a text editor that is included with Microsoft Windows. TextEdit is distributed with the Mac OS X operating system. BBEdit is another popular editing program for Mac users. An alternative to using a simple text editor or word processor is to use a commercial Web authoring tool, such as Microsoft Expression Web or Adobe Dreamweaver. There are also many free or shareware editors available, including PageBreeze and Emacs. Netscape Composer is a Web page editor built into the Netscape Navigator browser. Regardless of the tool you use, having a solid foundation in XHTML will be useful. The examples in this text use Notepad.

The final version of the basic anatomy of a Web page follows. Note that the first five lines will usually be the same on every Web page that you create.

```
<?xml version="1.0" encoding="UTF-8"?>
<!DOCTYPE html PUBLIC "-//W3C//DTD XHTML 1.0 Transitional//EN"
   "http://www.w3.org/TR/xhtml1/DTD/xhtml1-transitional.dtd">
<html xmlns="http://www.w3.org/1999/xhtml">
<head>
... header information goes here
</head>
<body>
... body information goes here
</body>
</html>
```

HANDS-ON PRACTICE 2.1

Launch Notepad or another text editor and type in the following XHTML:

```
<?xml version="1.0" encoding="UTF-8"?>
<!DOCTYPE html PUBLIC "-//W3C//DTD XHTML 1.0 Transitional//EN"
   "http://www.w3.org/TR/xhtml1/DTD/xhtml1-transitional.dtd">
<html xmlns="http://www.w3.org/1999/xhtml">
<head>
<title>My First Web Page</title>
</head>
<body>
Hello World
</body>
</html>
```

Notice that the first lines in the file contain the XML declaration and the DTD. The XHTML code begins with an opening `<html>` tag and ends with a closing `</html>` tag. The purpose of these tags is to indicate that the content between the tags makes up a Web page. The head section is delimited by `<head>` and `</head>` tags and happens to contain a pair of title tags with the words "My First Web Page" in between. The body section is delimited by `<body>` and `</body>` tags. The words "Hello World" are typed on a line between the body tags. See Figure 2.1 for a screenshot of the code as it would appear in Notepad. You have just created the source code for a Web document.

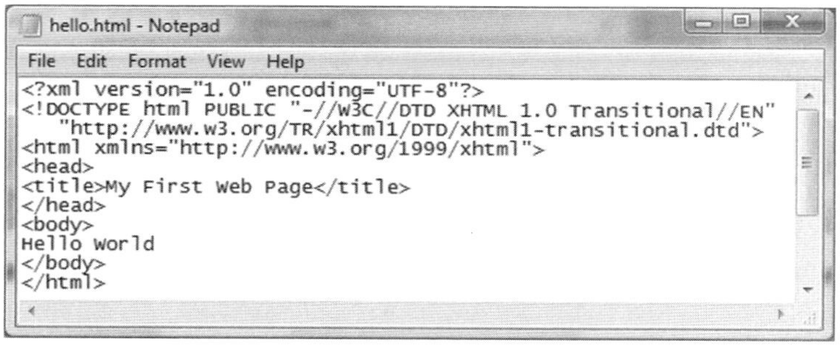

Figure 2.1
Source code of
hello.html

```
hello.html - Notepad
File  Edit  Format  View  Help
<?xml version="1.0" encoding="UTF-8"?>
<!DOCTYPE html PUBLIC "-//W3C//DTD XHTML 1.0 Transitional//EN"
    "http://www.w3.org/TR/xhtml1/DTD/xhtml1-transitional.dtd">
<html xmlns="http://www.w3.org/1999/xhtml">
<head>
<title>My First Web Page</title>
</head>
<body>
Hello World
</body>
</html>
```

Do I have to start each tag on its own line?

No. A browser can display a page even if all the tags follow each other on one line with no spaces. Humans, however, find it easier to write and read XHTML if line breaks and indentation (more on this later) are used.

Save Your File

You will save your file with the name of hello.html. Web pages use either an .htm or .html file extension. Select File from the menu bar, and then select Save As. The Save As dialog box appears. Using Figure 2.2 as an example, type the file name.

Figure 2.2
The Save As dialog box

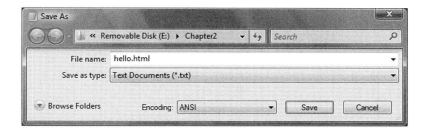

Why does my file have a .txt file extension?

In some older versions of Windows, Notepad will automatically append a .txt file extension. If this happens, type the name of the file within quotes, "hello.html", and save your file again.

Click the Save button after you type the file name. Sample solutions for the Hands-On Practice exercises are available in the student files. If you would like, compare your work with the solution (Chapter2/hello.html) before you test your page.

Test Your Page

There are two ways to test your page as follows:

1. **Launch Windows Explorer.** Navigate to your hello.html file. Double-click hello.html. The default browser will launch and will display your hello.html page. Your page should look similar to the one shown in Figure 2.3.

Figure 2.3
Web page displayed by Internet Explorer

2. **Launch Internet Explorer.** (If you are using Internet Explorer 7, select Tools, Menu Bar.) Select File, Open, Browse, My Computer, and then select your drive. Double-click hello.html and click OK. If you used Internet Explorer, your page should look similar to the one shown in Figure 2.3. A display of the page using Firefox is shown in Figure 2.4.

Figure 2.4
Web page displayed by Firefox

Examine your page. Look carefully at the browser window. What do you think is the purpose of the `<title>` tag? If you guessed that it's to display the title in the browser window, you are correct! Some search engines need the text surrounded by the `<title>` and `</title>` tags to help determine relevancy of keyword searches, so make certain that your pages contain descriptive titles. The `<title>` tag is also used when viewers bookmark your page or add it to their Favorites. An engaging and descriptive page title may entice a visitor to revisit your page. If your Web page is for a company or an organization, it's a good idea to include the name of the company or organization in the title.

You might be thinking "Hmmm … white background, black text, no images, can't we make the page look more interesting?" Sure we can. That's what you'll begin to learn in the next section.

CHECKPOINT 2.1

1. Describe the origin, purpose, and features of HTML.
2. Explain why you would use XHTML instead of HTML.
3. Describe the purpose of the header and body sections of a Web page.

2.5 XHTML—Body and Text Basics

Have you noticed the wide variety of page designs on Web sites? Whether a Web page contains mostly text, uses blocks of color, displays images, employs animation, or is interactive, the foundation of the page is the `<body>` tag.

The Body Element

The purpose of the `<body>` element is to contain the text and XHTML elements that will display in the browser window. As you noticed when you created your first Web page, any text that you type in the body section of a Web page document will be displayed by the browser in the actual Web page. Often, this text is organized by structural elements that indicate important headings, text paragraphs, and lists. These structural elements are **block-level elements**—they control blocks of text such as headings, paragraphs, and lists. Tags that affect individual sections of text are called **inline-level elements**. Web development is a skill—the more you practice, the better you get. Why not try each example as you read?

The Heading Element

Headings are block-level elements that are organized into levels h1 through h6. The size of the text is largest for **`<h1>`** and smallest for **`<h6>`**. Depending on the font being used (more on fonts in Chapter 3), text contained in `<h5>` and `<h6>` tags may be displayed smaller than the default text size.

HANDS-ON PRACTICE 2.2

Launch Notepad or another text editor and type in the following XHTML:

```
<?xml version="1.0" encoding="UTF-8"?>
<!DOCTYPE html PUBLIC "-//W3C//DTD XHTML 1.0 Transitional//EN"
  "http://www.w3.org/TR/xhtml1/DTD/xhtml1-transitional.dtd">
<html xmlns="http://www.w3.org/1999/xhtml">
<head>
<title>Sample Heading Tags</title>
</head>
<body>
  <h1>Heading Level 1</h1>
  <h2>Heading Level 2</h2>
  <h3>Heading Level 3</h3>
  <h4>Heading Level 4</h4>
  <h5>Heading Level 5</h5>
  <h6>Heading Level 6</h6>
</body>
</html>
```

Save the file as heading.html. Launch a browser such as Internet Explorer or Firefox to test your page. It should look similar to the page shown in Figure 2.5. You can compare your work with the solution found in the student files (Chapter2/heading.html).

Notice that each heading in Figure 2.5 is on its own line and that there is a blank line between headings. The heading tag is a container tag. Notice how there are always corresponding opening `<h#>` and closing `</h#>` tags. It's a good idea to use headings to emphasize important topics or sections on a Web page.

Figure 2.5
Sample
heading.html

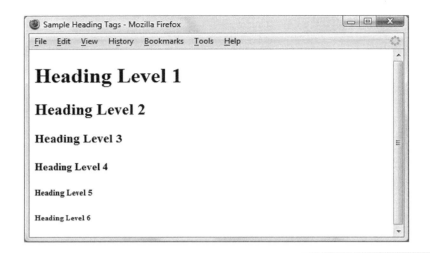

Accessibility and Headings

Focus on Accessibility

Heading tags can help to make your pages more accessible and usable. To indicate areas within a page hierarchically, code heading tags numerically as appropriate (h1, h2, h3, and so on) and include page content in block-level elements such as paragraphs and lists. Visually challenged visitors who are using a screen reader can configure the software to display a list of the headings used on a page to focus on the topics that interest them. Your well-organized page will be more usable for every visitor to your site, including those who are visually challenged.

The Paragraph Element

Paragraph elements are block-level elements used to group sentences and sections of text together. Text that is contained by **<p>** and </p> tags will have a blank line above and below it.

HANDS-ON PRACTICE 2.3

Open your heading.html file in a text editor. Use the following sample code and add a paragraph of text to your page below the line with the <h1> tags and above the line with the <h2> tags. Save your page as heading2.html.

```
<?xml version="1.0" encoding="UTF-8"?>
<!DOCTYPE html PUBLIC "-//W3C//DTD XHTML 1.0 Transitional//EN"
  "http://www.w3.org/TR/xhtml1/DTD/xhtml1-transitional.dtd">
<html xmlns="http://www.w3.org/1999/xhtml">
<head>
<title>Sample Heading Tags</title>
</head>
<body>
```

```
    <h1>Heading Level 1</h1>
    <p>This is a sample paragraph about HTML and XHTML. XHTML is the
newest version of HTML. XHTML uses the tags and attributes of HTML
along with the syntax of XML.</p>
    <h2>Heading Level 2</h2>
    <h3>Heading Level 3</h3>
    <h4>Heading Level 4</h4>
    <h5>Heading Level 5</h5>
    <h6>Heading Level 6</h6>
</body>
</html>
```

Launch a browser to test your page. It should look similar to the page shown in Figure 2.6 and to the solution in the student files (Chapter2/heading2.html).

Figure 2.6
Web page using headings and a paragraph

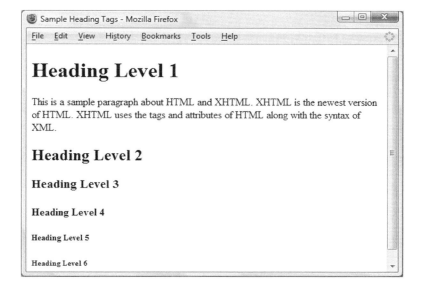

Notice how the text wraps automatically as you resize your browser window. If you wanted to have the second sentence in the paragraph begin on its own line, you would need to add a line break. The next section describes **
**, the tag used to create line breaks.

The Line Break Element

The line break tag, `<br />`, is used to force a new line when the text on the Web page document is displayed by a browser. The line break tag is used alone—it is not used as a pair of opening and closing tags. It is considered to be a stand-alone or self-contained tag. If you were using HTML syntax, the line break tag would be coded as `<br>`. Because you are using XHTML (which follows XML syntax), the line break tag is coded as `<br />` (the ending `/>` indicates a self-contained tag).

HANDS-ON PRACTICE 2.4

Open your heading2.html file in Notepad. Place your cursor after the first sentence in the paragraph (after "This is a sample paragraph about HTML and XHTML."). Press the ⟨Enter⟩ key. Save your page. Test your page in a browser and notice that even though your source code showed the "This is a sample paragraph about HTML and XHTML." sentence on its own line, the browser did not render it that way. A <br /> tag is needed to configure the browser. Open the heading2.html file in Notepad and add a <br /> tag after the first sentence in the paragraph. Save your page as heading3.html. Your source code should look similar to the following:

```
<?xml version="1.0" encoding="UTF-8"?>
<!DOCTYPE html PUBLIC "-//W3C//DTD XHTML 1.0 Transitional//EN"
   "http://www.w3.org/TR/xhtml1/DTD/xhtml1-transitional.dtd">
<html xmlns="http://www.w3.org/1999/xhtml">
<head>
<title>Sample Heading Tags</title>
</head>
<body>
   <h1>Heading Level 1</h1>
   <p>This is a sample paragraph about HTML and XHTML.<br /> XHTML is
the newest version of HTML. XHTML uses the tags and attributes of
HTML along with the syntax of XML.</p>
   <h2>Heading Level 2</h2>
   <h3>Heading Level 3</h3>
   <h4>Heading Level 4</h4>
   <h5>Heading Level 5</h5>
   <h6>Heading Level 6</h6>
</body>
</html>
```

Launch a browser to test your page. It should look similar to the page shown in Figure 2.7. You can compare your work with the solution found in the student files (Chapter2/heading3.html).

As you tested your Web pages, you may have noticed that the headings and text begin near the left margin. This is called **left alignment** and is the default alignment for Web pages. There are times when you want a paragraph or heading to be centered or right-aligned (justified). The align attribute can be used for this. The purpose of an **attribute** is to modify the properties of an XHTML element. In this case, the align attribute modifies the element's horizontal alignment (left, center, or right) on a Web page. To center an element on a Web page use the attribute align="center". To right-justify an element on a Web page, use align="right". The default alignment is left. The align attribute can be used with a number of block level elements, including the paragraph (<p>) and heading (<h1> through <h6>) tags.

Figure 2.7
A `<br />` tag creates the line break after the first sentence

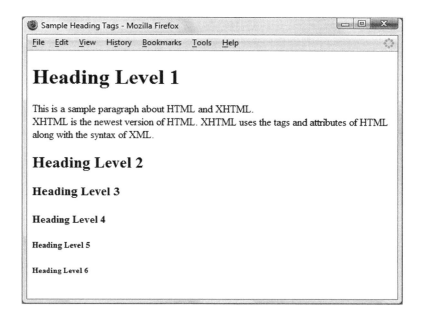

FAQ

FAQ

Why does my Web page still look the same?

Often, students make changes to a Web page but get frustrated because their browser shows an older version of the page. The following troubleshooting tips are helpful when you know you modified your Web page but the changes do not show up in the browser:

1. Make sure you save your page after you make the changes.
2. Verify the location that you are saving your page to—the hard drive, a particular folder.
3. Verify the location that your browser is requesting the page from—the hard drive, a particular folder.
4. Be sure to click the Refresh or Reload button in your browser.

Open your heading3.html file in Notepad. Modify the heading to be centered. Change the `<h1>` tag to `<h1 align="center">` but do not change the closing `</h1>` tag. Also modify the paragraph to be centered on the Web page. Change the `<p>` tag to `<p align="center">`, but do not change the closing `</p>` tag. Save your page as heading4.html and test it in a browser. Your page should look similar to the page shown in Figure 2.8. You can compare your work with the solution found in the student files (Chapter2/heading4.html).

Legacy Alert. You will find many Web pages that use the `align` attributes to center block-level elements such as paragraphs and headings. Be aware that the `align` attribute is supported in XHTML 1.0 Transitional but is deprecated. In Chapters 3 and 6, you will learn to use Cascading Style Sheets (CSS) to configure alignment of text on a Web page.

Figure 2.8
Using the `align` attribute to center the first heading and paragraph

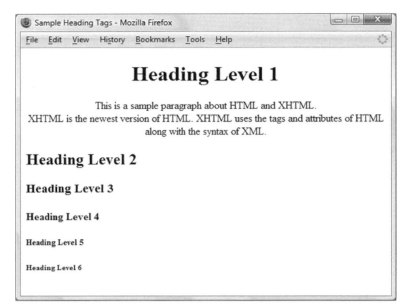

The Blockquote Element

Besides organizing text in paragraphs and lists, sometimes it is useful to indent a block of text for special emphasis. Items often found indented in this manner include quotations, lists, and instructions. A block of indented text begins with a **`<blockquote>`** tag and ends with a `</blockquote>` tag.

HANDS-ON PRACTICE 2.5

Launch Notepad or another text editor and type in the following XHTML:

```
<?xml version="1.0" encoding="UTF-8"?>
<!DOCTYPE html PUBLIC "-//W3C//DTD XHTML 1.0 Transitional//EN"
   "http://www.w3.org/TR/xhtml1/DTD/xhtml1-transitional.dtd">
<html xmlns="http://www.w3.org/1999/xhtml">
<head>
<title>Blockquote Example</title>
</head>
<body>
  <h1>Markup Languages</h1>
    <blockquote>
       HTML HyperText Markup Language<br />
       DHTML Dynamic HyperText Markup Language<br />
       XHTML eXtensible HyperText Markup Language<br />
       XML eXtensible Markup Language
    </blockquote>
```

```
</body>
</html>
```

Save your file as blockquote.html. Launch a browser and test your file. Your page should look similar to the page shown in Figure 2.9 and the solution in the student files (Chapter2/blockquote.html). Notice how the text that was entered between `<blockquote>` tags is indented.

Figure 2.9
Sample
blockquote.html

2.6 XHTML—List Basics

Lists are used on Web pages to organize information. When writing for the Web, remember that headings and bulleted lists make your pages clear and easy to read. XHTML can be used to create three types of lists: **definition lists, ordered lists,** and **unordered lists.**

Definition Lists

Definition lists help to organize terms and their definitions. The terms stand out and their definitions can be as long as needed to convey your message.

Definition lists are also handy for organizing Frequently Asked Questions (FAQs) and their answers. The questions and answers are offset with indentation. Each defined term begins on its own line at the margin. Each definition begins on its own line and is indented. See Figure 2.10 for an example of a Web page that uses a definition list.

Any type of information that consists of a number of corresponding terms and longer descriptions is well suited to being organized in a definition list.

Definition lists begin with the **`<dl>`** tag and end with the `</dl>` tag. Each defined term in the list begins with the **`<dt>`** tag and ends with the `</dt>` tag. Each term definition (data definition) begins with the **`<dd>`** tag and ends with the `</dd>` tag. A definition list is created in the following Hands-On Practice.

Figure 2.10
Sample
definitionlist.html

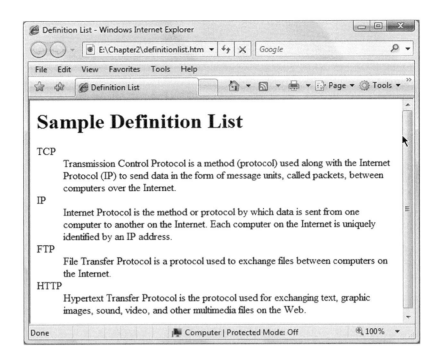

HANDS-ON PRACTICE 2.6

Open a new file in Notepad. Use the following sample code to create a definition list.

```
<?xml version="1.0" encoding="UTF-8"?>
<!DOCTYPE html PUBLIC "-//W3C//DTD XHTML 1.0 Transitional//EN"
   "http://www.w3.org/TR/xhtml1/DTD/xhtml1-transitional.dtd">
<html xmlns="http://www.w3.org/1999/xhtml">
<head>
<title>Definition List</title>
</head>
<body>
  <h1>Sample Definition List</h1>
    <dl>
      <dt>TCP</dt>
        <dd>Transmission Control Protocol is a method (protocol) used
along with the Internet Protocol (IP) to send data in the form of
message units, called packets, between computers over the
Internet.</dd>
        <dt>IP</dt>
        <dd>Internet Protocol is the method or protocol by which data
is sent from one computer to another on the Internet. Each computer
on the Internet is uniquely identified by an IP address.</dd>
        <dt>FTP</dt>
```

```
        <dd>File Transfer Protocol is a protocol used to exchange
files between computers on the Internet.</dd>
        <dt>HTTP</dt>
        <dd>Hypertext Transfer Protocol is the protocol used for
exchanging text, graphic images, sound, video, and other multimedia
files on the Web.</dd>
    </dl>
</body>
</html>
```

Save your file as definitionlist.html and test it in a browser. Your page should look similar to the one shown in Figure 2.10 and to the solution in the student files (Chapter2/definitionlist.html). Don't worry if the word wrap is a little different—the important formatting is that each <dt> term should be on its own line and the corresponding <dd> definition should be indented under it. Try resizing your browser window and notice how the word wrap on the definition text changes.

Ordered Lists

Ordered lists use a numbering or lettering system to organize the information contained in the list. An ordered list can be organized by the use of numerals (the default), uppercase letters, lowercase letters, uppercase Roman numerals, and lowercase Roman numerals. See Figure 2.11 for a sample ordered list.

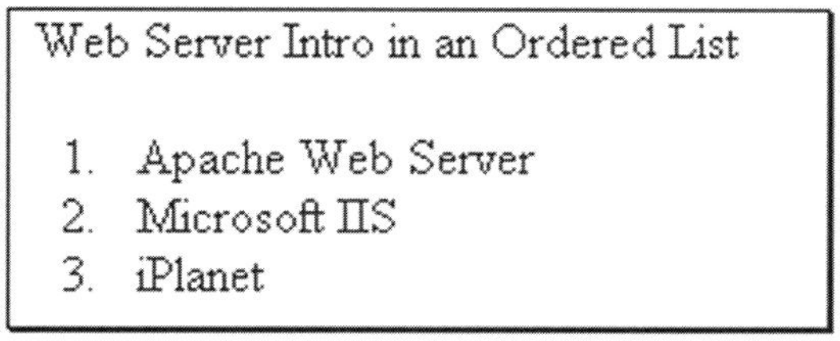

Figure 2.11
Sample ordered list

Web Server Intro in an Ordered List

1. Apache Web Server
2. Microsoft IIS
3. iPlanet

Ordered lists begin with an **<ol>** tag and end with an </ol> tag. Each list item begins with an **<li>** tag and ends with an </li> tag. The type attribute can be used to change the symbol used for ordering the list. For example, to create an ordered list organized by uppercase letters, use <ol type="A">. Table 2.2 documents the type attribute and its values for ordered lists.

Table 2.2 type attributes for ordered lists

Attribute	Value	Symbol
type	1	Numerals (the default)
	A	Uppercase letters
	a	Lowercase letters
	I	Roman numerals
	i	Lowercase Roman numerals

The XHTML code to create the ordered list shown in Figure 2.11 follows:

```
Web Server Intro in an Ordered List
<ol>
  <li>Apache Web Server</li>
  <li>Microsoft IIS</li>
  <li>iPlanet</li>
</ol>
```

Unordered Lists

Unordered lists show a bullet before each entry in the list. This bullet can be one of several types: disc (the default), square, and circle. See Figure 2.12 for a sample unordered list.

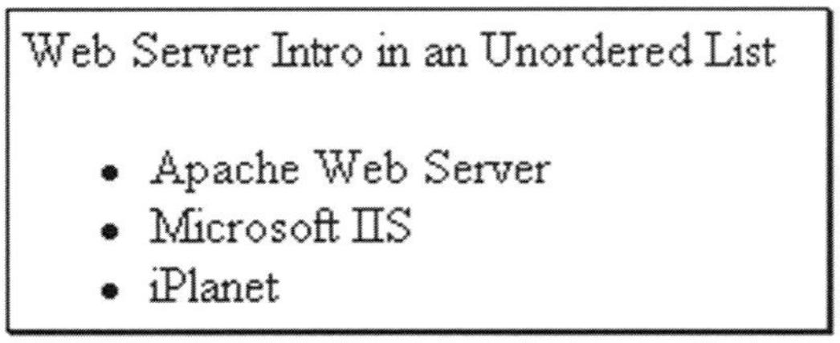

Figure 2.12
Sample unordered list

Web Server Intro in an Unordered List

- Apache Web Server
- Microsoft IIS
- iPlanet

Unordered lists begin with an **`<ul>`** tag and end with an `</ul>` tag. Each list item begins with an `<li>` tag and ends with an `</li>` tag. The `type` attribute can be used to change the type of bullet. For example, to create an unordered list organized with square bullets, use `<ul type="square">`. Table 2.3 documents the `type` attribute and its values for unordered lists.

Table 2.3 `type` attributes for unordered lists

Attribute	Value
type	disc (the default)
	square
	circle

The XHTML code to create the unordered list shown in Figure 2.12 follows:

```
Web Server Intro in an Unordered List
<ul>
   <li>Apache Web Server</li>
   <li>Microsoft IIS</li>
   <li>iPlanet</li>
</ul>
```

HANDS-ON PRACTICE 2.7

In this Hands-On Practice you will use heading tags and lists on the same page. Launch Notepad or another text editor and type in the following XHTML:

```
<?xml version="1.0" encoding="UTF-8"?>
<!DOCTYPE html PUBLIC "-//W3C//DTD XHTML 1.0 Transitional//EN"
   "http://www.w3.org/TR/xhtml1/DTD/xhtml1-transitional.dtd">
<html xmlns="http://www.w3.org/1999/xhtml">
<head>
<title>Headings and Lists</title>
</head>
<body>
   <h1>Web Servers and Web Browsers</h1>
     <h2>Popular Web Servers</h2>
        <ol>
           <li>Apache Web Server</li>
           <li>Microsoft IIS</li>
           <li>iPlanet</li>
        </ol>
     <h2>Popular Web Browsers</h2>
        <ul>
           <li>Internet Explorer</li>
           <li>Firefox</li>
           <li>Opera</li>
        </ul>
</body>
</html>
```

Save your file as heading5.html. Launch a browser and test your page. It should look similar to the pages shown in Figure 2.13. Notice that the Firefox browser configures unordered lists with a diamond bullet point by default instead of the disc as specified by the W3C. You can compare your work with the solution in the student files (Chapter2/heading5.html).

Figure 2.13
Web page using an
ordered and
unordered list

Take a few minutes to experiment with the `type` attribute. Configure the unordered list to use square bullets. Configure the ordered list to use uppercase letters instead of numerals. Save your page as heading6.html. Test your page in a browser. It should look similar to the page shown in Figure 2.14 and the solution in the student files (Chapter2/heading6.html).

Figure 2.14
Using the `type`
attribute with
unordered and
ordered lists

CHECKPOINT 2.2

1. Describe the features of a heading element and how it configures the text.
2. Describe the difference between ordered lists and unordered lists.
3. Describe the purpose of the blockquote element.

2.7 XHTML—Text Formatting

Text can be formatted in various ways using **logical style elements, physical style elements,** and **special characters.** These are considered to be inline-level elements because they can apply to either a section of text or a single character of text. This is not the only method for formatting text; Cascading Style Sheets (introduced in Chapter 3) is commonly used for this purpose.

FAQ

What about the font tag?

The `<font>` tag allows you to configure the typeface, color, and size of the text between the `<font>` and `</font>` container tags. However, the `<font>` tag is deprecated. A **deprecated** XHTML element or attribute is still supported by XHTML 1.0 Transitional and currently popular browsers, but may not be supported in the future. The W3C recommends using Cascading Style Sheets (see Chapter 3) to format text instead of using the `<font>` tag. If you'd like more information about the `<font>` tag, see Appendix A, XHTML Reference.

XHTML Logical Style Elements

Logical style elements, sometimes called phrase elements, indicate the logical style used to display the text between the container tags. It is up to each browser to interpret that style. For example, the `<strong>` element indicates that the text associated with it be displayed in a "strong" manner in relation to normal text on the page. Usually, but not always, the browser (or other user agent) will display <strong> text in bold. A screen reader, such as Jaws or Window-Eyes, might interpret <strong> text to indicate that the text should be more strongly spoken. With more and more devices used to access the Web, the use of logical style elements instead of physical style elements (whenever possible) is preferred. Both are still used on the Web.

Note that all logical style elements are container tags—an opening and a closing tag should be used. For example, if you wanted the phone number in the following line to have a strong logical style

```
Call for a free quote for your Web development needs: 888.555.5555
```

the XHTML would look like

```
<p>Call for a free quote for your Web development needs:
<strong>888.555.5555</strong></p>
```

Notice that the `<strong>` opening and closing tags are contained within the paragraph tags (`<p>` and `</p>`). This XHTML code is nested properly, follows XML syntax, and is considered to be well formed. An example of improper nesting follows:

```
<p>Call for a free quote for your Web development needs:
<strong>888.555.5555</p></strong>
```

When improperly nested, the `<p>` and `<strong>` tag pairs overlap each other instead of being nested within each other. Appendix D, Comparison of HTML and XHTML, contains a list of the key syntax rules of XML.

Table 2.4 lists logical style tags and examples of their use.

Table 2.4 Logical style elements

Element	Example	Usage
`<strong>`	**strong** text	Causes text to be emphasized or to stand out from surrounding text; usually displayed in bold
`<em>`	*emphasized* text	Causes text to be emphasized in relation to other text; usually displayed in italics
`<cite>`	*cite* text	Identifies a citation or reference; usually displayed in italics
`<code>`	`code` text	Identifies program code samples; usually a fixed-space font
`<dfn>`	*dfn* text	Identifies a definition of a word or term; usually displayed in italics
`<kbd>`	`kbd` text	Identifies user text to be typed; usually a fixed-space font
`<samp>`	`samp` text	Shows program sample output; usually a fixed-space font
`<var>`	*var* text	Identifies and displays a variable or program output; usually displayed in italics

Why do the displays look so similar?

As you look at Table 2.4, you may notice that some tags, such as `<cite>` and `<dfn>`, result in the same type of display (italics) as the `<em>` tag in today's browsers. These tags are logically describing the text as a citation or definition, but the physical display is usually italics in both cases. Cascading Style Sheets (see Chapter 3) are a better way to format elements than logical style tags. However, logical style tags are preferred over physical style tags. If you find this a little confusing and think that there are too many tags with similar purposes, you are correct. Please keep in mind that Cascading Style Sheets is the preferred method to format text—not physical style and logical style elements. However, we introduce physical style and logical style elements in this chapter because they are still used on the Web.

XHTML—Physical Style Elements

Physical style elements are sometimes called font style elements because they provide specific font instructions for the browser. This type of tag is still commonly used and generated by some Web authoring tools. Be aware that logical style elements and Cascading Style Sheets provide for a wider range of Web access. Physical style elements are covered in this book because many existing Web pages use them. Table 2.5 lists physical style tags and examples of their use.

Table 2.5 Physical style elements

Element	Example	Usage
`<b>`	**bold** text	Displays text as bold
`<i>`	*emphasized* text	Displays text in italics
`<big>`	big text	Displays text larger than normal size
`<small>`	small text	Displays text smaller than normal size
`<sub>`	sub text	Displays small text below the baseline
`<sup>`	sup text	Displays small text above the baseline
`<strike>`	~~strike~~ text	Displays text with a line through it (deprecated)
`<u>`	u text	Displays text underlined; avoid using this because underlined text can be confused with hyperlinks (deprecated)
`<tt>`	`teletype` text	Displays text in teletype or fixed-space font

You may have noticed that the `<strong>` logical style tag usually has the same effect as the `<b>` physical style tag. Also, the **`<em>`** logical style tag usually has the same effect as the `<i>` physical style tag. In order to create XHTML that describes logical styles instead of font instructions for browsers, use `<strong>` instead of `<b>` and use `<em>` instead of `<i>`. As you continue to study Web development, you will learn about Cascading Style Sheets and their use in text formatting.

Special XHTML Characters

In order to use special characters such as quotation marks, greater than (>), lesser than (<), and the copyright symbol (©) in your Web document, you need to use special characters, sometimes called entity characters. For example, if you wanted to include a copyright line on your page as follows:

© Copyright 2008 My Company. All rights reserved.

You would use the special character **`&copy;`** to display the copyright symbol. The XHTML would look as follows:

`<p>&copy; Copyright 2008 My Company. All rights reserved.</p>`

Another useful special character is **` `**, which stands for nonbreaking space. You may have noticed that Web browsers treat multiple spaces as a single space. If you need a small number of spaces in your text, you may use ` ` multiple times to indicate multiple blank spaces. This is acceptable if you simply need to tweak the position of an element a little. If you find that your Web pages contain many ` ` special characters in a row, you should use a different method to align elements, such as a table or Cascading Style Sheets.

See Table 2.6 and Appendix B, Special Characters, for a description of special characters and their codes.

Table 2.6 Common special characters

Character	Entity Name	Code
"	Quotation mark	`&quot;`
©	Copyright symbol	`&copy;`
&	Ampersand	`&amp;`
Empty space	Nonbreaking space	` `

HANDS-ON PRACTICE 2.8

Figure 2.15 shows the Web page you will create. Launch Notepad and open one of the Web page files that you have already created, such as blockquote.html from Hands-On Practice 2.5. Modify the title of the Web page by changing the text between the `<title>` and `</title>` tags to Web Design Steps. Since our Web Design Steps page will be quite different from the previous page you created, delete the code between the `<body>` and `</body>` tags. Save the file as design.html.

Figure 2.15
Sample design.html

The sample page shown in Figure 2.15 contains a heading, an ordered list, and copyright information.

Configure the heading Web Design Steps as a level 1 heading (`<h1>`) as follows:

```
<h1>Web Design Steps</h1>
```

Now create the unordered list. The first line of each bulleted item is the title of the Web design step. In the sample, each step title should be strong, or stand out from the rest of the text. The subsequent lines in each bulleted item should be emphasized. The code for the beginning of the unordered list follows:

```
<ul>
  <li>Determine the Intended Audience</strong><br />
  <em>The colors, images, fonts, and layout should be tailored to the
preferences of your audience. The type of site content (reading
level, amount of animation, etc.) should be appropriate for your
chosen audience.</em>
  </li>
```

Edit your design.html file and code the entire ordered list. Remember to code the closing `</ul>` tag at the end of the list. Don't worry if your text wraps a little differently—your screen resolution or browser window size may be different.

Finally, configure the copyright information. This should be smaller than the rest of the text. Use the special character, `&copy;`, for the copyright symbol. The code for the copyright line follows:

```
<p><small>Copyright &copy; 2008 Your name. All Rights Reserved.
</small></p>
```

How did you do? Compare your work to the sample in the student files (Chapter2/design.html).

2.8 XHTML—Hyperlinks

The Anchor Element

The **anchor element** can be used to specify a hyperlink reference (`href`) to a Web page you want to display. Each **hyperlink** begins with an `<a>` tag and ends with an `</a>` tag. The opening and closing anchor tags surround the text to click to perform the hyperlink.

You have probably seen many links on the Web but may have never thought about how they are created. To create an **absolute link** to a Web site such as Yahoo!, you would create a hyperlink with the URL for Yahoo! for the value of the **`href` attribute** as follows:

```
<a href="http://yahoo.com">Yahoo!</a>
```

"Yahoo!", the text contained between the anchor tags, is displayed in the browser window. By default, this text is underlined and blue. Figure 2.16 shows an example of a hyperlink to the Yahoo! Web site in a browser.

Figure 2.16
A hyperlink to the Yahoo! Web site

Absolute and Relative Links

The link to Yahoo! you just created is an absolute link. Notice that the XHTML code for the link indicates the protocol being used, http://, and continues with the domain name, yahoo.com. This indicates the absolute location of the Web resource. Use absolute links when you are creating links to other Web sites.

When you need to link to Web pages within your site, use a **relative link**. This link does not begin with http://. It only contains the file name or file name and folder of the Web page you want to display. The link location is relative to the page currently being displayed. For example, if you had a home page called index.html and wanted to link to a page with your resumé (called resume.html) located in the same folder as index.html, the XHTML for the relative link would be as follows:

```
<a href="resume.html">My Resume</a>
```

HANDS-ON PRACTICE 2.9

The best way to learn XHTML is by writing it. Let's experiment with the anchor tag and create a sample Web site to use to practice creating hyperlinks.

First, create a new folder called mywebsite.

- **Windows XP Users.** Launch Windows Explorer by selecting Start, Programs, Windows Explorer with your pointing (mouse) cursor. Click your drive to select it. Select File, New, Folder.
- **Windows Vista Users.** Launch the Computer folder by selecting Start, Computer with your pointing (mouse) cursor. Click your drive to select it. Select Organize, New Folder.

Name your folder mywebsite. This site could be a personal Web site. It will contain a home page called index.html and two content pages called resume.html and favorites.html. A sample site map that was created using Adobe Dreamweaver (see Figure 2.17) shows the architecture of the site—a home page (index.html) with major links to two pages (resume.html and favorites.html).

Figure 2.17
Site map

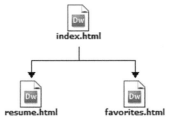

Now create the home page for your mywebsite Web site. Launch Notepad or another text editor and type in the tags found on every Web page (XML declaration, DTD, html, head, title, body). In the body of the Web page create the following:

- A heading: My Web Site
- An absolute link to Yahoo!

- An absolute link to the Web site of your school
- A relative link to resume.html
- A relative link to favorites.html

Save your page as index.html in the mywebsite folder. Display your page in a browser. It should look similar to the page shown in Figure 2.18. Compare your work to the sample in the student files (Chapter2/2.9/index.html). *Hint*: Check Appendix B, Special Characters, for the XHTML code for the "é".

Figure 2.18
Sample index.html

Test your page by clicking each link. When you click the absolute links to Yahoo! and your school you should see those pages displayed if you are connected to the Internet. The relative links should not work yet—let's create those pages next.

Create the resume.html page. Launch Notepad or another text editor and type in the tags found on every Web page (XML declaration, DTD, html, head, title, body). In the body of the Web page place the following:

- A heading of Resumé
- Some text that describes your job objective
- A navigation bar that contains a relative link to the Home page (index.html), and a relative link to the Favorites page (favorites.html)

FAQ   What if my absolute links don't work?

Check the following:

- Are you currently connected to the Internet?
- Are you certain that you spelled the URLs of the Web sites correctly?
- Did you begin with http://?
- When you place your mouse over a link, the URL will display in the status bar in the lower edge of the browser window. Verify that this is the correct URL.
- *Hint*: When you are about to put an absolute link in a Web page, display the Web site in a browser, then copy and paste the URL. Don't rely on typing the URL accurately.

See Figure 2.19 for a sample Resumé page. Save your Resumé page as resume.html in your mywebsite folder.

Figure 2.19
Sample resume.html

Test your index.html page again. This time when you click the Resumé link, your new page should display. Use the Home link on your resume.html page to redisplay your home page.

Create the favorites.html page. Launch Notepad or another text editor and type in the tags found on every Web page (XML declaration, DTD, html, head, title, body). In the body of the Web page place the following:

- A heading: Favorite Sites
- An unordered list that contains the following categories:
  Hobbies
  XHTML
  JavaScript
  Professional Groups
- A navigation bar that contains a relative link to the Home page (index.html) and a relative link to the Resumé page (resume.html)

See Figure 2.20 for a sample Favorites page. Save your page as favorites.html in your mywebsite folder.

Figure 2.20
Sample
favorites.html

Test your index.html page again and try the links between the Home page, Resumé page, and Favorites pages. Don't worry if the links don't work perfectly the first time. If you have problems, carefully examine the source code of the pages and verify the existence of the files using Windows Explorer.

FAQ

What if my relative links don't work?

Check the following:

- Did you save your index.html and resume.html pages in your mywebsite folder?

- Did you save the files with the names as requested? Use Windows Explorer or My Computer to verify the actual names of the files you saved.

- Did you type the file names correctly in the link's `href` property? Check for typographical errors.

- When you place your mouse over a link, the file name of a relative link will display in the status bar in the lower edge of the browser window. Verify that this is the correct file name.

- On many operating systems such as UNIX or Linux, the use of uppercase and lowercase in file names matters—make sure that the file name and the reference to it are in the same case. It's a good practice to always use lowercase for file names used on the Web.

- *Hint*: Tiny details such as spelling file names correctly and consistently are very important in Web development.

E-Mail Links

The anchor tag can also be used to create e-mail links. An **e-mail link** will automatically launch the default mail program configured for the browser. It is similar to an external hyperlink with the following two exceptions:

- It uses mailto: instead of http://.
- It launches the default e-mail application for the visitor's browser with your e-mail address as the recipient.

For example, to create an e-mail link to the e-mail address help@terrymorris.net, code the following:

```
<a href="mailto:help@terrymorris.net">help@terrymorris.net</a>
```

It is good practice to place the e-mail address both on the Web page and within the anchor tag. Not everyone has an e-mail program configured with his or her browser. By placing the e-mail address in both places, you increase usability for all your visitors.

HANDS-ON PRACTICE 2.10

Open the home page of your mywebsite Web site and add an e-mail link to the bottom of the page. Save and test it in a browser. The page should look similar to the page shown in Figure 2.21. Compare your work with the sample in the student files (Chapter2/2.10/index.html).

Figure 2.21
E-mail link added to
index.html

This section provided a quick introduction to the anchor element. You should now be able to code different types of text hyperlinks: e-mail links, links relative to a Web page, and absolute links to other Web sites. As you continue to study, you will learn to use images as hyperlinks (Chapter 4), to code links internal to a Web page (Chapter 7), and to target specific windows (Chapter 7).

Accessibility and Links

Focus on Accessibility

Visually challenged visitors who are using a screen reader can configure the software to display a list of the hyperlinks in the document. In addition, some popular browsers, such as Opera (visit http://www.opera.com for free download information), provide this feature as a convenience for all users. However, a list of links is only useful if the text describing each link is actually helpful and descriptive. For example, on your college Web site a "Search the course schedule" link would be more useful than a link that simply says "More information." Keep this in mind as you are coding hyperlinks in your Web pages.

FAQ **Can you share some tips on using links?**

- Make your link names descriptive and brief to minimize possible confusion.

- Avoid using the phrase "Click here for" in your links. In the beginning of the Web, this phrase was needed because clicking links was a new experience for Web users. Now that the Web is a daily part of our lives, this phrase seems slightly redundant and almost archaic.

- Try not to bury links in large blocks of text—use bullets or definition lists. It is more difficult to read Web pages than printed pages.

- Be careful when linking to external Web sites. The Web is dynamic and it's possible that the external site may change the name of the page or even delete the page. If this happens, your link will be broken.

CHECKPOINT 2.3

1. Provide a reason for using logical style tags rather than physical style tags.
2. Describe the purpose of special characters.
3. Describe when to use an absolute link. Is the http protocol used in the `href` value?
4. Describe when to use a relative link. Is the http protocol used in the `href` value?

2.9 XHTML Validation

The W3C has a free Markup Validation Service available at http://validator.w3.org/ that will validate your XHTML code and check it for syntax errors. **XHTML validation** provides students with quick self-assessment—you can prove that your code uses correct syntax. In the working world, XHTML validation serves as a quality assurance tool. Invalid code may cause browsers to render the pages slower than otherwise.

HANDS-ON PRACTICE 2.11

In this Hands-On Practice you will use the W3C Markup Validation Service to validate a Web page. This example uses the design.html page completed in Hands-On Practice 2.8 (student files Chapter2/design.html). Locate design.html and open it in Notepad. We will add an error to the design.html page. Delete the first closing `</li>` tag. This modification should generate several error messages. The first error message will be a direct result of the incorrect syntax.

Next, attempt to validate the design.html file. At the time this was written, the W3C warns that their validator may not work with all versions of Internet Explorer browsers. Therefore, launch a Mozilla-based browser such as Firefox or Netscape and visit the W3C Markup Validation Service file upload page at http://validator.w3.org/#validate_by_upload. Click the Browse button and select the Chapter2/design.html file from your computer. Select More Options. Verify that the check boxes next to Show Source and Verbose Output are checked, as shown in Figure 2.22. Click the Check button to upload the file to the W3C site.

Figure 2.22
Use Firefox or Netscape to validate your page

Your display should be similar to that shown in Figure 2.23. Notice the "Result: Failed validation, 8 Errors" message.

Figure 2.23
The validation
results indicate
errors

You can view the errors by scrolling down the page, as shown in Figure 2.24.

Figure 2.24
The error indicates
line 16

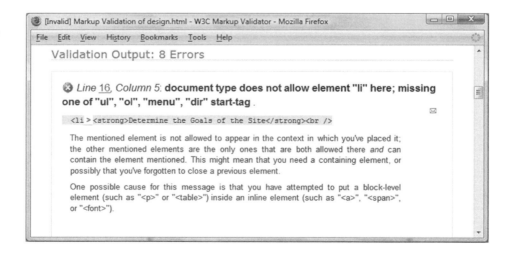

Notice that the message indicates line 16—which is the first line after the missing clos-ing `</li>` tag. XHTML error messages often point to the line that follows the error. The text of the message 'document type does not allow element "li" here; missing one of "ul", "ol", "menu", "dir" start-tag' lets you know that something is wrong. It's up to you to figure out what it is. A good place to start is to check your container tags and make sure they are in pairs. In this case, that is the problem. You can scroll down to view the other errors. However, since multiple error messages are often displayed after a single error occurs, it's a good idea to fix one item at a time and then revalidate.

Edit the design.html file in Notepad and add the missing `</li>` tag. Save the file. Launch Firefox or Netscape and visit http://validator.w3.org/#validate_by_upload. Select your file, select More Options, and verify the Show Source and Verbose Output check boxes are checked. Click the Check button to begin the validation.

Your display should be similar to that shown in Figure 2.25. Notice the "Result: Passed validation" message. This means your page passed the validation test. Congratulations, your design.html page is a valid XHTML page! It's a good practice to validate your Web pages. However, when validating code use common sense. Since Web browsers still do not completely follow W3C recommendations, there will be situations, such as when adding multimedia to a Web page, when XHTML code configured to work reliably across a variety of browsers and platforms will not pass XHTML validation.

Figure 2.25
The page has passed the validation test

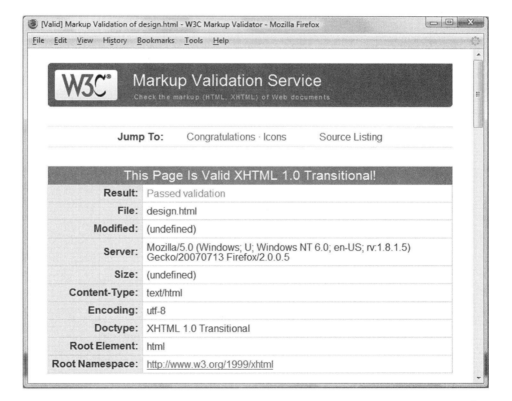

CHAPTER SUMMARY

This chapter provided an introduction to XHTML. It began with an introduction to HTML, discussed the transition to XHTML, continued with the anatomy of a Web page, introduced inline- and block-level formatting, and demonstrated coding anchor elements to link Web pages. If you worked along with the samples in the chapter, you should be ready to create some Web pages on your own. The Hands-On Exercises and Web Case Studies that follow will provide some practice.

Visit the textbook Web site at http://www.webdevfoundations.net for the links listed in this chapter and for updated information.

Key Terms

&copy;	<ul>	Hypertext Markup Language (HTML)
	absolute link	inline-level element
<a>	anchor element	left alignment
<blockquote>	attribute	logical style element
<body>	block-level element	ordered list
 	body	paragraph element
<dd>	definition list	physical style element
<dl>	deprecated	relative link
<dt>	DOCTYPE	special characters
<em>	document type definition (DTD)	tag
<font>	element	unordered list
<h1>	e-mail link	well-formed document
<h6>	eXtensible HyperText Markup Language (XHTML)	XHTML 1.0 Frameset
<head>	head	XHTML 1.0 Strict
<html>	header	XHTML 1.0 Transitional
<li>	headings	XHTML validation
<ol>	href attribute	XML (eXtensible Markup Language)
<p>	hyperlink	XML namespace (xmlns)
<strong>		
<title>		

Review Questions

Multiple Choice

1. Which tag pair is used to create a new paragraph?

a. `<new paragraph> </new paragraph>`
b. `<paragraph> </paragraph>`
c. `<p> </p>`
d. `<para> </para>`

2. Which tag pair is used to create the smallest heading?

a. `<h1> </h1>`
b. `<h9> </h9>`
c. `<h type="smallest"> </h>`
d. `<h6> </h6>`

3. Which tag is used to force the browser to display the next text or element on a new line?

   a. `<new line />`

   b. `<nl />`

   c. `<br />`

   d. `<line />`

4. Which tag is used to link Web pages to each other?

   a. `<link>` tag

   b. `<hyperlink>` tag

   c. `<a>` tag

   d. `<body>` tag

5. What is the default alignment for headings and paragraphs?

   a. `center`

   b. `left`

   c. `right`

   d. wherever you type them in the source code

6. Which type of XHTML list will automatically number the items for you?

   a. numbered list

   b. ordered list

   c. unordered list

   d. definition list

7. Which type of XHTML list contains bullets?

   a. bullet list

   b. ordered list

   c. unordered list

   d. definition list

8. When do you need to use a fully qualified URL in a hyperlink?

   a. always

   b. when linking to a Web page file on the same site

   c. when linking to a Web page file on an external site

   d. never

9. Which tag pair contains the items in an ordered or unordered list?

   a. `<item> </item>`

   b. `<li> </li>`

   c. `<dd> </dd>`

   d. all of the above

10. What does an e-mail link do?

   a. automatically sends you an e-mail message with the visitor's e-mail address as the reply-to field

   b. launches the default e-mail application for the visitor's browser with your e-mail address as the recipient

   c. displays your e-mail address so that the visitor can send you a message later

   d. links to your mail server

Fill in the Blank

11. The `<blockquote>` element is used to _____.

12. _____ can be used to display characters such as the copyright symbol.

13. The _____ is the preferred element to use when you need to emphasize text.

14. The _____ is used to place a nonbreaking space on a Web page.

Short Answer

15. Explain why it is good practice to place the e-mail address on the Web page and within the anchor tag when creating an e-mail link.

Apply Your Knowledge

1. **Predict the Result.** Draw and write a brief description of the Web page that will be created with the following XHTML code:

```
<?xml version="1.0" encoding="UTF-8"?>
<!DOCTYPE html PUBLIC "-//W3C//DTD XHTML 1.0 Transitional//EN"
    "http://www.w3.org/TR/xhtml1/DTD/xhtml1-transitional.dtd">
```

```
<html xmlns="http://www.w3.org/1999/xhtml">
<head>
<title>Predict the Result</title>
</head>
<body>
  <h1><em>Favorite Sites</em></h1>
  <ol>
    <li><a href="http://myspace.com">My Space</a></li>
    <li><a href="http://google.com">Google</a></li>
  </ol>
  <p><small>Copyright &copy; 2008 Your name here</small></p>
</body>
</html>
```

2. **Fill in the Missing Code.** This Web page should display a heading and a definition list, but some XHTML tags, indicated by < _> are missing. Fill in the missing code.

```
<?xml version="1.0" encoding="UTF-8"?>
<!DOCTYPE html PUBLIC "-//W3C//DTD XHTML 1.0 Transitional//EN"
   "http://www.w3.org/TR/xhtml1/DTD/xhtml1-transitional.dtd">
<html xmlns="http://www.w3.org/1999/xhtml">
<head>
<title>Door County Wild Flowers</title>
</head>
<body>
  < _>Door County Wild Flowers< _>
  <dl>
    <dt>Trillium< _>
      < _>This white flower blooms from April through June in
wooded areas.< _>
      < _>Lady Slipper< _>
      < _>This yellow orchid blooms in June in wooded areas.</dd>
    < _>
</body>
</html>
```

3. **Find the Error.** Why won't this page display in a browser?

```
<?xml version="1.0" encoding="UTF-8"?>
<!DOCTYPE html PUBLIC "-//W3C//DTD XHTML 1.0 Transitional//EN"
   "http://www.w3.org/TR/xhtml1/DTD/xhtml1-transitional.dtd">
<html xmlns="http://www.w3.org/1999/xhtml">
<head>
<title>Find the Error<title>
</head>
<body>
  <h1>Why don't I display?</h1>
</body>
</html>
```

Hands-On Exercises

1. Write the XHTML to display your name in the largest size heading element.

2. Write the XHTML to create an absolute link to a Web site whose domain name is yahoo.com.

3. Write the XHTML for an unordered list to display the days of the week.

4. Write the XHTML for an ordered list that uses uppercase letters to order the item. This ordered list will display the following terms: HTML, XML, and XHTML.

5. Think of a favorite quote by someone you admire. Write the XHTML code to display the person's name in a heading and the quote in a paragraph.

6. Modify the following code snippet to use logical style tags instead of physical style tags.

```
<p>A diagram of the organization of a web site is called a <b>site
map</b> or <b>storyboard</b>. <i>Creating the <b>site map</b> is
one of the initial steps in developing a web site.</i></p>
```

7. Create a Web page about your favorite movie. Include the name of the movie, the actors and actresses, a hyperlink to a Web site that displays a review of the movie, and a brief description of the movie. Use an unordered list to organize the names of the actors and actresses. Save the page as movie.html. Open your file in Notepad and print the source code for the page. Display your page in a browser and print the page. Hand in both printouts to your instructor.

8. Create a Web page that uses a definition list to display three network protocols (see Chapter 1) and their descriptions. Include a hyperlink to a Web site that provides information about the protocols. Add an appropriate heading to the page. Save the page as network.html. Open your file in Notepad and print the source code for the page. Display your page in a browser and print the page. Hand in both printouts to your instructor.

9. Create a Web page about your favorite musical group. Include the name of the group, the individuals in the group, a hyperlink to the group's Web site, your favorite three (or fewer if the group is new) CD releases, and a brief review of each CD.

- Use an unordered list to organize the names of the individuals.
- Use a definition list for the names of the CDs and your reviews.

Save the page as band.html. Open your file in Notepad and print the source code for the page. Display your page in a browser and print the page. Hand in both printouts to your instructor.

10. Create a Web page about your favorite recipe. Use an unordered list for the ingredients and an ordered list to describe the steps needed to prepare the food. Include a hyperlink to a Web site that offers free recipes. Save the page as recipe.html. Open your file in Notepad and print the source code for the page. Display your page in a browser and print the page. Hand in both printouts to your instructor.

Web Research

1. There are many HTML and XHTML tutorials on the Web. Use your favorite search engine to discover them. Choose two that are helpful. For each, print out the home page or other pertinent page and create a Web page that contains the answers to the following questions:

    a. What is the URL of the Web site?

    b. Is the tutorial geared toward the beginner level, intermediate level, or both levels?

    c. Would you recommend this site to others? Why or why not?

    d. List one or two concepts that you learned from this tutorial.

    Open your file in Notepad and print the source code for the page. (*Hint*: Select File, Print.) Display your page in a browser and print the page. Hand in both printouts to your instructor.

Focus on Web Design

1. You are learning the syntax of XHTML. However, coding alone does not make a Web page—design is very important. Surf the Web and find two Web pages—one that is appealing to you and one that is unappealing to you. Print each page. Create a Web page that answers the following questions for each of your examples.

    a. What is the URL of the Web site?

    b. Is the page appealing or unappealing? List three reasons for your answer.

    c. If the page is unappealing, what would you do to improve it?

    Open your file in Notepad and print the source code for the page. Display your page in a browser and print the page. Hand in both printouts to your instructor.

WEB SITE CASE STUDY

Each of the following case studies continues throughout most of the text. This chapter introduces each Web site scenario, presents the site map or storyboard, and directs you to create two pages for the site.

JavaJam Coffee House

Julio Perez is the owner of the JavaJam Coffee House, a gourmet coffee shop that serves snacks, coffee, tea, and soft drinks. Local folk music performances and poetry readings are held a few nights during the week. The customers of JavaJam are mainly college students and young professionals. Julio would like a Web presence for his shop that will display his services and provide a calendar for the performances. He would like a home page, menu page, music performance schedule page, and job opportunities page.

A site map for the JavaJam Coffee House Web site is shown in Figure 2.26.

The site map describes the architecture of the Web site, a Home page with three main content pages: Menu, Music, and Jobs.

Figure 2.26
JavaJam site map

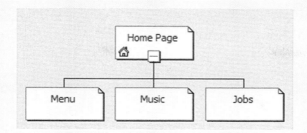

Figure 2.27 displays a sample layout for the pages. It contains a site logo, a navigation area, a content area, and a footer area for copyright information.

Figure 2.27
JavaJam page layout

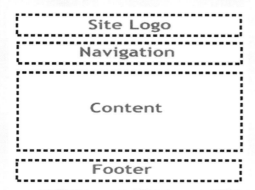

You have two tasks in this case study:

1. Create the Home page: index.html.
2. Create the Menu page: menu.html.

Hands-On Practice Case

Create a folder called javajam to contain your JavaJam Web site files.

1. **The Home Page.** You will use Notepad to create the Home page for the JavaJam Coffee House Web site. The Home page is shown in Figure 2.28.

Figure 2.28
JavaJam index.html

Launch Notepad and create a Web page with the following specifications:

- **Web page:** Use a descriptive page title—the company name is a good choice for a business Web site.
- **Logo area:** Use `<h1>` for the JavaJam Coffee House logo.
- **Navigation:** Place the following text within a paragraph:

  Home   Menu   Music   Jobs

  Code anchor tags so that Home links to index.html, Menu links to menu.html, Music links to music.html, and Jobs links to jobs.html.
- **Content:** Place the following content in an unordered list:

  Specialty Coffee and Teas

  Bagels, Muffins, and Organic Snacks

  Music and Poetry Readings

  Open Mic Night
- **Contact information:** Place the address and phone number information within a paragraph below the unordered list. *Hint*: Use line break tags to help you configure this area.

  12312 Main Street

  Mountain Home, CA 93923

  1-888-555-5555
- **Footer:** Place the following information in a small text size (use the `<small>` physical style element) and emphasized font style (use the `<em>` logical style element):

  Copyright © 2008 JavaJam Coffee House

  Place your name in an e-mail link on the line under the copyright information.

The page in Figure 2.28 may seem a little sparse, but don't worry, as you gain experience and learn to use more advanced techniques, your pages will look more professional. White space (blank space) on the page can be added with `<br />` tags where needed. Your page does not need to look exactly the same as the sample. Your goal at this point should be to practice and get comfortable using XHTML.

Save your page in the javajam folder and name it index.html.

2. **The Menu Page.** Create the Menu page shown in Figure 2.29. A productivity technique is to create new pages based on existing pages—so you can benefit from your previous work. Your new Menu page will use the index.html page as a starting point.

Open the index.html page for the JavaJam Web site in Notepad. Select File, Save As, and save the file with the new name of menu.html in the javajam folder. Now you are ready to edit the page.

- Modify the page title. Change the text contained between the `<title>` and `</title>` tags to JavaJam Coffee House Menu.
- Delete the unordered list and the contact information.
- Add the menu content to the page using a definition list. Use the `<dt>` element to contain each menu item name. Configure the menu item name to display in bold text (use the `<strong>` element). Use the `<dd>` element to contain the menu item description.

Figure 2.29
JavaJam menu.html

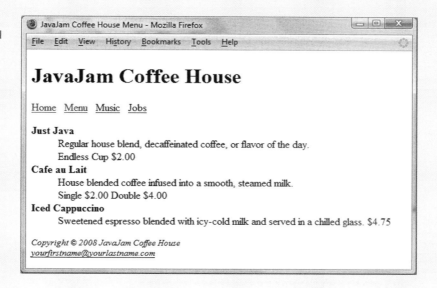

- The menu items names and descriptions are as follows:

Just Java
Regular house blend, decaffeinated coffee, or flavor of the day.
Endless Cup $2.00

Cafe au Lait
House blended coffee infused into a smooth, steamed milk.
Single $2.00 Double $4.00

Iced Cappuccino
Sweetened espresso blended with icy-cold milk and served in a chilled glass.
$4.75

Save your page and test it in a browser. Test the hyperlink from the menu.html page to index.html. Test the hyperlink from the index.html page to menu.html. If your links do not work, review your work with close attention to these details:

- Verify that you have saved the pages with the correct names in the correct folder.
- Verify your spelling of the page names in the anchor tags.
- After you make changes, test again.

Fish Creek Animal Hospital

Magda Patel is a veterinarian and owner of the Fish Creek Animal Hospital. Her customers are local pet owners who range in age from children to senior citizens. Magda would like a Web site to provide information to her current and potential customers. She has requested a home page, a services page, an ask the vet page, and a contact page.

A site map for the Fish Creek Animal Hospital Web site is shown in Figure 2.30.

The site map describes the architecture of the Web site, a Home page with three main content pages: Services, Ask the Vet, and Contact.

Figure 2.30
Fish Creek site map

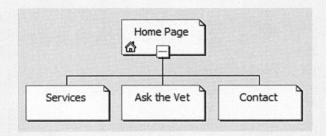

Figure 2.31 displays a sample page layout. It contains a site logo, a navigation area, a content area, and a footer area for copyright information.

Figure 2.31
Fish Creek page layout

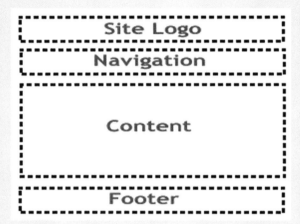

You have two tasks in this case study:

1. Create the Home page: index.html.
2. Create the Services page: services.html.

Hands-On Practice Case

Create a folder called fishcreek to contain your Fish Creek Web site files.

1. **The Home Page.** You will use Notepad to create the Home page for the Fish Creek Animal Hospital Web site. The Home page is shown in Figure 2.32.

   Launch Notepad and create a Web page with the following specifications:

   - **Web page:** Use a descriptive page title—the company name is a good choice for a business Web site.
   - **Logo area:** Use `<h1>` for the Fish Creek Animal Hospital logo.
   - **Navigation:** Place the following text using the `<strong>` logical style element within a paragraph:

     Home   Services   Ask the Vet   Contact

   Code anchor tags so that Home links to index.html, Services links to services.html, Ask the Vet links to askvet.html, and Contact links to contact.html.

Figure 2.32
Fish Creek
index.html

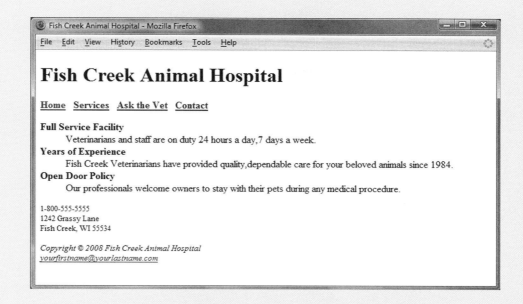

- **Content:** Place the following content in a definition list:

    Full Service Facility

    Veterinarians and staff are on duty 24 hours a day, 7 days a week.

    Years of Experience

    Fish Creek Veterinarians have provided quality, dependable care for your beloved animals since 1984.

    Open Door Policy

    Our professionals welcome owners to stay with their pets during any medical procedure.

- **Contact information:** Place the address and phone number information within a paragraph below the unordered list. *Hints*: Use line break tags to help you configure this area. The text size is configured with the `<small>` physical style element.

    1-800-555-5555

    1242 Grassy Lane

    Fish Creek, WI 55534

- **Footer:** Place the following information in a small text size (use the `<small>` physical style element) and emphasized font style (use the `<em>` logical style element):

    Copyright © 2008 Fish Creek Animal Hospital

    Place your name under the copyright information.

The page in Figure 2.32 may seem a little sparse, but don't worry, as you gain experience and learn to use more advanced techniques, your pages will look more professional. White space (blank space) on the page can be added with `<br />` tags where needed. Your page does not need to look exactly the same as the sample. Your goal at this point should be to practice and get comfortable using XHTML.

Save your page in the fishcreek folder and name it index.html.

2. **The Services Page.** Create the Services page shown in Figure 2.33. A productivity technique is to create new pages based on existing pages—so you can benefit from your previous work. Your new Services page will use the index.html page as a starting point.

Figure 2.33
Fish Creek
services.html

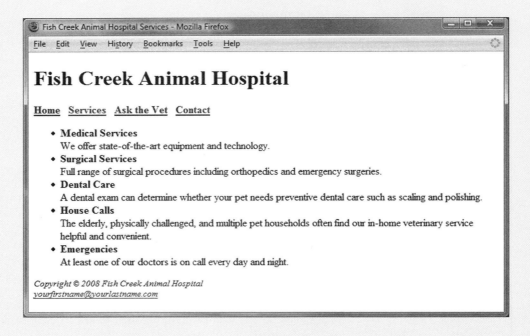

Open the index.html page for the Fish Creek Web site in Notepad. Select File, Save As, and save the file with the new name of services.html in the fishcreek folder. Now you are ready to edit the page.

- Modify the page title. Change the text contained between the `<title>` and `</title>` tags to Fish Creek Animal Hospital Services.

- Delete the definition list and the contact information.

- Add the services content to the page using an unordered list. Configure the name of each services category to be bold (use the `<strong>` logical style element). Code line breaks after each category name.

- The service categories and descriptions are as follows:

    Medical Services
    We offer state-of-the-art equipment and technology.

    Surgical Services
    Full range of surgical procedures including orthopedics and emergency surgeries.

    Dental Care
    A dental exam can determine whether your pet needs preventive dental care such as scaling and polishing.

    House Calls
    The elderly, physically challenged, and multiple pet households often find our in-home veterinary service helpful and convenient.

    Emergencies
    At least one of our doctors is on call every day and night.

Save your page and test it in a browser. Test the hyperlink from the services.html page to index.html. Test the hyperlink from the index.html page to services.html. If your links do not work, review your work with close attention to these details:

- Verify that you have saved the pages with the correct names in the correct folder.
- Verify your spelling of the page names in the anchor tags.
- After you make changes, test again.

Pete the Painter

Pete Johnson is an independent home painter and decorator. He would like to have a Web site to advertise his business. His clients are mainly homeowners in the middle-class suburbs of a large city. They range in age from thirties to fifties. Pete would like a site that contains a home page, a services page, a free estimates page, and a testimonial page.

A site map for the Pete the Painter Web site is shown in Figure 2.34.

Figure 2.34
Pete the Painter site map

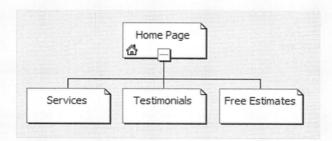

The site map describes the architecture of the Web site, a Home page with three main content pages: Services, Testimonials, and Free Estimates.

Figure 2.35 displays a sample page layout. It contains a site logo, a navigation area, a content area, and a footer area for copyright information.

You have two tasks in this case study:

1. Create the Home page: index.html.
2. Create the Services page: services.html.

Figure 2.35
Pete the Painter page layout

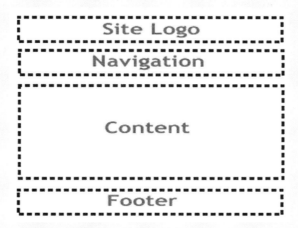

Hands-On Practice Case

Create a folder called painter to contain your Pete the Painter Web site files.

1. **The Home Page.** You will use Notepad to create the Home page for the Pete the Painter Web site. The Home page is shown in Figure 2.36.

Figure 2.36
Pete the Painter
index.html

Launch Notepad and create a Web page with the following specifications:

- **Web page:** Use a descriptive page title—the company name is a good choice for a business Web site.

- **Logo area:** Use <h1> for the Pete the Painter logo. The motto and phone number should be contained within an <h3> element. Emphasize the motto: Serving the Northwest Chicago Suburbs since 1986.

- **Navigation:** Place the following text using the <strong> logical style element within a paragraph:

    Home   Services   Testimonials   Free Estimate

    Code anchor tags so that Home links to index.html, Services links to services.html, Testimonials links to testimonials.html, and Free Estimate links to estimate.html.

- **Content:** Place this sentence in a paragraph: Pete's Design Specialists will work with you to create the home of your dreams.

    Place the following content in an unordered list:

    Interior Painting

    Exterior Painting

    Wallpaper Removal

    Wallpaper Installation

    Drywall

- **Footer:** Place the following information in a small text size (use the `<small>` physical style element) and emphasized font style (use the `<em>` logical style element):

    Copyright © 2008 Pete the Painter

    Place your name in an e-mail link on the line under the copyright information.

    The page in Figure 2.36 may seem a little sparse, but don't worry, as you gain experience and learn to use more advanced techniques, your pages will look more professional. White space (blank space) on the page can be added with `<br />` tags where needed. Your page does not need to look exactly the same as the sample. Your goal at this point should be to practice and get comfortable using XHTML.

    Save your page in the painter folder and name it index.html.

2. **The Services Page.** Create the Services page shown in Figure 2.37. A productivity technique is to create new pages based on existing pages—so you can benefit from your previous work. Your new Services page will use the index.html page as a starting point.

Figure 2.37
Pete the Painter
services.html

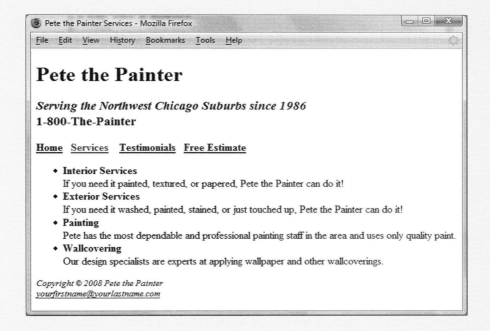

Open the index.html page for the Pete the Painter Web site in Notepad. Select File, Save As, and save the file with the new name of services.html in the painter folder. Now you are ready to edit the page.

- Modify the page title. Change the text contained between the `<title>` and `</title>` tags to Pete the Painter Services.
- Delete the content paragraph and unordered list.
- Add the services content to the page using an unordered list. Configure the name of each services category to be bold (use the `<strong>` logical style element). Code line breaks after each category name.

- The service categories and descriptions are as follows:

  Interior Services
  If you need it painted, textured, or papered, Pete the Painter can do it!

  Exterior Services
  If you need it washed, painted, stained, or just touched up, Pete the Painter can do it!

  Painting
  Pete has the most dependable and professional painting staff in the area and uses only quality paint.

  Wallcovering
  Our design specialists are experts at applying wallpaper and other wallcoverings

Save your page and test it in a browser. Test the hyperlink from the services.html page to index.html. Test the hyperlink from the index.html page to services.html. If your links do not work, review your work with close attention to these details:

- Verify that you have saved the pages with the correct names in the correct folder.
- Verify your spelling of the page names in the anchor tags.
- After you make changes, test again.

Prime Properties

Prime Properties is a small real estate company that specializes in residential properties. The owner, Maria Valdez, would like a Web site to showcase her listings and provide a point of contact for her clients, who are mainly middle-class working adults who are looking for a home in the northwest Chicago suburbs. Maria would like a home page, a listings page that contains information about her properties, a financing page, and a contact page.

A site map for the Prime Properties Web site is shown in Figure 2.38.

Figure 2.38
Prime Properties site map

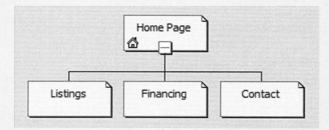

The site map describes the architecture of the Web site, a Home page with three main content pages: Listings, Financing, and Contact.

Figure 2.39 displays a sample page layout. It contains a site logo, a navigation area, a content area, and a footer area for copyright information.

You have two tasks in this case study:

1. Create the Home page: index.html.
2. Create the Financing page: financing.html.

Figure 2.39
Prime Properties
page layout

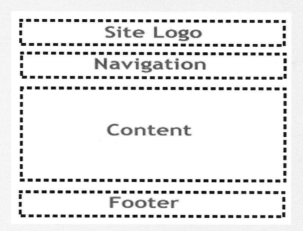

Hands-On Practice Case

Create a folder called prime to contain your Prime Properties Web page files.

1. **The Home Page.** You will use Notepad to create the Home page for the Prime Properties Web site. The Home page is shown in Figure 2.40.

Figure 2.40
Prime Properties
index.html

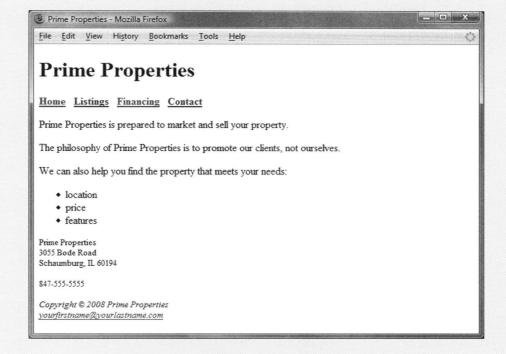

Launch Notepad and create a Web page with the following specifications:

- **Web page:** Use a descriptive page title—the company name is a good choice for a business Web site.

- **Logo area:** Use `<h1>` for the Prime Properties logo.

- **Navigation:** Configure the following text to display in bold font (use the `<strong>` logical style element) within a paragraph:

    Home   Listings   Financing   Contact

Code anchor tags so that Home links to index.html, Services links to services.html, Financing links to financing.html, and Contact links to contact.html.

- **Content:** Place each line of text shown below in its own paragraph.

  Prime Properties is prepared to market and sell your property.

  The philosophy of Prime Properties is to promote our clients, not ourselves.

  We can also help you find the property that meets your needs:

  Place the following content in an unordered list:

  location

  price

  features

- **Contact information:** The address and phone information should display in small text (use the `<small>` physical style element).

  Prime Properties

  3055 Bode Road

  Schaumburg, IL 60194

  847-555-5555

- **Footer:** Place the following information in a small text size and emphasized font style (use `<small>` and `<em>` elements):

  Copyright © 2008 Prime Properties

  Place your name in an e-mail link on the line under the copyright information.

The page in Figure 2.40 may seem a little sparse, but don't worry, as you gain experience and learn to use more advanced techniques, your pages will look more professional. White space (blank space) on the page can be added with `<br />` tags where needed. Your page does not need to look exactly the same as the sample. Your goal at this point should be to practice and get comfortable using XHTML.

Save your page in the prime folder and name it index.html.

2. **The Financing Page.** Create the Financing page shown in Figure 2.41. A productivity technique is to create new pages based on existing pages—so you can benefit from your previous work. Your new Financing page will use the index.html page as a starting point.

Open the index.html page for the Prime Properties Web site in Notepad. Select File, Save As, and save the file with the new name of financing.html in the prime folder. Now you are ready to edit the page.

- Modify the page title. Change the text contained between the `<title>` and `</title>` tags to Prime Properties :: Financing.

- Delete the content paragraphs, unordered list, and contact information.

- Add the financing content to the page.

  First, configure the following text in an `<h2>` element: Financing.

  Next, place the following sentence in a paragraph:

  We work with many area mortgage and finance companies.

  Finally, configure the following phrase with an `<h4>` element:

  Mortgage FAQs

Figure 2.41
Prime Properties
financing.html

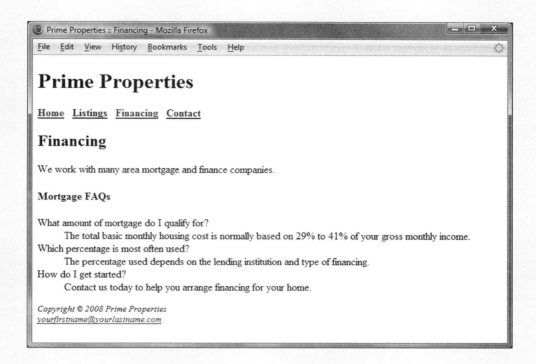

Use a definition list to configure the FAQs. Use `<dt>` elements for the questions and `<dd>` elements for the answers. The FAQ questions and answers are as follows:

> What amount of mortgage do I qualify for?
>
> The total basic monthly housing cost is normally based on 29% to 41% of your gross monthly income.
>
> Which percentage is most often used?
>
> The percentage used depends on the lending institution and type of financing.
>
> How do I get started?
>
> Contact us today to help you arrange financing for your home.

Save your page and test it in a browser. Test the hyperlink from the financing.html page to index.html. Test the hyperlink from the index.html page to financing.html. If your links do not work, review your work with close attention to these details:

- Verify that you have saved the pages with the correct names in the correct folder.
- Verify your spelling of the page names in the anchor tags.
- After you make changes, test again.

Configuring Color and Text with CSS

Chapter Objectives In this chapter, you will learn how to ...

- Describe the evolution of style sheets from print media to the Web
- List advantages of using Cascading Style Sheets
- Use color on Web pages
- Create style sheets that configure common color and text properties

- Apply inline styles
- Use embedded style sheets
- Use external style sheets
- Create CSS `class` and `id` selectors
- Validate CSS

Now that you have been introduced to XHTML, you are ready to explore **Cascading Style Sheets (CSS)**. CSS is not new—it was first proposed as a standard by the W3C in 1996. However, browsers and other user agents have only supported this technology consistently for the past few years. Now that there is fairly steady support, Web developers have begun to use CSS to separate the presentation style of a Web page from the information on the Web page itself. CSS is used to configure text, color, and page layout.

This chapter introduces you to the use of CSS on the Web as you explore configuring color and text.

3.1 Overview of Cascading Style Sheets

For years, style sheets have been used in desktop publishing to apply typographical styles and spacing instructions to printed media. CSS provides this functionality (and much more) for Web developers. It allows Web developers to apply typographic styles (typeface, font size, and so on) and page layout instructions to a Web page. The CSS Zen Garden, http://www.csszengarden.com, exemplifies the power and flexibility of CSS. Visit this site for an example of CSS in action. Notice how the content looks dramatically different depending on the design (CSS style rules) you select. Although the designs on CSS Zen Garden are created by CSS masters, at some point these designers were just like you—starting out with CSS basics.

CSS is a flexible, cross-platform, standards-based language developed by the W3C. Its description of CSS can be found at http://www.w3.org/Style/. Be aware that CSS, even though it has been in use for many years, is still considered an emerging technology and the two most popular browsers do not support it in exactly the same way. There are CSS reference pages at http://web.archive.org/web/20040202153928/http://devedge. netscape.com/library/xref/2003/css-support/css1/mastergrid.html and http://www. westciv.com/style_master/academy/browser_support that list the way styles are supported by various browsers and platforms. This chapter concentrates on those aspects of CSS that are well supported by popular browsers.

Advantages of Cascading Style Sheets

There are several advantages to using CSS:

- **Typography and page layout can be better controlled.** These features include font size, line spacing, letter spacing, indents, margins, and element positioning.
- **Style is separate from structure.** The format of the text and colors used on the page can be configured and stored separately from the body section of the Web page document.
- **Styles can be stored.** You can store styles in a separate document and associate them with the Web page. When the styles are modified, the XHTML remains intact. This means that if your client decides to change the background color from red to white you only need to change one file that contains the styles, instead of each Web page document.
- **Documents are potentially smaller.** The formatting is separate from the document; therefore, the actual documents should be smaller.
- **Site maintenance is easier.** Again, if the styles need to be changed it's possible to complete the modifications by changing the style sheet only.

Do you see that there might be advantages to using CSS? You may be wondering if there are any disadvantages to using CSS. In fact, there is one large disadvantage—CSS technology is not yet uniformly supported by browsers. This disadvantage will be less of an issue in the future as browsers comply with standards.

Types of Cascading Style Sheets

There are four methods used to incorporate CSS technology in a Web site: inline, embedded, external, and imported.

- **Inline styles** are coded in the body of the Web page as an attribute of an XHTML tag. The style only applies to the specific element that contains it as an attribute.
- **Embedded styles** are defined in the header of a Web page. These style instructions apply to the entire Web page document.
- **External styles** are coded in a separate text file. This text file is associated with the Web page by using a `<link />` element in the header section.
- **Imported styles** are similar to external styles in that they can connect styles coded in a separate text file with a Web page document. An external style sheet can be imported into embedded styles or into another external style sheet by using the @import directive. The @import directive is only supported by version 5.0 and later browsers. This chapter concentrates on the other three uses of CSS.

Introduction to CSS Syntax

Style sheets are composed of rules that describe the styling to be applied. Each **rule** contains a **selector** and a **declaration**. The selector can be an XHTML element, a class name (that you create yourself), or an id name (that you create yourself). This example concentrates on applying styles to XHTML elements. The declaration is the **property** you are setting (such as color or typeface) and the value you are assigning to it.

For example, the CSS rule shown in Figure 3.1 would set the color of the text used on a Web page to blue. The selector is the XHTML body tag and the declaration sets the `color` **property** to the value of blue.

Figure 3.1
Using CSS to set the text color to blue

If you wanted the background color of the Web page to be yellow, the CSS rule could be expanded as follows:

```
body { color: blue; background-color: yellow; }
```

This could also be written using hexadecimal color values as follows:

```
body { color: #0000FF; background-color: #FFFF00; }
```

Notice that both the `background-color` and text `color` properties were configured in the previous example. To avoid surprising results caused by default browser colors, the W3C recommends that the **background-color** property is set when the text color is configured.

Have you ever wondered why some text-based links are not underlined? This can be accomplished with a style applied to the anchor tag. The following style rule selects the anchor tag (denoted by a) and sets the **text-decoration** property (the underline) to none:

```
a { text-decoration: none }
```

You might be asking yourself how you would know what properties and values are allowed to be used. This chapter introduces you to some of the CSS properties commonly used to configure color and text. Table 3.1 presents a summary of the CSS properties used in this chapter. Appendix C, CSS Property Reference, contains a more detailed list. In the next sections, we'll take a look at how color is used on Web pages and we'll explore how to use CSS to configure color.

Table 3.1 CSS properties used in this chapter

Property	Description	Values
background-color	Background color on the Web page	Any valid color
color	Text color	Any valid color
font-family	Name of a font or font family	Any valid font or a font family such as `serif`, `sans-serif`, `fantasy`, `monospace`, or `cursive`
font-size	The size of the text font	This varies; `pt` (standard font point sizes), `px` (pixels), the unit `em` (which corresponds to the width of the capital M of the current font), or percentages; the text values `xx-small`, `small`, `medium`, `large`, `x-large`, and `xx-large` are also valid
font-style	The style of the font	`normal`, `italic`, `oblique`
font-weight	The "boldness" or weight of the font	This varies; the text values `normal`, **`bold`**, **`bolder`**, and `lighter` can be used; the numeric values `100`, `200`, `300`, `400`, `500`, `600`, `700`, `800`, and `900` can be used
line-height	The spacing allowed for the line of text	It is most common to use a percentage for this value; for example, a value of 200% would be double-spaced
margin	Shorthand notation to configure the margin surrounding an element	A numeric value (**`px`** or **`em`**); for example, `body { margin: 0px}` will set the page margins in the document to zero
margin-left	Configures the space in the left margin of the element	A numeric value (**`px`** or **`em`**) or `auto`
margin-right	Configures the space in the right margin of the element	A numeric value (**`px`** or **`em`**) or `auto`
text-align	The alignment of text	`center`, `justify`, `left`, `right`
text-decoration	Determines whether text is underlined; this style is most often applied to hyperlinks	The value **`none`** will cause a hyperlink not to be underlined in a browser that normally processes in this manner
width	The width of an element	A numeric value (**`px`** or **`em`**), numeric percentage, or `auto` (default)

3.2 Using Color on Web Pages

Monitors display color as a combination of different intensities of red, green, and blue, also known as **RGB color**. RGB intensity values are numerical from 0 to 255. Each

RGB color will have three values, one each for red, green, and blue. These are always listed in that order (red, green, blue) and specify the numerical value of each color used. For example, the RGB values for red are (255,0,0)—all red, no green and no blue. The RGB values for blue are (0,0,255)—no red, no green, and all blue. These colors can also be specified using hexadecimal values.

Hexadecimal is the name for the Base 16 numbering system, which uses the characters 0, 1, 2, 3, 4, 5, 6, 7, 8, 9, A, B, C, D, E, and F to specify numeric values. When a hexadecimal value is used to specify RGB color, the numeric value pairs range from 00 to FF (0 to 255 in Base 10). The hexadecimal value contains three numeric value pairs written sequentially as one number. Each pair is associated with the amount of red, green, and blue displayed. Using this notation, the color red would be specified as `#FF0000` and the color blue as `#0000FF`. The # symbol signifies that the value is in hexadecimal. You can use either uppercase or lowercase letters in **hexadecimal color values**–`#FF0000` and `#ff0000` both configure the color red.

Don't worry—you won't need to do calculations to work with Web colors. Just become familiar with the numbering scheme. See Figure 3.2 (shown also in the color insert section) for an excerpt from the color chart at http://webdevfoundations.net/color.

Figure 3.2
Partial color chart

#FFFFFF	#FFFFCC	#FFFF99	#FFFF66	#FFFF33	#FFFF00
#FFCCFF	#FFCCCC	#FFCC99	#FFCC66	#FFCC33	#FFCC00
#FF99FF	#FF99CC	#FF9999	#FF9966	#FF9933	#FF9900

See the center color insert

Take a few moments to examine the color chart. You will observe a display of colors and their associated hexadecimal RGB values in hexadecimal. You may notice that there is a pattern to the hexadecimal numbers (pairs of 00, 33, 66, 99, CC, or FF). This pattern signifies a color on the **Web Safe Color Palette** (more on this later). As you examine the color chart further, you will see a list of colors using color names. Some Web developers find it easier to use the color names. However, the names are not uniformly supported by all versions of all browsers, so the W3C recommends using numeric color values instead of color names.

Web Color Palette

A Web developer usually has no way of knowing what type of computer or browser the Web site visitors will be using. The various operating systems and browsers display colors differently, and sometimes not at all. The Web Safe Color Palette, also known as the Web Color Palette, is a collection of 216 colors that display the same on both the Windows and Mac OS platforms. It is easy to tell if a color is on the Web Color Palette when you consider the individual hexadecimal RGB value pairs. The values of 00, 33, 66, 99, CC, and FF are the only values for hexadecimal RGB value pairs on the Web Color Palette. Take another look at the color chart at http://webdevfoundations.net/color and note that all the colors listed by RGB follow this numbering scheme—they comprise the Web Color Palette. See Figure 3.3 (shown also in the color insert section) for a comparison of a Web Safe Color, `#CC0000`, and a non-Web safe color, `#880000`. Both are a shade of red; however, the Web safe color will display predictably across

Figure 3.3
Web safe colors
display predictably

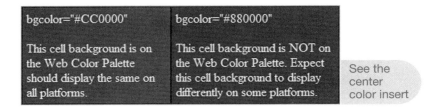

Windows and Mac OS platforms and the other color will not. Using Web safe colors has become less important now that most monitors display billions of colors. The Web Color Palette is rather limited and it is common for today's Web designers to choose colors creatively rather than select them from the Web Color Palette.

Making Color Choices

You may be wondering how to select colors to display on Web pages. One easy way to choose colors is to use a monochromatic color scheme—all shades or tints of the same color. Try the Color Blender at http://meyerweb.com/eric/tools/color-blend to select colors for a monochromatic color scheme. Another way to create a color scheme is to base it on a photograph or image. Visit http://www.colr.org to generate a color scheme based on an image from the Web or one that you upload. If you have a favorite color and would like to create a color scheme around it, visit one of the following sites that suggest color schemes:

- http://colorsontheweb.com/colorwizard.asp
- http://kuler.Adobe.com
- http://www.steeldolphin.com/color_scheme.html
- http://wellstyled.com/tools/colorscheme2/index-en.html
- http://www.colors4webmasters.com/safecolor/index.htm

Accessibility and Color

Focus on Accessibility

While using color can help you create a compelling Web page, keep in mind that not all your visitors will see or be able to distinguish between colors. Some visitors will use a screen reader and will not experience your colors, so your information must be clearly conveyed even if colors cannot be viewed. Other visitors may be challenged with color vision deficiency (color blindness) and will not see the colors as you intended. According to Vischeck (http://www.vischeck.com/vischeck/) about 1 out of 20 people experience some type of color deficiency. To increase Web page accessibility, choose background and text colors with a high amount of contrast. The choice of colors is important—avoid using red, green, brown, gray, or purple next to each other. White, black, and shades of blue and yellow are easier for individuals with color vision deficiencies to differentiate. Visit http://www.vischeck.com/vischeck/vischeckURL.php to simulate how a person with a color deficiency experiences the colors on a Web page. Using color on Web pages will be revisited in Chapter 5, Web Design.

3.3 Configuring Color with Inline CSS

Now that you are aware of how color on Web pages is specified and where to get ideas for color schemes on Web pages, let's start configuring color with inline styles. **Inline styles** are coded as attributes on XHTML tags.

The Style Attribute

The **style** attribute is used with the value of the style rule declaration you need to set. Recall that a declaration consists of a property and a value. Each property is separated from its value with a colon (:). The following code will set the text color of an `<h1>` tag to a shade of red:

```
<h1 style="color:#cc0000">This is displayed as a red heading</h1>
```

If there is more than one property, they are separated by a semicolon (;). The following code sets the text in the heading to red and italic:

```
<h1 style="color:#cc0000;background-color:#cccccc">This is displayed
as a red heading on a gray background</h1>
```

The following code example uses an inline style to set the background color to green and text color to white:

```
<p style="background-color:green;color:white">This paragraph is using
an inline style.</p>
```

Are there different ways to configure colors using CSS?

CSS syntax allows you to configure colors in a number of ways, including hexadecimal color values, color names, and decimal color values. For example, Table 3.2 shows the syntax for setting the color of text in a paragraph to red.

The examples in this book use either hexadecimal color value or color name to configure colors using CSS. The color chart on this textbook's companion Web site at http://webdevfoundations.net/color provides examples of the color created by hexadecimal values in the Web Color Palette.

Table 3.2 Syntax for setting the color of text in a paragraph to red

CSS Syntax	Color Type
`p { color: red }`	Color name
`p { color: #FF0000 }`	Hexadecimal color value
`p { color: #F00 }`	Shorthand hexadecimal (one character for each hexadecimal pair)
`p { color: rgb(255,0,0) }`	Decimal color value (RGB triplet)

HANDS-ON PRACTICE 3.1

By now you are aware that the best way to learn new coding technologies is to practice them. In this Hands-On Practice you will configure a paragraph using inline styles. The styles will specify a green background with white text. A sample is shown in Figure 3.4.

Figure 3.4
Web page using inline styles

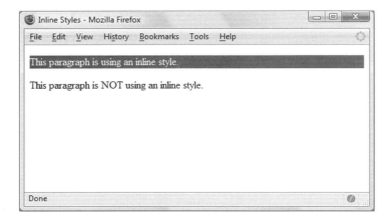

Launch Notepad and type in the following XHTML:

```
<?xml version="1.0" encoding="UTF-8"?>
<!DOCTYPE html PUBLIC "-//W3C//DTD XHTML 1.0 Transitional//EN"
  "http://www.w3.org/TR/xhtml1/DTD/xhtml1-transitional.dtd">
<html xmlns="http://www.w3.org/1999/xhtml">
<head>
<title>Inline Styles</title>
</head>
<body>
<p style="background-color:#00FF00;color:#FFFFFF">This paragraph is
using an inline style.</p>
<p>This paragraph is NOT using an inline style.</p>
</body>
</html>
```

Save your file as inline.html. Test your page in a browser and compare it with Figure 3.4. The student files contain a sample solution at Chapter3/inline.html. Note that the paragraph that used a style has the green background and white text. The paragraph that does not use a style is displayed using default browser settings.

3.4 Configuring Color with Embedded Styles

In the previous Hands-On Practice you added inline styles for one of the paragraphs. You needed to code a style attribute on the paragraph element. But what if you needed to configure the styles for ten or twenty paragraphs instead of just one. Using inline styles, you might be doing a lot of repetitive coding! While inline styles apply to one XHTML element, embedded styles apply to an entire Web page.

The Style Element

Embedded styles are placed within a **`<style>` element** located in the header section of a Web page. The opening `<style>` tag begins the embedded style rules and the closing `</style>` tag ends the area containing embedded style rules. When using the `<style>` tag, you do not need the `style` attribute. However, the `<style>` tag does use a **type attribute** that should have the value of `"text/css"`.

The following code is an example of a `<style>` tag that uses embedded styles to set the text color and background color of the page.

```
<style type="text/css">
body {  background-color: #000000;
        color: #FFFFFF;
}
</style>
```

The indentation is not required for the styles to work, but it makes the styles more readable and easier to maintain than one long row of text. The styles are in effect for the entire Web page document because they were applied to the `<body>` tag using the body selector.

HANDS-ON PRACTICE 3.2

Now let's see a working example. Launch Notepad and open the starter.html file from the Chapter3 folder in the student files.

Save your page as embedded.html and test it in a browser. Your page should look similar to the one shown in Figure 3.5.

Figure 3.5
The Web page without any styles

Open the file in Notepad and view the source code. Notice that the XHTML code uses the `<h1>`, `<h2>`, `<p>`, `<ul>`, and `<li>` elements. In this Hands-On Practice you'll code embedded styles to configure selected background and text colors. You'll use the `body` selector to configure the default background color (`#E6E6FA`) and default text color (`#191970`) for the entire page. You'll also use the `h1` and `h2` selectors to configure different background and text colors for the heading areas.

Edit the embedded.html page in Notepad and add the following code below `<title>` element in the head section of the Web page.

```
<style type="text/css">
body {  background-color: #E6E6FA;
        color: #191970;
}
h1 {  background-color: #191970;
      color: #E6E6FA;
}
h2 {  background-color: #AEAED4;
      color: #191970;
}
</style>
```

Save and test your file in a browser. Figure 3.6 (shown also in the color insert section) displays the Web page along with color swatches. The monochromatic color scheme was chosen using the Color Blender at http://meyerweb.com/eric/tools/color-blend. Notice how the repetition of a limited number of colors adds interest and unifies the design of the Web page.

Figure 3.6
embedded.html with
styles applied

See the
center
color insert

View the source code for embedded.html and review the CSS and XHTML code. Note that all the styles were located in a single place on the Web page. Since embedded styles are coded in a specific location, they are easier to maintain over time than inline styles. Also notice that you only needed to code the styles for the h2 selector once (in the head section) and *both* of the <h2> XHTML elements applied the h2 style. This is more efficient than coding the same inline style on each <h2> element.

FAQ

My CSS doesn't work, what can I do?

Coding CSS is a detail-oriented process. There are several common errors that can cause the browser not to apply CSS correctly to a Web page. With a careful review of your code and the following tips, you should get your CSS working:

- Verify that you are using the : and ; symbols in the right spots—they are easy to confuse. The : should separate the properties from their values, the ; should be placed between each *property:value* configuration.

- Check that you are not using = signs instead of : between each property and its value.

- Verify that the { and } symbols are properly placed around the style rules for each selector.

- Check the syntax of your selectors, their properties, and property values for correct usage.

- If part of your CSS works, and part doesn't—read through the CSS and check to determine the first rule that is not applied. Often the error is in the rule above the rule that is not applied.

- Use a program to check your CSS code. The W3C has a free CSS code validator at http://jigsaw.w3.org/css-validator. The W3C's CSS validator can help you find syntax errors. See Section 3.9 for an overview of how to use this tool to validate your CSS.

CHECKPOINT 3.1

1. List three reasons to use CSS on a Web page.

2. When designing a page that uses colors other than the default colors for text and background, explain why it is a good reason to configure both properties: text color and background color.

3. Describe one advantage to using embedded styles instead of inline styles.

3.5 Configuring Text with CSS

In Chapter 2 you discovered how to use XHTML to configure some characteristics of text on Web pages, including logical style tags (such as the <strong> element) and physical style tags (such as the <small> element). You've also already configured text color using the CSS color property. In this section you'll learn how to use CSS to configure additional characteristics of text, including font typeface, font weight, font style, and font size. Using CSS to configure text is more flexible (especially when using an external style sheet as you'll discover later in the chapter) than using XHTML elements and is the method preferred by today's Web developers.

CSS and Fonts

Let's take a closer look at the CSS properties useful for configuring fonts: `font-weight`, `font-style`, `font-size`, and `font-family`.

The **font-weight** property configures the boldness of the text. You can use either numeric values (`100`, `200`, `300`, `400`, `500`, `600`, `700`, `800`, and `900`) or text values (including `normal` (default), `bold`, `bolder`, and `lighter`). Configuring the CSS rule `font-weight:bold` has a similar effect as the `<strong>` or `<b>` XHTML element.

The **font-style** property typically is used to configure text displayed in italics (the same visual effect as an `<i>` or `<em>` XHTML element). The `font-style` property values are `normal` (default), `italic`, and `oblique`.

The **font-size** property sets the size of the font. There are a wide variety of text and numeric values. Text values for `font-size` include `xx-small`, `x-small`, `small`, `medium` (default), `large`, `x-large`, and `xx-large`. Valid numeric values include units of `px` (**pixels**), `pt` (standard font **point** sizes), percentage values, and `em`. Figure 3.7 demonstrates examples of text with various `font-size` configurations displayed in the Firefox browser on a monitor set to 1440×900 screen resolution. Compare font sizes on your own computer— launch a browser and view chapter3/fonts.html in the student files.

Figure 3.7
A sampling of CSS font-size values

Text Values	Em Units	Px Units	Pt Units	Percentage
xx-small	.5 em	10 px	6 pt	50%
x-small	.60 em	11 px	8 pt	60%
small	.75 em	13 px	10 pt	75%
medium	1 em	16 px	12 pt	100%
x-large	1.5 em	24 px	18 pt	150%
xx-large	2 em	28 px	24 pt	200%

Be aware that the text values and the `pt` (**point**) unit size are browser dependent. For example, text configured with the CSS rule `font-size: 12pt` may look different when various browsers are used to display Web pages. The `px` (pixel) unit is monitor resolution dependent and looks different depending on the screen resolution used. The **em unit** is a relative font unit that has its roots in the print industry. Recall that printers used to set type manually with blocks of characters. An em unit is the width of a square block of type (typically the uppercase M) for a particular font and type size. On Web pages an em unit corresponds to the width of the font and size used in the parent element (typically the body element). With this in mind, the size of an em unit is relative to the font typeface and default size. Percentage values work in a similar manner to em units. For example, font-size: 100% and font-size: 1em should render the same in a browser.

Focus on Accessibility

With all these available choices, what's the best way to configure font-sizes? The W3C recommends the use of em units or percentages in their specification for CSS2 at http://www.w3.org/TR/REC-CSS2/fonts.html. So, usually the best choice is either em units or percentages. However, the W3C's Web Accessibility Initiative WCAG 1.0 lists the use of relative font size values such as em units and percentages to be a Priority 2 level guideline (a "should" not a "must"). In addition, modern browsers such as

Firefox and Opera allow visitors to increase (or "zoom") the text size on the page easily even if nonrelative units, such as px, are used to configure font size. Expect to see more browser support of page customization and zoom features in the future. For certain graphic-dependent designs that require "pixel-perfect" rendering, px units might be more appropriate than em units or percentages— it's up to you to choose. As you work through the Hands-On Practice and Case Study exercises in this book, you'll gain experience using a variety of font-size configurations. In all cases, it is crucial to test your Web pages in a variety of client platforms (including browser and monitor resolution). This testing is part of the Web design and development process. Statistics available at http://thecounter.com indicate that at the time this was written Internet Explorer at 1028×768 or 1280×1024 resolution is most commonly used, although use of the Firefox browser continues to grow.

The **font-family** property configures font typefaces. A Web browser displays text using the fonts that have been installed on the user's computer. For example, the CSS rule font-family: Arial causes the browser to display text using Arial instead of the default browser font. When a font is specified that is not installed on the Web visitor's computer, the default font is substituted. Times New Roman is the default font displayed by most Web browsers. You can list multiple fonts and categories for the value of the font face attribute. The browser will attempt to use the fonts in the order listed. When processing a CSS rule such as font-family: Arial, Verdana, sans-serif, the browser will use Arial if it is installed. If Arial is not installed, the browser will use Verdana if it is installed. If neither Arial nor Verdana are installed, the browser will use any sans-serif font installed on the computer. Finally, if no sans-serif fonts are installed on the computer, the default font face will be used. Table 3.3 shows font family categories and some common font typefaces.

Table 3.3 Common fonts

Font-family Category	Font Typeface
serif	Times New Roman, Georgia, Times
sans-serif	Arial, Verdana, Geneva
monospace	Courier New, Lucida Console
cursive	Brush Script MT, Comic Sans MS
fantasy	Jokerman, Curlz MT

Now that you are familiar with font configuration using CSS, we'll quickly explore three other CSS properties that modify the appearance of text: text-align, text-decoration, and line-height.

As you already know, the default alignment of text on a Web page is at the left margin, called left alignment. The **text-align property** is used to specify the alignment of text. Values for the text-align property are left (default), right, and center.

Have you ever seen a hyperlink on a Web page that was not underlined? This is typically configured with the **text-decoration property** (text-decoration: none CSS rule). See Table 3.1 for additional values that are less commonly used with the text-decoration property.

The **line-height property** modifies the default height of a line of text. For example, code `line-height: 200%` to configure text to appear double-spaced.

HANDS-ON PRACTICE 3.3

Now that you've got a collection of new CSS properties for font and text configuration, let's try them out and modify the embedded.html page. Launch Notepad and open embedded.html. You'll code additional CSS style rules to configure the text on the page. When complete, your Web page will look similar to the one shown in Figure 3.8.

Figure 3.8
CSS configures the text on the Web page

Set Default Font Properties for the Page

As you have already seen, CSS rules applied to the `body` selector apply to the entire page. Modify the CSS for the `body` selector to display most text using a sans-serif font. The new font typeface style rule will apply to the entire Web page unless more specific styles rules are applied to a selector (such as `h1` or `p`), a class, or an id (more on classes and ids later).

```
body {  background-color: #E6E6FA;
        color: #191970;
        font-family: Arial, Verdana, sans-serif;
}
```

Save your page as embedded2.html and test it in a browser. Your page should look similar to the one shown in Figure 3.9. Notice that just a single line of CSS changed the font typeface of all the text on the page!

Figure 3.9
Text is displayed using a sans-serif font

Configure the `h1` Selector

You will configure the `line-height` and `font-family` CSS properties. Set the `line-height` property to 200%—this will add a bit of empty space above and below the heading text. (In Chapter 6 you'll explore other CSS properties, such as the margin, border, and padding that are more commonly used to configure space surrounding an element.) Next, modify the `h1` selector to use a serif font. When a font name contains spaces, type quotes as indicated in the code below. While it is generally recognized that blocks of text using sans-serif fonts are easier to read, it is common to use a serif font to configure page or section headings.

```
h1 {  background-color: #191970;
      color: #E6E6FA;
      line-height: 200%;
      font-family: Georgia, "Times New Roman", serif;
}
```

Save and test your page in a browser. If you notice that the Trillium Media Design text seems to crowd the left margin, add a ` ` nonbreaking space special character in the body of the Web page after the opening `<h1>` tag.

Configure the `h2` Selector

Configure the CSS rule to use the same font typeface as the `h1` selector.

```
h2 {  background-color: #AEAED4;
      color: #191970;
      font-family: Georgia, "Times New Roman", serif;
}
```

Add a New Paragraph Element Selector

Configure text in paragraphs to display just slightly smaller than the default text size. Use the `font-size` property set to `.90em`.

```
p { font-size: .90em; }
```

Configure the Unordered List

Configure the text displayed in the unordered list to be bold.

```
ul { font-weight: bold; }
```

Save your page as embedded2.html and test it in a browser. Your page should look similar to the one shown in Figure 3.8. The student files contain a sample solution at Chapter3/embedded2.html. CSS is quite powerful—just a few lines of code significantly changed the appearance of the Web page. You may be wondering if even more customization is possible. For example, what if you did not want all the paragraphs to display in exactly the same way? While you could add inline styles to the Web page code, that's usually not the most efficient technique. The next section introduces the CSS `class` and `id` selectors, which are widely utilized to configure specific page elements.

FAQ | **Is there a quick way to apply the same styles to more than one XHTML tag or more than one class?**

Yes, you can apply the same style rules to multiple selectors (such as XHTML elements, `class`es, or `id`s) by listing the selectors in front of the rule. The code sample below shows the `font-size` of `1em` being applied to both the paragraph and line item elements.

```
p, li { font-size: 1em; }
```

3.6 The `Class` and `Id` Selectors

The `class` Selector

There are times when you'd like to apply a CSS rule to a certain class of elements on a Web page and not necessarily tie the style to a particular XHTML tag. This is when you use the **class** selector. For example, perhaps you would prefer if the paragraph containing the navigation area information in embedded.2html was displayed with large, bold text. When setting a style for a class, configure the class name as the selector. Place a dot or period (.) in front of the class name in the style sheet. The following code configures a class called `nav` in a style sheet.

```
nav {  font-weight: bold;
       font-size: 1.25em;
}
```

The styles set in the `nav` class can be applied to any XHTML element you wish. You do this by using the **`class` attribute**, such as `class="nav"`. Do not write the dot in front of the class value in the XHTML tag where the class is being applied. The following code will apply the `nav` class styles to a `<p>` element:

```
<p class="nav">This paragraph will be displayed using the styles in
the nav class.</p>
```

FAQ

Why is the class called `nav`?

You can choose almost any name you wish for a CSS class. However, CSS class names are more flexible and easier to maintain over time if they are descriptive of the structure rather than of specific formatting. For example, a class name of `largeBold` would no longer be meaningful if the design was changed to display the area differently; but a structural class name such as `nav`, `logo`, `footer`, `content`, or `subheading` is meaningful regardless of how the area is configured. Here are more hints for class names:

- Use short but descriptive names.
- Avoid class names that are the same as XHTML element names—they could be confusing to anyone working on the page.
- Both letters and numbers may be used.
- Avoid spaces in class names.
- Class names are not case sensitive, but consistency will make page maintenance easier.

A final tip about CSS classes is to be wary of "classitis"— that is, creating a brand new class each time you need to configure text a bit differently. Decide ahead of time how you will configure page areas, code your classes, and apply them. The result will be a more cohesive and better organized Web page.

The `Id` Selector

Use an **`id` selector** instead of a `class` selector if you plan to identify and apply a CSS rule uniquely to a single area on a Web page. For example, perhaps you would prefer if the paragraph containing the copyright information in the page footer area of embedded2.html was displayed with small italics text. While a `class` selector could be used, an `id` selector is more appropriate if your page layout contains a single footer area. For example, you can create a style for an `id` named `footer` to configure the footer area to use small, italicized text. When setting a style for an `id`, place a hash mark (#) in front of the `id` name in the style sheet. The following code will configure an `id` called new in a style sheet:

```
#footer {  font-size: .75em;
           font-style: italic;
}
```

The styles set in the `footer` id can be applied to any XHTML element you wish by using the **`id` attribute**, `id="footer"`. Do not write the # in front of the class value in the XHTML tag.

The following code will apply the `footer` id styles to a `<p>` tag:

```
<p id="footer">This paragraph will be displayed using styles
configured in the footer id.</p>
```

Using CSS with an `id` selector is similar to using CSS with a `class` selector. It's common practice to use an `id` selector to refer to a *single* XHTML element and a `class` selector to refer to multiple XHTML elements.

HANDS-ON PRACTICE 3.4

In this Hands-On Practice you will modify the CSS and the XHTML in the Trillium Technologies page—configuring the navigation and page footer areas. Launch Notepad and open embedded2.html.

Configure the Navigation Area

The navigation links would be more prominent if they displayed in a larger and bolder font. Create a class named nav, which sets the `font-size` and `font-weight` properties. The code follows:

```
.nav { font-weight: bold;
       font-size: 1.25em;
}
```

Modify the opening paragraph tag of the navigation area. Add a `class` attribute that associates the paragraph with the nav class as follows:

```
<p class="nav"><a href="index.html">Home</a>
<a href="services.html">Services</a>
<a href="contact.html">Contact</a></p>
```

Configure the Footer Area

Create an `id` named `footer`, which sets the `font-size` and `font-style` properties.

```
#footer { font-size: .75em;
          font-style: italic;
}
```

Modify the opening paragraph tag of the `footer` area. Add an `id` attribute that associates the paragraph with the `id` class.

```
<p id="footer">Copyright &copy; 2007 Your Name Here</p>
```

Save your file embedded3.html and test it in a browser. Your page should look similar to the image shown in Figure 3.10. The student files contain a sample solution at Chapter3/embedded3.html. Notice how the `class` and `id` styles are applied.

Figure 3.10
Using classes and ids

3.7 The `Div` and `Span` XHTML Elements

The **`<div>`** and **`<span>`** XHTML elements are used along with CSS to format page areas. The block-level `<div>` element configures a section or division on a Web page with a line break above and below. Use the `<div>` tag when you need to format a section that is separated from the rest of the Web page by line breaks. The `<div>` element is also useful to define a section that contains block-level elements, such as `<p>`, `<blockquote>`, `<ul>`, `<ol>`, and even other `<div>` elements within it. In Chapter 6 you will see how `<div>` elements are used to configure a page layout with CSS.

In contrast, the `<span>` element defines a section on a Web page that is *not* physically separated from other areas by line breaks. Use the `<span>` tag if you need to format an area that is contained within another, such as within a `<p>`, `<blockquote>`, `<li>`, or `<div>` element.

HANDS-ON PRACTICE 3.5

You will experiment with the `<div>` and `<span>` elements in this Hands-On Practice. First, you will place the navigation area within a `<div>` element. Next, you will configure a new class to format the company name when displayed within the text on the page and use the `<span>` element to apply this class. Open the embedded3.html file in Notepad. Your Web page will look similar to the one shown in Figure 3.11 after the changes are complete.

Configure the Navigation Area

View the source code of embedded3.html and notice that the hyperlinks (anchor elements) in the navigation area are contained within a paragraph element. While this is valid XHTML, it isn't the best choice *semantically* since the navigation is a list of hyperlinks and not a true paragraph of text. Replace the <p> tags with <div> tags as follows:

```
<div class="nav"><a href="index.html">Home</a>
<a href="services.html">Services</a>
<a href="contact.html">Contact</a></div>
```

Save your file as embedded4.html and test in a browser. You'll notice that the navigation area does not look any different— however, "under the hood" the code is better semantically (see Chapter 7 for more information about this topic).

Configure the Company Name

View Figure 3.11 and notice that the company name, Trillium Technologies, is displayed in bold and serif font within the first paragraph. You'll code both CSS and XHTML to accomplish this. First, create a new CSS rule that configures a class called companyname as bold, serif font, and 1.25em in size. The code follows:

```
.companyname {  font-weight: bold;
                font-family: Georgia, "Times New Roman", serif;
                font-size: 1.25em;
}
```

Next, modify the beginning of the first paragraph of XHTML to use the <span> element to apply the class as follows:

```
<p><span class="companyname">Trillium Media Design</span> will bring
```

Save your file and test in a browser. Your page should look similar to the one shown in Figure 3.11. The student files contain a sample solution at Chapter3/embedded4.html.

Figure 3.11
This Web page uses
<div> and <span>
elements

3.8 Using External Style Sheets

External style sheets are contained in a text file separate from the XHTML documents. The `<link />` element is a self-contained tag used in the header section of an XHTML document to associate the style sheet with the Web page. This allows multiple Web pages to link to the same external style sheet file. The external style sheet text file is saved with the file extension .css and contains style rules only—it does not contain any XHTML tags.

The advantage of this technique is that styles are configured in a single file. This means that when styles need to be modified only one file needs to be changed, instead of multiple Web pages. On large sites this can save a Web developer much time and increase productivity. Let's get some practice with this useful technique.

HANDS-ON PRACTICE 3.6

Launch Notepad and type in the style rules to set the `background-color` of a page to blue and the text to white. Save it as color.css. The code is as follows:

```
body {  background-color: #0000FF;
        color: #FFFFFF;
}
```

Figure 3.12 shows the external color.css style sheet displayed in Notepad. Notice that there is no XHTML in this file. `<style>` tags are not coded within an external style sheet. Only CSS rules (selectors, properties, and values) are coded in an external style sheet.

Figure 3.12
The external style sheet `color.css`

Next, associate that style to a Web page using the `<link />` element in the header section of the page. Three attributes are used with the `<link />` element to associate a Web page with an external style sheet: `rel`, `href`, and `type`. The value of the **rel attribute** is `stylesheet`. The value of the `href` attribute is the name of the style sheet file. The value of the `type` attribute is `text/css`, which is the MIME type for a style sheet. The XHTML code to link color.css to a Web page is as follows:

```
<link rel="stylesheet" href="color.css" type="text/css" />
```

Ready to try it out? Launch Notepad and type in the following XHTML:

```
<?xml version="1.0" encoding="UTF-8"?>
<!DOCTYPE html PUBLIC "-//W3C//DTD XHTML 1.0 Transitional//EN"
  "http://www.w3.org/TR/xhtml1/DTD/xhtml1-transitional.dtd">
```

```
<html xmlns="http://www.w3.org/1999/xhtml">
<head>
<title>External Styles</title>
   <link rel="stylesheet" href="color.css" type="text/css" />
</head>
<body>
   <p>This web page uses an external style sheet.</p>
</body>
</html>
```

Save the file as external.html in the same folder as color.css. Test your page in a browser. Your file should look similar to Figure 3.13.

Figure 3.13
This page is associated with an external style sheet

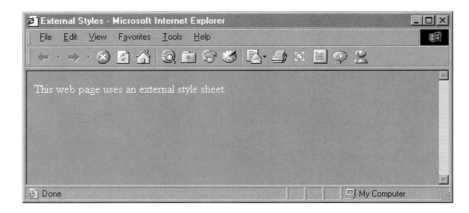

The color.css style sheet can be associated with any number of Web pages. If you ever need to change the style of formatting, you only need to change a single file (color.css) instead of multiple files (all the Web pages). As mentioned earlier, this technique can boost productivity on a large site.

This is a simple example, but the advantage of having only a single file to update is significant for both small and large Web sites. In the next Hands-On Practice you'll modify the Trillium Technologies home page to use an external style sheet.

HANDS-ON PRACTICE 3.7

In this Hands-On Practice you continue to gain experience using external style sheets as you create the external style sheet file named trillium.css, modify the Trillium Technologies home page to use external styles instead of embedded styles, and associate a second Web page with the trillium.css style sheet.

A version of the Trillium home page is in the student files. Open the embedded4.html file in a browser. The display should be the same as the Web page shown in Figure 3.11 from Hands-On Practice 3.5.

Now that you've seen what you're working with let's begin. Launch Notepad and save the file as index.html in a folder called trillium. You are ready to convert the embedded

CSS to external CSS. Select the CSS rules (all the lines of code between, but not including, the opening and closing `<style>` tags). Use Edit, Copy or press the `Ctrl`+`C` keys to copy the CSS code to the clipboard. You will place the CSS in a new file. Launch Notepad, paste the CSS style rules (use Edit, Paste or press the `Ctrl`+`V` keys), and save the file as trillium.css. See Figure 3.14 for a screenshot of the new trillium.css file in Notepad. Notice that there are no XHTML elements in trillium.css— not even the `<style>` element. The file contains CSS rules only.

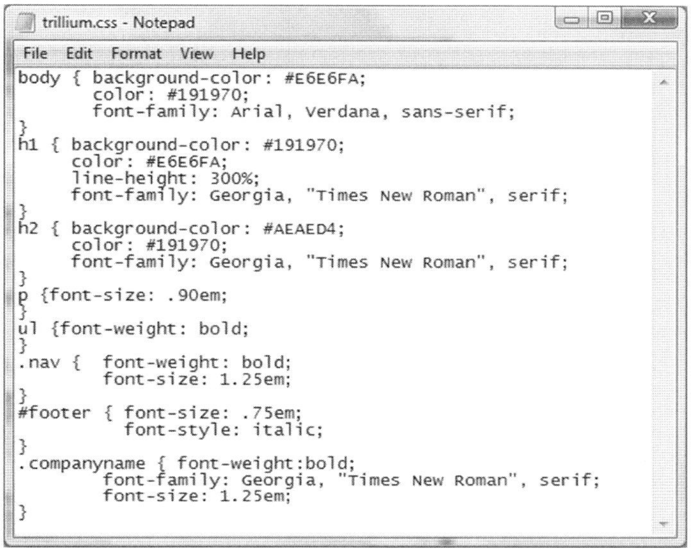

Figure 3.14
The external style sheet named trillium.css

Next, edit the index.html file in Notepad. Delete the CSS code you just copied. Delete the closing `</style>` tag. Replace the opening `<style>` tag with a `<link>` element to associate the style sheet named `trillium.css`. The `<link>` element code follows:

```
<link href="trillium.css" rel="stylesheet" type="text/css" />
```

Save the file and test in a browser. Your Web page should look just like the one shown in Figure 3.11. Although it looks the same, the difference is in the code—the page now uses external instead of embedded CSS.

Now, for the fun part—you'll associate a second page with the style sheet. The student files contain a services.html page for Trillium at Chapter3/services.html. When you display this page in a browser it should look similar to the one shown in Figure 3.15. Notice that although the structure of the page is similar to the home page, the styling of the text and colors are absent.

Launch Notepad to edit the services.html file. If you view the XHTML code you'll notice that this page is ready for our trillium.css styles—for example, the `nav` class and `footer` id have been coded as attributes in the corresponding navigation and page footer areas. All that's left for you to do is to code an XHTML `<link>` element to associate the services.html Web page with the trillium.css external style sheet. Place the following code in the header section above the closing `</head>` tag:

```
<link href="trillium.css" rel="stylesheet" type="text/css" />
```

Save your file and test in a browser. Your page should look similar to Figure 3.16—the CSS rules have been applied!

Figure 3.15
The services.html page is not associated with a style sheet

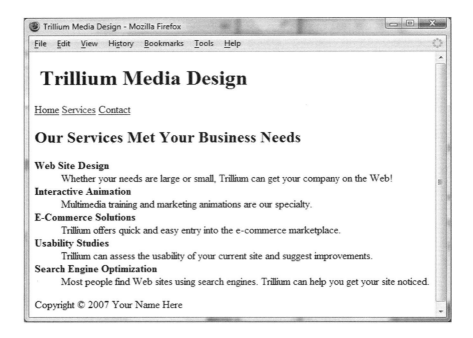

Figure 3.16
The services.html page has been associated with trillium.css

If you click the Home and Services hyperlinks, you can move back and forth between the index.html and services.html pages in the browser. The student files contain a sample solution in the Chapter3/3.7 folder.

Notice that when using an external style sheet, if the use of color or fonts on the page ever needs to be changed, modifications only need to be made to the external style sheet. Think about how this can improve productivity on a site with many pages. Instead of modifying hundreds of pages to make a color or font change, only a single file—the CSS external style sheet— needs to be updated. Becoming comfortable with CSS and other technologies such as Extensible Style Sheet Language (XSL) will be important as you develop your skills and increase your technical expertise.

CHECKPOINT 3.2

1. Describe a reason to use embedded styles. Explain where embedded styles are placed on a Web page.

2. Describe a reason to use external styles. Explain where external styles are placed and how Web pages indicate they are using external styles.

3. Write the code to configure a Web page to associate with an external style sheet called `mystyles.css`.

When designing a new Web page or Web site, how do I begin to work with CSS?

The following guidelines can be helpful when configuring a page using CSS:

- Review the design of the page—check if common fonts are used. Define global properties (the default for the entire page) for characteristics such as fonts and colors attached to the `body` selector.

- Identify typical elements used for organization in the page (such as `<h1>`, `<h3>`, and so on) and declare style rules for these if different from default.

- Identify various page areas such as logo, navigation, footer, and so on—and list any special configurations needed for these areas. You may decide to configure classes or ids in your CSS to configure these areas.

- Create one prototype page that contains most of the elements you plan to use and test. Revise your CSS as needed.

- Plan and test. These are important activities when designing a Web site.

3.9 Centering XHTML Elements with CSS

Recall that by default, XHTML elements are left-aligned— they begin at the left margin. In Chapter 2 (Hands-On Practice 2.4) you used the XHTML `align="center"` attribute to center text on a Web page. While this is valid, it is more efficient to configure the alignment using CSS. The CSS `text-align` property configures the alignment of text. The CSS code sample below configures an `<h1>` XHTML element to have centered text.

```
h1 { text-align:center;
}
```

While it can be quite effective to center the text displayed in Web page headings, be careful about centering text in paragraphs. According to WebAIM (http://www.webaim .org/techniques/textlayout), studies have shown that centered text is more difficult to read than left-aligned text.

Center the Page Content

A popular page layout design that is easy to accomplish with just a few lines of CSS is to center the entire content of a Web page within a browser window. The Web page shown in Figure 3.17 uses this type of page layout.

Figure 3.17
The Web page content is centered in the browser window

Compare the left and right margins of Figure 3.17 to the Web page displayed in Figure 3.11. It's easy to configure this centered layout. Create a <div> to contain, or wrap, the page content and then configure it with the CSS **margin-left** property, **margin-right** property, and **width** property. As will be discussed further in Chapter 6, the margin is the empty space surrounding an element. In the case of the body element, the margin is the empty space between the page content and the edges of the browser window. As you might expect, the `margin-left` and `margin-right` properties configure the space in the left and right margins. The margins can be set to 0, pixel units, em units, percentages, or `auto`. When `margin-left` and `margin-right` are both set to `auto`, the browser calculates the amount of space available and divides it evenly between the left and right margins. The `width` property configures the width of a block-level element. The CSS code sample below sets the width of an `id` named `wrapper` to 700 pixels and centered (using `margin-left:auto` and `margin-right:auto`).

```
#wrapper { width: 700px;
        margin-left: auto;
        margin-right: auto;
}
```

The XHTML code follows:

```
<body>
  <div id="wrapper">
  ... page content goes here
  </div>
</body>
```

HANDS-ON PRACTICE 3.8

In this Hands-On Practice you will code CSS properties to configure a centered page layout. We'll use the files from Hands-On Practice 3.7 as a starting point. Create a new folder called trillium2. Locate the Chapter3/3.7 folder in the student files. Copy the index.html, services.html, and trillium.css files to your trillium2 folder. Open the trillium.css file in a text editor. Create an id named `container`. Add the `margin-left`, `margin-right`, and `width` style properties to the style rules as follows:

```
#container { margin-left: auto;
          margin-right: auto;
          width:80%;
}
```

Save the file.

Open the index.html file in a text editor. Add the XHTML code to configure a `<div>` assigned to the id `container` that "wraps" or contains the code within the body section. Save the file. When you test your index.html file in a browser, it should look similar to the one shown in Figure 3.17. The student files contain a sample solution in the Chapter3/3.8 folder.

3.10 CSS Validation

The W3C has a free Markup Validation Service (http://jigsaw.w3.org/css-validator/) that will validate your CSS code and check it for syntax errors. **CSS validation** provides students with quick self-assessment—you can prove that your code uses correct syntax. In the working world, CSS validation serves as a quality assurance tool. Invalid code may cause browsers to render the pages slower than otherwise.

HANDS-ON PRACTICE 3.9

In this Hands-On Practice you will use the W3C CSS Validation Service to validate an external CSS style sheet. This example uses the color.css file completed in Hands-On Practice 3.6 (student files Chapter3/color.css). Locate color.css and open it in Notepad.

We will add an error to the color.css file. Find the `body` selector style rule and delete the first "r" in the `background-color` property. Remove the `#` from the `color` property value. Save the file.

Next, attempt to validate the color.css file. Visit the W3C CSS Validation Service page at http://jigsaw.w3.org/css-validator/ and select the "by File Upload" tab. Click the Browse button and select the color.css file from your computer. Click the Check button. Your display should be similar to that shown in Figure 3.18. Notice that two errors were found. The selector is listed followed by the reason an error was noted.

Figure 3.18
The validation results indicate errors

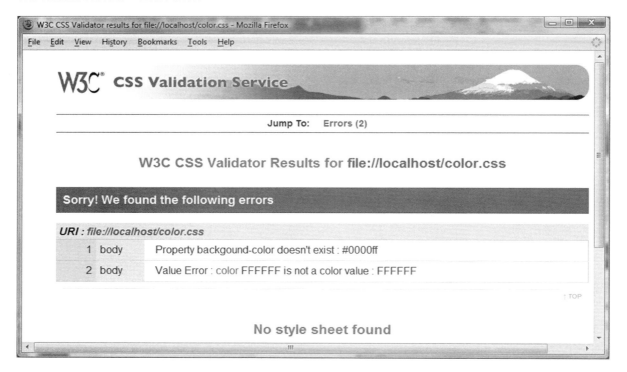

Notice that the first message indicates that the "backgound-color" property does not exist. This is a clue to check the syntax of the property name. Edit color.css and correct the error. Test and revalidate your page. Your browser should now look similar to the one shown in Figure 3.19 and report only one error.

The error reminds you that FFFFFF is not a color value and expects you to already know that you need to add a "#" character to code a valid color value, #FFFFFF. Notice how any valid CSS rules are displayed below the error messages. Correct the color value, save the file, and test again.

Your results should look similar to those shown in Figure 3.20. There are no errors listed. The Valid CSS Information contains all the CSS style rules in color.css. This means your file passed the CSS validation test. Congratulations, your color.css file is valid CSS syntax! It's a good practice to validate your CSS style rules. The CSS validator can help you to identify code that needs to be corrected quickly and indicate which style rules a browser is likely to consider valid. Validating CSS is one of the many productivity techniques that Web developers commonly use.

Figure 3.19
The valid CSS is displayed below the errors (and warnings, if any)

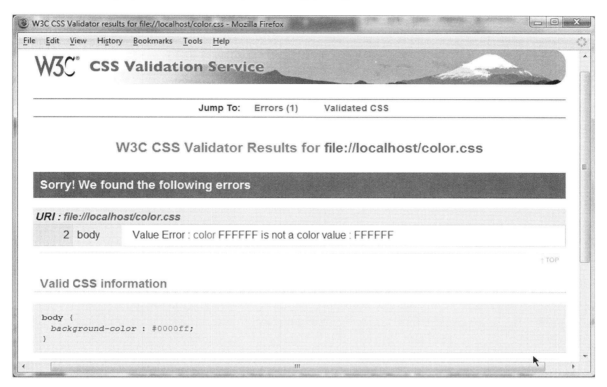

Figure 3.20
The CSS is valid!

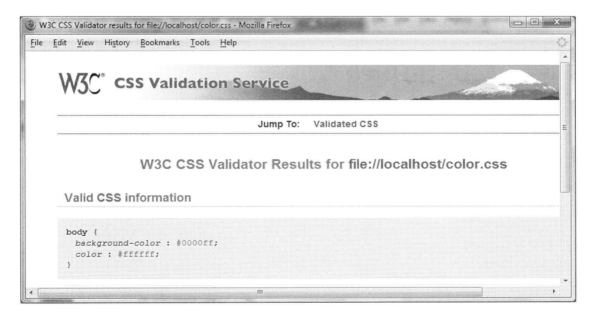

CHAPTER SUMMARY

This chapter introduced Cascading Style Sheet rules associated with color and text on Web pages. There is much more that you can do with CSS: positioning, hiding and showing page areas, formatting margins, and formatting borders. As you continue your study of Web development with this textbook, you will study these additional uses. To learn more about CSS, check out the tutorials at http://echoecho.com/css.htm and http://www.mako4css.com, or visit the W3C site for official specifications.

Visit the textbook Web site at http://www.webdevfoundations.net for examples, the links listed in this chapter, and updated information.

Key Terms

`<div>`	external styles	pixels
`<link />`	`font-family` property	point
`<span>`	`font-size` property	property
`<style>`	`font-style` property	rel attribute
`background-color` property	`font-weight` property	RGB color
Cascading Style Sheets (CSS)	hexadecimal color values	rule
class attribute	id attribute	selector
class selector	id selector	style attribute
color property	imported styles	`text-align` property
CSS validation	inline styles	`text-decoration` property
declaration	`line-height` property	type attribute
em unit	`margin-left` property	Web Safe Color Palette
embedded styles	`margin-right` property	`width` property

Review Questions

Multiple Choice

1. Which type of CSS is coded in the body of the Web page as an attribute of an XHTML tag?
   a. embedded
   b. inline
   c. external
   d. imported

2. Which of the following describe two components of CSS rules?
   a. selectors and declarations
   b. properties and declarations
   c. selectors and attributes
   d. none of the above

3. Which of the following can be a CSS selector?
   a. an XHTML element
   b. a class name
   c. an id name
   d. all of the above

4. Which of the following is the declaration property used to set the background color of a Web page?
   a. `bgcolor`
   b. `background-color`
   c. `color`
   d. none of the above

5. Which of the following do you configure to apply a style to a certain group of elements on a Web page?

   a. group
   b. id
   c. class
   d. none of the above

6. Which of the following is the declaration property used to set the font typeface for an area of a Web page?

   a. `font-face`
   b. `face`
   c. `font-family`
   d. `size`

7. Which of the following is the file extension for an external style sheet?

   a. ess
   b. css
   c. htm
   d. no file extension is necessary

8. Which of the following is the element used to associate a Web page with an external style sheet?

   a. `<target>`
   b. `<a>`
   c. `<include>`
   d. `<link />`

9. Which of the following configures a background color of `#FFF8DC` for a Web page using CSS?

   a. `body { background-color: #FFF8DC; }`
   b. `document { background: #FFF8DC; }`
   c. `body { background: #FFF8DC'}`
   d. none of the above

10. Which of the following configures a class called special with red text, 24px, and Arial or a sans-serif font using CSS?

    a. `special {  color: red;`
    `          font-size: 24px;`
    `          font-family: Arial,`
    `             sans-serif;}`

    b. `.special {  color: red;`
    `          font-size: 24px;`
    `          font-family: Arial,`
    `             sans-serif;}`

    c. `.special {  text: red;`
    `          font-size: 24px;`
    `          font-family: Arial,`
    `             sans-serif;}`

    d. `.#special { text: red;`
    `          font-size: 24px;`
    `          font-family: Arial,`
    `             sans-serif;}`

Fill in the Blank

11. The _____ element is useful for creating logical areas on a Web page that are embedded within paragraphs or other block formatting elements.

12. CSS is a technology that is _____ supported by browsers.

13. The _____ CSS property can be used to center text on a Web page.

14. The _____ element is useful for creating areas on a Web page that are physically separated from other areas.

15. CSS was first proposed as a standard by the W3C in _____.

Apply Your Knowledge

1. **Predict the Result.** Draw and write a brief description of the Web page that will be created with the following XHTML code:

```
<?xml version="1.0" encoding="UTF-8"?>
<!DOCTYPE html PUBLIC "-//W3C//DTD XHTML 1.0 Transitional//EN"
   "http://www.w3.org/TR/xhtml1/DTD/xhtml1-transitional.dtd">
<html xmlns="http://www.w3.org/1999/xhtml">
<head>
<title>Predict the Result</title>
<style type="text/css">
```

```
body {    background-color: #000066;
          color: #CCCCCC;
          font-family: Arial,sans-serif;
          font-size: 12px;
}
h1 {    background-color: #FFFFFF;
        color: #000066;
        font-size: 20px;
}
.footer {  font-size: 10px;
           font-style: italic;
}
</style>
</head>
<body>
   <div align="center">
      <h1>Trillium Media Design</h1>
      <br />
      <p>Home <a href="about.html">About</a>
        <a href="services.html">Services</a>
      </p>
   </div>
<p>Our professional staff takes pride in its working relationship
with our clients by offering personalized services that listen to
their needs, develop their target areas, and incorporate these
items into a well presented Web site that works.</p>
<p> </p>
<p> </p>
   <div align="center">
   <p class="footer">Contact <a
     href="mailto:web@trilliumtechnologies.com">
     web@trilliumtechnologies.com</a><br />
   Copyright &copy; 2008 Trillium Media Design</p>
   </div>
</body>
</html>
```

2. **Fill in the Missing Code.** This Web page should be configured so that the background and text colors have good contrast. The <h2> tag should use Arial. Some CSS properties and values, indicated by " _ " (underscore), are missing. Some XHTML tags, indicated by < _ >, are missing. Fill in the missing code.

```
<?xml version="1.0" encoding="UTF-8"?>
<!DOCTYPE html PUBLIC "-//W3C//DTD XHTML 1.0 Transitional//EN"
   "http://www.w3.org/TR/xhtml1/DTD/xhtml1-transitional.dtd">
<html xmlns="http://www.w3.org/1999/xhtml">
<head>
<title>Trillium Media Design</title>
<style type="text/css">
body {  background-color: #0066CC;
        color: "_";
}
```

```
h2 { "_": "_"
}
<_>
<_>
<body>
  <h2>Trillium Media Design</h2>
  <p> Our professional staff takes pride in its working
relationship with our clients by offering personalized services
that listen to their needs, develop their target areas, and
incorporate these items into a well presented Web site that works.
  </p>
</body>
</html>
```

3. Find the Error. Why won't this page display properly in a browser?

```
<?xml version="1.0" encoding="UTF-8"?>
<!DOCTYPE html PUBLIC "-//W3C//DTD XHTML 1.0 Transitional//EN"
   "http://www.w3.org/TR/xhtml1/DTD/xhtml1-transitional.dtd">
<html xmlns="http://www.w3.org/1999/xhtml">
<head>
<title>Trillium Media Design</title>
<style type="text/css">
body {  background-color: #000066;
        color: #CCCCCC;
        font-family: Arial,sans-serif;
        font-size: 12px
}
<style>
</head>
<body>
  <h2>Trillium Media Design</h2>
  <p> Our professional staff takes pride in its working
relationship with our clients by offering personalized services
that listen to their needs, develop their target areas, and
incorporate these items into a well presented Web site that works.
  </p>
</body>
</html>
```

Hands-On Exercises

1. Write the XHTML for a large heading that uses inline styles to configure the background color of red and the text color of white.

2. Write the XHTML and CSS code for an embedded style sheet that configures a background color of white and a text color of green.

3. Write the CSS code for an external style sheet that configures the text to be brown, 14 px in size, and in Arial, Verdana, or a sans-serif font.

4. Write the XHTML and CSS code for an embedded style sheet that configures a class called new, that is bold and italic.

5. Write the XHTML and CSS code for an embedded style sheet that configures links without underlines; background color of white; text color of black; is in Arial, Helvetica, or a sans-serif font; and has a class called new that is bold and italic.

6. Write the CSS code for an external style sheet that configures a page background color of #FFF8DC; has a text color of #000099; is in Arial, Helvetica, or a sans-serif font; and has an id called new that is bold and italic.

7. **Practice with External Style Sheets.** In this exercise you will create two external style sheet files and a Web page. You will experiment with linking the Web page to the external style sheets and note how the display of the page is changed.

   a. Create an external style sheet (call it format1.css) to format as follows: document background color of white, document text color of #000099, and document font family of Arial, Helvetica, or sans-serif. Hyperlinks should have a background color of gray (#CCCCCC). <h1> elements should use the Times New Roman font with red text color.

   b. Create an external style sheet (call it format2.css) to format as follows: document background color of yellow, document text color of green. Hyperlinks should have a background color of white. <h1> elements should use the Times New Roman font with white background color and green text color.

   c. Create a Web page about your favorite movie that displays the movie name in an <h1> tag, a description of the movie in a paragraph, and an unordered (bulleted) list of the main actors and actresses in the movie. The page should also have a hyperlink to a Web site about the movie. Place an e-mail link to yourself on the Web page. This page should be associated with the format1.css file. Save the page as moviecss1.html. Be sure to test your page in more than one browser. Hand in printouts of format1.css, the movieccs1.html source code (print in Notepad), and the browser display of your moviecss1.html to your instructor.

   d. Modify the moviecss1.html page to link to the format2.css external style sheet instead of the format1.css file. Save the page as moviecss2.html and test it in a browser. Notice how different the page looks! Hand in printouts of format2.css, the moviecss2.html source code (print in Notepad), and the browser display of your moviecss2.html.

8. **Practice with the Cascade.** In this exercise you will create two Web pages that link to the same external style sheet. After modifying the configuration in the external style sheet, you will test your pages again and find that they automatically pick up the new style configuration. Finally, you will add an inline style to one of the pages and find that it takes effect and overrides the external style.

   a. Create a Web page that includes an unordered list describing at least three advantages of using CSS. The text CSS Advantages should be contained within <h1> tags. This page should include a hyperlink to the W3C Web site. Write the XHTML code so that one of the advantages is configured to be a class called news. Place an e-mail link to yourself on the Web page. The Web page should use the external style sheet called ex3.css. Save the page as advantage.html.

   b. Create a Web page that includes an unordered list describing at least three disadvantages of utilizing Cascading Style Sheets. The text CSS Disadvantages should be contained within <h1> tags. This page should include a hyperlink to the W3C Web site. Write the XHTML code so that one of the disadvantages is configured to be a class called news. Place an e-mail link to yourself on the Web page. The Web page should use the external style sheet called ex3.css. Save the page as disadvantage.html.

c. Create an external style sheet (call it ex3.css) to format as follows: document background color of white, document text color of #000099 and document font family of Arial, Helvetica, or sans-serif. Hyperlinks should have a background color of gray (#CCCCCC). <h1> elements should use the Times New Roman font with black text color. The news class should use red italic text.

d. Launch a browser and test your work. Display the advantage.html page. It should use the formatting configured in ex3.css. Modify the Web page and/or the css file until your page displays as requested. Display the disadvantage.html page. It should also use the formatting configured in the ex3.css file. Create printouts of ex3.css, advantage.html, disadvantage.html source code (print in Notepad), the browser display of advantage.html, and the browser display of disadvantage.html. Label these printouts Exercise 8d.

e. Change the configuration of the external style sheet (ex3.css) to use a document background color of black, document text color of white, and <h1> text color of gray (#CCCCCC). Save the file. Launch a browser and test the advantage.html and disadvantage.html pages. Notice how they each pick up the styles from the external style sheet. Create printouts of the advantage.html and disadvantage.html browser display and label them Exercise 8e.

f. Modify the advantage.html file to use an inline style. The inline style should be applied to the <h1> tag and configure it to have red text. Save the advantage.html page and test in a browser. Notice how the <h1> text color specified in the style sheet is overridden by the inline style. Print the browser display of advantage.html and label it Exercise 8f.

9. **Practice Validating CSS.** Choose a CSS external style sheet file to validate—perhaps you have created one for your own Web site. Otherwise, use an external style sheet file that you worked with in this chapter. Use the W3C free CSS validator. Visit http://jigsaw.w3.org/css-validator/. If your CSS does not immediately pass the validation test, modify it and test again. Repeat this process until the W3C validates your CSS code. Write a one or two paragraph summary about the validation process. Answer the following questions. Was it easy to use? Did anything surprise you? Did you encounter a number of errors or just a few? How easy was it to determine how to correct the CSS file? Would you recommend this to other students? Why or why not?

Web Research

1. This chapter introduced you to using CSS to configure Web pages. Use a search engine to search for CSS resources. The following resources can help you get started:

   - http://www.w3.org/Style/CSS/
   - http://positioniseverything.net
   - http://www.dezwozhere.com/links.html
   - http://www.westciv.com/style_master/academy/browser_support

Create a Web page that provides a list of at least five CSS resources on the Web. For each CSS resource provide the URL, Web site name, and a brief description. Your Web page should contain a table and use color. Place your name in the e-mail address at the bottom of the Web page. Print the source code (from Notepad) and the browser view of your Web page.

2. There is still much for you to learn about CSS. A great place to learn about Web technology is the Web itself. Use a search engine to search for CSS tutorials. The following resources can help you get started:

- http://www.echoecho.com/css.htm
- http://www.mako4css.com
- http://www.htmlgoodies.com/beyond/css.html

Choose a tutorial that is easy to read. Select a section that discusses a CSS technique that was not covered in this chapter. Create a Web page that uses this new technique. The Web page should provide the URL of your tutorial, the name of the Web site, and a description of the new technique you discovered. Place your name in the e-mail address at the bottom of the Web page. Print the external style sheet (if you used one), the Web page source code (from Notepad), and the browser view of your Web page.

Focus on Web Design

In this chapter you learned how to configure color and text with CSS. In this activity you will design a color scheme, code an external CSS file for the color scheme, and code an example Web page that applies the styles you configured. Use any of the following sites to help you get started with color and Web design ideas:

Psychology of Color

- http://www.infoplease.com/spot/colors1.html
- http://coe.sdsu.edu/eet/Articles/wadecolor/start.htm
- http://iit.bloomu.edu/vthc/Design/psychology.htm
- http://www.my-photoshop.com/bydesign/id-tutorials/color-psychology.html

Color Theory

- http://www.colormatters.com/colortheory.html
- http://colortheory.liquisoft.com/
- http://www.digital-web.com/articles/color_theory_for_the_colorblind/

Color Scheme Generators

- http://meyerweb.com/eric/tools/color-blend
- http://colorschemer.com/schemes/
- http://www.colr.org
- http://colorsontheweb.com/colorwizard.asp
- http://www.steeldolphin.com/color_scheme.html
- http://wellstyled.com/tools/colorscheme2/index-en.html

You have the following tasks:

    a. Design a color scheme. List three hexadecimal color values (in addition to white (#FFFFFF) or black (#000000) in your design.

    b. Describe the process you went through as you selected the colors. Describe why you chose these colors. What type of Web site would they be appropriate for? List the URLs of any resources you used.

    c. Create an external CSS file name color1.css that configures font properties, text color, and background color selections for the document, h1 selector, p selector, and footer class using the colors you have chosen.

    d. Create a Web page named color1.html that shows examples of the CSS style rules.

Open your files in Notepad and print the source code for color1.css and color1.html. Display your page in a browser; print the page. Hand in all printouts to your instructor.

WEB SITE CASE STUDY:
Implementing CSS

Each of the following case studies continues throughout most of the text. This chapter implements CSS in the Web sites.

JavaJam Coffee House

See Chapter 2 for an introduction to the JavaJam Coffee House Case Study. Figure 2.26 shows a site map for the JavaJam Web site. The Home page and Menu page were created in Chapter 2. You will use the existing Web site as a start while you create a new version that uses an external style sheet to configure text and color.

You have the following tasks:

    1. Create an external style sheet named javajam.css that configures the color and text for the JavaJam Web site.

    2. Modify the Home page to utilize an external style sheet to configure colors and fonts. The new Home page and color swatches are shown in Figure 3.21 (also shown in the color insert section).

    3. Modify the Menu page to be consistent with the new Home page.

    4. Configure centered page layout.

Figure 3.21
New JavaJam
index.html

See the center
color insert

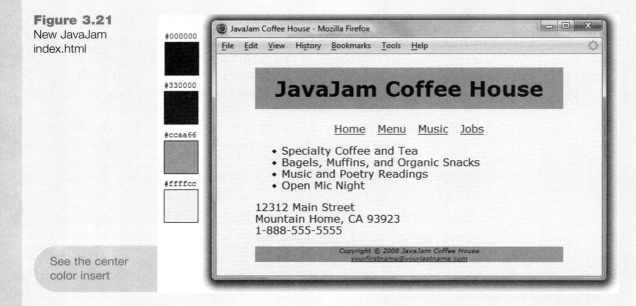

#000000

#330000

#ccaa66

#ffffcc

Hands-On Practice Case

Create a folder called javajamcss. Copy all the files from your javajam folder into the javajamcss folder.

1. **The External Style Sheet.** Launch Notepad. You will create an external style sheet named javajam.css. Code the CSS to configure the following:

   - Global styles for the document background color (`#ffffcc`), text color (`#330000`), and Verdana, Arial, or any sans-serif font

   - Style rules for the `h1` selector that configure background color (`#ccaa66`), text color (`#000000`), 200% line height, and centered text

   - Style rules for the centered navigation area (use an id named `nav`)

   - Style rules for the page footer area (use an id named `footer`) for background color (`#ccaa66`), text color (`#000000`), small font size (.60em), italics, and centered

   Save the file as javajam.css in the javajamcss folder. Check your syntax with the CSS validator (http://jigsaw.w3.org/css-validator). Correct and retest if necessary.

2. **The Home Page.** Launch Notepad and open the index.html file. You will modify this file to apply styles from the javajam.css external style sheet as follows:

   - Add a `<link />` element to associate the Web page with the javajam.css external style sheet file. Save and test your index.html page in a browser and you'll notice that the styles configured with the body and `h1` selectors are already applied!

   - Configure the navigation area. Since the navigation is not semantically a "paragraph" (a collection of sentences about a central topic), replace the `<p>` element with a `<div>` element. Assign this `<div>` to the id named `nav`.

   - Configure the page footer area. Replace the `<p>` elements with `<div>` elements. Remove the `<small>` and `<em>` elements because the `font-size` and `font-style` are configured as part of the `footer` id. Assign this `<div>` to the id named `footer`.

- Save the index.html file and test in a browser. Your page should look similar to the one shown in Figure 3.21 except that your page content will be left-aligned instead of centered. Don't worry—you'll center your page layout in Step 4 of this case study.

3. **The Menu Page.** Launch Notepad and open the menu.html file. You will modify this file in a similar manner—add the `<link />` element, configure the navigation area, and configure the page footer area. Save and test your new menu.html page. It should look similar to the one shown in Figure 3.22 except for the alignment.

Figure 3.22
New menu.html
page

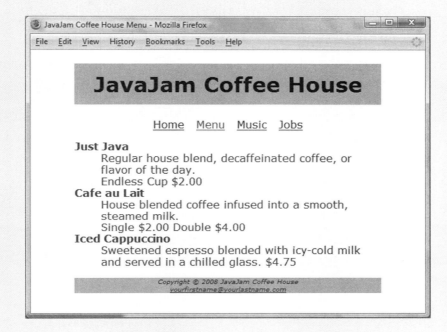

4. **Centered Page Layout with CSS.** Modify javajam.css, index.html, and menu.html to configure page content that is centered with width set to 80%. Refer to Hands-On Practice 3.8 if necessary. Save your files and retest your pages. The index.html and menu.html pages should closely match the samples shown in Figures 3.21 and 3.22.

Experiment with modifying the javajam.css file. Change the page background color, the font family, and so on. Test your pages in a browser. Isn't it amazing how a change in a single file can affect multiple files when external style sheets are used?

Fish Creek Animal Hospital

See Chapter 2 for an introduction to the Fish Creek Animal Hospital Case Study. Figure 2.30 shows a site map for the Fish Creek Web site. The Home page and Services page were created in Chapter 2. You will use the existing Web site as a start while you create a new version that uses an external style sheet to configure text and color.

You have the following tasks:

1. Create an external style sheet named fishcreek.css that configures the color and text for the Fish Creek Web site.

2. Modify the Home page to use an external style sheet to configure colors and fonts. The new Home page and color swatches are shown in Figure 3.23 (shown also in the color insert section).

Figure 3.23
New Fish Creek
index.html

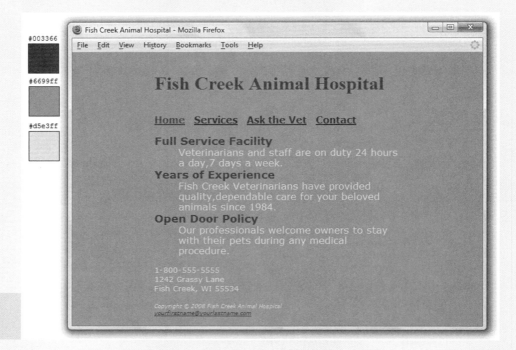

See the center
color insert

3. Modify the Services page to be consistent with the new Home page. Configure centered page layout.

Hands-On Practice Case

Create a folder called fishcreekcss. Copy all the files from your fishcreek folder into the fishcreekcss folder.

1. **The External Style Sheet.** Launch Notepad. You will create an external style sheet named fishcreek.css. Code the CSS to configure the following:

   - Global styles for the document background color (#6699ff), text color (#d5e3ff), and Verdana, Arial, or any sans-serif font

   - Style rules for the h1 selector that configure background color (#6699ff), text color (#003366), and 200% line height

   - Style rules for a navigation area (use an id named nav) that displays text in bold

   - Style rules for a class named category with bold font, background-color (#6699ff), text color (#003366), and larger font size (1.1em)

   - Style rules for the page footer area (use an id named footer) with a small font size (.70em) and italic text

   Save the file as fishcreek.css in the fishcreekcss folder. Check your syntax with the CSS validator (http://jigsaw.w3.org/css-validator). Correct and retest if necessary.

2. **The Home Page.** Launch Notepad and open the index.html file. You will modify this file to apply styles from the fishcreek.css external style sheet.

- Add a `<link />` element to associate the Web page with the fishcreek.css external style sheet file. Save and test your index.html page in a browser and you'll notice that the styles configured with the `body` and `h1` selectors are already applied!

- Configure the navigation area. Since the navigation is not semantically a "paragraph" (a collection of sentences about a central topic), replace the `<p>` element with a `<div>` element. Assign this `<div>` to the id named `nav`. Remove the `<strong>` element from this area.

- Configure each `<dt>` element to apply the `category` class. Remove the `<strong>` elements from this area.

- Configure the page footer area. Replace the `<p>` elements with `<div>` elements. Assign this `<div>` to the id named `footer`. Remove the `<small>` and `<em>` elements because the `font-size` and `font-style` are configured as part of the `footer` id.

- Save the index.html file and test in a browser. Your page should look similar to the one shown in Figure 3.23 except that your page content will be left-aligned instead of indented from the margins. Don't worry—you'll configure your page layout in Step 4 of this case study.

3. **The Services Page.** Launch Notepad and open the services.html file. You will modify this file in a similar manner—add the `<link />` element, configure the navigation area, configure the `category` classes (use `<span>` elements), and configure the page footer area. Save and test your new services.html page. It should look similar to the one shown in Figure 3.24 except for the alignment.

Figure 3.24
New services.html page

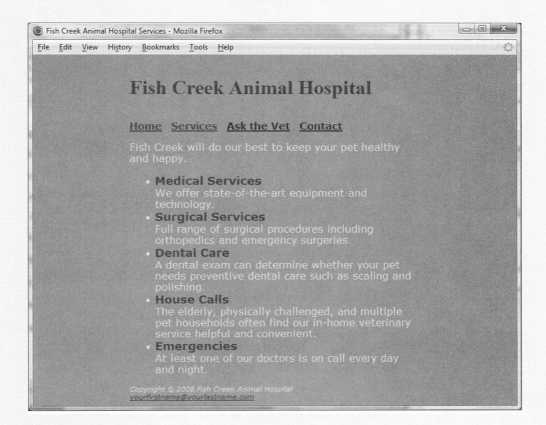

4. **Centered Page Layout with CSS.** Modify fishcreek.css, index.html, and services.html to configure page content that is centered with width set to 80%. Refer to Hands-On Practice 3.8 if necessary. Save your file and retest your pages. The index.html and services.html pages should closely match the samples shown in Figures 3.23 and 3.24.

Experiment with modifying the fishcreek.css file. Change the page background color, the font family, font color, and so on. Test your pages in a browser. Notice that multiple pages display differently because they link to the single file (fishcreek.css) that configures their formatting.

Pete the Painter

See Chapter 2 for an introduction to the Pete the Painter Case Study. Figure 2.34 shows a site map for the Pete the Painter Web site. The Home page and Services page were created in Chapter 2. You will use the existing Web site as a start while you create a new version of this Web site that uses an external style sheet to configure text and color.

You have the following tasks:

1. Create an external style sheet named painter.css that configures the color and text for the Pete the Painter Web site.

2. Modify the Home page to utilize an external style sheet to configure colors and fonts. The new Home page and color swatches are shown in Figure 3.25 (shown also in the color insert section).

Figure 3.25
New Pete the Painter
index.html

See the center
color insert

3. Modify the Services page to be consistent with the new Home page.

Hands-On Practice Case

Create a folder called paintercss. Copy all the files from your painter folder into the paintercss folder.

1. **The External Style Sheet.** Launch Notepad. You will create an external style sheet named painter.css. Code the CSS to configure the following:
   - Global styles for the document background color (#ffffff), text color (#000000), and Verdana, Arial, or any sans-serif font
   - Style rules for the logo class that configure background color (#ffffff), text color (#336633), and Georgia, Times New Roman, or any serif font
   - Style rules for a navigation area (use an id named nav) that displays text in bold
   - Style rules for a class named category with a bold font, background-color (#ffffff), text color (#336633), and a larger font size (1.2em)
   - Style rules for the page footer area (use an id named footer) with a small font size (.60em) and italic text

   Save the file as painter.css in the paintercss folder. Check your syntax with the CSS validator (http://jigsaw.w3.org/css-validator). Correct and retest if necessary.

2. **The Home Page.** Launch Notepad and open the index.html file. You will modify this file to apply styles from the painter.css external style sheet.
   - Add a <link /> element to associate the Web page with the painter.css external style sheet file. Save and test your index.html page in a browser and you'll notice that the styles configured with the body selector are already applied!
   - Configure the logo area. Code a <div> element that contains the <h1> and <h3> elements in the logo area. Assign the <div> to the logo class.
   - Configure the navigation area. Since the navigation is not semantically a "paragraph" (a collection of sentences about a central topic), replace the <p> element with a <div> element. Assign this <div> to the id named nav. Remove the <strong> element from this area.
   - Configure the <ul> to apply the category class.
   - Configure the page footer area. Replace the <p> elements with <div> elements. Assign this <div> to the id named footer. Remove the <small> and <em> elements because the font-size and font-style are configured as part of the footer id.
   - Save the index.html file and test in a browser. Your page should look similar to Figure 3.25.

3. **The Services Page.** Launch Notepad and open the services.html file. You will modify this file in a similar manner— add the <link /> element, configure the logo area, configure the navigation area, configure the category classes (use <span> elements and remove the <strong> element from this area), and configure the page footer area. Save and test your new services.html page. It should look similar to the one shown in Figure 3.26.

Experiment with modifying the painter.css file. Change the page background color, the font family, and so on. Test your pages in a browser. Notice how a change in a single file can affect multiple files when external style sheets are used.

Figure 3.26
New services.html page

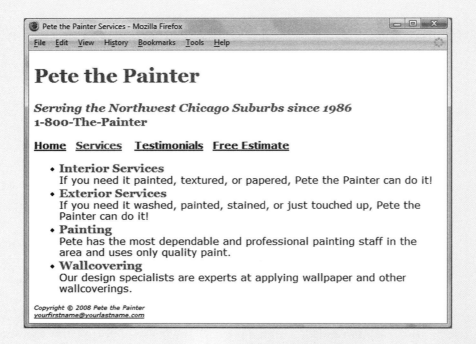

Prime Properties

See Chapter 2 for an introduction to the Prime Properties Case Study. Figure 2.38 shows a site map for the Prime Properties Web site. The Home page and Financing page were created in Chapter 2. You will use the existing Web site as a start while you create a new version of this Web site that uses an external style sheet to configure text and color.

You have the following tasks:

1. Create an external style sheet named prime.css that configures the color and text for the Prime Properties Web site.

2. Modify the Home page to use an external style sheet to configure colors and fonts. The new Home page and color swatches are shown in Figure 3.27 (shown also in the Color Insert Section).

3. Modify the Financing page to be consistent with the new Home page.

Hands-On Practice Case

Create a folder called primecss. Copy all the files from your prime folder into the primecss folder.

1. **The External Style Sheet.** Launch Notepad. You will create an external style sheet named painter.css. Code the CSS to configure the following:

   - Global styles for the document background color (#ffffcc), text color (#003300), and Arial, Helvetica, or any sans-serif font

   - Style rules for the h2 selector that configure background color (#ffffcc) and text color (#003366)

   - Style rules for the h4 selector that configure background color (#ffffcc) and text color (#006600)

Figure 3.27
New Prime Properties
index.html

See the center
color insert

- Style rules for the dd selector that configure italic, smaller than the default (.90em), with 200% line height
- Style rules for the logo class that configure background color (#ffffcc) and text color (#48751A)
- Style rules for a navigation area (use an id named nav) that displays text in bold, large (1.2em) font
- Style rules for a class named contact with bold, smaller than the default (.90em) using the Times New Roman or any serif font
- Style rules for the page footer area (use an id named footer) with small font size (.60em) and italic text

Save the file as prime.css in the primecss folder. Check your syntax with the CSS validator (http://jigsaw.w3.org/css-validator). Correct and retest if necessary.

2. **The Home Page.** Launch Notepad and open the index.html file. You will modify this file to apply styles from the prime.css external style sheet.

- Add a <link /> element to associate the Web page with the painter.css external style sheet file. Save and test your index.html page in a browser and you'll notice that the styles configured with the body selector are already applied!
- Configure the logo area. Assign the <h1> element to the class named logo.
- Configure the navigation area. Since the navigation is not semantically a "paragraph" (a collection of sentences about a central topic), replace the <p> element with a <div> element. Assign this <div> to the id named nav. Remove the <strong> element from this area.
- Configure the paragraph containing the address and phone information. Assign this area to the class named contact. Remove the <small> element from this area.

- Configure the page footer area. Replace the `<p>` elements with `<div>` elements. Assign this `<div>` to the id named `footer`. Remove the `<small>` and `<em>` elements because the `font-size` and `font-style` are configured as part of the `footer id`.
- Save the index.html file and test in a browser. Your page should look similar to the one shown in Figure 3.27.

3. **The Financing Page.** Launch Notepad and open the financing.html file. You will modify this file in a similar manner—add the `<link />` element, configure the logo area, configure the navigation area, and configure the page footer area. Save and test your new financing.html page. It should look similar to the one shown in Figure 3.28.

Figure 3.28
New financing.html page

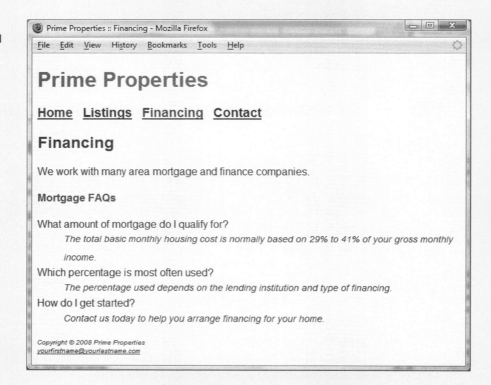

Experiment with modifying the prime.css file. Change the page background color, the font family, and so on. Test your pages in a browser. Notice how a change in a single file can affect multiple files when external style sheets are used.

Visual Elements and Graphics

CHAPTER 4

Chapter Objectives   In this chapter, you will learn how to ...

- Create and format lines and borders on Web pages
- Decide when to use graphics and what graphics are appropriate
- Apply the image element to add graphics to Web pages

- Configure images as backgrounds on Web pages
- Configure images as hyperlinks
- Find free and fee-based graphics sources
- Follow recommended Web design guidelines when using graphics on Web pages

A key component of a compelling Web site is the use of interesting and appropriate graphics. This chapter introduces you to working with visual elements on Web pages.

When you include images on your Web site, it is important to remember that not all Web users are able to view them. Some users may have vision problems and need assistive technology such as a screen reader application that reads the Web page to them. In addition, search engines send out spiders and robots to walk the Web and catalog pages for their indexes and databases; such programs do not access your images. As a Web developer, you should create pages that are enhanced by graphical elements but that are usable without them.

4.1 Configuring Lines and Borders

Web designers often use visual elements such as lines and borders to separate or define areas on Web pages. In this section you'll explore two coding techniques to configure a line on a Web page: the XHTML horizontal rule element and the CSS `border` and `padding` properties.

The Horizontal Rule Element

A horizontal rule or line visually separates areas of a page. The **`<hr />`** element configures a horizontal line across a Web page. Since the horizontal rule element does not contain any text, it is coded as a stand-alone tag, and not in a pair of opening and closing tags.

HANDS-ON PRACTICE 4.1

Open the Web page found at chapter4/starter1.html in the student files in a text editor. This file should be familiar to you; it is similar to the Web page you worked with in Chapter 3 (see Figure 3.11). Add an `<hr />` tag above the paragraph that contains the page footer (id="footer").

Save your file as hr.html and test it in a browser. The lower portion of your Web page should look similar to the partial screenshot shown in Figure 4.1. Compare your work with the solution in the student files (Chapter4/hr.html).

Figure 4.1
The `<hr />` element configures a horizontal line

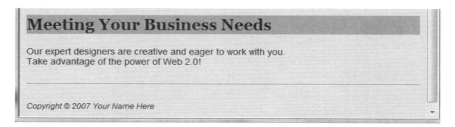

Horizontal rules are centered within their container element (in this case the Web page body) by default. A number of attributes exist for the `<hr />` tag but they are deprecated or not officially supported by the W3C. Appendix A contains a list of these attributes and descriptions.

While a horizontal rule can be easily created using XHTML, a more modern technique is to use CSS to configure a border for a Web page element.

The `border` and `padding` Properties

As you may have noticed when you configured background colors for heading elements in Chapter 3, block-level XHTML elements form the shape of a rectangular box on a Web page. This is known as the CSS box model, which you will explore in detail in

Chapter 6. For now, let's focus on two CSS properties that can be configured for the "box"—the `border` and `padding` properties.

The `border` Property. The `border` property configures the border, or boundary, around an element. By default, the border has a width set to 0 and does not display. You can set the **border-width**, **border-color**, and **border-style**. And there's more—you can even configure individual settings for `border-top`, `border-right`, `border-bottom`, and `border-left`. You'll get some practice configuring properties for just the top border (`border-top`) in the next Hands-On Practice.

The `border-style` property also offers a variety of formatting options including `inset`, `outset`, `double`, `groove`, `ridge`, `solid`, `dashed`, and `dotted`. Be aware that these property values are not all uniformly applied by browsers. Figure 4.2 shows how Firefox 2 and Internet Explorer 7 render various `border-style` values.

Figure 4.2
Not all `border-style` properties are rendered the same way by popular browsers

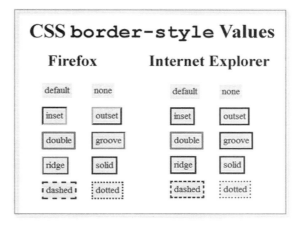

The CSS to configure the borders shown in Figure 4.2 uses a `border-color` of #000033, `border-width` of 3 pixels, and the value indicated for the `border-style` property. For example, the style rule to configure the dashed border follows:

```
.dashedborder {  border-color:  #000033;
                 border-width:  3px;
                 border-style:  dashed;
}
```

A shorthand notation allows you to configure all the `border` properties in one style rule by listing the values of `border-width`, `border-style`, and `border-color`. An example follows:

```
.dashedborder { border: 3px #000033 dashed }
```

The `padding` Property. The `padding` property configures empty space between the content of the XHTML element (usually text) and the border. By default, the padding is set to 0. If you configure a background color for an element, the color is applied to both the padding and the content areas. You'll apply the `padding` property in the next Hands-On Practice. You may want to refer to Table 4.1, which presents a description of the CSS properties introduced in Chapter 4, as you work through the Hands-On Practice exercises.

Table 4.1 New CSS properties introduced in this chapter

Property	Description	Values
background-image	Background image on an element	url (imagename.gif) or url (imagename.jpg)
background-position	Position of the background image	Two percentage values or numeric pixel values. The first value configures the horizontal position and the second configures the vertical position starting from the upper-left corner of the container's box. Text values can also be used: left, top, center, bottom, right.
background-repeat	Controls how the background image will repeat	Text values repeat (default), repeat-y, (vertical repeat), repeat-x (horizontal repeat) , no-repeat (no repeat)
border	Shorthand notation to configure the values for border-width, border-style, and border-color of an element	The values for border-width, border-style, and border-color separated by spaces; for example: border: 1px solid #000000;
border-bottom	Shorthand notation to configure the bottom border of an element	The values for border-width, border-style, and border-color separated by spaces; for example: border-bottom: 1px solid #000000;
border-color	The color of the border around an element	Any valid color
border-left	Shorthand notation to configure the left border of an element	The values for border-width, border-style, and border-color separated by spaces; for example: border-left: 1px solid #000000;
border-right	Shorthand notation to configure the right border of an element	The values for border-width, border-style, and border-color separated by spaces; for example: border-right: 1px solid #000000;
border-style	The type of border around an element	Text values double, groove, inset, none (the default), outset, ridge, solid, dashed, dotted, hidden
border-top	Shorthand notation to configure the top border of an element	The values for border-width, border-style, and border-color separated by spaces; for example: border-top: 1px solid #000000;
border-width	The width of a border around an element	A numeric pixel value (such as 1px) or the text values thin, medium, thick

Table 4.1 New CSS properties introduced in this chapter (*continued*)

Property	Description	Values
`padding`	Shorthand notation to configure the amount of padding—the blank space between the element and its border	1. A single numeric value (px or em); configure padding on all sides of the element. 2. Two numeric values (px or em); the first value configures the top and bottom padding, the second value configures the left and right padding; for example: `padding: 20px 10px;` 3. Four numeric values (px or em) or percentages. The values configure the padding in the following order: `padding-top`, `padding-right`, `padding-bottom`, `padding-left`.
`padding-bottom`	Blank space between an element and its bottom border	A numeric value (px or em) or percentage
`padding-left`	Blank space between an element and its left border	A numeric value (px or em) or percentage
`padding-right`	Blank space between an element and its right border	A numeric value (px or em) or percentage
`padding-top`	Blank space between an element and its top border	A numeric value (px or em) or percentage

HANDS-ON PRACTICE 4.2

In this Hands-On Practice you will work with the `border` and `padding` properties. Launch a text editor and open the Web page found at chapter4/starter2.html in the student files. You will modify the CSS style rules for the `h1` selector, `h2` selector and `footer` id. When you are finished, your page should look similar to the one shown in Figure 4.3.

Modify the CSS style rules as follows:

- Modify the style rules for the `h1` selector. Remove the `line-height` style rule because you will configure the empty space using `padding`. Add a style rule to set the `padding` to 15 pixels. The code follows:

  `padding: 15px;`

- Add a style rule to the `h2` selector to configure a 2 pixel, dashed, bottom border in the color #191970. The code follows:

  `border-bottom: 2px dashed #191970;`

- Add style rules to the `footer` id to configure a thin, solid, top border in the color #aeaed4 along with 10 pixels of top padding. The code follows:

  `border-top: thin solid #aeaed4;`
  `padding-top: 10px;`

Save your file as border.html.

Figure 4.3
CSS `border` and `padding` properties add visual interest to the page

Test in multiple browsers. Expect your page to look slightly different in browsers such as Internet Explorer and Firefox. See Figure 4.3 for a screenshot of the page using Firefox. Figure 4.4 shows the page displayed in Opera. The student files contain a sample solution (Chapter4/border.html).

Figure 4.4
Opera renders the dashed border and bullet points differently than Firefox

My page looks different in various browsers. What can I do?

Do not expect your Web pages to always look the same in every browser and every browser version. Web pages that look different in various browsers are a frustrating part of life in the world of Web developers. The good news is that browser manufacturers are finally beginning to be less inventive and more compliant with the W3C standards. Also, organizations such as The Web Standards Project at http://www.webstandards.org have lobbied for standards compliance in browsers. Look for more compliance in the future!

Notice how objects even as simple as bullet points and dashed borders appear different depending on the way the browsers display the page. To deal with this, remember the following:

- Design for the browser you think most of your visitors will use.
- Design the page so that it looks okay (degrades gracefully) in other browsers.

Perhaps the most exciting way to add visual interest to a Web page is to add graphics. The next section continues with a discussion of types of graphics used on Web pages.

CHECKPOINT 4.1

1. Is it reasonable to try to code a Web page that looks exactly the same on every browser and every platform? Explain your answer.

2. When a Web page containing the style rules below is rendered in a browser, the border does not display. Describe what is incorrect with the following code:

```
h2 { background-color: #ff0000
     border-top: thin solid #000000
}
```

3. True or False? CSS can be used to configure visual elements such as rectangular shapes and lines on Web pages.

4.2 Types of Graphics

Graphics help to make Web pages compelling. Unfortunately, they can also make pages very slow to load. This section discusses types and features of graphic files used on the Web: **GIF**, **JPEG**, and **PNG**.

Browsers render, or display, Web page documents in order, line-by-line, starting at the top of the document. They also display standard images as the files are read in order from top to bottom. The top of a standard image begins to display after 50 percent of the image has been read by a browser. As you read about types of images, look for techniques you can use to make your pages load faster.

GIF Images

Graphic interchange format (GIF) is best used for flat line drawings containing solid tones and simple images such as clip art. The maximum number of colors in a GIF file is 256 (although most do not use more than the 216 colors in the Web Color Palette). GIF images have a .gif file extension.

Transparency. The format GIF89A used by GIF images supports image **transparency**. In a graphics application such as Adobe Photoshop or Adobe Fireworks one color (usually the background color) of the image can be set to be transparent. This helps the image to blend in with the Web page background or table background. Figure 4.5 shows two GIF images, one that does not use transparency and one with a background color configured to be transparent.

Figure 4.5
Comparison of nontransparent and transparent GIFs

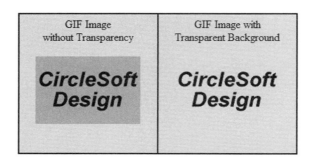

When working with transparent GIFs you should also be aware of the **halo effect**—a fringe of color around parts of the transparent image. Transparent GIFs are usually optimized for display on a particular background color. Displaying them on a background other than the type they were designed for can produce the halo effect.

The GIF used in Figure 4.6 was created to display on a light background. When it is shown on a dark background, the halo of light pixels is noticeable. This halo can only be fixed by modifying the image in a graphics application such as Adobe Photoshop or Adobe Fireworks and saving a version that is optimized for display on a dark background.

Figure 4.6
Notice the halo effect on the dark background

Animation. Animated GIF images also use the .gif file extension. They are contained in a GIF file that consists of several images or frames, each of which is slightly different. When the frames flash on the screen in order, the image appears animated—**animated GIFs** can be created in a graphics application such as Adobe Fireworks or Adobe

ImageReady. Shareware GIF animation applications such as the GIF Construction Set are also commonly used. There are advantages to using an animated GIF to add action to your Web page. This format is widely supported, does not require a browser plug-in, and is relatively easy to create.

When you decide to add an animated GIF to your Web page, try to use the image for special emphasis only. If you're like most people, at some time you have been annoyed by a flashing ad banner at the top of a Web page. Use animated gifs sparingly.

Compression. When a GIF file is saved, **lossless compression** is used. This means that nothing in the original image is lost and that the compressed image, when rendered by a browser, will contain the same pixels as the original.

Optimization. To avoid slow-loading Web pages, graphic files should be optimized for the Web. **Image optimization** is the process of creating an image with the lowest file size that still renders a good quality image—balancing image quality and file size. GIF images are typically optimized by reducing the number of colors in the image. The image shown in Figure 4.6 was created using 235 colors and is 12KB in size. A graphics application such as Adobe Photoshop can be used to optimize the image for the Web—reducing the number of colors, which decreases the file size. The image shown in Figure 4.7 uses only eight colors and has a file size less than 5KB. However, the image quality is unacceptable.

Figure 4.7
This GIF image is less than 5KB but is poor quality

Figure 4.8 shows the optimized image with acceptable quality using 128 colors and a file size of 9KB—the best balancing of quality and file size for this particular image.

Figure 4.8
Optimization is a trade-off between file size and image quality

Interlacing. When a GIF graphic file is created it can be configured as interlaced. This changes the way that browsers render the image. Remember that browsers display standard (noninterlaced) images as the file is read from top to bottom and only begin to display the image after 50 percent of the file has been downloaded by a browser. An **interlaced image** progressively displays and seems to fade in as it downloads. The image first appears fuzzy but gradually becomes clearer and sharper. Interlaced images are repeatedly scanned from left to right. The first time about 13 percent of the image is displayed. The next pass renders about 25 percent. This process continues until the image is completely displayed. When you are using complex GIF images, consider interlacing to improve the perceived load time of your page.

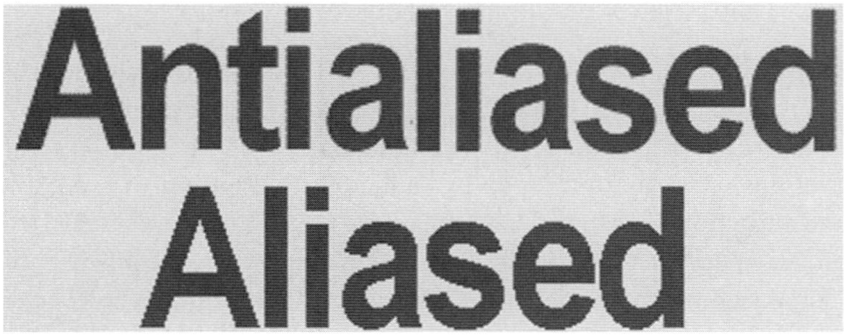

Figure 4.9
Notice the smoother look of the top line of text

Antialiased
Aliased

JPEG Images

Joint Photographic Experts Group (JPEG) images are best used for photographic images. In contrast to a GIF image, a JPEG image can contain 16.7 million colors. However, JPEG images cannot be made transparent and they cannot be animated. JPEG images usually have a .jpg or .jpeg file extension.

Compression. Another difference between GIF and JPEG images is that when JPEG images are saved **lossy compression** is used. This means that some pixels in the original image are lost or removed from the compressed file. When a browser renders the compressed image, the display is similar but not exactly the same as the original image.

Optimization. There are trade-offs between the quality of the image and the amount of compression. An image with less compression will have higher quality and result in a larger file size. An image with more compression will have lower quality and result in a smaller file size. Most graphics applications allow you to preview the quality/compression trade-off and choose the image that best suits your needs.

Figure 4.10 shows a JPEG image (photograph taken by Karen Felke) that is stored in a 78KB file. The same image was saved at various quality levels: Figure 4.11 was saved with 80 percent quality and is 26KB; Figure 4.12 was saved with 20 percent quality and is 6KB, but its quality is unacceptable. View these images to gain a perspective on the quality/size trade-off. You should notice that the quality of the image degrades as the file size decreases. The square blockiness you see in the smallest file is called **pixelation**.

Another method to optimize JPEG images is to use a graphics application to reduce the dimensions of the images. Figure 4.13 shows a small version, or thumbnail, image of acceptable quality.

Figure 4.10
Initial JPEG image
(78KB file size)
photo courtesy of
Karen Felke

Figure 4.11
JPEG saved at 80
percent quality
(26KB file size)

Figure 4.12
JPEG saved at 20
percent quality (6KB
file size)

Figure 4.13
This small image is only 6KB

Progressive JPEG. When a JPEG file is created it can be configured as progressive. A **progressive JPEG** is similar to an interlaced GIF in that the image progressively displays and seems to fade in as it downloads. Consider using this for complex images since the general shapes will initially appear and then sharpen as the file is progressively scanned and displayed by the browser.

PNG Images

PNG, pronounced "ping," stands for portable network graphic. Browsers have only recently begun to support this type of image. It combines the best of GIF and JPEG images and will be a replacement for the GIF in the future. PNG graphics can support millions of colors. They can support variable transparency levels and use lossless compression. PNG images also support interlacing. PNG is the native file format of some graphics applications, such as Adobe Fireworks.

4.3 Using Graphics

Now that you've been introduced to the types of graphic files displayed on Web pages, we'll discuss how to place graphics on your Web pages.

The Image Element

The `<img />`, pronounced image, element is used to place graphics on a Web page. These graphics can be photographs, banners, company logos, navigation buttons—you are limited only by your creativity and imagination.

The image tag is used alone, not in a pair of opening and closing tags. The image file should be either in the same folder as your Web site or in a subfolder of your site. For example, to place an image called logo.gif on your Web page, you would use the following XHTML code:

```
<img src="logo.gif" height="200" width="500" alt="CircleSoft Logo" />
```

The **src attribute** is used to specify the file name of the image. A number of optional attributes can be applied to images. It is a good idea to include the `height`, `width`, and `alt` attributes. The **height attribute** and **width attribute** can cause the Web page to load more efficiently and quickly. The **alt attribute** provides a text replacement, typically a text description, of the image. Table 4.2 lists attributes and their values. Commonly used attributes are shown in bold.

Table 4.2 Attributes of the `<img />` tag

Attribute	Value
align	`right`, `left` (default), `top`, `middle`, `bottom` (Deprecated)
alt	Text phrase that describes the image
border	Image border size in pixels (Deprecated) 0 will prevent the border from being displayed.
height	Height of image in pixels
hspace	Amount of space that is blank to the left and right of the image in pixels (Deprecated)
id	Text name, alphanumeric, beginning with a letter, no spaces—the value must be unique and not used for other id values on the same XHTML document
longdesc	URL of a Web page that contains a text description of the image
name	Text name, alphanumeric, beginning with a letter, no spaces—this attribute names the image so that it can be easily accessed by client-side scripting languages such as JavaScript. This attribute is deprecated in XHTML but is used to provide backward compatibility with browsers that support HTML.
src	The URL or file name of the image
title	A text phrase containing advisory information about the image—typically more descriptive than the `alt` text
vspace	Amount of space that is blank above and below the image in pixels (Deprecated)
width	Width of image in pixels

Use `height` and `width` attributes to help the browser render your page more efficiently. If you omit the attributes, the browser must often adjust and shift the other page elements after your images load. This slows down the loading of your Web page. The browser reserves the correct amount of space for your image if you use the `height` and `width` attributes with values either equal to or approximately the size of the image.

What if I don't know the height and width of an image?

Most graphics applications can display the height and width of an image. If you have a graphics application such as Adobe Photoshop or Adobe Fireworks handy, launch the application and open the image. These applications include options that will display the properties of the image, such as height and width.

If you don't have a graphics application available, you can determine the dimensions of an image using a browser. Display the image on a Web page. Right-click on the image to display the context-sensitive menu. Select properties and view the dimensions (height and width) of the image. (*Warning*: if the height and width are specified on the Web page, those values will be displayed even if the image's actual height and width are different.)

Accessibility and Images

Focus on Accessibility

Use the `alt` attribute to provide accessibility. Recall from Chapter 1 that Section 508 of the Rehabilitation Act requires the use of accessibility features for new information technology (including Web sites) associated with the federal government. The `alt` attribute configures an alternative text description of the image. This `alt` text is used by the browser in two ways. The browser will show the `alt` text in the image area before the graphic is downloaded and displayed. Some browsers will also show the `alt` text as a tool tip whenever the Web page visitor places a mouse over the image area. Applications such as screen readers will read the text in the `alt` attribute out loud.

Standard browsers such as Internet Explorer and Safari are not the only type of application or user agent that can access your Web site. Major search engines run programs called spiders or robots; these programs index and categorize Web sites. They cannot process images, but some process the value of the `alt` attributes in image tags.

Focus on Accessibility

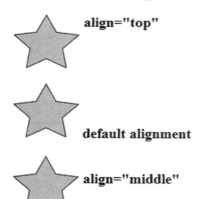

The **`longdesc` attribute** is used to provide accessibility when the `alt` text description is too short to convey the meaning of the image. The value of the `longdesc` attribute is the URL of a Web page that contains a detailed text description and explanation of the image. Most current browsers do not support this attribute but you can expect expanded support in the future.

Legacy Alert. The `align`, `vspace`, and `hspace` attributes help position the image on the page relative to text. Examples of formatting images and text using vertical alignment properties are shown in Figure 4.14.

Figure 4.15 provides examples of horizontal alignments, the **`hspace` attribute**, and the **`vspace` attribute**. The `hspace` and `vspace` attributes are used to add space around an image symmetrically.

Since you'll find many pages on the Web coded using the deprecated attributes of the image element (`align`, `hspace`, `vspace`, `border`), it's a good idea to become familiar with them. CSS techniques that replicate the functionality of these attributes will be discussed in Chapter 6.

Figure 4.14
Examples of vertical alignment

Vertical Alignment

align="top"

default alignment

align="middle"

Figure 4.15
Examples of horizontal alignment

Horizontal Alignment

The XHTML tag for this star image is coded with align="right". This causes the text to be placed to the left and wrap around the image. If text continues, it will wrap under the image.

The XHTML tag for this star image is coded with align="left". This causes the text to be placed to the right and wrap around the image. If text continues, it will wrap under the image.

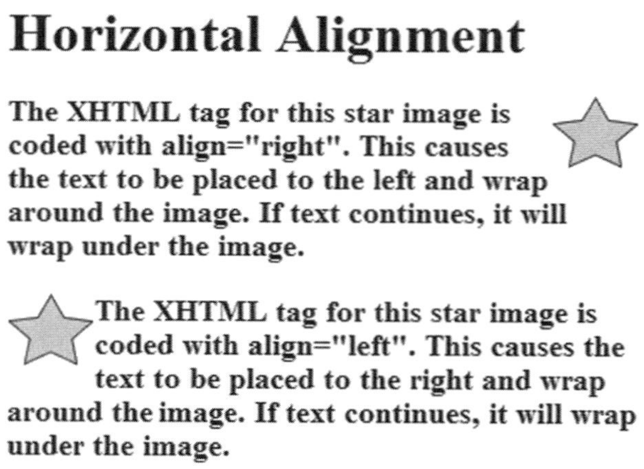

HANDS-ON PRACTICE 4.3

In this Hands-On Practice you will place a graphical logo banner on a Web page. Create a new folder called trilliumch4. The graphic used in this Hands-On Practice is located in the student files: Chapter4/starters folder. Save trilliumbanner.jpg file in your trilliumch4 folder. A starter version of the Trillium Media Design Home page is ready for you in the student files. Save the chapter4/starter3.html file to your trilliumch4 folder. Launch a browser to display the starter3.html Web page—notice a monochromatic green color scheme has been configured with CSS. When you are finished with this Hands-On Practice, your page will look similar to the one shown in Figure 4.16—with a logo banner.

Figure 4.16
The new Trillium Home page with a logo banner

Launch a text editor and open starter3.html in the Chapter4 folder.

Configure the image as follows:

> Replace the text contained between the `<h1>` opening and closing tags. Code an `<img />` element to display trilliumbanner.jpg in this area. Remember to include the `src`, `alt`, `height`, and `width` attributes. Sample code follows:

```
<img src="trilliumbanner.jpg" alt="Trillium Media Design"
width="700" height="86" />
```

Modify the `h2` selector as follows:

Let's review working with the CSS `padding` property. Add a style rule to configure 10 pixels of padding on the left side of the `h2` element. The new style rule follows:

```
padding-left: 10px;
```

Save your page as index.html in the trilliumch4 folder. Launch a browser and test your page. It should look similar to the one shown in Figure 4.16. *Note*: if the image did not display on your Web page, verify that you have saved the trilliumbanner.jpg file in the trilliumch4 folder and that you have spelled the file name correctly in the `<img />` element. The student files contain a sample solution in the Chapter4/4.3 folder. Isn't it interesting how just one image can add visual interest to a Web page?

Image Links

The XHTML to make an image function as a hyperlink is very easy. To create an **image link** all you need to do is surround your `<img />` element with anchor tags. For example, to place a link around an image called home.gif, use the following XHTML code:

```
<a href="index.html"><img src="home.gif" height="19" width="85"
alt="Home" /></a>
```

When an image is used as a hyperlink, the default is to show a blue outline (border) around the image. If you would prefer not to display this outline, you could use the `border="0"` attribute in your image tag as follows:

```
<a href="index.html"><img src="home.gif" height="19"
width="85"alt="Home" border="0" /></a>
```

A more modern approach is to use CSS to configure the border on the `img` selector. The next Hands-On Practice will demonstrate this technique as you add image links to a Web page.

HANDS-ON PRACTICE 4.4

You will add image links to the Trillium Media Design Home page in this Hands-On Practice. You should already have the index.html and trilliumbanner.jpg files in your trilliumch4 folder. The graphics used in this Hands-On Practice are located in the student files: Chapter4/starters folder. Save the home.gif, services.gif, and contact.gif files to your trilliumch4 folder. View Figure 4.17 to see how your page should look after you are done with this Hands-On Practice.

Focus on Accessibility

Let's get started. Launch a text editor and open index.html. Notice that the anchor tags are already coded—you'll just need to convert the text links to image links! However, before you start changing the code, let's take a minute to discuss accessibility. Whenever

Figure 4.17
The new Trillium Home page navigation with image links

the main navigation consists of media, such as an image, some individuals may not be able to see the images (or may have images turned off in their browser). To provide navigation that is accessible to all, configure a set of plain text navigation links in the page footer area as follows:

1. Copy the `<div>` element containing the navigation area to the lower portion of the page and paste it above the page footer.

2. Modify the style rules in the `nav` class. Change the font size to `.75em`.

3. Now, focus on the top navigation area. Replace the text contained between each pair of anchor tags with an image element. Use home.gif for the link to index.html, services.gif for the link to services.html, and contact.gif for the link to contact.html. A sample follows:

   ```
   <a href="index.html"><img src="home.gif" alt="Home" width="120"
   height="40" /></a>
   ```

4. Create a new style rule that configures no border for the `img` selector. The code follows:

   ```
   img {border:0 }
   ```

Save your page as index.html. Launch a browser and test your page. It should look similar to the one shown in Figure 4.17. The student files contain a sample solution in the Chapter4/4.4 folder.

What if my images don't show?

The following are common reasons for images not displaying on a Web page:

- Are your images really in the Web site folder? Use Windows Explorer to double-check.
- Did you code the XTHML and CSS correctly? Check for common mistakes such as typing `scr` instead of `src` and missing quotation marks.
- Do your images have the exact file names that you have used in the background or `src` attributes in your XHTML code? Attention to detail and consistency will be very helpful here.

Hints for naming image files:

- Use all lowercase letters.
- Do not use punctuation symbols and spaces.
- Do not change the file extensions (should be .gif, .jpg, .jpeg, or .png).
- Keep your file names short but descriptive.

    i1.gif is probably too short

    myimagewithmydogonmybirthday.gif is too long

    dogbday.gif may be just about right

Background Images

Using the CSS `background-color` property to configure the background color of a Web page was introduced in Chapter 3. The W3C recommends that Web developers use the hexadecimal numeric value rather than the color name when setting a background color. For example, the following CSS code configures the background of a Web page to be a soft yellow:

```
body { background-color: #ffff99; }
```

In addition to a background color, you can also choose to use an image for the background of a Web page. Be careful not to choose an image that is too busy; it could interfere with your text and graphics. Use the CSS **background-image property** to configure a background image for a Web page. For example, the following CSS code configures the background of a Web page to be the image background1.gif located in the same folder as the Web page:

```
body { background-image: url(background1.gif); }
```

You can use a graphics application to create your own backgrounds or find a free background image on the Web.

Legacy Alert. If you work with Web pages created by others you may find that the XHTML attributes `bgcolor` and `background` have been used to configure the page instead of CSS properties. See Appendix A for more information on the `<body>` element and these attributes.

FAQ

Can I use both a `background-color` and a `background-image` attribute on the `body` selector?

Yes, you can! The background color (specified by the **`background-color`** property) will display first. Then the image specified as the Web page background will be loaded and tiled across the page. It's a good idea to choose a background color of a hue similar to the major color in your Web page background image. By coding both a background color and a background image you provide your visitor with a more pleasing visual experience. If the background image does not load for some reason, the page background will still have the expected contrast with your text color. If the background image is smaller than the Web browser window and the Web page is configured with CSS to not automatically tile (repeat), the page background color will display in areas not covered by the background image. The CSS for a page with both a background color and a background image is as follows:

```
body {  background-color: #cccccc;
        background-image: url(mybackground.gif);
}
```

You may think that a graphic created to be the background of a Web page would always be about the size of a browser window. This can be done; however, often the background image is actually much smaller than the typical browser window. The shape of a background image is usually either a long, thin rectangle or a small rectangular block. Unless otherwise specified in a style rule, Web browsers repeat, or tile, these images to cover the page background. The images have small file sizes so that they download as quickly as possible. Figure 4.18 shows a long, thin rectangular image that will repeat down the page. The Web page shown in Figure 4.19 uses a small rectangular image that is repeated or tiled on the page. In each of these cases, the small background image has the effect of a much larger image that fills the screen.

Figure 4.18
A long, thin background image tiles down the page

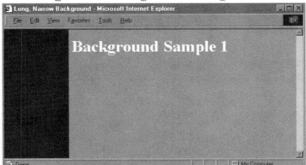

Figure 4.19
A small rectangular background is repeated to fill the Web page window

Configuring Background Images with CSS

The default behavior of a browser is to repeat, or tile, background images to cover the entire element's background. Figures 4.18 and 4.19 display examples of this type of tiling for a Web page background. This behavior also applies to other elements, such as backgrounds for headings, paragraphs, and so on. You can change this tiling behavior with the CSS **background-repeat** property. The background-repeat property has a number of values: repeat (default), repeat-y (vertical repeat of background image), repeat-x (horizontal repeat of background image), and no-repeat (background image does not repeat). Figure 4.20 provides examples of the actual background image and the result of applying various background-repeat property values.

You will explore configuring image backgrounds in the next Hands-On Practice.

Figure 4.20
Examples of the CSS background-repeat property

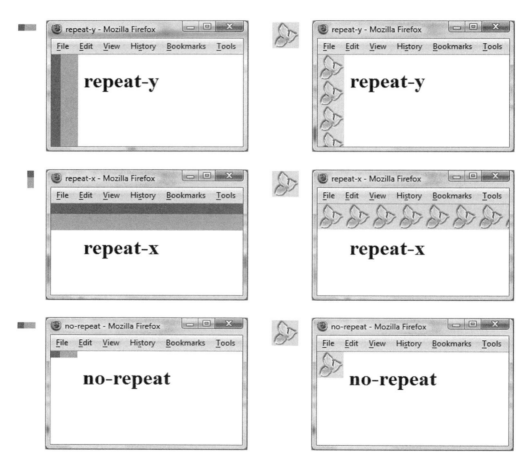

HANDS-ON PRACTICE 4.5

You will update the index.html file from the previous Hands-On Practice (shown in Figure 4.17). In this Hands-On Practice you will configure the h2 selector with a background image that does not repeat. Obtain the trilliumbullet.gif image from the student files in the Chapter4/starters folder. Save the images in your trilliumch4 folder. When you are completed with this exercise, your page should look similar to the one shown in Figure 4.21.

Figure 4.21
The background image in the `<h2>` areas is configured with
`background-repeat: no-repeat`

Launch Notepad and open index.html.

Modify the style rule for the `h2` selector and configure the `background-image` and `background-repeat` properties. Set the background image to be trilliumbullet.gif. Set the background to not repeat. The `h2` selector style rules follow:

```
h2 {  background-color: #d5edb3;
      color: #5c743d;
      font-family: Georgia, "Times New Roman", serif;
      padding-left: 30px;
      background-image: url(trilliumbullet.gif);
      background-repeat: no-repeat;
}
```

Save your page as index.html. Launch a browser and test your page. It should look similar to the one shown in Figure 4.21. The student files contain a sample solution in the Chapter4/4.5 folder.

What if my images are in their own folder?

It's a good idea to organize your Web site by placing all your images in a folder separate from your Web pages. Notice that the CircleSoft Web site shown in Figure 4.22 has a folder called images, which contains a number of GIF files. To refer to these files in XHTML or CSS code, you also need to refer to the images folder. The following are some examples:

- The CSS code to configure the background.gif file from the images folder as the page background is as follows:

```
body { background-image: url(images/background.gif); }
```

- XHTML to display the logo1.gif file from the images folder is as follows:

```
<img src="images/logo1.gif" alt="CircleSoft" width="588"
height="120" />
```

Figure 4.22
A folder named "images" contains the graphic files

CHECKPOINT 4.2

1. Describe the CSS to configure a graphic named circle.jpg to display once in the background of all `<h1>` elements. Code sample CSS to demonstrate this.

2. Describe the CSS that configures a file named bg.gif to repeat vertically down the background of a Web page. Code sample CSS to demonstrate this.

3. True or False? When coding image links, you must configure the image tag with `border="0"` to avoid the default blue border.

4.4 XHTML Images and More

This section introduces additional XHTML coding techniques associated with using images on Web pages. Topics discussed include image maps, thumbnail images, and image slicing.

Image Maps

An **image map** is an image that can be used as one or more hyperlinks. An image map will have at least one clickable area and usually multiple clickable areas that link to another Web page or Web site. The clickable areas are sometimes called **hotspots**. You have probably used image maps many times but never realized it. One common use of image maps is to create real clickable maps that Web site visitors can manipulate to choose a location. Figure 4.23 shows the home page of Recreation.gov with a map of the United States. Visitors use the map to select the state they are interested in. You can also visit the textbook's Web site at http://webdevfoundations.net to try out an image map.

Figure 4.23
An image map is used to select a location on this Web site

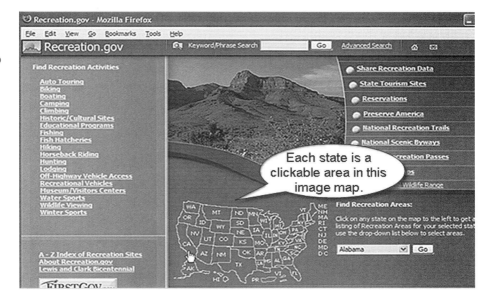

Most Web authoring software, such as Adobe Dreamweaver, have wizards or other tools to help you create image maps quickly and easily. If you don't have access to a Web authoring tool to create an image map, the most difficult part is determining the pixel coordinates of the hyperlink area. The coordinates are in pairs of numbers that signify the number of pixels from the top and the number of pixels from the left edge of the image. If you are working with a graphic artist, he or she may be able to supply you with the coordinates. Another option is to open the image in a graphics application such as Adobe Fireworks, Adobe Photoshop, or even MS Paint to obtain approximate coordinates. You can modify these coordinate values as you work with the XHTML on your Web page. Image maps can be used to create clickable areas in three shapes: rectangles, circles, and polygons.

An image map uses two new elements: <map> and <area />. The **<map>** tag is a container tag and is used to begin and end the image map. The name attribute is used to correspond the <map> tag with its associated image. The image tag uses the **usemap attribute** to indicate which <map> to use. For example, <img src="fishingboat.jpg" usemap="#boat" /> will be associated with the image map described by <map name="boat" id="boat">. The id attribute is part of XHTML. The name attribute is required for backward compatibility with older browsers that were written to process HTML.

The **<area />** tag is used to define the coordinates or edges of the map area and uses shape, coords, alt, and href attributes. Table 4.3 describes the type of coordinates (coords) needed for each shape value.

Table 4.3 Shape coordinates

Shape	Coordinates	Meaning
rect	"x1,y1, x2,y2"	The coordinates at point (x1,y1) represent the upper-left corner of the rectangle. The coordinates at point (x2,y2) represent the lower-right corner of the rectangle.
circle	"x,y,r"	The coordinates at point (x,y) indicate the center of the circle. The value of r is the radius of the circle in pixels.
polygon	"x1,y1, x2,y2, x3,y3", etc.	The values of each (x,y) pair represent the coordinates of a corner point of the polygon.

This text focuses on rectangular image maps. For a rectangular image map, the value of the shape attribute is rect and the coordinates indicate the pixel positions as follows: upper-left corner distance from top of image, upper-left corner distance from left side of image, lower-right corner distance from top of image, and lower-right corner distance from left edge of image.

Figure 4.24 shows an image with a fishing boat. The dotted rectangle around the fishing boat indicates the location of the hotspot. The coordinates shown (24, 188) indicate that the top-left corner is 24 pixels from the left edge of the image and 188 pixels from the top of the image. The pair of coordinates in the lower-right corner (339, 283) indicates that this corner is 339 pixels from the left image edge and 283 pixels from the image top. The XHTML code to create this image map follows:

```
<map name="boat" id="boat">
<area href="http://www.doorcountyvacations.com" shape="rect"
coords="24, 188, 339, 283" alt="Door County Fishing" />
</map>
<img src="fishingboat.jpg" usemap="#boat" alt="Door County"
width="416" height="350" />
```

Figure 4.24
Sample image map

This example is for a client-side image map. No special Web server processing is needed for this image map to work. Another, more complex type of image map is a server-side image map. This type requires a program on the Web server to coordinate the linking. Server-side maps are no longer commonly used because they require resources on the Web server. It is more efficient to distribute processing to be on the Web browser client whenever possible. This way, the resources of the Web server can be reserved for the tasks that only it can perform.

Most Web developers do not hand-code image maps. As mentioned previously, the easiest way to create a client-side image map is to use a Web authoring tool. Some shareware programs, such as CoffeeCup Image Mapper (http://www.coffeecup.com) and HTML Map Designer Pro (http://www.imagecure.com/) also provide this feature.

Thumbnail Images

A **thumbnail image** is a smaller version of an image you would like to include on a Web site. It is usually placed within anchor tags that link to the larger, more detailed version of the image. Large images can significantly increase the load time of a Web page. If you are creating a page with multiple detailed images, consider displaying thumbnail images instead. This way, visitors who are interested in the images and willing to wait can use the thumbnail image to link to the larger image. Most graphics applications can create thumbnail images.

Advanced Techniques: Image Slicing

Graphic artists and designers can create complex Web page images. Sometimes parts of these images are better optimized as GIFs than as JPEGs. Some parts of these images may be better optimized as JPEGs than as GIFs. By **image slicing** the single, complex images into multiple, smaller images, you can optimize all portions for the most efficient display. There may be times when you plan special mouse rollover effects for parts of a large, complex image. In this case, parts of the image need to be individually accessible to scripting languages and the image needs to be sliced. When an image is sliced, it is broken into multiple graphic files. These multiple graphic files are formatted using an XHTML table. Most graphics applications, such as Macromedia Fireworks and Adobe Photoshop, have features for image slicing that automatically create the XHTML for you. Visit the textbook Web site at http://webdevfoundations.net/4e/chapter4.html for more information on image slicing.

4.5 Sources and Guidelines for Graphics

How do you obtain graphics for your pages? What are recommended ways to use graphics? This section will help you answer these questions and discuss sources of graphics as well as guidelines for using images on Web pages.

Sources of Graphics

There are many ways to obtain graphics: you can create them using a graphics application, download them from a free site, purchase and download them from a graphics site, purchase a graphics collection on a CD, take digital photographs, scan photographs, scan drawings, or hire a graphic designer to create graphics for you. Popular graphic applications include Adobe Photoshop, Adobe Fireworks, and Jasc Paint Shop Pro. These applications usually include tutorials and sample images to help you get started. Visit the textbook Web site at http://webdevfoundations.net/4e/chapter4.html, for tutorials on using Adobe Fireworks and Adobe Photoshop to create a logo banner image.

Focus on Ethics

However, one thing that you should definitely not do is right-click and download graphics that others have created without first obtaining their permission. Materials on a Web site are copyrighted (even if a copyright symbol or notice does not appear) and are not free to use unless the owner of the site permits it.

There are many Web sites that offer free graphics, although some graphics are free for nonprofit use only. Choose a search engine and search for "free graphics"—you'll get more results than you have time to view. The following are a few sites that you may find helpful when looking for images:

- Microsoft Clip Art: http://office.microsoft.com/clipart/default.aspx
- FamFamFam: http://www.famfamfam.com
- Free Stock Photos: http://free-stock-photos.com
- Free Images: http://www.freeimages.co.uk

Some sites offer graphics and photographs for a fee. A selection is listed here. Search for "stock photos" to find others.

- The Stock Solution: http://www.tssphoto.com
- SuperStock: http://www.superstock.com
- Getty Images: http://creative.gettyimages.com

It is also possible to create a banner or button image online. There are a number of sites that offer this feature—some include advertising with your free image, some offer paid memberships, others are simply free. Search for "create free online banner" to find sites offering this service.

- Animation Online: http://www.animationonline.com
- 3D Textmaker: http://www.3dtextmaker.com
- Cooltext.com: http://www.cooltext.com
- Ad Designer.com: http://www.addesigner.com

Guidelines for Using Images

Images can help your Web page by creating an engaging, interesting user experience. Images can hurt your Web pages by slowing down their performance to a crawl and discouraging visitors.

Consider Image Load Time. Be careful when using images on Web pages—it takes time for them to load. A suggested maximum file size for both the Web page and all the media files used by it is 60KB. If your banner graphic is 25KB, that does not leave much room for other images or even for your Web page XHTML. Use images when they are necessary to convey a message or complement a Web site's look and feel. Table 4.4 lists the download time for file sizes of 30KB, 60KB, and 90KB at various connection speeds.

Table 4.4 Download times

File Size	Connection Speed				
	28.8KB	33.6KB	56KB	ISDN (128KB)	T-1 (1.544MB)
30KB	8 seconds	7 seconds	4 seconds	1 second	Less than 1 second
60KB	17 seconds	14 seconds	8 seconds	3 seconds	Less than 1 second
90KB	25 seconds	21 seconds	13 seconds	5 seconds	Less than 1 second

Reuse Images. Once an image from your site is requested for a Web page, it is stored in the cache on your visitor's hard drive. Subsequent requests for the image will use the file from the hard drive instead of another download. This results in faster page loads for all pages that also use the image. It is recommended that you reuse common graphics such as logos and navigation buttons on multiple pages instead of creating different versions of these common graphics.

Consider the Size/Quality Issue. When using a graphics application to create an image, you can choose among varying levels of image quality. There is a correspondence between the quality of the image and the size of the image file—the higher the quality, the larger the file size. Choose the smallest file that gives you appropriate quality. You may need to experiment until you get the right match. Also be aware of the file size when using graphics created by others—the image may look great but if it is 300KB, you really shouldn't use it on a Web page.

Use Appropriate Resolution. Web browsers display images at relatively low resolution—72ppi (pixels per inch) or 96ppi. Many digital cameras and scanners can create images with much higher resolution. Of course, higher resolution means larger file size. Even though the browser does not display the depth of resolution, more bandwidth is still used for the large file size. Be careful when taking digital photographs or scanning. Use a resolution setting appropriate for Web pages. A one-inch image saved at 150ppi will appear close to two inches wide on a 72ppi monitor.

Specify Dimensions. Always use accurate `height` and `width` attributes on image tags. This will allow the browser to allocate the appropriate space on the Web page for the image and load the page faster. Do not try to resize the appearance of an image by modifying the settings of the `height` and `width` attributes. While this will work, your page will load slower and your image quality may suffer. Instead, use a graphics application to create a smaller or larger version of the graphic when needed.

Be Aware of Brightness and Contrast. Gamma refers to the brightness and contrast of the monitor display. Monitors used with Macintosh and Windows operating systems use a different default gamma setting (Macintosh 1.8, Windows 2.2). Images that have good contrast on a computer running Windows may look slightly washed out on a Macintosh. Images created on a Macintosh may look darker with less contrast when displayed on a computer with a Windows operating system. Be aware that even monitors on the same operating system may have slightly different gamma values than the default for the platform. A Web developer cannot control gamma, but should be aware that images will look different on various platforms because of this issue.

Web Accessibility

Even though images help to create a compelling, interesting Web site, remember that not all your visitors will be able to view your images. The Web Accessibility Initiative has a number of guidelines for Web developers in the use of color and images.

- Don't rely on color alone. Some visitors may have color perception deficiencies. Use high contrast between background and text color.
- Provide a text equivalent for every nontext element. Use the `alt` attribute on your image tags.
- If your site navigation uses image links, provide simple text links at the bottom of the page.

Vinton Cerf, the coinventor of TCP/IP and the former Chairman of the Internet Society, said, "The Internet is for everyone." Follow Web accessibility guidelines to ensure that this is true.

CHECKPOINT 4.3

1. Search for a site that uses image links to provide navigation. List the URL of the page. What colors are used on the image links? If the image links contain text, is there good contrast between the background color and letters on the image links? Would the page be accessible to a visitor who is sight-challenged? How have accessibility issues been addressed? Is the `alt` attribute used to describe the image link? Is there a row of text links in the footer section of the page? Answer these questions and discuss your findings.

2. When configuring an image map, describe the relationship between the image, map, and area tags.

3. True or False? Save your images using the smallest file size possible.

CHAPTER SUMMARY

This chapter introduced the use of visual elements and graphics on Web pages. As you continue to create Web pages, refer to the guidelines and accessibility issues related to graphics. The number one reason visitors leave Web pages is long download times. When using images, be careful to minimize download time. Also, provide alternatives to images (such as text links) and use the `alt` attribute on your pages.

Visit the textbook Web site at http://www.webdevfoundations.net for examples, the links listed in this chapter, and updated information.

Key Terms

`<area />`	gamma	lossless compression
`<hr />`	GIF	lossy compression
`<img />`	halo effect	`padding` property
`<map>`	`height` attribute	pixelation
`alt` attribute	hotspots	PNG
animated GIFs	`hspace` attribute	progressive JPEG
antialiasing	image link	resolution
`background-image` property	image map	`src` attribute
`background-repeat` property	image optimization	thumbnail image
`border` property	image slicing	transparency
`border-color` property	interlaced image	`usemap` attribute
`border-style` property	JPEG	`vspace` attribute
`border-width` property	`longdesc` attribute	`width` attribute

Review Questions

Multiple Choice

1. Why should you include `height` and `width` attributes on an `<img />` tag?
   a. They are required attributes and must always be included.
   b. They help the browser render the page faster because it reserves the appropriate space for the image.
   c. They help the browser display the image in its own window.
   d. none of the above

2. If you use CSS to configure both the background image and the background color, the browser will do which of the following?
   a. display the background color instead of the background image.
   b. display no background for the page because it is confused.
   c. display the background color while the background image loads and while the background image is displayed.
   d. none of the above

3. Which of the following creates an image link to the index.html page when the home.gif graphic is clicked?

a. `<a href="index.html"`
   `src="home.gif"></a>`
b. `<a href="index.html"><img`
   `src="home.gif" /></a>`
c. `<img src="home.gif"`
   `href="index.html">`
d. none of the above

4. What XHTML element is used to place an image on a Web page?

a. `<a href>`
b. `<img />`
c. `<image>`
d. `<graphic>`

5. Which attribute specifies text that is available to browsers and other user agents that do not support graphics?

a. `alt`
b. `text`
c. `src`
d. none of the above

6. Which of the following configures the size, color, and display style of an element's border?

a. `border-edge` property
b. `padding` property
c. `border` property
d. none of the above

7. Which of the following graphic types is best suited to photographs?

a. GIF
b. photo
c. PNG
d. none of the above

8. Which of the following graphic types can be made transparent and is most commonly used on the Web?

a. GIF
b. JPG
c. PNG
d. photo

9. Which of the following configures empty space between the content of the XHTML element (usually text) and the border?

a. `vspace` property
b. `padding` property
c. `margin` property
d. none of the above

10. Which of the following configures a graphic to repeat vertically down the side of a Web page?

a. `hspace="10"`
b. `background-repeat:repeat;`
c. `valign="left"`
d. `background-repeat: repeat-y;`

Fill in the Blank

11. A background image will automatically be repeated, or _____, by a Web browser.

12. If your Web page uses graphic links, include _____ at the bottom of the page to increase accessibility.

13. A _____ image is a smaller version of a larger image that usually links to the larger image.

14. One method to obtain graphics for your Web site is to _____.

15. A(n) _____ is an image that can be used as one or more hyperlinks.

Apply Your Knowledge

1. **Predict the Result.** Draw and write a brief description of the Web page that will be created with the following XHTML code:

```
<?xml version="1.0" encoding="UTF-8"?>
<!DOCTYPE html PUBLIC "-//W3C//DTD XHTML 1.0 Transitional//EN"
   "http://www.w3.org/TR/xhtml1/DTD/xhtml1-transitional.dtd">
<html xmlns="http://www.w3.org/1999/xhtml">
<head>
```

```
<title>Predict the Result</title>
</head>
<body>
  <div>
    <img src="logo.gif" alt="CircleSoft Design"
    height="150" width="600" />    <br />
    <p>Home <a href="about.html">About</a>
      <a href="services.html">Services</a>
    </p>
  </div>
    <p><img src="people.jpg" alt="Professionals at CircleSoft
Design" height="300" width="300" align="right" /> Our professional
staff takes pride in its working relationship with our clients by
offering personalized services which listen to their needs,
develop their target areas, and incorporate these items into a
well presented Web Site that works.</p>
    <p> </p>
    <p> </p>
    <div>
    <p>Contact
      <a href="mailto:web@circlesoft.com">web@circlesoft.com</a><br />
      Copyright &copy; 2008 CircleSoft Design</p>
    </div>
</body>
</html>
```

2. **Fill in the Missing Code.** This Web page contains an image link and should be configured so that the background and text colors have good contrast. The image used on this Web page should link to a page called services.html. Some XHTML attribute values, indicated by "_" are missing. Some CSS style rules indicated by "_" are incomplete.

```
<?xml version="1.0" encoding="UTF-8"?>
<!DOCTYPE html PUBLIC "-//W3C//DTD XHTML 1.0 Transitional//EN"
    "http://www.w3.org/TR/xhtml1/DTD/xhtml1-transitional.dtd">
<html xmlns="http://www.w3.org/1999/xhtml">
<head>
<title>CircleSoft Design</title>
<style type="text/css">
.body { "_": "_";
        color: "_";
}
</style>
</head>
<body>
<div>
  <a href="_"><img src="logo.gif" alt="_" height="100" width="600" />
  <br />Enter CircleSoft Design</a>
</div>
</body>
</html>
```

3. Find the Error. This page displays an image called trillium.jpg. The image is 100 pixels wide by 200 pixels high. When this page is displayed, the image does not look right. Find the error. Describe the attributes that you would code in the `<img />` tag to provide accessibility.

```
<?xml version="1.0" encoding="UTF-8"?>
<!DOCTYPE html PUBLIC "-//W3C//DTD XHTML 1.0 Transitional//EN"
    "http://www.w3.org/TR/xhtml1/DTD/xhtml1-transitional.dtd">
<html xmlns="http://www.w3.org/1999/xhtml">
<head>
<title>Find the Error<title>
</head>
<body>
<img src="trillium.jpg" height="100" width="100" />
</body>
</html>
```

Hands-On Exercises

1. Write the XHTML to place an image called mylogo.gif on a Web page. The image is 100 pixels high by 600 pixels wide.

2. Write the XHTML to create an image hyperlink. The image is called myfamily.jpg. It is 200 pixels high by 300 pixels wide. The image should link to a Web page called family.htm. There should be no border on the image.

3. Write the XHTML to create a `<div>` containing three images used as navigation links. Table 4.5 provides information about the images and their associated links.

Table 4.5

Image Name	Link Page Name	Image Height	Image Width
home.gif	index.html	50	200
products.gif	products.html	50	200
order.gif	order.html	50	200

4. Experiment with page backgrounds.

a. Locate the twocolor.gif file in the student files chapter4/starters folder. Design a Web page that uses this file as a background image that repeats down the left side of the browser window. Save your file as bg1.html. Hand in printouts of the source code (print in Notepad) and the browser display of your page to your instructor.

b. Locate the twocolor1.gif file in the student files chapter4/starters folder. Design a Web page that uses this file as a background image that repeats across the top of the browser window. Save your file as bg2.html. Hand in printouts of the source code (print in Notepad) and the browser display of your page to your instructor.

5. Visit one of your favorite Web sites. Note the colors used for background, text, headings, images, and so on. Write a paragraph that describes how the site uses color for these elements and if the Web Safe Color Palette is used. Code a Web page (either a new page or you can use the index.html file from the student files, Chapter4/index.html) that uses colors in a similar manner.

6. Think of one of your favorite quotes by someone you admire. Design a Web page that displays the person's name in a heading, their photo, and the quote in a paragraph. Configure the photo to be an image link to a Web site about the person.

   (*Note*: It is unethical to steal an image from another Web site. Some Web sites have a link to their copyright policy. Most Web sites will give permission for you to use an image in a school assignment. If there is no available policy, e-mail the site's contact person and request permission to use the photo. If you are unable to obtain permission, you may substitute with clip art or an image from a free site.)

Focus on Ethics

7. Design a new Web page about your favorite movie. Configure a background color for the page, and either background images or background colors for at least two sections of the page. Search the Web for a photo of a scene from the movie, an actress in the movie, or an actor in the movie.

   Include the following information on your Web page:

   - Title of the movie
   - Director or producer
   - Leading actor
   - Leading actress
   - Rating (R, PG-13, PG, G, NR)
   - A brief description of the movie
   - An absolute link to a review about the movie

   Save the page as movie3.html. Hand in printouts of both the source code (print in Notepad) and the browser display of your page to your instructor.

   (*Note*: It is unethical to steal an image from another Web site. Some Web sites have a link to their copyright policy. Most Web sites will give permission for you to use an image in a school assignment. If there is no available policy, e-mail the site's contact person and request permission to use the photo. If you are unable to obtain permission, you may substitute with clip art or an image from a free site instead.)

Focus on Ethics

8. Design a Web page that provides a list of resources for free clip art and free photographs. The list should contain at least five different Web sites. Use your favorite graphic sites, the sites suggested in this chapter, or sites you have found on the Web. Save the page as freegraphics.html. Hand in printouts of both the source code (print in Notepad) and the browser display of your page to your instructor.

9. Design a Web page about your favorite musical group. Use a background color for the page and either background images or background colors for at least two sections of the page. Search the Web for a photo of the group.

   Include the following information about the group on your Web page:

   - Name of group
   - Type of music
   - Names of principle group members
   - Photo of group
   - Link to another Web page with information about the group.

   Save the page as band3.html. Hand in printouts of the source code (print in Notepad) and the browser display of your page to your instructor.

Focus on Ethics

(*Note*: It is unethical to steal an image from another Web site. Some Web sites have a link to their copyright policy. Most Web sites will give permission for you to use an image in a school assignment. If there is no available policy, e-mail the site's contact person and request permission to use the photo. If you are unable to obtain permission, you may substitute clip art or an image from a free site.)

10. Visit the textbook Web site at http://webdevfoundations.net/4e/chapter4.html and follow the link to the Adobe Fireworks or Adobe Photoshop tutorial. Follow the instructions to create a logo banner. Hand in the printouts described in the tutorial to your instructor.

Web Research

Providing access to the Web for all people is an important issue. Visit the W3C's Web Accessibility Initiative and explore their WCAG 2.0 Quick Reference at http://www.w3 .org/WAI/WCAG20/quickref/ (the textbook Web site at http://webdevfoundations.net/ 4e/chapter4.html has an updated link if needed). View additional pages at the W3C's site as necessary. Explore the checkpoints that are related to the use of color and images on Web pages. Create a Web page that uses color, uses images, and includes the information that you discovered. Print both the source code (from Notepad) and the browser view of your Web page.

Focus on Web Design

Visit a Web sites that interests you. Print the home page or one other pertinent page from the site. Write a one-page summary and reaction to the Web site you chose to visit. Address the following topics:

    a. What is the purpose of the site?

    b. Who is the intended audience?

    c. Do you believe the site reaches its audience?

    d. Was this site useful to you? Why or why not?

    e. List the colors that were used on the home page of this Web site: background, backgrounds of page sections, text, logo, navigation buttons, and so on.

    f. How did the use of color enhance the Web site?

WEB SITE CASE STUDY
Using Graphics

Each of the following case studies continues throughout most of the text. This chapter adds images to the Web sites, creates a new page, and modifies existing pages.

JavaJam Coffee House

See Chapter 2 for an introduction to the JavaJam Coffee House Case Study. Figure 2.26 shows a site map for the JavaJam Web site. The Home page and Menu page were created in earlier chapters. You will continue to work with this Web site here.

You have the following tasks:

1. Modify the Home page to display a logo, a JPEG image, and additional text, as shown in Figure 4.25 (shown also in the color insert section).

Figure 4.25
New JavaJam Home page

See the center color insert

2. Modify the Menu page to be consistent with the Home page.
3. Create a new Music page, as shown in Figure 4.26.
4. Modify the style rules in the javajam.css file as needed.

Figure 4.26
JavaJam music.html

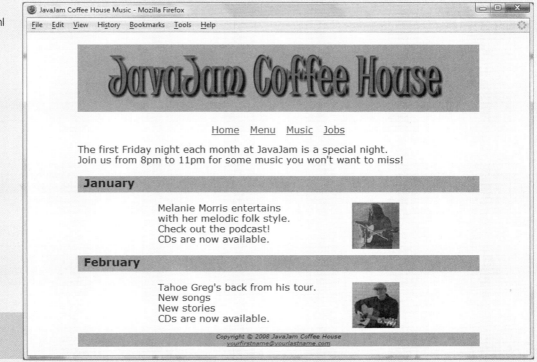

See the center color insert

Hands-On Practice Case

Obtain the images used in this case study from the student files. The images are located in the Chapter4/CaseStudyStarters folder. The images are: melanie.jpg (Figure 4.27), melaniethumb.jpg (Figure 4.28), greg.jpg (Figure 4.29), gregthumb.jpg (Figure 4.30), javalogo.gif (Figure 4.31), and windingroad.jpg (Figure 4.32). Save them in your javajam folder.

Figure 4.27
Melanie Morris (melanie.jpg)

Figure 4.28
Melanie Morris thumbnail (melaniethumb.jpg)

Figure 4.29
Greg (greg.jpg)

Figure 4.30
Greg thumbnail (gregthumb.jpg)

Figure 4.31
JavaJam logo (javalogo.gif)

Figure 4.32
Winding road (windingroad.jpg)

1. **The Home Page.** Launch Notepad and open the index.html file from your javajam folder. Modify the index.html file to look similar to the Web page shown in Figure 4.25.

   - Replace the JavaJam Coffee House heading with the javalogo.gif, Figure 4.31. Be sure to include the `alt`, `height`, and `width` attributes on the `<img />` tag for the graphic.
   - Configure windingroad.jpg, Figure 4.32, to display on the right side of the paragraph. Be sure to include the `alt`, `height`, and `width` attributes. *Hint*: Use the `align="right"` attribute on the `<img />` tag. *Note*: In Chapter 6 you'll learn to use CSS to configure this alignment.

   Save and test your new index.html page.

2. **The Menu Page.** Launch Notepad and open the menu.html page from your java-jam folder. Modify the menu.html page in a similar manner—adding the logo banner. Save and test your new menu.html page.

3. **The Music Page.** Use the Menu page as the starting point for the Music page. Launch Notepad and open the menu.html file in the javajam folder that you previously created. Save the file as music.html.

Modify the music.html file to look similar to the Music page, as shown in Figure 4.26:

- Change the page title to an appropriate phrase.
- Delete the definition list from the page.
- The main content in the page will consist of an introductory paragraph below the navigation and two sections describing music performances.
- The content of the paragraph is as follows:

  The first Friday night each month at JavaJam is a special night. Join us from 8pm to 11pm for some music you won't want to miss!

  Place a line break tag after the first sentence.

- The section describing each music performance consists of an `<h3>` element, a paragraph, and an image link. You'll need to configure the paragraph, so assign it to a class named `content`.

- January Music Performance:

  Configure an `<h3>` with the following text: January

  Configure a paragraph assigned to the `content` class with the following text:

  Melanie Morris entertains

  with her melodic folk style.

  Check out the podcast!

  CDs are now available.

  Add line breaks as indicated above.

- Configure the melaniethumb.jpg as an image link to melanie.jpg. Code appropriate attributes on the `<img />` element, including `align="right"`

- February Music Performance:

  Configure an `<h3>` with the following text: February

  Configure a paragraph assigned to the `content` class with the following text:

  Tahoe Greg's back from his tour.

  New songs

  New stories

  CDs are now available.

  Add line breaks as indicated above.

- Configure the gregthumb.jpg as an image link to greg.jpg. Code appropriate attributes on the `<img />` element, including `align="right"`

- Save the music.html file. If you test your page in a browser you'll notice that it looks different from Figure 4.26—you still need to configure style rules.

4. **Configure the CSS.** Open javajam.css in Notepad. Edit the style rules as follows:

- Modify the `h1` selector. Remove the line-height style rule.
- Add a new style rule for the `h3` selector that configures a background color (#ccaa66), left padding (10px) and bottom padding (5px). The style rules follow:

```
background-color: #ccaa66;
padding-left: 10px;
padding-bottom: 5px;
```

- Configure the class named `content` to add 20 percent left and right padding (use `padding-left` and `padding-right`). Notice how this adds empty space either side of the music performance description and image.
- Configure the `img` selector not to display a border.

Save the javajam.css file. Test it in a browser. If your images do not appear or your image links do not work, examine your work carefully. Use Windows Explorer to verify that the images are saved in your javajam folder. Examine the `src` attribute on the `<img />` tags to be sure you spelled the image names correctly. Another useful troubleshooting technique is to validate the XHTML and CSS code. See Chapters 2 and 3 for Hands-On Practice exercises that describe how to use these validators.

Fish Creek Animal Hospital

See Chapter 2 for an introduction to the Fish Creek Animal Hospital Case Study. Figure 2.30 shows a site map for Fish Creek. The Home page and Services page were created in earlier chapters. You will continue to work with this Web site in this case study, creating the Ask the Vet page, shown in Figure 4.33 (shown also in the color insert section). You will then modify the other pages so they are consistent with the new design.

Figure 4.33
Fish Creek
askvet.html

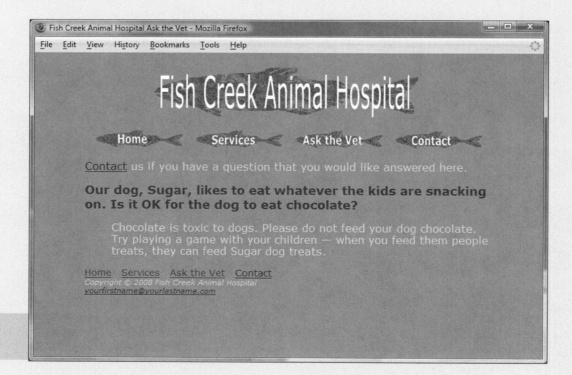

See the center
color insert

Hands-On Practice Case

Obtain the images used in this case study from the student files. The images are located in the Chapter4/CaseStudyStarters folder. The images are: fishcreeklogo.gif (Figure 4.34), home.gif (Figure 4.35), services.gif (Figure 4.36), askthevet.gif (Figure 4.37), and contact.gif (Figure 4.38). Save the files in your fishcreek folder.

Figure 4.34
Fish Creek logo
(fishcreeklogo.gif)

Figure 4.35
Home button
(home.gif)

Figure 4.36
Services button
(services.gif)

Figure 4.37
Ask the Vet button
(askthevet.gif)

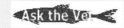

Figure 4.38
Contact button
(contact.gif)

1. **The Ask the Vet Page.** Use the Services page as the starting point for the Ask the Vet page. Launch Notepad and open the services.html file in the fishcreek folder that you previously created. Save the file as askvet.html.

   Modify your file to look similar to the Ask the Vet page, as shown in Figure 4.33.

   - Change the page title to an appropriate phrase.

   - Replace the Fish Creek Animal Hospital heading with the fishcreeklogo.gif, as shown in Figure 4.34. Be sure to include the `alt`, `height`, and `width` attributes on the `<img />` tag for the graphic.

   - Move the text links to the bottom of the page right above the copyright information (see Figure 4.33).

   - See Figure 4.33 and add image links under the logo area. Use a `<div>` element to contain this area. Assign the `<div>` to a class named `imgnav`. The home.gif (Figure 4.35) should link to index.html. The services.gif (Figure 4.36) should link to services.html. The askthevet.gif (Figure 4.37) should link to askvet.html. The contact.gif (Figure 4.38) should link to contact.html. Use appropriate attributes on the `<img />` tag: `alt`, `height`, `width`.

   - Delete the unordered list that was part of the services.html page.

   - The page content consists of a paragraph of text followed by a definition list that contains a question and answer.

   - Replace the text in the paragraph as follows:

     Contact us if you have a question that you would like answered here.

     The word "Contact" should link to the contact.html page.

   - The definition list displays the question and answer. The `<dt>` element configures the question. Assign the `<dt>` element to the `category` class used on the Services page. The `<dd>` element configures the answer.

- The content of the definition list is as follows:

  Question: Our dog, Sugar, likes to eat whatever the kids are snacking on. Is it OK for the dog to eat chocolate?"

  Answer: Chocolate is toxic to dogs. Please do not feed your dog chocolate. Try playing a game with your children—when you feed them people treats they can feed Sugar dog treats.

2. **Configure the CSS.** Open fishcreek.css in Notepad. Edit the style rules as follows:

   - The fish navigation image area is quite wide. Modify the style rules and change the width of the page content `container` id from 80 percent to 700 pixels.

   - Modify the style rules for the `h1` selector. Delete the existing style rules. Add a new style rule to center the image (use `text-align:center`).

   - Configure the class named `imgnav` to be centered (use `text-align:center`).

   - Configure the `img` selector not to display a border.

   Save the fishcreek.css file.

3. **Save and Test.** Save your page and test it in a browser. If your images do not appear or your image links do not work, examine your work carefully. Use Windows Explorer to verify that the images are saved in your fishcreek folder. Examine the `src` attribute on the image tags to be sure you spelled the image names correctly. Another useful troubleshooting technique is to validate the XHTML and CSS code. See Chapters 2 and 3 for Hands-On Practice exercises that describe how to use these validators.

4. **The Home and Services Pages.** Modify the Home page (index.html) and Services page (services.html) to look similar to the Ask the Vet page you just created. Save and test your pages. Notice how the use of coordinating logo and navigation images helped to unite the Web site visually. To provide accessibility, the original text navigation links were not deleted. Instead, they were moved to the bottom of the page. It is common for sites that use images for main navigation to provide simple text links at the lower portion of each Web page.

Pete the Painter

See Chapter 2 for an introduction to the Pete the Painter Case Study. Figure 2.34 shows a site map for Pete the Painter. The Home page and Services page were created in earlier chapters. You will continue to work with this Web site in this case study and create the Testimonials page, as shown in Figure 4.39 (shown also in the color insert section). You will then modify the other pages so they are consistent with the new design.

Hands-On Practice Case

Obtain the images used in this case study from the student files. The images are located in the Chapter4/CaseStudyStarters folder. The images are: painterlogo.gif (Figure 4.40), paintroom.jpg (Figure 4.41), paintroom_small.jpg (Figure 4.42), undecorated.jpg (Figure 4.43), and undecorated_small.jpg (Figure 4.44). Save the files in your painter folder.

1. **The Testimonials Page.** Use the Services page as the starting point for the Testimonials page. Launch Notepad and open the services.html file in the painter

Figure 4.39
Pete the Painter
testimonials.html

See the center
color insert

Figure 4.40
Pete the Painter logo
(painterlogo.gif)

Figure 4.41
Painted room
(paintroom.jpg)

Figure 4.42
Painted room thumbnail
(paintroom_small.jpg)

Figure 4.43
Undecorated room
(undecorated.jpg)

Figure 4.44
Undecorated room thumbnail
(undecorated_small.jpg)

folder that you previously created. Save the file as testimonials.html Modify your file to look similar to the Testimonials page, as shown in Figure 4.39:

- Change the page title to an appropriate phrase.
- Replace the Pete the Painter heading with the painterlogo.gif, Figure 4.40. Be sure to include the `alt`, `height`, and `width` attributes on the `<img />` tag for the graphic.
- Delete the unordered list that was copied as part of the services.html page.
- The main content consists of two sections describing testimonials with an `<h4>` element, a paragraph, and an image hyperlink.

Painting Testimonial

- Configure an `<h4>` with the following text: Painting
- Configure a paragraph with the following text:

    We were selling our home and needed a room painted quickly. Pete's team promptly came out and gave an estimate. It was quite reasonably priced.

    They started and finished the very next day!—The Morris Family.

- Configure the paintroom_small.jpg as an image link to paintroom.jpg. Code appropriate attributes on the `<img />` element, including `align="left"`. *Note*: In Chapter 6 you'll learn to use CSS to configure this alignment.

Remodeling Testimonial

- Configure an `<h4>` with the following text: Remodeling
- Configure a paragraph with the following text:

    We needed to "undecorate" a room — the previous owners had been a little too creative. Pete's team provided an estimate, promptly began work, and within a few days our room was looking great! — The Felkes.

- Configure the undecorated_small.jpg as an image link to undecorated.jpg. Code appropriate attributes on the `<img />` element, including `align="left"`.

Save the testimonials.html file. If you test your page in a browser you'll notice that it looks different from Figure 4.39 — you still need to configure style rules.

2. **Configure the CSS.** Open painter.css in Notepad. Edit the style rules as follows:
   - Add a new style rule for the h4 selector that configures a background color (#336633), text color (#ffffff), font typeface (Georgia, Times New Roman, or serif), left padding (10px), and bottom padding (5px).
   - Modify the CSS to configure an id named `container` with width set to 620 pixels.
   - Configure the `img` selector as follows: 10 pixels of right padding and do not display a border.

   Save the painter.css file.

3. **Configure the `container` id on each page.** Modify the index.html, services.html, and testimonials.html pages to utilize a wrapper `<div>` that configures the page width as indicated. On each page, assign the `container` id to a `<div>` element that contains the page content (see Section 3.9 for a review). Configure this `<div>` on each page as follows:

```
<body>
  <div id="container">
  ... page content goes here
  </div>
</body>
```

4. **Test.** Test your pages in a browser. If your images do not appear or your image links do not work, examine your work carefully. Use Windows Explorer to verify that the images are saved in your painter folder. Examine the `src` attribute on the `<img />` tags to be sure you spelled the image names correctly. Another useful troubleshooting technique is to validate the XHTML and CSS code. See Chapters 2 and 3 for Hands-On Practice exercises that describe how to use these validators.

5. **The Home and Services Pages.** Modify the Home page (index.html) and Services page (services.html) to display the Pete the Painter logo (painterlogo.gif) image and look similar to the Testimonials page you just created. A cohesive Web site uses color and images in a consistent manner. Save and test your pages.

Prime Properties

See Chapter 2 for an introduction to the Prime Properties Case Study. Figure 2.38 shows a site map for Prime Properties. A Home page and Financing page were created in earlier chapters. You will continue to work with this Web site in this case study and create the Listings page, as shown in Figure 4.45 (shown also in the color insert section). You will then modify the other pages so that they are consistent with the new design.

Hands-On Practice Case

Obtain the images used in this case study from the student files. The images are located in the Chapter4/CaseStudyStarters folder. The images are: primelogo.gif (Figure 4.46), primehomenav.gif (Figure 4.47), primehomebtn.gif (Figure 4.48), primelistingsnav.gif (Figure 4.49), primelistingsbtn.gif (Figure 4.50), primefinancingnav.gif (Figure 4.51), primefinancingbtn.gif (Figure 4.52), primecontactnav.gif (Figure 4.53), primecontactbtn.gif (Figure 4.54), schaumburg.jpg (Figure 4.55), schaumburgthumb.jpg (Figure 4.56), libertyville.jpg (Figure 4.57), and libertyvillethumb.jpg (Figure 4.58). Save the files in your prime folder.

Figure 4.45
Prime Properties
listings.html

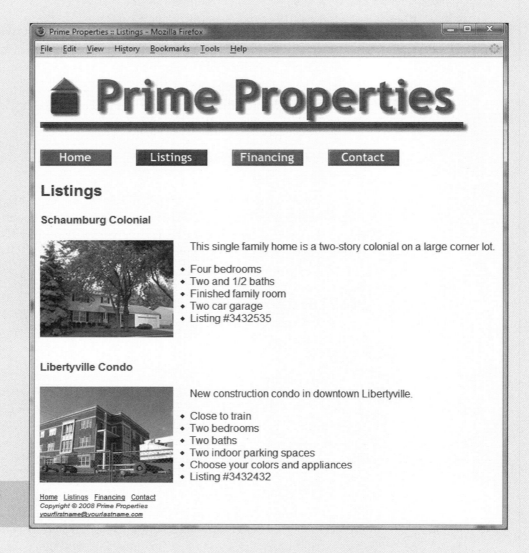

See the center
color insert

Figure 4.46
Prime Properties logo
(primelogo.gif)

Figure 4.47
Home navigation
button
(primehomenav.gif)

Figure 4.48
Home page
placeholder button
(primehomebtn.gif)

Figure 4.49
Listings navigation
button
(primelistingsnav.gif)

Figure 4.50
Listings page
placeholder button
(primelistingsbtn.gif)

Figure 4.51
Financing
navigation button
(primefinancingnav.gif)

Figure 4.52
Financing page
placeholder button
(primefinancingbtn.gif)

Figure 4.53
Contact navigation
button
(primecontactnav.gif)

Figure 4.54
Contact page
placeholder button
(primecontactbtn.gif)

Figure 4.55
Schaumburg listing photo (schaumburg.jpg)

Figure 4.56
Schaumburg listing thumbnail
(schaumburgthumb.jpg)

Figure 4.57
Libertyville listing photo (libertyville.jpg)

Figure 4.58
Libertyville listing thumbnail
(libertyvillethumb.jpg)

1. **The Listings Page.** Use the Financing page as the starting point for the Listings page. Launch Notepad and open the financing.html file in the prime folder that you previously created. Save the file as listings.html. Modify your file to look similar to the Listings page, as shown in Figure 4.45.

   - Change the title to an appropriate phrase.
   - Replace the Prime Properties heading with the primelogo.gif, Figure 4.46. Be sure to include the `alt`, `height`, and `width` attributes on the `<img />` tag for the graphic.

     Move the text links to the bottom of the page right above the copyright information (see Figure 4.45).

   - See Figure 4.45 and add image links under the logo area. The navigation buttons use color as a visual cue for visitors. The navigation button links use a green background. The button for the current page is not a link and uses a blue background. To configure this area for the Listings page, use primehomenav.gif (link to index.html), primelistingsbtn.gif (no link), primefinancingnav.gif (link to financing.html), and primecontactnav.gif (link to contact.html). Place each image within its own paragraph. Use appropriate attributes on the `<img />` tag: `alt`, `height`, and `width`.
   - Replace the heading Financing with the heading Listings.
   - Delete the text between the Listings heading and the text navigation near the footer section of the Web page.
   - The section describing each listing consists of an `<h4>` element, a paragraph, an image link, and an unordered list.

   Schaumburg Colonial Listing
   - Configure an `<h4>` with the following text: Schaumburg Colonial
   - Configure a paragraph with the following text:

     This single family home is a two-story colonial on a large lot.
   - Configure the schaumburgthumb.jpg as an image link to schaumburg.jpg. Assign the `<img />` element to a class named property. Code appropriate attributes on the `<img />` element, including `align="left"`. *Note*: In Chapter 6 you'll learn to use CSS to configure this alignment.
   - Configure an unordered list with the following text:

     Four bedrooms

     Two and 1/2 baths

     Finished family room

     Two car garage

     Listing #3432535
   - Code a line break between the two listings.

   Libertyville Condo Listing
   - Configure an `<h4>` with the following text:

     Libertyville Condo
   - Configure a paragraph with the following text:

     New construction condo in downtown Libertyville.

- Configure the libertyvillethumb.jpg as an image link to libertyville.jpg. Assign the `<img />` element to a class named property. Code appropriate attributes on the `<img />` element, including `align="left"`.

- Configure an unordered list with the following text:

  Close to train

  Two bedrooms

  Two baths

  Two indoor parking spaces

  Choose your colors and appliances

  Listing #3432432

Save the listings.html file. If you test your page in a browser you'll notice that it looks different from Figure 4.45—you still need to configure style rules.

2. **Configure the CSS.** Open prime.css in Notepad. Edit the style rules as indicated.

   - Configure the `img` selector to not display a border.

   - Configure a class named property to have 25 pixels of right padding.

   Save the prime.css file.

3. **Test.** Test the listings.html page in a browser. If your images do not appear or your image links do not function, examine your work carefully. Use Windows Explorer to verify that the images are saved in your prime folder. Examine the `src` attributes on the `<img />` tags to be sure you spelled the image names correctly.

4. **The Home and Financing Pages.** Modify the Home page (index.html) and Financing page (financing.html) to be similar to the Listings page you just created. Pay close attention to the navigation buttons. Refer to Step 2 if necessary. Save and test your pages. Isn't it interesting how just a few images can add a professional look to a Web site?

Web Design

Chapter Objectives   In this chapter, you will learn how to . . .

- Describe the most common types of Web site organization
- Create clear, easy Web site navigation
- Design user-friendly Web pages
- Improve the readability of the text on your Web pages
- Use graphics appropriately
- Create accessible Web pages
- Describe design principles
- Describe Web page design techniques
- Apply best practices of Web design

As a Web site visitor, you have probably found that certain Web sites are appealing and easy to use while others seem awkward or just plain annoying. What separates the good from the bad? This chapter discusses recommended Web site design practices. The topics include site organization, site navigation, page design, text design, graphic design, and accessibility considerations.

Whatever your personal preferences, your Web site should be designed to appeal to your **target audience**—the people who will use your Web site. They may be teens, shoppers, college students, young couples, the list goes on and on. You should follow all of the recommended Web site design practices with an eye toward your target audience.

For example, NASA's site, http://www.nasa.gov (Figure 5.1), features compelling graphics and has a different look and feel from the text-based, link-intensive Bureau of Labor Statistics site (see http://www.bls.gov, Figure 5.2).

Figure 5.1
The compelling graphics draw you in

Figure 5.2
This Web site offers numerous choices

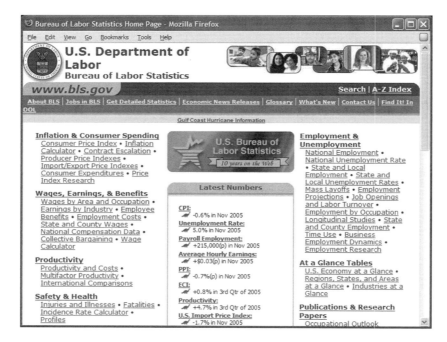

The first site engages you and draws you in. The second site provides you with a wide range of choices so that you can quickly get down to work. With your target audience in mind, take a look at some common recommended Web site design practices.

5.1 Web Site Organization

How will visitors move around your site? How will they find what they need? This is largely determined by the Web site's organization or architecture. There are three common types of Web site organization:

- Hierarchical
- Linear
- Random (sometimes called Web organization)

A diagram of the organization of a Web site is called a **site map** or **storyboard**. Creating the site map is one of the initial steps in developing a Web site (more on this in Chapter 10).

Hierarchical Organization

Most Web sites use **hierarchical organization**. A site map for hierarchical organization, such as the one shown in Figure 5.3, is characterized by a clearly defined home page with links to major site sections. Web pages within sections are placed as needed.

Figure 5.3
Hierarchical site organization

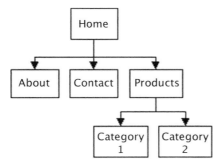

It is important to be aware of pitfalls of hierarchical organization. Figure 5.4 shows a site design that is too shallow—there are too many major site sections.

Figure 5.4
This site design uses a shallow hierarchy

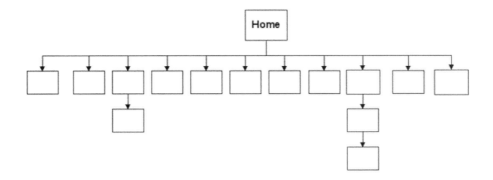

This site design needs to be broken down into small, easily managed topics or units, a process called **chunking**. In the case of Web page design, each unit of information is a page. George A. Miller, a research psychologist for Princeton University's WorldNet (http://www.cogsci.princeton.edu/~wn/) found that humans can store only five to nine chunks of information at a time in short-term memory (see http://www.well.com/user/smalin/miller.html). He called this the "seven plus or minus two" principle. Following this principle, many Web designers try not to place more than nine major navigation links on a page, unless they are creating a very large site. Even then, they may try to chunk the navigation links into visually separate sections on the page with each group having no more than nine links.

Another design pitfall is designing a site that is too deep. Figure 5.5 shows an example of this. The interface design "three click rule" says that a Web page visitor should be able to get from any page on your site to any other page on your site with a maximum of three hyperlinks. In other words, a visitor who cannot get what they want in three mouse clicks will begin to feel frustrated and may leave your site. This rule may be very difficult to satisfy on a large site, but in general, the goal is to organize your site so that your visitors can easily navigate from page to page within the site structure.

Figure 5.5
This site design uses a deep hierarchy

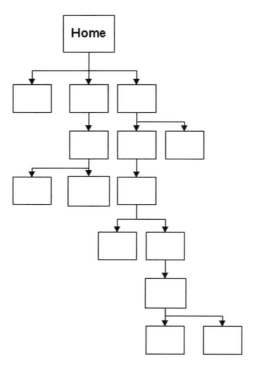

An example of hierarchical organization is the Map Collections area of the Library of Congress site at http://memory.loc.gov/ammem/gmdhtml/gmdhome.html. A partial site map is shown in Figure 5.6.

The Map Collections Home Page contains navigation to the main map areas. It functions as a map to the site (see Figure 5.7) and it is intentionally different from the content pages.

The main section content pages of a site usually have a similar look and feel. Two content pages are shown in Figure 5.8.

Figure 5.6
Map Collections site map

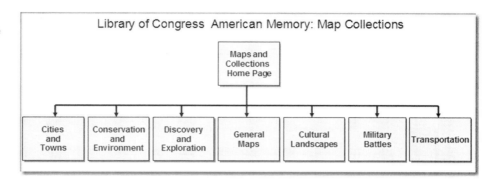

Figure 5.7
Map Collections Home page

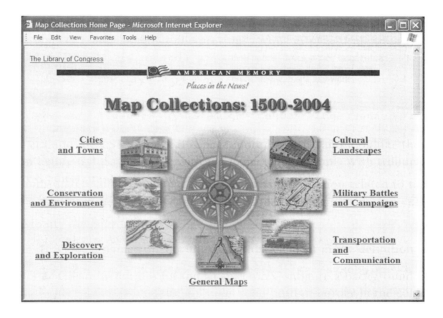

Figure 5.8
Sample content pages

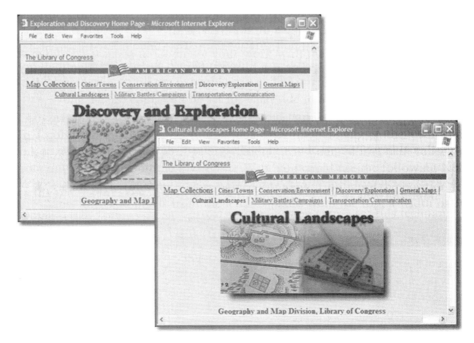

Each main section may have one or more subpages. Some sites with a hierarchical organization may use a consistent design for the home page and the content pages. Either method is acceptable. Most commercial sites, such as http://amazon.com and http://ebay.com use hierarchical site organization.

Linear Organization

When the purpose of a site or series of pages on a site is to provide a tutorial, tour, or presentation that needs to be viewed sequentially, **linear organization**, as shown in Figure 5.9, is useful.

Figure 5.9
Linear site organization

In linear organization, the pages are viewed one after another. Some Web sites use hierarchical organization in general, but with linear organization in a few small areas. An example of this is the National Library of Medicine site at http://www.nlm.nih.gov. The main site organization is hierarchical with linear organization used for tutorials. Notice the "Next" link in Figure 5.10; it's the link to the next page in the linear presentation.

Figure 5.10
Tutorial linear organization using the "Next" link

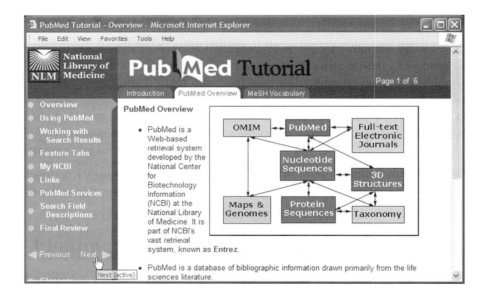

Random Organization

Random organization (sometimes called Web organization) offers no clear path through the site, as shown in Figure 5.11 There is often no clear home page and no discernable structure. Random organization is not as common as hierarchical or linear organization and is usually found only on artistic sites or sites that strive to be especially different and original. This type of organization is typically not used for commercial Web sites.

Figure 5.11
Random site
organization

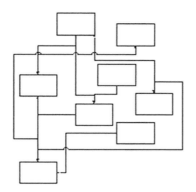

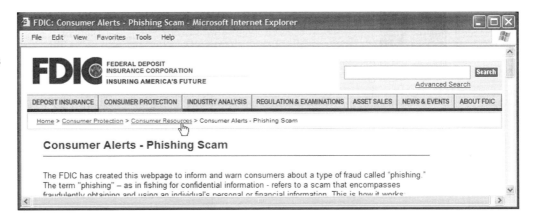

FAQ

Where do I begin?

Sometimes it is difficult to begin creating a site map for a Web site. Some design teams meet in a room with a blank wall and a package of large Post-it® Notes. They write the titles of topics and subtopics needed on the site on the Post-it® Notes. They arrange the notes on the wall and discuss until the site structure becomes clear and there is consensus within the group. If you are not working in a group, you can try this on your own and then discuss the way you have chosen to organize the Web site with a friend or fellow student.

5.2 Web Site Navigation—Best Practices

Ease of Navigation

Sometimes Web developers are so close to their sites that they can't see the forest for the trees. A new visitor will wander on to the site and not know what to click or how to find out what it offers. Clearly labeled navigation on each page is helpful—it should be in the same location on each page for maximum usability. A visitor should not feel lost in the site. Jakob Nielsen, a well-known Web usability and Web design professional, favors what he calls **breadcrumb trails** for larger sites. Figure 5.12 shows a page from http://www.fdic.gov, a site that has a well-organized navigation area near the top of the page in addition to personalized breadcrumb trails for each visitor. To access the

Figure 5.12
Visitors can follow the "breadcrumbs" to retrace their steps through the site

Phishing Scam page currently displayed, the visitor has already viewed the Home, Consumer Protection, and Consumer Alerts pages. Note the breadcrumb navigation at the top of the main content area: Home > Consumer Protection > Consumer Resources > Consumer Alerts-Phishing Scam. Visitors can easily retrace their steps or jump back to a previously viewed page.

Navigation Bars

Clear navigation bars, either graphic- or text-based, make it obvious to Web site users where they are and where they can go next. The site shown in Figure 5.13 includes a vertical text navigation bar down the left side of the page.

Figure 5.13
Vertical text-based navigation is used at http://www.doj.gov

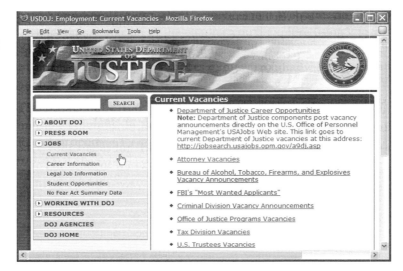

The display of the Current Vacancies link shown on a contrasting background color, provides a visual cue that the visitor is at that location. The page header and page title also display the text "Current Vacancies." The **navigation bar** indicates other choices available to the Web site visitor.

Sometimes graphics are used to convey navigation, as in the Web site for the Department of Transportation (http://www.dot.gov), as shown in Figure 5.14.

Figure 5.14
The tabs provide horizontal graphics-based navigation

The "text" for the navigation is actually stored in image files. This technique of placing text in navigation images is used to create interactive Web pages. In this case, JavaScript is used to detect when the Web page visitor has placed the mouse over an image of text, which then displays an alternate image. Even though images provide the main navigation of the site, the site is still accessible: a row of text links appear in the footer section of the page (not shown in Figure 5.14) and the image tags are configured with text descriptions using the `alt` attribute. Combinations of text with graphic images can be helpful to your visitors and add visual interest. Figure 5.15 shows a graphical navigation bar at http://www.genome.gov.

Figure 5.15
The graphical navigation bar adds visual interest

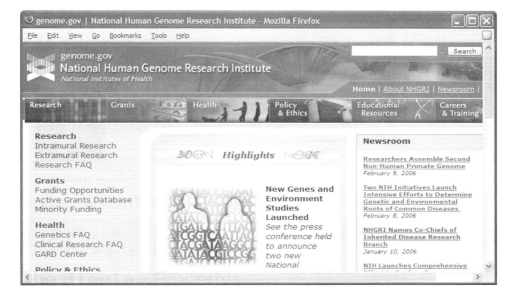

Technologies such as Adobe Flash can be combined with XHTML to create interactive, interesting navigation. See the screenshot in Figure 5.16 of http://www.loc.gov/wiseguide. The designers of this site used Flash to create the dynamic navigation and interactive images.

Figure 5.16
Flash navigation

Java applets and Dynamic HTML (DHTML) can also be used to create similar interactive effects. Chapter 11 discusses using these technologies to create interactive Web pages.

In Figure 5.17, Programs has been selected causing the vertical menu to appear. This type of navigation on a large complex site keeps the visitor from feeling overwhelmed by choices. The visitor first chooses a major menu category, and then sees the individual additional choices that can be made.

Figure 5.17
The Take Pride in America (http://www.takepride.gov) Web site uses DHTML to create dynamic navigation menus

Short Pages

A Web page is considered long if it is three or more screen lengths. Long pages are usually slow to load. Your visitors are probably only interested in portions of a long page, so consider breaking a long page into multiple short pages—possibly using linear organization to link the ideas.

Table of Contents

When a long Web page must be kept as a single file, a **table of contents** or bulleted list at the top of the page can provide links to specific parts of the page. This will help visitors find exactly what they need. An example of this is the page shown in Figure 5.18. Note the list of questions near the lower right of the page—they all link to corresponding answers at another location on the same page.

Site Map and Site Search Features

The city of San Diego Web site shown in Figure 5.19 has a **site search** and site map on the same page. The site map allows a visitor to scan the contents of the site visually. The search helps visitors find information that is not apparent from the navigation or

Figure 5.18
A list of FAQ links to answers on the page

Figure 5.18
A list of FAQ links to answers on the page

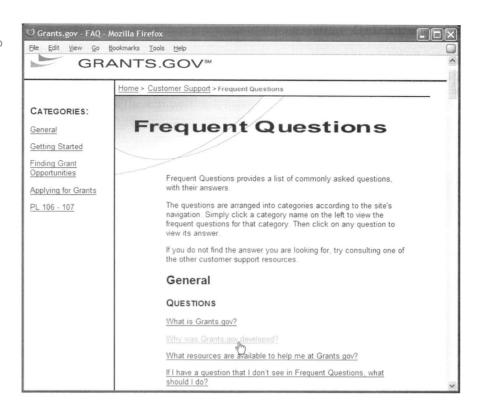

Figure 5.19
This large site offers a site search and a site map to visitors

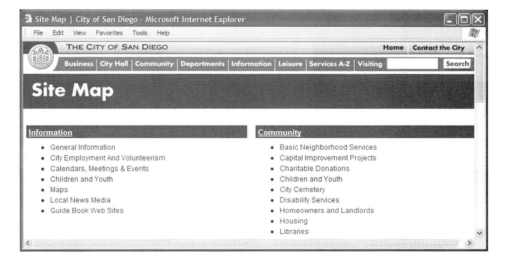

the site map features. A Web developer could add the `title` attribute to these anchor tags to provide a brief text description.

Commercial site search applications are available, including FreeFind (http://www .freefind.com) and FusionBot (http://www.fusionbot.com), which provide a free service for sites that are under a certain number of pages.

You are now familiar with Web site organization and navigation. The next section continues with a discussion of visual design principles.

5.3 Design Principles

There are four visual design principles that you can apply to the design of just about anything: **repetition**, **contrast**, **proximity**, and **alignment**. Whether you are designing a Web page, a button, a logo, a CD cover, a brochure or a software interface—the design principles of repetition, contrast, proximity, and alignment will help to create the "look and feel" of your project and will determine whether your message is effectively communicated.

Repetition: Repeat Visual Elements throughout Design

When applying the principle of repetition, the designer repeats one or more elements through the product. The repeating aspect ties the work together. Figure 5.20 displays the home page of Starbucks (http://www.starbucks.com). The repetition of the square icons with rounded corners helps to unify the navigation area. Page content areas are divided using a number of rounded rectangles—again repeating the shape. Each rounded rectangle uses the same background color. This color is also present in the subtle vertical stripe on the page background. Whether it is color, shape, font, or image, repetition of elements helps to unify a design.

Figure 5.20
The design principles of repetition, contrast, proximity, and alignment are well used on this site

Contrast: Add Visual Excitement and Draw Attention

To apply the principle of contrast, the designer should make elements very different (add contrast) in order to make the design interesting and direct attention. When designing Web pages, there should be good contrast between the background color and the text. Notice how the navigation area in Figure 5.20 pops out of the upper-left rounded rectangle due to the contrast change in background color. The Starbucks site uses dark text on a medium or light background to provide good visual contrast and easy reading.

Proximity: Group-Related Items

When designers apply the principle of proximity, related items are placed physically close together. Unrelated items should have space separating them. The placing of interface items close together gives visual clues to the logical organization of the information or functionality. In Figure 5.20, the vertical navigation links are all placed in close proximity to each other. This creates a visual group on the page and makes the navigation easier to use. Notice the proximity of the account and shopping cart related links in the top right corner of the page. Proximity is used well on this page to group related elements.

Alignment: Align Elements to Create Visual Unity

Another principle that helps to create a cohesive Web page is alignment. When applying this principle, the designer organizes the page so that each element placed has some alignment (vertical or horizontal) with another element on the page. The Starbucks page shown in Figure 5.20 also applies this principle. Notice how the rounded rectangles are aligned with each other. Within each rounded rectangle, alignment is again used—the vertical navigation links, the placement of the content links/descriptions in the upper-right rounded rectangle, and the two columns of site-related links in the lower-right rounded rectangle. Notice also the horizontal alignment of the links in the top right side of the page. Good alignment is used throughout the Starbucks home page.

Repetition, contrast, proximity, and alignment are four principles that can greatly improve your Web page designs. If you apply these principles effectively, your Web pages will look more professional and you will communicate your message more clearly. Keep these visual design principles in mind as you explore recommended Web site design practices related to **page layout**, text, graphic, and accessibility in the next section.

5.4 Web Page Design—Best Practices

The major components of Web page design are as follows:

- Page layout design
- Text design

- Graphic design
- Accessibility considerations

Web sites that look great and are easy to use don't happen by accident. Outstanding Web sites are carefully planned and created by using recommended design practices. (They also require a little bit of talent!) There are a number of factors to consider when designing a Web page. Some factors relate to the usability, accessibility, and appeal of the site to the target audience—use of color, text, graphics, and animations. Other factors relate to the medium of the Web itself—**load time** issues, browser support, and monitor **screen resolution**.

Load Time

The last thing you want to happen is for your visitors to leave your page before it has even finished loading! Make sure your pages load as quickly as possible. How long do you generally wait for a page to load? Many Web page visitors will not wait more than several seconds. It's a good practice to limit the total file size of a Web page and all of its associated images and media files to under 60KB. It takes about eight seconds at 56KB for a browser to display a Web page and associated files of 60KB.

According to a recent study by the PEW Internet and American Life Project http://www .pewinternet.org/PPF/r/184/report_display.asp, the percentage of U.S. Internet users with a broadband (cable, DSL, and so on) connection at home or at work is rising. Forty-two percent of adult Americans have access to broadband at home. Even with the trend of increasing bandwidth available to your visitors, keep in mind that approximately one-half of households do not have broadband Internet access. For the most up-to-date statistics, visit http://www.pewinternet.org and http://www.clickz.com.

The 60KB per page limit is a guideline—it's better if the file size of your home page and associated media files is smaller. Go over the limit for content pages only when you are sure your visitors will be interested enough to wait to see what your site is presenting. The chart shown in Figure 5.21 compares file sizes and connection speed download times.

Figure 5.21
File size download times and Internet connection speeds

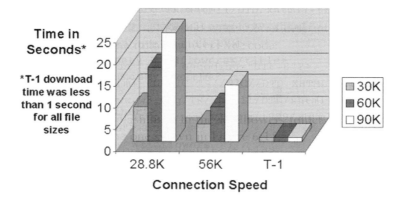

One method to help determine if the load time of your page is acceptable is to view the size of your Web site files in Windows Explorer. Calculate the total file size of your Web page plus all its associated images and media. If the total file size for a single page and its associated files is over 60KB, take a closer look at your design. Consider if you really need to use all the images to convey your message. Perhaps the images can be better optimized for the Web or the content of the page should be divided into multiple pages. This is a time for some decision making!

Popular Web authoring tools such as Microsoft Expression Web and Adobe Dreamweaver will calculate load time at various transmission speeds.

Perceived Load Time

Perceived load time is the amount of time a Web page visitor is aware of waiting while your page is loading. Since visitors often leave a Web site if a page takes too long to load, it is important to shorten their perception of waiting. A common technique is to shorten the perceived loading time by breaking the long page into multiple smaller pages using the methods described earlier. This might even aid in the organization of your Web site.

Web pages containing large graphics may appear to load very slowly. Image slicing— dividing or slicing large images into multiple smaller images (see Chapter 4), divides large images into several smaller graphics. Since each graphic displays as it loads, the perceived load time is shorter than it is for a single large graphic. Even though the total download time is about the same, the visitor sees the browser window changing and perceives the wait as being shorter.

Above the Fold

Placing important information **above the fold** is a technique borrowed from the newspaper industry. When newspapers are placed on counters and in vending machines waiting to be sold, the portion above the fold in the page is viewable. Publishers noticed that more papers were sold when the most important, attention-getting information was placed in this location. You may use this technique to attract and keep visitors on your Web pages. Arrange interesting content above the fold—the area the visitor sees before scrolling down the page. At a commonly used screen resolution, 800 pixels wide by 600 pixels high, the amount of screen viewable above the fold (after accounting for Web browser menus and controls) is about 410 pixels.

Web Page "Real Estate"

There is a saying in the real estate field that the three most important factors about a property are location, location, and location. The Web page location you choose for high-profile components such as logo banners, page headings, and navigation is also important. Web page visitor eye tracking studies reported by The Poynter Institute (http://www.poynterextra.org/eyetrack2004/main.htm) indicate that "eyes most often fixated first in the upper-left of the page, then hovered in that area before going left to right." This makes the most valuable Web page "real estate" the upper-left side and top center of the page. Avoid placing important information and navigation on the far right side—this area may not be initially displayed by browsers at some screen resolutions.

Horizontal Scrolling

In order to make it easy for Web page visitors to view and use your Web pages, avoid creating pages that are too wide to be displayed in the browser window. These pages require the user to scroll horizontally. Using a common screen resolution, 800 pixels wide by 600 pixels high, the amount of viewable screen (after accounting for area used by the Web browser) is about 760 pixels. An easy way to make sure your page will not require **horizontal scrolling** is to place the page contents in a layout table that uses a percentage width of 100 percent or less. Another method is to use a fixed table width set to 760 pixels or less. If you expect your pages to be printed often, set the width to 560 or less pixels.

Adequate White Space

This term **white space** is also borrowed from the publishing industry. Placing blank or white space (because paper is usually white) in areas around blocks of text increases the readability of the page. Placing white space around graphics helps them to stand out. Allow for some blank space between blocks of text and images. How much is adequate? It depends—experiment until the page is likely to look appealing to your target audience.

Target Audience

Use of Color.   Younger audiences, such as children and preteens, prefer bright, lively colors. The United States Mint's Site for Kids home page (http://usmint.gov/kids/) shown in Figure 5.22 (shown also in the color insert section), features bright graphics, lots of color, and interactivity.

Figure 5.22
A typical site for children

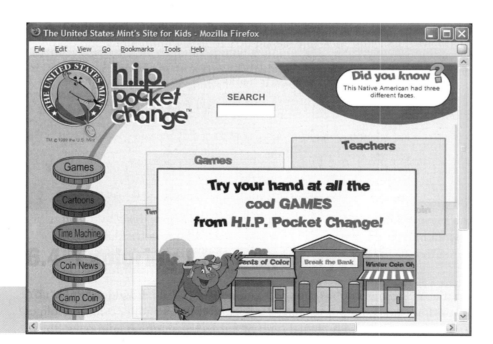

See the center color insert

Individuals in their late teens and early twenties generally prefer dark background colors with occasional use of bright contrast, music, and dynamic navigation. Figure 5.23 (shown also in the color insert section) shows http://www.cnccz.com, a gaming Web site designed for this age group.

Figure 5.23
Many teens and young adults find dark sites appealing

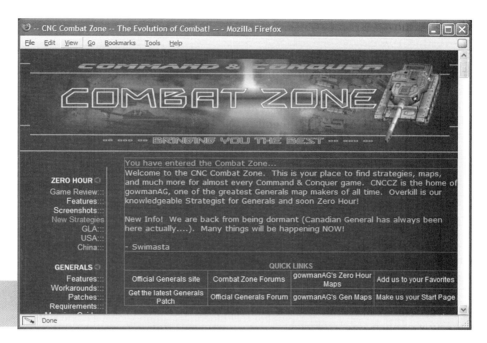

See the center color insert

Note how it has a completely different look and feel from the site designed for children.

If your goal is to appeal to everyone, follow the example of the popular Amazon.com and eBay.com Web sites in their use of color. These sites use a neutral white background with splashes of color to add interest and highlight page areas. Use of white as a background color was also reported by Jakob Nielsen and Marie Tahir in Homepage Usability: 50 Websites Deconstructed, a book that analyzed 50 top Web sites. According to this study, 84 percent of the sites used white as the background color and 72 percent used black as the text color. This maximized the contrast between text and background—providing maximum readability.

For an older target audience, light backgrounds, well-defined images, and large text are appropriate. The screenshot of the http://www.drs.wa.gov shown in Figure 5.24 (shown also in the color insert section) is an example of a site intended for the over 50 group.

Focus on Accessibility

Another issue related to color is the fact that many individuals experience color deficiency (color blindness). The inability to differentiate between red and green, called deuteranopia, is the most common type of color deficiency. To increase the accessibility of Web pages for these individuals, a Web designer can use high contrast between background and text. The choice of colors is important—avoid using red, green, brown, gray, or purple next to each other. White, black, and shades of blue and yellow are easier for these individuals to differentiate. To see what your pages look like to a person with color blindness, try the online simulator at http://www.vischeck.com/vischeck/.

Figure 5.24
A site designed
specifically for the 50
and over age range

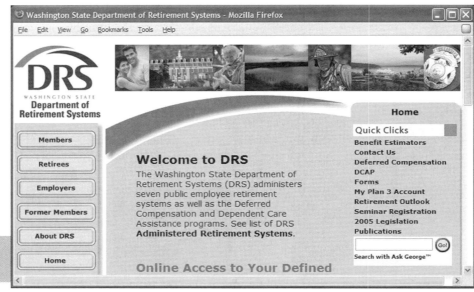

See the center
color insert

Reading Level. Match the reading level and style of writing to your target audience. Use vocabulary that they will be comfortable with.

Animation. Use animation only if it adds to your site. Don't include an animated GIF just because you have one. In general, animation appeals more to younger audiences than to older audiences. The United States Mint's Site for Kids (Figure 5.22) is geared to children and uses lots of animation. This would be too much animation for a Web site targeted to adult shoppers. However, a well-done navigation animation or an animation that describes a product could be appealing to almost any target group. Adobe Flash is frequently used on the Web to add animation to Web pages and even to create entire animated Web sites.

FAQ   **Which browser is everyone using?**

A recent survey by Janco Associates' IT Productivity Center (http://www.itproductivity.org/browser.htm) indicates that while Microsoft's Internet Explorer is still the most popular Web browser, the Firefox open source browser has been gaining ground. The survey reports that 64 percent of users use Internet Explorer and 17 percent use Firefox (http://www.mozilla.org/products/firefox/). However, even though Internet Explorer seems to have the market cornered, it is still important to test your site in the major browsers (and versions). You never know which browser your next client will favor!

If you are developing for an intranet, ask what browser (and version) is installed at the organization. If you are developing for a client, ask what browser he or she regularly uses.

Browser-Friendly

Just because your Web page looks great in your favorite browser, doesn't automatically mean that all browsers will render it well. Determine the browser most likely to be used by your target audience. A good source of statistics is http://www.thecounter.com/stats. Develop the site so that it looks great in your target audience's most popular browser and looks acceptable (degrades gracefully) in other browsers. Visit http://www.upsdell .com/BrowserNews/ for timely information about current browsers.

Always try to test your pages in the most popular versions of browsers and in the newest versions. At the time of this writing, these are Firefox 2, Internet Explorer 7, Safari (both Mac and Windows versions), Opera 9, and Netscape 9. While it is possible to install multiple versions of Netscape on the same computer, dual installs cannot easily be done with Internet Explorer. Unless you have multiple computers to work with, test with the most popular version of Internet Explorer. If you can, it is also a good idea to test your pages on both the Mac and PC platforms.

Large information technology departments and Web design firms will dedicate a number of computers with various operating systems and browser versions for compatibility testing. Many Web page components, including default text size and default margin size, are different among browsers, browser versions, and operating systems.

Screen Resolution

Most users have their monitors configured for 1024×768, 1280×1024, or 800×600 screen resolution. You should design your page to avoid horizontal scrolling at these resolutions. Higher resolutions are becoming more popular. However, depending on your target audience, you still may have some visitors using 640×480 screen resolution! One way to create a page that looks good in multiple screen resolutions is to center the entire page. A code sample follows:

```
<html>
<head>
... header section of Web page document
</head>
<body>
  <div style="text-align: center">
  ... page content goes here
  </div>
</body>
</html>
```

FAQ

Which screen resolution is everyone using?

A recent survey by The Counter (http://www.thecounter.com) about Web visitors for sites monitored by their service reported 1024×768 is currently the most popular screen resolution. Of visitors surveyed, 51 percent use 1024×768, 25 percent use 1280×1024, 11 percent use 800×600, 3 percent use 1152×864, and less than 1 percent use 640×480.

Wireframes and Page Layout

A **wireframe** is a sketch or blueprint of a Web page that shows the structure (but not the detailed design) of basic page elements such as the logo, navigation, content, and footer. Depending on the purpose of a particular Web site, the wireframe may incorporate additional components including pull quotes, news items, and interactive features such as a login or search function. Wireframes are used as part of the design process to experiment with various page layouts, develop the structure and navigation of the site, and provide a basis for communication among project members. Figures 5.25 through 5.27 can be considered very basic wireframes. See the textbook website at http://www.webdevfoundations.net/4e/chapter5.html, for more detailed examples.

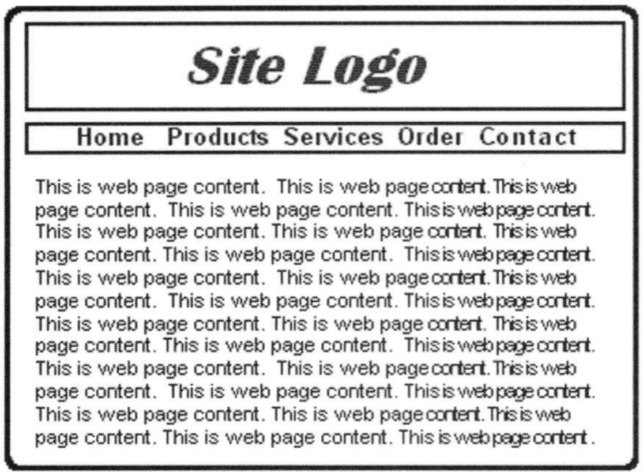

Figure 5.25
An adequate page layout

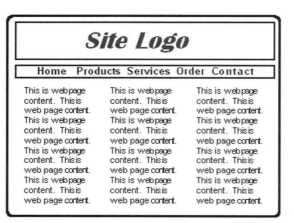

Figures 5.25, 5.26, and 5.27 show diagrams of three possible Web page layouts. Note that the exact content (text, images, logo, and navigation) does not need to be placed in the diagram in order to illustrate this concept. The page area where the content will appear is indicated. This type of sketch, called a wireframe, can be used to experiment with page structures and find the one that will work best for a site. Figure 5.25 shows a diagram of a Web page with a logo, navigation area, and content area.

Figure 5.26
The columns make this page layout more interesting

This layout is adequate and may be appropriate for some content, but it's not very interesting. Figure 5.26 shows a diagram of a Web page containing the same content, but formatted in three-columns.

This is an improvement, but something is still missing. Figure 5.27 shows a diagram of the same content but formatted in three columns of varying widths, with graphics interspersed.

Figure 5.27
This page layout uses images and columns of varied widths

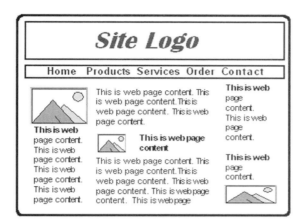

This is the most interesting page layout of the three. Notice how images and tables make the same content more appealing. Try using this concept when designing your pages. In Chapters 6 and 7 you'll learn how to use CSS to configure Web pages with multiple columns.

Often the page layout (sometimes called a storyboard) for the home page is different from the page layout used for the content pages. Even when this is the case, a consistent logo and color scheme will produce a more cohesive Web site. Using style sheets to create interesting page layouts can keep visitors interested in your Web site. Web authoring tools such as Microsoft Expression Web and Adobe Dreamweaver offer templates and example sites to assist you with layout ideas.

5.5 Page Layout Design Techniques

Now that you have been introduced to Web page design best practices and page layout, it's time to consider three popular techniques of Web page layout design: ice, jello, and liquid.

Ice Design

The **ice design** technique is sometimes referred to as a solid or fixed design. The page hugs the left margin and generally either CSS is used to configure a fixed-width block-level element or an XHTML table (see Chapter 8) is used to format the page. A CSS style rule is shown below that configures an id named `wrapper` in this manner.

```
#wrapper { width: 700px; }
```

Due to the fixed width, the designer has much control over the layout and formatting—configuring the page to look best at a certain screen resolution (often 800×600) and degrade gracefully when other screen resolutions are used. The right-hand side of the browser window will often contain much empty space—especially at higher screen resolutions.

The students.gov site (http://www.students.gov), shown in Figure 5.28, is an example of ice design. This particular page is formatted with one or more fixed width tables. Other sites that currently use this technique include http://www.cabelas.com and http://www.league.org.

Figure 5.28
This page is configured with a fixed width and demonstrates ice design

Jello Design

The **jello design** technique configures content that is centered and may be of a fixed width or a percentage width such as 80 percent. A CSS style rule that configures an id named `wrapper` in this manner follows:

```
#wrapper { width: 80%;
           margin-left: auto;
           margin-right: auto;
}
```

Jello design pages typically are more pleasing to view at higher screen resolutions than ice design pages. No matter the screen resolution, the content is centered in the page with even margins on both sides. The Department of Energy site (http://energy.gov), as shown in Figure 5.29, uses jello design. Other sites currently using this technique include http://www.pbs.org and http://www.officedepot.com.

Figure 5.29
The left and right margins are balanced on this page using jello design

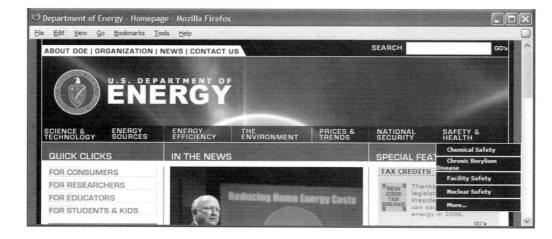

Liquid Design

The **liquid design** technique results in a fluid Web page with content that takes up 100 percent of the browser window regardless of the screen resolution. There is no blank margin on the left or right—the multicolumn content will flow to fill whatever size window is used to display it. This type of design can be created with CSS or with XHTML using a table with width set to 100 percent (see Chapter 8). Figure 5.30 shows a page from the State of Illinois site at http://www.illinois.gov/tech/. Other sites currently using this technique include http://www.amazon.com and http://moodle.org.

Figure 5.30
This page uses liquid design to adjust content to fill the browser window

Digital Web (http://digital-web.com), an online magazine, uses liquid design to position the elements on the page. Using CSS instead of a table to configure Web page layout has a number of advantages, including smaller Web page document file sizes, quicker loading pages, and more accessible pages that are easier for screen readers to access. The home page of the NSA, as shown in Figure 5.31, uses CSS to configure the page layout.

Figure 5.31
This page is configured using CSS

Sites designed using ice, jello, and liquid techniques can be found throughout the Web. Ice and jello designs using a fixed-width layout provide the Web developer the most control over the page configuration but result in pages with large empty areas when viewed at higher screen resolutions.

Figure 5.32 shows the National Park Service (http://nps.gov) site viewed using 1280×1024 screen resolution. Note how more than one-third of the browser window is empty. Liquid design avoids this awkwardness and takes advantage of the entire browser window.

Figure 5.32
At 1280×1024 resolution the right side of this page is empty

See the liquid-designed Census Bureau (http://www.census.gov) site using 1280×1024 screen resolution in Figure 5.33—the site still fills the browser window. Since liquid design pages are intended to stretch, it's very important to test pages using this technique at various screen resolutions.

Figure 5.33
This page stretches to fill the browser window—even at 1280×1024 resolution

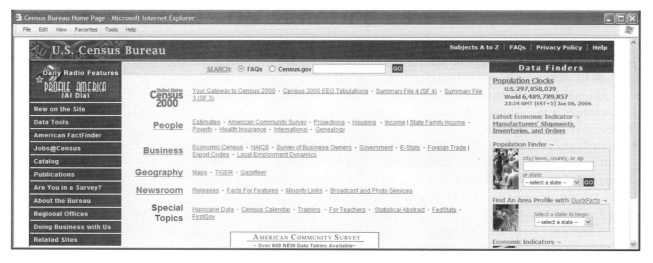

Ice, jello, and liquid designs using CSS for page layout can be displayed on most browsers used today. Be aware that older browsers, such as Netscape 4.x, do not support CSS used for positioning and will not display your site as you intend. Keep the preferences of your target audience in mind as you make design choices.

CHECKPOINT 5.1

1. List the four basic principles of design. View the home page of your school and describe how each principle is applied.

2. View http://www.walmart.com, http://www.mugglenet.com/, and http://www.sesameworkshop.org/sesamestreet/. Describe the target audience for each site. How do their designs differ? Do the sites meet the needs of their target audiences?

3. View your favorite Web site (or a URL provided by your instructor). Maximize and resize the browser window. Decide whether the site uses ice, jello, or liquid design. Adjust the screen resolution on your monitor (Start, Control Panel, Display, Settings) to a different resolution than you normally use. Does the site look similar or very different? List two recommendations for improving the design of the site.

5.6 Text Design—Best Practices

Long blocks of text and long paragraphs are difficult to read on the Web. Use the text equivalent of sound bytes—short sentences and phrases. It's important to be concise. Bulleted lists stand out on the page and are easily read. Long-winded sentences and explanations are often found in academic textbooks and romance novels, but they really are not appropriate on a Web page.

You may be wondering how to know if a page is easy to read. The following are some suggestions that will help increase the readability of your pages:

- Use common fonts such as Arial, Verdana, or Times New Roman. Remember that the Web page visitor must have the font installed on his/her computer in order for that particular font to appear. Your page may look great with Gill Sans Ultra Bold Condensed, but if your visitor doesn't have the font, the browser's default font will be displayed.

- Serif fonts, such as Times New Roman, were originally developed for printing text on paper—not for displaying text on a computer monitor. Research shows that sans serif fonts, such as Arial, are easier to read than serif fonts when displayed on a computer screen (see http://www.alexpoole.info/academic/literaturereview.html or http://www.wilsonweb.com/wmt6/html-email-fonts.htm for details). The sans serif Verdana font, designed by Microsoft specifically for display on a computer screen, may be more readable than Arial due to the increased width and openness of the letters.

- Be careful with the size of the fonts—12 point font size is the same as "Medium" size and is the same as 1 em. Be aware that fonts display smaller on a Mac than on a PC. Even within the PC platform, the default font size for Netscape is larger than the default font size for Internet Explorer. Consider creating prototype pages of your font size settings to test on a variety of browsers and screen resolution settings.

- Use appropriate color combinations. Students often choose color combinations for Web pages that they would never dream of using in their wardrobe. An easy way to choose colors that contrast well and look good together is to select colors from an image or logo you will use for your site. Make sure your page background color properly contrasts with your text and hyperlink colors. Refer to Chapter 3 for additional color scheme ideas.

- Be aware of line length and alignment—use white space and multiple columns if possible. Review Figures 5.24, 5.25, and 5.26 for examples of text placement on a Web page.

- Bold (use the <strong> element) or emphasize (use the <em> element) important text.

- Hyperlink keywords or phrases—do not hyperlink entire sentences.

- Avoid the use of the words "click here"—users know what to do by now.

Finally, check spelling and grammar. Many Web sites every day contain misspelled words. Most Web authoring tools have built-in spell checkers; consider using this feature. Also, be sure that you proofread and test your site thoroughly. It is very helpful if you can find Web developer buddies—you check their sites and they check yours. It's always easier to see someone else's mistake than your own.

5.7 Graphic Design—Best Practices

Chapter 4 discussed the use of graphics on Web pages. This section summarizes and adds to the recommended practices discussed in that chapter.

- Choose colors on the Web Color Palette. If you would like your site to look consistent when displayed on various monitors using various computer platforms, choose from the 216 colors on the Web Color Palette.

- Use **antialiased text** in images. Antialiasing introduces intermediate colors to smooth jagged edges in digital images. Graphic applications such as Adobe Photoshop and Adobe Fireworks can be used to create antialiased text images. The graphic shown in Figure 5.34 was created using antialiasing.

Figure 5.34
Antialiased text

Antialiased

Figure 5.35 contains an image that did not use antialiasing; note the jagged edges.

Figure 5.35
This graphic has a jagged look and was not saved using antialiasing

Aliased

The only letters not affected are the i and I because the edges of these letters are perfectly horizontal and vertical.

- Use only necessary images. Don't use extra images, just because you have them. Oh, by the way, isn't my dog (see Figure 5.36) cute?

Figure 5.36
This is Sparky—but do you really need to see a picture of my dog in this book? Use necessary images only.

Focus on Accessibility

- Keep images as small as possible. Try to display only exactly what is needed to get your point across. Use a graphic application to crop an image or create a thumbnail image that links to a larger version of the image.
- Make sure the site is usable if images are not displayed. If a Web page visitor is using an assistive technology, such as screen reader, he or she will not see your images but will still want to navigate through your Web site. If your main navigation uses images, DHTML, Flash, or other interactive technologies, place a plain text navigation bar at the bottom of each page. The Studentjobs.gov Web site, http://www.studentjobs.gov/, shown in Figure 5.37, uses this technique.

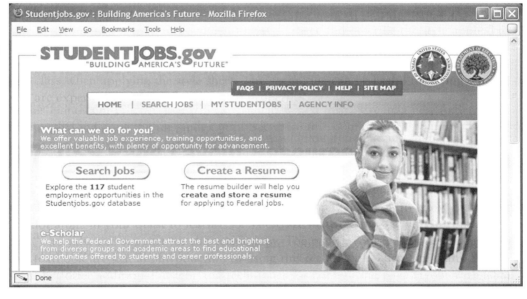

Figure 5.37
Scrolling to the bottom of this page will display simple text links, which provide accessibility

Image links are used for the main navigation in the upper-left column on the page. There are plain text links to the main site categories at the bottom of the page. These text links provide for accessibility.

Focus on Accessibility

It is also a good idea to include text descriptions of important concepts or key points that your site is trying to communicate. Don't rely on images alone—some individuals may not be able to see them—they may have set their browser not to display images or use an assistive technology such as a screen reader to visit your page.

- Use alternate text for images. Place the `alt` attribute with descriptive text on each `<img />` tag. (See Chapter 4 for a discussion of the `<img />` tag and use of the `alt` attribute.)

- Limit the use of animated items. Only use animation if it makes the page more effective. Consider limiting how long an animation plays.

- Create a text only version of the page. If there are a large number of images, or the images are integral to your content, consider creating an alternate version of the page that contains text only. Keep in mind that this means double maintenance for all future page modifications. Figure 5.38 displays both the standard and text-only versions of the U.S Fish & Wildlife Service Birds page, http://www.fws.gov/birds/.

Figure 5.38
The standard page provides a link to the text-only version

Focus on Accessibility

- Provide a method to skip repetitive navigation links. It is easy for visitors without vision and mobility challenges to scan a Web page and quickly focus on the page content. However, long, repetitive navigation bars quickly become tedious to access when utilizing a screen reader or a keyboard to visit a Web page. Consider adding a Skip Navigation or Skip to Content hyperlink before your main navigation bar that links to a named anchor (see Chapter 7, Internal Links) at the beginning of the content section of your page. The Department of Transportation site, as shown in Figure 5.14, uses a transparent image link to provide this feature. Since the image is "invisible," visitors using a graphical browser are not even aware of the additional functionality.

Figure 5.39 shows comparison screenshots of the page when viewed with Internet Explorer and Firefox's Web Developer extension (available at https://addons.mozilla.org/extensions/moreinfo.php?id=60) to display image `alt`

Figure 5.39
The Firefox Web Developer extension can display the text descriptions of each image

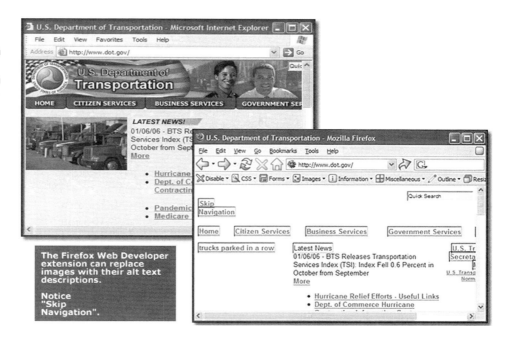

attribute text instead of images. Notice the Skip Navigation alternate text displayed in the upper-left-hand corner—convenient for visitors using screen readers or nongraphical browsers.

Figure 5.40 shows another way to implement this feature. Notice the subtle Skip Navigation link in the upper-right side of the Web page. Other Web sites, such as http://studentjobs.gov, provide this functionality using a text link the same color as the page background.

Figure 5.40
The Skip Navigation link is subtle

5.8 Design to Provide Accessibility

Focus on Accessibility

Vinton Cerf, the coinventor of TCP/IP and the former chairman of the Internet Society, proclaimed that "The Internet is for everyone" (see http://www.isoc.org/isoc/media/speeches/foreveryone.shtml). Tim Berners-Lee, the inventor of the World Wide Web, states that "The power of the Web is in its universality. Access by everyone regardless of disability is an essential aspect" (see http://www.w3.org/WAI/).

Who benefits from increased accessibility? Consider the following scenarios:

- Maria, a young woman in her twenties with physical challenges who cannot manipulate a mouse and who uses a keyboard with much effort
- Leotis, a college student who is deaf and wants to be a Web developer
- Jim, a middle-aged man who has a dial-up Internet connection and is using the Web for personal enjoyment
- Nadine, a mature woman with age-related macular degeneration who has difficulty reading small print
- Karen, a college student using a different type of user-agent, such as a cell phone, to access the Web
- Prakesh, a man in his thirties who is legally blind and needs access to the Web to do his job

All these individuals benefit from Web pages designed with accessibility in mind. A Web page that is designed to be accessible is typically more usable for all—even a person who has no physical challenges and is using a broadband connection benefits from the improved presentation and organization of a well-designed Web page.

The Internet and Web are such a pervasive part of our culture that accessibility is protected by laws in the United States. Section 508 of the Rehabilitation Act requires electronic and information technology, including Web pages, used by federal agencies to be accessible to people with disabilities.

The accessibility recommendations presented in this text are intended to satisfy the Section 508 standards and the W3C Web Accessibility Initiative guidelines See http://www.access-board.gov/sec508/guide/1194.22.htm for an informative, descriptive list of the Section 508 Standards for Web pages (Web-based intranet and Internet information and applications).

The federal government is promoting accessibility by law and the private sector is following its lead.

The W3C is also active in this cause and has created the Web Accessibility Initiative (WAI) (see http://www.w3.org/WAI/) to create guidelines and standards applicable to Web content developers, authoring tool developers, and browser developers. The Web Content Accessibility Guidelines 1.0 (WCAG 1.0) created by the WAI are organized in three groups of guidelines; Priority 1, Priority 2, and Priority 3.

- Priority 1 guidelines must be met by Web developers to ensure accessibility of page content.
- Priority 2 guidelines are stricter in nature—they should be met by Web developers to ensure that all visitors can access their pages.
- Priority 3 guidelines are the most stringent and may be met by Web developers.

In addition to satisfying the Section 508 guidelines, the accessibility recommendations discussed in this textbook are also intended to fully satisfy the WCAG 1.0 Priority 1 guidelines and partially satisfy the Priority 2 and Priority 3 guidelines. See http://www.w3.org/TR/WCAG10/full-checklist.html for a descriptive checklist of these guidelines.

The WAI (http://www.w3.org/WAI/References/QuickTips/)has developed a collection of materials designed to promote accessibility, including the following quick tips:

- **Images and Animations.** Use the `alt` attribute to describe the function of each visual.
- **Image Maps.** Use the client-side map and text for hotspots.
- **Multimedia.** Provide captioning and transcripts of audio, and descriptions of video. (See Chapter 11 for information on multimedia)
- **Hypertext Links.** Use text that makes sense when read out of context. For example, avoid "click here."
- **Page Organization.** Use headings, lists, and consistent structure. Use Cascading Style Sheets (see Chapter 3) for layout and style where possible.
- **Graphs and Charts.** Summarize or use the `longdesc` attribute.
- **Scripts, Applets, and Plug-ins.** Provide alternative content in case active features such as JavaScript, Java applets, and Flash are inaccessible or unsupported.
- **Frames.** Use the `<noframes>` element and meaningful titles.
- **Tables.** Make line-by-line reading sensible. Summarize.
- **Check Your Work.** Validate. Use the tools, checklists, and guidelines at http://www.w3.org/TR/WCAG.

At the time this was written, the WAI has released a working draft of the WCAG 2.0 guidelines at http://www.w3.org/TR/WCAG20. The purpose of this new version of Web content accessibility guidelines is to address a variety of different Web technologies, be easier to understand, and be more precisely tested. Check the WAI's WCAG Overview page (http://www.w3.org/WAI/intro/wcag.php) and the textbook Web site (http://webdevfoundations.net) for updates on WCAG 2.0.

Developing accessible Web sites is an important aspect of Web site design. Web authoring tools such as Adobe Dreamweaver provide extensions that will help you create accessible sites. Watchfire's WebXACT (http://webxact.watchfire.com) is a free Web page validator that will check your Web page for common accessibility issues. The Cynthia Says Portal (http://www.cynthiasays.com) also provides a free accessibility validation service. This portal was developed as a joint effort by Hisoftware and the Internet Society's Disability and Special Needs Chapter. Both online validators test one page at a time.

Finally, the Section 508 Standards require that if a Web page cannot comply with accessibility requirements, then a separate text-only version of the Web page must be provided and regularly updated. Although the text pages could be coded manually, other options exist to provide this functionality. The LIFT Text Transcoder server, available from UsableNet (http://www.usablenet.com), dynamically generates text-only, accessible pages that comply with accessibility standards. For a live example of this technology in action, compare the graphical University of Illinois home page (http://www.uiuc.edu) with the text-only version generated by UsableNet at (http://transcoder.usablenet.com/tt/http://www.uiuc.edu).

5.9 Best Practices Checklist

Table 5.1 contains a checklist of recommended Web design practices. Use this as a guide to help you create easy to read, usable, and accessible Web pages.

Table 5.1 Web Design Best Practices Checklist

		Page Layout
❏	1.	Appealing to target audience
❏	2.	Consistent site header/logo
❏	3.	Consistent navigation area
❏	4.	Informative page title that includes the company/organization/site name
❏	5.	Page footer area—copyright, last update, contact e-mail address
❏	6.	Good use of basic design principles: repetition, contrast, proximity, and alignment
❏	7.	Displays without horizontal scrolling at 800×600 and higher resolutions
❏	8.	Balance of text/graphics/white space on page
❏	9.	Good contrast between text and background
❏	10.	Repetitive information (header/logo and navigation) takes up no more than one-quarter to one-third of the browser window at 800×600 resolution
❏	11.	Home page has compelling, interesting information above the fold (before scrolling down) at 800×600 resolution
❏	12.	Home page downloads within 10 seconds on dial-up connection
		Browser Compatibility
❏	1.	Displays on current versions of Internet Explorer (6+)
❏	2.	Displays on current versions of Firefox (2+)
❏	3.	Displays on current versions of Netscape (7+)
❏	4.	Displays on current versions of Opera (9+)
❏	5.	Displays on current versions of Safari (both Mac and Windows)
		Navigation
❏	1.	Main navigation links are clearly and consistently labeled
❏	2.	Navigation is easy to use for target audience
❏	3.	If image, Flash, or DHTML is the main navigation, clear text links are in the footer section of the page (accessibility)
❏	4.	Navigational aids, such as site map, skip navigation link, or breadcrumbs, are used
❏	5.	All navigation hyperlinks work
		Color and Graphics
❏	1.	Use of different colors in page backgrounds/text is limited to a maximum of three or four
❏	2.	Color is used consistently
❏	3.	Color has good contrast with associated text
❏	4.	Color is not used alone to convey meaning (accessibility)
❏	5.	Use of color and graphics enhances rather than distracts from the site
❏	6.	Graphics are optimized and do not slow download significantly
❏	7.	Each graphic used serves a clear purpose
❏	8.	Image tags use the `alt` attribute to configure alternate text to display if the browser or user agent does not support images (accessibility)
❏	9.	Animated images do not distract from the site and either do not repeat or only repeat a few times

Table 5.1 Web Design Best Practices Checklist (*continued*)

		Multimedia (See Chapter 11)
❏	1.	Each audio/video/Flash file used serves a clear purpose
❏	2.	The audio/video/Flash files used enhance rather than distract from the site
❏	3.	Captions are provided for each audio or video file used (accessibility)
❏	4.	Download times for audio or video files are indicated
❏	5.	Links to downloads for media plug-ins are provided

		Content Presentation
❏	1.	Common fonts such as Arial or Times New Roman are used
❏	2.	Techniques of writing for the Web are used: headings, bullet points, short sentences in short paragraphs, use of white space, and so on
❏	3.	Fonts, font sizes, and font colors are consistently used
❏	4.	Content provides meaningful, useful, information
❏	5.	Content is organized in a consistent manner
❏	6.	Information is easy to find (minimal clicks)
❏	7.	Timeliness: The date of the last revision and/or copyright date is accurate
❏	8.	Content does not include outdated material
❏	9.	Content is free of typographical and grammatical errors
❏	10.	Content provides links to other useful sites
❏	11.	Avoids the use of "Click here" when writing text for hyperlinks
❏	12.	If standard link colors are not used, all links use a consistent set of colors to indicate visited/nonvisited status
❏	13.	If graphics and/or media is used to convey meaning, the alternate text equivalent of the content is provided (accessibility)

		Functionality
❏	1.	All internal hyperlinks work
❏	2.	All external hyperlinks work
❏	3.	All forms function as expected
❏	4.	No JavaScript (see Chapters 11 and 14) errors are generated by the pages

		Accessibility
❏	1.	If image, Flash, or DHTML is the main navigation, clear text links are in the footer section of the page
❏	2.	Color is not used alone to convey meaning
❏	3.	Image tags use the `alt` attribute to configure alternate text replacement
❏	4.	Captions are provided for each audio or video file used
❏	5.	Use attributes designed to improve accessibility such as `longdesc`, `title`, and `summary` where appropriate
❏	6.	If the site uses frames, use frame titles and place meaningful content in the noframes area
❏	7.	*Optional*: To assist screen readers, the html element's lang and xml:lang attributes indicate the spoken language of the page.

Note: Web Design Best Practices Checklist is copyrighted by http://terrymorris.net. Used by permission.

CHECKPOINT 5.2

1. View the home page of your school. Use the Best Practices Checklist (Table 5.1) to evaluate the page. Describe the results.

2. List three best practices of writing text for the Web. The following text was found on a real Web site. The company name and city have been changed. Use the hints in the text design best practices described earlier in the chapter to rewrite the following content for the Web:

   "Acme, Inc. is a new laboratory instrument repair and service company. Our staff at this time has a combined total of 30 plus years of specimen preparation instrumentation service and repair.

   Our technicians are EPA refrigeration certified. We are fully insured and all of our workers are fully covered by workman's compensation insurance. A proof of insurance certificate can be provided upon request.

   We are located in Chicago, Illinois. Which houses shop repair facilities and offices. Acme, Inc. technicians are factory trained and equipped with the best diagnostic and repair equipment available.

   We keep a separate file on every piece of equipment we work on. When a technician is sent on a repair, he has a file which lists the whole repair history on that piece of equipment. These files also help us answer any of your questions about past repairs.

   Our rates are $100.00 per hour for Labor and Travel with a 2 hour minimum. $0.40 per mile and all related expenses PARTS are not included."

3. List three best practices of using graphics on Web pages. View the home page of your school. Describe the use of graphic design best practices on this page.

CHAPTER SUMMARY

This chapter introduced recommended Web site design practices. The choices you make in the use of color, graphics, and text should be based on your particular target audience. Developing an accessible Web site should be the goal of every Web developer.

Visit the textbook Web site at http://www.webdevfoundations.net for examples, the links listed in this chapter, and updated information.

Key Terms

above the fold	jello design	repetition
alignment	linear organization	screen resolution
antialiased text	liquid design	site map
breadcrumb trails	load time	site search
chunking	navigation bar	storyboard
contrast	page layout	table of contents
hierarchical organization	perceived load time	target audience
horizontal scrolling	proximity	white space
ice design	random organization	wireframe

Review Questions

Multiple Choice

1. Which of the following recommended design practices apply to a Web site that uses images for its main site navigation?

   a. provide alternative text for the images
   b. place text links at the bottom of the page
   c. both a and b
   d. no special considerations are needed

2. Which of the following are the three most common methods of organizing Web sites?

   a. horizontal, vertical, and diagonal
   b. hierarchical, linear, and random
   c. accessible, readable, maintainable
   d. none of the above

3. To avoid overly long load times for your pages, try not to let the file size of the page and its associated media exceed which of the following?

   a. 30KB
   b. 60KB
   c. 1MB
   d. 60MB

4. Which of the following is not a Web design recommended practice?

   a. design your site to be easy to navigate
   b. colorful pages appeal to everyone
   c. design your pages to load quickly
   d. limit the use of animated items

5. Which of the following would a consistent Web site design *not* have?

   a. the same fonts on each content page
   b. the same logo in the same location on each content page
   c. a similar navigation area on each content page
   d. a different background color on each page

6. Which of the following are influenced by the intended or target audience of a site?

   a. the amount of color used on the site
   b. the font size and styles used on the site
   c. the overall look and feel for the site
   d. all of the above

7. Which of the following should the main site navigation or a section offering navigation choices contain?

   a. no more than nine links
   b. as many links as you need
   c. only the most important pages
   d. none of the above

8. Which of the following is known as white space?

   a. the empty screen area around blocks of text and images
   b. the background color of white used for a page
   c. both a and b
   d. none of the above

9. Which of the following should you do when creating text hyperlinks?

   a. create the entire sentence as a hyperlink
   b. include the words "click here" in your text
   c. use a key phrase as a hyperlink
   d. none of the above

10. Which of the following is the design technique used to create pages that stretch to fill the browser window?

    a. ice
    b. liquid
    c. jello
    d. none of the above

Fill in the Blank

11. The most common Web site structure used for commercial Web sites is _____ Web site organization.

12. Placing _____ around graphics and headings helps them to stand out.

13. Animation should be used only if it _____ to your Web site.

14. All browsers and browser versions _____ display Web pages in exactly the same way.

15. The _____ is a group whose mission is to create guidelines and standards for Web accessibility.

Hands-On Exercises

1. Practice creating site maps for the following situations. You may either draw your site map using a pencil and a ruler or use software such as Microsoft Visio, Microsoft Word, or Microsoft PowerPoint.

   a. Doug Kowalski is a freelance photographer specializing in nature photography. He often gets work on contract, shooting photos for textbooks and journals. Doug would like a Web site that showcases his talents and that provides publishers with an easy way to contact him. He would like a home page, a few pages with samples of his nature photographs, and a contact page. Create a site map based on this scenario.

   b. Mary Ruarez owns a business, named Just Throw Me, that handcrafts specialty pillows. She currently sells at craft fairs and local gift shops but would like to expand her business to the Web. She would like a Web site with a home page, a page that describes her products, a page for each of her seven pillow styles, and an order page. She has been advised that since she is collecting information from individuals, a page describing her privacy policy would be a good idea. Create a site map based on this scenario.

   c. Prakesh Khan owns a dog-grooming business named A Dog's Life. He would like a Web site that includes a home page, a page about grooming services, a page with a map to his shop, a contact page, and a section that explains how to select a good pet. The content for the part of the Web site on selecting a pet will be a step-by-step presentation. Create a site map based on this scenario.

2. Practice creating wireframe page layouts with the following situations. Use the style for page layout composition shown in Figures 5.25, 5.26, and 5.27, where places for logo, navigation, text, and images are indicated. Do not worry about exact wording or exact images. Use a pencil, ruler, and paper to draw the diagrams.

   a. Create sample page layout diagrams for Doug Kowalski's photography business, described in 1(a). Create one page layout diagram for the home page. Create another page layout diagram for the content pages.

   b. Create sample page layout diagrams for the Just Throw Me Web site described in 1(b). Create one page layout diagram for the home page. Create another page layout diagram for the content pages.

   c. Create sample page layout diagrams for the A Dog's Life Web site described in 1(c). Create one page layout diagram for the home page and the regular content pages. Create another page layout diagram for the presentation pages.

3. Choose two sites that are similar in nature or have a similar target audience such as the following:

   - http://amazon.com and http://bn.com
   - http://kohls.com and http://jcpenney.com
   - http://cnn.com and http://msnbc.com

   Describe how the two sites you chose to review exhibit the design principles of repetition, contrast, alignment, and proximity.

4. Choose two sites that are similar in nature or have a similar target audience such as the following:

   - http://www.crateandbarrel.com and http://www.potterybarn.com
   - http://www.harpercollege.edu and http://www.clcillinois.edu
   - http://chicagobears.com and http://greenbaypackers.com

   Describe how the two sites you chose to review exhibit Web design best practices. How would you improve these sites? Recommend three improvements for each site.

5. Think about the following scenarios and how you would design a home page using the ice design technique. Describe the advantages this technique provides for the Web developer. Describe the advantages this technique provides for the Web site visitor. Create a wireframe page layout for the home page.

   a. See 1(a) for the description of Doug Kowalski's photography business.

   b. See 1(b) for the description of Just Throw Me.

   c. See 1(c) for the description of A Dog's Life.

6. Think about the following scenarios and how you would design a home page using the jello design technique. Describe the advantages this technique provides for the Web developer. Describe the advantages this technique provides for the Web site visitor. Create a wireframe page layout for the home page.

   a. See 1(a) for the description of Doug Kowalski's photography business.

   b. See 1(b) for the description of Just Throw Me.

   c. See 1(c) for the description of A Dog's Life.

7. Think about the scenarios described below and how you would design a home page using the liquid design technique. Describe the advantages this technique provides for the Web developer. Describe the advantages this technique provides for the Web site visitor. Create a wireframe page layout for the home page.

   a. See 1(a) for the description of Doug Kowalski's photography business.

   b. See 1(b) for the description of Just Throw Me.

   c. See 1(c) for the description of A Dog's Life.

Web Research

This chapter offered suggestions for organizing text on Web pages. In this research exercise, take this topic a step further and investigate writing for the Web. A few resources are listed here:

- http://useit.com. Search for the article "Writing for the Web."
- http://www.efuse.com/Design/web_writing_basics.html. Explore the article "Writing for the Web."
- http://www.webreference.com/content/writing. If you cannot find that page, visit webreference.com and search for "writing for the Web."
- http://www.webwritingthatworks.com
- http://www.alistapart.com/articles/writeliving

If these resources are no longer available, search the Web for information on "writing for the Web." Read one or more articles. Select five techniques that you would like to share with others. Write a one-page summary of your findings. Include the URLs of your resources.

Focus on Web Design

1. This chapter discusses recommended Web design practices. Sometimes it is helpful to learn about good design by examining poor design. Visit http://www. webpagesthatsuck.com and read about their examples of poor design. Try to think of Web sites that you have visited on the Web. Do any of them have similar qualities? Find two Web sites that use poor Web design practices. Write a one-page report that includes an introduction about the design practices not followed at the Web sites, a link to each site, and a description of how each site has practiced poor Web site design.

2. Visit any of the Web sites referenced in this chapter that interested you. Print the home page or one other pertinent page from the site. Write a one-page summary and reaction to the Web site you chose to visit. Address the following topics:

   - What is the purpose of the site?
   - Who is the intended audience?
   - Do you think the site reaches the intended audience?
   - List three examples of how this Web site uses recommended Web design guidelines.
   - How could this site be improved?

WEB SITE CASE STUDY
Web Design Best Practices

Each of the following case studies continues throughout most of the text. This chapter asks you to analyze the design of the Web sites.

JavaJam Coffee House

See Chapter 2 for an introduction to the JavaJam Coffee House case. Figure 2.26 shows a site map for the JavaJam Web site. Three pages for this site were created in earlier chapters. In this case study you will review the site for recommended Web site design practices.

Hands-On Practice Case

1. Examine the site map in Figure 2.26. What type of site organization is used for the JavaJam Web site? Is it the most appropriate organization for the site? Why or why not?

2. Review the recommended Web page design practices from this chapter. Use the Web Design Best Practices Checklist (Table 5.1) to evaluate the JavaJam site that you created in earlier chapters. Cite three design practices that have been well implemented. Cite three design practices that could be implemented in a better way. How else would you improve the Web site?

Fish Creek Animal Hospital

See Chapter 2 for an introduction to the Fish Creek Animal Hospital Case. Figure 2.30 shows a site map for the Fish Creek Web site. Three pages for the site were created in earlier chapters. In this case study you will review the site for recommended Web site design practices.

Hands-On Practice Case

1. Examine the site map in Figure 2.30. What type of site organization is used for the Fish Creek Web site? Is it the most appropriate organization for the site? Why or why not?

2. Review the recommended Web page design practices from this chapter. Use the Web Design Best Practices Checklist (Table 5.1) to evaluate the Fish Creek site that you created in earlier chapters. Cite three design practices that have been well implemented. Cite three design practices that could be implemented in a better way. How else would you improve the Web site?

Pete the Painter

See Chapter 2 for an introduction to the Pete the Painter Case. Figure 2.34 shows a site map for the Pete the Painter Web site. Three pages for the site were created in earlier chapters. During this case study you will review the site for recommended Web site design practices.

Hands-On Practice Case

1. Examine the site map in Figure 2.34. What type of site organization is used for the Pete the Painter Web site? Is it the most appropriate organization for the site? Why or why not?

2. Review the recommended Web page design practices from this chapter. Use the Web Design Best Practices Checklist (Table 5.1) to evaluate the Pete the Painter site that you created in earlier chapters. Cite three design practices that have been well implemented. Cite three design practices that could be implemented in a better way. How else would you improve the Web site?

Prime Properties

See Chapter 2 for an introduction to the Prime Properties Case. Figure 2.38 shows a site map for the Prime Properties Web site. Three pages for the site were created in earlier chapters. During this case study you will review the site for recommended Web site design practices.

Hands-On Practice Case

1. Examine the site map in Figure 2.38. What type of site organization is used for the Prime Properties Web site? Is it the most appropriate organization for the site? Why or why not?

2. Review the recommended Web page design practices from this chapter. Use the Web Design Best Practices Checklist (Table 5.1) to evaluate the Prime Properties site you created in earlier chapters. Cite three design practices that have been well implemented. Cite three design practices that could be implemented in a better way. How else would you improve the site?

Web Project

The purpose of this Web Project Case Study is to design a Web site using recommended design practices. Your Web site might be about a favorite hobby or subject, your family, a church or club you belong to, a company that a friend owns, the company you work for, and so on. Your Web site will contain a home page and at least six (but no more than ten) content pages. In the Chapter 5 Web Project Case Study you will complete the following documents: Topic Approval, Site Map, and Page Layout Design. You will not develop Web pages as part of the Chapter 5 Web Project Case Study—you will complete that task in later chapters.

Hands-On Practice Case

1. **Web Project Topic Approval.** The topic of your Web site must be approved by your instructor. Complete the following:
   - What is the purpose of the site?

     List the reason you are creating the site.

- What do you want the site to accomplish?

  List the goals you have for the site.

  Describe what needs to happen for you to consider your site a success.

- Who is your target audience?

  Describe your target audience by age, gender, socio-economic characteristics, and so on.

- What opportunity or issue is your site addressing? *Note*: Your site might be addressing the opportunity of providing information about a topic to others, creating an initial Web presence for a company, and so on.

- What type of content might be included in your site?

  Describe the type of text, graphics, and media you will need for the site.

- List at least two related or similar sites found on the Web.

  Hand in this document to your instructor for approval of your Web project topic.

2. **Web Project Site Map.** Use the drawing features of a word processing program, a graphic application, or paper and pencil to create a site map of your Web site that shows the hierarchy of pages and relationships between pages. Hand in this document to your instructor.

3. **Web Project Page Layout Design.** Use the drawing features of a word processing program, a graphic application, or paper and pencil to create wireframe page layouts for the home page and content pages of your site. Unless otherwise directed by your instructor, use the style for page layout composition shown in Figures 5.25, 5.26, and 5.27. Indicate where the logo, navigation, text, and images will be located. Do not worry about exact wording or exact images. Hand in these documents to your instructor.

Page Layout with CSS

Chapter Objectives In this chapter, you will learn how to ...

- Describe reasons to use CSS for page layout
- Use relative and absolute positioning
- Apply the CSS Box Model

- Configure basic page layouts using CSS
- Configure two-column page layouts using CSS
- Locate CSS page layout resources

Now that you are familiar with using CSS to format text and color, you are ready to explore using CSS to configure Web page layout. This method relies on CSS properties rather than tables to design a Web page. The technology for this layout is called **CSS-P**, for CSS positioning. This chapter introduces you to configuring page layouts using CSS.

6.1 CSS Page Layout Overview

You've been using CSS to configure presentation (fonts, colors, and so on) of the structural XHTML elements including headings, paragraphs, divs, and lists. You may have noticed that using CSS results in smaller Web page documents (html files), which saves on bandwidth and eases site maintenance. You will soon see that using CSS to configure page layout enhances these advantages.

First, here is a little background about CSS and some acronyms you should be familiar with. As you already know, the W3C produced a recommendation for CSS (http://www.w3.org/TR/REC-CSS1-961217.html), now called CSS Level 1 (CSS1), in 1996. They continued their work and produced a recommendation for CSS Level 2 or CSS2, (http://www.w3.org/TR/1998/REC-CSS2-19980512/) in 1998. CSS2 built on CSS1 and introduced new properties needed for positioning—known as CSS-P.

Even though CSS2 was introduced in the last millennium, commercial Web sites have only recently begun to utilize its features. You may wonder why it has taken so long. The reason is lack of browser support of the W3C recommendations. Only very recently have the most current versions of commonly used browsers begun to support these recommendations reliably and consistently. Even so, you will encounter differences in rendering when displaying pages coded using CSS-P in various browsers. Keep in mind that not all Web page visitors will be using the most current browser version. There are a number of ways to handle this issue—including coding alternate pages or allowing the browser display to degrade gracefully. Visitors using an older browser will see a usable, but not highly formatted Web page. Let's take a look at an example of a Web site that uses CSS to configure page layout.

Figure 6.1 shows the DisabilityInfo.gov (http://www.disabilityinfo.gov) home page rendered by Firefox. The Web site uses CSS for page layout to configure a page with multiple columns.

Figure 6.1
The DisabilityInfo.gov home page displayed in Firefox, a modern browser

A visitor using an outdated, older browser such as Netscape 4.7 experiences a plain vanilla version of the site, as shown in Figure 6.2. The content is displayed in the order

Figure 6.2
The DisabilityInfo.gov home page displayed in Netscape 4.79, an outdated browser

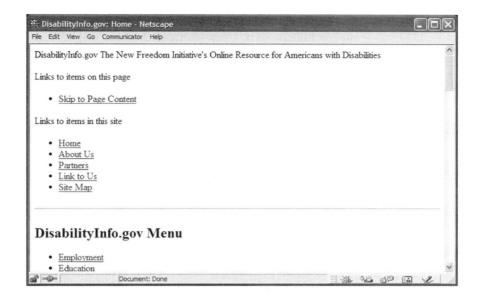

it is coded in the Web page. Because the site configures most of its graphics as background images within the external CSS style sheet, these graphics are unavailable to the older browser. The visitor experience is not exactly compelling when using an out-of-date browser. However, the site can still be navigated and information can be obtained.

Figure 6.3 shows the same page displayed in an Opera browser configured to simulate a text browser. The text content is displayed in the order it is coded in the Web page. Notice how even with the newer CSS page layout techniques utilized, the page is usable when rendered in a text browser.

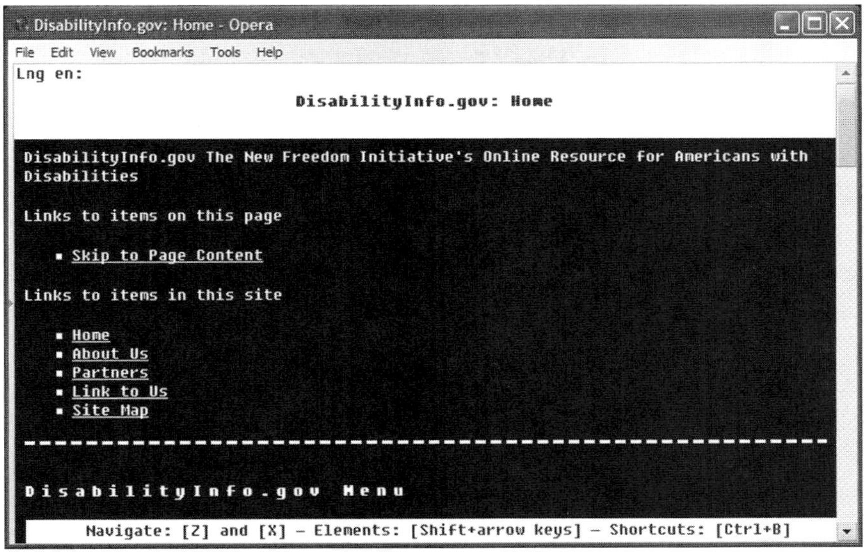

Figure 6.3
A text browser simulation of DisabilityInfo.gov's home page

Web developers have long delayed using CSS for page layout because of these rendering issues. What has recently changed? As modern browser support of CSS has increased, the number of Web visitors who use older browsers has decreased. For a typical Web site, less than 1 percent of visitors use these older browsers. Depending on your site's target audience, this figure could be higher or lower—your Web logs (see Chapter 13) will provide this information. For example, TruGreen (http://trugreen.com) and wired (http://wired.com) are two organizations that use CSS for page layout. Although many existing Web sites use XHTML tables (see Chapter 8) to configure page layout, most Web sites developed today use CSS for this purpose.

Advantages of Using CSS for Page Layout

When CSS is used to configure page layout in addition to formatting text and color, the following advantages of using CSS for formatting are enhanced:

- **Greater Typography Control.** This includes font size, line spacing, letter spacing, indents, margins, and element positioning without using the XHTML table element (discussed in Chapter 8).

- **Style Is Separate from Structure.** The formatting and page layout can be configured and stored separately from the body section of the Web page document. When the styles are modified, the XHTML remains intact. This means that if your client decides to change something as small as the background color or as potentially huge as the page layout, you may only need to change one file that contains the styles, instead of each Web page document. For a look at how very powerful this can be, visit http://www.csszengarden.com and be amazed at how different pages with the same content and XHTML code (but different CSS) can look!

- **Potentially Smaller Documents.** Since both the formatting and page layout are separate from the document, the actual .html documents should be smaller.

- **Easier Site Maintenance.** Again, if the styles or page layout need to be changed it may be possible to complete the modifications by changing a single file only—the style sheet.

- **Increased Page Layout Control.** CSS used in conjunction with modern standards-compliant browsers provides a variety of positioning options (even down to the pixel) along with an ability to overlap elements. This gives the Web developer more control over the layout compared to the use of the previously popular XHTML tables.

- **Increased Accessibility.** Pages designed using XHTML tables for layout are easy to view with a traditional browser but can be very tedious when using a screen reader or other assistive technology. By reserving the use of XHTML tables for organizing tabular information and using CSS for page layout—the pages become more accessible.

- **Ability to Define Styles for Multiple Media Types.** Since presentation is separated from content, CSS can be used to set a separate style for printing, or possible use of a screen reader.

- **Support of the Semantic Web.** The Semantic Web is Tim Berners-Lee's vision of the future of the Internet (http://www.w3.org/2001/sw/). According to Berners-Lee, "The Semantic Web is an extension of the current Web in which information is given well-defined meaning, better enabling computers and people to work in cooperation." While much development is being done in this area, Web developers can take small steps, including using XHTML syntax and using CSS to separate styles from structure.

Disadvantages of Using CSS for Page Layout

If you review the screenshots of a site that uses CSS for page layout (Figures 6.1 and 6.2) you'll see a very obvious disadvantage. Visitors using older browsers will not experience your Web site in the same way as visitors using modern browsers. If you are using tables for page layout, this is not an issue. Why then are developers beginning to code mainstream Web sites using CSS for page layout? With good support of CSS by modern browsers and the increasing use of modern browsers, the advantages of using CSS to configure page layout usually outweigh the disadvantages. Of course, the target audience of a Web site should be a deciding factor. For example, if your target audience for an intranet site is a company that has standardized on Netscape 4.7 for the desktop, none of the advantages would be realized and it would be better to design the site using tables for page layout. The projected (and eventually actual) target audience should be considered when deciding on a page layout technique.

Even with the increased CSS support of modern browsers, there are still differences and bugs in their implementation of the W3C Recommendations. This is a disadvantage for Web developers, since coding and testing time is increased. Leading developers have created Web sites that document and discuss these issues (see http://www.quirksmode.org and http://www.positioniseverything.net). The CSS techniques in this chapter have been tested with Internet Explorer 7, Opera 9.21, Firefox 2, and Apple's Safari for Windows beta.

Another potential disadvantage is the fact that experienced Web developers who are adept at coding pages using XHTML tables for layout will see productivity drop temporarily as they learn about CSS techniques and properties. Using CSS positioning is different from configuring pages with tables. Time and practice are needed when learning something new.

At this point you've seen some examples of using CSS for page layout and are aware of the issues related to using this technology. The next section discusses the **CSS Box Model**—a crucial building block of CSS positioning.

Should XHTML tables never be used?

Many commercial Web sites still use XHTML tables for page layout. This is for a very good reason—tables are widely supported by browsers. As a Web developer you will most likely work on sites that use XHTML layout tables and you'll work with these in Chapter 8. However, a growing trend is to configure pages using CSS (sometimes called table-less layout). This does not mean that tables are bad, ineffective, or that they are never coded on Web sites that use CSS for page layout. Even Web sites with so-called "table-less" layouts may include tables to present information in a tabular manner or facilitate design of a small portion of the page.

6.2 The Box Model

Each element in a document is considered to be a rectangular box. As shown in Figure 6.4, this box consists of a content area surrounded by padding, a border, and margins. This is known as the Box Model.

Figure 6.4
The CSS box
model

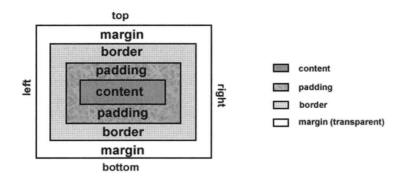

- The **content** area can consist of a combination of text and Web page elements such as images, paragraphs, headings, lists, and so on. The **visible width** of the element on a Web page is the total of the content width, the padding width, and the border width.

- The **padding** area is between the content and the border. The default padding value is zero. When configuring the background of an element, the background is applied to both the padding and the content areas.

- The **border** area is between the padding and the margin. The default border has a value of 0 and does not display. You have already worked with borders in Hands-On Practice 4.2. As shown in Figure 4.2, this area can be set to various styles.

- The **margin** determines the empty space between the element and any adjacent elements. The margin is always transparent. The solid line in Figure 6.4 that contains the margin area does not display on a Web page. Keep in mind that browsers often have default margin values set for the Web page document and for certain elements such as paragraphs, headings, forms, and so on. Use the `margin` property to override the default browser values.

Figures 6.5 and 6.6 display `<div>` elements containing text content. Let's take a closer look. Figure 6.5 shows a screenshot of two `<div>` elements placed one after another on a Web page. In Figure 6.6 the boxes are nested inside each other. In both cases, the

Figure 6.5
Two `<div>`
elements displaying
the box model

Figure 6.6
Nested elements
showing the box
model

browser used **normal flow** (the default) and displayed the elements in the order that they appeared in the source code. As you've worked through the exercises in the previous chapters, you created Web pages that the browser rendered using normal flow. You'll practice this a bit more in the next Hands-On Practice, then later in the chapter you'll experiment with positioning to configure the flow, or placement, of elements on a Web page.

HANDS-ON PRACTICE 6.1

You will explore the box model in this Hands-On Practice as you create the Web pages shown in Figure 6.5 and Figure 6.6.

Practice with Normal Flow

Launch a text editor and open the Chapter6/starter1.html file from the student files. Save the file with the name box1.html. This page is displayed in Figure 6.5. Edit the body of the Web page and add the following code to configure two <div> elements:

```
<div class="div1">
This is the first box.
</div>
<div class="div2">
This is the second box.
</div>
```

Now let's add the CSS to configure the "boxes." Add a new style rule for a class named div1 to configure a light gray background, dashed border, width of 200, height of 200, and 5 pixels of padding. The code follows:

```
.div1 {  width: 200px;
         height: 200px;
         background-color: #cccccc;
         border: dashed;
         padding: 5px;
}
```

Create a style rule for a class named div2 to configure a width and height of 100, ridged border, 10 pixel margin, and 5 pixels of padding. The code follows:

```
.div2 {  width: 100px;
         height: 100px;
         background-color: #ffffff;
         border: ridge;
         padding: 5px;
         margin: 10px;
}
```

Save the file. Launch a browser and test your page. It should look similar to the one shown in Figure 6.5. The student files contain a sample solution at Chapter6/box1.html.

Practice with Normal Flow and Nested Elements

Launch a text editor and open the box1.html file from the student files. Save the file with the name box2.html. This page is displayed in Figure 6.6.

Edit the code. You will not modify the CSS but you will edit the XHTML. Delete the content from the body section of the Web page. Add the following code to configure two `<div>` elements— one nested inside the other.

```
<div class="div1">
This is the outer box.
  <div class="div2">
  This is the inner box.
  </div>
</div>
```

Save the file. Launch a browser and test your page. It should look similar to the one shown in Figure 6.6. Notice how the browser renders the nested `<div>` elements— this is an example of normal flow. The student files contain a sample solution at Chapter6/box2.html.

The examples in the Hands-On Practice happened to use two `<divs>`. However, the box model applies to XHTML elements in general—not just to `<divs>`. You will get more practice using the box model in this chapter. Notice that since the CSS did not use any configurations for positioning, normal flow was used and the second box is nested within the first box because it is coded inside the first `<div>` in the XHTML. Next, we will take a look at some properties that affect positioning: `position`, `float`, `display`, and `z-index`.

6.3 CSS Positioning Properties

You've seen how normal flow causes the browser to render the elements in the order that they appear in the XHTML source code. When using CSS for page layout there are times where you will want to specify the location of an element on the page—either the absolute pixel location, the location relative to where the element would normally display, or floating on the page. There are even times when you will want to modify the way an element displays or cause an element to appear partially or completely over another element. The CSS properties used to accomplish these tasks are discussed next.

Relative and Absolute Positioning

Use **relative positioning** to change the location of an element slightly, relative to where it would otherwise appear in normal flow. Use the `position:relative` property along with either a left, right, and/or top property. The **left** property configures the position of the element in relation to the left side of the browser window. The **right** property sets the position of the element in relation to the right side of the browser window. The **top** property indicates the position of the element in relation to the top of the document area in the browser window.

Figure 6.7 shows a Web page (see the student files, Chapter6/relative.html) that uses relative positioning and the `left` property to configure the placement of a `<div>` (assigned to the `id mycontent`) to the left of the normal flow.

Figure 6.7
The paragraph is configured using relative positioning

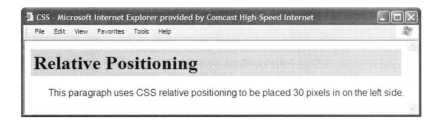

The result is that the content of the `<div>`—the paragraph—is rendered 30 pixels in from the left where it would normally be placed at the browser's left margin. W3C Recommendations call for positioning to be applied to any element and Internet Explorer follows this recommendation. However, cross-browser support of positioning is more reliable when the `<div>` element is used for positioning. Notice also how the `padding` and `background-color` properties configure the heading element. The CSS follows:

```
#myContent { position: relative;
             left: 30px;
             font-family: Arial,sans-serif;
}
h1 { background-color: #cccccc;
     padding: 5px;
     color: #000000;
}
```

The XHTML source code follows:

```
<h1>Relative Positioning</h1>
<div id="myContent">
  <p>This paragraph uses CSS relative positioning to be placed 30
pixels in on the left side.</p>
</div>
```

Use **absolute positioning** to specify the location of an element precisely in a browser window. The `position:absolute` property along with either a `left`, `right`, and/or `top` property is needed to configure the placement.

Figure 6.8 shows a screenshot of a Web page that uses absolute positioning to configure a `<div>` (see the student files, Chapter6/absolute.html).

The `<div>` is assigned to the `content id` which is positioned 200 pixels in from the left margin and 100 pixels down from the top of the browser window. The result is that the paragraph contained within the `<div>` is rendered 200 pixels in from the left side and 100 pixels down from the top of the document area in the browser window. The width of the `<div>` is set to 300 pixels. Again, `padding` and `background-color` are used to configure the heading element. The CSS follows:

Figure 6.8
The paragraph is
configured using
absolute positioning

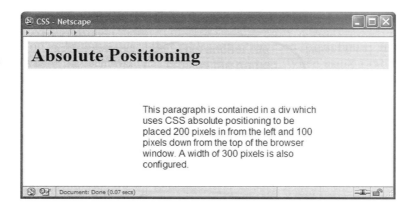

Figure 6.8
The paragraph is
configured using
absolute positioning

```
#content { position: absolute;
           left: 200px;
           top: 100px;
           font-family: Arial,sans-serif;
           width: 300px;
}
h1 { background-color: #cccccc;
     padding: 5px;
     color: #000000;
}
```

The XHTML source code follows:

```
<h1>Absolute Positioning</h1>
<div id="content">
<p>This paragraph is contained in a div which uses CSS absolute
positioning to be placed 200 pixels in from the left and 100 pixels
down from the top of the browser window. A width of 300 pixels is
also configured.</p>
</div>
```

When working with absolute positioning it is important to be aware that elements not absolutely positioned will be rendered following normal flow by the browser. Elements that are absolutely positioned are rendered outside of normal flow. You'll explore this behavior in the next Hands-On Practice.

HANDS-ON PRACTICE 6.2

Figure 6.9 shows screenshots of two Web pages with similar XHTML content. The Web page in the upper screenshot does not have any CSS applied. The Web page in the lower screenshot uses CSS to configure text, color, and the absolute position of a paragraph element. Launch a text editor and open the Chapter6/starter2.html found in the student files. When a browser renders the page it will use normal flow and display the XHTML elements in the same order as they are coded: <h1>, <div>, <p>, and <ul>. Launch a browser and display the page to verify.

Figure 6.9
The lower Web page uses CSS absolute positioning

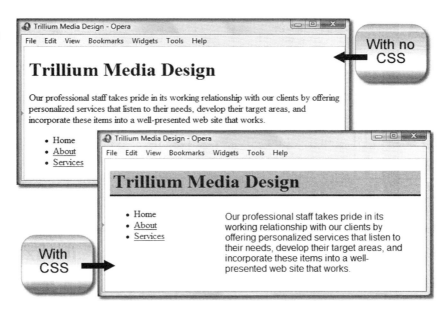

Let's add the CSS to make this page more "stylish" and look like the lower screenshot in Figure 6.9. Save the file with the name trillium.html. With trillium.html open in a text editor, modify the code as follows:

1. This page uses embedded styles. Code opening and closing `<style>` tags in the header section.

```
<style type="text/css">
</style>
```

2. Create style rules for the `h1` selector. Configure a background color (`#B0C4DE`), text color (`#000080`), a 3 pixel solid bottom border in the color `#000080`, and 5 pixels of padding on the bottom and left sides.

```
h1 { border-bottom: 3px solid #000080;
     color: #000080;
     background-color: #B0C4DE;
     padding: 0 0 5px 5px;
}
```

Note: The padding can be set for each side individually using the `padding-top`, `padding-right`, `padding-bottom`, and `padding-left` properties. You can use shorthand notation to set all four values in one `padding` property. The order of the numeric values determines which box side is configured (top, right, bottom, left).

3. Create style rules for a class named `content`. Configure the position to be absolute, 200 pixels from the left, 75 pixels from the top, a width of 300 pixels, and Arial or sans serif font typeface.

```
.content { position: absolute;
           left: 200px;
           top: 75px;
           font-family: Arial,sans-serif;
           width: 300px;
}
```

4. Assign the paragraph to the `content` class. Add `class="content"` to the opening paragraph tag in the body of the Web page.

Save the file. Launch a browser and test your page. It should look similar to the lower Web page shown in Figure 6.9. The student files contain a sample solution at Chapter6/trillium.html. Note that even though the unordered list is coded in the page after the paragraph, it's displayed immediately after the heading. This is because the paragraph is absolutely positioned (`position: absolute`). Browsers render absolutely positioned elements *outside* of normal flow.

Note: This Hands-On Practice used embedded CSS for ease of editing. However, for an actual Web site with more than one page the most efficient solution is to use an external CSS file. See Chapter 3 if you'd like to review using external style sheets. You'll use external style sheets later in this chapter.

FAQ

What's a good name for a class?

A class name should be descriptive of the purpose (such as `nav`, `news`, `footer`, and so on) rather than being descriptive of the presentation (such as `redText`). According to Google's Web Authoring Statistics Study, http://code.google.com/webstats, the 10 most commonly used class names are `footer`, `menu`, `title`, `small`, `text`, `content`, `header`, `nav`, `copyright`, and `button`.

The `float` Property

Elements that seem to float on the right or left side of either the browser window or another element are often configured using the **`float`** property. The browser renders these elements using normal flow, and then shifts them as far as possible within their container (usually either the browser window or a `<div>`) to either the right or left. Other content will flow around the float. To stop this flow, use the **`clear`** property. When floating an image, the `margin` property is useful to configure empty space between the image and text on the page.

Figure 6.10 shows a Web page (see the student files, Chapter6/float.html) with an image that has been configured with `float:right`.

Figure 6.10
The image is configured with `float:right`

Floating an Image

The heading and paragraph follow normal flow. The Yellow Lady Slipper pictured on the right is a wildflower. It grows in wooded areas and blooms in June each year. The Yellow Lady Slipper is a member of the orchid family.

Notice how the text in the paragraph wraps around the image. An `id` called `yls` was created that applies the `float`, `margin`, and `border` properties. The attribute `id="yls"` was placed on the image tag. The CSS follows:

```
h1 { background-color: #cccccc;
     padding: 5px;
     color: #000000;
}
p { font-family:Arial,sans-serif;
}
#yls { float: right;
       margin: 0 0 5px 5px;
       border: solid;
}
```

The XHTML source code follows:

```
<img id="yls" src="yls.jpg" alt="Yellow Lady Slipper" height="100"
width="100" />
<h1>Floating an Image</h1>
<p>The heading and paragraph follow normal flow. The Yellow Lady
Slipper pictured on the right is a wildflower. It grows in wooded
areas and blooms in June each year. The Yellow Lady Slipper is a
member of the orchid family.</p>
```

There are times when you want to clear the effect of the float. In these cases you use the `clear` property.

The Web page displayed in Figure 6.11 uses the `clear` property set to `clear:right`. The images each clear the float that precedes them and float to the right of the browser window (see the student files, Chapter6/float2.html).

Figure 6.11
Using both the `float` and `clear` properties

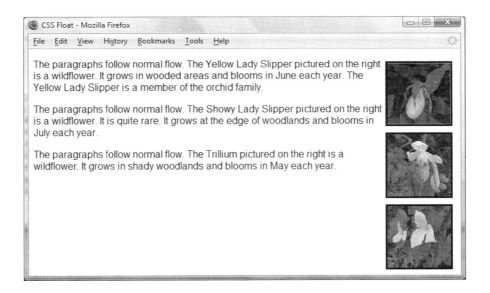

The CSS follows:

```
.rightfloat { float: right;
              margin: 5px;
              clear: right;
              border: solid;
}
```

The XHTML source code follows:

```
<img class="rightfloat" src="yls.jpg" alt="Yellow Lady Slipper"
height="100" width="100" />
<p>The paragraphs follow normal flow. The Yellow Lady Slipper
pictured on the right is a wildflower. It grows in wooded areas and
blooms in June each year. The Yellow Lady Slipper is a member of the
orchid family.</p>
<img class="rightfloat" src="pls.jpg" alt="Showy Lady Slipper"
height="100" width="100" />
<p>The paragraphs follow normal flow. The Showy Lady Slipper pictured
on the right is a wildflower. It is quite rare. It grows at the edge
of woodlands and blooms in July each year.</p>
<img class="rightfloat" src="trillium.jpg" alt="Trillium" height="100"
width="100" />
<p>The paragraphs follow normal flow. The Trillium pictured on the
right is a wildflower. It grows in shady woodlands and blooms in May
each year.</p>
```

The `float` and `clear` properties will also be useful when configuring page layouts with multiple columns. In the next Hands-On Practice you'll gain experience using the CSS `float` property.

How do I know when to configure a `class` or an `id`?

If the style can be used on more than one element on a page, configure the style as a `class`. Use the **.** (dot) notation in the style sheet. Use the `class` attribute in the XHTML.

If the style is specific to only one element or if the element will be manipulated using DHTML (see Chapter 11), configure the style as an `id`. Use the **#** notation in the style sheet. Use the `id` attribute in the XHTML.

HANDS-ON PRACTICE 6.3

In this Hands-On Practice you'll practice using the CSS `float` and `clear` properties as you configure the Web page shown in Figure 6.12.

Create a folder named ch6float. Copy the starter3.html and yls.jpg files from the chapter6 folder in the student files into your ch6float folder. Launch a text editor and open the starter3.html file. Notice the order of the images and paragraphs. Notice that there is no CSS configuration for floating the images. Display starter3.html in a browser. The browser renders the page using normal flow and displays the XHTML elements in the order they are coded.

Let's add CSS to float the images and look more similar to Figure 6.12. Save the file with the name floatyls.html. With floatyls.html open in a text editor, modify the code as follows:

1. Add a style rule for a class name `float` that configures `float`, `margin`, and `border` properties.

```
.float { float:left;
         margin-right:10px;
         border:ridge;
}
```

   2. Assign the image element to the class named float (use `class="float"`).

Save the file. Launch a browser and test your page. It should look similar to the Web page shown in Figure 6.12. The student files contain a sample solution at Chapter6/floatyls.html.

Figure 6.12
The CSS `float` property left-aligns the image

The `display` Property

Recall from Chapter 2 that some XHTML elements, such as the paragraph and heading elements, are block elements. A division (`<div>`) is also a block element. The browser renders these elements with 100 percent of the available width and displays a line break above and below—forming a "block." Other elements, such as anchor tags and span tags, are rendered directly inline—with no line break before or after them. These are called inline elements.

The **display property** configures if and how an element is displayed. An element configured with `display:none` will not be displayed. This is sometimes used when configuring styles to print a Web page. An element configured with `display:block` will be rendered as a block element (even if it is actually an inline element, such as an anchor tag). You will work with the `display` property in Chapter 7.

The `z-index` Property

The **z-index property** is used to modify the stacking order of elements on a Web page. When using only XHTML there is no easy way to "stack" elements other than configuring backgrounds for pages or tables. The `z-index` property provides flexibility in the display of elements. The default `z-index` value is `"0"`. Elements with higher `z-index` values will appear stacked on top of elements with lower `z-index` values rendered on the same position of the page. Figure 6.13 is configured using absolute positioning and `z-index` properties.

Figure 6.13
This page uses
absolute positioning
and `z-index`
properties

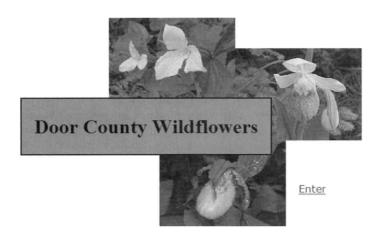

Notice how the three flower photos and the logo are arranged. It would be difficult to recreate this just using XHTML. This type of page design may be appropriate for the splash page of a Web site. You will recreate this Web page when you complete the next Hands-On Practice . The term splash page originates from client-server applications that display an introductory (or splash) screen while the program loads. Splash pages, sometimes called splash screens, can set the tone or introduce a Web site.

You have been introduced to the `position`, `float`, `display`, and `z-index` properties. For your reference, Table 6.1 contains a list of CSS properties often used with formatting and page layout.

Table 6.1 CSS properties used with formatting and page layout

Property	Description	Commonly Used Values
`background-color`	Background color on an element	Any valid color
`background-image`	Background image on an element	`url(imagename.gif)` or `url(imagename.jpg)`
`background-position`	Position of the background image	Two percentage values or numeric pixel values. The first value configures the horizontal position and the second configures the vertical position starting from the upper-left corner of the container's box. Text values can also be used: `left`, `top`, `center`, `bottom`, `right`.
`background-repeat`	Controls how the background image will repeat	Text values `repeat` (default), `repeat-y` (vertical repeat), `repeat-x` (horizontal repeat), `no-repeat` (no repeat)
`border`	Shorthand notation to configure the `border-width`, `border-style`, and `border-color` of an element	The values for `border-width`, `border-style`, and `border-color` separated by spaces. For example: `border:1px solid #000000;`
`border-color`	Color of the border around an element	Any valid color
`border-style`	Type of border around an element	Text values `double`, `groove`, `inset`, `none` (the default), `outset`, `ridge`, `solid`, `dashed`, `dotted`, `hidden`

Table 6.1 CSS properties used with formatting and page layout (*continued*)

Property	Description	Commonly Used Values
`border-width`	Width of a border around an element	A numeric pixel value (such as `1px`), percentage value, or the text values `thin`, `medium`, `thick`
`clear`	Specifies the display of an element in relation to floating elements	Text values `left`, `right`, `both`, `none` (default)
`color`	Text color	Any valid color
`display`	Controls how and if the element will display	Text values `none`, `block`, `inline`, `list-item`. Display set to `"none"` causes the element not to display.
`font-family`	Name of a font or font family	Any valid font or a font family such as `serif`, `sans-serif`, `fantasy`, `monospace`, or `cursive`
`font-size`	Size of the text font	This varies; `pt` (standard font point sizes), `px` (pixels), the unit `em` (which corresponds to the width of the capital M of the current font), or percentages; the text values `xx-small`, `small`, `medium`, `large`, `x-large`, and `xx-large` are also valid
`font-style`	Style of the font	`normal` (default), `italic`, `oblique`
`font-weight`	Boldness or weight of the font	This varies: the text values `normal`, `bold`, `bolder`, and `lighter` can be used; the numeric values `100`, `200`, `300`, `400`, `500`, `600`, `700`, `800`, and `900` can be used
`height`	Height of an element	A numeric value (`px` or `em`), numeric percentage, or `auto` (default)
`left`	Distance in from the left to display an element	A numeric pixel value or percentage
`line-height`	Spacing allowed for the line of text	It is most common to use a percentage for this value. For example, a value of `200%` is double space.
`list-style-image`	Image used to replace "bullets" in an XHTML list	`url(imagename.gif)` or `url(imagename.jpg)`
`list-style-type`	Indicates the type of list item marker	Text values `none`, `disc`, `circle`, `square`, `decimal`, `lower-roman`, `upper-roman`, `lower-alpha`, `upper-alpha`
`margin`	Shorthand notation to configure the margin surrounding an element	A numeric value (`px` or `em`) or percentage; for example: `body { margin: 10px;}` will set page margins in the document to 10 pixels. If you set a value to 0 pixels, omit the `px`. Four numeric values (`px` or `em`) can be specified. The values configure the margins in the following order (`margin-top`, `margin-right`, `margin-bottom`, `margin-left`).

continued

Table 6.1 CSS properties used with formatting and page layout (*continued*)

Property	Description	Commonly Used Values
margin-bottom	Size of an element's bottom margin	A numeric value (**px** or **em**) or percentage
margin-left	Size of an element's left margin	A numeric value (**px** or **em**) or percentage
margin-right	Size of an element's right margin	A numeric value (**px** or **em**) or percentage
margin-top	Size of an element's top margin	A numeric value (**px** or **em**) or percentage
min-width	The minimum width of an element	A numeric value (**px** or **em**) or percentage
overflow	Controls the display of a block-level element if the element exceeds its set height or width	Text values **visible**, **hidden**, **auto**, **scroll**
padding	Shorthand notation to configure the amount of padding—the blank space between the element and its border	Two numeric values (**px** or **em**) or percentages. The first value configures the top and bottom padding, the second value configures the left and right padding: **padding: 20px 10px;** Four numeric values (**px** or **em**) or percentages. The values configure the padding in the following order: **padding-top**, **padding-right**, **padding-bottom**, **padding-left**.
padding-bottom	Blank space between an element and its bottom border	A numeric value (**px** or **em**) or percentage
padding-left	Blank space between an element and its left border	A numeric value (**px** or **em**) or percentage
padding-right	Blank space between an element and its right border	A numeric value (**px** or **em**) or percentage
padding-top	Blank space between an element and its top border	A numeric value (**px** or **em**) or percentage
position	Configures the positioning of an element	The value **relative** will position the element in relation to the normal flow. The value **absolute** will position the element at the exact pixel location.
right	Distance in from the right to display an element	A numeric pixel value or percentage
scrollbar-arrow-color	Color of the arrow on the scroll bar (IE only)	Any valid color
scrollbar-face-color	Color of the sliding scroll bar (IE only)	Any valid color
scrollbar-track-color	Color of the track the scroll bar slides in (IE only)	Any valid color
text-align	The alignment of text	Text values **center**, **justify**, **left**, **right**
text-decoration	Determines whether text is underlined; this style is most often applied to hyperlinks	The text value **none** will cause a hyperlink not to be underlined in a browser that normally processes in this manner. The text value **underline** will configure hyperlink to be underlined.

Table 6.1 CSS properties used with formatting and page layout (*continued*)

Property	Description	Commonly Used Values
text-indent	Indents first line of a block element	A numeric value (**em** or **px**), percentage
text-transform	Modifies appearance of text	Text values none (default), capitalize, uppercase, lowercase
top	Distance down from the top to display an element	A numeric pixel value or percentage
vertical-align	Modifies the alignment of an inline element	Text values middle, bottom, text-bottom, text-top, top, super, sub, or a percentage value
visibility	Controls whether an element displays and takes up space on a Web page	Text values visible, hidden, inherit
width	Width of an element	A numeric value (px or em), percentage
z-index	The stack order of an element on a Web page; a higher value will display in front of elements with lower values	A numeric value; the default value is 0. May be negative although this can cause problems in Netscape.

HANDS-ON PRACTICE 6.4

Of course, the best way to learn new coding technologies is to practice them. In this Hands-On Practice you will configure two files: an external style sheet (wildflower.css), and a splash page similar to the one shown in Figure 6.13. You will use CSS to format and position the page elements.

Getting Started

Locate the yls.jpg, pls.jpg, showy.jpg, and trillium.jpg files in the Chapter6 folder in the student files. Create a new folder called wildflowers. Copy the files to the wildflowers folder.

Part 1—Code the Splash Page

Review Figure 6.13 and notice the page elements: three images (yls.jpg, pls.jpg, and trillium.jpg), a logo, and a link. Figure 6.14 shows a wireframe of these elements arranged on the page.

In this part of the Hands-On Practice you will code each page element using XHTML and wrap it in a <div> that is assigned to an id. Then, in Part 2 you will code CSS to configure a number of properties including the absolute position, border, font-family, and so on. As you code the splash page, splash.html, you will place the elements on the page and assign id values. In essence, you are configuring a set of boxes (using the box model). Launch Notepad and type in the following XHTML:

Figure 6.14
A sketch of the splash page elements

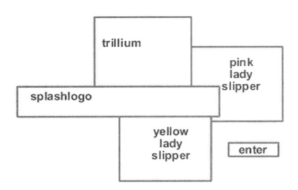

```
<?xml version="1.0" encoding="UTF-8"?>
<!DOCTYPE html PUBLIC "-//W3C//DTD XHTML 1.0 Transitional//EN"
   "http://www.w3.org/TR/xhtml1/DTD/xhtml1-transitional.dtd">
<html xmlns="http://www.w3.org/1999/xhtml">
<head>
  <title>Door County Wildflowers</title>
  <link rel="stylesheet" href="wildflower.css" type="text/css" />
</head>
<body>
<div id="splashlogo">
  <h1>Door County Wildflowers</h1>
</div>
<div id="trillium">
  <img src="trillium.jpg" alt="Trillium" width="200" height="150" />
</div>
<div id="yls">
  <img src="yls.jpg" alt="Yellow Lady Slipper" width="200" height="150" />
</div>
<div id="pls">
  <img src="pls.jpg" alt="Pink Lady Slipper" width="200" height="150" />
</div>
<div id="enter">
  <a href="page1.html">Enter</a>
</div>
</body>
</html>
```

Save your file as splash.html in the wildflowers folder. Test your page in a browser and compare it with the one shown in Figure 6.15.

The browser has displayed the page using normal flow—following the order of the elements in the source code. Don't worry that your elements are not positioned as they should be. Next, you'll configure the positioning properties as you create the wildflower.css.

Part 2—Code the External Style Sheet

Let's take a moment to consider what type of positioning is needed for the splash page: the splash screen logo, the three images, and the link. Refer to the wireframe sketch in

Figure 6.15
The splash page before the styles are coded

Figure 6.14 and to the screenshot shown in Figure 6.13. Type the CSS in your wildflower.css file as the styles are discussed as follows:

- **Splash Screen Logo Area.** This should be configured with the id value of splashlogo. This id will use absolute positioning, appear 210 pixels from the top of the browser window, use the background color of #e8b9e8, use a text color of black, display in Times New Roman or serif font with center-aligned text, have about 5 pixels of padding on the top and bottom sides, and have 20 pixels of padding on the left and right sides. There should be a 2 pixel solid border. This element will overlap the images so it must have a higher z-index value than the three images. The CSS follows:

```
#splashlogo { background-color: #e8b9e8;
              padding: 5px 20px;
              color: #000000;
              font-family: "Times New Roman", serif;
              position: absolute;
              text-align: center;
              z-index: 4;
              top: 210px;
              left: 80px;
              border: 2px solid #000000;
}
```

- **Trillium Image Area**

```
#trillium { position: absolute;
            z-index: 3;
            left: 20px;
            top: 80px;
}
```

- **Pink Lady Slipper Image Area**

```
#pls { position: absolute;
       z-index: 2;
       left: 420px;
       top: 130px;
}
```

- **Yellow Lady Slipper Image Area**

```
#yls { position: absolute;
       z-index: 3;
       left: 300px;
       top: 270px;
}
```

- **Hyperlink Area**

```
#enter { position: absolute;
         left: 520px;
         top: 350px;
         font-family: Verdana,sans-serif;
}
```

Save the wildflower.css file in the wildflowers folder.

How do I know exactly what values to use for absolute positioning?

Lots of testing! When hand-coding a page that uses absolute positioning there is a lot of trial and error. It is helpful to sketch the page or create a prototype using a graphics application. Be patient—make your best guess, test, and repeat until the configuration is complete. The good news is that Web authoring tools such as Adobe Dreamweaver provide a visual editor that greatly streamlines this process.

Part 3—Test the Splash Page

Now that your styles are coded, test the splash.html page again. Your page should be similar to the screenshot shown in Figure 6.13. If there are differences, verify the id values in your XHTML and check the syntax of your CSS. You may find the W3C CSS validator at http://jigsaw.w3.org/css-validator helpful when verifying CSS syntax. The student files contain a copy of wildflower.css and splash.html in the Chapter6 folder.

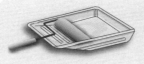

CHECKPOINT 6.1

1. State three reasons to use CSS for page layout on a commercial site being developed today.

2. Describe the difference between relative and absolute positioning.

3. Describe the purpose of the `z-index` CSS property.

6.4 Exploring CSS Page Layout

You've just configured a Web page using CSS to position elements. You'll continue to explore using CSS for page layout as you create another page for the Door County Wildflowers site. As discussed earlier in this chapter, the CSS `float` property causes the browser to display XHTML elements outside of the normal flow. Elements configured with the `float` property appear to float on the right or left side of either the browser window or another XHTML element such as a paragraph. For best results, elements that float should have an intrinsic width (such as an image element) or have their width configured. In the next Hands-On Practice you'll gain more practice using floats.

HANDS-ON PRACTICE 6.5

In the previous Hands-On Practice you created the splash page for the Door County Wildflowers Web site. In this Hands-On Practice you'll add to this site—create a new content page (page1.html) and modify the wildflower.css external CSS file to configure page1.html to display similar to the one shown in Figure 6.16 (shown also in the color insert section).

Figure 6.16
The image is floating on the page

See the center color insert

Getting Started

Locate the wildflowers folder you created in the previous Hands-On Practice. Copy the showy.jpg from the Chapter6 folder in the student files to the wildflowers folder.

Part 1—Code the Content Page

Review Figure 6.16 and notice the page elements: the logo, navigation area, floating right image, page content, and page footer. Figure 6.17 shows a wireframe sketch of these elements on the page.

In this part of the Hands-On Practice, you will code each element in an XHTML document. These will be coded to use `ids` and `classes` that correspond to CSS, which configures a number of properties including the `margin`, `padding`, `border`, `font-family`, and so on. As you code the content page, page1.html, you will place the elements on the page and assign `id` and `class` values. You are creating a combination of nested boxes, instead of coding tables and cells. Launch Notepad and type in the following XHTML:

Figure 6.17
Note how the elements are arranged on the page

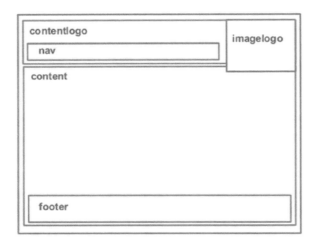

```
<?xml version="1.0" encoding="UTF-8"?>
<!DOCTYPE html PUBLIC "-//W3C//DTD XHTML 1.0 Transitional//EN"
   "http://www.w3.org/TR/xhtml1/DTD/xhtml1-transitional.dtd">
<html xmlns="http://www.w3.org/1999/xhtml">
<head>
   <title>Door County Wildflowers</title>
   <link rel="stylesheet" href="wildflower.css" type="text/css" />
</head>
<body>
<img id="imagelogo" src="pls.jpg" alt="Pink Lady Slipper"
width="200" height="150" />
<div id="contentlogo">
   <h1>Door County Wildflowers</h1>
   <a class="nav" href="home.html">Home</a>
   <a class="nav" href="spring.html">Spring</a>
   <a class="nav" href="summer.html">Summer</a>
   <a class="nav" href="fall.html">Fall</a>
   <a class="nav" href="winter.html">Winter</a>
</div>
<div class="content">
   <p>Wisconsin&#39;s Door County Peninsula is a unique, ecologically
diverse place with upland and boreal forest, bogs, swamps, sand and
rock beaches, limestone escarpments, and farmlands. A wide array of
wildflowers grow in the county because of this variety of
ecosystems.</p>
   <p>Explore the beauty of Door County Wildflowers....</p>
   <div class="footer">
     Copyright &copy; 2007 Door County Wild Flowers<br />
     Last Updated on 07/02/07
   </div>
</div>
</body>
</html>
```

Save your page in the wildflowers folder and test it in a browser. It will not look like Figure 6.16 since you have not yet configured all the `ids` and classes in the external style sheet. Your page should look similar to the one shown in Figure 6.18.

Figure 6.18
The page before
CSS for positioning
is configured

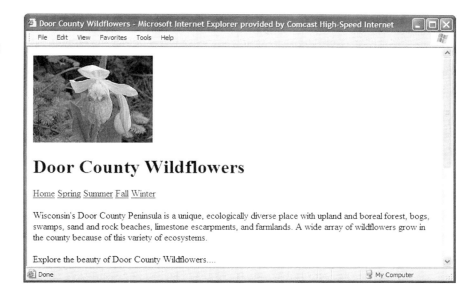

Part 2—Add Styles to the External Style Sheet

Open your wildflower.css file with Notepad and prepare to add additional styles to configure the page1.html page. Let's take a moment to consider what type of positioning is needed for the page shown in Figure 6.16, the page1.html page. Locate the following areas on the sketch in Figure 6.17: logo area, logo image, navigation links, content, and footer. Type the CSS in your wildflower.css file as the styles are discussed as follows:

- **Logo Area.** This should be configured with the `id` value of `contentlogo`. Configure this `id` so that the `background-color` is #e8b9e8, the text color is black, the `font-size` is larger, and the padding is 10 pixels. The CSS to configure this follows:

```
#contentlogo { background-color: #e8b9e8;
               font-size: larger;
               padding: 10px;
               color: #000000;
}
```

- **Logo Image.** Notice how this image floats at the right edge of the browser window. Configure the id `imagelogo` with a right float. We have most often set the margin to be the same for all sides of an element's box. The margins can be set for each side individually using the `margin-top`, `margin-right`, `margin-bottom`, and `margin-left` properties. A short-hand version of this is to set all four values in one `margin` property. The order of the numeric values determines which box side is configured (top, right, bottom, left). In this page layout the margin at the top and right of the `imagelogo` should be set to 0; the bottom and left margins should be set to 5 pixels. Configure a solid border. The CSS follows:

```
#imagelogo { float: right;
             margin: 0 0 5px 5px;
             border: solid;
}
```

- **Navigation Links.** Configure the nav class to use 5 pixel padding, a background color of #e8b9e8, text color of dark blue (#000066), no underline (text-decoration:none), Verdana, Arial or other sans-serif font, and center-aligned text. The CSS follows:

```
.nav { padding: 5px;
       background-color: #e8b9e8;
       color: #000066;
       text-decoration: none;
       font-family: Verdana, Arial, sans-serif;
       text-align: center;
}
```

- **Overall Content.** Configure the content class to use Verdana, Arial, or sans-serif font and have a margin of 10 pixels.

```
.content { font-family: Verdana,Arial,sans-serif;
           margin: 10px;
}
```

- **Page Footer.** Configure a class called footer with xx-small font that is centered as follows:

```
.footer { font-size: xx-small;
          text-align: center;
}
```

Save the wildflower.css file in the wildflowers folder.

Part 3—Test the Content Page

Now that your styles are coded, test the page1.html page again. Your display should be similar to the screenshot shown in Figure 6.16. If there are differences, verify the id and class values in your XHTML. Also check the syntax of your CSS. You may find the W3C CSS validator at http://jigsaw.w3.org/css-validator helpful when verifying CSS syntax. The student files contain a copy of splash.html, page1.html, and wildflower.css in the Chapter6/wildflowers folder.

6.5 Two-Column Page Layout

A common design for a Web page is a two-column layout with left-column navigation and right-column logo and content. Figure 6.19 shows a page designed in this format using CSS.

The page contains a number of elements, as shown in Figure 6.19. Compare the wireframe sketch in Figure 6.20 with the page displayed in Figure 6.19 (shown also in the color insert section).

Figure 6.19
A two-column page configured using CSS

See the center color insert

Figure 6.20
The two-column page layout

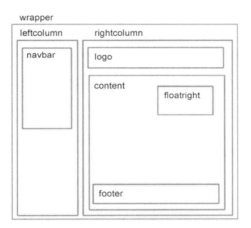

The page is designed with a number of boxes that correspond to the following page areas: wrapper, left column, right column, logo, navigation bar, content, right-floating image, and footer. Each of these areas will correspond to a `class` or `id` configured using CSS. The key to this layout is that the left column is coded to float to the left using `float:left`. With the left column navigation area floating to the left, the browser renders the other content down the page using normal flow. In the next Hands-On Practice you will code the XHTML and CSS to create the page shown in Figure 6.19.

HANDS-ON PRACTICE 6.6

In this Hands-On Practice you will develop your first two-column Web page using CSS. As you create the Web page and CSS, keep in mind that using this technique is like creating a series of nested boxes. Refer to the Web page screenshot shown in Figure 6.19 and the page layout sketch in Figure 6.20 as you complete this Hands-On Practice.

Getting Started

Locate the showy.jpg file in the Chapter6 folder in the student files. Create a new folder called wildflowers2. Copy the file to the folder.

Part 1—Code the XHTML

Review Figures 6.19 and 6.20. Notice the following page elements: wrapper, left column, right column, logo, navigation bar, content, right-floating image, and footer. Each of these areas will be coded to use an `id` and `class` that corresponds to CSS, which configures a number of properties including the `padding`, `border`, `font-family`, and so on. As you code the XHTML document, you will place the elements on the page, assigning `id` and `class` values that correspond to the areas in the sketch shown in Figure 6.20. Launch Notepad and type in the following XHTML:

```
<?xml version="1.0" encoding="UTF-8"?>
<!DOCTYPE html PUBLIC "-//W3C//DTD XHTML 1.0 Transitional//EN"
  "http://www.w3.org/TR/xhtml1/DTD/xhtml1-transitional.dtd">
<html xmlns="http://www.w3.org/1999/xhtml">
<head>
  <title>Door County Wildflowers</title>
</head>
<body>
<div id="wrapper">
  <div id="leftcolumn">
    <a class="navBar" href="index.html">Home</a>
    <a class="navBar" href="spring.html">Spring</a>
    <a class="navBar" href="summer.html">Summer</a>
    <a class="navBar" href="fall.html">Fall</a>
    <a class="navBar" href="winter.html">Winter</a>
  </div>
  <div id="rightcolumn">
    <div id="logo">
      <h1>Door County Wildflowers</h1>
    </div>
    <div class="content">
      <img src="showy.jpg" width="200" height="150" id="floatright"
        alt="Showy Lady Slippers" />
      <p>Wisconsin&#39;s Door County Peninsula is a unique,
ecologically diverse place with upland and boreal forest, bogs,
swamps, sand and rock beaches, limestone escarpments, and farmlands.
</p>
      <p>A wide array of wildflowers grow in the county because of
this variety of ecosystems.</p>
      <h3>Explore the beauty <br />of Door County Wildflowers</h3>
    </div>
    <div class="footer">
```

```
            Copyright &copy; 2007 Door County Wild Flowers<br />
            Last Updated on 07/07/07
        </div>
      </div>
    </div>
  </body>
</html>
```

Save your page as twocolumn.html in your wildflowers2 folder. Test the page in a browser. Your display will not look like the one shown in Figure 6.19 because you have not yet configured the CSS. Your page should look similar to the page shown in Figure 6.21.

Figure 6.21
The two-column page before CSS is applied

Part 2—Configure the CSS

For ease of editing, in this Hands-On Practice you will code the CSS as embedded styles in the header section of the Web page. However, if you were creating an entire Web site you would most likely use an external style sheet as you did in the previous Hands-On Practice.

Launch Notepad and open twocolumn.html. Let's take a moment to consider what type of layout is needed for the page shown in Figure 6.19: wrapper, left column, right column, logo, navigation bar, content, right-floating image, and footer. Locate these areas on the sketch shown in Figure 6.20. Notice that the same font is used throughout the page and the page begins right at the browser margin. Launch Notepad and open your twocolumn.html file. In the header section of your Web page document, add a tag to begin the embedded styles: `<style type="text/css">`.

Now let's consider the CSS configuration. Type the CSS in your document as it is discussed as follows:

- **Body Tag.** This should be configured with the default fonts of Verdana, Arial, or any sans-serif font. The page margin should be set to 0 pixels.

```
body { font-family: Verdana,Arial,sans-serif;
    margin: 0;
}
```

- **Wrapper.** Configure a container, or wrapper, area to contain the two columns and configure default background (#e8b9e8) and text (#000066) colors.

```
#wrapper { background-color: #e8b9e8;
    color: #000066;
}
```

- **Left Column.** The key to this two-column page layout is that the left 100 pixel wide column is designed to float to the left. The left column uses the background and text colors configured in the wrapper id.

```
#leftcolumn { float: left;
    width: 100px;
}
```

- **Right Column.** Since the left column is 100 pixels wide and floats on the left side, assign a 100 pixel wide left margin to the right column. Configure a background (#ffffff) and text (#000000) color.

```
#rightcolumn { margin-left: 100px;
    background-color: #ffffff;
    color: #000000;
}
```

- **Logo.** The logo is configured with a background color of #eeeeee, text color of #cc66cc, an extra large font size, 10 pixels of padding, and a solid black border that is 1 pixel wide.

```
#logo { background-color: #eeeeee;
    color: #cc66cc;
    font-size: x-large;
    border-bottom: 1px solid #000000;
    padding: 10px
}
```

- **Content.** The content area will be easier to read if there is additional empty space on the top, right, and left sides. This can be configured using the padding property. Typically, you have set the same padding value for all four sides of the element's box. The padding set for the logo is an example of this. Padding can be set for each side individually using the padding-top, padding-right, padding-bottom, and padding-left properties. A short-hand version of this is to set all four values in one padding property. The order of the numeric values determines which box side is configured (top, right, bottom, left). In this page layout the padding at the top, right, and left sides of the content should be set to 20 pixels.

```
.content { padding: 20px 20px 0 20px;
}
```

- **Image Floating at the Right.** Configure the image with a 10 pixel margin and float:right.

```
#floatright { margin: 10px;
              float: right;
}
```

- **Footer.** Configure the page footer with very small text that is centered. A `clear:right` is needed to clear the float of the image. Configure 20 pixels of padding on the bottom of the footer.

```
.footer { font-size: xx-small;
          text-align: center;
          clear: right;
          padding-bottom: 20px;
}
```

- **Navigation Area.** Configure the class for the navigation with no underlines (`text-decoration:none`), a 15 pixel margin, and to use `display:block`, which will allow each anchor tag act as a block element and be displayed on a separate line.

```
.navBar { text-decoration: none;
          margin: 15px;
          display: block;
}
```

Type the closing XHTML style tag as follows.

```
</style>
```

Save the twocolumn.html file in the wildflowers2 folder.

Part 3—Test the Page

Now that your styles are coded, test the twocolumn.html page again. Your page should be similar to the screenshot shown in Figure 6.19. If there are differences, verify the `id` and `class` values in your XHTML and check the syntax of your CSS. You may find the W3C CSS validator at http://jigsaw.w3.org/css-validator helpful when verifying CSS syntax. The student files contain a copy of twocolumn.html in the Chapter6/wildflowers2 folder.

This is just one of many ways that a two-column page layout can be coded. The best way to learn is to experiment by changing some of the properties and noting the result. It is a very good idea to test your pages in more than one browser. The pages in this chapter were tested using Internet Explorer 7, Opera 9, Safari for Windows beta, and Firefox 2.

FAQ

How do I create a custom-color scroll bar?

It can be fun to color-coordinate the scroll bar with your Web site! Keep in mind that not all your Web visitors will see your handiwork. While this effect is supported by Internet Explorer, it is not supported by all browsers. To configure a scroll bar with colors that you choose, add the following styles to the body tag: `scrollbar-face-color`, `scrollbar-arrow-color`, `scrollbar-track-color`. For example:

```
body {  scrollbar-face-color: #cc66cc;
        scrollbar-arrow-color: #006600;
        scrollbar-track-color: #cccccc;
}
```

Note: Your CSS will not pass W3C validation tests if you use these Internet Explorer only properties.

6.6 CSS Debugging Tips

Using CSS for page layout requires some patience. It takes a while to get used to it. One of the biggest issues is that even modern browsers implement CSS in slightly different ways. Testing is crucial. Don't make it your goal that the pages must look exactly the same on every browser. Expect your pages to look slightly different on various browsers. Design so they look best on the most commonly used browser (currently Internet Explorer) and display acceptably well on other browsers. There are Web pages devoted to CSS bugs and browser support of CSS. The following are a few that you will find helpful:

- http://web.archive.org//20040202153928/http://devedge.netscape.com/library/xref/2003/css-support/css1/mastergrid.html

  The original "Master List" created by Eric Meyer

- http://www.westciv.com/style_master/academy/browser_support/index.html

  A comprehensive browser compatibility list

- http://www.positioniseverything.net

  John and Holly Bergevin's site focuses on CSS bugs in modern browsers—it contains some great sample CSS page layouts

- http://www.quirksmode.org

  Peter-Paul Koch's site is dedicated to studying and defeating browser incompatibilities related to CSS and JavaScript

CSS Debugging Techniques

Debugging CSS can be frustrating. The following are helpful techniques to use:

- **Manually Check Syntax Errors.** Sometimes a CSS style does not apply due to a syntax error. Carefully check your code. Many times the error is in the line above the style that is not correctly applied.

- **Programmatically Check Syntax Errors.** As mentioned earlier, you can use the W3C's CSS Validator at http://jigsaw.w3.org/css-validator to verify your syntax.

- **Configure Temporary Background Colors.** Sometimes your code is valid but the browser window is not configured the way you would expect. If you temporarily assign distinctive background colors such as red or yellow and test again, it should be easier to see where the "boxes" are ending up.

- **Configure Temporary Borders.** Similar to the temporary background colors, you could temporarily configure an element with a 3 pixel red solid border—this will really jump out at you and help you recognize the issue sooner.

- **Use Comments to Find the Unexpected Cascade.** Styles and XHTML attributes configured farther down the page can override earlier styles. If your styles are misbehaving, try commenting out (see below) some styles and test with a smaller group of statements. Then add the styles back in one by one to see where or when the breakdown occurs. Work patiently and test the entire style sheet in this manner.

Note that Comment Areas Are Ignored by Browsers. A style sheet comment begins with /* and ends with */. Comments can span multiple lines. A code snippet with CSS comments follows:

```
/* Set Page Margins to Zero */
body { margin: 0
}
/* temporarily commented out during testing
.nav { text-decoration: none;
}
*/
```

The first comment is used to document the style sheet and describe the style applied to the body tag. The second comment spans multiple lines. It begins on the line above the nav class and ends on the line below the nav class. This causes the browser to skip the nav class when applying the style sheet. This technique can be useful in testing when you are experimenting with a number of properties.

6.7 CSS Page Layout Resources

This chapter introduces you to using CSS for page layout configuration and should get you started in your exploration of this technology. It may help you to know that you are not alone in your quest to learn CSS. There are many resources with documentation, tutorials, and support for this technology. The page layout techniques discussed in this textbook are just an introduction to using this technology. There are many Web sites that offer additional insight and techniques for configuring page layout with CSS. The following are a few that you may find useful:

- http://glish.com/css

  Large collection of CSS page layouts and links to tutorials

- http://www.websitetips.com/css/index.shtml

  Comprehensive list of tutorials and CSS-related sites

- http://www.meyerweb.com/eric/css

  The site of Eric Meyer, a leading-edge Web developer

- http://www.w3.org/Style/CSS/learning

  W3C's list of CSS resources

- http://www.bluerobot.com/web/layouts

  A "reservoir" of CSS page layouts

- http://www.blooberry.com/indexdot/css

  CSS syntax reference list

- http://www.w3.org/TR/1998/REC-CSS2-19980512

  W3C CSS Level 2 Recommendation

- http://www.w3.org/TR/REC-CSS1-961217.html

  W3C CSS Level 1 Recommendation

CHECKPOINT 6.2

1. The two-column layouts you created in the previous Hands-On Practice did not use absolute positioning. Open the twocolumn.html page in a browser. Resize the browser window. Describe what happens. What type of page design layout (ice, jello, or liquid) is being used?

2. Describe one CSS debugging tip that you have found helpful.

3. Describe how to choose whether to configure an XHTML tag, create a class, or create an id when working with CSS.

CHAPTER SUMMARY

This chapter introduced Cascading Style Sheet rules associated with page layout. Techniques for positioning and floating elements and configuring two-column page layouts were demonstrated. This topic is very deep and you have much to explore. Visit the resources in the chapter to continue learning about this technology.

Visit the textbook Web site at http://www.webdevfoundations.net for examples, the links listed in this chapter, and updated information.

Key Terms

absolute positioning
border
clear property
content
CSS Box Model
CSS-P

display property
float property
left property
margin
normal flow
padding

relative positioning
right property
top property
visible width
z-index property

Review Questions

Multiple Choice

1. When using absolute positioning, which of the following properties may be used to determine the placement of the element?

   a. top and left
   b. z-index and display
   c. float and clear
   d. none of the above

2. Which of the following, from outermost to innermost, are components of the box model?

   a. margin, border, padding, content
   b. content, padding, border, margin
   c. content, margin, padding, border
   d. margin, padding, border, content

3. Which of the following is the default value of the border and padding properties for an element?

   a. 1 pixel
   b. 0 pixels
   c. 3 pixels
   d. 10 pixels

4. Which of the following configures a class called sidebar to float to the right?

   a. .sidebar { right: float; }
   b. .sidebar { float: right; }
   c. .sidebar { float-right: 200px; }
   d. none of the above

5. Which of the following is the rendering flow used by a browser by default?

   a. XHTML flow
   b. normal display
   c. browser flow
   d. normal flow

6. Which of the following is used to change the location of an element slightly in relation to where it would otherwise appear on the page?

   a. the float property
   b. absolute positioning
   c. relative positioning
   d. this cannot be done with CSS

7. Which of the following will configure padding that is 10 pixels on the top, 0 pixels on the left and right, and 5 pixels on the bottom?

   a. `margin: 0px 5px 0px 10px;`
   b. `margin:top-10, left-0, right-0, bottom-5;`
   c. `padding: 10px 0 5px 0;`
   d. none of the above

8. Which of the following is used along with the `left`, `right` and/or `top` property to configure the position of an element precisely?

   a. `position: relative`
   b. `position: absolute`
   c. `position: float`
   d. none of the above

9. Which of the following configures a margin for an element with the following values: top margin 20 pixels, left margin 300 pixels, right margin 0 pixels, and bottom margin 0 pixels?

   a. `margin: 300px 20px 0px 300px;`
   b. `margin: top-20, left-300, right-0, bottom-0;`
   c. `margin: 20px 0 0 300px;`
   d. none of the above

10. Which of the following will configure a class called `news` to stack on top of other elements that have a z-index of 5?

    a. `.news { z-index: high}  ;`
    b. `.news { z-index:6}  ;`
    c. `.news { z-index:4}  ;`
    d. none of the above

Fill in the Blank

11. Configure a style with a(n) _____ if the style will only apply to one element on a page.

12. If an element is configured with `float:right`, the other content on the page will appear to its _____.

13. The _____ is always transparent.

14. Use the `position:relative` property along with the _____, _____, and/or _____ property to configure the position of an element in relation to the normal flow.

15. Configure a style with a_____ if the style could apply to more than one element on a page.

Apply Your Knowledge

1. **Predict the Result.** Draw and write a brief description of the Web page that will be created with the following XHTML code:

```
<html>
<head>
   <title>CircleSoft Web Design</title>
   <style type="text/css">
   h1 { border-bottom: 1px groove #333333;
        color: #006600;
        background-color: #cccccc
   }
   #content { position: absolute;
              left: 200px;
              top: 75px;
              font-family: Arial,sans-serif;
              width: 300px;
   }
   .nav { font-weight: bold;
   }
   </style>
</head>
```

```
<body>
  <h1>CircleSoft Web Design</h1>
  <div id="content">
    <p>Our professional staff takes pride in its working
relationship with our clients by offering personalized services
that listen to their needs, develop their target areas, and
incorporate these items into a well-presented Web site that
works.</p>
  </div>
  <ul>
    <li class="nav">Home</li>
    <li class="nav"><a href="about.html">About</a></li>
    <li class="nav"><a href="services.html">Services</a></li>
  </ul>
  </div>
</body>
</html>
```

2. **Fill in the Missing Code.** This Web page should be configured as a two-column page layout with a right column 150 pixels wide. The right column should have a 1 pixel border. The padding in the left column content area needs to allow for the room that will be used by the right column. Some CSS properties and values, indicated by "_", are missing. Fill in the missing code.

```
<?xml version="1.0" encoding="UTF-8"?>
<!DOCTYPE html PUBLIC "-//W3C//DTD XHTML 1.0 Transitional//EN"
   "http://www.w3.org/TR/xhtml1/DTD/xhtml1-transitional.dtd">
<html xmlns="http://www.w3.org/1999/xhtml">
<head>
<title>Trillium Media Design</title>
<style type="text/css">
body { margin: 0;
       font-family: Verdana, Arial, sans-serif;
}
#rightcolumn { "_":"_";
               width: "_";
               background-color: #cccccc;
               height: 400px;
               border: "_";
}
#leftcolumn {
}
#logo { background-color: #cccccc;
       color: #663333;
       font-size: x-large;
       border-bottom: 1px solid #333333;
}
.content { padding: "_";
}
```

```
.footer { font-size: xx-small;
          text-align: center;
          clear: "_";
}
.navBar { color: #000066;
          text-decoration: none;
          padding: 3px;
          margin: 15px;
          display: "_";
}
</style>
</head>
<body>
<div id="rightcolumn">
  <a class="navBar" href="index.html">Home</a>
  <a class="navBar" href="products.html">Products</a>
  <a class="navBar" href="services.html">Services</a>
  <a class="navBar" href="about.html">About</a>
</div>
<div id="leftcolumn">
  <div id="logo">
    <h1>Trillium Media Design</h1>
  </div>
  <div class="content">
    <p>Our professional staff takes pride in its working
relationship with our clients by offering personalized services
that listen to their needs, develop their target  areas, and
incorporate these items into a well-presented Web site that
works.</p>
  </div>
  <div class="footer">
    Copyright &copy; 2008 Trillium Media Design<br />
    Last Updated on 01/15/08
  </div>
</div>
</body>
</html>
```

3. **Find the Error.** When this page is displayed using Internet Explorer 7, the heading information obscures the paragraph text. Correct the errors and describe the process you followed.

```
<?xml version="1.0" encoding="UTF-8"?>
<!DOCTYPE html PUBLIC "-//W3C//DTD XHTML 1.0 Transitional//EN"
"http://www.w3.org/TR/xhtml1/DTD/xhtml1-transitional.dtd">
<html xmlns="http://www.w3.org/1999/xhtml">
<head>
<title>CSS Float</title>
<style type="text/css">
```

```
h1 { background-color: #eeeeee;
    padding: 5px;
    color: #666633;
    position: absolute;
    left: 200px;
    top: 20px;
}
p { font-family: Arial,sans-serif;
    position;
    absolute;
    left: 100px;
    top: 100px;
}
#yls { float:right;
    margin: 0 0 5px 5px;
    border: solid;
}
</style>
</head>
<body>
<img id="yls" src="yls.jpg" alt="Yellow Lady Slipper" height="100"
  width="100" />
<h1>Floating an Image</h1>
<p> The Yellow Lady Slipper pictured on the right is a wildflower.
It grows in wooded areas and blooms in June each year. The Yellow
Lady Slipper is a member of the orchid family.</p>
</body>
</html>
```

Hands-On Exercises

1. Write the CSS for a class with the following attributes: a light blue background color, Arial or sans-serif font, dark blue text color, 10 pixels of padding, and a narrow dashed border in a dark blue color.

2. Write the CSS for an id with the following attributes: float to the left of the page, light beige background, Verdana or sans-serif large font, and 20 pixels of padding.

3. Write the CSS to configure a class that will produce a headline with a dotted line underneath it. Choose a color that you like for the text and dotted line.

4. Write the CSS for an id that will be absolutely positioned on a page 20 pixels from the top and 40 pixels from the right. This area should have a light gray background and a solid border.

5. Write the CSS for a class that is relatively positioned. This class should appear 15 pixels in from the left. Configure the class to have a light green background.

6. **Extending Hands-On Practice 6.6.** Design a two-column page layout with the navigation on the right side. Use the twocolumn.html file from Hands-On Practice 6.6 as a starting point. This file is in the Chapter6/wildflowers2folder in the student files.

Code an external style sheet file called rightcolumn.css and a Web page called rightcolumn.html. The Web page should have two columns. The right column will be the navigation column and the left column will be the content column. Hand in printouts of rightcolumn.css, the rightcolumn.html source code (print in Notepad), and the browser display of your rightcolumn.html to your instructor.

7. **Extending Hands-On Practice 6.6.** Design a two-column page layout with a logo area across the top. Review the Hands-On Practice 6.6 twocolumn.html file for some examples. These files are in the Chapter6/wildflowers2 folder in the student files. Code an external style sheet file called mydesign.css and a Web page called mydesign.html. The Web page should have two columns and a logo area across the top. Hand in printouts of mydesign.css, the mydesign.html source code (print in Notepad), and the browser display of your mydesign.html to your instructor.

8. **Extending Hands-On Practice 6.6.** In Hands-On Practice 6.6 you created two files for a version of the Door County Wildflowers Web site. The files are available in the Chapter6/wildflowers2 folder in the student files. You will create two additional content pages for the Door County Wildflowers site, called spring.html and summer.html, in this exercise. Be sure that all CSS is placed in an external style sheet, called mywildflower.css. (Modify pre-existing pages to use this style sheet.) Here is some content to include on the new pages:

Spring Page (spring.html):

- Use the trillium.jpg image (see the Chapter6 folder in the student files).
- Trillium facts: 8–18 inches tall, perennial, native plant, grows in rich moist deciduous woodlands, white flowers turn pink with age, fruit is a single red berry, protected flower species.

Summer Page (summer.html):

- Use the yls.jpg image (see the Chapter6 folder in the student files).
- Yellow Lady's Slipper facts: 4–24 inches tall, perennial, native plant, grows in wet shaded deciduous woods, swamps, and bogs, an orchid, official flower of Door County.

Hand in printouts of mywildflower.css, spring.html source code (print in Notepad), summer.html source code, the browser display of spring.html, and the browser display of summer.html to your instructor.

9. **Extending Hands-On Practice 6.2.** Modify the twocolumn.html page you created in Hands-On Practice 6.2. This file is in the Chapter6/wildflowers2 folder in the student files. Recall from Chapter 5 that a Web page using jello design has content in the center of the Web page with blank margins on either side. You can code this using CSS by configuring the margin property of the body tag to use percentages for the left and right. For example:

```
body { margin: 0 10% 0 10%; }
```

Hand in printouts of the source code (print in Notepad) and browser display for the Web page to your instructor.

10. Design a splash page called moviesplash.html about your favorite movie. Use absolute positioning and z-index to create an interesting display. First sketch the areas for images, text, and link to the first page on the site. Search the Web for

photos of the movie. Next, locate images from the movie. When you code your page use embedded CSS unless your instructor directs you otherwise. Hand in printouts of the moviesplash.html source code (print in Notepad), and the browser display of moviesplash.html to your instructor.

(*Note*: It is unethical to steal an image from another Web site. Some Web sites have a link to their copyright policy. Most Web sites will give permission for you to use an image in a school assignment. If there is no available policy, e-mail the site's contact person and request permission to use the photo. If you are unable to obtain permission, you may substitute clip art or an image from a free site.)

Focus on Ethics

Web Research

This chapter introduced using CSS to configure Web page layout. Use the resources listed in the text as a starting point. You can also use a search engine to search for CSS resources.

Create a Web page that provides a list of at least five CSS resources on the Web. For each CSS resource provide the URL, Web site name, and a brief description. Your Web page should use absolute positioning. Print both the source code (from Notepad) and the browser view of your Web page.

Focus on Web Design

There is still much for you to learn about CSS. A great place to learn about Web technology is on the Web itself. Use a search engine to search for CSS page layout tutorials. Choose a tutorial that is easy to read. Select a section that discusses a CSS technique that was not covered in this chapter. Create a Web page that uses this new technique. Consider how the suggested page layout follows (or does not follow) principles of design such as contrast, repetition, alignment, and proximity (see Chapter 5). The Web page should provide the URL of your tutorial, the name of the Web site, a description of the new technique you discovered, and a discussion of how the technique follows (or does not follow) principles of design. Print the external style sheet (if you used one), the Web page source code (from Notepad), and the browser view of your Web page.

WEB SITE CASE STUDY
Implementing CSS Two-Column Page Layout

Each of the following case studies continues throughout most of the text. This chapter implements CSS two-column page layout in the Web sites.

JavaJam Coffee House

See Chapter 2 for an introduction to the JavaJam Coffee House case. Figure 2.26 shows a site map for the JavaJam Web site. The pages were created in earlier chapters. In this case study you will implement a new two-column CSS page layout for JavaJam. You will modify the external style sheet and the Home, Menu, Music, and Jobs pages. Unless your instructor directs you otherwise, use the Chapter 4 JavaJam Web site as a starting point for this case study.

Figure 6.22 displays a wireframe for the two-column page layout with a page container, logo, left column, navigation, right column, floating, and footer areas.

Figure 6.22
JavaJam two-column page layout

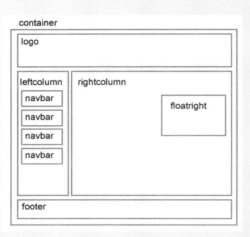

Hands-On Practice Case

1. **Create a Folder.** Create a folder called javajamcss. Copy all the files from your Chapter 4 javajam folder into the javajamcss folder. You will modify the java-jam.css file and each Web page file (index.html, menu.html, and music.html) to implement the two-column page layout shown in Figure 6.22. See the new JavaJam Home page, as shown in Figure 6.23 (shown also in the color insert section).

2. **Configure the CSS.** Open javajam.css in Notepad. Edit the style rules as follows:

   - Modify the `container` id to have a minimum width of 700 pixels (use `min-width: 700px`), background (#e8d882) and text (#000000) color, 80% width, and a 2 pixel black double border (`border: 2px double #000000`).

   - Configure the logo area. Remove the `h1` selector and style rules. Create a new id named `logo` with a background (#ccaa66) and text (#000000) color, center alignment (`text-align: center`) and a bottom border that is 2 pixels, double, and black (`border-bottom: 2px double #000000`).

   - Configure the left column area. Add a new style rule for the `leftcolumn` id to configure an area that floats to the left, is 100 pixels wide, and has 10 pixels of padding on the top side.

     ```
     #leftcolumn { float: left;
                   width: 100px;
                   padding-top: 10px;
     }
     ```

   - Configure the navigation area. Remove the `nav` id. Add a new style rule for the `navbar` class to configure an area with no underlines on hyperlinks, a 15

Figure 6.23
The new JavaJam two-column index.html

pixel margin, and is displayed as a block element (with line breaks above and below) by the browser.

```
.navBar{ text-decoration: none;
        margin: 15px;
        display: block;
}
```

- Configure the right column area. Add a new style rule for the `rightcolumn` id to configure an area with a 150 pixel left margin, background (`#f1e8b0`) and text (`#000000`) color, and 10 pixels of padding.

```
#rightcolumn { margin-left: 150px;
             background-color: #f1e8b0;
             color: #000000;
             padding: 10px;
}
```

- Configure an area that floats to the right. Notice how the winding road graphic shown in Figure 6.23 floats on the right side—this is configured with the `floatright` class. Images are more compelling when separated from other elements (such as text) by empty space. Add 40 pixels of padding to the left side of this area.

```
.floatright { padding-left: 40px;
            float: right;
}
```

- Modify the `footer` id to display a 2 pixel double black top border (`border-top: 2px double #000000`).

Save the javajam.css file.

3. **Modify the index.html File.** Add `<div>` elements and modify the code as follows:

   - Configure the logo area. Remove the `<h1>` opening and closing tags surrounding the JavaJam logo image. Code a `<div>` that surrounds the JavaJam logo image element. Assign the `<div>` to the id `logo`.

   - Configure the left column. The navigation links are the only content in the left column. Change `<div id="nav">` to `<div id="leftcolumn">`. Assign each anchor element in this area to the `navbar` class (`class="navbar"`).

   - Configure the right column. This area contains the remaining page content, including the footer area. Add a `<div>` that surrounds the text, winding road image, and footer area. Assign the `<div>` to the id `rightcolumn`.

   - Configure the area that floats to the right. Modify the winding road image element. Remove the `align="right"` attribute and add `class="floatright"` to the winding road image element.

   Save the index.html file. It should look similar to the Web page shown in Figure 6.23. Remember that validating your XHTML and CSS can help you find syntax errors. Test and correct this page before you continue.

4. **Modify the menu.html and music.html Files.** Modify the code in these Web page files in a similar manner as you did in Step 3. Save and test your pages in a browser. As you test your pages, use the CSS and XHTML validators to help you find syntax errors.

5. **Bonus Style: `text-transform`.** Figure 6.24 shows an alternate design for the music.html page. Notice how the `<h3>` elements are styled differently—with all uppercase text (using a new property, `text-transform`) different background and text colors, font size, bottom border, and margin. Open javajam.css in a text editor and replace the `h3` selector style rules with the following:

```
h3 { text-transform: uppercase;
     background-color: #ffffcc;
     color: #663300;
     font-size: 20px;
     border-bottom: 1px solid #000000;
     margin-right: 20px;
}
```

Save the javajam.css file. Test your pages in a browser. Your music.html page should look similar to the one shown in Figure 6.23. The other pages do not use `<h3>` elements and should appear as they did at the end of Step 4.

In this case study you changed the page layout of the JavaJam Web site pages. Notice that with just a few changes in the CSS and XHTML code, you configured a two-column page layout.

Figure 6.24
New style rules for the **h3** selectors

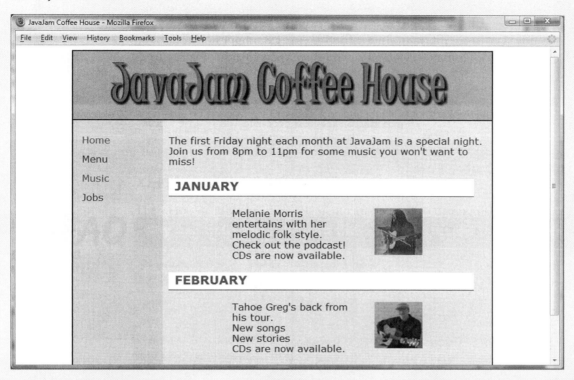

Fish Creek Animal Hospital

See Chapter 2 for an introduction to the Fish Creek Animal Hospital Case Study. Figure 2.30 shows a site map for the Fish Creek Web site. The pages were created in earlier chapters. In this case study you will implement a new two-column CSS page layout. You will modify the external style sheet and the Home, Services, and Ask the Vet pages. Unless your instructor directs you otherwise, use the Chapter 4 Fish Creek Web site as a starting point for this case study.

Figure 6.25 displays a wireframe for the two-column page layout with a page container, logo, left column, navigation, right column, and footer areas.

Figure 6.25
Fish Creek two-
column page layout

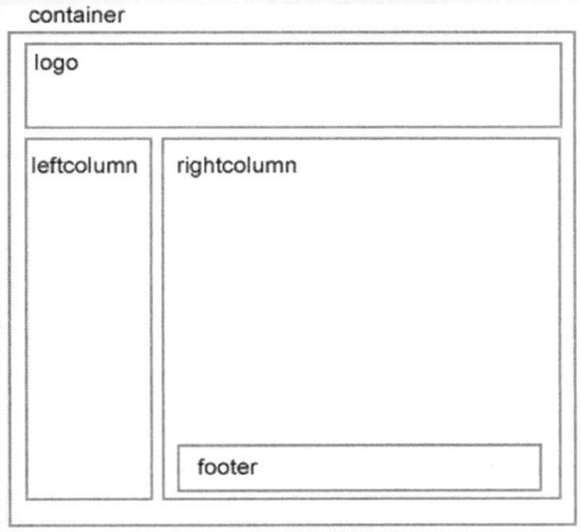

Hands-On Practice Case

1. **Create a Folder.** Create a folder called fishcreekcss. Copy all the files from your Chapter 4 fishcreek folder into the fishcreekcss folder. You will modify the fishcreek.css file and each Web page file (index.html, services.html, and askvet.html) to implement the two-column page layout, as shown in Figure 6.25. See the new Fish Creek home page, as shown in Figure 6.26 (shown also in the color insert section).

Figure 6.26
The new Fish Creek two-column index.html

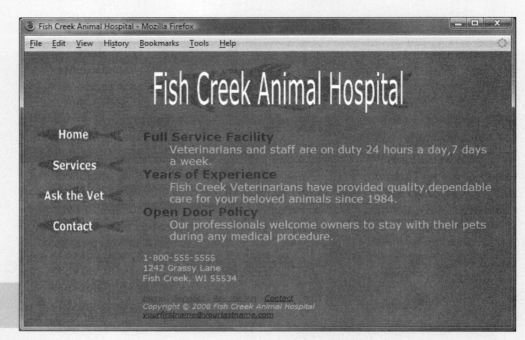

See the center color insert

2. **Configure the CSS.** Open fishcreek.css in Notepad. Edit the style rules as follows:
   - Modify the container id style rules. Notice that the new page layout aligns with the left margin. Remove the properties previously used to center the content (`margin-left` and `margin-right`).
   - Configure the logo area. Remove the `h1` selector and style rules. Create a new id named `logo` with 70 pixels of padding on the left side (`padding-left: 70px`).
   - Configure the left column area. Add a new style rule for the `leftcolumn` id to configure an area that floats to the left and is 140 pixels wide.

     ```
     #leftcolumn { float: left;
                   width: 140px;
     }
     ```
   - Configure the navigation area. Remove the `imgnav` id. Add a property to the style rules for the `img` selector—configure 10 pixels of padding (`padding: 10px`).
   - Configure the right column area. Add a new style rule for the `rightcolumn` id to configure an area with a 170 pixel left margin.
   - Configure the footer area. Remove the `nav` id.

   Save the fishcreek.css file.

3. **Modify the index.html File.** Add `<div>` elements and modify the code as follows:

   - Configure the logo area. Remove the `<h1>` opening and closing tags surrounding the Fish Creek image. Code a `<div>` that surrounds the Fish Creek logo image element. Assign the `<div>` to the id `logo`.

   - Configure the left column. The navigation image links are the only content in the left column. Change `<div id="imgnav">` to `<div id="leftcolumn">`.

   - Configure the right column. This area contains the definition list and the paragraph with the contact information. Code a `<div>` that surrounds this area. Assign the `<div>` to the id `rightcolumn`.

   - Configure the page footer area. You need to adjust the starting location of the `footer` id. Locate `<div id="footer">` in the code and remove the assignment to the id from the `<div>`. Next, change `<div id="nav">` to `<div id="footer">`. The area assigned to the `footer` id now includes the text navigation, copyright information, and e-mail link.

   Save the index.html file. It should look similar to the Web page shown in Figure 6.26. Remember that validating your XHTML and CSS can help you find syntax errors. Test and correct this page before you continue.

4. **Modify the services.html and askvet.html Files.** Modify these Web page files in a similar manner as you did in Step 3. Save and test your pages in a browser. As you test your pages, use the CSS and XHTML validators to help you find syntax errors.

In this case study you changed the page layout of the Fish Creek Web site pages. Notice that with just a few changes in the CSS and XHTML code, you configured a two-column page layout.

Pete the Painter

See Chapter 2 for an introduction to the Pete the Painter Case Study. Figure 2.34 shows a site map for the Pete the Painter Web site. The pages were created in earlier chapters. In this case study you will implement a new two column CSS page layout for Pete the Painter. You will modify the external style sheet and of the Home, Services, and Testimonials, pages. Unless your instructor directs you otherwise, use the Chapter 4 Pete the Painter Web site as a starting point for this case study.

Figure 6.27 displays a wireframe for the two-column page layout with a page container, logo, left column, navigation, right column, and footer areas.

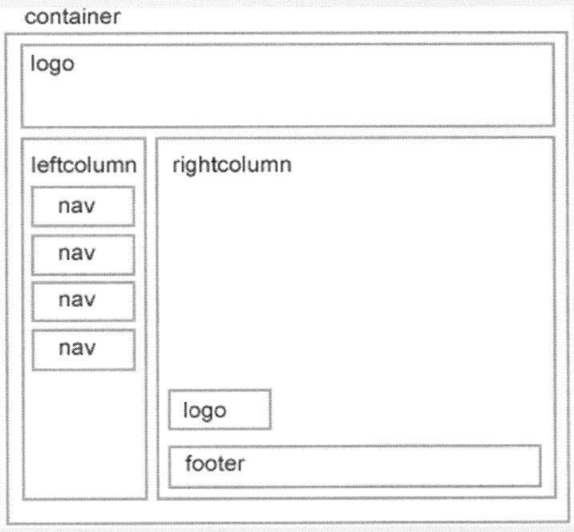

Figure 6.27
Pete the Painter two-column page layout

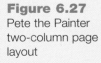

Hands-On Practice Case

1. **Create a Folder.** Create a folder called paintercss. Copy all the files from your Chapter 4 folder into the paintercss folder. You will modify the painter.css file and each Web page file (index.html, services.html, and testimonials.html) to implement the two-column page layout shown in Figure 6.27. See the new Pete the Painter home page, as shown in Figure 6.28 (shown also in the color insert section).

Figure 6.28
The new Pete the Painter two-column index.html

See the center color insert

2. **Configure the CSS.** Open painter.css in Notepad. Edit the style rules as follows:

   • Configure the left column area. Add a new style rule for the `leftcolumn` id to configure an area that floats to the left and is 150 pixels wide.

   ```
   #leftcolumn { float: left;
                 width: 150px;
   }
   ```

   • Configure the navigation area. Remove the nav id. Add a new style rule for the `nav` class to configure an area with bold font, a 15 pixel margin on the right, bottom, and left sides, and is displayed as a block element (with line breaks above and below) by the browser.

   ```
   .nav { font-weight: bold;
          margin: 0 15px 15px 15px;
          display: block;
   }
   ```

   • Configure the right column area. Add a new style rule for the `rightcolumn` id to configure an area with a 150 pixel left margin and a 10 pixel top margin (margin: 10px 0 0 150px).

   • Configure an area that floats to the right. Add a new style rule for the `floatright` class.

   ```
   .floatright { float: right;
   }
   ```

   Save the painter.css file.

3. **Modify the index.html File.** Add `<div>` elements and modify the code as follows:

- Configure the logo area. Remove the `<h1>` opening and closing tags surrounding the Pete the Painter image. Code a `<div>` that surrounds the Painter logo image element. Assign the `<div>` to the id `logo`.

- Configure the left column. The navigation links are the only content in the left column. Change `<div id="nav">` to `<div id="leftcolumn">`. Assign each anchor element in this area to the nav class (`class="nav"`).

- Configure the right column. This area contains the content (paragraph, unordered list, and heading 3 elements) and the footer section. Code a `<div>` that surrounds this area. Assign the `<div>` to the `rightcolumn` id.

- Assign the `<h3>` element to the `logo` class.

Save the index.html file. It should look similar to the Web page shown in Figure 6.28. Remember that validating your XHTML and CSS can help you find syntax errors. Test and correct this page before you continue.

4. **Modify the services.html and testimonials.html Files.** Modify these Web page files in a similar manner as you did in Step 3. Configure the room images on the testimonials.html page—on the opening image tag for each room photo, remove the `align="right"` attribute and add `class="floatright"`.

5. **Save and Test Your Pages in a Browser.** As you test your pages, use the CSS and XHTML validators to help you find syntax errors.

6. **Bonus Style.** Figure 6.29 shows an alternate design for the testimonials.html page. Notice how the `<h4>` elements are styled differently—it is set to float and is configured with a *negative* top margin. This allows the dark green box to stand out better on the page. The paragraph elements in this area are each assigned to a class that configures a top border of the same color green and extra padding.

Figure 6.29
New style rules for the `h4` selector

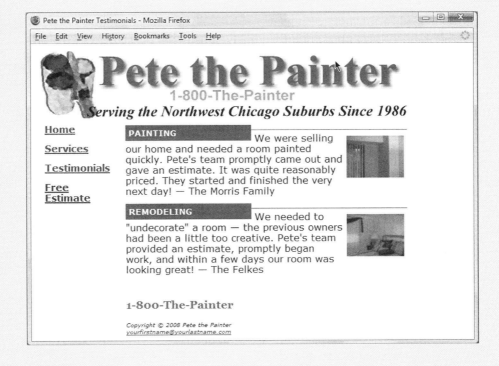

Open painter.css in a text editor and update the style rules with the following:

```
h4 { margin: -10px 5px 5px 0px;
     padding: 5px;
     font-family: Verdana, sans-serif;
     font-size: 14px;
     float: left;
     width: 200px;
     background-color: #336600;
     color: #ffffff;
     text-transform: uppercase;
}
.desc { padding: 5px 0 20px 0;
        border-top: 1px solid #336600;
}
```

Save the painter.css file. Test your pages in a browser. Your testimonials.html page should be similar to the one shown in Figure 6.29. The other pages should display as they did at the end of Step 4. Consider modifying the unordered list on the Services page (services.html) to use <h4> and <p> elements (assigned to the desc class) instead—the result will be a more cohesive design for your Web site.

In this case study you changed the page layout of the Pete the Painter Web site pages. Notice that with just a few changes in the CSS and XHTML code, you configured a two-column page layout.

Prime Properties

See Chapter 2 for an introduction to the Prime Properties Case Study. Figure 2.38 shows a site map for the Prime Properties Web site. The pages were created in earlier chapters. In this case study you will implement a new two-column CSS page layout for Prime Properties. You will modify the external style sheet and the Home, Listings, and Financing pages. Unless your instructor directs you otherwise, use the Chapter 4 Prime Properties Web site as a starting point for this case study.

Figure 6.30 displays a wireframe for the two-column page layout with a page wrapper, logo, left column, navigation, right column, and footer areas.

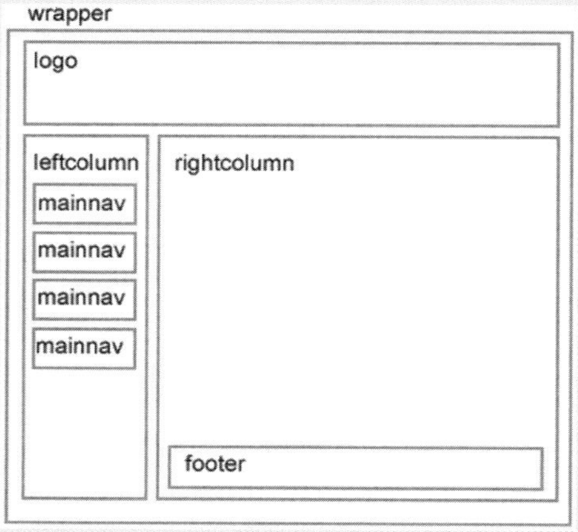

Figure 6.30
Prime Properties two-column page layout

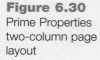

Hands-On Practice Case

1. **Create a Folder.** Create a folder called primecss. Copy all the files from your Chapter 4 prime folder into the primecss folder. You will modify the prime.css file and each Web page file (index.html, listings.html, and financing.html) to implement the two-column page layout shown in Figure 6.30. See the new Prime Properties Home page, as shown in Figure 6.31 (shown also in the color insert section).

Figure 6.31
The new Prime Properties two-column index.html

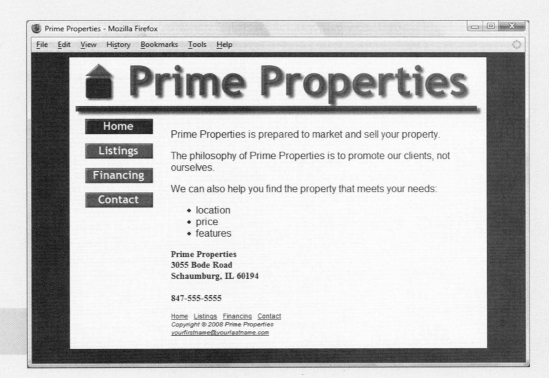

See the center color insert

2. **Configure the CSS.** Open prime.css in Notepad. Edit the style rules as follows:
   - Configure the page background color. Modify the style rules for the body selector. Set the `background-color` property to #003366. Set the text color to #ffffcc.
   - Create a new `wrapper` id to contain the page content. Configure the area with a width of 680 pixels and centered (`margin:0 auto`). Set the minimum width to 680 pixels, also. Configure the background (#ffffcc) and text (#003300) colors. Set the left padding to 10 pixels.

```
#wrapper { width: 680px;
           min-width: 680px;
           margin: 0 auto;
           background-color: #ffffcc;
           color: #003300;
           padding-left: 10px;
}
```

- Configure the left column area. Add a new style rule for the `leftcolumn` id to configure an area that floats to the left and is 150 pixels wide.

```
#leftcolumn { float: left;
              width: 150px;
}
```

- Configure the navigation area. Add a new style rule for the `mainnav` class to configure an area that is displayed as a block element with a 15 pixel right, bottom, and left margin.

```
.mainnav{ display: block;
          margin: 0 15px 15px 15px;
}
```

- Configure the right column area. Add a new style rule for the `rightcolumn` id to configure an area with a 150 pixel left margin and 20 pixels of right and bottom padding (`padding: 0 20px 20px 0`).

- Configure the images on the listings.html page to float to the left. Add a new float:left style rule to the property class.

Save the prime.css file.

3. **Modify the index.html File.** Add `<div>` elements and modify the code as indicated below.

- Configure the logo area. Remove the `<h1>` opening and closing tags surrounding the Prime Properties logo image. Code a `<div>` that surrounds the Prime Properties logo image element. Assign the `<div>` to the id `logo`.

- Configure the left column. The navigation image links are the only content in the left column. Assign the `<div>` that contains the image links to the `leftcolumn` id, `<div id="leftcolumn">`. Assign each anchor element in this area to the `mainnav` class (`class="mainnav"`).

- Configure the right column. This area contains the content (paragraphs, unordered list, and text navigation links) and the footer section. Code a `<div>` that surrounds this area. Assign the `<div>` to the `rightcolumn` id.

Save the index.html file. It should look similar to the Web page shown in Figure 6.31. Remember that validating your XHTML and CSS can help you find syntax errors. Test and correct this page before you continue.

4. **Modify the listings.html and financing.html Files.** Modify these Web page files in a similar manner as you did in Step 3. Configure the property images on the listings.html page—on the opening image tag for each property photo, remove the `align="left"` attribute and add `class="floatleft"`. Save and test your pages in a browser. As you test your pages, use the CSS and XHTML validators to help you find syntax errors.

5. **Bonus Style.** Figure 6.32 shows an alternate design for the financing.html page. Notice the image near the center of the content with the text "Mortgage FAQs." This was configured with CSS using an interesting technique. The XHTML is straightforward:

```
<h4 class="home">Mortgage FAQs</h4>.
```

Figure 6.32
New style rules for
the Mortgage FAQs
heading

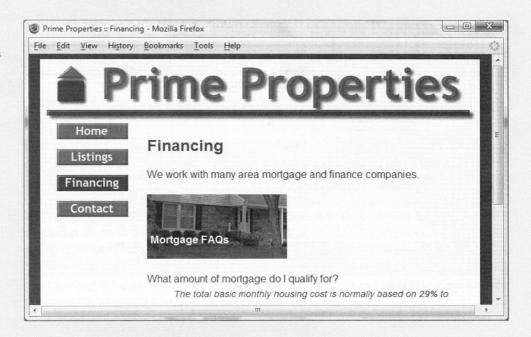

CSS creates the effect. Styles are declared for the home class with the following properties: a background image that does not repeat and is positioned very carefully, a width of 200 pixels, light text, and generous padding.

```
.home { background-image: url(schaumburg.jpg);
        background-position: -100px -260px;
        background-repeat: no-repeat;
        color: #ffffcc;
        padding: 60px 5px 20px 5px;
        width: 200px;
}
```

Notice that the background-position property is used with carefully chosen values. As indicated in Table 6.1, the background-position property can use two numeric pixel values—horizontal and vertical. The *negative number*s cause the background image to shift 100 pixels to the left and 260 pixels down from the top. The effect is somewhat abstract and ends up displaying just part of the image. In this case, it is a part of a house to tie in with the home financing theme. Padding is set quite high to allow room for the image to display around the text. The text color is light in order to contrast well with the image.

Save the prime.css file. Modify the financing.html page as indicated above—add class="home" to the <h4> element. Save the financing.html file. Test your pages in a browser. Your financing.html page should look similar to the one shown in Figure 6.32. The other pages should display as they did at the end of Step 4.

In this case study you changed the page layout of the Prime Properties Web site pages. Notice that with just a few changes in the CSS and XHTML code, you configured a two-column page layout.

Web Project

See Chapter 5 for an introduction to the Web Project case. As you completed the Chapter 5 Web Project Case Study activities you completed a Web Project Topic Approval, Web Project Site Map, and Web Project Page Layout Design. In this case study you will use your design documents as a guide as you develop the pages for your Web Project using CSS (external style sheet) for both formatting and page layout.

Hands-On Practice Case

1. Create a folder called project. All your project files and graphics will be organized in this folder and subfolders as needed.

2. Refer to your Site Map to view the pages that you need to create. Jot down a list of the file names. Add these to the Site Map.

3. Refer to the Page Layout Design. Make a list of the common fonts and colors used on the pages. These may become the CSS you configure for the body element. Note where typical elements used for organization (such as headings, lists, paragraphs, and so on) may be used. You may want to configure CSS for these elements. Identify various page areas such as logo, navigation, footer, and so on—and list any special configurations needed for these areas. These will be configured as classes in your CSS. Create an external style sheet, called project.css, which contains these configurations.

4. Using your design documents as a guide, code a representative page for your site. Use CSS to format text, color, and layout. Be sure to apply classes and ids where appropriate. Associate the Web page to the external style sheet.

   Save and test the page. Modify both the Web page and the project.css file as needed. Test and modify until you have achieved the look you want.

5. Using the completed page as a template wherever possible, code the rest of the pages on your site. Test and modify them as needed.

6. Experiment with modifying the project.css file. Change the page background color, the font family, and so on. Test your pages in a browser. Notice how a change in a single file can affect multiple files when external style sheets are used.

More on Links, Lists, and Layout

Chapter Objectives In this chapter, you will learn how to ...

- Code relative hyperlinks to Web pages in folders within a Web site
- Configure a hyperlink to a named anchor internal to a Web page
- Add interactivity to Web pages with CSS pseudo-classes

- Configure a navigation layout list with CSS
- Configure three-column page layouts using CSS
- Configure CSS for both screen and print display
- Utilize the "cascade" in CSS

Now that you've had some experience coding XHTML and CSS, you're ready to explore a variety of techniques in this chapter including XHTML relative hyperlinks and internal hyperlinks, CSS pseudo-classes, navigation list layout, three-column page layout, styling for print, and an overview of the "cascade" in CSS.

7.1 Another Look at XHTML Hyperlinks

Hyperlinks make the Web a "web" of interconnected information. In this section you'll revisit the topic of hyperlinks and explore coding relative links, using the target attribute to open Web pages in a new browser window, and coding hyperlinks that are internal to a Web page.

More on Relative Linking

As indicated earlier in Chapter 2, a relative link is used to link to Web pages within your site. You've been coding relative links to display Web pages within the same folder. There are times when you need to link to files in other folders on your Web site. Let's consider the example of a Web site for a dog groomer that highlights services and products. The Web developer for this site created separate folders called services and products in order to organize the site. See the folder and file listing shown in Figure 7.1.

Figure 7.1
The dog groomer site contains the images, products, and services folders

groomer
index.html
contact.html

    images

    products
    collars.html
    shampoo.html

    services
    bathing.html
    daycare.html

Relative Link Examples

- To review, when linking to a file in the same folder or directory, the value of the href is the name of the file. For example, to link to the contact.html page from the home page (index.html), code the anchor element as follows:

  ```
  <a href="contact.html">Contact</a>
  ```

- When linking to a folder located within the current directory, use both the folder name and the file name in the relative link. For example, to link to the collars.html page in the products folder from the home page (index.html), code the anchor element as follows:

  ```
  <a href="products/collars.html">Collars</a>
  ```

- In Figure 7.1 the collars.html page is located in a subfolder of the groomer folder. The home page for the site, index.html is located in the groomer folder. When linking to a file that is up one directory level from the current page use "../" notation. To link to the home page for the site from the collars.html page, code the anchor element as follows:

  ```
  <a href="../index.html">Home</a>
  ```

- When linking to a file that is in a folder on the same level as the current folder, the `href` value will use the `"../"` notation to indicate moving up one level and then down to the chosen folder. For example, to link to the bathing.html page in the services folder from the collars.html page in the products folder, code the anchor element as follows:

```
<a href="../services/bathing.html">Dog Bathing</a>
```

Don't worry if the use of `"../"` notation and linking to files in different folders seems new and different. In most of the exercises in this book you will code either absolute links to other Web sites or relative links to files in the same folder.

Opening a Link in a New Browser Window

The **`target` attribute** can be used on the anchor to open a link in a new browser window. For example,

```
<a href="http://yahoo.com" target="_blank">Yahoo!</a>
```

will open Yahoo!'s home page in a new window. Why not create a test page and try it? The `target` attribute with the value `"_blank"` configures the Web page to open in a new browser window.

By now you should be comfortable with hyperlinks. You may have noticed that these links display the top of the Web page. Sometimes it is helpful to link to an exact position on a Web page instead of to the top of the page. Internal links are used for this function.

Internal Links

Internal links are sometimes called bookmarks, **named anchors**, or named fragments. They can be very useful when you need to provide the capability to link to a specific portion of a Web page. Lists of frequently asked questions (FAQs) often use this technique.

When using internal links remember that there are two components:

1. The anchor tag that identifies a bookmark or **named fragment** of a Web page. This requires two attributes: the `id` attribute (supported by modern browsers) and the `name` attribute (used for compatibility with old browsers such as Netscape 4).
2. The anchor tag that links to the bookmark or named fragment of a Web page. This uses the `href` attribute.

To see how these two components are used, consider that Web pages sometimes have links to the top of a page (see Figure 7.2). This is accomplished in two steps as follows:

1. **Establish Target.** Type an anchor element that configures the `id` and `name` attributes on a blank line under the `<body>` tag. The value of the `id` and `name` attributes should describe the bookmark. It's a good idea to use lowercase letters and avoid punctuation, symbols, and spaces. The value given to the `id` attribute should be unique within the document. Place the following code near the top of a Web page document:

```
<a id="top" name="top"></a>
```

Figure 7.2
Notice how the anchor tags are used

```
<?xml version="1.0" encoding="UTF-8"?>
<!DOCTYPE html PUBLIC "-//W3C//DTD XHTML 1.0 Transitional//EN"
    "http://www.w3.org/          -transitional.dtd">
<html xmlns="http:/
<head>
<title>Favorite Site
</head>
<body bgcolor="#FFFF
<a id="top" name="top"></a><h1 align="center">Favorite Sites</h1>
<dl>
   <dt>Running</dt>
      <dd><a href="http://www.running.com">running.com</a></dd>
   <dt>Cooking</dt>
      <dd><a href="h         oking.com">cooking.com</a></dd>

   The page

   <dt>Internet
      <dd><a hre          ternet.com">internet.com</a></dd>
</dl>
<p><a href="#top">Back to Top</a></p>
</body>
</html>
```

This anchor tag creates the named fragment for the top of the page.

This anchor tag indicates the link to the top of the page.

2. **Reference Target.** At the point of the page where you want to place a link to the top, type another anchor element. Use the `href` attribute and place a # (sometimes called a hash mark) before the name of the bookmark. The XHTML for a hyperlink to the named anchor `"top"` is

```
<a href="#top">Top of Page</a>
```

The hash mark indicates that the browser should search for an anchor tag on the same page. If you forget to type the hash mark, the browser will not look on the same Web page; it will look for an external file. A bookmark or named anchor does not have to be at the top of a page; it can be just about anywhere.

If you are coding only for an XHTML-compliant browser such as Internet Explorer 5 (or later), Mozilla Firefox, or Netscape 6 (or later), you can use the `id` attribute with any container tag, such as a `<p>` or a `<h1>`, to create a named fragment or bookmark. The top of page example uses the anchor element to provide for backward compatibility with Netscape 4.

HANDS-ON PRACTICE 7.1

You will work with internal links in this Hands-On Practice. Locate the Chapter7/starter1.html file in the student files. Figure 7.3 shows a partial screenshot of this Web page.

Launch Notepad and open the starter1.html file. Save the file as favorites.html. Examine the source code and notice that the top portion of the page contains an unordered list with categories of interest (such as Hobbies, XHTML, CSS, and Professional Organizations) that correspond to the text displayed in the `<h2>` elements below. After each `<h2>` element is a definition list of topics and URLs related to that category. It might be helpful to Web page visitors if they can click a category item and

Figure 7.3
You will add internal links to this Web page

immediately jump to the page area that has information related to that item. This could be a useful application of internal links!

Modify the page as follows:

1. Code a named anchor for each `<h2>` element in the definition list. For example:

   `<h2><a id="hobbies" name="hobbies"></a>Hobbies</h2>`

2. Add hyperlinks to the items in the unordered list so that each entry will link to its corresponding `<h2>`.

3. Add a named fragment near the top of the page.

4. Near the bottom of the favorites.html page add a link to the top of the page.

Save the file and test it. Compare your work with the sample found in the student files (Chapter7/favorites.html).

There may be times when you need to link to a named fragment on another Web page. To accomplish this, place the internal link after the file name in the anchor tag. So, to link to the "Professional Groups" (given that it is a named fragment called "groups") from any other page on the mywebsite Web, you could use the following XHTML:

`<a href="favorites.html#groups">Professional Organizations</a>`

FAQ

Why don't some of my internal links work?

A Web browser cannot display less than the height of the browser window. If there is not enough space left on the bottom of the page below the named reference, it cannot be displayed at the top of the page. Try adding some blank lines (use the `<br />` tag) to the lower portion of the Web page. Save your work and test your internal links again.

7.2 CSS Pseudo-Classes and Links

Have you ever visited a Web site and found that the text hyperlinks changed color when you moved the mouse pointer over them? Often, this is accomplished using a special technique in CSS called a pseudo-class. The four pseudo-classes that can be applied to the anchor tag are shown in Table 7.1. The **link pseudo-class** configures the appearance of the hyperlink before it is clicked. The **visited pseudo-class** configures the appearance

Table 7.1 Commonly used CSS pseudo-classes

Pseudo-class	When Applied
link	Default state for a link that has not been visited
visited	Default state for a visited link
hover	Triggered when the mouse moves over the link
active	Triggered when the link is actually clicked

of the hyperlink after it is clicked. The **hover pseudo-class** configures the hyperlink as the mouse is held or "hovered" over it. The **active pseudo-class** configures the appearance of the hyperlink while it is being clicked. Notice the order in which the pseudo-classes are listed in Table 7.1. Anchor element pseudo-classes must be coded in this order (although it's okay to omit one or more of those listed). If you code the pseudo-classes in a different order, the styles will not be reliably applied. Some students find the order easier to remember if they think of the mnemonic device "**lovehate**" – **l**ink, **v**isited, **h**over, **a**ctive.

The syntax of pseudo-classes uses a colon (:) to apply the **pseudo-class** to the anchor tag. The following code sample will configure text hyperlinks to be red initially. The sample also uses the hover pseudo-class, a:hover, to configure the links to change their appearance when the visitor places the mouse pointer over them so that the underline disappears and the color changes.

```
<style type="text/css">
a:link {   color: #ff0000;
}
a:hover {   text-decoration: none;
        color: #000066;
}
</style>
```

Figure 7.4 shows part of a Web page that uses this technique. Note the position of the mouse pointer over the Print this Page link—the link color has changed and has no underline.

While some Web design experts, such as Jakob Nielsen, recommend that Web developers not change the default look of text links, this technique is often used. Most modern browsers (since Internet Explorer 4+ and Netscape 6+) support CSS pseudo-classes. Netscape 4.x does not support the hover pseudo-class, but the technique degrades gracefully and the hyperlink is still usable.

Figure 7.4
Using the hover
pseudo-class

Text links are underlined by default.

The "hover" pseudo-class is triggered
by the mouse. The browser no longer
displays the underline below the link.

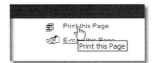

The tooltip was configured by using
a title attribute on the anchor tag.

HANDS-ON PRACTICE 7.2

You will use pseudo-classes to create interactive hyperlinks in this Hands-On Practice as
you create a series of pages that contain hyperlinks styled in different ways.

Part 1

The first page contains text links that you will configure to use CSS pseudo-classes. A
sample is shown in Figure 7.5. When the mouse hovers over a link, it will change color
and the underline will disappear. You will code embedded CSS to configure the link,
visited, and hover pseudo-classes for the anchor selector.

Figure 7.5
The hyperlink's
underline disappears
when the mouse
hovers

Launch Notepad and type the following XHTML:

```
<?xml version="1.0" encoding="UTF-8"?>
<!DOCTYPE html PUBLIC "-//W3C//DTD XHTML 1.0 Transitional//EN"
   "http://www.w3.org/TR/xhtml1/DTD/xhtml1-transitional.dtd">
<html xmlns="http://www.w3.org/1999/xhtml">
<head>
<title>CSS Pseudo-class Example 1</title>
<style type="text/css">
body {   margin: 0 auto;
         width: 400px;
         text-align: center;
}
```

```
a:link {    background-color: #ffffff;
            color: #ff0000;
}
a:visited {  background-color: #ffffff;
              color: #00ff00;
}
a:hover {  background-color: #ffffff;
           color: #000066;
           text-decoration: none;
}
</style>
</head>
<body>
<div align="center">
  <h2>Navigation Links</h2>
  <p><a href="http://yahoo.com">Yahoo!</a>
  <a href="http://google.com">Google</a></p>
</div>
</body>
</html>
```

Save your file as link1.html. Test your page in a browser and compare it with Figure 7.5. The student files contain a sample solution at Chapter7/link1.html. The browser applies the CSS pseudo-class rules to every link on the page. In this example, the CSS was coded using embedded styles, but an external style sheet also could have been used.

Part 2

Now you will create a page that uses CSS and pseudo-classes to configure navigation links that look like buttons. These can be used in place of image links to save on the bandwidth used by graphics. See the sample in Figure 7.6. When the mouse hovers over a navigation button, the text color and border change.

Figure 7.6
The hyperlink's appearance changes when the mouse hovers

You will use the following CSS properties to configure the buttons: width, border, and padding. Let's review these properties. The width property configures the amount of horizontal space used by the element in the browser window. The border property configures the width (border-width), style (border-style), and color (border-color) of the border around an element. The padding property configures the amount of padding—the blank space between the element and its border.

Launch Notepad and type the following XHTML:

```
<?xml version="1.0" encoding="UTF-8"?>
<!DOCTYPE html PUBLIC "-//W3C//DTD XHTML 1.0 Transitional//EN"
  "http://www.w3.org/TR/xhtml1/DTD/xhtml1-transitional.dtd">
<html xmlns="http://www.w3.org/1999/xhtml">
<head>
<title>CSS Pseudo-class Example 2</title>
<style type="text/css">
body {   margin: 0 auto;
         width: 550px;
         text-align: center;
}
.button {  border: 2px inset #CCCCCC;
           width: 100px;
           padding: 3px 15px;
           color: #FFFFFF;
           background-color: #006600;
           font-family: Arial,Helvetica,sans-serif;
           font-size: 16px;
           font-weight: bold;
           text-align: center;
           text-decoration: none;
}
a.button: link { color : #FFFFFF; }
a.button: visited { color : #CCCCCC; }
a.button: hover { color : #66CC33;
                  border: 2px outset #CCCCCC;
}
</style>
</head>
<body>
<div align="center">
  <h2>CSS Buttons!</h2>
  <a href="index.htm" class="button">Home</a>
  <a href="products.htm" class="button">Products</a>
  <a href="services.htm" class="button">Services</a>
  <a href="contact.htm" class="button">Contact</a>
  <a href="about.htm" class="button">About</a>
</div>
</body>
</html>
```

Save your file as link2.html. Test your page in a browser and compare it with Figure 7.6. The student files contain a sample solution at Chapter7/link2.html. The new technique here is to configure a class called `button`, which has all the initial properties of the navigation link. Because this example produced a button look, the `width`, `border`, and `padding` attributes were used. Then, CSS rules using an `anchor` selector with the `button` class and `link`, `visited`, and `hover` pseudo-classes were configured. The W3C prefers that the normal class names precede pseudo-classes in the selector. That is why the selector for the pseudo-classes use the `a.button:hover` notation. Finally, the `class` attribute in the XHTML anchor tags connects the link on the page with the CSS style rules in the header.

Part 3

It is often the case that the design of the Web page requires the main navigation links to look different from the links within the content of the pages. You have already created a page, link2.html, with specially configured navigation links. You used the class called `button` to configure these links. In this part of the Hands-On Practice, you will add a line of text containing a hyperlink to the page to verify that the hyperlink retains the default browser appearance and behavior. Figure 7.7 shows a sample page.

Figure 7.7
The link to Yahoo! retains the default hyperlink properties

Launch Notepad and open your link2.html file. Save the file as link3.html. Modify the title to be "CSS Pseudo-class Example 3" and add the following paragraph under the navigation links:

```
<p>Visit <a href="http://yahoo.com">Yahoo!</a>.</p>
```

Save your file, test your page in a browser, and compare it with the one shown in Figure 7.7. The student files contain a sample solution at Chapter7/link3.html. Because the new link is not part of the defined class `button`, it retains the default hyperlink characteristics. If you needed yet another set of characteristics for links in another section of the page such as the footer, you could define a new class with a unique name and configure pseudo-classes, as was done in Part 2 of this Hands-On Practice.

As you can see, pseudo-classes—along with careful configuration of classes, can be a powerful tool for a Web developer.

7.3 CSS Navigation Layout Using Lists

One of the advantages of using CSS for page layout involves the use of semantically correct code. Writing semantically correct code means using the markup tag that most accurately reflects the purpose of the content. Using the various levels of heading tags for content headings and subheadings, or placing paragraphs of text within paragraph tags (rather than using line breaks) are examples of writing semantically correct code. This type of coding is a step in the direction to support the Semantic Web. Leading Web developers such as Eric Meyer, Mark Newhouse, Jeffrey Zeldman, and others have promoted the idea of using unordered lists to configure navigation menus. After all—a navigation menu is a list of links—semantically speaking it's a much better fit than coding links in separate paragraphs or using the `display:block` property on anchor tags.

Figure 7.8 shows the top portion of a revised twocolumn.html (the page you created in Hands-On Practice 6.6). In this version the CSS declaration for the `navBar` class was changed (`display:block` and `margin:15px` were removed), the left column was widened a bit, and the navigation links were coded in an unordered list. An XHTML code snippet follows:

```
<ul class="navBar">
  <li><a class="navBar" href="home.html">Home</a></li>
  <li><a class="navBar" href="spring.html">Spring</a></li>
  <li><a class="navBar" href="summer.html">Summer</a></li>
  <li><a class="navBar" href="fall.html">Fall</a></li>
  <li><a class="navBar" href="winter.html">Winter</a></li>
</ul>
```

Figure 7.8
An unordered list to configure the navigation menu

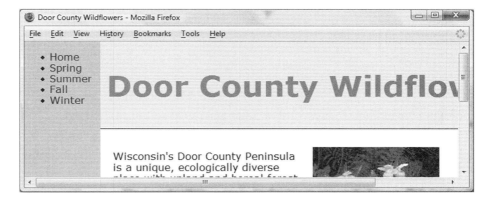

Perhaps you would prefer that the bullets in the unordered list were not displayed. Use the **list-style-type** property to configure the list-item markers (bullets). The property `list-style-type:none` prevents the browser from displaying the bullets.

Figure 7.9 shows the effect of adding `list-style-type:none` to the `navBar` class.

If you would like a custom image to replace the bullet, use the **list-style-image** property. In Figure 7.10 an image named arrow.gif was configured to replace the bullets using: `list-style-image:url(arrow.gif)`. View the twocolumn1.html file in the Chapter7 folder in the student files to examine the code.

Figure 7.9
An unordered list with `list-style-type:none`

Figure 7.10
An unordered list with an image replacing the bullet

You may be wondering how to apply this technique to a horizontal navigation menu such as the one coded on the page1.html page used in Hands-On Practice 6.5. The answer is CSS! List items are block elements. They need to be configured as inline elements to display in a single line. The `display:inline` property is used to accomplish this. Figure 7.11 displays a new version of the page using this technique. The page looks about the same as the original (Figure 6.16) when displayed in a browser even though the XHTML and CSS are configured to use a list.

Figure 7.11

Horizontal navigation using an unordered list configured with CSS

The XHTML code snippet is the same as the one used for the vertical navigation menus shown at the beginning of this section. For the horizontal list to display properly, you must add a CSS configuration for the `<li>` element within the nav class as follows:

```
.nav li {  display: inline;
        list-style-type: none;
}
```

Focus on Accessibility

View the home0.html and wildflower0.css files in the Chapter7 folder in the student files to experiment with this technique. See Chapter7/skipnav.html for a version of this page that includes a transparent image configured as an internal link to the named fragment maincontent. This "skip navigation" method allows visitors using screen readers to easily skip repetitive navigation links.

7.4 Three-Column CSS Page Layout

Often a Web page layout will consist of a header across the top of the page with three columns below: navigation, content, and sidebar. If you are thinking about this layout as a series of boxes—you're thinking correctly for configuring pages using CSS! Figure 7.12 shows a wireframe sketch of this page layout design. Figure 7.13 (shown also in the color insert section) shows a Web page configured using this design. You will create this page in the next Hands-On Practice.

Figure 7.12
Sketch of three-column page layout

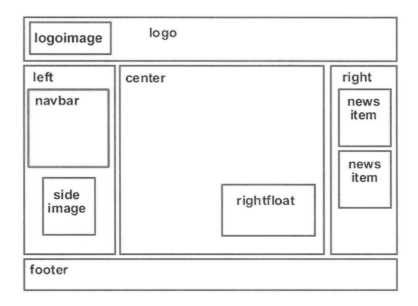

Figure 7.13
This three-column page layout is designed using CSS and no tables

See the center color insert

HANDS-ON PRACTICE 7.3

In this Hands-On Practice you will develop your first three-column Web page using CSS. The same techniques that you used to configure the two-column page will apply here—think of the page as a series of elements or boxes. Assign ids or classes to the elements as you code the XHTML. Configure the CSS to correspond to the ids and classes. Recall that a key technique in creating a two-column page with left column navigation was to design the left column to float to the left. A key technique in our three-column page is to code the left column with `float:left` and the right column with `float:right`. The center column occupies the middle of the browser window. Refer to Figures 7.12 and 7.13 as you complete this Hands-On Practice.

Getting Started

Locate the showybg.jpg, plsthumb.jpg, and trillium.jpg files in the Chapter 7 folder in the student files. Create a new folder called wildflowers3. Copy the files to the folder.

Part 1—Code the XHTML

Review Figures 7.12 and 7.13. Notice the page elements: a logo area with both a logo and a background image that repeats; a left column with a navigation area and an image; a center column with paragraphs of text, a heading, and an image that floats to the right; a right column with two news items; and a footer. These will all be coded to use ids and classes corresponding to CSS, which configures a number of properties including the `float`, `margin`, `border`, `font-family`, and so on. The navigation menu links will be configured using an unordered list. As you code the XHTML document, you will place the elements on the page and assign `id` and `class` values that correspond to the areas in the sketch in Figure 7.12. Launch Notepad and type in the following XHTML:

```
<<?xml version="1.0" encoding="utf-8"?>
<!DOCTYPE html PUBLIC "-//W3C//DTD XHTML 1.0 Transitional//EN"
  "http://www.w3.org/TR/xhtml1/DTD/xhtml1-transitional.dtd">
<html xmlns="http://www.w3.org/1999/xhtml">
<head>
<title>Door County Wildflowers</title>
</head>
<body>
<div id="container">
  <div id="logo">
    Door County Wildflowers
  </div>
  <div id="left">
    <ul class="navBar">
      <li><a class="nav" href="home.html">Home</a></li>
      <li><a class="nav" href="spring.html">Spring</a></li>
      <li><a class="nav" href="summer.html">Summer</a></li>
      <li><a class="nav" href="fall.html">Fall</a></li>
      <li><a class="nav" href="winter.html">Winter</a></li>
    </ul>
```

```
      <img class="sideimages" src="plsthumb.jpg" width="100"
      height="100" alt="Showy Pink Lady Slipper" />
   </div>
   <div id="right">
      <h4>The Ridges</h4>
      <p class="newsitem">The Ridges Nature Sanctuary offers wild
      orchid hikes during the summer months. For more info, visit
      <a href="http://www.ridgesanctuary.org">The Ridges</a>.</p>
      <h4>Newport State Park</h4>
      <p class="newsitem">The Newport Wilderness Society sponsors
      free meadow hikes at 9am every Saturday. Stop by the park
      office to register.</p>
   </div>
   <div id="center">
      <p>Wisconsin's Door County Peninsula is a unique,
      ecologically diverse place with upland and boreal forest,
      bogs, swamps, sand and rock beaches, limestone escarpments, and
      farmlands.</p>
      <p>A wide array of wildflowers grow in the county because
      of this variety of ecosystems.</p>
      <img src="trillium.jpg" width="200" height="150" alt="Trillium"
      id="floatright" />
      <h3>Explore the beauty <br />of Door County Wildflowers....</h3>
      <p>With five state parks, tons of county parks, and private
      nature sanctuaries, Door County is teeming with natural areas
      for you to stalk your favorite wildflowers.</p>
   </div>
   <div class="footer">
      Copyright &copy; 2007 Door County Wild Flowers<br />
      Last Updated on 07/07/07
   </div>
</div>
</body>
</html>
```

Save your page as threecolumn.html in your wildflowers3 folder. Test the page in a browser. Your display will not look like Figure 7.13 since you have not yet configured the CSS. The top of your page should look similar to the page shown in Figure 7.14.

Part 2—Code the Basic CSS

For ease of editing, in this Hands-On Practice you will code the CSS as embedded styles in the header section of the Web page. However, if you were creating an entire Web site you would most likely use an external style sheet as you did in Hands-On Practice 6.5.

Launch Notepad and open threecolumn.html. Let's take a moment to consider the main elements used on the page shown in Figure 7.13: logo, left column, right column, center column, and footer. The left column will contain a navigation area and a small image. The center column will contain paragraphs, a heading, and a right-floating image. The right column will contain a series of headings and news items. Locate these areas on the sketch in Figure 7.12. Notice also that the same font is used throughout

Figure 7.14
The three-column page before CSS is applied

the page and the page begins right at the browser margin. Launch Notepad and open your threecolumn.html file. In the header section of your Web page document, add a tag to begin the embedded styles:

```
<style type="text/css">
```

Now let's consider the CSS configuration. Type the CSS in your document as it is discussed as follows:

1. **Body Selector.** Set the margin to 0 pixels. Configure the background color to #ffffff.

   ```
   body {   margin:0;
            background-color: #ffffff;
   }
   ```

2. **Container.** Configure this area with background (#eeeeee) and text (#006600) colors, a minimum width of 700 pixels, and with font family of Verdana, Arial or sans-serif.

   ```
   #container {   background-color: #eeeeee;
                  color: #006600;
                  min-width: 700px;
                  font-family: Verdana, Arial, sans-serif;
   }
   ```

3. **Logo.** Code this area so that the image showybg.jpg will repeat using background-image:url(showybg.jpg). The text should be set to 2.5em font size and bold. The height of the logo area is 100 pixels—this corresponds to the height of the background image. Although it will most likely never display, configure the background color to #eeeeee. The text color should be #cc66cc. Set the left padding to 20 pixels. Configure a 2 pixel solid black border across the bottom of this area as follows:

   ```
   #logo {   color: #cc66cc;
             background-color: #eeeeee;
             font-size: 2.5em;
   ```

```
        font-weight: bold;
        border-bottom: 2px solid #000000;
        height: 100px;
        background-image: url(showybg.jpg);
        padding-left: 20px;
}
```

4. **Left Column.** One of the keys to this three-column page layout is that the left column is designed to float to the left of the browser window. Configure a width of 150.

```
#left { float: left;
        width: 150px;
}
```

5. **Right Column.** One of the keys to this three-column page layout is that the right column is designed to float to the right of the browser window. Configure a width of 200 pixels.

```
#right { float: right;
         width: 200px;
}
```

6. **Center.** The center column will take up all the room that is available after the left and right columns float. The content area has a special need for margins since the left and right columns are floating on either side. Set the left margin to 150 pixels, the right margin to 200 pixels, and the remaining side margins to 0. Configure padding for this area, also. Set the background (#ffffff) and text (#006600) colors for this area.

```
#center { margin: 0 200px 0 150px;
          padding: 1px 10px 20px 10px;
          background-color: #ffffff;
          color: #006600;
}
```

7. **Footer.** Configure the page footer with very small text that is centered. Configure the background (#ffffff) and text (#006600) colors for this area. Set the top padding to 10 pixels. A clear:both is needed to clear the float of the right and left columns as follows:

```
.footer { font-size: .70em
          text-align: center;
          color: #006600;
          background-color: #ffffff;
          padding-top: 10px;
          clear:both;
}
```

At this point you have configured the main elements of the three-column page layout. It's a good idea to save and do a quick test to make sure you are on the right track. Code the closing XHTML style tag: </style>.

Save the threecolumn.html file in the wildflowers3 folder. Test your page in a browser. It should look similar to the one shown in Figure 7.15. Note that there is still some detail work to do but you are well on your way!

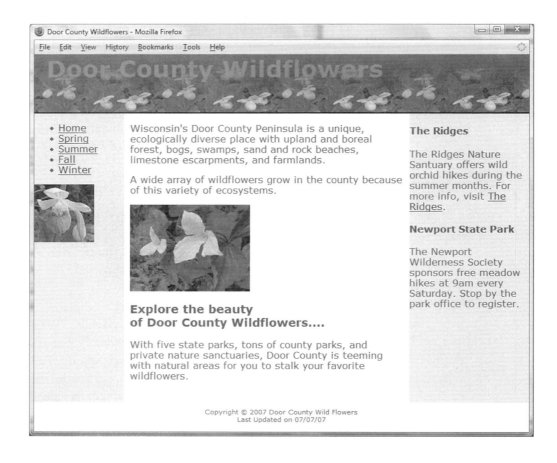

Part 3—Continue Coding CSS

Now you are ready to continue with your styles. Open the threecolumn.html page in Notepad and position your cursor on a blank line above the closing style tag. First we will configure the components in the left column as follows:

1. **Navigation Menu.** Configure the unordered list to provide for a 20 pixel top margin and not to display any bullets.

```
.navBar { margin-top: 20px;
        list-display-type: none;
}
```

Configure the navigation links to have no underline (`text-decoration:none`). Configure the font size to 1.2em. Pseudo-classes should be configured for link, visited, and hover with different text colors as follows:

```
.nav {  text-decoration: none;
        font-size: 1.2em;
}
a.nav:link {  color:#006600;}
            background-color: #eeeeee; }
a.nav:visited {  color: #003300;}
              background-color: #eeeeee; }
a.nav:hover {  color: #cc66cc;}
            background-color: #eeeeee; }
```

2. **Left Column Image (`sideimages`).** Configure this class with a margin of 30 pixels as follows:

```
.sideimages { margin: 30px;}
```

Next, we'll configure the contents of the center column. Styles for paragraphs, `heading elements`, and an image that floats to the right need to be constructed.

3. **`p`:** Configure the paragraph selector to use a margin of 20 pixels as follows:

```
p { margin: 20px; }
```

4. **`h3`:** Configure the `h3` selector with the same text color as the logo and the same background color as the main body of the page as follows:

```
h3 {   color: #cc66cc;
       background-color: #FFFFFF;
}
```

5. **Image Floating at the Right.** Set the `floatright` id to use a 10 pixel margin and `float:right` as follows:

```
#floatright {   margin: 10px;
                float: right;
}
```

Now, we'll configure the styles for the contents of the right column. The announcements consist of a heading (contained within <h4> tags) and a paragraph (assigned to a class called `newsitem`).

6. **`h4`:** Configure the heading to have a 1 pixel black solid bottom border, 2 pixels of padding at the bottom, a 10 pixel margin, the same text color as the logo, and the same background color as the right column:

```
h4 {   padding-bottom: 2px;
       border-bottom: 1px solid #000000;
       margin: 10px;
       color: #cc66cc;
       background-color: #eeeeee;
}
```

7. **News Items.** Configure a class called `newsitem` that uses a small font and has a 10 pixel margin as follows:

```
.newsitem {   font-size:.9em;
              margin: 10px;
}
```

Save the threecolumn.html file in the wildflowers3 folder.

Part 4—Test the Page

Now that your styles are coded, test the threecolumn.html page again. Your page should look similar to the screenshot shown in Figure 7.13. If there are differences, verify the `id` and `class` values in your XHTML. Also check the syntax of your CSS. You may find the W3C CSS validator at http://jigsaw.w3.org/css-validator helpful when verifying CSS syntax. The student files contain a copy of threecolumn.html in the Chapter7 folder.

How do I create a custom-color scroll bar?

It can be fun to color-coordinate the scroll bar with your Web site! Keep in mind that not all your Web visitors will see your handiwork. While this effect is supported by Internet Explorer, it is not supported by all browsers. To configure a scroll bar with colors that you choose, add the following styles to the body tag: `scrollbar-face-color`, `scrollbar-arrow-color`, and `scrollbar-track-color`. For example:

```
body {  scrollbar-face-color:#cc66cc;
        scrollbar-arrow-color:#006600;
        scrollbar-track-color:#cccccc;
}
```

Note: Your CSS will not pass W3C validation tests if you use these Internet Explorer only properties.

CHECKPOINT 7.1

1. Describe a reason to organize the files in a Web site using folders and subfolders.

2. State a reason to use an unordered list to configure navigation links.

3. You are using CSS pseudo-classes on a Web page to configure the navigation links to look like buttons. You want the "regular" links in the Web page content to be configured as they normally would (not look like a button). Describe how you could configure the styles and XHTML to accomplish this.

7.5 CSS Styling for Print

Even though the advent of the "paperless society" has been talked about for decades, the fact is that many people still love paper and you can expect your Web pages to be printed. CSS offers you some control over what gets printed and how the printouts are configured.

This is easy to do using external style sheets. Create one external style sheet with the configurations for browser display and a second external style sheet with the special printing configurations. Associate both of the external style sheets to the Web page using two `<link>` elements. The `<link>` elements will utilize a new attribute, called `media`. Configure the link element for your browser display with `media="screen"`. Configure the link element for your printout with `media="print"`. Modern browsers will use the correct style sheet depending on whether they are rendering a screen display or preparing to print a document. An example of the XHTML follows:

```
<link rel="stylesheet" href="wildflower.css" type="text/css"
  media="screen" />
<link rel="stylesheet" href="wildflowerprint.css" type="text/css"
  media="print" />
```

Often `display:none` is used in the print style sheet to prevent banner ads, navigation, or other extraneous areas from appearing on the printout. Another common practice is to configure the font sizes on the print style sheet to use `pt` sizes—this will better control the text on the printout. You can also use styles to configure areas in the document, such as detailed contact info, that are only printed out and do not appear in the browser window. Figure 7.16 shows the print preview of the content page you created in Hands-On Practice 6.5 (see Figure 6.16). Notice that the print preview includes the navigation area. Figure 7.17 displays an alternate version of the page that uses CSS to prevent the navigation area from printing. You will explore this technique in the next Hands-On Practice.

Figure 7.16
Print preview of the page displayed in Figure 6.16

Figure 7.17
Print preview using CSS to remove the navigation from the printout

HANDS-ON PRACTICE 7.4

In this Hands-On Practice you will code special styles to use when printing a Web page. We will use the page1.html and wildflower.css files that you created in Hands-On Practice 6.5 as a starting point. Figure 6.16 shows the browser display of the page1.html file. You will create a new version of the page1.html file and a new style sheet configured for printing. When printed, the logo will be configured using a 24 pt size and the navigation will not display.

Getting Started

Locate the pls.jpg, wildflower.css, and page1.html files in the student files, Chapter7 folder. Create a new folder called wildflowersPrint. Copy the files to the folder.

Part 1—Code the XHTML

Launch Notepad and open page1.html. This page is associated with an external style sheet called wildflower.css. The styles in wildflower.css should be used when the Web page is displayed on the screen. Add the **media attribute** with the value of screen to the link element for wildflower.css. Code a new link element to invoke an external style sheet called wildflowerprint.css for printing (media="print"). The XHTML follows:

```
<link rel="stylesheet" href="wildflower.css" type="text/css"
    media="screen" />
<link rel="stylesheet" href="wildflowerprint.css" type="text/css"
    media="print" />
```

Save the page1.html file in the wildflowersPrint folder.

Part 2—Code the New CSS

Launch Notepad and open wildflower.css. Since you want to keep most of the styles for printing, you will start by creating a new version of the external style sheet. Save wildflower.css with the name of wildflowerprint.css in the wildflowersPrint folder. You will modify three areas on this style sheet: the contentlogo id, the content id, and the nav class configuration.

1. Modify the contentlogo id so that the printer will use 24 point font size. The CSS follows:

```
#contentlogo { color: #000000;
               font-size: 24pt;
               padding: 10px;
}
```

2. Modify the content id so that the printer will use 12 point font size. The CSS follows:

```
.content { font-family: Verdana,Arial,sans-serif;
           font-size: 12pt;
           margin: 10px;
}
```

3. Configure the nav class to not be printed with the page. Delete all styles associated with the nav class and replace them with the following CSS:

```
.nav { display: none;
}
```

Save your file in the wildflowersPrint folder.

Part 3—Test Your Work

Test your page1.html file in a browser. Select Print, Preview. Your display should look similar to the page shown in Figure 7.17. The logo and content font sizes have been configured. The navigation does not display. The student files contain a copy of page1.html and wildflowerprint.css in the Chapter7/wildflowersPrint folder.

7.6 The "Cascade"

Figure 7.18 shows the "cascade" (**rules of precedence**) that applies the styles in order from outermost (external styles) to innermost (actual XHTML coded on the page). This way site-wide styles can be configured but overridden when needed by more granular (or page-specific) styles.

Figure 7.18
The "cascade" of Cascading Style Sheets

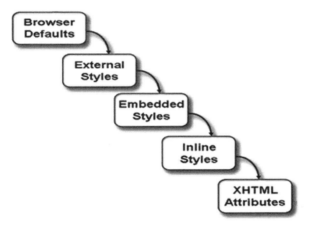

External styles can apply to multiple pages. If a Web page contains both a link to an external style sheet and embedded styles, the external styles will be applied first, and then the embedded styles will be applied. This allows a Web developer to override global external styles on selected pages.

If a Web page contains both embedded styles and inline styles, the embedded styles are applied first, and then the inline styles are applied. This allows a Web developer to override page-wide styles for particular XHTML tags or classes.

Any XHTML tag or attribute will override styles. For example, a `<strong>` tag will override corresponding font-related styles configured for the page. If no attribute or style is applied to an element, the browser default is applied. The appearance of the browser default may vary by browser and you might be disappointed with the result. Specify the properties of your text and Web page elements using CSS. Avoid depending on the browser default.

The overall CSS cascade was described above. In addition to this general cascade of CSS types, the style rules themselves follow rules of precedence. Style rules applied to more local elements (such as a paragraph) take precedence over those applied to more global elements (such as a `<div>` which contains the paragraph).

Let's look at an example of the cascade. The CSS and XHTML code is shown below. The CSS has two style rules: a rule creating a class named `content` which configures text using the Arial (or generic sans-serif) font family, and a rule configuring all paragraphs to use the Times New Roman (or generic serif) font family. The CSS follows:

```
.content { font-family:Arial, sans-serif; }
p { font-family: "Times New Roman", serif;}
```

The XHTML on the page contains a `<div>` with multiple elements, such as headings and paragraphs. Partial code follows:

```
<div class="content">
  <h1>Main Heading</h1>
  <p>This is a paragraph. Notice how the paragraph is contained in
  the div.</p>
</div>
```

Here's how the browser would render the code:

1. The text contained in the heading is displayed with Arial font because it is part of the `<div>` assigned to the `content` class. It inherits the properties from its parent (`<div>`) class.

2. The text contained in the paragraph is displayed with Times New Roman font because the browser applied the styles associated with the most local element (the paragraph). Even though the paragraph was contained in (and is considered a child of) the `content` class, the local paragraph style rules took precedence and were applied by the browser.

Don't worry if CSS and rules of precedence seem a bit overwhelming at this point. CSS definitely becomes easier with practice. You'll get a chance to practice with the "cascade" as you complete the next Hands-On Practice.

HANDS-ON PRACTICE 7.5

You will experiment with the "cascade" in this Hands-On Practice as you work with a Web page that uses external, embedded, and inline styles. Begin by creating an external style sheet called site.css that sets the `background-color` of the Web page to a shade of yellow (#FFFF66) and the `font-size` to 24px. The code follows:

```
body { background-color: #FFFF66;
       font-size: 24px;
}
```

Next, create a Web page called mypage1.html that is associated with the file site.css and has an embedded style that sets the text color to blue. The file mypage1.html will contain two paragraphs of text. The XHTML used to code the first paragraph will not use any styles. The XHTML used to code the second paragraph will use inline styles to set the text color to red and the `font-size` to 14px. The code for mypage1.html follows:

```
<?xml version="1.0" encoding="utf-8"?>
<!DOCTYPE html PUBLIC "-//W3C//DTD XHTML 1.0 Transitional//EN"
   "http://www.w3.org/TR/xhtml1/DTD/xhtml1-transitional.dtd">
<html xmlns="http://www.w3.org/1999/xhtml">
<head>
<title>External Styles</title>
   <link rel="stylesheet" href="site.css" type="text/css" />
   <style type="text/css">
   body { color: #0000FF;
   }
   </style>
</head>
<body>
<p>This paragraph does not contain inline styles.</p>
<p style="color:#FF0000;font-size:14px">This paragraph contains inline
styles and should be red with 14 px font</p>
</body>
</html>
```

Save both site.css and mypage1.html in the same folder. Display mypage1.html in a browser. Your page should look similar to the sample shown in Figure 7.19. The student files contain a sample solution at Chapter7/mypage1.html.

Figure 7.19
Mixing external, embedded, and inline styles

Take a moment to examine the mypage1.html Web page and compare it with its source code. The Web page picked up the yellow background and the 24px font size from the external style. The embedded style configured the text to be the color blue. The first paragraph in the Web page does not contain any inline styles, so it inherits the style rules in the external and embedded style sheets. The second paragraph contains an inline style of red text color and 14px font size—these settings override the corresponding external and embedded styles.

FAQ

Is there a quick way to apply the same styles to more than one XHTML tag or more than one class?

Yes, you can apply the same style rules to multiple selectors (such as XHTML elements, classes, or ids) by listing the selectors in front of the rule. The code sample below shows the `font-size` of `1em` being applied to both the paragraph and line item elements.

```
p, li { font-size: 1em; }
```

CHECKPOINT 7.2

1. State an advantage of using CSS to style for print.

2. Describe how to choose whether to configure an XHTML tag, create a class, or create an id when working with CSS.

3. List the following terms in the order that the properties and attributes are applied when using CSS.

    Inline styles
    External styles
    XHTML attributes
    Embedded styles

CHAPTER SUMMARY

This chapter explored a variety of Web development topics including XHTML relative hyperlinks and internal hyperlinks, CSS pseudo-classes, navigation list layout, three-column page layout, styling for print, and an overview of the "cascade" in Cascading Style Sheets.

Visit the textbook Web site at http://www.webdevfoundations.net for examples, the links listed in this chapter, and updated information.

Key Terms

active pseudo-class
the "cascade"
hover pseudo-class
internal links
link pseudo-class

`list-style-type` property
`list-style-image` property
media attribute
named anchor
named fragment

pseudo-class
rules of precedence
`target` attribute
visited pseudo-class

Review Questions

Multiple Choice

1. Which of the following anchor tag attributes define an internal bookmark or named reference in a page?
   a. `id` and `name`
   b. `name` and `bookmark`
   c. `internal` and `id`
   d. `id` and `bookmark`

2. How would you link to the bookmark `#jobs` on the page employ.html from the home page of the site?
   a. `<a href="employ.html#jobs">Employment Opportunities</a>`
   b. `<a name="employ.html#jobs">Employment Opportunities</a>`
   c. `<a link="employ.html#jobs">Employment Opportunities</a>`
   d. none of the above

3. Which of the following causes an object not to display either in the browser window or on a printed page?
   a. `display:block;`
   b. `display: 0px;`
   c. `display:none;`
   d. this cannot be done with CSS

4. Which property and value is used to configure an unordered list item so that the bullet does not display?
   a. `list-bullet:none;`
   b. `list-style-type:none;`
   c. `list-style-type:off;`
   d. `list-marker:none;`

5. How would you define an internal bookmark or named fragment at the top of a page, called "top"?
   a. `<a name="top" id="top"></a>`
   b. `<a bookmark="top"></a>`
   c. `<a name="#top" id="#top"></a>`
   d. `id` and `bookmark`

6. Which of the following is true if a Web page contains both a link to an external style sheet and embedded styles?
   a. embedded styles will be applied first, then the external styles will be applied
   b. the inline styles will be used
   c. external styles will be applied first, and then the embedded styles will be applied
   d. Web page will not display

7. Which of the following is the file extension for an external style sheet?

a. ess
b. css
c. html
d. no file extension is necessary

8. Which of the following elements is used to associate a Web page with an external style sheet?

a. `<target>`
b. `<a>`
c. `<include>`
d. `<link />`

9. Which of the following properties configures an image to use as a bullet point in an unordered list?

a. `bullet-image`
b. `image-style`
c. `list-style-image`
d. `bullet-style-image`

10. Which style rule below causes other page content to appear at the left of the element?

a. `position:left;`
b. `position:relative;`
c. `float:left;`
d. `float:right;`

Fill in the Blank

11. To indicate that an external style sheet is used to configure printing, code _____ on the `<link>` element.

12. The _____ is always transparent.

13. The _____ pseudo-class can be used to modify the display of a hyperlink when a mouse passes over it.

14. _____ is an attribute of the anchor element that can cause the new Web page to open in its own browser window.

15. The rules of _____ describe how Cascading Style Sheet rules, XHTML attributes, and browser defaults are applied.

Apply Your Knowledge

1. Predict the Result. Draw and write a brief description of the Web page that will be created with the following XHTML code:

```
<?xml version="1.0" encoding="utf-8"?>
<!DOCTYPE html PUBLIC "-//W3C//DTD XHTML 1.0 Transitional//EN"
"http://www.w3.org/TR/xhtml1/DTD/xhtml1-transitional.dtd">
<html xmlns="http://www.w3.org/1999/xhtml">
<head>
<title>Predict the Result</title>
<style type="text/css">
body { background-color: #000066;
       color: #CCCCCC;
       font-family: Arial,sans-serif;
}
h1 { background-color: #FFFFFF;
     color: #000066;
     padding: 20px;
}
.navBar { list-style-type: none;
          display: inline;
          padding: 20px;
}
```

```
.nav { text-decoration: none;
       font-size: 1.2em;
}
a.nav:link {color: #eeeeee; }
a.nav:visited {color: #778899; }
a.nav:hover {color: #3399CC; }
</style>
</head>
<body>
<h1>Trillium Media Design</h1>
<ul>
  <li class="navBar"><a class="nav" href="index.html">
  Home</a></li>
  <li class="navBar"><a class="nav" href="about.html">
  About</a></li>
  <li class="navBar"><a class="nav" href="services.htm">
  Services</a></li>
</ul>
<p>Our professional staff takes pride in its working
relationship with our clients by offering personalized services
that listen to their needs, develop their target areas, and
incorporate these items into a well presented web site that
works.
</p>
<div>Contact <a
href="mailto:web@trilliumtechnologies.com">Trillium</a><br />
Copyright &copy; 2008 Trillium Media Design
</div>
</body>
</html>
```

2. **Fill in the Missing Code.** This Web page should be configured so that the left naviga-tion column has a light pastel background color and floats on the left side of the browser window. Instead, the navigation displays with a white background color. CSS properties and values, indicated by "_" (underscore), are missing. Fill in the missing code to correct the error.

```
<?xml version="1.0" encoding="utf-8"?>
<!DOCTYPE html PUBLIC "-//W3C//DTD XHTML 1.0 Transitional//EN"
"http://www.w3.org/TR/xhtml1/DTD/xhtml1-transitional.dtd">
<html xmlns="http://www.w3.org/1999/xhtml">
<head>
<title>Fill in the Missing</title>
<style type="text/css">
body { background-color: #d5edb3;
       color: #000066;
       font-family: Verdana, Arial, sans-serif;
}
#leftcolumn { float: left;
              width: 120px;
}
```

```
#rightcolumn {  "_": "_";
                background-color: #ffffff;
                color: #000000;
                padding: 20px;
}
</style>
</head>
<body>
<div id="leftcolumn">
  <ul>
    <li><a href="home.html">Home</a></li>
    <li><a href="spring.html">Spring</a></li>
    <li><a href="summer.html">Summer</a></li>
    <li><a href="fall.html">Fall</a></li>
    <li><a href="winter.html">Winter</a></li>
  </ul>
</div>
<div id="rightcolumn">
  <h1>Trillium Media Design</h1>
  <p>Our professional staff takes pride in its working
  relationship with our clients by offering personalized
  services that listen to their needs, develop their target
  areas, and incorporate these items into a well presented web
  site that works.
  </p>
  <div>
  Contact <a href="mailto:web@trilliumtechnologies.com">
  web@trilliumtechnologies.com</a>
  <br />Copyright &copy; 2008 Trillium Media Design
  </div>
</div>
</body>
</html>
```

3. **Find the Error.** The page below is intended for the navigation area to display on the right side of the browser window. What needs to be changed to make this happen?

```
<?xml version="1.0" encoding="utf-8"?>
<!DOCTYPE html PUBLIC "-//W3C//DTD XHTML 1.0 Transitional//EN"
"http://www.w3.org/TR/xhtml1/DTD/xhtml1-transitional.dtd">
<html xmlns="http://www.w3.org/1999/xhtml">
<head>
<title>Find the Error</title>
<style type="text/css">
body {  background-color: #d5edb3;
        color: #000066;
        font-family: Verdana, Arial, sans-serif;
}
#rightcolumn {  float: left;
                width: 120px;
}
```

```
#maincontent {  padding: 20px 150px 20px 20px;
                background-color: #ffffff;
                color: #000000;
}
</style>
</head>
<body>
<div id="rightcolumn">
  <ul>
    <li><a href="home.html">Home</a></li>
    <li><a href="spring.html">Spring</a></li>
    <li><a href="summer.html">Summer</a></li>
    <li><a href="fall.html">Fall</a></li>
    <li><a href="winter.html">Winter</a></li>
  </ul>
</div>
<div id="maincontent">
  <h1>Trillium Media Design</h1>
  <p>Our professional staff takes pride in its working
  relationship with our clients by offering personalized
  services that listen to their needs, develop their target
  areas, and incorporate these items into a well presented web
  site that works.</p>
  <div>Contact <a href="mailto:web@trilliumtechnologies.com">
  web@trilliumtechnologies.com</a>
  <br />Copyright &copy; 2008 Trillium Media Design
  </div>
</div>
</body>
</html>
```

Hands-On Exercises

1. Write the XHTML to create a named anchor or bookmark at the beginning of a Web page designated by "top".

2. Write the XHTML to create an internal link to the named anchor designated by "top".

3. Write the XHTML to associate a Web page with an external style sheet named myprint.css to configure a printout.

4. Write the CSS to configure an image file named myimage.gif as the "bullet" in an unordered list.

5. Write the CSS to configure an unordered list not to display a "bullet".

6. **Extending Hands-On Practice 7.3.** In Hands-On Practice 7.3 you created files for a version of the Door County Wildflowers Web site. These files are also available in the Chapter7 folder in the student files. In this exercise, you will create two additional content pages for the Door County Wildflowers site, called spring.html and summer.html. Be sure that all CSS is placed in an external style sheet, called

mywildflower.css. (Modify pre-existing pages to use this style sheet). Rename threecolumn.html as appropriate. The following is some content to include on the new pages:

Spring Page (spring.html):

- Use the trillium.jpg image (see the Chapter7 folder in the student files).
- Trillium facts: 8–18 inches tall, perennial, native plant, grows in rich moist deciduous woodlands, white flowers turn pink with age, fruit is a single red berry, protected flower species.

Summer Page (summer.html):

- Use the yls.jpg image (see the Chapter7 folder in the student files).
- Yellow Lady's Slipper facts: 4–24 inches tall, perennial, native plant, grows in wet shaded deciduous woods, swamps, and bogs, an orchid, official flower of Door County.

Hand in printouts of mywildflower.css, spring.html source code (print in Notepad), summer.html source code, the browser display of spring.html, and the browser display of summer.html to your instructor.

7. **Configure Printing for Hands-On Practice 7.3.** Configure special printing for the threecolumn.html file created in Hands-On Practice 7.3. Use the threecolumn.html file from Hands-On Practice 7.3 as a starting point. This file is in the Chapter7 folder in the student files. Save a copy of this file as threecolumnprint.html. Modify the file so that it links to an external style sheet called threecolumn.css instead of using embedded styles. Save and test your page. Create a new style sheet, called myprint.css, which will prevent the navigation from displaying when the page is printed. Modify the threecolumnprint.html page to link to this file. Review the use of the `media` attribute on the link element. Save all files and test your page. Select File, Print Preview to test the print styles. Hand in printouts of myprint.css, threecolumn.css, threecolumnprint.html source code (print in Notepad), and the browser display of threecolumprint.html to your instructor.

8. **Modify the Design of Hands-On Practice 7.3.** Locate the threecolumn.html page you created in Hands-On Practice 7.3. This file is in the Chapter7 folder in the student files. Recall from Chapter 5 that a Web page using jello design has content in the center of the Web page with blank margins on either side. Configure the style rules for threecolumn.html to display the page in this manner. Refer to Chapter 5 for CSS style rule suggestions. Hand in printouts of the source code (print in Notepad) and browser display for the Web page to your instructor.

9. **Practice Validating CSS.** Choose a CSS external style sheet file to validate—perhaps you have created one for your own Web site. Otherwise, use an external style sheet file that you worked with in this chapter. Use the W3C free CSS validator (http://jigsaw.w3.org/css-validator/). If your CSS does not immediately pass the validation test, modify it and test again. Repeat this process until the W3C validates your CSS code. Write a one or two paragraph summary about the validation process. Answer the following questions. Was it easy to use? Did anything surprise you? Did you encounter a number of errors or just a few? How easy was it to determine how to correct the CSS file? Would you recommend this to other students? Why or why not?

Web Research

You've been working a lot with navigation links in this chapter. There is one aspect that we did not discuss—using background images in navigation links. There are numerous tutorials on the Web that present this technique. Visit the following sites and choose a tutorial you find easy to read.

- http://www.cssplay.co.uk/menus/menu5teen.html
- http://superfluousbanter.org/archives/2004/05/navigation-matrix-reloaded
- http://www.alistapart.com/articles/sprites
- http://www.wpdfd.com/issues/73/film-strip_rollovers_a_simpler_way_to_do_rollovers
- http://css.maxdesign.com.au/listutorial/roll_introduction.htm
- http://www.shapeshed.com/journal/overlapping_tabbed_navigation_in_css/

Choose and follow one of the tutorials listed above. Create a Web page that uses this new technique. The Web page should provide the URL of your tutorial, the name of the Web site, and a description of the new technique you discovered. Place your name in the e-mail address at the bottom of the Web page. Print the external style sheet (if you used one), the Web page source code (from Notepad), and the browser view of your Web page.

Focus On Web Design

Take a few moments and visit the CSS Zen Garden at http://www.csszengarden.com. Explore the site and note the widely different designs. What thought processes and decisions are needed as a person creates a new design for this site? Visit http://www.stopdesign.com/articles/process, http://www.mikepick.com/news/archives/000086.html, or http://www.bobbyvandersluis.com/articles/gardenparty.php for a behind-the-scenes look at how Web developers have approached this task. Reflect on their stories and suggestions. Write a one page (double-spaced) essay that describes ideas about the design process you'll be able to use as you begin to design Web sites for personal or professional use. Be sure to include the URL of the resources you used.

WEB SITE CASE STUDY:
Navigation Links in a List

Each of the following case studies continues throughout most of the text. This chapter configures the main navigation in your Web sites to utilize an unordered list.

JavaJam Coffee House

See Chapter 2 for an introduction to the JavaJam Coffee House Case Study. Figure 2.26 shows a site map for the JavaJam Web site. The pages were created in earlier chapters. You will use the existing Web site in the javajamcss folder (unless your instructor specifies otherwise) as a start and create a new version that configures the main navigation using an unordered list.

Hands-On Practice Case

1. Review Section 7.2 CSS Pseudo-classes and Links and Section 7.3 CSS Navigation Layout using Lists.

2. Modify the javajam.css file as needed to configure the main navigation links in an unordered list without "bullets". Also configure the main navigation links to change color when a mouse hovers over them.

3. Modify the index.html, menu.html, and music.html Web pages to display the main navigation links in an unordered list.

4. Launch a browser and test the pages in the javajamcss folder. Modify your java.css file as needed to configure your pages. Be sure to test in more than one browser.

Fish Creek Animal Hospital

See Chapter 2 for an introduction to the Fish Creek Animal Hospital Case Study. Figure 2.30 shows a site map for the Fish Creek Web site. The pages were created in earlier chapters. You will use the existing Web site in the fishcreekcss folder (unless your instructor specifies otherwise) as a start and create a new version that configures the main navigation using an unordered list.

Hands-On Practice Case

1. Review Section 7.3 CSS Navigation Layout using Lists.

2. Modify the fishcreek.css file as needed to configure the main navigation links in an unordered list without "bullets". *Hint*: To eliminate the extra space on the left side of the fish navigation links, use CSS to configure the unordered list to have 0 margin and padding on the left side.

3. Modify the index.html, services.html, and askvet.html Web pages to display the main navigation links in an unordered list.

4. Launch a browser and test the pages in the fishcreekcss folder. Modify your fishcreek.css file as needed to configure your pages. Be sure to test in more than one browser.

Pete the Painter

See Chapter 2 for an introduction to the Pete the Painter Case Study. Figure 2.34 shows a site map for the Pete the Painter Web site. The pages were created in earlier chapters. You will use the existing Web site in the paintercss folder (unless your instructor specifies otherwise) as a start and create a new version that configures the main navigation using an unordered list.

Hands-On Practice Case

1. Review Section 7.2 CSS Pseudo-classes and Links and Section 7.3 CSS Navigation Layout using Lists.

2. Modify the painter.css file as needed to configure the main navigation links in an unordered list without "bullets". Also configure the main navigation links to change color when a mouse hovers over them. *Hint*: To eliminate the extra space

on the left side of the main navigation links, use CSS to configure the unordered list to have 0 margin and padding on the left side.

3. Modify the index.html, services.html, and testimonials.html Web pages to display the main navigation links in an unordered list.

4. Launch a browser and test the pages in the paintercss folder. Modify your painter.css file as needed to configure your pages. Be sure to test in more than one browser.

Prime Properties

See Chapter 2 for an introduction to the Prime Properties Case Study. Figure 2.38 shows a site map for the Prime Properties Web site. The pages were created in earlier chapters. You will use the existing Web site as in the primecss folder (unless your instructor specifies otherwise) as a start and create a new version that configures the main navigation using an unordered list.

Hands-On Practice Case

1. Review Section 7.2 CSS Pseudo-classes and Links and Section 7.3 CSS Navigation Layout using Lists.

2. Modify the prime.css file as needed to configure the main navigation links in an unordered list without "bullets". Also remove the image buttons and, instead, configure CSS buttons with text that changes color when the mouse hovers over them. *Hint*: To eliminate the extra space on the left side of the main navigation links, use CSS to configure the unordered list to have 0 margin and padding on the left side.

3. Modify the index.html, financing.html, and listings.html Web pages to display the main navigation links in an unordered list.

4. Launch a browser and test the pages in the primecss folder. Modify your prime.css file as needed to configure your pages. Be sure to test in more than one browser.

Web Project

See Chapters 5 and 6 for an introduction to the Web Project case. You will modify the main navigation to use an unordered list. If appropriate, also add interactivity to the main navigation area with CSS pseudo-classes.

Hands-On Practice Case

1. Review Section 7.2 CSS Pseudo-Classes and Links and Section 7.3 CSS Navigation Layout Using Lists.

2. Modify your project's external CSS file and Web page files as needed to configure the main navigation in an unordered list.

3. Optional: Modify your project's external style sheet to configure CSS link and hover pseudo-classes for your main navigation hyperlinks.

4. Launch a browser and test the Web pages. Modify your files as needed to configure your pages. Be sure to test in more than one browser.

Tables

Chapter Objectives   In this chapter, you will learn how to ...

- Create a table on a Web page
- Apply attributes to format tables, table rows, and table cells
- Format an entire Web page within a table
- Use nested tables
- Use CSS to configure an XHTML table

Tables can be used to organize Web page content. They can also be used to provide structure and format the layout of an entire Web page. In this chapter, you will become familiar with coding XHTML tables to both organize information and format page layout. You'll configure tables using both XHTML and CSS.

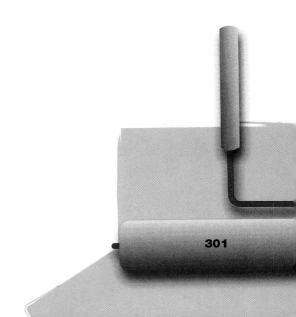

8.1 Using Tables on Web Pages

Tables are commonly used on Web pages in two ways:

- To organize information
- To format the layout of an entire Web page

Although it is increasingly common to use CSS to configure page layout, some well-known sites, such as http://www.cdw.com, http://www.gamestop.com, and http://jcpenney.com use the older method of XHTML tables for this function.

Overview of an XHTML Table

An XHTML table is composed of rows and columns, like a spreadsheet. Each individual table **cell** is at the intersection of a specific row and column. Each table begins with a **`<table>`** tag and ends with a `</table>` tag. There are a number of optional attributes for the `<table>` element, such as `border`, `width`, `height`, `cellspacing`, and `cellpadding`. Each table row begins with a **`<tr>`** tag and ends with a `</tr>` tag. Each cell (table data) begins with a **`<td>`** tag and ends with a `</td>` tag. Table cells can contain text and graphics. In fact, table cells usually contain other XHTML tags such as paragraphs, headings, and tables. Be very careful to use opening and closing tags when working with tables. If you omit or misplace a tag the results are unpredictable and your page may not display at all. Figure 8.1 shows a sample table with three rows, four columns, and a border.

Figure 8.1
Table with three rows, four columns, and a border

Name	Birthday	Phone	E-mail
Jack	5/13	857-555-5555	jack04521@gmail.com
Sparky	11/28	303-555-5555	sparky@iname.com

The following is the sample XHTML code for the table shown in Figure 8.1:

```
<table border="1">
  <tr>
    <td>Name</td>
    <td>Birthday</td>
    <td>Phone</td>
    <td>E-mail</td>
  </tr>
  <tr>
    <td>Jack</td>
    <td>5/13</td>
    <td>857-555-5555</td>
    <td>jack04521@gmail.com</td>
  </tr>
  <tr>
    <td>Sparky</td>
    <td>11/28</td>
    <td>303-555-5555</td>
    <td>sparky@iname.com</td>
  </tr>
</table>
```

Notice how the table is described row by row. Also, each row is described cell by cell. This attention to detail is crucial to the successful use of tables.

What if you don't want a border on your table? The **border** attribute is optional. The table shown in Figure 8.1 uses a border with its width set to 1. If you omit the border attribute, the table displays with no visible border. Figure 8.2 shows the same table with the border attribute omitted.

Figure 8.2
Table with no visible border

Name	Birthday	Phone	E-mail
Jack	5/13	857-555-5555	jack04521@gmail.com
Sparky	11/28	303-555-5555	sparky@iname.com

XHTML Table Headings

The **<th>**, or table heading, element can be used to distinguish column headings from table content. Figure 8.3 shows a table that uses the <th> element.

Figure 8.3
Using <th> tags on a table

Name	Birthday	Phone	E-mail
Jack	5/13	857-555-5555	jack04521@gmail.com
Sparky	11/28	303-555-5555	sparky@iname.com

The XHTML for the table shown in Figure 8.3 is shown below. Notice that the first row uses <th> instead of <td> tags.

```
<table border="1">
  <tr>
    <th>Name</th>
    <th>Birthday</th>
    <th>Phone</th>
    <th>E-mail</th>
  </tr>
  <tr>
    <td>Jack</td>
    <td>5/13</td>
    <td>857-555-5555</td>
    <td>jack04521@gmail.com</td>
  </tr>
  <tr>
    <td>Sparky</td>
    <td>11/28</td>
    <td>303-555-5555</td>
    <td>sparky@iname.com</td>
  </tr>
</table>
```

XHTML Table Captions

The **<caption>** element is often used with a data table to describe its contents. The table shown in Figure 8.4 uses <caption> tags to set the caption to Birthday List.

Figure 8.4
The caption for this table is Birthday List

Birthday List

Name	Birthday	Phone	E-mail
Jack	5/13	857-555-5555	jack04521@gmail.com
Sparky	11/28	303-555-5555	sparky@iname.com

The XHTML for the table follows:

```
<table border="1">
<caption>Birthday List</caption>
   <tr>
      <th>Name</th>
      <th>Birthday</th>
      <th>Phone</th>
      <th>E-mail</th>
   </tr>
   <tr>
      <td>Jack</td>
      <td>5/13</td>
      <td>857-555-5555</td>
      <td>jack04521@gmail.com</td>
   </tr>
   <tr>
      <td>Sparky</td>
      <td>11/28</td>
      <td>303-555-5555</td>
      <td>sparky@iname.com</td>
   </tr>
</table>
```

Notice how the `<caption>` element was placed after the beginning `<table>` tag but before the first `<tr>` tag.

HANDS-ON PRACTICE 8.1

You will work with a new version of the Trillium Web site. Create a new folder called trilliumch8 and copy the files index.html, services.html, trillium.css, trilliumbanner.jpg, and trilliumbullet.gif files from the student files Chapter8/starters folder. You will modify the services page to look similar to the display shown in Figure 8.5.

Launch a text editor and open the services.html page from your trilliumch8 folder. You will modify the services page to look similar to the display shown in Figure 8.5. Locate the `<h2>` element. Create a table under this element with four rows and two columns. Configure the first cell in each column as a table heading. Use Figure 8.5 as a guide and type text in the table cells. Save your page and test it in a browser. A solution is located in the student files Chatper8/8.1 folder.

Figure 8.5
Table added to services.html

XHTML Table Attributes

Common `<table>` element attributes include `align`, `border`, `bordercolor`, `width`, `height`, `cellspacing`, `cellpadding`, `bgcolor`, `summary`, and `title`. The default display of rows and cells in tables can also be modified using attributes. The most commonly used attributes with the `<td>` element to configure table cells are `bgcolor`, `valign`, `rowspan`, and `colspan`. Since XHTML table attributes are widely used on the Web, it's a good idea to become familiar with them. You'll discover how to configure most of these features using CSS later in this chapter. Let's take a closer look at attributes used with `<table>` elements.

Why doesn't my table display?

While Internet Explorer will display a table even if you forget about a closing tag here or there, other browsers such as Firefox can be very picky. Be sure to use Firefox to test pages that contain tables. Internet Explorer will often ignore a missing or misspelled tag and display your table. However, when Firefox encounters missing or unmatched table tags, it sometimes will not display parts of your Web page or display only a portion of the table.

As you read about each `<table>` element attribute, experiment with the Birthday List table. The best way to learn to write XHTML is to practice it.

The `align` Attribute. This attribute specifies the alignment of the table with the values `right`, `center`, and `left`. The table shown in Figure 8.6 has the `align` attribute set to `center`.

Figure 8.6
Centered table with `width` set to 75%

Even though it is still often used, the W3C has deprecated the use of the `align` attribute with the `<table>` tag. Later in this chapter you'll use CSS to replace the functionality of most of the table attributes—including configuring the horizontal alignment, borders, width, padding, and background color of XHTML tables.

The `border` Attribute. This attribute specifies whether and what type of visible border the table will have. The value ranges from 0 to 100, with 0 indicating that no border will be visible. The values between 1 and 100 determine the thickness of the visible border, where 1 indicates a relatively thin border and 100 indicates a very thick border. The table shown in Figure 8.7 has a border set to `10`.

Figure 8.7
Table with a border set to `10`

Name	Birthday	Phone	E-mail
Jack	5/13	857-555-5555	jack04521@gmail.com
Sparky	11/28	303-555-5555	sparky@iname.com

The browser determines the border color and shading based on the page background color. If you want a specific color, also use the `bordercolor` attribute.

The `bordercolor` Attribute. This attribute specifies the color of the border. The values can be a color name or numeric value. See the color chart at http://webdevfoundations.net/color. The browser displays the border color as a solid color and does not shade the border when the `bordercolor` attribute is used. The bordercolor attribute is not part of the official W3C Recommendations but is included here because it is widely used and well supported by browsers. The table shown in Figure 8.8 has a border set to 5 and bordercolor set to a dark color.

Figure 8.8
Table with bordercolor set to a dark color

Name	Birthday	Phone	E-mail
Jack	5/13	857-555-5555	jack04521@gmail.com
Sparky	11/28	303-555-5555	sparky@iname.com

The width Attribute. This attribute specifies the width of the table in either pixels or in a percentage of the Web page. The table will stretch to fit the entire width of the page if 100% is used. If width is not specified, the browser determines the width of a particular table by calculating the width of the elements and text it contains. Use the width attribute when you want more control over your Web page. The table shown in Figure 8.6 is centered and has a width set to 75%. The XHTML code for the table tag is <table border="1" align="center" width="75%">

FAQ

Which is better, specifying width by pixels or by percentage?

It depends. Keep in mind that visitors to your Web page will use monitors with different screen resolutions. If you need your table to have a fixed width that you specify, use pixels. If you'd like your table to be flexible and to resize with the browser window, use percentages. It's a good idea to test your Web pages using different screen resolutions.

The height Attribute. This attribute specifies the height of the table in either pixels or in a percentage of the Web page. This is more commonly used on <tr> and <td> tags. The height attribute is not part of the official W3C Recommendation for the <table> element, but is included here because it is widely used and well supported by browsers.

The cellspacing Attribute. This attribute specifies the distance between the cells in pixels. If you omit the cellspacing attribute, the default value (usually around 2 pixels) is determined by the browser. The table shown in Figure 8.9 has cellspacing set to 10. The XHTML code for the <table> tag follows:

```
<table border="1" cellspacing="10">
```

Figure 8.9
Table with cellspacing set to 10

Name	Birthday	Phone	E-mail
Jack	5/13	857-555-5555	jack04521@gmail.com
Sparky	11/28	303-555-5555	sparky@iname.com

The cellpadding Attribute. This attribute specifies the distance in pixels between the cell contents and the edge of the cell. If you omit the cellpadding attribute, the default value is 1 pixel. An example with cellpadding set to 10 is shown in Figure 8.10. The XHTML code for the <table> tag follows:

```
<table border="1" cellpadding="10">
```

Figure 8.10
Table with `cellpadding` set to 10

Name	Birthday	Phone	E-mail
Jack	5/13	857-555-5555	jack04521@gmail.com
Sparky	11/28	303-555-5555	sparky@iname.com

FAQ   Can I mix and match fixed widths and percentages?

Yes. The width attribute can be applied to table cells (`<td>` elements) as well as to the entire table (`<table>` element). If you are using a table to format an entire page, you might want a particular column used for navigation links to have a fixed width while the entire table uses a percentage width. As always, test your Web pages using different screen resolutions to make sure that you achieve your desired effect.

The `bgcolor` Attribute.   This deprecated attribute specifies a background color for the table. The values can be a color name or numeric value. See the color chart at http://webdevfoundations.net/color. An example with a background color, no border, and `cellpadding` of 10 is shown in Figure 8.11. The XHTML code for the `<table>` tag follows:

```
<table border="0" bgcolor="#99CCFF" cellpadding="10">
```

Figure 8.11
Borderless table using `cellpadding` set to 10 along with a background color

Name	Birthday	Phone	E-mail
Jack	5/13	857-555-5555	jack04521@gmail.com
Sparky	11/28	303-555-5555	sparky@iname.com

Focus on Accessibility

The `summary` Attribute.   This attribute specifies a summary of the table contents that can be accessed by a screen reader. The Web Accessibility Initiative (WAI) suggests using the `summary` attribute with tables containing data. For example:

```
<table border="0" width="75%" title="Birthday List"
  summary="This table contains a list of names, birthdates, phone
number, and e-mail addresses.">
```

Focus on Accessibility

The `title` Attribute.   This attribute specifies a title of the table that can be accessed by a screen reader. The value of the `title` attribute is displayed by some browsers, such as Internet Explorer 5.x (or later) and Netscape 6 (or later), when the mouse passes over the table area. The WAI suggests using the `title` attribute with tables containing data.

Applying Attributes to Rows and Cells

Many of the `<table>` element attributes discussed above can also be applied to the `<tr>` and `<td>` tags to customize the look of your table. In particular, the `bgcolor`, `align`, and `width` attributes are most often used. The following are commonly used attributes for `<tr>` and `<td>` elements. Later in the chapter you'll use CSS to configure the background color, alignment, and width of these page areas.

The `align` Attribute. This attribute can be used to align the contents of a table row or table cell within a table. In Figure 8.12, the cells containing birthday information are configured to be centered by the `align` attribute on the `<td>` elements containing the birthday information.

Figure 8.12
Table with selected cells center-aligned

Name	Birthday	Phone	E-mail
Jack	5/13	857-555-5555	jack04521@gmail.com
Sparky	11/28	303-555-5555	sparky@iname.com

The XHTML code for the table follows:

```
<table border="1">
  <tr>
    <th>Name</th>
    <th>Birthday</th>
    <th>Phone</th>
    <th>E-mail</th>
  </tr>
  <tr>
    <td>Jack</td>
    <td align="center">5/13</td>
    <td>847-555-5555</td>
    <td>jack04521@gmail.com</td>
  </tr>
  <tr>
    <td>Sparky</td>
    <td align="center">11/28</td>
    <td>303-555-5555</td>
    <td>sparky@iname.com</td>
  </tr>
</table>
```

The `bgcolor` Attribute. This deprecated attribute can be used to apply a background color to a table row or cell. See Figure 8.13 for an example of applying a background color to alternating rows of a table using this attribute.

Figure 8.13
Table using a background color on alternate rows

Name	Birthday	Phone	E-mail
Jack	5/13	857-555-5555	jack04521@gmail.com
Sparky	11/28	303-555-5555	sparky@iname.com

The XHTML code for the table follows:

```
<table border="0" cellpadding="10" cellspacing="0">
  <tr bgcolor="#CCCCCC">
    <th>Name</th>
    <th>Birthday</th>
```

```
      <th>Phone</th>
      <th>E-mail</th>
    </tr>
    <tr>
      <td>Jack</td>
      <td>5/13</td>
      <td>857-555-5555</td>
      <td>jack04521@gmail.com</td>
    </tr>
    <tr bgcolor="#CCCCCC">
      <td>Sparky</td>
      <td>11/28</td>
      <td>303-555-5555</td>
      <td>sparky@iname.com</td>
    </tr>
</table>
```

FAQ

What if I want a more interesting table?

You can alter the gridlike look of a table by applying the `colspan` and `rowspan` attributes to `<td>` elements. As you get into more complex table configurations like these, be sure to sketch the table on paper before you start typing the XHTML code.

The `colspan` Attribute. This attribute specifies the number of columns that a cell will occupy. Figure 8.14 shows a row that spans two columns.

<table border="1"><tr><td colspan="2">This spans two columns</td></tr><tr><td>Column 1</td><td>Column 2</td></tr></table>

Figure 8.14 Table with a row that spans two columns

The XHTML code for the table follows:

```
<table border="1">
  <tr>
    <td colspan="2">This spans two columns</td>
  </tr>
  <tr>
    <td>Column 1</td>
    <td>Column 2</td>
  </tr>
</table>
```

The `rowspan` Attribute. This attribute specifies the number of rows that a cell will occupy. An example of a column that spans two rows is shown in Figure 8.15.

<table border="1"><tr><td rowspan="2">This spans two rows</td><td>Row 1 Column 2</td></tr><tr><td>Row 2 Column 2</td></tr></table>

Figure 8.15 Table with a column that spans two rows

The XHTML code for the table follows:

```
<table border="1">
  <tr>
    <td rowspan="2">This spans two rows</td>
    <td>Row 1 Column 2</td>
  </tr>
  <tr>
    <td>Row 2 Column 2</td>
  </tr>
</table>
```

The `valign` Attribute.   This attribute specifies the alignment of the text or image in the cell. The default vertical alignment is `middle`, shown in the `rowspan` example in Figure 8.15. Use the `valign` attribute when you need the contents of a cell to be vertically aligned at the top or bottom of a cell. Common values for the `valign` attribute are `top`, `middle`, and `bottom`. Figure 8.16 shows the `valign` attribute used to top align the contents of the first cell.

Figure 8.16
The first cell in this table uses the `valign` attribute

This spans two rows	Row 1 Column 2
	Row 2 Column 2

The XHTML code for the table follows:

```
<table border="1">
  <tr>
    <td rowspan="2" valign="top">This spans two rows</td>
    <td>Row 1 Column 2</td>
  </tr>
  <tr>
    <td>Row 2 Column 2</td>
  </tr>
</table>
```

HANDS-ON PRACTICE 8.2

You will continue to work with the Trillium Web site. Launch Notepad or another text editor and open the services.html page from your trilliumch8 folder. Center the table on the page with the `align="center"` attribute. Configure the width of the table to `75%`. Set the `cellpadding` to `5` and the `cellspacing` to `0`. See Figure 8.17 for an example.

Be sure to use the table attributes recommended for accessibility. Save your page and test it in a browser. Compare your work to the sample in the student files (Chapter8/8.2).

Figure 8.17
Sample services.html

Accessibility and Tables

Focus on Accessibility

This chapter has introduced three methods to increase the accessibility of tables:

- Use `<th>` elements to indicate column or row headings.
- Use the `summary` attribute on the table element to provide an overview of the table contents.
- Use the `title` attribute on the table element to provide a brief description of the table.

Another method to increase the accessibility of an informational table is to associate table cell values with their corresponding headers. This technique uses the `id` attribute (usually in a `<th>` element) to identify a specific header cell and the **headers attribute** in a `<td>` element. Figure 8.18 shows a table that has been configured in this manner.

Figure 8.18
This informational table was coded with techniques to improve accessibility

School Attended	Years	Subject	Degree Awarded
Schaumburg High School	2000 - 2005	College Prep	H.S. Diploma
William Rainey Harper College	2006 - 2008	Internet & Web Development	Web Developer Certificate

The XTHML code for the table follows:

```
<table border="1" width="75%" title="Educational Background"
    summary="This table lists my educational background including
    school attended, years, subject, and degree awarded (column
    headings). Schaumburg High School is presented first. Harper
    College is presented second.">
  <tr>
    <th id="school">School Attended</th>
    <th id="years">Years</th>
    <th id="subject">Subject</th>
    <th id="degree" >Degree Awarded</th>
  </tr>
  <tr>
    <td headers="school">Schaumburg High School</td>
    <td headers="years">2000 - 2005</td>
    <td headers="subject">College Prep</td>
    <td headers="degree">H.S. Diploma</td>
  </tr>
  <tr>
    <td headers="school">William Rainey Harper College</td>
    <td headers="years">2006 - 2008</td>
    <td headers="subject">Internet &amp; Web Development</td>
    <td headers="degree">Web Developer Certificate</td>
  </tr>
</table>
```

CHECKPOINT 8.1

1. Describe two reasons to use tables on a Web page.
2. Describe the difference between the `cellpadding` and `cellspacing` table attributes.
3. Describe one coding technique that increases the accessibility of an XHTML table.

8.2 XHTML—Table Page Layout

You may be wondering about the title of this section because you've been configuring page layout using CSS. While CSS **page layout** configuration is a more modern and preferred method, many current Web sites are still designed with table-based page layouts. You'll explore this coding technique in this section. Let's take a look at some well-known sites that at the time this was written use tables to format their Web pages—http://www.cdw.com, http://www.gamestop.com, and http://www.jcpenney.com. As you surf the Web and analyze these and other sites, look for a Web page layout that appeals to you. View the source code by selecting View, Source from the browser menu bar (for IE7 select Page, View Source). Examine how the page was formatted. You will find that many of the pages use tables. It is important not to copy a page, but rather to get ideas from many sources and organize them in a fresh, new way that is all your own. When designing a new Web page, it's a good idea to sketch your ideas on paper first.

Figure 8.19 shows a sketch of a common format consisting of a horizontal banner and three columns. Notice that the middle cell in the second row is used for spacing purposes only—to separate the navigation area from the content area. Sample XHTML code for this type of table layout follows:

```
<table border="0" width="80%">
  <tr>
    <td colspan="3"><h1>This is the banner area</h1></td>
  </tr>
  <tr>
    <td width="20%" valign="top">Place Navigation here</td>
    <td width="10"> </td>
    <td>Page content goes here</td>
  </tr>
</table>
```

Figure 8.19
Using a table to format a Web page

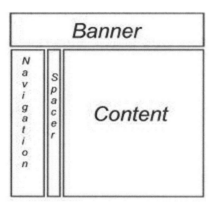

A Web page using this type of table layout is shown in Figure 8.20 and can be found in the student files (Chapter8/tables/table1.html).

The   character is coded in the table displayed by Figure 8.20 as a placeholder in the cell used for a spacer. Recall from Chapter 2 that   is a special character that creates a nonbreaking space.

The alignment of the table will be to the left by default. This can sometimes make the page look unbalanced when it is viewed with a monitor set to a higher resolution, such as 1280×1024. To prevent this display issue, use the align attribute to center the table. Assign the table a percentage width of the Web page. These techniques will cause all browsers of varying resolutions to display the table centered and extended across 80 percent of the Web page.

Figure 8.21 shows a similar Web page layout—only the cellspacing and cellpadding attributes on the table tag were changed. This layout uses cellspacing set to 0 and cellpadding set to 10. Note how the cellspacing value of 0 merges the table cell backgrounds while the cellpadding value configures additional empty space around the text. Examine the source code in the student files (Chapter8/tables/table1a.html).

Figure 8.20
Page layout using a table

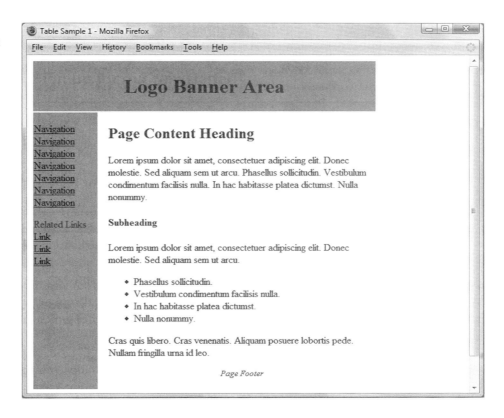

Figure 8.21
This table is centered and uses `cellspacing` set to `0`

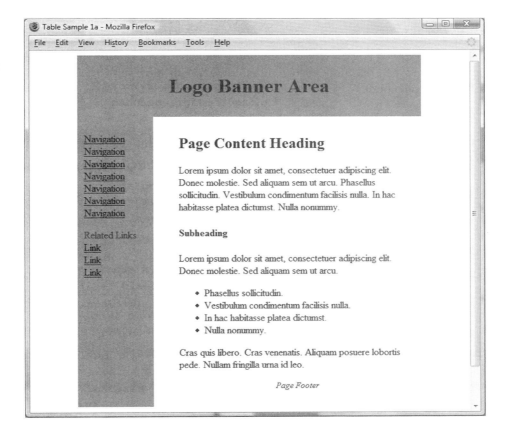

Accessibility and Layout Tables

You've become aware that tables are often used to configure Web page layouts on the Web. This technique has been used for years. When using a table in this manner it is important to understand that screen readers and other assistive technologies typically access a table in a *linear manner*—that is, they "read" the table row by row.

Review the table layout sketch shown in Figure 8.19. A screen reader would access the table row by row, from top to bottom. The order of the areas "read" would be: banner, navigation, spacer, and content. This would occur on each page configured in this manner. One major disadvantage of the layout shown in Figure 8.19 is that the navigation links would be "read" over and over as each page on the Web site is rendered. Refer to the Internal Links section in Chapter 7 for a coding technique that allows visitors to skip the repetitive navigation.

As you explore other table layout designs in this chapter and create your own, keep in mind the way a screen reader would access the content. You may want to download a free screen reader and listen yourself! Try free trial versions of JAWS (http://www.freedomscientific.com/fs_downloads/jaws.asp) and Window-Eyes (http://www.gwmicro.com/Window-Eyes/Demo/).

More Sample Page Layout Tables

There are a variety of commonly used designs for page layout tables. This section contains examples of three commonly used page layouts to get you started using this technique.

The layout shown in Figure 8.22 shows banner, horizontal navigation, and two content columns. The narrower content column on the right (called a sidebar) is commonly used for advertisements or to showcase products and services offered. A page using this layout can be found in the student files (Chapter8/tables/table2.html). Sample code for this type of table layout follows:

```
<table border="0" width="80%" cellpadding="5">
  <tr>
    <td colspan="2" ><h1 align="center">Logo Banner</h1></td>
  </tr>
  <tr>
    <td colspan="2" ><h3 align="center">Navigation</h3></td>
  </tr>
  <tr>
    <td valign="top">Main Content</td>
    <td width="100" valign="top">Sidebar</td>
  </tr>
</table>
```

There are many ways to combine table rows and columns to create interesting, usable Web pages. The page layout shown in Figure 8.23 uses a vertical left-side navigation, center main content area, and right sidebar area.

Figure 3.2
Partial color chart

#FFFFFF	#FFFFCC	#FFFF99	#FFFF66	#FFFF33	#FFFF00
#FFCCFF	#FFCCCC	#FFCC99	#FFCC66	#FFCC33	#FFCC00
#FF99FF	#FF99CC	#FF9999	#FF9966	#FF9933	#FF9900

Figure 3.3
Web safe colors
display predictably

bgcolor="#CC0000"	bgcolor="#880000"
This cell background is on the Web Color Palette should display the same on all platforms.	This cell background is NOT on the Web Color Palette. Expect this cell background to display differently on some platforms.

Figure 3.6
embedded.html with
styles applied

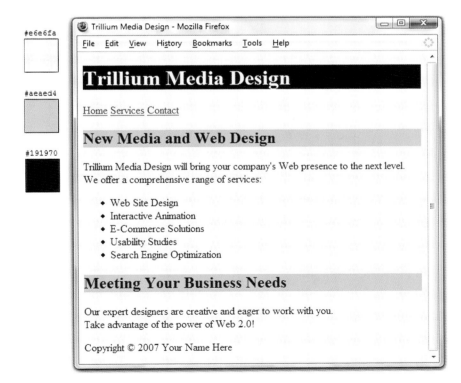

#e6e6fa

#aeaed4

#191970

Trillium Media Design - Mozilla Firefox

File   Edit   View   History   Bookmarks   Tools   Help

Trillium Media Design

Home Services Contact

New Media and Web Design

Trillium Media Design will bring your company's Web presence to the next level. We offer a comprehensive range of services:

- Web Site Design
- Interactive Animation
- E-Commerce Solutions
- Usability Studies
- Search Engine Optimization

Meeting Your Business Needs

Our expert designers are creative and eager to work with you. Take advantage of the power of Web 2.0!

Copyright © 2007 Your Name Here

Figure 3.21
New JavaJam index.html

Figure 3.23
New Fish Creek index.html

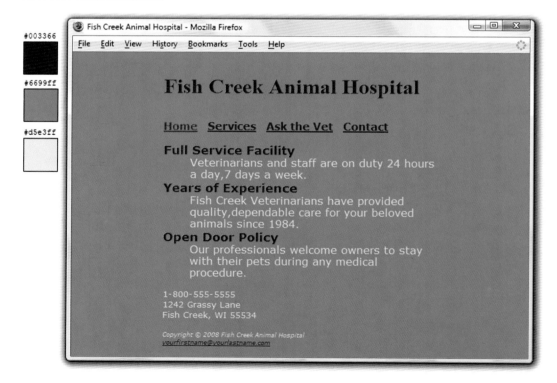

Figure 3.25
New Pete the Painter index.html

Figure 3.27
New Prime Properties index.html

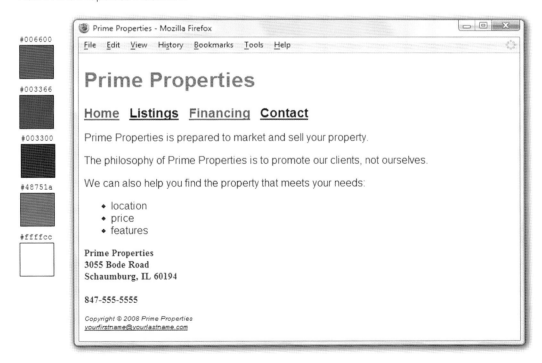

Figure 4.16

The new Trillium Home page with a logo banner

Figure 4.25

New JavaJam Home page

Figure 4.26
JavaJam music.html

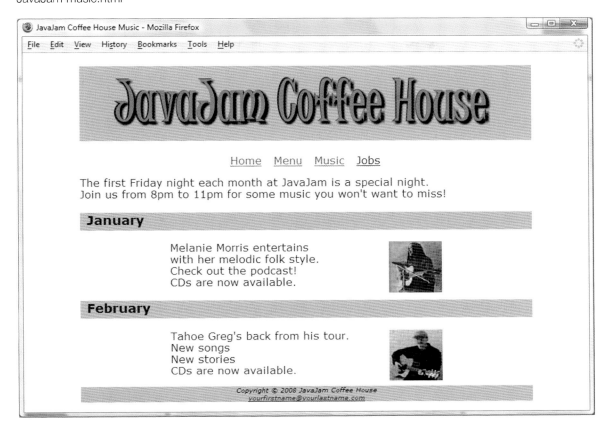

Figure 4.33
Fish Creek askvet.html

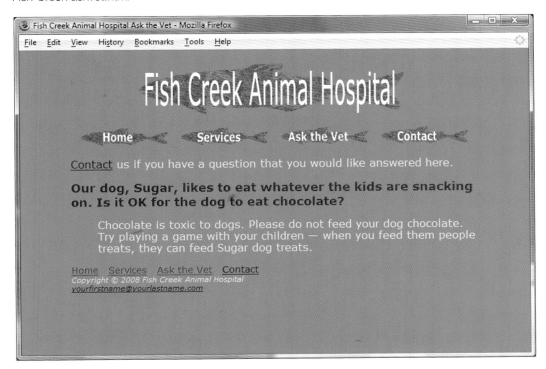

Figure 4.39
Pete the Painter testimonials.html

Figure 4.45

Prime Properties listings.html

Figure 5.22
A typical site for children

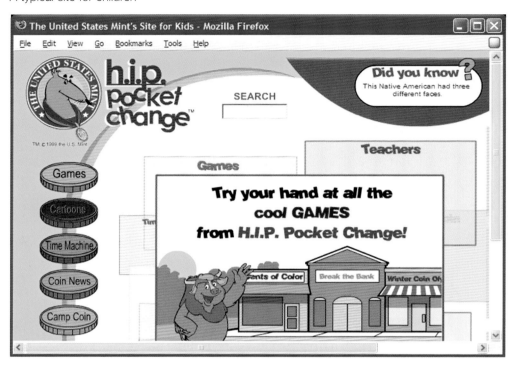

Figure 5.23
Many teens and young adults find dark sites appealing

Figure 5.24
A site designed
specifically for the 50
and over age range

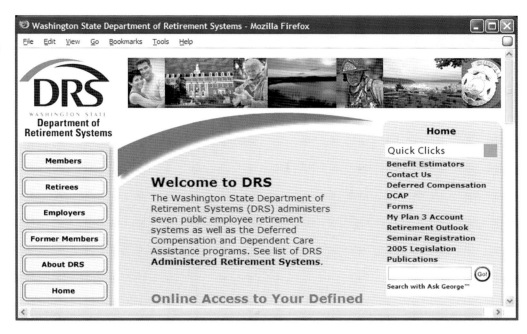

Figure 6.16
The image is floating
on the page

Figure 6.19
A two-column page
configured using
CSS

Figure 6.23
The new JavaJam two-column index.html

Figure 6.26
The new Fish Creek two-column index.html

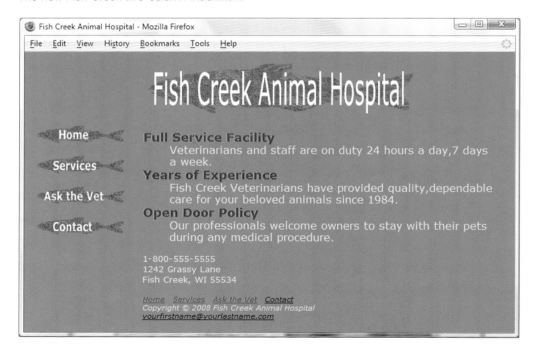

Figure 6.28

The new Pete the Painter two-column index.html

Figure 6.31

The new Prime Properties two-column index.html

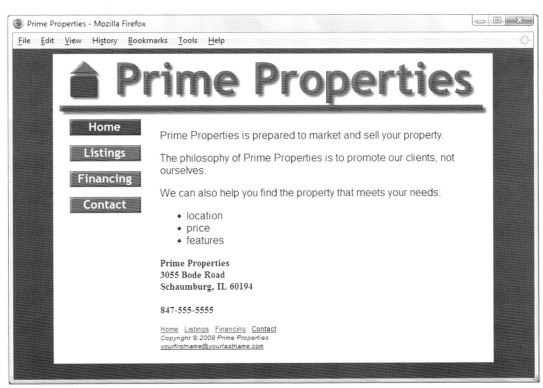

Figure 7.13
This three-column page layout is designed using CSS and no tables

Figure 8.25
New index.html using a table for layout

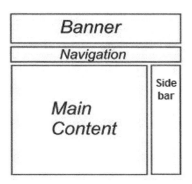

The vertical navigation area allows room to display a wide variety of links and is more useful for a large site than the previous layout. A page using this layout can be found in the student files (Chapter8/tables/table3.html). Sample code follows:

```
<table border="0" width="80%" cellpadding="5">
  <tr>
    <td colspan="3" ><h1 align="center">Logo Banner</h1></td>
  </tr>
  <tr>
    <td width="100" valign="top">Navigation</td>
    <td>Main Content</td>
    <td width="100" valign="top">Sidebar</td>
  </tr>
</table>
```

Flexible and Fixed Table Widths

The examples in the section above use a percentage table width of 80%. This creates a **flexible-width table** that the browser stretches to take up 80% of the browser window regardless of the screen resolution or window size. Review the table page layout examples in the student files (Chapter8/tables). In these examples, the columns used for navigation or sidebars are configured with a fixed width. The table cells used for the banner and main content are not configured with a width—this will cause the browser to stretch these cells to fill the available space. This provides a pleasing look on most browsers at most screen resolutions.

You do not have to use 80% for the percentage width. A table width set to 100% is used when you want the page to fill the entire browser window. See http://cdw.com for an example of a page configured in this manner.

You can also use a fixed value for a table width. This will provide a more consistent look across different browsers and platforms. Often the **fixed-width table** is centered on the page. The GameStop site, http://www.gamestop.com, uses this technique with a width set to 945 pixels. The content is displayed in the center of the browser window with a balanced margin of white background on either side.

At this point you should have a basic understanding of the use of tables on Web pages. The best way to learn is to practice. Why not create a few experimental pages of your own?

HANDS-ON PRACTICE 8.3

You will work with the Chapter 4 Trillium Web site you created in Hands-On Practice 4.5. Create a new folder called trilliumch8table and copy the contents of the Chapter4/4.5 folder found in the student files. You will create an alternate version of the home page that uses a table for the page layout. Launch Notepad or another text editor and open the index.html page from your trilliumch8table folder. Save the file as newindex.html. Your page will look similar to the one shown in Figure 8.24.

Figure 8.24
The Trillium Home page before changes

In Notepad, you will modify this page so that it uses a table for layout. See Figure 8.19 for a layout sketch containing a top banner row that spans three columns and a second row with three columns: navigation area, spacer, and main content. The sample page is shown in Figure 8.25 (shown also in the color insert section).

Compare it with the previous version of index.html page shown in Figure 8.24. The content is very similar but the pages look quite different! The table layout with vertical navigation creates visually separate areas. The page still uses the embedded style sheet.

Figure 8.25
New index.html using a table for layout

The page content has been moved into a table. The XHTML code for the table follows:

```
<table border="0" width="80%">
  <tr>
    <td colspan="3"><h1>This is the banner area</h1></td>
  </tr>
  <tr>
    <td width="120" valign="top">Place Navigation here</td>
    <td width="10"> </td>
    <td>Page content goes here</td>
  </tr>
</table>
```

The layout of the new version of the home page is configured as follows:

- The table has `border`, `cellspacing`, and `cellpadding` set to 0; and a width of 80%.
- The background color on the table cell used for the banner area is set to #d5edb3.
- The background color on the table cell that contains the main navigation is set to #5c743d.
- The `summary` table attribute is set to the value "" since the table configures the page layout.

Move the page contents into the table as indicated below:

- Replace `This is the banner area` with the logo image trilliumlogo.gif. Remove the `<h1>` tags that surround the logo image.
- Replace `Place navigation here` with the `div` that contains the navigation images.
- Replace `Page content goes here` with the remaining code for the page. After making these modifications, save the newindex.html page and test it in a browser. Your page should look similar to the one shown in Figure 8.25. Compare your work to the sample in the student files (Chapter8/8.3/newindex.html).

Are you surprised at the way the content of the Web page was transformed just by using a table page layout and some color? While configuring page layout using CSS is a more modern and preferred method, many current Web sites are designed with table-based page layouts. Later on in the chapter you'll explore using CSS to configure properties of XHTML tables. In the next section, you'll get some practice coding nested tables.

Nested Tables

Recall that tables have two common uses on Web pages—to organize information and to format the page layout. Figure 8.26 shows a Web page that uses two tables—the school history table used in Figure 8.18 and the page layout table from Figure 8.19.

The technique used to nest a table within another is to place the interior table within a table cell (`<td>`) of the exterior table. Sample code for this type of table nesting follows. Examine the source code of the Web page shown in Figure 8.26 in the student files (Chapter8/tables/table4.html).

Figure 8.26
The school history table is nested inside the page layout table

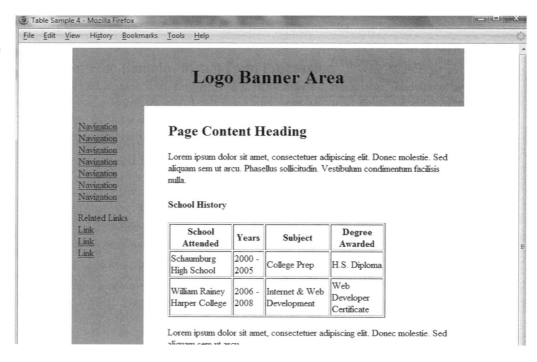

```
<table width="80%" border="0" cellpadding="10" cellspacing="0"
align="center">
  <tr bgcolor="#9999cc">
    <td colspan="3"><h1 align="center">Logo Banner Area</h1></td>
  </tr>
  <tr>
    <td width="100" valign="top" bgcolor="#9999cc">Navigation</td>
    <td width="10"> </td>
    <td valign="top"><h2>Page Content Heading</h2>
      <h4>School History</h4>
      <table width="90%" border="1" title="Educational Background"
      summary="This table lists my educational background
      including school attended and subject (column headings).
      Schaumburg High School is presented first. Harper College is
        presented second.">
        <tr>
          <th>School Attended</th>
          <th>Subject</th>
        </tr>
        <tr>
          <td>Schaumburg High School</td>
          <td>College Prep</td>
        </tr>
        <tr>
          <td>William Rainey Harper College</td>
          <td>Internet &amp; Web Development</td>
        </tr>
      </table>
    </td>
  </tr>
</table>
```

Use this technique when a Web page layout is configured with a table and you also want to use a table to further organize information on the page. Be careful to nest tables only when needed because **nested tables** can slow the browser display of Web pages. When designing a page with nested tables it is helpful to sketch your page on paper before hand-coding. You can nest more than one set of tables inside one another.

When HTML was developed it was not intended to be a page layout language—the table element was intended to display tabular data and to organize information. Disadvantages to using multiple levels of nested tables on a Web page include complicated and difficult to read source code (resulting in a larger .html file size and a slower browser display). Some browsers, such as Netscape, have difficulty displaying complicated nested tables. Even with these disadvantages, tables are still widely used for page layout.

Legacy Alert.   Although page layout tables will continue to be used on the Web for many years, a newer and preferred design technique uses CSS to configure Web page layouts instead of tables. That is the reason why some of the attributes used with `<table>` (align and bgcolor), `<tr>` (bgcolor), and `<td>` (bgcolor, width) elements are deprecated. Throughout most of this textbook, you've been using CSS to configure page layout. There are advantages to using CSS—easier-to-read source code, smaller

.html file sizes, and more efficient display by browsers that support this technology. Today's Web developers must be aware of both legacy page layout coding techniques (such as tables), and newer techniques such as CSS. In the next section you'll explore using CSS to configure properties associated with table elements.

CHECKPOINT 8.2

1. Describe a reason to use a percentage width for a table that configures a Web page layout. Provide an example of a page that uses this technique.

2. Describe a reason to use a fixed pixel width for a table that configures a Web page layout. Provide an example of a page that uses this technique.

3. True or False? Tables can be nested within other tables.

8.3 Using CSS to Style a Table

Earlier in this chapter you used XHTML attributes such as `align`, `width`, `cellpadding`, `cellspacing`, and `bgcolor` to configure the display of a table. In this section you'll explore using CSS to replace the functionality of these attributes. Table 8.1 lists corresponding CSS properties with XHTML attributes used to style tables. These properties are also described in Appendix C.

Table 8.1 CSS properties used to style tables

XHTML Attribute	CSS Property

align	To align a table, configure the `width` and `margin` properties for the `table` selector. For example, to center a table:
	
	`table { width: 75%;`
	`        margin: auto; }`
	
	To align items within table cells:
	
	`text-align`

width	width
height	height
cellpadding	padding
cellspacing	To configure the table cells to share a common border and eliminate the default space between table cells configure the `border-collapse` property for the `table` selector. For example: `table { border-collapse: collapse; }`
bgcolor	background-color
valign	vertical-align
border, bordercolor	border, border-style

HANDS-ON PRACTICE 8.4

In this Hands-On Practice you will code CSS style rules to configure an informational table on a Web page. Create a new folder named trilliumtableCSS. Copy the following files from the Chapter8/starters folder to your trilliumtableCSS folder: myservices.html, trilliumbanner.jpg, and trilliumbullet.gif files. We'll use embedded styles for ease of editing and testing your page. Display the myservices.html file in a browser; the file should look similar to the one shown in Figure 8.17. Launch Notepad or another text editor and open the myservices.html file from your trilliumtableCSS folder. Locate the opening `<table>` tag as follows:

```
<table border="1" width="75%" align="center" cellpadding="5"
cellspacing="0">
```

Notice that the attributes configure the `border`, `width`, `alignment`, `cellpadding`, and `cellspacing` of the table. Delete the attributes from the `<table>` tag. You will code CSS to replace the functionality of these attributes.

1. Configure the `table` selector. Locate the embedded styles in the header section of the Web page. Add a style rule for the `table` selector in this area that configures the table to be centered, have a border, and a width of 75%.

```
table { border: 1px solid #5c743d;
        width: 75%;
        margin: auto; }
```

Save the file and display your page in a browser. The table area will look similar to the one shown in Figure 8.27. Notice that this configures a border surrounding the entire table but not surrounding each table cell.

Figure 8.27
The border outlines the table

Web Site Design	Whether your needs are large or small, Trillium can get your company on the Web!
Interactive Animation	Multimedia training and marketing animations are our specialty.
E-Commerce Solutions	Trillium offers quick and easy entry into the e-commerce marketplace.
Usability Studies	Trillium can assess the usability of your current site and suggest improvements.

2. Configure the `td` and `th` selectors. Add a style rule that configures a border and padding.

```
td, th { border: 1px solid #5c743d;
         padding: 5px; }
```

Save the file and display your page in a browser. The table area should look similar to the one shown in Figure 8.28. Each table cell is now outlined with a border.

Figure 8.28
CSS configures border and padding for each table cell

Web Site Design	Whether your needs are large or small, Trillium can get your company on the Web!
Interactive Animation	Multimedia training and marketing animations are our specialty.
E-Commerce Solutions	Trillium offers quick and easy entry into the e-commerce marketplace.
Usability Studies	Trillium can assess the usability of your current site and suggest improvements.

3. Notice the empty space between the table cells borders. The **border-collapse property** can be used to eliminate this space and "collapse" the table border. Add a style rule with the `border-collapse` property to the table selector as shown below.

```
table { border: 1px solid #5c743d;
        width: 75%;
        margin: auto;
        border-collapse: collapse;
}
```

Save the file and display your page in a browser. The table area should look similar to the one shown in Figure 8.29.

Web Site Design	Whether your needs are large or small, Trillium can get your company on the Web!
Interactive Animation	Multimedia training and marketing animations are our specialty.
E-Commerce Solutions	Trillium offers quick and easy entry into the e-commerce marketplace.
Usability Studies	Trillium can assess the usability of your current site and suggest improvements.

4. Let's experiment with a slightly different design that uses background colors for the rows instead of cell borders. Modify the style rules, configuring the `td` and `th` selectors to have padding but without configuring a border.

```
td, th { padding:5px; }
```

Create a new class called `altrow` that sets a background color.

```
.altrow { background-color:#d5edb3; }
```

Modify the `<tr>` elements in the XHTML: assign the first and third `<tr>` elements to the `altrow` class.

Display your page in a browser. The table area should look similar to the one shown in Figure 8.30.

Web Site Design	Whether your needs are large or small, Trillium can get your company on the Web!
Interactive Animation	Multimedia training and marketing animations are our specialty.
E-Commerce Solutions	Trillium offers quick and easy entry into the e-commerce marketplace.
Usability Studies	Trillium can assess the usability of your current site and suggest improvements.

Notice how the background color of the alternate rows adds subtle interest to the Web page. Compare your work with the sample located in the student files (Chapter8/8.4/myservices.html). In this Hands-On Practice you configured the display of an XHTML table using CSS. You'll see this coding technique used increasingly in the future.

CHAPTER SUMMARY

This chapter introduces both the XHTML techniques used to code tables to organize information and configure page layout and the CSS properties that configure the display of tables on Web pages. As you use these skills to design Web pages, keep in mind that while you'll see many examples of table page layout on the Web, configuring page layout with CSS is the preferred method.

Visit the textbook Web site at http://www.webdevfoundations.net for examples, the links listed in this chapter, and updated information.

Key Terms

`<caption>`	border-collapse property	headers attribute
`<table>`	cell	nested tables
`<td>`	cellpadding attribute	rowspan attribute
`<th>`	cellspacing attribute	summary attribute
`<tr>`	colspan attribute	title attribute
align attribute	fixed-width table	vertical-align property
border attribute	flexible-width table	valign attribute

Review Questions

Multiple Choice

1. Which XHTML attribute specifies the distance between the edges of each cell?

   a. cellpad

   b. cellpadding

   c. cellspacing

   d. cellborder

2. Which XHTML attribute specifies the distance between the cell text and the cell border?

   a. cellpad

   b. cellpadding

   c. cellspacing

   d. cellborder

3. Which XHTML tag pair is used to start and end a table?

   a. `<td>` `</td>`

   b. `<tr>` `</tr>`

   c. `<table>` `</table>`

   d. none of the above

4. Which XHTML element uses a border attribute to display a table with a border?

   a. `<td>`

   b. `<tr>`

   c. `<table>`

   d. `<tableborder>`

5. Which XHTML tag pair is used to specify table headings?

   a. `<td> </td>`

   b. `<th> </th>`

   c. `<head> </head>`

   d. none of the above

6. Which XHTML attribute specifies the background color of a table?

   a. `background`

   b. `bgcolor`

   c. `background-color`

   d. none of the above

7. Which XHTML tag pair is used to begin and end a table row?

   a. `<td> </td>`

   b. `<tr> </tr>`

   c. `<table> </table>`

   d. none of the above

8. Which of the following are common uses of tables on Web pages?

   a. configuring the layout of an entire page

   b. organizing information

   c. forming hyperlinks

   d. both a and b

9. Which CSS property specifies the background color of a table?

   a. `background`

   b. `bgcolor`

   c. `background-color`

   d. none of the above

Fill in the Blank

10. The CSS _____ property can be used to configure the color and width of a table border.

11. The _____ attribute specifies the vertical alignment of the contents of a cell in a table.

12. A table with a width set to 600 pixels will look _____ on a monitor with resolution set to 640×480 than on a monitor with resolution set to 1024×768.

13. _____ is an attribute of the `<table>` element that provides accessibility.

14. _____ is a CSS property that can be used to configure the padding of table cells.

Short Answer

15. Explain why it is a good practice to use CSS to configure page layout instead of an XHTML table.

Apply Your Knowledge

1. Predict the Result. Draw and write a brief description of the Web page that will be created with the following XHTML code:

```
<?xml version="1.0" encoding="UTF-8"?>
<!DOCTYPE html PUBLIC "-//W3C//DTD XHTML 1.0 Transitional//EN"
  "http://www.w3.org/TR/xhtml1/DTD/xhtml1-transitional.dtd">
<html xmlns="http://www.w3.org/1999/xhtml">
<head>
<title>Predict the Result</title>
</head>
<body>
  <table border="0" bgcolor="#cccccc" width="80%" align="center">
    <tr>
      <td bgcolor="#0000FF" colspan="3">
      <h1><font color="#FFFFFF">Trillium Media Design</font></h1>
      </td>
    </tr>
```

```
        <tr>
          <td width="150">
            <p> Home<br /><a href="about.html">About</a><br />
            <a href="services.html">Services</a><br />
            <a href="products.html">Products</a></p>
          </td>
          <td>  
          </td>
          <td>
            <p>More than just another web development firm, Trillium
Media Design strives to celebrate creativity and the efficient
flow of information.</p>
            <p> We aren&#39;t satisfied until every site we build is
the best in its class.</p>
          </td>
        </tr>
    </table>
</body>
</html>
```

2. **Fill in the Missing Code.** This Web page should have a table with a background color of #cccccc and a border. Some CSS properties and values, indicated by "_", are missing. Fill in the missing code.

```
<?xml version="1.0" encoding="UTF-8"?>
<!DOCTYPE html PUBLIC "-//W3C//DTD XHTML 1.0 Transitional//EN"
    "http://www.w3.org/TR/xhtml1/DTD/xhtml1-transitional.dtd">
<html xmlns="http://www.w3.org/1999/xhtml">
<head>
<title>CircleSoft Web Design</title>
<style type="text/css">
table { "_":"_";
        "_":"_";
}
</style>
</head>
<body>
<h1>CircleSoft Web Design</h1>
<table>
  <caption>Contact Information</caption>
  <tr>
    <th>Name</th>
    <th>Phone</th>
  </tr>
  <tr>
    <td>Mike Circle</td>
    <td>920-555-5555</td>
  </tr>
</table>
</body>
</html>
```

3. Find the Error. Why doesn't the table information display in the order it was coded?

```
<?xml version="1.0" encoding="UTF-8"?>
<!DOCTYPE html PUBLIC "-//W3C//DTD XHTML 1.0 Transitional//EN"
  "http://www.w3.org/TR/xhtml1/DTD/xhtml1-transitional.dtd">
<html xmlns="http://www.w3.org/1999/xhtml">
<head>
<title>CircleSoft Web Design</title>
</head>
<body>
<h1>CircleSoft Web Design</h1>
<table>
  <caption>Contact Information</caption>
  <tr>
    <th>Name</th>
    <th>Phone</th>
  </tr>
  <tr>
    <tr>Mike Circle</td>
    <td>920-555-5555</td>
  </tr>
</table>
</body>
</html>
```

Hands-On Exercises

1. Write the XHTML for a two-column table that contains the names of your friends and their birthdays. The first row of the table should span two columns and contain the following heading: Birthday List. Include at least two people in your table.

2. Write the XHTML for a three-column table to describe the courses you are taking this semester. The columns should contain the course number, course name, and instructor name. The first row of the table should use th tags and contain descriptive headings for the columns.

3. Write the XHTML for table with three rows, two columns and no border. The cell in the first column of each row will contain one of the following terms: HTML, XML, and XHTML. The corresponding cell in the second column of each row will contain a definition of the term. Configure alternating rows to use the background color #CCCCCC.

4. Use CSS to configure a table that has a border around both the entire table and the table cells. Write the XHTML to create a table with three rows and two columns. The cell in the first column of each row will contain one of the following terms: HTML, XML, and XHTML. The corresponding cell in the second column of each row will contain a definition of the term.

5. Think of one of your favorite quotes by someone you admire. Write the XHTML code for a table to display the person's name in a heading, their quote in a paragraph, and an absolute link to a Web site about them.

6. Modify the table you created in Hands-On Exercise 5 to be centered on the page, use a background color of #CCCC99, and display text in Arial or the browser default sans-serif font. Configure this table using CSS.

7. Create a Web page about your favorite movie that uses a two-column table containing details about the movie. The table should have no border and use background color to organize the information. Include the following in the table:

   - Title of the movie
   - Director or producer
   - Leading actor
   - Leading actress
   - Rating (R, PG-13, PG, G, NR)
   - A brief description of the movie
   - An absolute link to a review about the movie

   Place an e-mail link to yourself on the Web page. Save the page as movie8.html. Hand in printouts of the source code (print in Notepad) and the browser display of your page to your instructor.

8. Create a Web page that uses a table and describes two organizations that perform work related to Internet/Web standards and guidelines (see Chapter 1). Place the information in a table that comprises at least three columns and three rows. Include links to the Web site of each organization. Place an e-mail link to yourself on the Web page. Save the page as organization.html. Hand in printouts of both the source code (print in Notepad) and the browser display of your page to your instructor.

9. Create a Web page about your favorite music CD that uses a four-column table. The column headings should be as follows:

   - **Group:** Place the name of the group and the names of its principal members in this column.
   - **Tracks:** List the title of each music track or song.
   - **Year:** List the year the CD was recorded.
   - **Links:** Place at least two absolute links to sites about the group in this column.

   Include an e-mail link to yourself on the Web page. Save the page as band8.html. Hand in printouts of both the source code (print in Notepad) and the browser display of your page to your instructor.

10. Create a Web page about your favorite recipe. Organize the ingredients and directions in a single table. Use two columns for the ingredients. Use a row that spans two columns to contain the instructions for creating your culinary delight. Save the page as recipe8.html. Hand in printouts of both the source code (print in Notepad) and the browser display of your page to your instructor.

Web Research

Search the Web and find a Web page configured with one or more XHTML tables. Print the browser view of the page. Print out the source code of the Web page. (*Hint*: To print the source code, display the page using Internet Explorer 7, and select Page, View Source. Notepad will launch and display the page. Select File and Print.) On the printout, highlight or circle the tags related to tables. On a separate sheet of paper create some XHTML notes by listing the tags and attributes related to tables found on your sample page, along with a brief description of their purpose. Hand in the browser view of the page, source code printout, and your XHTML notes page to your instructor.

Focus on Web Design

Good artists view and analyze many paintings. Good writers read and evaluate many books. Similarly, good Web designers view and scrutinize many Web pages. Surf the Web and find two Web pages, one that is appealing to you and one that is unappealing to you. Print out each page. Create a Web page that answers the following questions for each of your examples:

    a. What is the URL of the Web site?

    b. Does this page use tables? If so, for what purpose—page layout, organization of information, or another reason?

    c. Does this page use CSS? If so, for what purpose—page layout, text and color configuration, or another reason?

    d. Is this page appealing or unappealing? List three reasons for your answer.

    e. If this page is unappealing, what would you do to improve it?

Open your file in Notepad and print the source code for the page. Display your page in a browser and print the page. Hand in both printouts to your instructor.

WEB SITE CASE STUDY
Using Tables

Each of the following case studies continues throughout most of the text. This chapter incorporates an XHTML table in the case study Web sites.

JavaJam Coffee House

See Chapter 2 for an introduction to the JavaJam Coffee House Case Study. Figure 2.26 shows a site map for JavaJam. The pages were created in earlier chapters. You will use the existing Web site in the javajamcss folder (unless your instructor specifies otherwise) for this case study. You will modify the menu page (menu.html) to display information in an XHTML table. You will use CSS to style the table. You have two tasks:

    1. Add style rules to the javajam.css file that will configure the new table.

    2. Modify the menu.html page to use a table to display information. Refer to Figure 8.31.

Hands-On Practice Case

    1. Configure the CSS. Modify the external style sheet, javajam.css. Review Figure 8.31 and note the menu descriptions, which are coded in an XHTML table. Add style rules to the javajam.css external style sheet to configure a table that is centered,

Figure 8.31
Menu page with table

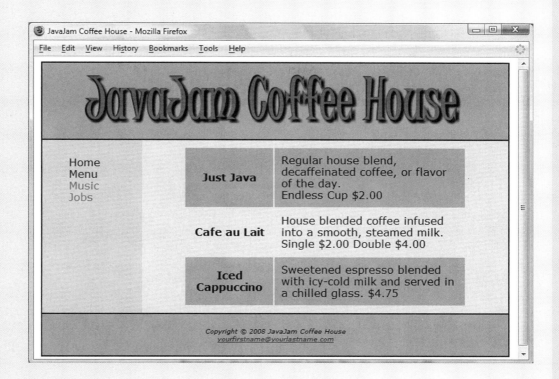

td and th selectors with 10 pixels of padding, and displays a background color of #ccaa66 in alternate rows (use a class). Save the javajam.css file.

2. **Modify the Menu Page.** Edit the Menu file (menu.html) in Notepad. The menu descriptions are configured with a definition list. Replace the definition list with a table that has three rows and two columns. Use <th> and <td> elements where appropriate.

Save your page and test it in a browser. If the page does not display as you intended, review your work, validate the CSS, validate the XHTML, modify as needed, and test again.

Fish Creek Animal Hospital

See Chapter 2 for an introduction to the Fish Creek Animal Hospital Case Study. Figure 2.30 shows a site map for Fish Creek. The pages were created in earlier chapters. You will use the existing Web site in the fishcreekcss folder (unless your instructor specifies otherwise). You will modify the services page (services.html) to display information in an XHTML table. You will use CSS to style the table. You have two tasks:

1. Add style rules to the fishcreek.css file that will configure the new table.
2. Modify the Services page (services.html) to use a table to display information. Refer to Figure 8.32.

Hands-On Practice Case

1. **Configure the CSS.** Modify the external style sheet, fishcreek.css. Review Figure 8.32 and note the services descriptions, which are coded in an XHTML table. Add style rules to the fishcreek.css external style sheet as indicated:

Figure 8.32
Services page with table

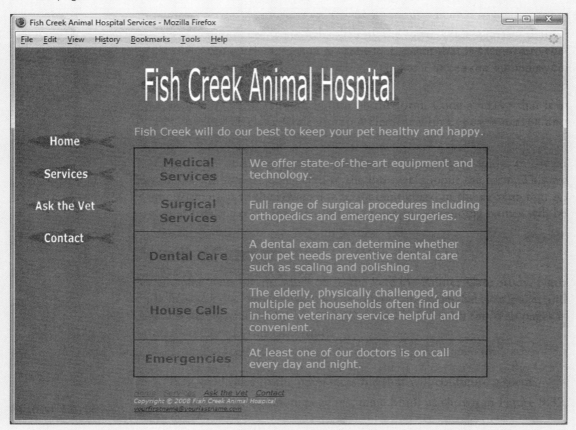

a. Configure a table that has a solid, dark blue, 2 pixel border.

b. Configure the borders in the table to collapse.

c. Configure `td` and `th` selectors with 10 pixels of padding and a solid, dark blue, 1 pixel border.

Save the fishcreek.css file.

2. **Modify the Services Page.** Edit the Services file (services.html) in Notepad. The services descriptions are configured with an unordered list. Replace the unordered list with a table that has five rows and two columns. Use `<th>` and `<td>` elements where appropriate. *Hint*: Assign the `<th>` element to the category class.

Save your page and test it in a browser.

If the page does not display as you intended, review your work, validate the CSS, validate the XHTML, modify as needed, and test again.

Pete the Painter

See Chapter 2 for an introduction to the Pete the Painter Case Study. Figure 2.34 shows a site map for Pete the Painter. The pages were created in earlier chapters. You will use the existing Web site in the paintercss folder (unless your instructor specifies otherwise).

You will modify the services page (services.html) to display information in an XHTML table. You will use CSS to style the table. You have two tasks:

1. Add style rules to the painter.css file that will configure the new table.

2. Modify the services.html file to use a table to display information. Refer to Figure 8.33.

Figure 8.33
Services page with table

Hands-On Practice Case

1. **Configure the CSS.** Modify the external style sheet, painter.css. Review Figure 8.33 and note the services descriptions, which are coded in an XHTML table. Add a style rule to the painter.css external style sheet that configures a class named `service`. The `service` class has a background color (#336633), text color (#ffffff), Georgia, Times New Roman, or serif font typeface, bold font, 3 pixels of padding, and a solid, black, 1 pixel bottom border. Save the painter.css file.

2. **Modify the Services Page.** Edit the services file (services.html) in Notepad. The names of the services are contained in <h4> elements. The descriptions of the services are each contained in a `div` assigned to the `desc` class. You will change the code to display the information using a table that has eight rows and one column with each service name and each service description is in its own row. Each table row (<tr> tag pair) contains one <td> tag pair. As you code the table, assign the <td> elements that contain the service names to the service class.

Save your page and test it in a browser.

If the page does not display as you intended, review your work, validate the CSS, validate the XHTML, modify as needed, and test again.

Prime Properties

See Chapter 2 for an introduction to the Prime Properties Case Study. Figure 2.38 shows a site map for Prime Properties. The pages were created in earlier chapters. You will use the existing Web site in the primecss folder (unless your instructor specifies otherwise). You will modify the listings page (listings.html) to display information in an XHTML table. You will use CSS to style the table. You have two tasks:

1. Add style rules to the prime.css file that will configure the new table.
2. Modify the listings.html page to use a table to display information. Refer to Figure 8.34.

Figure 8.34
Listings page with tables

Hands-On Practice Case

1. **Configure the CSS.** Modify the external style sheet, prime.css. Review Figure 8.34 and note the property listing information, which is coded in two XHTML tables. Add style rules to the prime.css external style sheet to configure the following:

   a. A table with a background color (#ffffff0) and 5 pixels of padding

   b. A th selector with left-aligned text in a green color (#006600)

   c. A td selector that is aligned vertically to the top

   Save the prime.css file.

2. **Modify the Listings Page.** Edit the Listings file (listings.html) in Notepad. The listings information currently uses the <h4>, image, paragraph and unordered lists elements. You will reconfigure this area with two tables—one for each real estate listing. Each table will have two rows. Refer to Figure 8.34. The first row in each table consists of one table cell that spans two columns—containing the real estate listing name. The second row in each table consists of two table cells. The first table cell in this row contains the image (remove the floatleft class from the image element). The second table cell contains the paragraph and unordered list.

Save your page and test it in a browser.

If the page does not display as you intended, review your work, validate the CSS, validate the XHTML, modify as needed, and test again.

Web Project

See Chapters 5 and 6 for an introduction to the Web Project case. You will modify the design of one of the pages to display information in an XHTML table. Use CSS to style the table.

Hands-On Practice Case

1. Choose one of your project Web pages to modify. Sketch a design of the table you plan to create. Decide on borders, background color, padding, alignments, and so on.

2. Modify your project's external CSS file (project.css) to configure the table (and table cells) as needed.

3. Update your chosen Web page and add the XHTML code for a table.

Save and test the page. Modify both the Web page and the project.css file as needed. Test and modify until you have achieved the look you want.

XHTML Forms

Chapter Objectives   In this chapter, you will learn how to ...

- Describe common uses of forms on Web pages
- Create forms on Web pages using the `<form>`, `<input />`, `<textarea>`, and `<select>` elements
- Create forms that provide additional accessibility features using the `accesskey` and `tabindex` attributes
- Associate form elements and element groups using `<label>`, `<fieldset>`, and `<legend>`

- Create custom image buttons and use the `<button>` element
- Use CSS to style a form
- Describe the features and common uses of CGI
- Invoke CGI server-side processing to handle form data
- Find free CGI resources on the Web

Forms are used for many purposes all over the Web.

They are used by search engines to accept keywords and by online stores to process e-commerce shopping carts. Web sites use forms to help with a variety of functions—accepting visitor feedback, encouraging visitors to send a news story to a friend or colleague, collecting e-mail addresses for a newsletter, and accepting order information. This chapter introduces a very powerful tool for Web developers—forms that accept information from Web page visitors.

337

9.1 Overview of Forms

Every time you use a search engine, place an order, or join an online mailing list, you use a **form**. A form is an XHTML element that contains and organizes other objects—such as text boxes, check boxes, and buttons—that can accept information from Web site visitors.

For example, look at Yahoo!'s search form shown in Figure 9.1. You may have used this many times but never thought about how it works. The form is quite simple; it contains just two elements: the text box that accepts the keywords used in the search, and the search button that submits the form and gets the search started.

Figure 9.1
The search form on Yahoo!'s home page contains a box to enter text and a button. Reproduced with permission of Yahoo! Inc. ©2006 Yahoo! Inc. Yahoo! and the Yahoo! logo are trademarks of Yahoo! Inc.

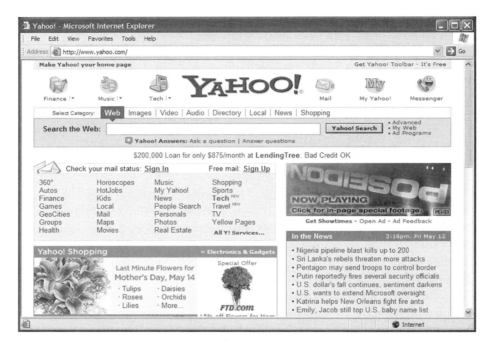

Figure 9.2 shows a more detailed form, used to enter shipping information at irs.gov. This form uses text boxes to accept information such as name and address. Select lists (sometimes called drop-down boxes) are used to capture information with a limited number of correct values, such as state and country information. When a visitor clicks the continue button, the form information is submitted and the ordering process continues. Whether a form is used to search for Web pages or to order a publication, the form alone cannot do all the processing. The form needs to invoke a program or script on the server in order to search a database or record an order. There are usually two components of a form:

1. The XHTML form itself, which is the Web page user interface

2. The server-side processing, called **Common Gateway Interface** (**CGI**), which works with the form data and sends e-mail, writes to a text file, updates a database, or performs some other type of processing on the server

Figure 9.2
This form accepts information needed to place an order

> **Shipping Address Entry**
>
> Name: [_____]
>
> Company: [_____]
>
> Address Line 1: [_____]
>
> Address Line 2: [_____]
>
> City: [_____]
>
> State: [v]
>
> Zip Code: [____] - [____]
>
> Country: [United States   v]
>
> [Continue] [Clear All]

9.2 XHTML—Using Forms

Now that you have a basic understanding of what forms do, let's focus on the XHTML code to create a form. The **<form>** element, **<input />** element, and their attributes will be introduced while you create a sample form page. Once you've experimented a little with this form, you will be ready for a detailed discussion of the elements and attributes.

HANDS-ON PRACTICE 9.1

In this Hands-On Practice you will experiment with a form. Create a new folder called trilliumch9 and copy the files index.html, services.html, contact.html, trillium.css, trilliumbanner.jpg, and trilliumbullet.gif files from the student files Chapter9/starters folder. You will add a form to the contact page (contact.html). The form, shown in Figure 9.3, is very simple and only contains two elements: a text box to accept the visitor's e-mail address, and a submit button.

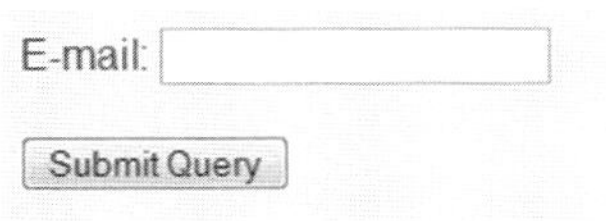

Figure 9.3
The initial version of the form

E-mail: [_____]

[Submit Query]

The form will be added to the contact.html page, as shown in Figure 9.4.

Figure 9.4
The contact page

Let's get started. Launch Notepad and open the contact.html file. Add a paragraph below the `<h2>` element that says "Complete this form and a Trillium representative will contact you."

You are ready to configure the form area. The first XHTML in a form is the `<form>` element. Place your cursor on a blank line under the paragraph you just added and type in a `<form>` tag as follows:

```
<form>
```

As you read through the chapter you will find that a number of attributes can be used with the `<form>` element. In your first form, we are using the minimal XHTML needed to create the form.

To create the area for the visitor's e-mail address to be entered, type the following XHTML:

```
E-mail: <input type="text" name="CustEmail" id="CustEmail" />
<br /><br />
```

This places the text "E-mail:" in front of the text box used to enter the visitor's e-mail address. The `<input />` tag has a `type` attribute with the value of text that causes the browser to display a text box. The `name` attribute assigns the name `CustEmail` to the information entered into the text box (the value) and could be used by server-side processing. The `id` attribute is included for forward compatibility with XHTML. Since the `<input />` tag is a self-contained tag, it needs to be closed with `/>`. The `<br />` elements configure line breaks.

Now you are ready to add the submit button to the form. The XHTML code is as follows:

```
<input type="submit" />
```

This causes the browser to display a button with the default value of "Submit Query." Finally, you are ready to enter the closing form tag, `</form>`. A sample with all of the XHTML for the form follows:

```
<form>
E-mail: <input type="text" name="CustEmail" id="CustEmail" />
<br /><br />
<input type="submit" />
</form>
```

Save your contact.html file. Test your page in a browser. It should look similar to the page shown in Figure 9.4.

You can compare your work with the solution found on the student files in the Chapter9/9.1 folder. Try entering some information into your form. Try clicking the button. Don't worry if the form redisplays but nothing seems to happen when you click the button—you haven't configured this form to work with any server-side processing. Connecting forms to server-side processing is demonstrated in the next Hands-On Practice. First, let's take a detailed look at the elements and attributes used to create forms.

The Form Element

The `<form>` tag specifies the beginning of a form area on a Web page. Its closing tag, `</form>`, specifies the ending of a form area on a Web page. There can be multiple forms on a Web page, but they cannot be nested inside each other. The `<form>` tag can be configured with attributes that specify what server-side program or file will process the form, how the form information will be sent to the server, and the name of the form. Attributes such as `name`, `method`, and `action` are used to configure these options. These attributes are listed in Table 9.1. The most commonly used attributes are shown in bold.

For example, to configure a form with the name of `order`, using the `post` method, and invoking a script called `order.php` in a folder called `cgi-bin` on your Web server, the XHTML is as follows:

```
<form name="order" method="post" id="order"
  action="cgi-bin/order.php">
form elements go here . . .
</form>
```

FAQ

What's the difference between the `get` and `post` methods?

You should usually use **post** as the value of the method on your forms. When you use get as the value the form data is appended to the end of the URL. This URL area (called the HTTP_REFERER) can be captured and stored in Web site logs. You probably don't want your visitor's form data showing up in someone else's Web server logs. This makes the **get** method much less private than the post message, which sends the form data in the entity body of the HTTP Request.

Table 9.1 `<form>` tag attributes

Attribute	Values	Purpose
`action`	When used to invoke server-side processing, the value should be a valid file name on a Web server. This is often a PHP script (.php extension), a Microsoft Active Server Pages (.asp extension), or a Sun JavaServer Pages (.jsp extension) file. When used to send an e-mail, the value should be `mailto:` followed by a valid e-mail address.	This attribute is optional. It is commonly used to specify what server-side program or script will process your form data using CGI. Although not recommended, this attribute can also be used to specify an e-mail address that the form information will be sent to. If no `action` attribute is present, the Web page containing the form is requested and redisplayed by the browser.
`id`	Alphanumeric, no spaces. The value must be unique and not used for other `id` values on the same XHTML document.	This attribute is optional. It provides a unique identifier for the form.
`method`	`get`	This attribute is optional, but defaults to a value of `get` if omitted. The value of `get` causes the form data to be appended to the URL and sent to the Web server.
	`post`	The post method is more private and transmits the form data in the body of the HTTP response. This method is preferred by the W3C.
`name`	Alphanumeric, no spaces, begins with a letter. Choose a form name value that is descriptive but short. For example, OrderForm is better than Form1 or WidgetsRUsOrderForm.	This attribute is optional. It names the form so that it can be easily accessed by client-side scripting languages, such as JavaScript, to edit and verify the form information before the server-side processing is invoked.

How can I send form information in an e-mail?

Forms usually need to invoke some type of server-side processing to perform functions such as sending e-mail, writing to text files, updating databases, and so on. Another option is to set up a form to send information using the e-mail program configured to work with the Web page visitor's browser. In what is sometimes called using a mailto: URL, the `<form>` tag is coded to use your e-mail address in the `action` attribute:

```
<form method="post" action="mailto:lsnblf@yahoo.com">
```

When a form is used in this manner the Web visitor will see a warning message. The warning message presents a nonprofessional image and is not the best way to inspire trust and confidence in your Web site or business.

Be aware that information sent in e-mail messages is not secure. Sensitive information, such as credit card numbers, should not be transmitted using e-mail. See Chapter 12 for information about using encryption to transmit data securely.

There are other reasons not to use the mailto: URL. For example, when people share a computer—they may not be using the default e-mail application. In this case, filling out the form is a waste of time. Even if the person using the computer also uses the default e-mail application, perhaps he or she may not want to divulge this particular e-mail address. Perhaps they have another e-mail address that is used for forms and newsletters, and do not want to waste time filling out your form. In either case, the result is an unhappy Web site visitor. So, while using the mailto: URL is easy, it does not always create the most usable Web form for your visitors. What's a Web developer to do? Use server-side processing (see Hands-On Practice 9.4) to handle form data instead of the mailto: URL.

Basic Form Elements

The purpose of a form is to gather information from a Web page visitor; form elements are the objects that accept the information. Types of form elements include text boxes, scrolling text boxes, select lists, radio buttons, check boxes, and buttons. XHTML tags that configure these form elements include the `<input />`, **`<textarea>`**, **`<select>`**, and **`<option>`** tags. Most form elements are configured with the `<input />` tag, which is self-contained. The **text box, password box, check box, radio button, scrolling text box, select list, submit button, reset button, button,** and **hidden form element fields** are introduced in the following sections.

Text Box. This form element is configured by the `<input />` tag and accepts text or numeric information such as names, e-mail addresses, phone numbers, and other text. A sample text box is shown in Figure 9.5.

Figure 9.5
The `<input />` tag with `type="text"` configures this form element

The XHTML code follows:

`E-mail: <input type="text" name="email" id="email" />`

Common text box attributes are listed in Table 9.2.

Table 9.2 Common text box attributes

Common Attributes	Values	Usage
`type`	`text`	Configures the text box.
`name`	Alphanumeric, no spaces, begins with a letter	Names the form element so that it can be easily accessed by client-side scripting languages (such as JavaScript) or by server-side processing. The name should be unique.
`id`	Alphanumeric, no spaces, begins with a letter	Provides a unique identifier for the form element.
`size`	Numeric	Configures the width of the text box as displayed by the browser. If size is omitted, the browser displays the text box with its own default size.
`maxlength`	Numeric	Configures the maximum length of data accepted by the text box.
`value`	Text or numeric characters	Assigns an initial value to the text box that is displayed by the browser. Accepts information typed in the text box. This value can be accessed by client-side scripting languages and by server-side processing.

Password Box. The `<input />` tag configures this element. The password box is similar to the text box but it accepts information that needs to be hidden as it is entered, such as a password. When the user types information in a password box, asterisks (*) are displayed instead of the characters that have been typed, as shown in Figure 9.6.

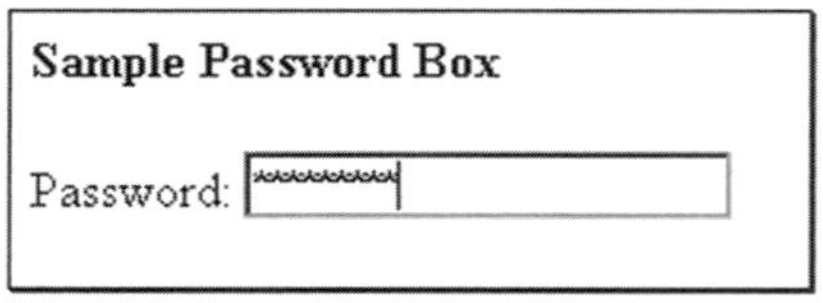

Figure 9.6
The characters secret999 were typed, but the browser displays ********* (*Note*: your browser may use a different symbol to "hide" the characters.)

```
Sample Password Box

Password: [*********]
```

This hides the information from someone looking over the shoulder of the person typing. The actual characters typed are sent to the server and the information is not really secret or hidden. See Chapter 12 for a discussion of encryption and security.

The XHTML code follows:

```
Password: <input type="password" name="myPassword"
  id="myPassword" />
```

Common password box attributes are listed in Table 9.3.

Table 9.3 Common password box attributes

Common Attributes	Values	Usage
type	password	Configures the password box.
name	Alphanumeric, no spaces, begins with a letter	Names the form element so that it can be easily accessed by client-side scripting languages or by server-side processing. The name should be unique.
id	Alphanumeric, no spaces, begins with a letter	Provides a unique identifier for the form element.
size	Numeric	Configures the width of the password box as displayed by the browser. If size is omitted, the browser displays the password box with its own default size.
maxlength	Numeric	Optional. Configures the maximum length of data accepted by the password box.
value	Text or numeric characters	Assigns an initial value to the text box that is displayed by the browser. Accepts the information typed in the password box. This value can be accessed by client-side and by server-side processing.

Check Box. This form element is configured by the `<input />` tag and allows the user to select one or more of a group of predetermined items. A sample check box is shown in Figure 9.7.

Figure 9.7
Use a check box when one or more selections is appropriate

Sample Check Box

Choose the browsers you use:
☐ Internet Explorer
☐ Netscape
☐ Opera

The XHTML code follows:

```
Choose the browsers you use:<br />
<input type="checkbox" name="IE" id="IE" value="yes" />
Internet Explorer<br />
<input type="checkbox" name="Netscape" id="Netscape" value="yes" />
Netscape<br />
<input type="checkbox" name="Opera" id="Opera" value="yes" /> Opera
```

Note that the value of all the check boxes just happened to be yes. You can set the value to be any meaningful word or phrase. The name of each check box should be unique.

Common check box attributes are listed in Table 9.4.

Table 9.4 Common check box attributes

Attribute	Values	Usage
type	checkbox	Configures the check box.
name	Alphanumeric, no spaces, begins with a letter	Names the form element so that it can be easily accessed by client-side scripting languages or by server-side processing. The name of each check box should be unique.
id	Alphanumeric, no spaces, begins with a letter	Provides a unique identifier for the form element.
checked	checked	Configures the check box to be checked by default when displayed by the browser.
value	Text or numeric characters	Assigns a value to the check box that is triggered when the check box is checked. This value can be accessed by client-side and by server-side processing.

Radio Button. The `<input />` tag configures this element. Radio buttons allow the user to select exactly one item from a group of predetermined items. Each radio button in a group is given the same name and a unique value. Because the name is the same, the elements are identified as part of a group and only one may be selected. A sample radio button group is shown in Figure 9.8.

Figure 9.8
Use radio buttons when only one choice is an appropriate response

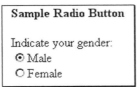

Sample Radio Button

Indicate your gender:
◉ Male
○ Female

The XHTML code follows:

```
Indicate your gender:<br />
<input type="radio" name="Gender" id="gm" value="Male"
   checked="checked" /> Male<br />
<input type="radio" name="Gender" id="gf" value="Female" /> Female
```

Notice that the name attributes all have the same value—Gender. This is what creates the group. Each radio button in the same group can be uniquely identified by its value attribute. Each radio button in the same group is configured with a different value.

Common radio button attributes are listed in Table 9.5.

Table 9.5 Common radio button attributes

Attribute	Values	Usage
type	radio	Configures the radio button.
name	Alphanumeric, no spaces, begins with a letter	Required. All radio buttons in a group must have the same name. This attribute also names the form element so that it can be easily accessed by client-side scripting languages or by server-side processing.
id	Alphanumeric, no spaces, begins with a letter	Provides a unique identifier for the form element.
checked	checked	Configures the radio button to be selected by default when displayed by the browser.
value	Text or numeric characters	Assigns a value to the radio button that is triggered when the radio button is selected. This should be a unique value for each radio button in a group. This value can be accessed by client-side and by server-side processing.

Scrolling Text Box. The <textarea> tag configures a scrolling text box. A scrolling text box is used for accepting free-form comments, questions, or descriptions. A sample scrolling text box is shown in Figure 9.9.

Figure 9.9
Scrolling text boxes accept free-form comments from Web page visitors

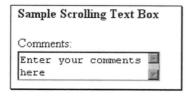

The XHTML code follows:

```
Comments:<br />
<textarea name="ordercomments" id="ordercomments" cols="40"
   rows="2">Enter your comments here</textarea>
```

Notice that the <textarea> tag is a container tag. The text that you place between the opening <textarea> and closing </textarea> will be initially displayed in the scrolling text box.

Common scrolling text box attributes are listed in Table 9.6.

Table 9.6 Common scrolling text box attributes

Common Attributes	Values	Usage
`name`	Alphanumeric, no spaces, begins with a letter	Names the form element so that it can be easily accessed by client-side scripting languages (such as JavaScript) or by server-side processing. The name should be unique.
`id`	Alphanumeric, no spaces, begins with a letter	Provides a unique identifier for the form element.
`cols`	Numeric	Configures the width in character columns of the scrolling text box. If `cols` is omitted, the browser displays the scrolling text box with its own default width.
`rows`	Numeric	Configures the height in rows of the scrolling text box. If `rows` is omitted, the browser displays the scrolling text box with its own default height.

Select List. The `<select>` container tag (along with `<option>` tags) configures a select list. This form element has several names: select list, select box, drop-down list, drop-down box, and option box. It allows the visitor to select one or more items from a list of predetermined choices. The `<option>` container tag configures the choices in a select list. Sample select lists are shown in Figures 9.10 and 9.11.

Figure 9.10
A select list with size set to **1** functions as a drop-down box when the arrow is clicked

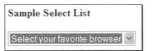

Figure 9.11
This select list has size set to **6**; since there are more than six choices, the browser displays a scroll bar

The XHTML code for Figure 9.10 follows:

```
<select size="1" name="favbrowser" id="favbrowser">
  <option selected="selected" >Select your favorite browser</option>
  <option value="Internet Explorer">Internet Explorer</option>
  <option value="Firefox">Firefox</option>
  <option value="Opera">Opera</option>
</select>
```

The XHTML code for Figure 9.11 follows:

```
<select size="6" name="jumpmenu" id="jumpmenu">
  <option value="cisdept.html">CIS Department</option>
  <option value="webdev1.html">Web Dev I</option>
  <option value="webdev2.html">Web Dev II</option>
  <option value="dreamweaver.html">Dreamweaver</option>
  <option value="ecommerce.html">E-Commerce</option>
  <option value="webmgt.html">Web Site Mgt</option>
  <option value="php.html">PHP Intro</option>
</select>
```

Common select list attributes are listed in Table 9.7.

Table 9.7 Common select list attributes

Common Attributes	Values	Usage
Select List `<select>` Tag		
name	Alphanumeric, no spaces, begins with a letter	Names the form element so that it can be easily accessed by client-side scripting languages (such as JavaScript) or by server-side processing. The name should be unique.
id	Alphanumeric, no spaces, begins with a letter	Provides a unique identifier for the form element.
size	Numeric	Configures the number of choices the browser will display. If set to 1, element functions as a drop-down list (see Figure 9.10). Scroll bars are automatically added by the browser if the number of options exceeds the space allowed.
multiple	multiple	Configures a select list to accept more than one choice. By default, only one choice can be made from a select list.
Select List `<option>` Tag		
value	Text or numeric characters	Assigns a value to the option. This value can be accessed by client-side and by server-side processing.
selected	selected	Configures an option to be initially selected when displayed by a browser.

Submit Button. This form element is configured by the `<input />` tag and is used to submit the form. It triggers the action method on the `<form>` tag and causes the browser to send the form data (the name and value pairs for each form element) to the Web server. The Web server will invoke the server-side processing program or script listed on the form's action property. A sample submit button is shown in Figure 9.12.

Figure 9.12
Clicking the submit button invokes the server-side processing configured in the action property of the `<form>` tag

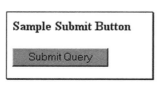

The XHTML code follows:

```
<input type="submit" />
```

Common submit button attributes are listed in Table 9.8.

Table 9.8 Common submit button attributes

Common Attributes	Values	Usage
type	submit	Configures the submit button.
name	Alphanumeric, no spaces, begins with a letter	Names the form element so that it can be easily accessed by client-side scripting languages (such as JavaScript) or by server-side processing. The name should be unique.
id	Alphanumeric, no spaces, begins with a letter	Provides a unique identifier for the form element.
value	Text or numeric characters	Configures the text displayed on the submit button. By default, the text "Submit Query" is displayed.

Reset Button. This form element is configured by the `<input />` tag and is used to reset the form fields to their initial values. A sample reset button is shown in Figure 9.13.

Figure 9.13
The reset button gives Web page visitors a chance to reset or clear their mistakes

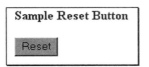

The XHTML code follows:

```
<input type="reset" />
```

Common reset button attributes are listed in Table 9.9.

Table 9.9 Common reset button attributes

Common Attributes	Values	Usage
type	reset	Configures the reset button.
name	Alphanumeric, no spaces, begins with a letter	Names the form element so that it can be easily accessed by client-side scripting languages (such as JavaScript) or by server-side processing. The name should be unique.
id	Alphanumeric, no spaces, begins with a letter	Provides a unique identifier for the form element.
value	Text or numeric characters	Configures the text displayed on the reset button. By default, the text "Reset" is displayed.

Button. This form element is configured by the `<input />` tag and offers a flexible user interface. There is no default action when the button is clicked. Form information is not sent to the Web server when this button is clicked.

This element is usually used with client-side scripting such as JavaScript, to cause some processing to occur on the client (see Chapters 11 and 14). Types of client-side processing may include calculations, edits, or other functions such as displaying a different page. A sample button is shown in Figure 9.14.

Figure 9.14
This button has no default action; it is often used with client-side scripting such as JavaScript

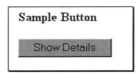

The XHTML code follows:

```
<input type="button" value="Show Details" name="myButton"
   id="myButton" />
```

Common button attributes are listed in Table 9.10.

Table 9.10 Common button attributes

Common Attributes	Values	Usage
type	button	Configures the button.
name	Alphanumeric, no spaces, begins with a letter	Names the form element so that it can be easily accessed by client-side scripting languages (such as JavaScript) or by server-side processing. The name should be unique.
id	Alphanumeric, no spaces, begins with a letter	Provides a unique identifier for the form element.
value	Text or numeric characters	Configures the text displayed on the button.

Hidden. This form element is configured by the `<input />` tag and is not displayed on the Web page. Hidden form fields can be accessed by both client-side and server-side scripting and sometimes contain information needed as the visitor moves from page to page.

The XHTML to create a hidden form element with the name `sendto` and the value of an e-mail address follows:

```
<input type="hidden" name="sendto" id="sendto"
   value="order@site.com"/>
```

Common hidden attributes are listed in Table 9.11.

Table 9.11 Common hidden attributes

Common Attributes	Values	Usage
type	hidden	Configures the hidden element.
name	Alphanumeric, no spaces, begins with a letter	Names the form element so that it can be easily accessed by client-side scripting languages (such as JavaScript) or by server-side processing. The name should be unique.
id	Alphanumeric, no spaces, begins with a letter	Provides a unique identifier for the form element.
value	Text or numeric characters	Assigns a value to the hidden element. This value can be accessed by client-side scripting languages and by server-side processing.

Why use both the name and the id attributes on the form elements?

The reason both attributes are used is for forward and backward compatibility with different versions of HTML and XHTML.

The **name** attribute is supported by both HTML and XHTML. It is used to name the form element so that it can be easily accessed by client-side scripting languages such as JavaScript or by server-side processing languages such as PHP or ASP. The value given to a **name** attribute for a form element should be unique for that form.

The **id** attribute is included for use with CSS and is supported by XHTML. The value of the **id** attribute should be unique to the entire Web page document that contains the form. Use the **id** attribute to be compatible with CSS and XHTML in the future.

Forward thinking Web developers use both the **name** and **id** attributes on their form elements. Typically, the values assigned to the **name** and **id** attribute on a particular form element are the same.

As you have seen, there are a number of form elements, each with a specific purpose. This would be a good time to visit a few Web sites and examine how they use forms. Take a look at sites such as http://yahoo.com, http://amazon.com, http://ebay.com, or one of your favorites and identify when and how they use forms and form elements.

HANDS-ON PRACTICE 9.2

In this Hands-On Practice you will modify the form you created in Hands-On Practice 9.1 (see Figure 9.3). Recall that the purpose of the form is to allow Web page visitors to request that a company representative contacts them. You will modify the form to include a reset button and to accept the customer's name, phone number, and a question or comment in addition to the e-mail address. This modified form is shown in Figure 9.15.

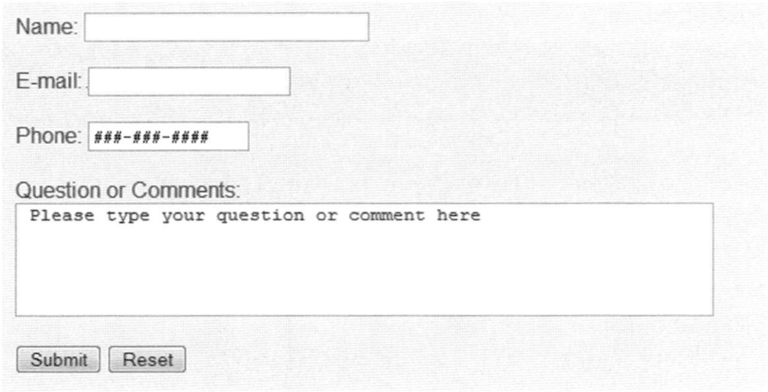

Figure 9.15
The new version of
the contact form

Name: [   ]

E-mail: [   ]

Phone: [###-###-####]

Question or Comments:
[Please type your question or comment here

]

[Submit] [Reset]

Launch Notepad and open the contact.html page that you created in Hands-On Practice
9.1. Perform the following edits:

1. Place the cursor after the `<form>` tag and press [Enter] to create a new line.
   Configure the area where the customer name will be entered. Type `Name:` to create the label for the text box. Now create an `<input />` tag that has type configured to `text`, name set to `CustName`, id set to `CustName`, and `size` configured to
   `30`. The label and text box should be on their own line. (*Hint*: Use two `<br />`
   elements.) The XHTML follows:

   ```
   Name: <input type="text" name="CustName" id="CustName" size="30" />
   <br /><br />
   ```

2. Verify that the e-mail form element you coded in Hands-On Practice 9.1 is on the
   next line. The XHTML follows:

   ```
   E-mail: <input type="text" name="CustEmail" id="CustEmail" />
   <br /><br />
   ```

3. Create a new line under the form area that configures the `CustEmail` text box
   and configure the area to accept the customer phone number. Type `Phone:` to
   create the label for the text box. Now create an `<input/>` tag that has `type` configured to `text`, `name` set to `CustPhone`, `id` set to `CustPhone`, `size` configured to
   `15`, and `maxlength` set to `12`. View Figure 9.16 and notice that the phone number
   text box initially displays the characters `###-###-####`. Configure this by setting
   the `value` attribute to `###-###-####`. The label and text box should be on their
   own line. The XHTML follows:

   ```
   Phone: <input type="text" name="CustPhone" id="CustPhone"
   size="15" maxlength="12" value="###-###-####" />
   <br /><br />
   ```

4. Now you will configure the area for customer comments or questions. On its
   own line, type `Question or Comments:` Use a `<br />` element to cause this
   text to display on its own line in the Web browser. Next, configure a scrolling
   text box with 4 rows, 60 columns, the `name` `CustComment`, and the `id` set to
   `CustComment`. Configure the default text to display between the `<textarea>` and
   `</textarea>` tags as `Please type your question or comment here`.

Figure 9.16
The new contact page

Configure a blank line underneath the scrolling text box. The XHTML follows:

```
Question or Comments:<br />
<textarea rows="4" cols="60" name="CustComment" id="CustComment">
Please type your question or comment here</textarea><br /><br />
```

5. Notice that in Figure 9.15 the submit button displays "Submit." Use the **value attribute** to configure this as follows:

```
<input type="submit" value="Submit" />
```

6. Add a blank space next to the submit button, and then add a reset button to the form. The XHTML follows:

```
<input type="reset" />
```

7. Save your contact.html file and test it in a browser. It should look similar to that shown in Figure 9.16. The solution can be found in the student files in the Chapter9/9.2 folder.

As you view your form (or Figure 9.16) you may notice that it looks a little messy—the form elements don't align under each other. A technique often used to align form elements is to format the form area with a table. See Figure 9.17 for a more orderly version of the form formatted with a table.

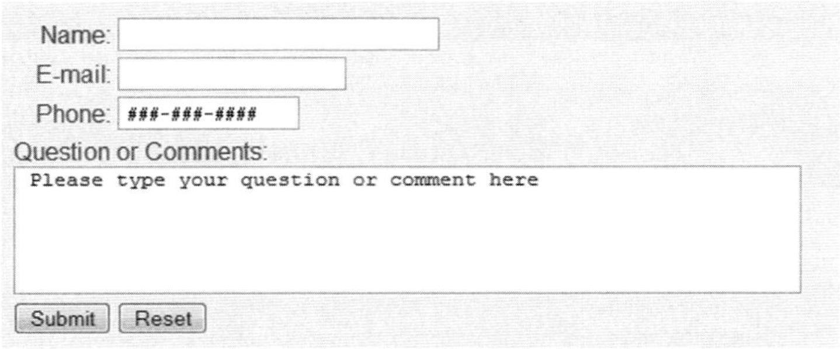

Figure 9.17
A table was used to
format this form

A table with five rows and two columns was added to the page in Figure 9.17, within the `<form>` and `</form>` container tags. The text labels for the `Name:`, `E-mail:`, and `Phone:` form elements were each placed in their own table cell and right-aligned. Each text box and button was placed in its own table cell. The scrolling text box was placed in a table cell that spans two columns. (See Chapter 8 to review tables.) The table was configured to have no border and to take up 75 percent of the browser window. The first column was configured to take up 10 percent of the table width. The revised XHTML for the form and table is shown here with the table code in color. Notice that since a table is used to format the form, fewer `<br />` tags are needed.

```
<form>
  <table border="0" width="75%">
    <tr>
      <td align="right" width="10%">Name: </td>
      <td><input type="text" name="CustName" id="CustName" size="30" />
      </td>
    </tr>
    <tr>
      <td align="right">E-mail: </td>
      <td><input type="text" name="CustEmail" id="CustEmail" /></td>
    </tr>
    <tr>
      <td align="right">Phone: </td>
      <td><input type="text" name="CustPhone" id="CustPhone"
        size="15" maxlength="12" value="###-###-####" /></td>
    </tr>
    <tr>
      <td colspan="2">Question or Comments:<br />
      <textarea rows="4" cols="60" name="CustComment"
        id="CustComment">Please type your question or comment
        here</textarea></td>
    </tr>
    <tr>
      <td align="right"><input type="submit" value="Submit" /></td>
      <td><input type="reset" /></td>
    </tr>
  </table>
```

Tables are often used to organize forms on Web pages. Modify your page as indicated here. Save the file with a new name, contact2.html, test in a browser, and compare your result with Figure 9.17. The solution can be found in the student files at Chapter9/9.2/contact2.html.

Now you are familiar with using forms on Web pages, with different elements that can be placed on forms, and with using a table to format a form. Additional detailed information on these form elements and their attributes may be found in Appendix A, XHTML Reference.

CHECKPOINT 9.1

1. You are designing a Web site for a client who sells items in a retail store. They want to create a customer list for e-mail marketing purposes. Your client sells to consumers and needs a form that accepts a customer's name and e-mail address. Would you recommend using two input boxes (one for the name and one for the e-mail) or three input boxes (one each for the first name, last name, and e-mail address)? Explain your answer.

2. You are designing a survey form for a client. One of the questions has 10 possible responses. Only one response can be selected per question. What type of form element would you use to configure this question on the Web page?

3. True or False? In a radio button group, the `value` attribute is used by the browser to process separate elements as a group.

9.3 Form Enhancements

There are additional XHTML tags that can enhance your forms by associating text labels with form elements and by visually grouping form elements together.

The Label Element

Focus on Accessibility

The `<label>` element is a container tag that is used to associate a text description with a form element. It is sometimes difficult for a person using a screen reader to match up the text descriptions on forms with their corresponding form elements. The purpose of the label element is to explicitly associate a form element with the text label that describes it. The label element also benefits individuals without fine motor control. Clicking anywhere on either a form field or its associated text label will set the cursor focus to the form field. In addition, the label element can serve as a fragment identifier or bookmark and allow the form element to be directly linked to other parts of the Web page (or other Web pages, if needed).

There are two ways to associate a label with a form element. The first method places the <label> tag as a container around both the text description and the form element. The code follows:

```
<label>E-mail: <input type="text" name="CustEmail" id="CustEmail" />
</label>
```

The second method uses the id attribute to associate the label with a particular form element. This is more flexible and is better suited for forms that are formatted with a table. The code follows:

```
<label for="email">E-mail: </label>
   <input type="text" name="email" id="email" />
```

Notice that the value of the **for attribute** on the <label> tag is the same as the value of the id attribute on the <input> tag. This creates the association between the <label> and the form element. The <input> tag uses both the name and id attributes for different purposes. The name attribute can be used by client-side and by server-side scripting. The id attribute creates an identifier that can be used by the <label> and anchor tags.

The Fieldset and Legend Elements

You have seen an example using a table to format a form. Another technique that can be used to create a more visually pleasing form is to group elements with the **<fieldset>** tag. Browsers that support this feature will place a visual cue, such as an outline or a border, around form elements grouped in a <fieldset>. The **<legend>** tag can be used to provide a label for this grouping. Figure 9.18 shows the CustName, CustEmail, and CustPhone elements grouped in this manner.

Figure 9.18
A <fieldset> organizes the customer information area

The XHTML to create the grouping shown in Figure 9.18 follows:

```
<fieldset><legend>Customer Information</legend>
<label>Name:
   <input type="text" name="CustName" id="CustName" size="30" />
   </label> <br /><br />
<label>E-mail:
   <input type="text" name="CustEmail" id="CustEmail" />
   </label><br /></br />
<label>Phone: <input type="text" name="CustPhone" id="CustPhone"
   size="15" maxlength="12" value="###-###-####" /></label>
   <br /></fieldset>
```

The grouping and visual effect of the `<fieldset>` element creates an organized and appealing Web page containing a form. Be aware that older browsers, such as Netscape 4, do not support the `<fieldset>` and `<legend>` tags. If you decide to use them, make sure that your form is easy to use and understand even if the visual grouping is not displayed.

The `tabindex` Attribute

Some of your Web page visitors may have difficulty using the mouse and will access your form with a keyboard. They may use the `Tab` key to move from one form element to another. The default action for the `Tab` key is to move to the next form element in the order the form elements are coded in the XHTML. This is usually appropriate. However, if the tab order needs to be changed for a form, use the **tabindex attribute** on each form element. For each form element (`<input>`, `<select>`, `<textarea>`), code a `tabindex` attribute with a numeric value, beginning with 1, 2, 3, and so on in numerical order. The XHTML code to configure the customer e-mail text box as the initial position of the cursor is: `<input type="text" name="CustEmail" id="CustEmail" tabindex="1" />`. The `tabindex` attribute is not supported in older browsers such as Netscape 4. If you assign a form element with `tabindex="0"`, it will be visited after all other form elements that are assigned `tabindex`. If you happen to assign two elements the same `tabindex` value, the one that is coded first in the XHTML will be visited first.

The `accesskey` Attribute

Another technique that can make your form keyboard-friendly is the use of the **accesskey attribute** on form elements. Assigning the `accesskey` a value of one of the characters (letter or number) on the keyboard will create a hot key that your Web page visitor can press to move the cursor immediately to a form element. The method used to access this hot key varies depending on the operating system. Windows users will press the `Alt` key and the character key. The combination is the ⌘ key and the character key for Mac users. For example, if the form shown in Figure 9.18 had the customer e-mail text coded with an `accesskey="E"`, the Web page visitor using Windows could press the `Alt` and `E` keys to move the cursor immediately to the e-mail text box. The XHTML code for this follows:

```
<input type="text" name="CustEmail" id="CustEmail" accesskey="E" />
```

The `accesskey` attribute is not supported in older browsers such as Netscape 4. Even when browsers do support the `accesskey` feature, you cannot rely on the browser to indicate that a character is an access key, also called a hot key. You will have to manually code information about the hot key. A visual cue may be helpful. The W3C suggests underlining the letter in each text label that is used as a hot key; however, these underlined letters could be confused with hyperlinks. Other options include displaying the hot key in bold or by placing a message such as `Alt`+`E` after a form element that uses a hot key. When choosing `accesskey` values, avoid combinations that are already used by the operating system (such as `Alt`+`F` to display the File menu). Testing hot keys is crucial.

Accessibility and Forms

Using the XHTML elements and attributes just discussed—`label`, `fieldset`, `legend`, `accesskey`, and `tabindex`—will increase the accessibility of your Web page forms.

This makes it easier for individuals with vision and mobility challenges to use your form pages. Often, these accessibility modifications, such as use of the `<fieldset>` and `<legend>` tags, increase the readability and usability of the Web form for all visitors. Be sure to include contact information (e-mail address and/or phone number) just in case a visitor is unable to submit your form successfully and requires additional assistance.

Image Buttons and the Button Element

As you have worked with forms in this chapter, you may have noticed that the standard submit button (see Figure 9.12) is a little plain. You can make the form area that you click to submit the form more compelling and visually interesting in two ways: by creating custom images that are configured with the `<input />` tag or by using the `<button>` tag.

Figure 9.19 shows an image used in place of the standard submit button. This is called an image button. When an image button is clicked, the form is submitted. The image button is coded using the `<input />` tag along with `type="image"` and a `src` attribute with the value of the name of the image file. For example, to use the image called login.gif as an image button the XHTML code is as follows:

```
<input type="image" src="login.gif" alt="Login Button" />
```

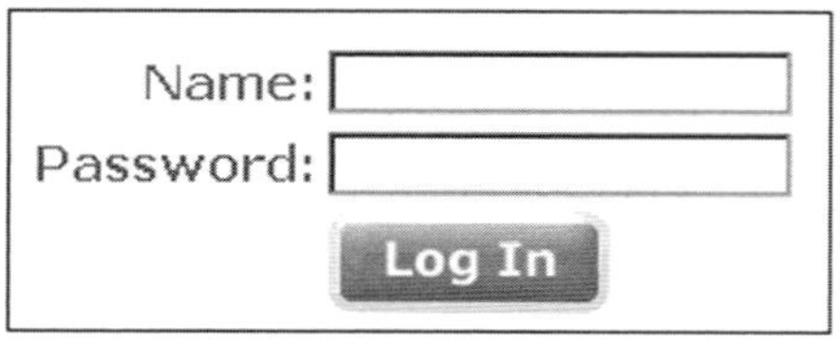

Figure 9.19
The Web page visitor will click the image button to submit the form

Another way to add more interest to a form is to use the `<button>` element. This element can be used to configure not only images but also blocks of text as the clickable area that can submit or reset a form. The `<button>` tag is a container tag. Any Web page content that is between the `<button>` and `</button>` tags is configured to be part of the button. Table 9.12 lists common attributes of the `<button>` tag.

Figure 9.20 shows a version of the contact form that has an image (contact.gif) configured as a submit button using the `<button>` element.

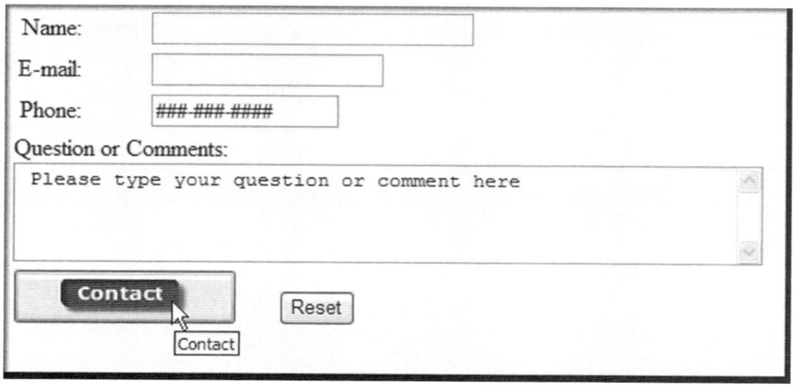

Figure 9.20
The `<button>` element configured as a submit button

Table 9.12 Common attributes of the `<button>` tag

Common Attributes	Values	Usage
type	submit	Functions as a submit button.
	reset	Functions as a reset button.
	button	Functions as a button.
name	Alphanumeric, no spaces, begins with a letter	Names the form element so that it can be easily accessed by client-side scripting languages (such as JavaScript) or by server-side processing. The name should be unique.
alt	Brief text description of the image	Provides accessibility to visitors unable to view the image.
id	Alphanumeric, no spaces, begins with a letter	Provides a unique identifier for the form element.
value	Text or numeric characters	A value given to a form element that is passed to the form handler.

The following XHTML code creates the button shown in Figure 9.20:

```
<button type="submit">
<img src="contact.gif" width="100" height="30" alt="Submit form" />
</button>
```

As you visit Web pages and look at their source code, you will find that the `<button>` element is not used as often as the standard submit button or the image button.

HANDS-ON PRACTICE 9.3

Focus on Accessibility

In this Hands-On Practice you will modify the contact form (contact.html) you worked with in Hands-On Practice 9.2 to use the `fieldset`, `legend`, and `label` elements (see Figure 9.21).

Launch Notepad and open the contact.html page that you created in Hands-On Practice 9.2. Perform the following edits:

1. Add an opening `<fieldset>` tag after the opening `<form>` tag.

2. Immediately after the opening `<fieldset>` tag code `<legend>` tags containing the following text: Customer Information.

3. Add a `<label>` element for each of the Customer Name, Customer E-mail, and Customer Comments form elements.

4. Choose an appropriate location to code the closing `<fieldset>` tag.

5. Save your contact.html file and test in a recent browser. It should look similar to the one shown in Figure 9.21. You can compare your work with the solution found in the student files (Chapter9/9.3). You may notice that when you activate the submit button, the form redisplays. This is because there is no action property in the `<form>` element. The next section focuses on the second component of using forms on Web pages—server-side processing.

Figure 9.21
This contact form uses the `label` element to provide for accessibility

CHECKPOINT 9.2

1. Describe the purpose of the `<fieldset>` and `<legend>` tags.

2. Describe the purpose of the `accesskey` attribute and how it supports accessibility.

3. When designing a form, should you use the standard submit button, an image button, or a button tag? Are these different in the way that they provide for accessibility? Explain your answer.

9.4 Using CSS to Style a Form

Many Web developers cruise along using CSS for page layout until they need to code a form. Tables (usually avoided when coding CSS page layouts) are traditionally used to configure forms. This section will show you two approaches to using CSS to style a form—the first uses a table whose attributes have been configured with CSS instead of with XHTML, the second is pure CSS-P and does not use a table.

Styling Forms with Tables and CSS

XHTML Tables Meet CSS Properties. This is considered to be a *transitional* approach. In this method, the form is organized by a table configured with CSS rather than with XHTML properties. While this is not completely table-less design and your instructor may be aghast at this suggestion, using a table to configure a small portion of a page that otherwise utilizes CSS is an alternate method to consider. It would be best to reserve the use of a table for pure tabular data—such as price lists and budgets. However, the purpose of this example is to show how CSS can be used to streamline even the XHTML needed by a table. Figure 9.22 shows a Web page (see Chapter9/form1.html in the student files) with the form area coded with a table.

Figure 9.22
This page uses a table styled with CSS

The table is configured with CSS rather than with XHTML attributes. CSS is used to configure the `<table>` and `<td>` properties that would otherwise be defined with XHTML attributes. CSS is also used to configure a class to right-align the text on the form.

The CSS follows:

```
table { border: solid 3px #000000;
        width: 100%;
}
td { padding: 5px;
}
.myLabel { text-align: right;
}
```

In the following XHTML code, the `<table>` and `<td>` tags have no attributes for table properties since these are all configured with CSS. The XHTML follows:

```
<form method="post">
  <table>
    <tr>
      <td class="myLabel"><label for="myName">Name:</label></td>
      <td><input type="text" name="myName" id="myName" /></td>
    </tr>
```

```
    <tr>
      <td class="myLabel"><label for="myEmail">E-mail:</label></td>
      <td><input type="text" name="myEmail" id="myEmail" /></td>
    </tr>
    <tr>
      <td class="myLabel"><label for="myComments">Comments:</label>
      </td>
      <td><textarea name="myComments" id="myComments" rows="2"
        cols="60"></textarea></td>
    </tr>
    <tr>
      <td colspan="2"><input type="submit" value="Get Newsletter" />
      </td>
    </tr>
  </table>
</form>
```

Styling Forms with Only CSS

Using "Pure" CSS to Style a Form. In this method, the CSS box model is used to create a series of boxes, as shown in Figure 9.23: the outermost box defining the form area, a series of boxes contained in the form area (one for each line in the form), and the innermost boxes to align the form text. CSS is used to configure each of the box types previously described. The myForm id declares properties for the entire form area. The myRow class sets the height of a typical line in the form. The myRowComments class configures the form area used to accept comments with a 20 pixel margin below the scrolling text box. The labelCol class is the key to aligning the text. The area has a width of 100 pixels and the text will align to the right.

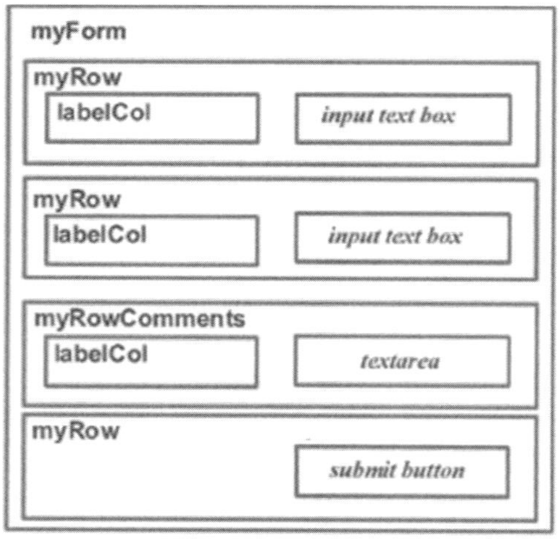

Figure 9.23
A sketch of the box model used to configure the form

Figure 9.24 displays a Web page with a form configured in this manner (see Chapter9/form2.html in the student files).

As you view the following CSS and XHTML, note that the labelCol class floats to the left side of the form and results in a neatly aligned text label for each input box.

Figure 9.24
This page does not use a table—just CSS

The CSS follows:

```
#myForm { border: 3px solid #000000;
          padding: 10px;
          margin: 10px;
          min-width: 500px;
}
.myRow { height: 30px;
}
.mySubmit{ margin-top: 10px;
           margin-left: 110px;
}
.labelCol { float: left;
            width: 100px;
            text-align: right;
            padding-right: 10px;
}
```

The XHTML code follows. Note the use of `<div>` elements.

```
<div id="myForm">
  <form method="post">
    <div class="myRow">
      <label class="labelCol" for="myName">Name:</label>
      <input type="text" name="myName" id="myName" />
    </div>
    <div class="myRow">
      <label class="labelCol" for="myEmail">E-mail:</label>
      <input type="text" name="myEmail" id="myEmail" />
    </div>
    <div>
      <label class="labelCol" for="myComments">Comments:</label>
      <textarea name="myComments" id="myComments" rows="2" cols="60">
      </textarea>
    </div>
```

```
      <div class="mySubmit">
        <input type="submit" value="Get Newsletter" />
      </div>
    </form>
</div>
```

This section provided you with two methods to configure forms. Both methods use advantages of CSS. Which method you choose for a particular Web site depends on the browsers used by the target audience. Testing the way that different browsers render the form is crucial. If in doubt about browser support, consider using the transitional approach of styling a table used for form configuration. After all, your form can't be used if it can't be seen by your visitors.

As you've coded and displayed the forms in this chapter, you may have noticed that when you click the submit button, the form just redisplays—the form doesn't "do" anything. This is because there is no action property in the `<form>` tag. The next section focuses on the second component of using forms on Web pages—server-side processing.

9.5 CGI Server-Side Processing

Your Web browser requests Web pages and their related files from a Web server. The Web server locates the files and sends them to your Web browser. Then the Web browser renders the returned files and displays the requested Web pages. Figure 9.25 illustrates the communication between the Web browser and the Web server.

Figure 9.25
The Web browser (client) works with the Web server

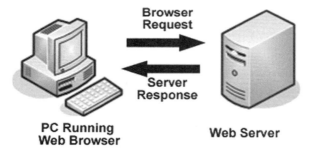

Sometimes a Web site needs more functionality than static Web pages—possibly a site search, order form, e-mail list, database display, or other type of processing. This is when server-side processing is needed, commonly known as the Common Gateway Interface (CGI). The term Common Gateway Interface refers to the fact that the two computers communicating do not need the same hardware or operating system—there is a common gateway between the different platforms.

CGI is a protocol, or standard method, for a Web server to pass a Web page user's request (which is typically initiated through the use of a form) to an application program and to accept information to send to the user. The Web server typically passes the form information to a small application program that processes the data, and it usually sends back a confirmation Web page or message. This specification for passing data back and forth between the server and the application is called CGI and is part of the Hypertext Transfer Protocol (HTTP) specification.

A Web page invokes CGI by either an **action attribute** on a form or a hyperlink—the URL of the CGI script or program is used. Any form data that exists is passed to the CGI script. The CGI script completes its processing and may create a confirmation or response Web page with the requested information. The Web server returns this page to the Web browser. Every time you perform a search using Yahoo! or other search engines, you are using CGI.

The CGI protocol can be used by many different programming or scripting languages including Perl, PHP, Active Server Pages, Adobe ColdFusion, and Sun JavaServer Pages. The actual script may be embedded within a Web page document saved with a file extension such as .pl (Perl), .php (PHP), .asp (Active Server Pages), .cfm (Adobe ColdFusion), or .jsp (Sun JavaServer Pages). Microsoft's .NET platform also uses the CGI protocol. ASP.Net pages coded using Visual Basic.Net typically use the .aspx file extension.

Steps in Utilizing CGI

1. Web page invokes CGI by a form or hyperlink.
2. Web server executes server-side script or program.
3. Server-side script accesses requested database, file, or process.
4. Web server returns Web page with requested information or confirmation of action.

The CGI protocol invokes **server-side scripts** and programs by their URL. This URL can be typed in the address bar of a browser window, coded in XHTML as the `href` on an anchor tag, or coded in XHTML as the action on a form tag.

When using CGI to invoke a server-side script from a form, the Web developer and the server-side programmer must communicate regarding the form **method attribute** (`get` or `post`), form `action` attribute (URL of the server-side script), and any special form element names expected by the server-side script. The value of the `name` attribute on each form element is passed to the server-side script and may be used as a variable name in the server-side processing. In the next Hands-On Practice, you will invoke an Active Server Pages server-side script from a form.

 HANDS-ON PRACTICE 9.4

In this Hands-On Practice you will modify the contact.html page that you created earlier in this chapter, configuring the form so that it uses the post method to invoke a server-side script. Please note that your computer must be connected to the Internet when you test your work.

Launch Notepad and open the contact.html file you created in Hands-On Practice 9.3. Modify the `<form>` tag to use the post method. The XHTML follows:

```
<form method="post">
```

The `post` method is recommended by the W3C and is more private than the `get` method. The `post` method does not pass the form information in the URL; it passes it in the entity-body of the HTTP Request, which makes it more private.

When using a server-side script you will need to obtain some information, or documentation, from the person or organization providing the script. You will need to know the location of the script, whether it requires any specific names for the form elements, and whether it requires any hidden form elements. The `action` attribute is used on the `<form>` tag to invoke a server-side script. A server-side script has been created at http://webdevfoundations.net/scripts/formdemo.asp for students to use for this exercise. The documentation for the server-side script is listed in Table 9.13.

Table 9.13 Server-side script documentation

Location of Script:	http://webdevfoundations.net/scripts/formdemo.asp
Purpose of Script:	This script will place all input from a form in the body of a Web page that is displayed. This is a sample script for student assignments. It demonstrates that server-side processing has been invoked. A script used by an actual Web site would perform a function such as sending an e-mail message or updating a database.

Now you will add the configuration required to use the formdemo.asp server-side processing with your form. Launch Notepad and open the contact.html file you created in Hands-On Practice 9.3, also found in the Chapter9/9.3 folder. Modify the `<form>` tag by adding an `action` attribute with a value of `"http://webdevfoundations.net/scripts/formdemo.asp"`. The XHTML code for the revised `<form>` tag follows:

```
<form method="post"
action="http://webdevfoundations.net/scripts/formdemo.asp" >
```

Save your page as contact.html and test it in a browser. Your screen should look similar to the one shown in Figure 9.21.

Now you are ready to test your form. You must be connected to the Internet to test your form successfully. Enter information in the form elements and click the submit button. You should see a confirmation page similar to the one shown in Figure 9.26.

Figure 9.26
The server-side script has created this page in response to the form

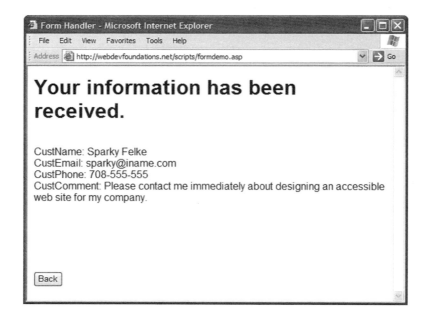

The formdemo.asp script creates a Web page that displays a message and the form information you entered. Where did this confirmation page originate? This confirmation page was created by the server-side script on the `action` attribute in the `<form>` tag. Sometimes students wonder what code is used in the formdemo.asp file. Writing scripts for server-side processing is beyond the scope of this textbook. However, if you are curious, visit http://webdevfoundations.net/4e/chapter9.html to see the source code for this script.

FAQ **What do I do if nothing happened when I tested my form?**

Try these troubleshooting hints:

- Verify that your computer is connected to the Internet.
- Verify the spelling of the script location in the `action` attribute.
- Attention to detail is crucial!

Privacy and Forms

Focus on Ethics

You've just learned how to collect information from your Web site visitors. Do you think your visitors may want to know how you plan to use the information you collect? The guidelines that you develop to protect the privacy of your visitors' information is called a **privacy policy**. Web sites either indicate this policy on the form page itself or create a separate page that describes the privacy policy (and other company policies). For example, the order form page at mymoney.gov (http://mymoney.gov/mymoneyorder .shtml) indicates the following:

"WE WILL NOT SHARE OR SELL ANY PERSONAL INFORMATION OBTAINED FROM YOU WITH ANY OTHER ORGANIZATION, UNLESS REQUIRED BY LAW TO DO SO."

For a more detailed example of a Web site's privacy notice, visit http://www.nps.gov/ privacy.htm, as shown in Figure 9.27. If you browse popular sites such as Amazon.com or eBay.com you'll find links to their privacy policies (sometimes called a privacy notice) in the page footer area.

If you've ever filled out a form on a Web site and suddenly received lots of annoying SPAM, you will most likely agree that you'd rather not have Web sites sharing your information with others and you'd like to know up front if this will occur. Your visitors probably feel the same way. Include a privacy notice in your site to inform your visitors how you plan to use the information they share with you. The Better Business Bureau provides a sample privacy notice at http://www.bbbonline.org/privacy/sample_privacy.asp.

CGI Resources

There are many CGI resources on the Web. If you'd like to see the official overview, go to http://hoohoo.ncsa.uiuc.edu/cgi/overview.html. The W3C has a resource page at http://www.w3.org/CGI/.

Figure 9.27
This privacy notice
describes what
information is
collected

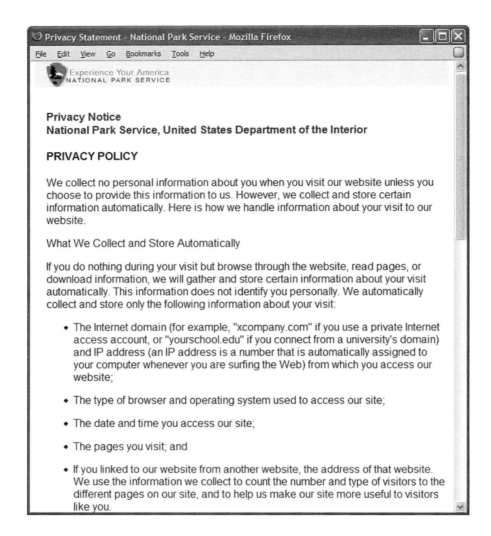

Sources of Free Remote-Hosted Form Processing. If your Web host provider does not support CGI, free remotely hosted scripts may be an option. The script is not hosted on your server so you don't need to worry about installing it or whether your Web host provider will support it. The disadvantage is that there usually is some advertising displayed. The following are a few sites that offer this service:

- http://formbuddy.com
- http://hostedscripts.com
- http://response-o-matic.com
- http://www.formmail.com
- http://www.master.com
- http://www.wufoo.com
- http://www.formassembly.com
- http://www.iceberg.com

Sources of Free CGI Scripts. To use free CGI scripts you need to have access to a Web server that supports the CGI language used by the script. Most free scripts use Perl. Contact your Web host provider to determine what is supported. Be aware that many free Web host providers do not support CGI (you get what you pay for!). The following are a few sites that offer free CGI scripts and other resources:

- http://www.scriptarchive.com/
- http://cgi.resourceindex.com/Programs_and_Scripts/
- http://www.extropia.com/
- http://www.asp101.com
- http://php.resourceindex.com

Other Server-Side Processing Technologies

Other types of technologies can be used for server-side scripting, form processing, and information sharing:

- JavaServer Pages (http://java.sun.com/products/jsp/)
- Active Server Pages (http://msdn.microsoft.com/ and search for "Active Server Pages")
- ColdFusion (http://www.adobe.com/products/coldfusion)
- PHP (http://www.php.net)
- Ruby on Rails (http://www.rubyonrails.org, http://tryruby.hobix.com)
- Microsoft's .NET Framework (http://www.microsoft.com/net)
- Web Services (http://www.webservicesarchitect.com, http://webservices.org, and http://www.uddi.xml.org/)

Any of these technologies would be a good choice for future study. Web developers often learn the client-side first (HTML, CSS, and JavaScript), and then progress to learning a server-side scripting or programming language.

CHECKPOINT 9.3

1. Describe CGI.

2. Code a Web page form that will use the post method to invoke a server-side script at http://webdevfoundations.net/scripts/subscribe.asp. The form will have three text boxes as described in Table 9.14.

3. Describe why communication is needed between the developer of a server-side script and the Web page designer.

Table 9.14 Form element names

Form Element	Name Attribute Value
First Name	`fname`
Last Name	`lname`
E-mail Address	`email`

CHAPTER SUMMARY

This chapter introduced the use of forms on Web pages. You learned how to configure form elements and provide for accessibility. You also learned how to configure a form to access server-side processing.

Visit the textbook Web site at http://www.webdevfoundations.net for examples, the links listed in this chapter, and updated information.

Key Terms

`<button>`	button	radio button
`<fieldset>`	check box	reset button
`<form>`	Common Gateway Interface	scrolling text box
`<input />`	(CGI)	select list
`<label>`	for attribute	server-side scripts
`<legend>`	form	submit button
`<option>`	hidden form element	`tabindex` attribute
`<select>`	method attribute	text box
`<textarea>`	name attribute	value attribute
`accesskey` attribute	password box	
action attribute	privacy policy	

Review Questions

Multiple Choice

1. Which XHTML tag configures a button that can be clicked to reset form fields to their default values automatically?

   a. `<input type="reset" />`

   b. `<button type="reset">Reset</button>`

   c. `<input type="button" value="Reset" />`

   d. both a and b

2. Which attribute of the `<form>` tag is used to specify the name and location of the script that will process the form field values?

   a. `action`

   b. `process`

   c. `method`

   d. none of the above

3. Which of the following form elements does not use the `<input>` tag?

   a. text box

   b. select list

   c. check box

   d. radio button

4. Choose the XHTML tag that would configure a text box with the name `"email"` and a width of 40 characters.

   a. `<input type="text" id="email" width="40" />`

   b. `<input type="text" name="email" size="40" />`

   c. `<input type="text" name="email" space="40" />`

   d. `<input type="text" width="40"/>`

5. Which of the following form elements would be appropriate for an area that your visitors can use to type in comments about your Web site?

   a. select list

   b. text box

   c. scrolling text box

   d. none of the above

6. You would like to conduct a survey and ask your Web page visitors to vote for their favorite search engine. Which of the following form elements is best to use for this purpose?

   a. check box

   b. radio button

   c. text box

   d. scrolling text box

7. You would like to conduct a survey and ask your Web page visitors to indicate the Web browsers that they use. Which of the following form elements is best to use for this purpose?

   a. check box

   b. radio button

   c. text box

   d. scrolling text box

8. An order form contains an area for Web visitors to select their preferred method of shipping. You need to limit the amount of space on the form that is used for this feature. Which of the following form elements is best to use for this purpose?

   a. check box

   b. radio button

   c. text box

   d. select list

9. Which XHTML tag would configure a scrolling text box with the name comments, 2 rows, and 30 characters?

   a. `<textarea name="comments" width="30" rows="2"></textarea>`

   b. `<input type="textarea" name="comments" size="30" rows="2" />`

   c. `<textarea name="comments" rows="2" cols="30"></textarea>`

   d. none of the above

10. Choose the XHTML that would associate a label displaying the text `Phone Number` with the text box named `orderPhone`. The letter `P` should function as a hot key for the text box.

    a. `Phone Number: <input type="textbox" name="orderPhone" id="orderPhone" />`

    b. `<label>Phone Number: <input type="text" name="orderPhone" id="orderPhone" accesskey="P" /> </label>`

    c. `<label for="Phone">Phone Number: </label><input type="text" name="orderPhone" id="Phone" accesskey="P" />`

    d. both b and c

Fill in the Blank

11. To limit the number of characters that a text box will accept, use the _____ attribute.

12. To group a number of form elements visually on the page, use the _____ element.

13. To cause a number of radio buttons to be treated as a single group, the value of the _____ attribute must be identical.

Short Answer

14. Explain why a Web developer should avoid using `mailto:` to process form information.

15. List one purpose of using a form on a Web page.

Apply Your Knowledge

1. **Predict the Result.** Draw and write a brief description of the Web page that will be created with the following XHTML code:

```
<?xml version="1.0" encoding="UTF-8"?>
<!DOCTYPE html PUBLIC "-//W3C//DTD XHTML 1.0 Transitional//EN"
    "http://www.w3.org/TR/xhtml1/DTD/xhtml1-transitional.dtd">
<html xmlns="http://www.w3.org/1999/xhtml">
<head>
<title>Predict the Result</title>
</head>
<body>
  <div align="center">
    <h1>Contact Us</h1>
    <form action="myscript.php">
      <fieldset><legend>Complete the form and a consultant will
      contact you</legend>
      Email: <input type="text" name="email" id="email" size="40"
      /><br />
      Please indicate which services you are interested in:<br />
        <select name="inquiry" id="inquiry" size="1">
          <option value="development">Web Development</option>
          <option value="redesign">Web Redesign</option>
          <option value="maintain">Web Maintenance</option>
          <option value="info">General Information</option>
        </select>
        <br />
        <input type="submit" />
      </fieldset>
    </form>
    <p><a href="index.htm">Home</a>
      <a href="services.htm">Services</a>
      Contact</p>
    <p>Contact <a href="mailto:web@trilliumtechnologies.com">
    web@trilliumtechnologies.com</a><br />
    Copyright &copy; 2008 Trillium Media Design</p>
  </div>
</body>
</html>
```

2. **Fill in the Missing Code.** This Web page configures a survey form to collect information on the favorite search engine used by Web page visitors. The form action should submit the form to the server-side script, called survey.php. Some XHTML tags and their attributes, indicated by <_>, are missing. Some XHTML attribute values, indicated by "_", are missing.

```
<?xml version="1.0" encoding="UTF-8"?>
<!DOCTYPE html PUBLIC "-//W3C//DTD XHTML 1.0 Transitional//EN"
    "http://www.w3.org/TR/xhtml1/DTD/xhtml1-transitional.dtd">
<html xmlns="http://www.w3.org/1999/xhtml">
<head>
```

```
      <title>Fill in the Missing Code</title>
    </head>
    <body>
      <h1>Vote for your favorite Search Engine</h1>
      <form method="_" action="_">
        <input type="radio" name="_" id="Ysurvey" value="Yahoo" />
        Yahoo!<br />
        <input type="radio" name="survey" id="Gsurvey" value="Google" />
        Google<br />
        <input type="radio" name="_" id="Asurvey" value="AltaVista" />
        Alta Vista<br />
        <_>
      </form>
    </body>
</html>
```

3. **Find the Error.** Find the coding errors in the following subscription form:

```
<?xml version="1.0" encoding="UTF-8"?>
<!DOCTYPE html PUBLIC "-//W3C//DTD XHTML 1.0 Transitional//EN"
  "http://www.w3.org/TR/xhtml1/DTD/xhtml1-transitional.dtd">
<html xmlns="http://www.w3.org/1999/xhtml">
<head>
<title>Find the Error</title>
</head>
<body>
  <p>Subscribe to our monthly newsletter and receive free
  coupons!</p>
  <form action="get" method="newsletter.php">
  E-mail: <input type="textbox" name="email" id="email" char="40">
  <br />
  <input type="button" /> <input type="reset" />
  </form>
</body>
</html>
```

Hands-On Exercises

1. Write the XHTML to create a text box named city that will be used to accept the name of a city from Web page visitors. The text box should allow a maximum of 30 characters to be entered.

2. Write the XHTML to create a group of radio buttons that Web site visitors can check to vote for their favorite day of the week.

3. Write the XHTML to create a select list that asks Web site visitors to select their favorite day of the week.

4. Write the XHTML to create a fieldset and legend with the text "Shipping Address" around the following form elements: AddressLine1, AddressLine2, City, State, ZIP.

5. Write the XHTML to configure an image called go.gif as an image button on a form.

6. Write the XHTML to configure a hidden form element with the name of `userid`.

7. Write the XHTML to configure a password form element with the name of `pword`.

8. Write the XHTML to configure a form tag to invoke server-side processing using http://webdevfoundations.net/scripts/mydemo.asp and the `post` method.

9. Write the XHTML to create a form that accepts requests for a brochure to be sent in the mail. Sketch out the form on paper before you begin.

10. Write the XHTML to create a form that accepts feedback from Web site visitors. Sketch out the form on paper before you begin.

11. Write a Web page that contains a music survey form similar to the example shown in Figure 9.28.

Figure 9.28
Sample music survey form

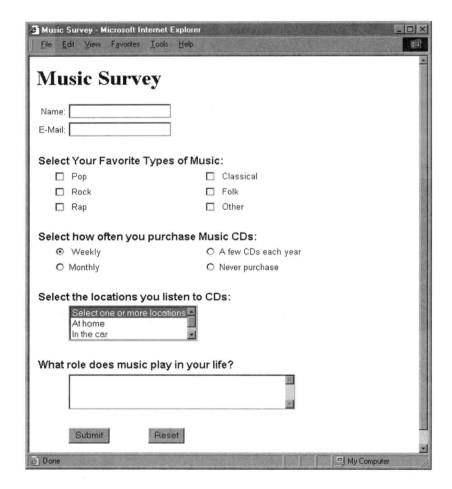

Include the following form elements:

• Text boxes for name and e-mail address

• A scrolling text box that is 60 characters wide and 3 rows high. (*Hint*: `<textarea>`)

- A radio button group with at least three choices
- A check box group with at least three choices
- A select box that initially shows three items but contains at least four items
- A submit button
- A reset button

Use a table to organize your form. Place your e-mail address at the bottom of the page. (*Hint*: Draw a sketch of your form and the table before you begin coding the XHTML.) Hand in printouts of both the source code (print in Notepad) and the browser display of your page to your instructor.

Web Research

1. This chapter mentioned a number of sources of free remotely hosted scripts, including http://formbuddy.com, http://hostedscripts.com, http://www.formmail.com, http://response-o-matic.com, and http://master.com. Visit two of these sites or use a search engine to find other resources for free remotely hosted scripts. Register (if necessary) and examine the Web site to see exactly what is offered. Most sites that provide remotely hosted scripts have a demo you can view or try. If you have time (or your instructor asks you to) follow the directions and access a remotely hosted script from one of your Web pages. Now that you've at least been through a demo of the product or tried it yourself (even better!), it's time to write your review.

   Create a Web page that lists the two resource sites you chose and provides a comparison of what they offer. Use a table to list the following:

   - Ease of registration
   - Number of scripts or services offered
   - Type of scripts or services offered
   - Site banner or advertisement
   - Ease of use
   - Your recommendation

   Provide links to the resource sites you reviewed and place your name in the e-mail address at the bottom of the page. Print the source code (from Notepad) and the browser view of your Web page.

2. Search the Web for a Web page that uses an XHTML form. Print the browser view of the page. Print out the source code of the Web page. Using the printout, highlight or circle the tags related to forms. On a separate sheet of paper, create some XHTML notes by listing the tags and attributes related to forms found on your sample page along with a brief description of their purpose. Hand in the browser view of the page, source code printout, and your XHTML notes page to your instructor.

3. Choose one server-side technology mentioned in this chapter: Perl, PHP, ASP, JSP, Ruby on Rails, or ASP.Net. Use the resources listed in the chapter as a starting point, but also search the Web for additional resources on the server-side technology you have chosen. Create a Web page that lists at least five useful resources along with information about each that provides the name of the site, the URL, a brief description of what is offered and a recommended page (such as a tutorial,

free script, and so on). Place your name in an e-mail link on the Web page. Print both the source code (from Notepad) and the browser view of your Web page.

Focus on Web Design

The design of a form, such as the justification of the labels, the use of background colors, and even the order of the form elements can either increase or decrease the usability of a form. Visit some of the following resources to explore form design:

- http://www.uie.com/articles/web_forms/
- http://particletree.com/features/10-tips-to-a-better-form/
- http://www.d.umn.edu/is/support/Training/Online/webdesign/usability.html#forms
- http://www.lukew.com/resources/articles/WebForms_LukeW.pdf

Create a Web page that lists the URLs of at least two useful resources along with a brief description of the information you found most interesting or valuable. Design a form on the Web page that applies what you've just learned in your exploration of form design. Place your name in an e-mail link on the Web page. Print both the source code (from Notepad) and the browser view of your Web page.

WEB SITE CASE STUDY
Adding a Form

Each of the following case studies continues throughout most of the text. This chapter adds a page containing a form that invokes server-side processing to the Web sites.

JavaJam Coffee House

See Chapter 2 for an introduction to the JavaJam Coffee House Case Study. Figure 2.26 shows a site map for the JavaJam site. The Home page, Menu page, and Music page were created in earlier chapters. You will work with the Web pages in the javajamcss folder in this case study.

You have two tasks:

1. Add style rules to the javajam.css file that will configure a form.
2. Create a Jobs page (jobs.html) as shown in Figure 9.29.

Hands-On Practice Case

1. **Configure the CSS.** Modify the external style sheet, javajam.css. The form is styled with CSS. Review Section 9.4. See Figures 9.29 and 9.30. Open javajam.css in Notepad. Add the style rules as follows:

    - Notice how the text labels for the form elements are on the left side of the content area but are right-aligned. Create a class called `labelCol` that will float to the left, has a width of 100 pixels, aligns text to the right, and has 10 pixels of padding on the right.

Figure 9.29
JavaJam jobs.html

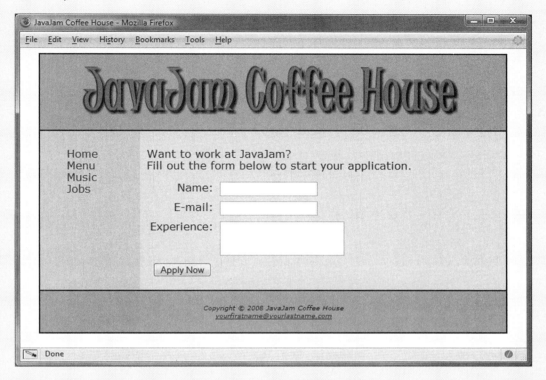

Figure 9.30
The box model of
the form

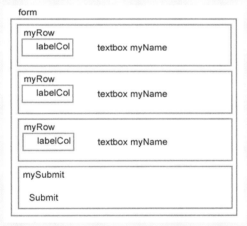

- Configure space around each form element. Create a class named `myRow` with 30 pixels of height.
- Configure extra space surrounding the submit button by creating a class called `mySubmit` with a 10 pixel margin.

Save the javajam.css file.

2. **The Jobs Page.** Use the Music page as the starting point for the Jobs page. Launch Notepad and open the music.html file in the javajamcss folder that you previously

created. Save the file as jobs.html. Modify your jobs.html file to look similar to the Jobs page, shown in Figure 9.29, as follows:

- Change the page title to an appropriate phrase.

- The Jobs page will contain a paragraph and a form in the `rightcol` div. Delete the current contents of the `rightcol` div (but leave the opening and closing `div` tags in place).

- Add a paragraph that contains the following text: Want to work at JavaJam? Fill out the form below to start your application.

- Prepare to code the XHTML for the form area. Begin with a `<form>` tag that uses the `post` method and the `action` attribute to invoke server-side processing. Unless directed otherwise by your instructor, configure the `action` attribute to send the form data to http://webdevfoundations.net/scripts/javajam.asp.

- Configure the Name area on the form. Code a `<div>` that is assigned to the `myRow` class. Create a `<label>` element that is assigned to the `labelCol` class. Code the text, `Name:`. Create a text box named `myName`.

- Configure the E-mail area on the form. Code a `<div>` that is assigned to the `myRow` class. Create a `<label>` element that is assigned to the `labelCol` class. Code the text, `E-mail:`. Create a text box named `myEmail`.

- Configure the Experience area on the form. Code a `<div>` that is assigned to the `myRow` class. Create a `<label>` element that is assigned to the `labelCol` class. Code the text, `Experience:`. Create a `textarea` named `myExperience` with rows set to `2` and cols set to `20`.

- Configure the submit button on the form. Code a `<div>` that is assigned to the `mySubmit` class. Code an input element with `type="submit"` and `value="Apply Now"`.

Save your page and test it in a browser. It should look similar to the page shown in Figure 9.29. If you are connected to the Internet, submit the form. This will send your form information to the server-side script configured in the `<form>` tag. A confirmation page that lists the form information and their corresponding names will be displayed.

Fish Creek Animal Hospital

See Chapter 2 for an introduction to the Fish Creek Animal Hospital Case Study. Figure 2.30 shows a site map for the Fish Creek site. The Home page, Services page, and Ask the Vet page were created in earlier chapters. You will work with the Web pages in the fishcreekcss folder in this case study.

You have two tasks:

1. Add style rules to the fishcreek.css file that will configure a form.
2. Create a Contact page (contact.html) as shown in Figure 9.31.

Hands-On Practice Case

1. **Configure the CSS.** Modify the external style sheet, fishcreek.css. The form is styled with CSS. Review Section 9.4. See Figures 9.30 and 9.31. Open

Figure 9.31
Fish Creek
contact.html

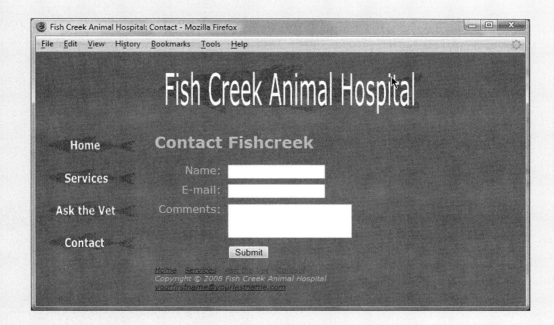

fishcreek.css in Notepad. Add the style rules as follows:

- Notice how the text labels for the form elements are on the left side of the content area but are right-aligned. Create a class called `labelCol` that will float to the left, has a width of 100 pixels, aligns text to the right, and has 10 pixels of padding on the right.

- Configure space around each form element. Create a class named `myRow` with 30 pixels of height.

- Configure extra space surrounding the submit button by creating a class called `mySubmit` with a left margin set to 110 pixels and all other margins set to 10 pixels.

Save the fishcreek.css file.

2. **The Contact Page.** Use the Ask the Vet page as the starting point for Contact page. Launch Notepad and open the askvet.html file in the fishcreekcss folder that you previously created. Save the file as contact.html. Modify your file to look similar to the Contact page, as shown in Figure 9.31, as follows:

- Change the page title to an appropriate phrase.

- The Contact page will contain an `<h2>` element and a form in the `rightcolumn div`. Delete the Ask the Vet page content from the `rightcolumn div` (but leave the page footer in place).

- Add an `<h2>` element that contains the following text: Contact FishCreek

- Prepare to code the XHTML for the form area. Begin with a `<form>` tag that uses the `post` method and the `action` attribute to invoke server-side processing. Unless directed otherwise by your instructor, configure the `action` attribute to send the form data to http://webdevfoundations.net/scripts/fishcreek.asp.

- Configure the Name area on the form. Code a `<div>` that is assigned to the `myRow` class. Create a `<label>` element that is assigned to the `labelCol` class. Code the text, `Name:`. Create a text box named `myName`.

- Configure the E-mail area on the form. Code a `<div>` that is assigned to the myRow class. Create a `<label>` element that is assigned to the `labelCol` class. Code the text, `E-mail:`. Create a text box named `myEmail`.
- Configure the Comments area on the form. Code a `<div>` that is assigned to the myRow class. Create a `<label>` element that is assigned to the `labelCol` class. Code the text, `Comments:`. Create a `textarea` named `myComments` with rows set to 2 and cols set to 20.
- Configure the submit button on the form. Code a `<div>` that is assigned to the mySubmit class. Code an input element with `type="submit"` and `value="Submit"`.

Save your page and display it in a browser. It should look similar to the page shown in Figure 9.31. If you are connected to the Internet, submit the form. This will send your form information to the server-side script configured in the `<form>` tag. A confirmation page that lists the form information and their corresponding names will be displayed.

Pete the Painter

See Chapter 2 for an introduction to the Pete the Painter Case Study. Figure 2.34 shows a site map for the Pete the Painter site. The Home page, Services page, and Testimonials page were created in earlier chapters. You will work with the Web pages in the paintercss folder in this case study.

You have two tasks:

1. Add style rules to the painter.css file that will configure a form.
2. Create a Free Estimate page (estimate.html) as shown in Figure 9.32.

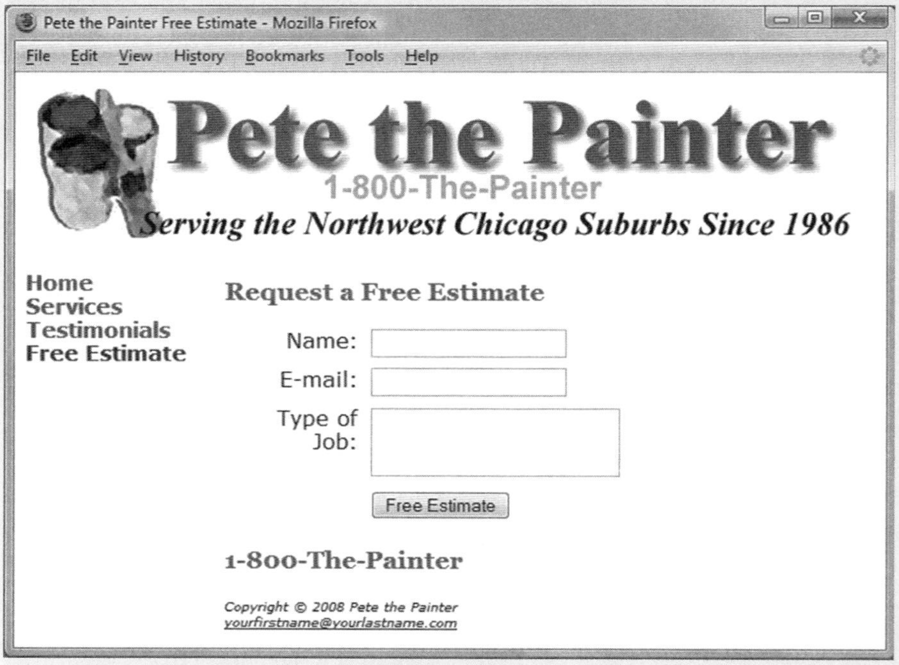

Figure 9.32
Pete the Painter
estimate.html

Hands-On Practice Case

1. **Configure the CSS.** Modify the external style sheet, painter.css. The form is styled with CSS. Review Section 9.4. See Figures 9.30 and 9.32. Open painter.css in Notepad. Add the style rules as follows:

   - Notice how the text labels for the form elements are on the left side of the content area but are right-aligned. Create a class called `labelCol` that will float to the left, has a width of 100 pixels, aligns text to the right, and has 10 pixels of padding on the right.

   - Configure space around each form element. Create a class named `myRow` with 30 pixels of height.

   - Configure extra space surrounding the submit button by creating a class called `mySubmit` with a left margin set to 110 pixels and all other margins set to 10 pixels.

   Save the painter.css file.

2. **The Free Estimate Page.** Use the Testimonials page as the starting point for the Free Estimate page. Launch Notepad and open the testimonials.html file in the paintercss folder that you previously created. Save the file as estimate.html. Modify your file to look similar to the Free Estimate page, shown in Figure 9.32, as follows:

   - Change the page title to an appropriate phrase.

   - The Estimate page will contain an `<h3>` element and a form in the `rightcolumn` div. Delete the Testimonials page content from the `rightcolumn` div (but leave the phone number and page footer in place).

   - Add an `<h3>` element that contains the following text: Request a Free Estimate. Assign the `<h3>` element to the `logo` class.

   - Prepare to code the XHTML for the form area. Begin with a `<form>` tag that uses the `post` method and the `action` attribute to invoke server-side processing. Unless directed otherwise by your instructor, configure the `action` attribute to send the form data to http://webdevfoundations.net/scripts/painter.asp.

   - Configure the Name area on the form. Code a `<div>` that is assigned to the `myRow` class. Create a `<label>` element that is assigned to the `labelCol` class. Code the text, `Name:`. Create a text box named `myName`.

   - Configure the E-mail area on the form. Code a `<div>` that is assigned to the `myRow` class. Create a `<label>` element that is assigned to the `labelCol` class. Code the text, `E-mail:`. Create a text box named `myEmail`.

   - Configure the Type of Job area on the form. Code a `<div>` that is assigned to the `myRow` class. Create a `<label>` element that is assigned to the `labelCol` class. Code the text, `Type of Job:`. Create a `textarea` named `myJob` with rows set to 2 and cols set to 20.

   - Configure the submit button on the form. Code a `<div>` that is assigned to the `mySubmit` class. Code an input element with `type="submit"` and `value="Free Estimate"`.

Save your page and test it in a browser. It should look similar to the page shown in Figure 9.32. If you are connected to the Internet, submit the form. This will send your form information to the server-side script configured in the `<form>` tag. A confirmation page that lists the form information and their corresponding names will be displayed.

Prime Properties

See Chapter 2 for an introduction to the Prime Properties Case Study. Figure 2.38 shows a site map for the Prime Properties site. The Home page, Listings page, and Financing page were created in earlier chapters. You will work on the Web pages in the primecss folder in this case study.

Figure 9.33
Prime Properties
contact.html

You have two tasks:

1. Add style rules to the prime.css file that will configure a form.
2. Create a Contact page (contact.html) as shown in Figure 9.33.

Hands-On Practice Case

1. **Configure the CSS.** Modify the external style sheet, prime.css. The form is styled with CSS. Review Section 9.4. See Figures 9.30 and 9.33. Open prime.css in Notepad. Add the style rules as follows:
   - Notice how the text labels for the form elements are on the left side of the content area but are right-aligned. Create a class called `labelCol` that will float to the left, has a width of 100 pixels, aligns text to the right, and has 10 pixels of padding on the right.
   - Configure space around each form element. Create a class named `myRow` with 30 pixels of height.

- Configure extra space surrounding the submit button by creating a class called mySubmit with margins set to 10 pixels.

Save the prime.css file.

2. **The Contact Page.** Use the Financing page as the starting point for the Contact page. Launch Notepad and open the financing.html file in the primecss folder that you previously created. Save the file as contact.html.

Modify your file to be similar to the Contact page, as shown in Figure 9.33, as follows:

- Change the page title to an appropriate phrase.
- Replace the Financing subheading with Contact.
- Delete the rest of the Financing page content from the rightcolumn div (but leave the navigation and page footer in place).
- Prepare to code the XHTML for the form area. Begin with a <form> tag that uses the post method and action attributes to invoke server-side processing. Unless directed otherwise by your instructor, configure the action attribute to send the form data to http://webdevfoundations.net/scripts/prime.asp.
- Configure the Name area on the form. Code a <div> that is assigned to the myRow class. Create a <label> element that is assigned to the labelCol class. Code the text, Name:. Create a text box named myName.
- Configure the E-mail area on the form. Code a <div> that is assigned to the myRow class. Create a <label> element that is assigned to the labelCol class. Code the text, E-mail:. Create a text box named myEmail.
- Configure the Comments area on the form. Code a <div> that is assigned to the myRow class. Create a <label> element that is assigned to the labelCol class. Code the text, Comments:. Create a textarea named myComments with rows set to 2 and cols set to 20.
- Configure the submit button on the form. Code a <div> that is assigned to the mySubmit class. Code an input element with type="submit" and value="Contact".

Save your page and test it in a browser. It should look similar to the page shown in Figure 9.33. If you are connected to the Internet, submit the form. This will send your form information to the server-side script configured in the <form> tag. A confirmation page that lists the form information and their corresponding names will be displayed.

Web Project

See Chapters 5 and 6 for an introduction to the Web Project case. You will either add a form to an existing page in your Web site or create a new page that contains a form. Use CSS to style the form.

Hands-On Practice Case

1. Choose one of your project Web pages to contain the form. Sketch a design of the form you plan to create.

2. Modify your project's external CSS file (project.css) to configure the form areas as needed.

3. Update your chosen Web page and add the XHTML code for the form.

4. The `<form>` tag should use the `post` method and `action` attributes to invoke server-side processing. Unless directed otherwise by your instructor, configure the `action` attribute to send the form data to http://webdevfoundations.net/scripts/formdemo.asp.

Save and test the page. If you are connected to the Internet, submit the form. This will send your form information to the server-side script configured in the `<form>` tag. A confirmation page that lists the form information and their corresponding names will be displayed.

Web Site Development

Chapter Objectives In this chapter, you will learn how to …

- Describe the skills, functions, and job roles needed for a successful Web project development
- Utilize the stages in the standard System Development Life Cycle
- Identify other common system development methodologies
- Apply the System Development Life Cycle to Web development projects
- Identify opportunities and determine goals during the Conceptualization phase
- Determine information topics and site requirements during the Analysis phase

- Create the site map, page layout, prototype, and documentation as part of the Design phase
- Complete the Web pages and associated files during the Production phase
- Verify the functionality of the Web site and use a test plan during the Testing phase
- Obtain client approval and launch a Web site
- Modify and enhance the Web site during the Maintenance phase
- Compare the goals of the Web site to the results as part of the Evaluation phase
- Find the right Web host provider for your Web site

This chapter discusses the skills needed for success-ful large-scale project development and introduces you to common Web development methods. It is important to realize that each project is unique; each has its own needs and requirements. Choosing the right people to work on a Web project team can make it or break it.

10.1 Successful Large-Scale Project Development

Large-scale projects are not completed by only one or two individuals. They are created by a group of people working together as a team. The job roles of project manager, information architect, marketing representative, copywriter, editor, graphic designer, database administrator, network administrator, and Web developer are usually needed for large projects. In smaller companies or smaller organizations each person can wear many hats and juggle his or her job roles. In a smaller-scale project, one of the Web developers may double as the project manager, graphic designer, database administrator, and/or information architect. Job roles necessary for successful projects are discussed in this section.

Project Manager

The **project manager** oversees the Web site development process and coordinates team activities. The project manager creates the project plan and schedule. This individual is accountable for reaching project milestones and producing results. Excellent organizational, managerial, and communication skills are required.

Information Architect

The **information architect** clarifies the mission and goals of the site, assists in determining the functionality of the site, and is instrumental in defining the site organization, navigation, and labeling. Web developers and/or the project manager sometimes take on this role themselves.

Marketing Representative

The **marketing representative** handles the organization's marketing plan and goals. The marketing representative works with the Web designers to create a **Web presence**, or look and feel, that aligns with the marketing goals of the organization. The marketing representative also helps to coordinate the Web site with other media used for marketing, such as print, radio, and television marketing.

Copywriter and Editor

The **copywriter** prepares and evaluates copy. When material from existing brochures, newsletters, and white papers will be used on the Web site, it must be repurposed or reworked for the Web media. The content manager or **editor** may work with the copywriter to check the text for correct grammar and consistency.

Content Manager

The **content manager** participates in the strategic and creative development and enhancements of the Web site. He or she oversees changes in content. The skill set of a successful content manager includes editing, copywriting, marketing, technology, and communication. The person in this dynamic job role must be able to facilitate change.

Graphic Designer

The **graphic designer** determines appropriate use of color and graphics on the site, creates page layouts, and designs graphics. The graphic designer may work closely with the Web developers to create graphic buttons used in mouseover effects.

Database Administrator

A **database administrator** is needed if the site accesses information stored in databases. Database administrators create databases, create procedures to maintain databases (including backup and recovery), and control access to databases.

Network Administrator

The **network administrator** configures and maintains the **Web server**, installs and maintains system hardware and software, and controls access security.

Web Developer

The **Web developer** writes XHTML code and client-side scripting such as JavaScript. The Web developer may develop server-side processing such as PHP or ASP. Typically, there are multiple Web developers assigned to a large project, each with his or her area of expertise.

Project Staffing Criteria

Whether the project is large or small, finding the right people to work on it is crucial. When selecting staff for a project, consider each individual's work experience, portfolio, formal education, and industry certifications.

Another option to staffing a Web project (or developing an entire Web site) is to outsource the project—that is, hire another company to do the work for you. Sometimes portions of a project are outsourced, such as graphics creation, multimedia animation, or server-side scripting. When this option is chosen, communication between the project manager and the external organization is crucial. The outsource team needs to be aware of the project goals and deadlines.

Large or small, developed in-house or outsourced, the success of a Web site project depends on planning and communication. Formal project development methodology is used to coordinate and facilitate the planning and communication needed for a successful Web project.

10.2 The Development Process

Large corporate and commercial Web sites don't just happen. They are carefully built, usually by following a project development methodology. A methodology is a step-by-step plan that encompasses the life cycle of a project from start to finish. It comprises of a series of **phases**, each having specific activities and deliverables. Most modern methodologies have their roots in the **System Development Life Cycle (SDLC)**, a process that has been used for several decades to build large-scale information systems. The SDLC comprises a set of phases, sometimes called steps or stages. Each phase is usually completed before beginning the activities in the next phase. The basic phases of the standard SDLC (see Figure 10.1) are systems investigation, systems analysis, systems design, systems implementation, and maintenance.

Figure 10.1
The System Development Life Cycle (SDLC)

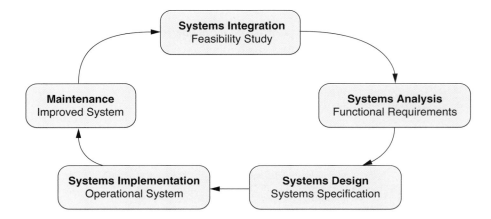

Web sites are often developed using a variation of the SDLC that is modified to apply to Web projects. Large companies and Web design firms usually create their own special methodology for use on projects. The Web Site Development Cycle is a guide to successful Web project management. Depending on the scope and complexity of a particular project, some steps can be completed in a single meeting; other steps can take weeks or months.

The Web Site Development Cycle, shown in Figure 10.2, usually consists of the following steps: Conceptualization, Analysis, Design, Production, Testing, Launch, Maintenance, and Evaluation.

Figure 10.2
The Web Site Development Cycle

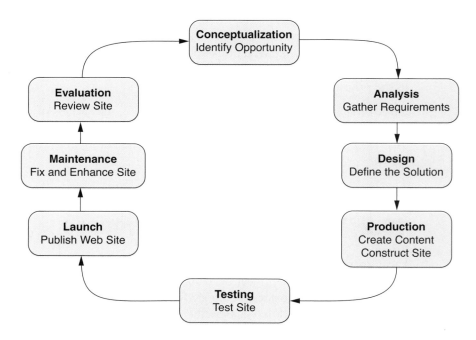

What about other Web site development methodologies?

The development methodology presented in this chapter is a version of the traditional SDLC modified for Web site development. Other development methods include the following:

- **Prototyping.** A small working model is created and shown to the client. It is continually revised by the developer until it is usable for the intended purpose. This method can easily be included in the Web Development Life Cycle during the Design phase.

- **Spiral System Development.** This is excellent for very large-scale or phased projects where it is important to reduce risk. Small portions of the project are completed one after the other in a spiral system of development.

- **Joint Application Development (JAD).** This type of development focuses on group meetings and collaboration between the users and developers of a Web site or system. It is generally used only with in-house development.

- **Agile Software Development.** This development methodology is viewed as innovative in that it stresses responsiveness based on generating and sharing knowledge within a development team and with the client. The philosophy emphasizes code over documentation and results in the project being developed in many small, iterative steps.

- **Organization-Specific Development Methodologies.** Large companies and Web development firms often create their own version or interpretation of site development methodology to be used on projects.

An important aspect of Web site development is that you are never finished—your site needs to be kept fresh and up-to-date, there will be errors or omissions that need to be corrected, and new components and pages will be needed. The first step is to decide why the Web site is needed in the first place.

Conceptualization

What opportunity or issue is the site addressing? What is the motivation for the site? Perhaps your client owns a retail store and wishes to sell products over the Internet. Perhaps your client's competitor just completed a Web site and your client needs to create one just to keep up. Perhaps you have a great idea that will be the next eBay!

Because the focus of your work is to make the site usable and appealing to your target audience, you must determine the site's intended audience. It is crucial to be aware of who your audience is and what their preferences are.

Another task during **conceptualization** is to determine the site's long-term and short-term goals or mission. Perhaps a short-term goal is simply to publish a home page. Perhaps a long-term goal is for 20 percent of a company's product sales to be made on the Web site. Or you may simply want a certain number of Web site visitors each month. Whatever they are, it is better if the objectives are measurable. Decide how you will measure the success (or failure) of your Web site.

Determining the purpose and goals of a site is usually done with the cooperation of the client, project manager, and information architect. In a formal project environment, a document that details the results of this step is created, and then approved by the client before development can proceed.

Analysis

The Analysis phase involves meetings and interviews with key client personnel. **Analysis** is usually completed by the project manager, information architect or other analyst, and the client's marketing representative and related personnel. The network administrator and database administrator may be interviewed depending on the scope of the project. Common tasks completed during the Analysis phase follow:

- **Determine Information Topics.** Organize the information to be presented on the site into categories and create a hierarchy. These **information topics** will be used later as a starting point for developing the site navigation.

- **Determine Functionality Requirements.** State what the site will do, not how it will do it. For example, state "the site will accept credit card orders from customers," not "the site will perform order processing using Active Server Pages to look up each price and sales tax information in Oracle databases and use real-time credit card verification supplied by somewebsite.com." Note the difference in the level of detail of these **functionality requirements**.

- **Determine Environmental Requirements.** What **environmental requirements**, such as hardware, operating system, memory capacity, screen resolution, and bandwidth will your site visitors be using? What type of hardware and software requirements will the Web server need? (See Section 10.3 Web Hosting and Section 10.4 Choosing a Virtual Host for help with this question.)

- **Determine Content Requirements.** Does content already exist in another format—brochures, catalogs, white papers? Determine who is responsible for creating and repurposing content for the site. Does the client company or marketing department have any **content requirements** that must be met? For example, is there a specific look and feel or corporate branding component that must be present on the site?

- **Compare the Old Approach to the New Approach.** Perhaps you are not creating a new Web site, but modifying an existing one. What benefits or added value will the new version provide?

- **Review Your Competitors' Sites.** A careful review of your competitors' Web presence will help you design a site that will stand out from the crowd and be more appealing to your shared customer base. Note the good and bad components of these sites.

- **Estimate Costs.** Create an estimate of the costs and time involved to create the site. A formal project plan is often created or modified at this point. Often, an application such as Microsoft Project is used to estimate costs and plan project schedules.

- **Do a Cost/Benefit Analysis.** Create a document that compares the costs and benefits of the site. Measurable benefits are the most useful and most appealing to clients. In a formal project environment, a document that details the results of this **cost/benefit analysis** must be approved by the client before the team can proceed.

Design

Once everyone knows what is needed, it is time to determine how it can be accomplished. The Design phase involves meetings and interviews with key client personnel. **Design** tasks are usually completed by the project manager, information architect or other analyst, graphic designer(s), senior Web developer(s), and the client's marketing representative and related personnel. Common tasks of the Design phase follow:

- **Choose a Site Organization.** As discussed in Chapter 5, common Web site organizational forms are hierarchical, linear, and random. Determine which is best for the project site and create a site map (sometimes called a flowchart or storyboard).

- **Prototype the Design.** Often, a graphics application is used to create sample Web page mock-ups, or wireframes, as page layouts are created. These can be shown to clients as a prototype, or working model, of the system for approval. They can also be shown to focus groups for **usability testing**.

- **Create a Page Layout Design.** The overall layout, or look and feel, of the site should be designed. The page layout design is used as a guideline for the Home page and Content page layouts. Items such as the site color scheme, size of logo graphics, button graphics, and text should be determined. Using the page layout design and site map, create sample layouts for the Home page and Content pages. Use a graphic application to create mock-ups of these pages to get a good idea of how the site will function. If you use a Web authoring tool, you run the risk of your manager or client thinking you already have the site half done and insisting on early delivery.

- **Document Each Page.** While this may seem unnecessary, lack of content is a frequent cause of Web site project delays. Prepare a content sheet for each page, such as the one shown in Figure 10.3, which describes the functionality of the document, text and graphic content requirements, source of content, and approver of content.

The site map and page design prototypes are usually approved by the client before the team can continue with the Production phase.

Figure 10.3
Sample content sheet

```
Page Title:

Basic Description:


Suggested Graphic Elements:



Other Special Features:


Special Informational Needs:


Information Sources:



_____

Content Provider(s):

File Format of Provided Content:
Deadline for Content:
Content Approval:
```

Production

During **production** all the previous work comes together (hopefully) in a usable and effective Web site. During the Production phase, the Web developers are on the critical path—their work must be done as scheduled or the project will be late. The other project members are consulted as needed for clarification and approval. Common tasks of the Production phase follow:

- **Choose a Web Authoring Tool.** The use of a Web authoring tool such as Adobe Dreamweaver or Microsoft Expression Web can greatly increase productivity. Specific productivity aids include designer notes, page templates, task management, and Web page check-in and check-out to avoid overlapping page updates. The use of an authoring tool will serve to standardize the XHTML used in the project pages. Any standards related to indentation, comments, and so on should be determined at this time.

- **Organize Your Site Files.** Consider placing images and media in their own folder. Also, place server-side scripts in a separate folder. Determine naming conventions for Web pages, images, and media.

- **Develop and Individually Test Components.** During this task the graphic designers and Web developers create and individually test their contributions to the site. As the images, Web pages, and server-side scripting are developed, they are individually tested. This is called **unit testing**. On some projects, a senior Web developer or the project manager will review the components for quality and standards compliance.

Once all components have been created and unit tested, it's time to put them together and begin the Testing phase.

Testing

The components should be published to a test Web server. This test Web server should have the same operating system and Web server software that the production (actual) Web server will be using. Some common site **testing** considerations follow:

- **Test on Different Browsers and Browser Versions.** Many Web pages look fine on Internet Explorer but will not even display on Netscape Navigator. It is very important to test your pages on commonly used browsers and versions of those browsers.

- **Test with Different Screen Resolutions.** Although as a Web developer, you may use a very high screen resolution, not everyone uses 1600×1200 screen resolution. The most commonly used screen resolutions at the time of this writing are 1024×768, 1280×1024, and 800×600. Be sure to test your Web pages on various resolutions—you might be surprised at the results.

- **Test Using Different Bandwidths.** If you live and work in a metropolitan area, everyone you know may have broadband access to the Internet. However, many people still use dial-up connections to access the Web. It is important to test your site on both slow and fast connections. Images that look great over your school's T3 line may load very slowly over a 56K modem.

- **Test from Another Location.** Be sure to test your Web site using a computer other than the one the Web site was developed on, in order to simulate the Web page visitor experience more closely.
- **Test, Test, Test.** There is no such thing as too much testing. Humans make mistakes. It is much better for you and your team to find the errors than for your client to point them out to you when they review the Web site.

Does this sound like a lot to keep track of? It is. That's why it's a good idea to create a **test plan**—a document that describes what will be tested on each page of a Web site. A sample test plan for a Web page, shown in Figure 10.4, can help you organize your testing as you check your document in different browsers and screen resolutions. The document validation section covers content, links, and any forms or scripting that are required for the page. The search engine optimization meta tags are discussed in Chapter 13. However, at this point you should be able to verify that the page title is descriptive and includes the company or organization name. Testing your page using different bandwidths is important because Web pages that take too long to download are often abandoned.

Figure 10.4
Sample test plan

Web Page Document Test Plan

File Name:		Date:	
Title:		Tester:	

Browser Compatibility

	1024x768	800x600	1280x1024	Other	PC	Mac	Linux	Images Off	Print	Other	Notes
Internet Explorer (Version #)											
Firefox (Version #)											
Safari (Version #)											
Opera (Version #)											
Netscape (Version #)											
Screen Reader											
Mobile											
Other											

Document Validation

	Pass	Fail	Notes
XHTML Validation			
Check Spelling			
Required Content			
Required Graphics			
Check Alt Attributes			
Test Links			
Accessibility Testing			
Form Processing			
Scripting/Dynamic Effects			
Usability Testing			

Search Engine Optimization

	Pass	Fail	Notes
Page Title			
Meta Tag (description)			
Meta Tag (keyword)			
Other			

Bandwidth Check

	Time	Notes
28.8 K		
56.6 K		
Broadband		
Other		

Notes

Automated Testing Tools and Validators. The Web authoring tool your project is using will have some built-in site reporting and testing features. Web authoring applications such as Adobe Dreamweaver and Microsoft Expression Web provide functions such as spell checks, link checks, and load time calculations. Each application has unique features. Dreamweaver's reporting includes link checking, accessibility, and code validation. There are other **automated testing** tools and **validators** available. Some are free, such as the W3C Validator and HTML Tidy. The W3C Validator (http://validator .w3.org) can be used to validate both HTML and XHTML. HTML Tidy (http://sourceforge.net/projects/tidy) will convert an HTML page to an XHTML page—correcting the tag syntax and replacing font tags with formatting using Cascading Style Sheets. An online version of HTML Tidy is available at http://valet.htmlhelp.com/tidy. Other testing tools that offer additional features such as page load time and broken-link checking are available from http://www.netmechanic.com/ and others. See http://www.softwareqatest.com/qatweb1.html for a partial list.

In addition to validating HTML and testing for broken links, consider using a tool such as HP Runner to load-test the Web server. The scope and complexity of your site will determine the amount of testing needed. For a simple site, validation and link checking will probably suffice. Other types of sites will benefit from more rigorous testing.

Focus on Accessibility

Accessibility Testing. In the design and coding process your team should have followed recommended techniques to provide accessibility. In fact, if your Web site will be used by an agency of the federal government, you are required to do so by law (Section 508 of the Rehabilitation Act). State governments have also begun to legislate accessibility requirements. For example, the recently passed Illinois Information Technology Act requires Illinois state agencies and universities to ensure that their information technology (including Web sites) is accessible. Prove your compliance by performing **accessibility testing** on your site. There are a variety of accessibility checkers available. Adobe Dreamweaver includes a built-in accessibility checker. Visit http://firefox.cita.uiuc.edu/ to download an accessibility extension for the FireFox browser. Popular online accessibility tests include Watchfire's WebXACT (http://webxact.watchfire.com) and Cynthia Says (http://www.cynthiasays.com).

Usability Testing. Testing how actual Web page visitors use a Web site is called usability testing. It can be conducted at any phase of a Web site's development and is often performed more than once. A usability test is conducted by asking users to complete tasks on a Web site, such as placing an order, looking up the phone number of a company, or finding a product. The exact tasks will vary depending on the Web site being tested. The users are monitored while they try to perform these tasks. They are asked to think out loud about their doubts and hesitations. The results are recorded (often on video tape) and discussed with the Web design team. Often changes are made to the navigation and page layouts based on these tests. Complete Hands-On Exercise 6 at the end of this chapter and perform a small-scale usability test to become more familiar with this technique.

If usability testing is done early in the development phase of a Web site, it may use the paper page layouts and site map. If the Web development team is struggling with a design issue, sometimes a usability test can help to determine which design idea is the better choice.

When usability is done during a later phase, such as the Testing phase, the actual Web site is tested. This can lead to a confirmation that the site is easy to use and well designed, to last minute changes in the Web site, or to a plan for Web site enhancements in the near future.

Launch

Your client—whether another company or another department in your organization—needs to review and approve the test Web site before the files are published to the live site. Sometimes this approval takes place at a face-to-face meeting. Other times, the test URL is given to the client and the client e-mails approval or requested changes.

Once the test Web site has been approved, it is published to your live production Web site (this is called a **launch**). If you think you are finished—think again! It is crucial to test all site components after publishing to make sure the site functions properly in its new environment. Marketing and promotion activities for the Web site (see Chapter 13) usually take place at this time.

Maintenance

A Web site is never finished. There are always errors or omissions that were overlooked during the development process. Clients usually find many new uses for a Web site once they have one and request modifications, additions, and new sections (this is called site **maintenance**). So at this point, the project team identifies the new opportunity or enhancement and begins another loop through the development process.

Other types of updates needed are relatively small—perhaps a link is broken, a word is misspelled, or a graphic needs to be changed. These small changes are usually made as soon as they are noticed. The question of who makes the changes and who approves them is often a matter of company policy. If you are a freelance Web developer, the situation is more straightforward—you will make the changes and your client will approve them.

Evaluation

Remember the goals set for the Web site in the Conceptualization phase? During **evaluation** it's time to review them and determine if your Web site meets them. If not, consider how you can enhance the site, and begin another loop through the development process.

CHECKPOINT 10.1

1. Describe the role of the project manager.
2. Explain why many different roles are needed on a large-scale Web project.
3. List three different techniques used to test a Web site. Describe each technique in one or two sentences.

10.3 Web Hosting

Where is the appropriate place for your Web project to "live"? Choosing the most appropriate **Web host** provider for your business or client could be one of the most important decisions you make. A good Web hosting service will provide a robust, reliable home for your Web site. A poor Web hosting service will be the source of problems and complaints. Which would you prefer?

Web Host Providers

The types of Web host providers range from local ISPs who have some empty space on their servers and Web developers who host sites on the side, to local hosting companies and national companies that guarantee 99.999 percent uptime. Understandably, the fees and the level of service are different. What does your business or client need? This section looks at needs of various size businesses.

One word of caution: Never consider using a "free" Web host provider for a business site. These free sites are great for kids, college students, and hobbyists, but they are unprofessional. The last thing you or your client wants is to be perceived as unprofessional or not serious about the business at hand.

As you consider different Web host providers, be sure to check references. Also, try contacting their support phone numbers and e-mail addresses to determine just how responsive they really are. It is common for Web host providers to charge a setup fee in addition to the monthly hosting fee. Hosting fees vary widely. The cheapest hosting provider is not necessarily the one to use. Word of mouth, Web searches, the local phone directory, and online directories such as http://webhosts.thelist.com/business are all resources in your quest for the perfect Web host provider.

Hosting Needs

Small- to Medium-Size Web Site. Suggested requirements include unlimited data transfer, 60MB or more of hard disk space, e-mail, and support of server-side scripting such as ASP or PHP. This type of hosting is usually **virtual hosting**. The Web host provider's server is divided into a number of virtual domains, and multiple Web sites are set up on the same computer.

Keep in mind that over time your Web site will grow and your processing needs will increase. Do you have access to your Web site log or will automatic reporting be included? Does the Web host provider offer an e-commerce package that you can use when you are ready? Does it offer CGI or database support? You may not need these technologies now, but keep your options open for the future. Moving a site from one Web host provider to another is not always an easy process. Choose a Web host provider that most likely will meet your future needs as well as your present needs.

Also consider the operating system and Web server application that your host offers. The UNIX operating system running an Apache Web server is quite common and very efficient. However, if the skill set of your organization is mainly Microsoft technologies, your staff will be more comfortable and more productive with a Web host that offers a Microsoft operating system running Internet Information Server as the Web server.

Consider local Web hosting providers as well as national Web host providers in your search.

Why do I care about knowing which operating system my Web host provider uses?
Knowing the operating system used by your Web host provider is important because it can help you with troubleshooting your Web site. Often, students' Web sites work great on their own PC (usually with a Windows-based operating system) but fall apart (with broken links and images that do not load) after being published on a free Web server that uses a different operating system.

Some operating systems, such as Windows, treat uppercase and lowercase letters in exactly the same way. Other operating systems, such as UNIX and Linux, consider uppercase and lowercase letters to be different. This is called being case-sensitive. For example, when a Web server running on a Windows operating system receives a request generated by an anchor tag coded as `<a href="MyPage.html">My Page</a>`, it will return a file named with any combination of uppercase or lowercase letters. The values MyPage.html, mypage.html, myPage.html can all be used. However, when the request generated by the same anchor tag is received by a Web server running on a UNIX system (which is case-sensitive) the file would only be found if it were really saved as MyPage.html. If the file were named mypage.html, a 404 (not found) error would result. This is a good reason to be consistent when naming files—consider always using lowercase letters for file names.

Large- to Enterprise-Size Web Site. If you are expecting a high traffic site that may support a chat room or streaming media content, consider large national Web hosting services. Generally, these provide a high bandwidth Internet connection (typically OC-1 or higher), 24-hour staffing, hardware and media redundancy, and enhanced security. Determine the guaranteed level of service and response time. Also consider using a dedicated or co-located Web server at a national Web host provider. A dedicated or co-located Web server will be running your Web site only—you do not share the processor or hard drive with any other organization. There is an additional charge, but the added security and guarantee of processing may be worth it to your organization.

A **dedicated Web server** refers to the rental and exclusive use of a computer and connection to the Internet that is housed on the Web hosting company's premises. A dedicated server is usually needed for a Web site that could have a considerable amount of traffic, such as tens of millions of hits a day. The server can usually be configured and operated remotely from the client company or you can pay the Web host provider to administer it for you.

A **co-located Web server,** sometimes referred to as colocated or collocated, is a computer that your organization has purchased and configured. Your organization effectively rents space at the Web host provider's location. Your server is kept and connected to the Internet at its location. Your organization administers this computer. This provides your organization with additional control over the Web server, but it also means that you need to staff or contract an individual with Web server administration experience.

Large, national Web host providers can supply dedicated T1 or T3 Internet access, 24/7 support, network utilization statistics and log access, hardware and media redundancy, and the ability to cluster Web servers, support Web farms, e-commerce, and streaming media delivery. A **Service-Level Agreement** (SLA) that details the level of support and response time is also usually supplied by large, national Web host providers.

For your Web site—small, medium, or large—selecting the right Web host can be crucial to its success.

10.4 Choosing a Virtual Host

A number of factors to consider when choosing a Web host, including bandwidth, disk storage space, technical support, and the availability of e-commerce packages have been discussed. For a handy list of these factors and others to consider in your quest for a virtual Web host, review the Web host checklist shown in Table 10.1.

Table 10.1 Web host checklist

Operating System	❏ UNIX ❏ Linux ❏ Windows	Some Web hosts offer a choice of these platforms. If you need to integrate your Web site with your business systems, choose the same operating system for both.
Web Server	❏ Apache ❏ IIS	These two Web server applications are the most popular. Apache usually runs on a UNIX or Linux operating system. IIS (Internet Information Services) is bundled with selected versions of Microsoft Windows.
Bandwidth	❏ _____ MB or GB ❏ _____ Charge for overage	Some Web hosts carefully monitor your data transfer bandwidth and charge you for overages. While unlimited bandwidth is great, it is not always available. A typical low-traffic Web site varies between 100 and 200MB per month. A medium-traffic site should be okay with about 20GB of data transfer bandwidth per month.
Technical Support	❏ E-mail ❏ Forum ❏ Phone	Review the description of technical support on the Web host's site. Is it available 24 hours a day, seven days a week? E-mail or phone a question to test it. If the organization is not responsive to you as a prospective customer, be leery about the availability of its technical support later.
Service Agreement	❏ Uptime guarantee ❏ Automatic monitoring	A Web host that offers an SLA (Service Level Agreement) with an uptime guarantee shows that they value service and reliability. The use of automatic monitoring will inform the Web host technical support staff when a server is not functioning.
Disk Space	❏ _____ MB ❏ _____ GB	Many virtual hosts routinely offer 100MB+ disk storage space. If you have a small site that is not graphic-intensive you may never even use 40MB of disk storage space.
E-mail	❏ _____ Mailboxes	Most virtual hosts offer multiple e-mail mailboxes per site. These can be used to filter messages—customer service, technical support, general inquiries, and so on.

Table 10.1 Web host checklist (*continued*)

Uploading Files	❏ FTP Access ❏ Web-based File Manager	A Web host that offers FTP access will allow you the most flexibility. Others only allow updates through a Web-based file manager application. Some Web hosts offer both options.
Canned Scripts	❏ Form processing ❏ _____	Many Web hosts supply canned, pre-written scripts to process form information.
Scripting Support	❏ ASP ❏ PHP ❏ .Net	If you plan to use server-side scripting on your site determine which, if any, scripting is supported by your Web host.
Database Support	❏ MySQL ❏ MS Access ❏ MS SQL	If you plan to access a database with your scripting, determine which, if any, database is supported by your Web host.
E-Commerce Packages	❏ _____	If you plan to enter into e-commerce (see Chapter 12) it may be easier if your Web host offers a shopping cart package. Check to see if one is available.
Scalability	❏ Scripting ❏ Database ❏ E-commerce	You probably will choose a basic (low-end) plan for your first Web site. Note the scalability of your Web host—are there other plans with scripting, database, e-commerce packages, and additional bandwidth or disk space available as your site grows?
Backups	❏ Daily ❏ Periodic ❏ No backups	Most Web hosts will back up your files regularly. Check to see how often the backups are made and if they are accessible to you. Be sure to make your own site backups as well.
Site Statistics	❏ Raw log file ❏ Log reports ❏ No log access	The Web server log contains useful information about your visitors, how they find your site, and what pages they visit. Check to see if the log is available to you. Some Web hosts provide reports about the log. See Chapter 13 for more information on Web server logs.
Domain Name	❏ Required to register with host ❏ OK to register on your own	Some Web hosts offer a package that includes registering your domain name. It is better if you register your domain name yourself (see http://register.com or http://networksolutions.com) and retain control of your domain name account.
Price	❏ _____ Set up fee ❏ _____ per month	Price is last in this list for a reason. Do not choose a Web host based on price alone—the old adage "you get what you pay for" is definitely true here. It is not unusual to pay a one-time set-up fee and then a periodic fee—either monthly, quarterly, or annually.

CHECKPOINT 10.2

1. Describe the type of Web host that would meet the needs of a small company for its initial Web presence.

2. Describe the difference between a dedicated Web server and a co-located Web server.

3. Explain why price is not the most important consideration when choosing a Web host.

CHAPTER SUMMARY

This chapter introduced the system development life cycle and its application to Web development projects. The job roles related to Web site development and issues related to Web hosting were also discussed.

Visit the textbook Web site at http://www.webdevfoundations.net for examples, the links listed in this chapter, and updated information.

Key Terms

accessibility testing
analysis
automated testing
co-located Web server
conceptualization
content manager
content requirements
copywriter
cost/benefit analysis
database administrator
dedicated Web server
design
editor

environmental requirements
evaluation
functionality requirements
graphic designer
information architect
information topics
launch
maintenance
marketing representative
network administrator
phases
production
project manager

Service Level Agreement (SLA)
System Development Life Cycle (SDLC)
test plan
testing
unit testing
usability testing
validators
virtual hosting
Web developer
Web host
Web presence
Web server

Review Questions

Multiple Choice

1. Which of the following should testing a site include?
   a. checking all of the hyperlinks within the site
   b. viewing the site in a variety of Web browsers
   c. viewing the site in a variety of screen resolutions
   d. all of the above

2. Which of the following does the role of an information architect include?
   a. being instrumental in defining the site organization, navigation, and labeling
   b. attending all meetings and collecting all information
   c. managing the project
   d. none of the above

3. Which methodology has long been used to develop information systems?
   a. System Development Life Cycle
   b. Service Delivery Life Cycle
   c. System Development Life Chain
   d. none of the above

4. Which methodology is usually used by Web project teams?
   a. the SDLC
   b. a derivative of the SDLC similar to the one discussed in this chapter
   c. decided on as the project is built
   d. no development methodology is necessary

5. What do team members do in the Analysis phase of a Web site project?

    a. determine what the site will do—not how it will be done

    b. determine the information topics of the site

    c. determine the content requirements of the site

    d. all of the above

6. In which phase is a prototype of the Web site often created?

    a. Design

    b. Conceptualization

    c. Production

    d. Analysis

7. Which of the following happens during the Production phase?

    a. a Web authoring tool is often used

    b. the graphics, Web pages, and other components are created

    c. the Web pages are individually tested

    d. all of the above

8. Which of the following happens during the Evaluation phase?

    a. the goals for the site are reviewed

    b. another loop through the development process may result

    c. both a and b

    d. none of the above

9. Which Web hosting option is appropriate for the initial Web presence of an organization?

    a. virtual hosting

    b. free Web hosting

    c. dedicated hosting

    d. co-located hosting

10. Which Web hosting option is appropriate for a large- to enterprise-size Web site?

    a. virtual hosting

    b. free Web hosting

    c. dedicated hosting

    d. none of the above

Fill in the Blank

11. _____ can be described as testing how actual Web page visitors use a Web site.

12. The _____ determines appropriate use of graphics on the site, and creates and edits graphics.

13. The _____ operating system(s) treat uppercase and lowercase letters differently.

Short Answer

14. Describe why the Web sites of competitors should be reviewed when designing a Web site.

15. Why should you try to contact the technical support of a Web host provider before you are one of its customers?

Hands-On Exercises

1. Skip this exercise if you have completed Hands-On Practice 2.11 in Chapter 2. In this exercise you will validate a Web page. Choose one of the Web pages that you have created. Launch a browser and visit the W3C HTML Validator page at http://validator.w3.org. Notice the Validate by File Upload area. Click the Browse button, select a file from your computer, and click the Check button to upload the file to the W3C site. Your page will be analyzed and a Results page generated, which shows a report of violations of the DTD that is used by your Web page. The error messages display the offending code along with the line number, column number, and description of the error. Don't worry if your Web page does not pass the validations the first time. Many well-known Web sites have pages that do not validate—even http://yahoo.com had validation errors at the time this was written. Modify your Web page document and revalidate it until you see a message that states "This page is valid XHTML 1.0 Transitional!" (See Figure 10.5.)

Figure 10.5
Message indicating that the Web page has passed the validation

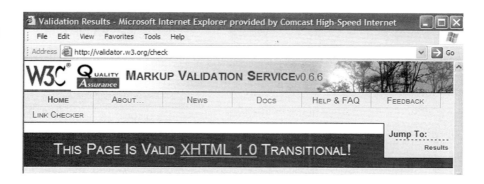

This page also provides you with some code and an image to display to tell the world that your page validated. Print the browser view of this page to hand in to your instructor.

You can also validate pages directly from the Web. Try validating the W3C's home page at http://w3.org, Yahoo! at http://yahoo.com, and your school's home page. Visit http://validator.w3.org and notice the Validate by URL area. Enter the URL of the Web page you would like to validate in the Address text box. Click the Check button. View the results. Experiment with the character encoding and `doctype` options. The W3C's page should pass the validation. Don't worry if the other pages do not validate. Validation is not required for Web pages. However, Web pages that pass the validation should display well in most browsers. (*Note*: If you have published pages to the Web, try validating one of them instead of your school's home page.)

2. The Cynthia Says site offers free accessibility testing at http://www.cynthiasays.com for your choice of Section 508 and WAI priority levels. Visit this site and test your school's home page for Section 508 compliance. After the Section 508 accessibility test is run, a report is displayed with categories corresponding to those listed at http://www.access-board.gov/sec508/guide/1194.22.htm. Print the browser view of the results page to hand in to your instructor. Were you surprised at the results? Did you notice that some criteria, such as "Web pages shall be designed so that all information conveyed with color is also available without color, for example from context or markup," cannot be checked automatically and must be verified manually by a person?

Next, check the Web page according to the W3C's WCAG Priority 1 accessibility criteria. Run the test again and select the WCAG – Priority 1 criteria. After the test is complete, a report is displayed with categories corresponding to those listed at http://www.w3.org/TR/WCAG10/full-checklist.html. Print out the browser view of the results page to hand in to your instructor.

Generally, it is easier to pass Section 508 validation than the WCAG criteria. Why do you think this is so? (*Note*: If you have published pages to the Web, try validating one of them instead of your school's home page.)

3. Watchfire offers a free WebXACT testing application at http://webxact.watchfire.com. Visit this site and test your school's home page. After the test is run, a report is displayed that shows the level of W3C WCAG compliance. In addition, information such as files size, download time, broken links, and so on is provided. Print out the browser view of the results page to hand in to your instructor. (*Note*: If you have

published pages to the Web, try validating one of them instead of your school's home page.)

4. NetMechanic offers a free sample of its HTML Toolbox Application at http://www.netmechanic.com/products/HTML_Toolbox_FreeSample.shtml. Visit this site and test your school's home page. After the test is run, a results page will be displayed with ratings related to link check, bad links, HTML check, browser compatibility, load time, and spell check. Each category has a link to a detailed display that describes the types of errors found. Print out the browser view of this results page to hand in to your instructor. (*Note*: If you have published pages to the Web, try validating one of them instead of your school's home page.)

5. The Dr. Watson site offers free Web page validation at http://watson.addy.com. Visit this site and test your school's home page. After the test is run, a report is displayed with categories including server response, estimated download speed, syntax and style analysis, spell check, link verifications, images, search engine compatibility (see Chapter 13), site link popularity (see Chapter 13), and source code. Print out the browser view of this report page to hand in to your instructor. (*Note*: If you have published pages to the Web, try validating one of them instead of your school's home page.)

6. Perform a small-scale usability test with a group of other students. Decide who will be the "typical users," the tester, and the observer. You will perform a usability test on your school's Web site.

- The "typical users" are the test subjects.
- The tester oversees the usability test and emphasizes that the users are not being tested—the Web site is being tested.
- The observer takes notes on the user's reactions and comments.

Step 1: The tester welcomes the users and introduces them to the Web site they will be testing.

Step 2: For each of the following scenarios, the tester introduces the scenario and questions the users as they work through the task. The tester should ask the users to indicate when they are in doubt, confused, or frustrated. The observer takes notes.

- Scenario 1: Find the phone number of the contact person for the Web development program at your school.
- Scenario 2: Determine when to register for the next semester.
- Scenario 3: Find the requirements to earn a degree or certificate in Web development or a related area.

Step 3: The tester and observer organize the results and write a brief report. If this were a usability test for an actual Web site, the development team would meet to review the results and discuss necessary improvements to the site.

Step 4: Hand in a report with your group's usability test results. Complete the report using a word processor. Write no more than one page about each scenario. Write one page of recommendations for improving your school's Web site.

Note: For more information on usability testing, see Keith Instone's classic presentation at http://instone.org/files/KEI-Howtotest-19990721.pdf. Another good resource is Steven Krug's book, *Don't Make Me Think*.

7. See the description of usability testing in Hands-On Exercise 6. In a small group of students, perform usability tests on two similar Web sites, such as the following:

- http://bn.com and http://powells.com
- http://accuweather.com and http://rainmaker.wunderground.com
- http://running.com and http://www.coolrunning.com

Decide on three scenarios. List them. Decide who will be the "users," the tester, and the observer. Follow the steps listed in Hands-On Exercise 6.

8. Pretend that you are on a job interview. Choose a role on a Web project team that interests you. In three to four sentences, describe why you would be an excellent addition to a Web development team in that role.

Web Research

1. This chapter discussed options for hosting Web sites. In this research exercise you will search for Web host providers and report on three that meet the following criteria:

- Support PHP and MySQL
- Offer e-commerce capabilities
- Provide at least 50MB hard disk space

Use your favorite search engine to find Web host providers or visit Web host directories such as http://webhosts.thelist.com/business.php and http://www.hostindex.com. Create a Web page that presents your findings. Include links to your three Web host providers. Your Web page should include a table of information such as set-up fees, monthly fees, domain name registration costs, amount of hard disk space, type of e-commerce package, and cost of e-commerce package. Use color and graphics appropriately on your Web page. Place your name and e-mail address at the bottom of your Web page. Print both the source code (from Notepad) and the browser view of your Web page.

2. This chapter discussed the different job functions that are needed to develop large Web sites. Choose a job role that interests you. Search for information about available jobs in your geographical area. Search for technology jobs with your favorite search engine or visit a job site such as http://monster.com, http://dice.com, http://hotjobs.com, or http://careerbuilder.com and search for your desired location and job type. Find three possible job positions that interest you and report on them. Create a Web page that includes a brief description of the job role you have chosen, a description of the three available positions, a description of the types of experience and/or educational background required for the job positions, and the salary range (if available). Organize your findings in a table. Use color and graphics appropriately on your Web page. Place your name and e-mail address at the bottom of your Web page. Print both the source code (from Notepad) and the browser view of your Web page.

Focus on Web Design

The U.S. Department of Health and Human Services offers a free online PDF book, *Research-Based Web Design & Usability Guidelines*, at http://www.usability.gov/pdfs/guidelines.html with PDF downloads for each chapter. The book suggests guidelines for a variety of topics including navigation, text appearance, scrolling and paging, writing Web content, usability testing, and accessibility, Choose one chapter topic that interests you. Read the chapter. Note four guidelines that you find intriguing or useful. In a one-page report, describe why you chose the chapter topic and the four guidelines you noted.

WEB SITE CASE STUDY
Testing Phase

This case study continues throughout the rest of the text. In this chapter you will test the Web Project case study.

Web Project

See Chapter 5 for an introduction to the Web Project. In this chapter you will develop a test plan for the project. You will review the documents created in the previous chapters' Web Project and create a test plan.

Hands-On Practice Case

Part 1: Review the Design Documents and Completed Web pages. Review the Topic Approval, Site Map, and Page Layout Design documents that you created in the Chapter 5 Web Project. Review the Web pages you have created and/or modified in the Chapter 6, Chapter 7, Chapter 8, and Chapter 9 Web Project activities.

Part 2: Prepare a Test Plan. See Figure 10.4 for a sample test plan document. Create a test plan document for your Web site. Include CSS validation, XHTML validation, and accessibility testing.

Part 3: Test Your Web Site. Implement your test plan and test each page that you have developed for your Web Project. Record the results. Write a list of suggested improvements.

Part 4: Perform Usability Testing. Describe three scenarios that typical visitors to your site may encounter. Using Hands-On Exercise 6 as a guide, conduct a usability test for these scenarios. Write a one-page report about your findings. What improvements can be suggested for the Web site?

Web Multimedia and Interactivity

Chapter Objectives   In this chapter, you will learn about ...

- Helper applications and plug-ins
- Audio file types and how to obtain them
- Adding sound to a Web page
- Podcasting
- Video file types and how to obtain them
- Adding video to a Web page
- Features and common uses of Adobe Flash
- Adding Flash animation to a Web page

- Features and common uses of Java applets
- Adding a Java applet to a Web page
- Features and common uses of JavaScript
- Features and common uses of DHTML
- Features and common uses of Ajax
- Free Flash, Java applets, JavaScript, DHTML, and Ajax resources on the Web

The saying goes, "A picture is worth a thousand words." You already are aware that graphics help to make Web pages compelling. Other types of **media,** such as audio and video are introduced in this chapter. Appropriate movies and sounds on your Web pages can make them more interesting and informative. Sources of these media types, the XHTML code needed to place the media on a Web page, and suggested uses of the media are discussed.

You have probably experienced **interactivity** on Web pages many times—moving the mouse to cause a new image to appear, clicking on radio buttons to take a survey, or clicking on a product while you watch and listen to a **Flash** movie about a company. These are all examples of Web page interactivity. Adding the right touch of interactivity to a Web page can make it engaging and compelling for your visitors.

Technologies commonly used to add interactivity to Web pages include Flash, **Java applets, JavaScript, DHTML,** and **Ajax.** This chapter introduces you to these techniques. Each of these topics is explored more fully in other books—each technology could be the sole subject of an entire book or college course. As you read this chapter and try the examples, concentrate on learning the features and capabilities of each technology, rather than trying to master the details.

11.1 Helper Applications and Plug-Ins

Web browsers are designed to display Web pages and GIF, JPG, and PNG images, among others. When the media is not one of these types, the browser searches for a **plug-in** or **helper application** configured to display the file type. If it cannot find a plug-in or helper application on the visitor's computer, the Web browser offers the visitor the option of saving the file to their computer. The visitor may have a program that can open the file or the visitor will simply be unable to experience the media file. This can be disappointing or frustrating to a Web page visitor. In order to provide your Web page visitors with a good experience, use media files that are supported by the most common helper applications and plug-ins (more on this later).

A helper application is a program that can handle a particular file type (such as .wav or .mp3) to allow the user to open the special file. The helper application runs in a window separate from the browser. A newer and more common method is for the browser to invoke a plug-in application. The plug-in can run directly in the browser window so that the visitor can open media objects directly within the Web page.

The most commonly used plug-ins include the following:

- **Adobe Flash Player (http://www.adobe.com/products/flashplayer).** The Flash Player displays **.swf** format files. These can contain audio, video, and animation, along with interactivity.
- **Adobe Shockwave Player (http://www.adobe.com/products/shockwaveplayer).** The Shockwave Player displays high-performance multimedia created using the Adobe Director application.
- **Adobe Reader (http://www.adobe.com/products/acrobat/readstep2.html).** Adobe Reader is commonly used to exchange information stored in .pdf format, such as printable brochures, documents, and white papers.
- **Java Runtime Environment (http://www.java.com/en/download/manual.jsp).** The JRE is used to run applications and applets utilizing Java technology.
- **RealPlayer 10 (http://real.com).** The RealPlayer plug-in plays streaming audio, video, animations, and multimedia presentations on the Web.
- **Windows Media Player (http://www.microsoft.com/windows/windowsmedia/download).** The Windows Media plug-in plays streaming audio, video, animations, and multimedia presentations on the Web.
- **Apple QuickTime (http://www.apple.com/quicktime/download).** The Apple QuickTime plug-in displays QuickTime animation, music, MIDI, audio, video, and VR panoramas and objects directly within the Web page.

You may be surprised at the number of plug-ins that exist. Mozilla provides a list of plug-ins and other browser extensions, or add-ons, used with its Firefox browser at http://addons.mozilla.org/en-US/firefox. Most plug-ins are free and can be easily downloaded and installed. As a Web developer, one of your goals should be usability. Some visitors will simply leave your page if you require them to download and install a new plug-in. Stick with audio and video files that use the most popular plug-ins because your visitors probably already have them.

Sounds can be used to set a mood for a Web site. They can also be used to provide additional information—an explanation of an image, a message from the company's chief executive officer, the pronunciation of a word, and so on. The next section discusses types of audio files used on the Web.

11.2 Multimedia File Types

The following file extensions are commonly used to designate **audio files:**

- **.wav (Wave file).** This format was originally created by Microsoft. It is a standard on the PC platform but is also supported by the Mac platform.
- **.aiff (Audio Interchange File Format).** This is one of the most popular audio file formats on the Mac platform. It is also supported on the PC platform (use the extension .aif).
- **.mid (Musical Instrument Digital Interface—MIDI).** These files contain instructions to recreate a musical sound rather than a digital recording of the sound itself. The advantage of this concise format is small file size, but the disadvantage is the limited number of types of sounds that can be reproduced.
- **.au (Sun UNIX Sound File).** This is an older type of sound file that generally has poorer sound quality than the newer audio file formats. It only uses 8-bit samples instead of the 16-bit samples used by some of the newer audio file types.
- **.mp3(MPEG-1 Audio Layer-3).** This sound file uses an advanced compression algorithm that results in the MP3 file being about one-twelfth the size of the original audio file. As mentioned in Chapter 1, podcasts typically use the MP3 audio file format.
- **.ogg (Ogg Vorbis).** This sound file format uses a relatively new audio compression format that is comparable to MP3. However, it is open source. This means it is not patented and free to use. Visit http://www.vorbis.com for more information about this technology.

The following file extensions are commonly used to designate **video files:**

- **.mov (QuickTime).** This format was originally created by Apple and used on the Macintosh platform. The QuickTime for Windows plug-in supports this file format on the Windows platform. Because it has universal support, this format is widely used on the Web. While other video file formats must download the entire video file before **playback**, QuickTime is smart enough to begin to play before the entire file is downloaded, giving the effect of streaming video.
- **.avi (Microsoft Audio Video Interleaved File for Windows).** This was the original standard video format for PC platforms and is still widely used.
- **.wmv (Windows Media Video).** This is a streaming video technology developed by Microsoft. The Windows Media Player supports this file format.

● **.mpg (MPEG).** The MPG technology standards were developed under the sponsor-ship of the Moving Picture Experts Group (MPEG), http://www.chiariglione.org/mpeg. This format is supported on both Windows and Mac platforms.

Obtaining Multimedia Files

There are a number of ways that you can obtain audio files. You can record your own sounds, download sounds or music from a free site, record music from a CD, or pur-chase a CD of sounds. There are some ethical issues related to using sounds and music created by others.

Focus on Ethics

You may only publish sounds or music that you have created yourself or for which you have obtained the rights (sometimes called a license) to publish.

The Windows and Mac operating systems contain audio recording utilities. You need a sound card and microphone. If you are using Windows XP, launch the Sound Recorder application by selecting Start, Programs, Accessories, Entertainment, Sound Recorder (Window Vista users select Start, All Programs, Accessories, Sound Recorder). This will allow you to create and edit sound files. As you can see in Figure 11.1, the controls are similar to those on a tape recorder. The Web is a great resource for tutorials on using Sound Recorder. Visit http://depts.washington.edu/trio/center/howto/media/audio/capture.html or http://www.musiknet.se/mla/encoding/wav_recording.htm to get started.

Figure 11.1
Windows Sound
Recorder

The recording process will be similar for other operating systems. If the built-in applica-tion is too tame for you, consider investigating the commercial software that is avail-able to edit media. Sonic Foundry (http://www.sonicfoundry.com) provides the software tools needed for the entire digital media production process, from content creation through final delivery. SourceForge.net Audacity (http://audacity.sourceforge.net) offers a free download of their Audacity digital audio editors. Audacity can record your voice for a podcast and mix in music loops to add interest. Once the .wav file is created, the LAME encoder (http://lame.sourceforge.net) or a similar application can be used to con-vert to MP3 format.

To create an MP3 from a CD, first use a program called a ripper to copy a selection from a CD onto your hard drive in a .wav file format. Then use an encoder application to convert the .wav file to an MP3 file. There are applications such as Media Box (http://www.e-soft.co.uk), Goldwave (http://www.goldwave.com), or Audio MP3 Maker (http://www.share2.com/mp3maker) that combine the ripper and encoder into a single program. **Copyright** and licensing are discussed later in this section.

A commercial CD can only be copied for personal use and not for publishing to the Web. Contact the owner of the copyright to request permission to use the music.

There are many sources of audio files on the Web. Some offer free files, such as Microsoft's Clip Art and Media (http://office.microsoft.com/clipart) and FreeAudioClips.com (http://www.freeaudioclips.com). Others, like SoundRangers (http://www.soundrangers.com), may offer one or two free sounds but ultimately are in the business of selling soundtracks and CDs. An interesting resource for free sound is at the Flash Kit site (http://www.flashkit.com); click on the Sound Loops link. While this site is intended for Adobe Flash developers, the sound files can be used without Flash. The Yahoo! (http://yahoo.com) and Google (http://google.com) search engines offer specific searches for both audio and video files.

Before you publish a media file on the Web, be sure to obtain the rights to use it from the creator or the copyright owner.

Audio files can be quite large and it is important to be aware of the amount of time required to download them for play. If you decide to use an audio file on a Web page, make it as brief as possible. If you are recording your own audio files, be aware that the sampling rate and bit depth will affect the file size. A **sampling rate** is a value related to the number of digital sound samples taken per second when the sound is recorded. It is measured in kilohertz (KHz). Common sampling rates vary from 8 KHz (AM radio quality sound or sound effects) to 11.025 KHz (most music) to 55.1 KHz (music CD quality sound). As you would expect, a sound recorded at 55.1 KHz has a much larger file size than a sound recorded at 8 KHz. Bit depth or resolution is another factor in audio file size. A sound recorded with 8-bit resolution (useful for a voice or other simple sounds) will have a smaller file size than a sound recorded using 16-bit resolution (music CD quality).

Just as with audio files, there are a number of ways that you can obtain video files, including recording your own, downloading videos, purchasing a CD that contains videos, or searching for video files on the Web (see http://yahoo.com or http://google.com).

Be aware that there are ethical issues related to using videos that you did not create yourself. You must obtain the rights or license to publish videos created by other individuals before publishing them on your Web site.

Many digital cameras have the capability to take still photographs as well as short MPG movies. This can be an easy way to obtain short video clips. Digital video cameras and webcams record digital videos. Use a video capture card to access analog VHS videos. Once you have created your video, software such as Adobe Premiere (http://www.adobe.com/products/premiere), Apple QuickTime (http://www.apple.com/quicktime), or Microsoft Movie Maker (http://www.microsoft.com/windowsxp/using/moviemaker/default.mspx) can be used to edit and configure your video masterpiece.

Now that you've got a sound or music file, what can you do with it? You can play an audio file as a **background sound** when the page loads. You can allow your Web page visitors to choose whether they want to listen to a sound. You can make the audio file available as a podcast. The XHTML code used to work with audio files is discussed in the next few sections.

11.3 Using Sound on a Web Page

One method to give your Web page visitors access to a sound is to create a simple hyperlink that references the sound file. The XHTML code to link to a sound file called ringing.wav follows:

```
<a href="ringing.wav"
title="Sound of a telephone ringing">telephone ringing</a>
```

If your Web site visitor clicks on the link, the plug-in for .wav files that is installed on the computer (possibly RealOne Player, Windows Media Player, or QuickTime) will display. Your Web page visitor can then use the plug-in to play the sound. This method is used for providing links to MP3 podcast files.

Another method to include sound on your page is to embed the sound in the page and optionally display a control panel for the sound. The `<embed />` element is usually used for this because it is well supported by browsers even though it is not part of the W3C XHTML 1.0 recommendation. The W3C XHTML 1.0 recommendation provides the `<object>` element as a means to present audio and other file types in a Web page. Examples of both elements are provided in this section. Because browser support of the `<embed />` element is nonstandard and browser support of the `<object>` element is uneven, you should test with the browsers and platforms your target audience will be using.

The Embed Element

The **`<embed />`** element configures sound and other media in a Web page. It is a self-contained tag and does not have a corresponding closing tag. Table 11.1 lists the attributes of the `<embed />` tag when it applies to media files.

In the following XHTML code, the `<embed />` tag configures the Web page to show a small console that can be used to control the sound. Because `autostart` is set to `false`, the sound does not play immediately when the page is loaded—it plays only when the Web page visitor uses the console to start the sound.

```
<embed src="catch.wav" autostart="false" controls="smallconsole"
height="25" width="100" />
```

Where did you get the sound file?

The sound file was found at http://flashkit.com and is used by permission of the author, Mikkel Meldgaard (mamp7@hotmail.com) who has recorded Mikkel Metal on the Echocord recording label (http://www.echocord.com/).

A Web page using the example `<embed />` tag can be found in the student files at Chapter11/audio1.html. A screenshot is shown in Figure 11.2.

Table 11.1 Attributes of media `<embed />` tags

Attribute	Value	Usage
`src`	Valid file name, name of media file	Required; provides the name of the file to be played
`controls`	`console`, `smallconsole`, `playbutton`, `pausebutton`, `stopbutton`, `volumelever`	Optional; configures the appearance of the media control console
`width`	Numeric, number of pixels	Optional; configures the width of media control console
`height`	Numeric, number of pixels	Optional; configures the height of media control console
`autostart`	`true`, `false`	Optional; determines if the media will play automatically when the page is loaded—if omitted, media may not automatically play
`autoplay`	`true`, `false`	Optional; determines if the media will play automatically when the page is loaded—if omitted, media may not automatically play
`loop`	Numeric value or true for continuous play (may not be uniformly supported)	Optional; repeats the media file
`align`	`baseline` (default), `left`, `right`, `center`, `top`	Optional; aligns the media control console
`hidden`	`true`	Optional; hides the default media console
`pluginspage`	A valid URL	Optional; location of download page for plugin
`controller`	`true`, `false`	Optional; indicates whether the media control console will display type
`type`	A valid MIME type such as audio/mpeg, audio/wav, and so on.	Optional; specifies the MIME type of the media file

Figure 11.2
Sample audio1.html

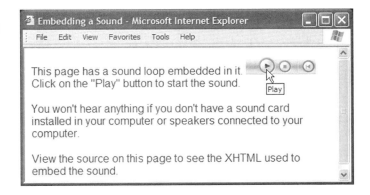

HANDS-ON PRACTICE 11.1

In this Hands-On Practice you will create a Web page that contains a control to let a visitor play a sound. Copy the catch.wav sound file from the Chapter11 folder in the student files and save it to disk. Launch Notepad or another text editor. Create a Web page with the heading "Playing Sounds with the Embed Tag" and an `<embed />` tag to play the sound file when the page loads. Use the sample code and list of `<embed />` tag attributes in Table 11.1 as a guide. Save your page as ch11page1.html and test it in a browser. Experiment with the `console`, `autostart`, `height`, `width`, and `loop` attributes. Try to test your page in different browsers and browser versions.

The Object Element

Another technique that can be used to place sound and other media on a Web page is the `<object>` element. It is a container tag and should be closed with an `</object>` tag. The `<object>` tag is part of the W3C standard and you should become familiar with its use. The attributes of the `<embed />` tag and the attributes of the `<object>` tag are quite similar. Depending on the media type and plug-in or player to be used, additional configuration values, called parameters, may need to be coded using the `<param />` element. The `<param />` tag is a self-contained tag with two attributes: name and value. All the `<param />` tags for the object appear before the ending `</object>` tag. The player's documentation will indicate if parameters are needed and the format you should use. Table 11.2 lists the attributes of the `<object>` tag when used with media files. Table 11.3 lists common `<param />` attribute values.

Table 11.2 Attributes of media `<object>` tags

Attribute	Value	Usage
data	Valid file name, name of audio file	Required; provides the name of the file to be played
type	A valid MIME type such as audio/midi, audio/wav, video/quicktime, and so on	Optional; specifies the MIME type of the media file
width	Numeric, number of pixels	Optional; configures the width of media control console
height	Numeric, number of pixels	Optional; configures the height of media control console
classid	Uniquely identifies the player software; for QuickTime, it must be set to `clsid: 02BF25D5-8C17-4B23-BC80-D3488ABDDC6B`; this unique code identifies an ActiveX control that must be installed on the user's PC before the movie can be played; if the user does not have the ActiveX control installed, the browser can automatically download and install it	The `classid` identifies an ActiveX control that must be installed on the visitor's PC; if the ActiveX control is not installed, the browser can automatically download and install it
codebase	Specifies a relative path for the location of the plug-in	For QuickTime and Internet Explorer, this value must be http://www.apple.com/qtactivex/qtplugin.cab —the location of the most recent version of the QuickTime player

Table 11.3 `<param />` media attribute values

Parameter Name	Parameter Value	Usage
`src`	Valid file name, name of media file	Required; provides the name of the file to be played
`loop`	Numeric value, or **`true`** for continuous play (not uniformly supported)	Optional; determines how many times the media file will repeat
`hidden`	**`true`** (not uniformly supported)	Optional; hides the default media console
`autoplay`	`true`, `false`	Optional; determines if the media will play automatically when the page is loaded—if omitted, media may not automatically play
`controller`	`true`, `false` (not uniformly supported)	Optional; indicates whether the media control console will display

The XHTML code to use the `<object>` tag to embed a sound loop in a Web page follows:

```
<object data="catch.wav" height="50" width="100" type="audio/wav">
  <param name="src" value="catch.wav" />
</object>
```

A sample page using this `<object>` tag can be found in the student files at Chapter11/audio2.html. See Figure 11.3 for a screenshot of this page. If you are using Internet Explorer and see warning messages when the `<object>` tag is used to play media, consult your network administrator or lab support staff for recommended security settings.

Figure 11.3
Sample audio2.html

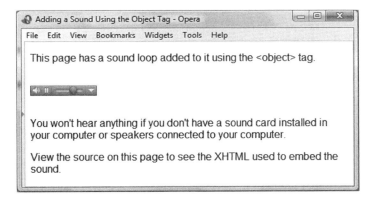

HANDS-ON PRACTICE 11.2

In this Hands-On Practice you will create a Web page that plays a sound when it is loaded by a browser. If you have not done so already, copy the catch.wav sound file from the Chapter11 folder in the student files and save it to disk. Launch Notepad or another text editor and create a Web page that contains the heading Playing Sounds with the Object Tag and uses the `<object>` tag and `<param />` tag to display a console that lets the Web page visitor control the catch.wav audio file. Use the sample code and the list of attributes and values in Table 11.2 and Table 11.3 as a guide.. Experiment with the `<object>` element's `height`, and `width` attributes. Explore the `<param />` element's `autoplay` value to configure the sound to not automatically play when the page loads. Use the `<param />` element's `loop` value to cause the sound to loop continuously. Save your page as ch11page2.html and test it in a browser. Try to test your page in different browsers and browser versions.

FAQ

Why doesn't my sound play?

Playing audio and video files on the Web depends on the plug-ins installed in your visitor's Web browsers. A page that works perfectly on your home computer may not work for all visitors—depending on the configuration of their computer. Some visitors will not have the plug-ins properly installed. Some visitors may have file types associated with incorrect plug-ins. Some visitors may be using low bandwidth and have to wait an overly long time for your media file to download. Are you detecting a pattern here? Sometimes media on the Web can be problematic.

The Flash player plug-in is available for multiple platforms and browsers. According to Adobe, a high percentage of browsers have this plug-in installed. For these reasons (and also due to built-in streaming capabilities of Flash) many Web developers use the Adobe Flash application to create .swf files that can deliver their audio and video. See the section about Adobe Flash later in this chapter for more information on this technology.

Background Sounds

Sometimes Web developers and clients would like a sound to play when a page loads. Use this technique with caution. If someone is listening to their favorite CD while they surf the Web, do they really want to hear the theme music from Gilligan's Island while the page loads? With that said, here's the lowdown on how to embed a sound in a Web page.

One common technique is to use an `<embed />` element. Although not part of the W3C XHTML 1.0 recommendation, `<embed />` tags are still widely used due to reliable browser support. As new versions of modern browsers increase their support of the `<object>` tag, expect to see increased use of this element.

FAQ

What about the `<bgsound>` tag?

As you surf the Web, you may find pages that use the `<bgsound>` tag. Earlier versions of Internet Explorer did not support the `<embed />` tag and instead supported a proprietary `<bgsound>` tag that was placed in the header section of the Web page. This tag is only supported by Internet Explorer and is not part of the W3C standard. The `<bgsound>` tag is no longer needed for a number of reasons. Current versions of Internet Explorer now support the `<embed />` tag and offer improved support of the `<object>` tag.

The XHTML code for a background sound loop in a Web page follows:

```
<embed src="catch.wav" autostart="true" hidden="true" loop="true" />
```

A sample page that uses the `<embed />` tag to hide the media console and play a background sound when the Web page loads can be found in the student files at Chapter11/audio3.html. A sample page that complies with the W3C XHTML 1.0 recommendation and uses the `<object>` element is located in the student files at Chapter11/audio4.html.

HANDS-ON PRACTICE 11.3

In this Hands-On Practice you will create a Web page that plays a sound when it is loaded by a browser. If you have not done so already, copy the catch.wav sound file from the Chapter11 folder in the student files and save it to disk. Create a Web page that contains the heading Playing Sounds in the Background (configure with `<h1>` or `<h2>` tags) and uses the `<embed />` tag to start the sound when the page is loaded without displaying a console. Use the sample code and list of `<embed />` tag attributes in Table 11.1 as a guide. Save your page as ch11page3.html and test it in a browser. Experiment with the `loop` attribute. Test your page in different browsers and browser versions.

By now you should have a feel for some of the issues involved with adding media to a Web page. If different browsers (and browser versions) offered uniform support for XHTML tags and attributes, a Web developer's job would be much easier.

Focus on Accessibility

Another consideration is accessibility for all your Web page visitors. Be aware that some of your visitors will not be able to hear the sounds or music. Include appropriate text descriptions or text transcriptions of these items.

11.4 Podcasting Overview

Recall from Chapter 1 that **podcasts** are audio files on the Web that may take the format of an audio blog, radio show, or interview. There are three steps in publishing a podcast: recording the podcast, uploading the podcast, and creating a Really Simple Syndication (RSS feed), which makes the podcast available. Section 11.2 discussed using a software application to record, edit, and convert your podcast to MP3 format. Upload the MP3 to your Web site. If your Web host does not permit MP3 files, an alternative is to upload to a site that accepts audio files at no cost such as http://archive.org or http://ourmedia.org. The next step is to make the podcast available. The most straightforward method is to code a hyperlink to the audio file (see Section 11.3). The hyperlink allows Web site visitors to access the podcast MP3 file but does not make the podcast available for subscription. An RSS feed must be created in order for your visitors to subscribe to your current and future podcasts. An **RSS feed** for a podcast is an XML file (with a .rss file extension) that lists information about your podcast. With a bit of patience, you can code your own RSS feed using a text editor (see http://www.downes.ca/cgi-bin/page.cgi?post=56 or http://www.masternewmedia.org/news/2006/03/09/how_to_create_a_rss.htm). However, a number of Web sites (including http://ponyfish.com, http://feedburner.com, and http://rss.icerocket.com) provide a service that generates and hosts the RSS feed for you. After the RSS feed is uploaded to the Web (either your own or the RSS feed generator's site), code a link to the file. Web visitors using software such as Apple's iTunes or a free RSS feed reader Web site (http://feedreader.com) can locate and automatically download your podcast.

The next section introduces the use of video on Web pages. Download time issues become even more important when video is included because both images and sounds are stored in the video file.

11.5 Using Video on a Web Page

The simplest method to give your Web page visitors access to a video is to create a hyperlink that references the video file. The XHTML code to link to a .mov video about my dog, Sparky, follows:

```
<a href="sparky.mov" title="Barking Dog Video">Sparky(.mov,1.2MB)</a>
```

If your Web site visitor clicks on the link, the plug-in associated with .mov files installed on the computer (probably QuickTime, Windows Media Player, or Real Player) will display. He or she will have the option of playing the video. It's a good practice to include the file type and file size in the link (as shown in the previous code sample). There are other methods available for including videos directly on your Web page: the `<embed />` tag, the `<object>` tag, and using the `dynsrc` attribute on an `<img />` tag (Internet Explorer only). All three methods are discussed next. Just as with audio files, testing in your target audience's environment is crucial to the successful use of video on the Web.

Focus on Accessibility

Also remember to supply text descriptions of videos in order to provide accessible pages for your Web site visitors. Visit http://www.webaim.org/techniques/captions for information about video captioning—creating synchronous text descriptions/transcripts for your videos.

The Embed Element

The `<embed />` element can be used to place a video control on a Web page just as it can be used to place a sound control. The attributes used by the `<embed />` tag were provided in the section on audio files. A sample page that uses the `<embed />` tag to display a video file is shown in Figure 11.4.

The XHTML code to embed this video follows:

```
<embed src="sparky.mov" autostart="false" width="160" height="120" />
```

A sample page using the code shown above can be found in the student files at Chapter11/video1.html. The values you use for the height and width should be as close to the actual size of the recorded video as possible. Don't try to stretch the video to make it larger—you won't be pleased with the results. Keep in mind that the `<embed />` element, although widely supported by browsers, does not comply with the W3C XHTML 1.0 recommendation.

Figure 11.4
Sample video1.html

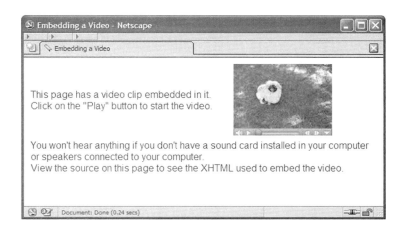

HANDS-ON PRACTICE 11.4

In this Hands-On Practice you will create a Web page that allows a visitor to play a video. Copy the sparky.mpg file from the Chapter11 folder in the student files and save it to disk. Launch Notepad or another text editor and create a Web page that contains the heading "Playing a Video" and uses the <embed /> tag. Use the sample code and list of <embed /> tag attributes in Table 11.1 as a guide. Save your page as ch11page4.html and test it in a browser. Try to test your page in different browsers and browser versions.

The Object Element

The <object> element can also be used to embed video files in Web pages. It is a container tag and should be closed with an </object> tag. The attributes used by the <object> tag are listed in Table 11.2. Use both the <object> and <param /> elements to display a video on a Web page. Refer to Table 11.3 for commonly used attribute values of the <param /> tag.

A sample page using the <object> element to display a video can be found in the student files at Chapter11/video2.html. Depending on your browser plug-ins, the video may not display on this page using the <object> tag. The sample pages were tested using the QuickTime plug-in for .mov files. This plug-in issue can be a problem for video components. Testing with your target audience in mind as well as giving your visitors hints on the most appropriate plug-ins will help. The basic XHTML code to use the <object> tag to display this video file in a Web page and use the QuickTime plug-in follows:

```
<object width="160" height="120"
  classid="clsid:02BF25D5-8C17-4B23-BC80-D3488ABDDC6B"
  codebase="http://www.apple.com/qtactivex/qtplugin.cab">
  <param name="src" value="sparky.mov" />
  <param name="autoplay" value="false" />
  <param name="controller" value="true" />
  A video of a cute Pekingese dog barking.
</object>
```

Notice how the name and value attributes are used on the parameter (`<param />`) tags to configure the file location, display of the plug-in controls, and plug-in action when the page loads.

Note that the text contained between the `<object>` and `</object>` tags is used to provide a text description of the video. This area will be read by some assistive technologies such as screen readers.

However, the `<object>` element shown above will only reliably display with Internet Explorer because of the `classid` and `codebase` attributes. One option to provide for display on all browsers is to also include an `<embed />` element as shown in the code below:

```
<object width="160" height="120"
  classid="clsid:02BF25D5-8C17-4B23-BC80-D3488ABDDC6B"
  codebase="http://www.apple.com/qtactivex/qtplugin.cab">
  <param name="src" value="sparky.mov">
  <param name="autoplay" value="false">
  <param name="controller" value="true">
  <embed src="sparky.mov" width="160" height="120"
  autoplay="false" controller="true"
  pluginspage="http://www.apple.com/quicktime/download/" />
  A video of a cute Pekingese dog barking.
</object>
```

The code shown above should reliably display the video on current versions of Internet Explorer and other popular browsers including Firefox, Opera, and Safari. However, the page will not pass W3C XHTML 1.0 validation due to the `<embed />` element.

In order to use the `<object>` element to display videos on current versions of Internet Explorer *and* other popular browsers such as Firefox, Safari, and Opera a technique of coding two `<object>` elements is used. In this technique, the conditional comments denoted by `<!--[if !IE]>-->` and `<!--<![endif]-->` direct browsers other than Internet Explorer to render an `<object>` tag without the `classsid` and `codebase` attributes. See Elizabeth Castro's discussion of `<object>` element coding at http://www.alistapart.com/articles/byebyeembed for more information. The code follows.

```
<object width="160" height="120" type="video/quicktime"
  classid="clsid:02BF25D5-8C17-4B23-BC80-D3488ABDDC6B"
  codebase="http://www.apple.com/qtactivex/qtplugin.cab">
  <param name="src" value="sparky.mov" />
  <param name="autoplay" value="false" />
  <param name="controller" value="true" />
  <!--[if !IE]>-->
    <object type="video/quicktime" data="sparky.mov"
    width="160" height="120">
      <param name="autoplay" value="false" />
      <param name="controller" value="true" />
      A video of a cute Pekingese dog barking.
    </object>
  <!--<![endif]-->
</object>
```

HANDS-ON PRACTICE 11.5

In this Hands-On Practice you will create a Web page that uses the <object> tag to play a video clip for a Web page visitor. If you have not already done so, copy the sparky.mov file from the Chapter11 folder in the student files and save it to disk. Launch Notepad or another text editor and create a Web page that contains the heading "Using the Object Tag to Play a Video" and that uses the <object> tag. Use the sample code and the list of attributes and values in Table 11.2 and Table 11.3 as a guide. Experiment with the <object> element's height and width attributes. Explore the <param /> element's, autoplay, and loop attributes. Save your page as ch11page5.html and test it in a browser. Try to test your page in different browsers and browser versions.

Internet Explorer Only Options

If you are creating Web pages for an intranet, you may have the luxury of knowing that all of the users will be using a certain browser, such as Internet Explorer. When this is the case, why not take advantage of a browser-specific feature? The dynsrc (dynamic source) attribute can be added to an <img /> tag to indicate a video. A screenshot of a sample page using this technique is shown in Figure 11.5.

Figure 11.5
This page uses the **dynsrc** attribute on the <img /> tag and is only supported by Internet Explorer

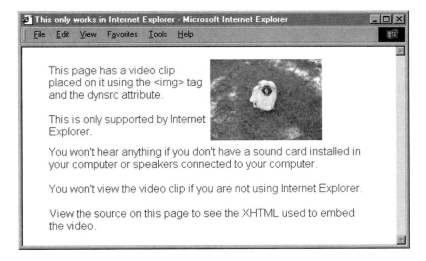

The XHTML code for the <img /> tag follows:

```
<img dynsrc="sparky.mov" autostart="true" width="160" height="120"
alt="Sparky Video 1.2 MB" />
```

A sample page using the code shown above can be found in the student files at Chapter11/dynsrc.html. While this is an interesting way to add video to your Web pages, it only works with Internet Explorer, so use it with caution.

11.6 Browser Compatibility and Accessibility

At this point, you should be familiar with adding standard audio and video to a Web page. The fact that both the `<object>` and the `<embed />` tags can be used to play media files is confusing for many Web developers. Keep in mind that while the `<embed />` tag seems to be well supported by current browser versions, the `<object>` tag is the W3C standard. It is important to be comfortable with both. Furthermore, not all the attributes are uniformly supported by current browser versions. This makes it critical that you test your page in the browsers (and browser versions) you expect your Web page visitors to use.

Focus on Accessibility

Also, in order to provide a positive experience for all your Web page visitors, you should provide alternate content or text descriptions of the media files you use on your Web site. Applications such as Media Access Generator (MAGpie) can add captioning to videos. See the National Center for Accessible Media's Web site at http://ncam.wgbh .org/webaccess/magpie for the most up-to-date information on the application.

Now that you are more knowledgeable about media and Web pages you may be wondering about copyright issues. What rights do you have as an author? What options do you have as a student? The next section discusses copyright as it applies to Web pages and media files. The concept of fair use of copyrighted materials is introduced.

11.7 Copyright Issues and Media Files

Focus on Ethics

It is very easy to copy and download an image, audio, or video file from a Web site. It may be very tempting to place someone else's file in one of your own projects, but that may not be ethical or lawful. Only publish Web pages, images, and other media that you have personally created or have obtained the rights or license to use. If another individual has created an image, sound, video, or document that you think would be useful on your own Web site, ask permission to use the material instead of simply taking it. All work (Web pages, images, sounds, videos, and so on) is copyrighted—even if there is no copyright symbol and date on the material.

Be aware that there are times when students and educators can use portions of another's work and not be in violation of copyright law. This is called **fair use**. Fair use is use of a copyrighted work for purposes such as criticism, reporting, teaching, scholarship, or research. Criteria used to determine fair use follow:

- The use must be educational rather than commercial.
- The nature of the work copied should be factual rather than creative.
- The amount copied must be as small of a portion of the work as possible.
- The copy does not impede the marketability of the original work.

Visit http://copyright.gov and http://www.copyrightwebsite.com for some additional insights on copyright issues.

Some individuals may want to retain ownership of their work but make it easy for others to use or adapt it. Creative Commons, http://creativecommons.org, provides a free service which allows authors and artists to register a type of a copyright license called a **Creative Commons license**. There are several licenses to choose from—depending on the rights you wish to grant as the author. The Creative Commons license informs others exactly what they can and cannot do with the creative work.

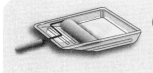

CHECKPOINT 11.1

1. List three common Web browser plug-ins and describe their use.

2. Describe issues involved with adding media such as audio or video to a Web page.

3. True or False? Visit the plug-in or player's Web site for the most current information on the XHTML needed to invoke a plug-in successfully.

11.8 Adobe Flash

Flash is a popular multimedia application often used to create animation and multimedia effects on Web pages. The animations can be as simple as the Flash effect shown in Figure 11.6 (see the student files at Chapter11/flash1.html). Flash can also be used to play audio files and video files, and to create many more complex effects, including full-screen animations, banner ads, and interactive site navigation using integrated audio clips.

Figure 11.6
Sample Flash Web page

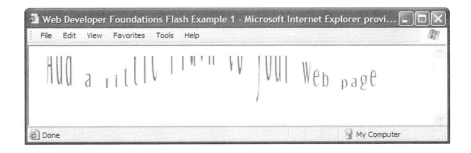

Flash animations are stored in a file with a .swf file extension. Unlike other media, .swf files play as they download and give the perception of speedy display of complex graphic animations. Flash animations can be interactive; they can be scripted, with a language called ActionScript, to respond to mouse clicks, accept information in text boxes, and invoke CGI or other server-side scripting.

Flash requires a browser plug-in, which is free and readily available for download from Adobe. According to Adobe, over 97 percent of Web browsers have a Flash plug-in installed. Recall that playing standard format audio and video files on Web pages is extremely dependent on the browser plug-ins visitors have installed. Recently, there has been an increasing use of Adobe Flash technology to play video (http://youtube.com) and audio (http://flashkit.com) files on Web pages. With the nearly ubiquitous Flash Player installed on most Web browsers, Web site developers are confident when using Flash technology.

Adobe licenses the Adobe Flash file format to third-party developers. This means that you can use applications other than Adobe Flash to create a Flash (.swf) effect. TechSmith's Cantasia (http://www.techsmith.com) and Swish (http://www.swishzone .com) are just two of the third-party tools that can be used to create media in the .swf format. Even Adobe Dreamweaver can be used to create Flash text and Flash button effects, which are stored in .swf files.

Common Uses of Flash

Navigation. Flash is often used to create an interactive navigation area on a Web page. See Figure 11.7 for the home page of the National Science Foundation (http://www.nsf .gov). It uses Flash to offer and describe main navigation choices. The site also uses the graphic animation features of Flash to provide a series of clickable images under the main navigation. These serve to highlight the site topics and create a more engaging user experience.

Figure 11.7
Flash is used to
provide navigation
and interactive
descriptions

The home page of the National Park Service (http://www.nps.gov) uses Flash to display a continuous slide show of beautiful scenery—drawing the visitor into the site. Notice how Flash components—such as navigation bars and slide shows can be combined with XHTML to create an engaging user experience.

Splash Page. The term splash screen originates from client-server applications that display an introductory (splash) screen while the program loads. Splash screens, sometimes called splash pages, can set the tone or introduce a Web site. Check out NASA's splash page, shown in Figure 11.8, for a display that gets you in the mood for a mission to Saturn. When using splash pages keep usability in mind—include a simple text link to the main page of your site that provides Web site visitors an easy option to skip the animation.

Figure 11.8
NASA uses a splash page to showcase the Saturn mission

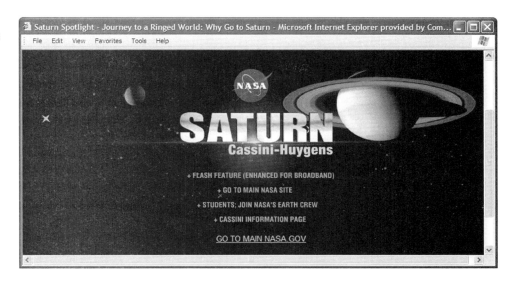

Rich Media Advertising. Flash can be used to create interactive ads on Web pages that respond to visitors' mouse movements with sound and animation. Adobe showcases best-of-breed ads that use Flash at http://www.adobe.com/devnet/rich_media_ads/feature/001.html. These ads are more engaging than simple GIF animated images. One featured ad garnered a 75 percent interaction rate—an amazing result considering that Web visitors often simply ignore Web page ads.

Entire Web Site. Flash can be used to create entire Web sites, including navigation, content, and forms. A compelling example is 2advanced Studios (http://www.2advanced.com/flashindex.htm). All the interactivity—navigation, animation, and content—is coded in the Flash .swf file. Visit Neon Sky (http://www.neonsky.com) for another example of this type of Web site.

Flash Innovation and Imagination. As you viewed the sample sites you may have noticed the creativity, innovation, and sheer imagination that some of them exhibit. Visit the textbook Web site at http://www.webdevfoundations.net for additional links to Flash Web sites.

Web Design and Flash

Some of the Flash examples above are quite compelling. However, not everyone is an advocate of Flash. While some Web developers and Web visitors love Flash effects, Jakob Nielsen—the noted Web design guru—has some serious concerns about Flash and usability. In his Alertbox article on Flash (http://www.useit.com/alertbox/20001029.html) Nielsen states, "Although multimedia has its role on the Web, current Flash technology tends to discourage usability for three reasons: it makes bad design more likely, it breaks with the Web's fundamental interaction style, and it consumes resources that would be better spent enhancing a site's core value." Adobe has responded to these concerns and has formed a strategic relationship with the Nielsen Norman Group to focus on improving the usability and accessibility of Flash media.

Focus on Accessibility
WWW

Adobe provides a variety of design guidelines and accessibility hints for Flash developers at http://www.adobe.com/resources/accessibility/flash8/best_practices.html. The Flash Player offers integrated support for Microsoft Active Accessibility (MSAA). This makes Flash content available to visitors using assistive technology such as the GW Micro Window-Eyes or Freedom Scientific JAWS screen reader. Expect more improvements in Flash and accessibility as Adobe Macromedia continues to focus on this area.

Today's Web developer needs to know how to add a Flash .swf file to a Web page. If you are working on a large project, a graphic designer may create the effect and pass it to you for placement on a page. If you are working on a small project, you may be expected to create Flash .swf files yourself. Adobe offers a free trial download of the Flash application, including a few tutorials and lessons on using Flash.

FAQ

What's Microsoft Silverlight?

According to Microsoft at http://silverlight.net, Silverlight is a plug-in for delivering media experiences and rich interactive applications for the Web. Microsoft Expression Blend is an application that creates interactive media for display by the Silverlight plug-in.

Adding a Flash Animation to a Web Page

You've seen some examples of Flash and are aware of issues related to Flash and Web usability. Now let's take a look at the XHTML that is needed to use Flash media on a Web page.

Both the `<object>` tag and the `<embed />` tag are used to place Flash media on a page because some versions of currently popular browsers such as Netscape support the `<embed />` tag and do not fully support the `<object>` tag. Use the **`<noembed>`** tag to contain a text description of the Flash media to improve accessibility.

The `<object>` tag specifies the beginning of Flash media on a Web page. Its closing tag, `</object>`, specifies the ending of Flash media. As previously discussed, the `<object>` tag is a multipurpose tag for adding various types of objects to a Web page. The `<object>` tag's attributes vary, depending on the type of object being referenced. The attributes required when working with Flash media are described in Table 11.4.

Table 11.4 Flash media attributes

`<object>` Attribute	Description and Value
`accesskey`	Specifies a hotkey for keyboard access, Windows users press the hotkey and the Ctrl key at the same time.
`classid`	The class id for the Flash plug-in; a recent value is `clsid:D27CDB6E-AE6D-11cf-96B8-444553540000`
`codebase`	The URL of the Flash plug-in (it allows for easy download if the Web page visitor does not have the Flash plug-in installed); a recent value is `http://download.macromedia.com/pub/shockwave/cabs/flash/swflash.cab#version=8,0,0,0`
`height`	Specifies the height of the object area in pixels
`tabindex`	A numeric value that specifies the tabbing order of the Flash media
`title`	Specifies a brief text description that may be displayed by browsers or assistive technologies
`width`	Specifies the width of the object area in pixels

The Flash object needs special values, called parameters, to configure the name of the .swf file, quality of the media, and background color of the page areas. These are configured with **`<param />`** or parameter tags. Parameters used with Flash media are shown in Table 11.5.

Table 11.5 Flash media parameters

Parameter Name	Parameter Value
movie	File name of the Flash media (.swf file)
quality	Describes the quality of the media; usually the value `high` is used
bgcolor	Background color of the Flash media area; uses a hexadecimal color value

I'm having problems validating the XHTML on my page after adding Flash. What can I do?

The code supplied by Adobe to add Flash .swf media to Web pages has been tested to work in multiple platforms and browsers. However, it does not pass W3C validation. Keep in mind that your clients are paying you to create Web pages that will display reliably regardless of the browser or operating system their potential customers are using. The nonstandards compliant code supplied by Adobe uses the syntax needed to achieve this goal.

With the trend toward XHTML validation, a number of individuals have developed various techniques to write W3C standards-compliant XHTML code to display Flash media. Some are intended to hide the Flash media code from the W3C validator! Visit http://www.adobe.com/devnet/flash/articles/fp8_detection.html for a summary of the coding techniques along with test results of their support on various platforms and browsers. Your instructor will inform you if he or she prefers a particular coding technique when placing Flash media on Web pages.

All the `<param />` tags for the object appear before the ending `</object>` tag. An example will be given later in this section. The `<embed />` tag is also used to provide for Web browsers that do not support the `<object>` tag. The `<embed />` tag is coded after the `<param />` tags, but before the ending `</object>` tag. An overview of this tag placement follows:

```
<object ... object attributes go here ...
   <param name="movie" ... value attribute goes here ... />
   <param name="quality" ... value attribute goes here ... />
   <param name="bgcolor" ... />
<embed ... object attributes go here ... />
<noembed> ... a brief description of the Flash media can go here
along with a link to alternate text content if appropriate ...
</noembed>
</object>
```

The required `<embed />` tag attributes for Flash media are described in Table 11.6.

Focus on Accessibility

The `<noembed>` tag is a container tag. Use it to provide a brief text description of the Flash media. Include a link to a Web page containing alternate text content if needed. While the developers of assistive technologies such as screen readers are working toward the support of Flash media, it is not yet the norm.

If this seems like a lot of tags and parameters to remember, it is! Most Web developers do not memorize this code. Instead, the Web developer obtains one example Web page file with XTHML code that displays Flash media, copies the code, and edits the code as needed on new pages. Some Web authoring applications, such as Adobe Dreamweaver, will automatically generate this code when you select to insert a Flash object on your page.

Table 11.6 Flash media `<embed>` tag attributes

`<embed>` Attribute	Description and Value
`src`	Name of the Flash media (.swf) file
`quality`	Describes the quality of the media; usually the value high is used
`pluginspage`	URL of the Flash plug-in (it allows for easy download if the Web page visitor does not have the Flash plug-in installed); a recent value is `http://www.macromedia.com/shockwave/download/index.cgi?P1_Prod_Version=ShockwaveFlash`
`type`	MIME type of the Flash media; the value is `application/x-shockwave-flash`
`bgcolor`	Background color of the Flash media area; uses a hexadecimal color value
`height`	Specifies the height of the object area in pixels
`width`	Specifies the width of the object area in pixels

HANDS-ON PRACTICE 11.6

In this Hands-On Practice you will launch Notepad and create a Web page that displays a Flash button. Your page will look like the one shown in Figure 11.9, which can be found in the student files at Chapter11/flash.html.

Figure 11.9
Flash sample

The Flash button on the page will animate when the mouse is placed on it and will link to the Adobe Web site when clicked (if you are connected to the Internet while viewing this page).

Let's get started. Create a folder called testflash on your disk. Copy the flashbutton.swf file from the student files Chapter11 folder and save it in your testflash folder.

Next, launch Notepad and create the page that will display this Flash button. The XHTML code follows:

```
<?xml version="1.0" encoding="UTF-8"?>
<!DOCTYPE html PUBLIC "-//W3C//DTD XHTML 1.0 Transitional//EN"
  "http://www.w3.org/TR/xhtml1/DTD/xhtml1-transitional.dtd">
<html xmlns="http://www.w3.org/1999/xhtml">
<head>
<title>Hands-On Practice 11.6</title>
</head>
<body bgcolor="#FFFFFF" text="#000000">
<h1>Flash Sample</h1>
<object classid="clsid:D27CDB6E-AE6D-11cf-96B8-444553540000"
codebase="http://download.macromedia.com/pub/shockwave/cabs/flash/
swflash.cab#version=8,0,0,0" width="147" height="34" accesskey="/"
tabindex="1" title="Button links to the Adobe Web site" >
<param name="movie" value="flashbutton.swf" />
<param name="quality" value="high" />
<param name="bgcolor" value="#FFFFFF" />
<embed src="flashbutton.swf" quality="high"
pluginspage="http://www.macromedia.com/shockwave/download/
index.cgi?P1_Prod_Version=ShockwaveFlash" type="application/
x-shockwave-flash" width="147" height="34" bgcolor="#FFFFFF" />
<noembed>This is a Flash button that links to the
<a href="http://www.adobe.com">Adobe Web site</a>
</noembed>
</object>
</body>
</html>
```

Save your file in the testflash folder as flash.html and test it in a browser. If this XHTML seems very tedious, don't worry—many Web authoring tools automate the process of writing code to place Flash effects on a Web page. All you do is point and click to the .swf file you are using. Adobe Dreamweaver also offers the option of creating Flash buttons and Flash text effects in this point-and-click manner.

Flash Resources

There are many sources of free Flash animations and Flash tutorials on the Web. In addition to resources at the Adobe Macromedia site, http://adobe.com, the following sites contain tutorials and news about Flash:

- http://flashkit.com
- http://www.actionscript.org
- http://www.scriptocean.com/flashn.html
- http://www.kirupa.com/developer/flash/index.htm

As you visit these and other Flash resource sites, keep in mind that some Flash media is copyrighted. Obtain permission from the creator of the media before using it on your site and follow any instructions for giving credit to the source. Some sites allow personal use of their Flash media for free but require licenses for commercial use.

Adobe has been working toward increasing the accessibility of Flash objects. Recent versions of Flash are accessible to assistive technologies, such as the Window-Eyes screen readers, enabling rich content for a wider audience of Web page visitors.

Flash supports Microsoft Active Accessibility, which provides both a standard method for client technology to communicate with assistive technologies and a technique for developers to ensure that the client software they create to this standard can include Adobe Flash support. Visit Adobe's Web site (http://www.adobe.com) for the most up-to-date information on the issue of Flash and accessibility. Keep in mind that while strides have been taken to provide accessible Flash media, not all of your Web page visitors using assistive technology will have the most recent applications—the <noembed> tag will provide alternate content for these visitors.

11.9 Java

Java is an object-oriented programming (OOP) language developed by Sun Microsystems. An object-oriented program consists of a group of cooperating objects that exchange messages for the purpose of achieving a common objective. Java is not the same language as JavaScript. It is more powerful and much more flexible than JavaScript. Java can be used to develop both stand-alone executable applications and applets that are invoked by Web pages. Java applets are platform independent; that means they can be written and run on any platform—Mac, UNIX, Linux, and Windows. Java applets are compiled (translated from the English-like Java statements to an encoded form) and saved as **.class** files, which contain byte code. The byte code is interpreted by the **Java Virtual Machine** (**JVM**) in the Web browser. The JVM interprets the byte code into the proper machine language for the operating system. The applet is then executed and appears on the Web page. See Figure 11.10 for a diagram that shows this process.

Figure 11.10
The Java Virtual Machine interprets the byte code into machine language

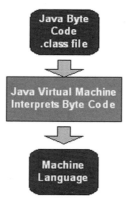

When a Java applet loads, the area reserved for it on the Web page displays a gray box until the applet begins to execute.

Common Uses of Java Applets

Processing Navigation Bars and Buttons. Java applets can process interactive navigation bars on Web pages. Visit http://javaboutique.internet.com/navigation/menu.html and http://www.apycom.com for a variety of navigation and menu Java applets.

Manipulating Images. Java can be used to manipulate images in a number of ways. Visit http://www.codebrain.com/java/codebrainslider for a sample slide show. Perhaps one of the best known Java applet images is the Lake Applet from http://javaboutique .internet.com/Lake, shown in Figure 11.11. This applet not only manipulates the lower portion of an image to make it look like a lake, it also functions as a hyperlink.

Figure 11.11
The classic lake applet

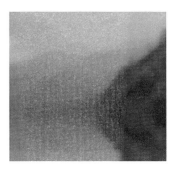

Creating Text Effects. Java applets can also be used to create text effects such as the sample applet shown in Figure 11.12 (see the student files, Chapter11/java1.html). Other text effects can be found at Web sites such as http://www.appletcollection.com/ text.html.

Figure 11.12
A Java applet that provides changing text

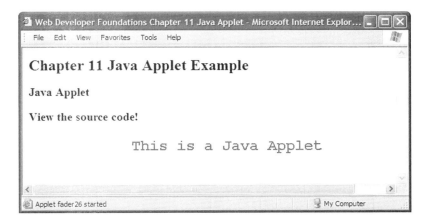

Creating Games. Another popular use of Java applets is to create games for Web pages. Figure 11.13 shows a word search game processed by a Java applet on the EPA's site (http://www.epa.gov/epaoswer/osw/kids/games/hiddenhints/wordsear.htm).

Try Java on the Brain (http://www.javaonthebrain.com/brain.html) for other examples of classic games as Java applets.

Figure 11.13
A Java applet game

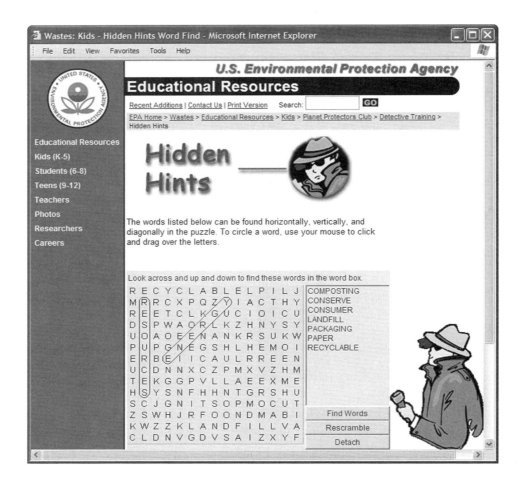

Using Web and Business Applications.   While image effects and games are fun, the use of Java applets in business applications has been increasing for functions such as financial calculations and visualization. The jars.com (http://www.jars.com) site provides a Java applet review service and describes applets that are useful in a business environment, such as NetCharts from http://visualmining.com. Quote.com (http://quote.com) offers a LiveCharts Java applet with real time stock quotes. These types of applets often connect to databases on a Web server and can be very powerful tools if you need to display live data visually.

You can see that Java applets can perform a variety of functions on Web pages. As a Web developer your usual role will not be that of a Java programmer—that is, you should not be expected to write Java applets. However, you could be asked to work with a Java programmer to place his or her applets on your Web site. Whether you obtain an applet from a coworker or find one on a free site, you need to code XHTML to display the applet.

Adding a Java Applet to a Web Page

The **`<applet>`** tag specifies the beginning of an applet area in the body of a Web page. Its closing tag, `</applet>`, specifies the ending of an applet area in the body of a Web page. The `<applet>` tag has a number of attributes described in Table 11.7.

Table 11.7 Attributes of the `<applet>` tag

Attribute	Value
code	Name of the applet file; this has a .class file extension
codebase	If the applet is not in the same folder as the Web page, the codebase indicates the folder that contains the applet
height	Specifies the height of the applet area in pixels
width	Specifies the width of the applet area in pixels
alt	A text description of the applet
id	Alphanumeric, no spaces; the value must be unique and not used for other id values on the same XHTML document

In addition, most applets need special values, or parameters, to configure their processing. An applet that shows images and handles navigation would need parameters to accept the file names of the images and the URLs for the hyperlinks. The programmer who creates an applet determines the parameter values and names required by a specific Java applet. Therefore, expect each applet to require different parameters. Parameters are configured with `<param />` tags. The `<param />` tag is a self-contained tag with two attributes: `name` and `value`. The parameter name is provided in the applet documentation. The parameter value will be different depending on the function of the applet. One parameter might be used to set a background color; another parameter could be used to contain a person's name. A description of the type of value expected should be contained in the applet documentation.

HANDS-ON PRACTICE 11.7

In this Hands-On Practice you will launch Notepad and create a Web page that contains a Java applet. This example will use the Fader26 applet (provided by Johannes Schellen). This applet displays text messages one at a time. The list of text messages is obtained from a text file (.txt file extension) that you will create. An example of this applet at work can be found in the student files at Chapter11/java1.html.

Let's get started. Create a folder called testapplet on your disk. Copy the applet file (fader26.class) from the student files at Chapter11/fader26.class and place it in the same folder as the Web page. Do not change the name of the applet.

Whether you obtain an applet from a free Web site or from a coworker, each applet should have some accompanying documentation that indicates what parameter it expects. Documentation for the Fader26 applet appears in Table 11.8.

Table 11.8 Documentation for Fader26 applet

Parameter Name	Parameter Value
AppletHome	http://www.crosswinds.net/~fader
Data	The name of the text file containing the message to be displayed; (*Note:* each line in the text file should begin with `text=`)
bgColor	This is the background color of the Java applet area; uses a hexadecimal color value

Launch Notepad and create a Web page that invokes this applet. The beginning XHTML is as follows:

```
<?xml version="1.0" encoding="UTF-8"?>
<!DOCTYPE html PUBLIC "-//W3C//DTD XHTML 1.0 Transitional//EN"
"http://www.w3.org/TR/xhtml1/DTD/xhtml1-transitional.dtd">
<html xmlns="http://www.w3.org/1999/xhtml">
<head>
<title>Hands-On Practice 11.7</title>
</head>
<body>
```

Now you are ready to add the XHTML to place the Java applet on your Web page. First, write the `<applet>` tag to reserve an area of the Web page that is 30 pixels high and 610 pixels wide for the fader26.class applet. The code follows:

```
<applet code="fader26.class" height="30" width="610">
```

Next, create the parameter tags. The code for the parameter tags follows:

```
<param name="AppletHome" value="http://www.crosswinds.net/~fader/" />
<param name="Data" value="mymessage.txt" />
<param name="bgColor" value="#FFFFFF" />
```

Finally, an ending applet tag `</applet>`, ending body tag `</body>`, and ending `</html>` tag are needed. The code shown in Notepad is displayed in Figure 11.14.

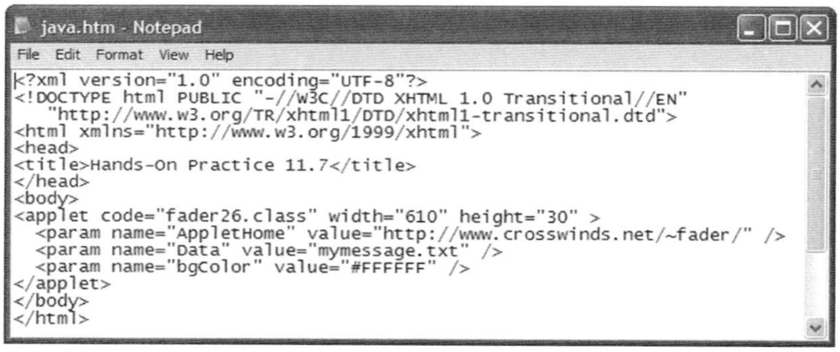

Figure 11.14
Sample Web page code using the fader26 Java applet

Save the file in the testapplet folder with the file name of java.html. You are not yet ready to test the page—you need to create and format the text file that the applet expects. This applet expects each line of text to begin with `text=`. Figure 11.15 shows a sample text file created using Notepad.

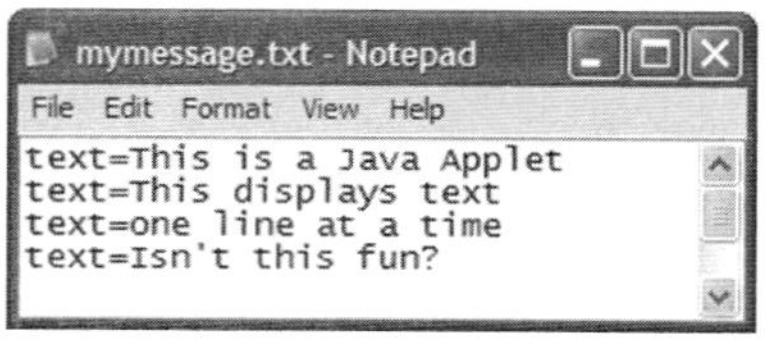

Figure 11.15
The text file needed by the fader26 Java applet

Use this as a guide to create your text file. Save your text file as mymessage.txt in the testapplet folder. The name of the text file must match the value of the "Data" parameter in the XHTML code. Now launch your page in a browser. The applet should display your text one line at a time.

To provide accessibility for all your Web page visitors, regardless of whether their browser or user-agent can process a Java applet, the `<applet>` tag should be modified to use an `alt` attribute and include a text description of the Java applet. The code is shown below:

```
<applet code="fader26.class" height="30" width="610"
alt="Java applet: displays a promotional message one line at a time">
<param name="AppletHome" value="http://www.crosswinds.net/~fader/" />
<param name="Data" value="mymessage.txt" />
<param name="bgColor" value="#FFFFFF" />
This Java applet displays a message one line at a time. Message:
This is a Java applet. This displays text one line at a time.
</applet>
```

FAQ

Why doesn't my Java applet work?

If your applet does not function as expected, verify the following:

- Are Java applets enabled in your browser?
- Is the applet saved in the testapplet folder?
- Is the applet saved with the name fader26.class (all letters must be in lowercase)?
- Are the java.html and mymessage.txt files saved in the testapplet folder?
- Does the code attribute on the `<applet>` tag have the value of fader26.class?

Be aware that the disadvantage of using Java applets is the lag between the time the Web page is initially loaded and the time the applet actually begins to execute. Your Web page visitor will see a box in the area reserved for the applet until it begins executing.

Free Java Applet Resources

Now that you are familiar with applets, you may be wondering how to write them. The organization that developed the Java programming language, Sun Microsystems, offers documentation and other resources on their Web site at http://java.sun.com. Be aware that the Java programming language is very powerful, but quite complex. There are many resources for free and commercial Java applets on the Web. Here are a few helpful sites:

- http://www.appletcollection.com
- http://www.javaonthebrain.com
- http://www.jars.com

As you visit these and other Java resource sites, keep in mind that some Java applets are copyrighted. Be sure to obtain permission from the creator of the applet before using it on your site. There may be some requirements for giving credit to the creator either by name or by linking to their Web site. Follow the instructions provided with the applet. Some applets are free to use in personal Web sites but require licenses for commercial use.

CHECKPOINT 11.2

1. Describe two uses of Flash on Web pages.

2. Describe two uses of Java applets on Web pages.

3. Describe two disadvantages of using interactive technologies such as Flash and Java applets on Web pages.

11.10 JavaScript

JavaScript is an object-based scripting language. In JavaScript you work with the objects associated with a Web page document: the window, the document, and the elements such as forms, images, and links. JavaScript, developed by Netscape, was originally called LiveScript. When Netscape collaborated with Sun Microsystems on modifications to the language, it was renamed JavaScript. JavaScript is not the same as the Java programming language. Unlike Java, JavaScript cannot be used to write standalone programs that can run outside of a Web browser. JavaScript statements can be placed in a separate file (with a .js extension) accessed by a Web browser, but JavaScript statements are more commonly embedded directly in the Web page along with the XHTML. In either case, the Web browser interprets the JavaScript statements. JavaScript is considered to be a client-side scripting language—it runs on the Web client (the browser) and not the Web server. Note that although some Web servers (such as the Sun Java System Web server) can process server-side JavaScript, the language is most commonly used for client-side scripting.

Don't all browsers support JavaScript?

Most modern browsers support JavaScript. However, they also offer the option to disable JavaScript, and some assistive technologies such as screen readers may not support JavaScript. You can't count on every person who visits your Web site to allow JavaScript. It's a good idea to offer your Web page visitors an alternative (plain text links, a phone number to call, and so on) if features of your Web site are dependent on JavaScript.

Common Uses of JavaScript

JavaScript is often used to respond to events such as moving the mouse, clicking a button, and loading a Web page. Figure 11.16 shows two screenshots from the Library of Congress Exhibitions site (http://www.loc.gov/exhibits). Notice how the image at the right is different depending on the position of the mouse. This "image swapping" is accomplished by using JavaScript. This technology is also often used to edit and verify information on XHTML form elements such as text boxes, check boxes, and radio buttons. JavaScript can be used to create pop-up windows, display the current date, perform calculations, and so on. There is an introduction to coding JavaScript in Chapter 14.

Figure 11.16
The Library of
Congress
Exhibitions page
uses JavaScript

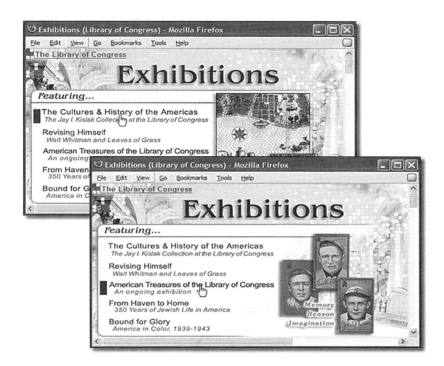

Free JavaScript Resources

There is a lot to learn about JavaScript, but there are many free resources for JavaScript code and JavaScript tutorials on the Web.

Here are a few sites that offer free tutorials or free scripts:

- JavaScript Tutorials (http://echoecho.com/javascript.htm)
- JavaScript Tutorials (http://www.pageresource.com/jscript/index4.htm)
- The JavaScript Source at Internet.com (http://javascript.internet.com/)

Focus on Ethics

As you visit these and other Web sites, be aware that it is unethical to copy and paste JavaScript that another person has written. Many Web sites that offer free JavaScript require that you link to them or place comments in the JavaScript to indicate the identity of the author. While it is unlikely that you would be sued for borrowing someone's JavaScript, the right thing to do is to ask permission, and if given, honor requests for links or identification.

Once you are comfortable with XHTML, the JavaScript language is a good technology to learn as you continue your studies. Try some of the resources listed and get your feet wet. The next section introduces Dynamic HTML, a technology that uses JavaScript.

11.11 Dynamic HTML (DHTML)

Dynamic HTML is not a single technology; it is a group of technologies that work together to change a Web page after it has been downloaded. These technologies allow the Web page to respond to user actions. The following technologies are used: Document Object Model, Cascading Style Sheets, and client-side scripting (JavaScript).

- **Document Object Model (DOM).** The DOM defines every object and element on a Web page. Its hierarchical structure can be used to access page elements and apply styles to page elements. A portion of a basic DOM common to most browsers is shown in Figure 11.17. A contributing factor to the complexity of DHTML is the fact that not all Web browsers use the same DOM. There are three different DOMs currently in use: the W3C DOM, the Microsoft DOM, and the Netscape DOM. The Netscape DOM is used by Netscape 4.x browsers only and has decreased in importance as the market share of that browser has decreased. It's good news for Web developers that current versions of browsers such as Internet Explorer, Firefox, and Opera follow the W3C DOM. Current versions of Internet Explorer support both the W3C DOM and the Microsoft DOM. The DHTML examples in this book support the W3C DOM and provide for other DOMs as appropriate.

Figure 11.17
The Document
Object Model
(DOM)

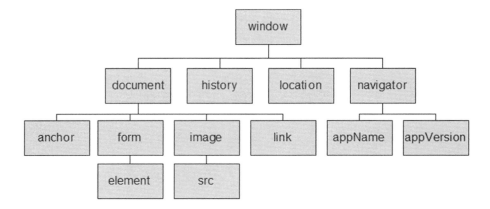

- **Cascading Style Sheets (CSS).** From previous chapters you already know that CSS can be used to apply formatting styles to Web page elements, position elements on a Web page, and even modify the visibility of elements. DHTML utilizes these features of CSS.
- **Client-side Scripting (JavaScript).** Scripting languages such as JavaScript, VBScript, or JScript are used to access the DOM and manipulate the elements.

DHTML frequently has a long learning curve because of the extent of the knowledge needed to combine the three technologies successfully. To further complicate matters, the DOM is implemented differently by major versions of the major browsers. Recently, there is better convergence between the DHTML implementations of modern browsers and it should become easier to write cross-browser DHTML in the future.

Common Uses of DHTML

Hiding and Showing Text. The appearance of text that describes anchor tags or images is another common effect that uses DHTML.

Navigation. The horizontal navigation shown in Figure 11.18 utilizes DHTML. This navigation type has become quite popular and is seen in both horizontal and vertical versions.

The lists of choices under each category (About USAID, Our Work, Locations, Policy, and so on) appear and disappear as you move your mouse pointer over the category

Figure 11.18
This Web site uses
DHTML navigation

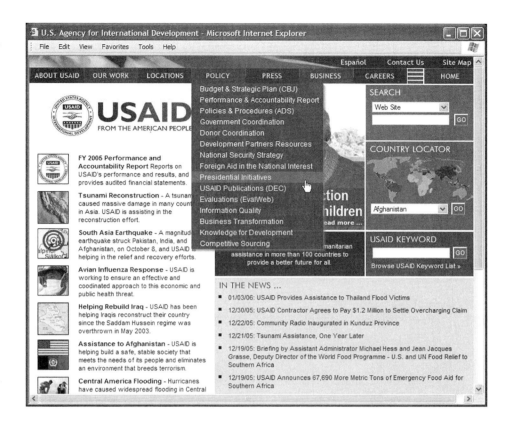

heading. A good source of DHTML code, including navigation menus, is the Dynamic Drive Web site at http://www.dynamicdrive.com.

Image Effects. Various image effects ranging from altering images to slide shows can be applied with DHTML. For several examples of using DHTML to create a slide show, visit http://dynamicdrive.com and search for "slide show."

Sources of Free DHTML

There are many available resources for DHTML on the Web. The following sites are helpful:

- http://dynamicdrive.com
- http://brainjar.com
- http://www.dhtmlgoodies.com

As you visit these and other DHTML resource sites, remember that some may be copyrighted. Be sure to obtain permission from the creator of the DHTML before using it on your site and follow any instructions for giving credit to the source. Some sites allow personal use of their DHTML free of charge but require licenses for commercial use.

If you choose to use free DHTML, be very careful about which browsers it is meant to work with. Some sites clearly indicate the browsers supported by each DHTML effect, such as dynamicdrive.com. Other sites, such as brainjar.com, contain code that is meant to work in the newer releases of browsers only and is not backward compatible to Netscape 4.x. Testing is crucial when you are using DHTML.

Focus on Ethics

Also, always offer your visitors an alternate method in case the DHTML does not work. For example, if you use DHTML for a navigation bar, offer plain text navigation at the bottom of the page.

11.12 Ajax

Ajax, like DHTML, is not a single technology, but a combination of different technologies. Ajax stands for Asynchronous JavaScript and XML. These technologies are not new, but recently have been used together to provide a better experience for Web visitors and create interactive Web applications. Jesse James Garrett of Adaptive Path (http://www.adaptivepath.com/publications/essays/archives/000385.php) is credited with coining the term "Ajax." He describes the technologies utilized in Ajax as the following:

- Standards-based XHTML and CSS
- Document Object Model
- XML (and the related XSLT technology)
- Asynchronous data retrieval using XMLHttpRequest
- JavaScript

Some of these technologies may be unfamiliar to you. That's okay at this point in your Web development career. You're currently creating a strong foundation in XHTML and CSS and may decide to continue your studies in the future and learn additional Web technologies. Right now, it's enough to know that these technologies exist and what they can be used for.

Ajax is part of the **Web 2.0** movement—the transition of the Web from isolated static Web sites to a platform that uses technology to provide rich interfaces and social networking opportunities for people. (See http://www.oreillynet.com/pub/a/oreilly/tim/news/2005/09/30/what-is-Web-20.html for an intriguing article about Web 2.0 by Tim O'Reilly, who was instrumental in the creation of the term "Web 2.0".) Ajax is a Web development technique for creating interactive Web applications. Recall the client/server model discussed in Chapters 1 and 9. The browser makes a request to the server (often triggered by clicking a link or a submit button) and the server returns an entire new Web page for the browser to display. Ajax pushes more of the processing on the client (browser) using JavaScript and XML and often uses "behind the scenes" requests to the server to refresh a portion of the browser display instead of the entire Web page. For example, as soon as a Web site visitor types a Zip code into a form the value could be looked up on a Zip code database and the city/state automatically populated using Ajax—and all this takes place while the visitor is entering the form information before they click the submit button. The result is that the visitor perceives the Web page as being more responsive and has a more interactive experience.

Common Uses of Ajax

Developers are using Ajax to support the Web applications that are part of Web 2.0—Flicker's photo sharing (http://www.flicker.com), del.icio.us's shared collection of favorite sites (http://del.icio.us), Google's e-mail (http://gmail.google.com), Amazon's A9 search engine (http://www.a9.com), and Microsoft Live (http://www.live.com).

Ajax Resources

Ajax is a very hot topic on the Web right now and there are many resources and articles available. Some helpful sites are listed here:

- http://www.ajaxdevelopersjournal.com
- http://www.ajaxpatterns.org
- http://www.webpasties.com/xmlHttpRequest
- http://dhtmlnirvana.com/ajax/ajax_tutorial

CHECKPOINT 11.3

1. Describe two uses of JavaScript.
2. Describe two uses of DHTML.
3. Describe two uses of Ajax.

11.13 Accessibility and Multimedia/Interactivity

Focus on Accessibility

WWW

Multimedia and interactivity can help to create a compelling, engaging experience for your Web site visitors. Please keep in mind that not every Web visitor will be able to experience these features.

- Provide links to free downloads for the plug-ins used by your multimedia. (The code provided to incorporate Flash media and Quicktime media includes these plug-in links.)
- Text descriptions and equivalent content (such as captions) of audio and video will provide access to those with hearing challenges.
- When you work with multimedia developers and programmers to create Flash animations or Java applets for your site, be sure to request features to provide accessibility—keyboard access, text descriptions, and so on. If you use Flash, a Java applet, or DHTML for site navigation—be sure it can be accessed with a keyboard and/or provide plain text navigation links in the footer section of the pages. Adobe provides a good resource for Web developers at their Accessibility Resource Center (http://www.adobe.com/resources/accessibility).
- Section 508 requires that certain rates of screen flickering (frequency greater than 2 Hz and lower than 55 Hz) are avoided. This is to prevent optically induced seizures. You may need to work with your multimedia developer to ensure that dynamic effects perform within a safe range.
- If you use JavaScript, be aware that some visitors may have JavaScript disabled or are unable to manipulate the mouse. Section 508 requires that your site is functional at a basic level even if your visitor's browser does not support JavaScript. A site using Ajax to redisplay a portion of the browser window may have issues when accessed using an assistive technology or text browser. The importance of testing cannot be overemphasized.

When you design with multimedia/interactivity accessibility in mind, you help those with physical challenges as well as those visitors using low bandwidth or who may have missing plug-ins on their browser. However, if the multimedia and/or interactivity used on a page cannot comply with accessibility guidelines, consider creating a separate text-only version of the page. Section 508 requires this feature for sites created for use by federal agencies.

CHAPTER SUMMARY

This chapter introduced technologies to add media and interactivity to Web pages. XHTML techniques used to configure sound, video, and streaming media files were discussed. Accessibility, usability, and copyright issues related to these technologies were addressed. Visit the textbook Web site at http://www.webdevfoundations.net for examples, the links listed in this chapter, and updated information.

Key Terms

.aiff	<noembed>	interactivity
.au	<object>	Java
.avi	<param />	Java applet
.class	Ajax	Java Virtual Machine (JVM)
.mid	audio files	JavaScript
.mov	background sound	media
.mp3	copyright	playback
.mpg	Creative Commons license	podcasting
.ogg	DHTML	plug-in
.swf	Document Object Model	RSS feed
.wav	(DOM)	sampling rate
.wmv	fair use	video files
<applet>	Flash	Web 2.0
<embed />	helper application	

Review Questions

Multiple Choice

1. What type of files are .wav, .aiff, .mid, and .au?

a. audio files

b. video files

c. both audio and video files

d. none of the above

2. Which code plays an audio file called hello.wav as a background sound as soon as the page loads?

a. `<embed src="hello.wav"`
   `background="true" hidden="true"`
   `loop="true"></embed>`

b. `<embed src="hello.wav"`
   `autostart="true" hidden="true"`
   `loop="true" />`

c. `<embed src="hello.wav"`
   `autostart="true" hidden="true"`
   `loop="true"></embed>`

d. `<embed src="hello.wav"`
   `background="true" hidden="true"`
   `loop="true" />`

3. Which of the following should you do to provide for usability and accessibility?

a. use video and sound whenever possible

b. supply text descriptions of audio and video files that appear in your Web pages

c. never use audio and video files

d. none of the above

4. Keeping in mind that it is easy to copy files from other's Web sites, which of the following is true?

   a. there is no copyright on the Web

   b. it is okay to use files created by others if you give them credit

   c. you should obtain permission before using files created by others

   d. none of the above

5. What is an XML file that lists information about your podcast called?

   a. subscription

   b. RSS Feed

   c. RSS blog

   d. none of the above

6. Which of the following can describe JavaScript?

   a. an object-based scripting language

   b. an easy form of Java

   c. a language created by Microsoft

   d. none of the above

7. Which of the following is true of Java applets?

   a. they are contained in files with the .class extension

   b. they are not copyrighted

   c. they must be saved in a different folder than Web pages

   d. none of the above

8. Which combination of technologies does DHTML use to create interactive Web pages?

   a. client-side scripting, Document Object Model, Web browser

   b. client-side Scripting, CSS, Java

   c. Document Object Model, CSS, Web browser

   d. Document Object Model, CSS, client-side scripting

9. Which of the following can create Animations in Flash format (.swf)?

   a. Adobe Flash only

   b. a number of applications, including Adobe Dreamweaver

   c. java

   d. none of the above

10. Which of the following can describe Ajax?

    a. an object-based scripting language

    b. the same as Web 2.0

    c. a Web development technique for creating interactive Web applications

    d. none of the above

Fill in the Blank

11. When recording human speech in an audio file, _____ resolution is sufficient.

12. Use of a copyrighted work for purposes such as criticism, reporting, teaching, scholarship, or research is called _____.

13. The _____ attribute for the image tag displays media but is only supported by Internet Explorer.

14. When displaying a Java applet, the browser invokes the _____ to interpret the bytecode into the appropriate machine language.

15. The _____ defines every object and element on a Web page.

Short Answer

16. List at least two reasons not to use audio or video on a Web page.

17. Describe a type of copyright license that empowers the author/artist to grant some but not all rights for using his or her work.

Apply Your Knowledge

1. Predict the Result. Draw and write a brief description of the Web page that will be created with the following XHTML code:

```
<?xml version="1.0" encoding="UTF-8"?>
<!DOCTYPE html PUBLIC "-//W3C//DTD XHTML 1.0 Transitional//EN"
```

```
      "http://www.w3.org/TR/xhtml1/DTD/xhtml1-transitional.dtd">
<html xmlns="http://www.w3.org/1999/xhtml">
<head>
<title>CircleSoft Designs</title>
<style type="text/css">
body { background-color: #FFFFCC;
       color: #330000;
       font-family Arial,Helvetica,sans-serif; }
.nav { margin: 10px;
       font-weight: bold;
       text-align: center; }
.content { width: 750px; }
.footer { font-size: smaller; }
</style>
</head>
<body>
  <div class="content">
  <div class="nav"><a href="index.html">Home</a> |
    <a href="services.html">Services</a> |
    <a href="about.html">About</a> |
    <a href="contact.html">Contact</a>
  </div>
  <div><strong>CircleSoft Designs will </strong>
    <ul>
      <li>work with you to create a Web presence that fits your
      company</li>
      <li>listen to you and answer your questions</li>
      <li>utilize the most appropriate technology for your sites:
      JavaScript, Java, PHP, databases, ASP, DHTML, XML, Flash and
      more</li>
    </ul>
    <p>Listen to what our clients say: <br />
      <object data="circlesoft.wav" height="50" width="100"
      type="audio/wav">
        <param name="src" value="circlesoft.wav" />
      </object>
    </p>
  </div>
  <div class="footer">Copyright &copy; 2008 CircleSoft Design
  </div>
  </div>
</body>
</html>
```

2. **Fill in the Missing Code.** This Web page should display a Java applet named slideshow.class that is 200 pixels wide and 175 pixels high. Some XHTML attributes, indicated by "_" are missing. Fill in the missing code.

```
<?xml version="1.0" encoding="UTF-8"?>
<!DOCTYPE html PUBLIC "-//W3C//DTD XHTML 1.0 Transitional//EN"
    "http://www.w3.org/TR/xhtml1/DTD/xhtml1-transitional.dtd">
```

```
<html xmlns="http://www.w3.org/1999/xhtml">
<head>
<title>Fill in the Missing Code</title>
</head>
<body>
<h2>Trillium Media Design</h2>
  <p>Visual Tour of Our Services </p><br />
<applet code="_" height="_" width="_">
  <param name="image1" value="service1.jpg" />
  <param name="image2" value="service2.jpg" />
  <param name="image3" value="service3.jpg" />
</applet>
</body>
</html>
```

3. **Find the Error.** The purpose of the following Web page is to display a video named products.mov. The video only displays on Internet Explorer. Why?

```
<?xml version="1.0" encoding="UTF-8"?>
<!DOCTYPE html PUBLIC "-//W3C//DTD XHTML 1.0 Transitional//EN"
   "http://www.w3.org/TR/xhtml1/DTD/xhtml1-transitional.dtd">
<html xmlns="http://www.w3.org/1999/xhtml">
<head>
<title>Find the Error<title>
</head>
<body>
<div align="center">
<img dynsrc="products.mov" autostart="true" width="160"
height="120" alt="Products Video 2MB" />
</div>
</body>
</html>
```

Hands-On Exercises

1. Practice working with media.

   a. Write the XHTML to add a video called demo1.mov to a Web page.

   b. Write the XHTML to add a background sound called message.wav to a Web page. It should only play once.

   c. Write the XHTML to add a background sound called theme.mid to a Web page that will loop repeatedly.

   d. Write the XHTML to add an audio file called lesson1.wav to a Web page that can be controlled by the visitor.

2. Practice writing XHTML.

   a. Write the XHTML to place a Java applet called mylink.class on a Web page. This applet needs an area that is 300 pixels wide and 40 pixels high. Its parameters are documented as follows:

Parameter Name	Parameter Value
LinkURL	Any URL
LinkDescription	Text describing the link

   b. Write the XHTML to add a Flash file called intro.swf to a Web page. The effect needs an area that is 500 pixels wide and 200 pixels high. Center the effect horizontally on the page.

3. Create a Web page about your favorite movie that contains one of the following: an audio file containing your review of the movie (use Windows Sound Recorder or a similar program to record your voice), an audio clip from the movie, a video clip from the movie, or an audio clip from the movie soundtrack. Place an e-mail link to yourself on the Web page. Save the page as movie11.html. Hand in printouts of both the source code (print in Notepad) and the browser display of your page to your instructor.

4. Create a Web page about your favorite music CD that contains either a brief audio file containing your review of the CD (use Windows Sound Recorder or a similar program to record your voice) or an audio clip from the CD. Place an e-mail link to yourself on the Web page. Save the page as cd11.html. Hand in printouts of both the source code (print in Notepad) and the browser display of your page to your instructor.

5. Create a Web page about a current political figure who you admire that contains one of the following: an audio file containing your thoughts about the political figure (use Windows Sound Recorder or a similar program to record your voice), an audio clip of an interview with the individual that you selected, or a brief video clip of the individual you selected. Place an e-mail link to yourself on the Web page. Save the page as political11.html. Hand in printouts of both the source code (print in Notepad) and the browser display of your page.

6. Create a Web page about your favorite music group that uses either the Java applet described in Hands-On Practice 11.7 or a Java applet of your choice. The applet should display the names of songs performed by the group. Place an e-mail link to yourself on the Web page. Save the page as java11.html. Hand in printouts of both the source code (print in Notepad) and the browser display of your page.

7. Visit the textbook Web site at http://webdevfoundations.net/flashcs3 and follow the instructions to create a Flash logo banner. Hand in the printouts described in the tutorial to your instructor.

Web Research

1. This chapter mentioned some software applications that can be used to create and edit media files. With those as a starting point, search for more applications on the Web. Create a Web page that lists at least five media authoring applications. Organize your page with a table that provides the name of the software application, the URL, a brief description, and the price. Place your name in an e-mail link on the Web page. Your page should play some background music. Include the sound loop (catch.wav) from this chapter, record your own, or find an appropriate sound file on the Web. Print both the source code (from Notepad) and the browser view of your page.

2. Issues related to copyright were discussed in this chapter. With the resources provided as a starting point, search for additional information related to copyrights and the Web. Create a Web page that provides five helpful facts about copyright and the Web. Provide the URLs of the Web sites you used as resources. Place a media console on the page to allow visitors to play an audio file while they read your page. Include the sound loop (catch.wav) from this chapter, record your own, or find an appropriate sound file on the Web. Print both the source code (from Notepad) and the browser view of your Web page.

3. Choose one method of Web interactivity discussed in this chapter: JavaScript, Java applets, DHTML, Flash, or Ajax. Use the resources listed in the chapter as a starting point, but also search the Web for additional resources on the interactivity method you have chosen. Create a Web page that lists at least five useful resources along with a brief description of each. Organize your Web page with a table that provides the name of the site, the URL, a brief description of what is offered, and a recommended page (such as a tutorial, free script, and so on) for each resource. Place your name in an e-mail link on the Web page. Print both the source code (from Notepad) and the browser view of the Web page.

4. Choose one method of Web interactivity discussed in this chapter: JavaScript, Java applets, DHTML, or Flash. Use the resources listed in the chapter as a starting point, but also search the Web for additional resources on the interactivity method you have chosen. Find either a tutorial or free download that uses the method of Web interactivity you are researching. Create a Web page that uses the code or download that you found. Describe the effect and list the URL of the resource on the Web page. Place your name in an e-mail link on the Web page. Print both the source code (from Notepad) and the browser view of the page.

Focus on Web Design

1. Ajax is a relatively new technology and there are Web design usability and accessibility issues associated with it. Visit the following sites to become aware of these issues:

   - http://ajaxian.com/archives/ajax-usability-mistakes
   - http://www.sitepoint.com/blogs/2005/03/10/usability-and-accessibility-with-ajax/
   - http://www.standards-schmandards.com/2005/ajax-and-accessibility/
   - http://www.clickz.com/showPage.html?page=3624207

   Write a one-page report that describes Ajax usability issues that Web designers should be aware of. Cite the URLs of the resources you used.

2. Read Jakob Nielson's (in)famous 2000 article about why Flash is 99 percent bad at http://www.useit.com/alertbox/20001029.html. Many years have passed, accessibility features have been built into Flash, and a new day has dawned. Some analysts say that Flash is 99 percent good (http://www.brajeshwar.com/2007/flash-99-good/). In an interview (http://www.guardian.co.uk/technology/2007/apr/05/adobe.newmedia) Mark Anders, the senior principal scientist at Adobe, recommended Flash as "a great platform for building the next generation of rich Internet applications."

   After you review the sources listed, decide on your own opinion of Flash and when, as a designer, you would recommend its use. Write a one-page paper that persuasively presents your opinion. Cite the URLs of your resources.

WEB SITE CASE STUDY
Adding Multimedia

Each of the following case studies continues throughout most of the text. This chapter adds media and interactivity to the Web sites.

JavaJam Coffee House

See Chapter 2 for an introduction to the JavaJam Coffee House Case Study. Figure 2.26 shows a site map for the JavaJam Web site. The pages were created in earlier chapters. Use the javajamcss folder. You have two tasks:

1. Add a background sound to the Home page (index.html).

2. Replace the javalogo.gif with a Flash animated banner called javalogo.swf on each page. The Flash media is 620 pixels in width and 117 pixels in length.

Hands-On Practice Case

1. Add a background sound to the Home page (index.html).
   - Copy the catch.wav file from the student files in the Chapter11 folder and save it to your javajamcss folder.
   - Launch Notepad and open the Home page (index.html) in the javajamcss folder. Modify index.html so that the sound file plays continuously when the page is loaded. See the Hands-On Practice exercises in this chapter for help Save your page. Test your page using several browsers. You should hear the sound.

2. Replace the logo image with a Flash animation on the Home page (index.html).
   - Copy the javalogo.swf file from the student files in the Chapter11 folder and save it to your javajamcss folder.
   - Launch Notepad and open the Home page (index.html) in the javajamcss folder. Modify index.html to display the Flash file (javalogo.swf) instead of the image (javalogo.gif). See the Hands-On Practice exercises in this chapter for help. Save your page. Test your page using several browsers. You should see the logo animate.
   - Modify the logo area on the rest of the JavaJam pages so that your Web site has a consistent design. Save and test your pages.

Fish Creek Animal Hospital

See Chapter 2 for an introduction to the Fish Creek Animal Hospital Case Study. Figure 2.30 shows a site map for the Fish Creek Web site. The pages were created in earlier chapters. Use the fishcreekcss folder. You have four tasks:

1. Add a background sound to the Home page (index.html).

2. Modify the fishcreek.css style rules to configure the placement of the Flash logo and Quicktime movie.

3. Add a video to the Ask the Vet page (askvet.html). See Figure 11.19 for a sample screenshot.

4. Replace the fishcreeklogo.gif with a Flash animated banner called fishcreeklogo.swf on each page. The Flash media is 400 pixels in width and 80 pixels in length.

Figure 11.19
Fish Creek Ask the Vet page

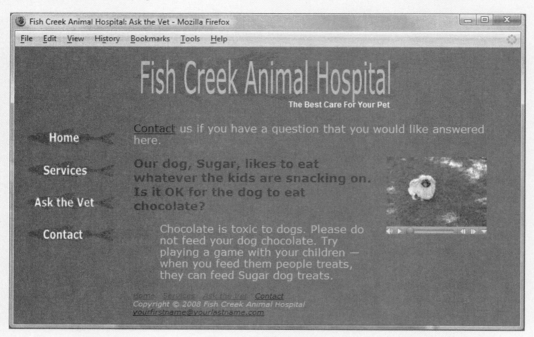

Hands-On Practice Case

1. Add a background sound to the Home page (index.html).
   - Copy the bark.wav sound file from the student files in the Chapter11 folder and save it to your fishcreekcss folder.
   - Launch Notepad and open the Home page (index.html) in the fishcreekcss folder. Modify index.html so that the sound file plays once when the page is loaded. See the Hands-On Practice exercises in this chapter for help Save your page. Test your page using several browsers. You should hear the sound.

2. Modify the fishcreek.css file.
   - Modify the `logo` class. Change the left padding to 170 pixels. This will align the new Flash logo with the right column.
   - Create a new id called `movie`. Configure the movie id to float to the right, have a 20 pixel left margin, and a 50 pixel bottom margin.

3. Add a video to the Ask the Vet page (askvet.html).
   - Copy the sparky.mov video file from the student files in the Chapter11 folder and save it to your fishcreekcss folder.
   - Launch Notepad and open the askthevet.html file in the fishcreekcss folder. Modify the questions and answers on the askthevet.htm page to display a

video along the right side of the page. See the screenshot shown in Figure 11.19 as a guide. Use the `<object>` and `<param />` elements to configure the video for display. See Hands on Practice 11.5 as a guide. Use the attributes and values listed in Table 11.9 as you configure your page.

Save your page. Test your page using several browsers.

Table 11.9 Configuration requirements for sparky.mov

Attribute	Value
src	sparky.mov
data	sparky.mov
height	120
width	150
autoplay	false
controller	true
classid	clsid:02BF25D5-8C17-4B23-BC80-D3488ABDDC6B
codebase	http://www.apple.com/qtactivex/qtplugin.cab
type	video/quicktime

4. Replace the logo image with a Flash animation on the Home page (index.html).
   - Copy the fishcreeklogo.swf file from the student files in the Chapter11 folder and save it to your fishcreekcss folder.
   - Launch Notepad and open the Home page (index.html) in the fishcreekcss folder. Modify index.html to display the Flash file (fishcreeklogo.swf) instead of the image (fishcreeklogo.gif). See the Hands-On Practice exercises in this chapter for help. Save your page. Test your page using several browsers. You should see the logo animate.
   - Modify the logo area on the rest of the Fish Creek Web pages to create a cohesive site with a consistent design. Save and test your pages.

Pete the Painter

See Chapter 2 for an introduction to the Pete the Painter Case Study. Figure 2.34 shows a site map for the Pete the Painter Web site. The pages were created in earlier chapters. Use the paintercss folder. You have two tasks:

1. Add a background sound to the Services page (services.html).
2. Modify the Home page to display a Flash slide show.

Hands-On Practice Case

1. Add a background sound to the Services page (services.html).
   - Copy the painter.wav sound file from the student files in the Chapter11 folder and save it to your paintercss folder.
   - Launch Notepad and open the Services page (services.html) in the paintercss folder. Modify services.html so that the sound file plays once when the page is

loaded. See the Hands-On Practice exercises in this chapter for help Save your page. Test your page using several browsers. You should hear the sound.

2. Modify the Home page to display a Flash slideshow file called painter.swf. See Figure 11.20.

- Copy the painter.swf file from the student files in the Chapter11 folder and save it to your paintercss folder. The Flash media is 213 pixels in width and 163 pixels in length.

- Launch Notepad and open the Home page (index.html) in the paintercss folder. Modify the content on index.html as follows:

   Write the XHTML needed in the right column to display the Flash slideshow painter.swf file. Assign the `<object>` tag to the `floatright` class.

Save your page and test it in a browser.

Figure 11.20
Pete the Painter new Home page

Prime Properties

See Chapter 2 for an introduction to the Prime Properties Case Study. Figure 2.38 shows a site map for the Prime Properties Web site. The pages were created in earlier chapters. Use the primecss folder. You have three tasks:

1. Add a background sound to the Contact page (contact.html).
2. Modify the prime.css style sheet to configure the placement of the Flash swf.
3. Modify the Home page to display a Flash slide show.

Hands-On Practice Case

1. Add a background sound to the Contact page (contact.html).
   - Copy the prime.wav sound file from the student files in the Chapter11 folder and save it to your primecss folder.
   - Launch Notepad and open the Contact page (contact.html) in the primecss folder. Modify contact.html so that the sound file plays once when the page is loaded. See the Hands-On Practice exercises in this chapter for help.

   Save your page and test it using several browsers. You should hear the sound.

2. Modify the prime.css file. Create a new class called `floatright`. Configure the `floatright` class to float to the right, have a 20 pixel left margin and a 60 pixel right margin.

3. Modify the Home page to display a Flash slideshow file called prime.swf. See Figure 11.21.
   - Copy the prime.swf file from the student files in the Chapter11 folder and save it to your primecss folder. The Flash media is 213 pixels in width and 163 pixels in length.
   - Launch Notepad and open the Home page (index.html) in the primecss folder. Write the XHTML needed in the right column (above the unordered list) to display the Flash slideshow prime.swf file. Assign the `<object>` tag to the `floatright` class.

   Save your page and test in a browser.

Figure 11.21
The Prime Properties Home page displays a Flash slideshow

Web Project

See Chapter 5 for an introduction to the Web Project Case. Review the goals of your Web site and determine if the use of media or interactivity would add value to your site. If so, you will add either media and/or interactivity to your project site. Check with your instructor for the required use of any specific media or technology that supports interactivity in your Web project.

Select one or more from the following:

1. Media: Choose one of the examples from the chapter, record your own audio or media file, or search the Web for royalty-free media.

2. Flash: Choose one of the examples from the chapter, create your own .swf file, or search the Web for additional .swf files.

3. Java applet: Choose one of the examples from the chapter, write your own if you have programming skills, or search the Web for free Java applets.

4. Decide where to apply the media and/or interactive technology to your site. Modify, save the page(s), and test in various browsers.

E-Commerce Overview

Chapter Objectives In this chapter, you will learn about ...

- E-commerce and the Web
- Benefits and risks of e-commerce
- E-commerce business models
- E-commerce security and encryption
- Electronic Data Interchange (EDI)

- Trends and projections for e-commerce
- Issues related to e-commerce
- Order and payment processing
- E-commerce solution options

E-commerce is the buying and selling of goods and
services on the Internet. Whether business-to-business, business-to-consumer, or
consumer-to-consumer, Web sites that support e-commerce are everywhere.
This chapter provides an overview of this topic.

12.1 What Is E-Commerce?

A formal definition of **e-commerce** is the integration of communications, data management, and security technologies, which allows individuals and organizations to exchange information related to the sale of goods and services. Major functions of e-commerce include the buying of goods, the selling of goods, and the performance of financial transactions on the Internet.

Advantages of E-Commerce

There are a number of advantages to both businesses and consumers when engaging in e-commerce. For businesses, the many advantages include the following:

- **Reduced Costs.** Online businesses can stay open 24 hours a day without the overhead of a brick-and-mortar facility. Many businesses establish a Web site before attempting e-commerce. When they add e-commerce functions to their Web site, the site becomes a source of revenue and, in many cases, pays for itself in short order.

- **Increased Customer Satisfaction.** Businesses can use their Web sites to improve communication with customers and increase customer satisfaction. E-commerce sites often contain an FAQ page. The availability of customer service representatives by e-mail, discussion forums, or even online chat (see http://liveperson.com) can improve customer relations.

- **More Effective Data Management.** Depending on the level of automation, e-commerce sites can perform credit card verification and authorization, update inventory levels, and interface with order fulfillment systems, thereby managing the organization's data more efficiently.

- **Potentially Higher Sales.** An e-commerce store that is open 24 hours a day, seven days a week and is available to everyone on the planet has the potential for higher sales than a traditional brick-and-mortar storefront.

Businesses aren't the only beneficiaries of e-commerce; consumers see some advantages as well, including the following:

- **Convenience.** Consumers can shop at any time of the day. There is no travel time to get to the store. Some consumers prefer Web site shopping over traditional catalog shopping because they can view additional images and join discussion forums about the products.

- **Easier Comparison Shopping.** There is no driving from store to store to check the price of an item. Customers can easily surf the Web and compare prices and value.

- **Wider Selection of Goods.** Since it is convenient to shop and compare, consumers have a wider selection of goods available for purchase.

As you can see, e-commerce provides a number of advantages for both businesses and consumers.

Risks of E-Commerce

There are risks involved in any business transaction, and e-commerce is no exception. Possible risk issues for businesses include the following:

- **Loss of Sales if Technology Fails.** If your Web site isn't available or your e-commerce form processing doesn't work, customers may not return to your site. It is always important to have a user-friendly, reliable Web site, but when you engage in e-commerce, reliability and ease of use are critical factors in the success of your business.

- **Fraudulent Transactions.** Fraudulent credit card purchases or crank orders placed by vandals (or thirteen-year-olds with time on their hands) are risks that businesses need to deal with.

- **Customer Reluctance.** Although more and more consumers are willing to purchase on the Web, the target market of your business may not be. However, by offering incentives such as free shipping or a "no questions asked" returns policy, your business may be able to attract these consumers.

- **Increased Competition.** Because the overhead for an e-commerce site can be much lower than that of a traditional brick-and-mortar store, a company operating out of a basement can be just as impressive as a long-standing organization if its Web site looks professional. Because it is much easier to enter the marketplace with an e-commerce store, your business will have increased competition.

Businesses are not alone in needing to deal with risks associated with e-commerce. Consumers may perceive the following risks:

- **Security Issues.** Later in this chapter you will learn how to determine whether a Web site has Secure Sockets Layer (SSL) for encryption and security of information. The general public may not know how to determine whether a Web site is using this encryption method and be wary of placing a credit card order. Another, possibly more important issue, is what the site does with information after it is transmitted over the Internet. Is the database secure? Are the database backups secure? These questions are difficult to answer. It's a good idea to purchase only from sites that you consider to be reputable.

- **Privacy Issues.** Many sites post privacy policy statements. These describe what the site will do (or will not do) with the information they receive. Some sites use the data for internal marketing purposes only. Other sites sell the data to outside companies. Web sites can and do change their privacy policies over time. Consumers may be leery of purchasing online because of the potential lack of privacy.

- **Purchasing Based on Photos and Descriptions.** There is nothing like holding and touching an item before you purchase it. Consumers run the risk of purchasing a product that they will not be happy with because they are making purchasing decisions based on photographs and written descriptions. If an e-commerce site has a generous return policy, consumers will feel more confident about purchasing.

- **Returns.** It is often more difficult to return an item to an e-commerce store than to a brick-and-mortar store. Consumers may not want to risk this inconvenience.

12.2 E-Commerce Business Models

Both businesses and consumers are riding the e-commerce wave. There are four common e-commerce business models: business-to-consumer, business-to-business, consumer-to-consumer, and business-to-government.

- **Business-to-Consumer (B2C).** Most of the business-to-consumer selling takes place in online stores. Some, like Amazon.com (http://amazon.com) are online only. Others are click-and-mortar—electronic storefronts for well-known brick-and-mortar stores such as Sears (http://sears.com).
- **Business-to-Business (B2B).** E-commerce between two businesses often takes the form of exchanging business supply chain information among vendors, partners, and business customers. Electronic Data Interchange (EDI) is also in this category.
- **Consumer-to-Consumer (C2C).** Individuals are selling to each other on the Internet. The most common format is that of the auction. The most well-known auction site is eBay (http://ebay.com), which was founded in 1995.
- **Business-to-Government (B2G).** Businesses are selling to the government on the Internet. There are very strict usability standards for businesses targeting governmental agencies. Section 508 of the Rehabilitation Act requires that electronic and information technology (including Web pages) used by federal agencies is accessible to people with disabilities. See http://www.section508.gov for more information.

Businesses began exchanging information electronically many years before the Web came into existence, using Electronic Data Interchange.

12.3 Electronic Data Interchange (EDI)

Electronic Data Interchange (EDI) is the transfer of data between companies over a network. This facilitates the exchange of standard business documents, including purchase orders and invoices. EDI is not new; it has been in existence since the 1960s. Organizations that exchange EDI transmissions are called trading partners.

The Accredited Standards Committee X12 (ASC X12) is chartered by the American National Standards Institute (ANSI) to develop and maintain EDI standards. These standards include transaction sets for common business forms, such as requisitions and invoices. This allows businesses to reduce paperwork and communicate electronically.

EDI messages are placed in transaction sets. A transaction set consists of a header, one or more data segments, which are strings of data elements separated by delimiters, and a trailer. Newer technologies such as XML and Web services are allowing trading partners virtually unlimited opportunities to customize their information exchange over the Internet.

Now that you are aware of possibilities of e-commerce and the types of business models, you may be wondering where the most money is being made. The next section discusses some statistics related to e-commerce.

12.4 E-Commerce Statistics

You may be surprised to discover that the most money is being made in B2B e-commerce—businesses selling to other businesses. According to Forrester Research, in 1998 business-to-business revenue in the United States amounted to $43 billion and total business-to-consumer revenue was only $8 billion.

E-commerce has experienced growth in these areas since that time. For example, Jupiter Research (http://www.jupitermedia.com/corporate/releases/06.02.06-newjupresearch.html) projected that online retail spending would increase from $81 billion in 2005 to $95 billion in 2006. According to the study, online retail spending is expected to increase to $144 billion in 2010. Clearly there is money to be made on the Internet! Some areas are growing faster than others, as shown by Figure 12.1. Clickz.com reports at http://www.clickz.com/showPage.html?page=3575456 that in 2005 the top five fastest growing retail categories are apparel and accessories, computer software, home and garden, toys and hobbies, and jewelry and watches. Although they didn't make the top five—other categories such as event tickets, furniture, and flowers/gifts each experienced over 20 percent growth in sales during this time.

Figure 12.1
E-commerce categories that experienced the most growth in 2005

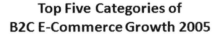
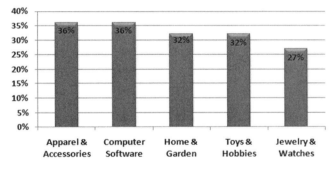

Jupiter Research projects optimistic growth for B2C e-commerce—predicting that by 2010 online purchases will be made by 71 percent of Internet users.

Who are your potential online consumers? A study by Harris Interactive discussed on ClickZ Stats (http://web.archive.org/web/20060225050858/http://www.clickz.com/stats/sectors/geographics/article.php/5911_1011491) indicates that Internet users in the United States generally mirror the U.S. population, but are slightly younger, more educated, and more affluent. Table 12.1 shows an excerpt of this research.

Table 12.1 Online population compared with U.S. population

	2002 Online Population	U.S. Population (2000 Census)
Male	49%	48%
Female	51%	52%
Household Income Less Than $25K	18%	25%
Household Income $25K to $50K	25%	29%
Household Income Higher Than $50K	46%	32%
Adults 18–49	74%	64%

12.5 E-Commerce Issues

Doing business on the Internet is not without its problems. The following are some common issues:

- **Intellectual Property.** There has been some recent controversy regarding intellectual property rights and domain names. **Cybersquatting** is the practice of registering a domain name that is a trademark of another entity in the hopes of profiting by selling the domain name to the entity. The Internet Corporation for Assigned Names and Numbers (ICANN) sponsors the Uniform Domain Name Dispute Policy at http://www.icann.org/udrp/udrp.htm, which can be used to combat cybersquatters.

- **Security.** Security is a constant issue on the Internet. Distributed denial of service (DDoS) attacks have shut down popular e-commerce sites. Some of these attacks are carried out by script kiddies (teenagers with technical knowledge and sometimes malicious intent) who literally have nothing better to do than cause havoc on the Web.

- **Fraud.** Fraudulent Web sites that ask for credit card numbers without any intent of delivering products or with fraudulent intent are an understandable source of concern for consumers.

- **Taxation.** State governments and local municipalities need sales taxes to fund education, public safety, health, and many other essential services. When an item is purchased at a retail store, the sales tax is collected from the purchaser by the seller at the time of sale and periodically remitted by the seller to the state in which the sale occurred.

  When an item is purchased on the Internet, the seller usually does not collect and remit the sales tax. In this situation, many states require that consumers file a use tax and pay the amount that would have been collected. In reality, few consumers do this and few states attempt to enforce it. Our local governments are losing revenue to fund worthwhile programs.

  There have been some movements to require that sales tax is collected on all Internet purchases. At the time this was written, the moratorium on Internet sales tax was still in effect. However, state and local governments are losing sources of revenue as more consumers turn to online shopping. Look for the topic of Internet sales tax to continue to be controversial.

- **International Commerce.** Web sites that target a global audience have additional concerns. If a site will be offered in multiple languages there are options of automatic translation programs (http://www.systranlinks.com) and companies that provide customized Web site translation services (http://www.worldlingo.com). Be aware that the graphical user interface (GUI) that works with English may not work with other languages. For example, comparable words and phrases often take quite a few more letters in German than in English. If your GUI doesn't have enough white space in the English version of the site, how will it look in the German version?

How will your international customers pay you? If you accept credit cards, the credit card company will perform the currency conversion. What about the culture of your target international audience? Have you studied the target countries and made certain that your site is appealing and not offensive? Another issue related to international commerce is the cost of shipping and the availability of delivery to remote destinations.

Now that you are familiar with the concept of e-commerce, let's take a closer look at encryption methods and security. The next section introduces encryption methods, SSL, and digital certificates.

12.6 E-Commerce Security

Encryption

Encryption is used to ensure privacy within an organization and on the Internet. **Encryption** is the conversion of data into an unreadable form, called a **ciphertext**. Ciphertext cannot be easily understood by unauthorized individuals. **Decryption** is the process of converting the ciphertext into its original form, called plain text or **clear text**, so that it can be understood. The process of encryption and decryption requires an algorithm and a key.

Encryption is important on the Internet because information in a packet can be intercepted as it travels the communications media. If a hacker or business competitor intercepts an encrypted packet, he or she will not be able to use the information (such as a credit card number or business strategy) because it cannot be read.

A number of types of encryption are commonly used on the Internet, including **symmetric-key encryption** and **asymmetric-key encryption**.

Symmetric-Key Encryption. Symmetric-key encryption, shown in Figure 12.2, is also called single-key encryption because *both* the encryption and decryption use the same key. Since the key must be kept secret from others, both the sender and receiver must know the key before communicating using encryption. An advantage of symmetric-key encryption is speed.

Figure 12.2
Symmetric-key encryption uses a single key

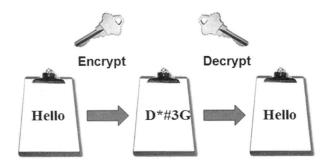

Asymmetric-Key Encryption. Asymmetric-key encryption is also called public-key encryption because there is no shared secret. Instead, two keys are created at the same time. This key pair contains a public key and a private key. The public key and the private key are mathematically related in such a way that it is unlikely anyone would guess one of the pair even with knowledge of the other. Only the public key can decrypt a message encrypted with the private key and only the private key can decrypt a message encrypted with the public key (see Figure 12.3). The public key is available via a digital

Figure 12.3
Asymmetric-key
encryption uses a
key pair

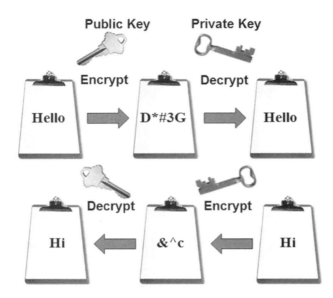

certificate (more on that later). The private key should be kept secure and secret. It is stored on the Web server (or other computer) of the key owner. Asymmetric-key encryption is much slower than symmetric-key encryption.

Integrity

The encryption methods described above help to keep the contents of a message secret. However, e-commerce security is also concerned with making sure that messages have not been altered or damaged during transmission. A message is said to have **integrity** if it can be proven that is has not been altered. **Hash functions** provide a way to ensure the integrity of messages. A hash function, or hash algorithm, transforms a string of characters into a usually shorter fixed-length value or key, called a **digest**, which represents the original string.

These security methods—especially the techniques of symmetric-key and symmetric-key encryption—are used as part of SSL, the technology that helps to make commerce on the Internet secure. The next section introduces this technology.

Secure Sockets Layer (SSL)

Secure Sockets Layer (SSL) is a protocol that allows data to be privately exchanged over public networks. It was developed by Netscape and is used to encrypt data sent between a client (usually a Web browser) and a Web server. SSL utilizes both symmetric and asymmetric keys.

SSL provides secure communication between a client and server by using the following:

- Server and (optionally) client digital certificates for authentication
- Symmetric-key cryptography with a "session key" for bulk encryption

- Public-key cryptography for transfer of the session key
- Message digests (hash function) to verify the integrity of the transmission

You can tell that a Web site is using SSL by the protocol in the Web browser address text box—it shows https instead of http. Also, Internet Explorer and Netscape browsers display a lock icon when SSL is used, as shown in Figure 12.4.

Figure 12.4
The browser indicates that SSL is being used

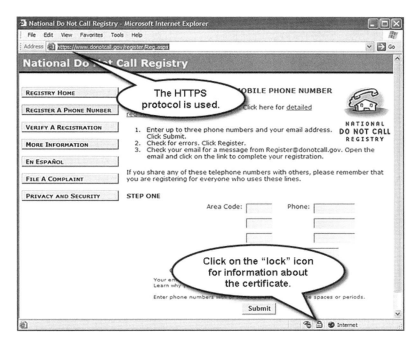

Digital Certificate

SSL enables two computers to communicate securely by posting a digital certificate for authentication. A **digital certificate** is a form of an asymmetric key that also contains information about the certificate, the holder of the certificate, and the issuer of the certificate. The contents of a digital certificate include the following:

- The public key
- Effective date of the certificate
- Expiration date of the certificate
- Details about the certificate authority—the issuer of the certificate
- Details about the certificate holder
- A digest of the certificate content

VeriSign (http://verisign.com) is a well-known certificate authority (CA). A recent version of its certificate is shown in Figure 12.5.

To obtain a certificate, you request a certificate from a certificate authority and pay the application fee. The certificate authority verifies your identity, issues your certificate, and supplies you with a public/private key pair. You store the certificate in your software—such as a Web server, Web browser, or e-mail application. The certificate authority makes your certificate publicly known.

Figure 12.5
VeriSign digital
certificate

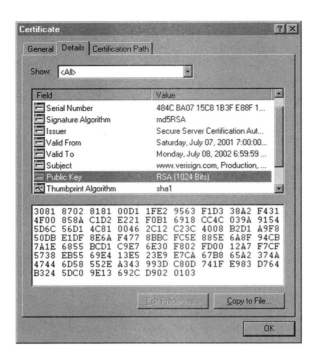

Certificate

General | Details | Certification Path |

Show: <All>

Field	Value
Serial Number	484C BA07 15C8 1B3F E88F 1...
Signature Algorithm	md5RSA
Issuer	Secure Server Certification Aut...
Valid From	Saturday, July 07, 2001 7:00:00...
Valid To	Monday, July 08, 2002 6:59:59 ...
Subject	www.verisign.com, Production, ...
Public Key	RSA (1024 Bits)
Thumbprint Algorithm	sha1

```
3081 8702 8181 00D1 1FE2 9563 F1D3 38A2 F431
4F00 858A C1D2 E221 F0B1 6918 CC4C 039A 9154
5D6C 56D1 4C81 0046 2C12 C23C 4008 B2D1 A9F8
50DB E1DF 8E6A F477 8BBC FC5E 885E 6A8F 94CB
7A1E 6855 BCD1 C9E7 6E30 F802 FD00 12A7 F7CF
5738 EB55 69E4 13E5 23E9 E7CA 67B8 65A2 374A
4744 6D58 552E A343 993D C80D 741F E983 D764
B324 5DC0 9E13 692C D902 0103
```

Edit Properties...   Copy to File...

OK

FAQ

Do I have to apply for a certificate?

If you are accepting any personal information on your Web site such as credit card numbers, you should be using SSL. One option is to visit a certificate authority (such as VeriSign or Thawte at http://www.thawte.com) and apply for your own certificate. There may be a waiting period and you will need to pay an annual fee.

As an alternative, your Web host provider may let you piggyback on its certificate. Normally, there is a setup and/or monthly fee for this service. Usually, the web host assigns you a folder on its secure server. You place the Web pages (and associated files such as images) that need to be securely processed in the folder. When linking to the Web pages you use "https" instead of "http" on your absolute links. Contact your Web host provider for details.

SSL and Digital Certificates

A number of steps are involved in the SSL authentication process. The Web browser and Web server go through initial handshaking steps, exchanging information about the server certificate and keys. Once trust is established, the Web browser encrypts the single secret key (symmetric key) that will be used for the rest of the communication. From this point on, all data is encrypted through the secret key. Table 12.2 shows this process.

At this point, you have a general idea of how SSL works to protect the integrity of information on the Internet, including the information exchanged in e-commerce transactions. The next section takes a closer look at order and payment processing in e-commerce.

Table 12.2 SSL encryption process overview

Browser	→	"hello"		→	Server
Browser	←	"hello" + server certificate		←	Server
Browser	←	The server's private key is used to encrypt a message. Only the public key can decrypt this message.		←	Server

The browser now verifies the identity of the Web server. It obtains the certificate of certificate authority (CA) that signed the server's certificate. Then the browser decrypts the certificate digest using the CA's public key (held in a root CA certificate). Next, it takes a digest of the server's certificate. The browser compares the two digests and checks the expiration date of the certificate. If all is valid, the next step occurs.

| Browser | → | The browser generates a session key and encrypts with the server public key. | | → | Server |
| Browser | ← | The server sends a message encrypted with the session key. | | ← | Server |

All future transmissions between the browser and server are encrypted with the session key.

How do I find out about the most recent security issues?

The CERT Coordination Center at http://www.cert.org is a federally funded research and development center operated by Carnegie Mellon University. CERT is an acronym for Computer Emergency Response Team. One of its functions is to act as a clearinghouse of information related to security issues and incidents. CERT issues advisories that describe security problems and offers suggestions for preventing or correcting them.

Security issues are a real and growing problem. In 1989 CERT handled 132 incident reports. That number has grown each year. There were 21,756 incidents reported in 2000 and over 137,529 incidents reported in 2003, the final year that this statistic was released by CERT.

CHECKPOINT 12.1

1. Describe three advantages of e-commerce for an entrepreneur just starting a business.
2. Describe three risks that businesses face when engaging in e-commerce.
3. Define SSL. Describe how an online shopper can tell that an e-commerce site is using SSL.

12.7 Order and Payment Processing

In B2C e-commerce, the products for sale are displayed in an online catalog. On large sites, these catalog pages are dynamically created using server-side scripts to access databases. Each item usually has a button or image that invites visitors to "Buy Me" or "Add to Cart." Items selected are placed in a virtual shopping cart. When visitors are finished shopping, they click a button or image link indicating that they want to "Check Out" or "Place Order." At this point, the items in their shopping cart are usually displayed on a Web page with an order form.

Secure ordering is facilitated through the use of SSL. Once an order is placed, there are a number of methods to pay for the merchandise or service; the payment methods, called payment models, are cash, check, credit, and smart card.

Cash Model

The **cash model** is the most difficult to implement—how do you send cash through a computer? You don't. You use e-cash. You purchase digital money from a bank and deposit it in a digital wallet. The transfer of funds is immediate. Vendors who provide this service include InternetCashCard (http://www.internetcashcard.com/) and ECash Direct (http://www.ecashdirect.net).

Check Model

In the **check model** the consumer writes a digital check to make the purchase. As with real-world checks, the availability of funds must be verified and the funds are not transferred immediately. One vendor that provides this service is CheckFree (http://www .checkfree.com).

Credit Model

Credit card payment processing is a very important component of an e-commerce Web site. Funds from the customer need to be transferred to the merchant's bank. In order to accept credit cards, the site owner must apply for a merchant account and be approved. A merchant account is an agreement between the business and the bank that allows you to take credit card orders. You may also need real-time credit card verification using a merchant gateway or third party such as Authorize.Net (http://www.authorizenet.com). A diagram of the **credit model** process is shown in Figure 12.6. **Secure Electronic Transactions (SET)** is a standard protocol that enables secure credit card transactions on the Internet. It provides security for credit card payments as they travel the Internet between merchant sites and processing banks. SET uses encryption and digital certificates.

Figure 12.6
The processing flow in credit card orders

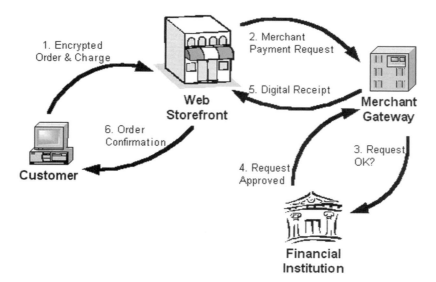

While merchant accounts can be expensive, there are low-cost solutions such as PayPal (http://www.paypal.com). Originally intended for consumer-to-consumer credit card sales, PayPal now offers credit card and shopping cart services for business Web site owners.

Smart Card

The **smart card** model is widely used in Europe, Australia, and Japan. A smart card is similar to a credit card, but it has an integrated circuit instead of a magnetic strip embedded in it. The smart card is inserted into a smart card reader. Expect to see more smart card applications in the United States in the coming years.

You have probably shopped at online stores and found some easy to work with and others difficult. A large problem for e-commerce sites is abandoned shopping carts—visitors who begin to shop but never place an order. The next section explores types of storefront solutions and shopping carts.

What about micropayments?

The term **micropayment** describes a payment model in which small amounts of currency (sometimes called microcents) are easily exchanged over the Internet by merchants and consumers. To download content, consumers pay in small increments ranging from just under a dollar to tiny fractions of a penny. It is not feasible for sellers to use the credit card payment model for these tiny amounts due to transaction processing fees. So, various micropayment methods have been introduced. Companies such as Cybercoin, Millicent, and Digicash arrived with fanfare but soon faded away. Factors contributing to their failure included the unwillingness of consumers to subscribe to these services and the unwillingness of consumers to pay for content.

12.8 E-Commerce Storefront Solutions

A number of different e-commerce storefront options are available to business owners and Web developers. They range from a simple instant online storefront supplied by another Web site, to building your own shopping cart system. This section examines some of the options.

Instant Online Storefront

You supply the products—the **instant online storefront** does the rest. There is no need to install software. All you do is use your Web browser to point and click your way to a virtual store. You use a template provided by the online storefront and choose features, configure settings, and add your products—upload images, descriptions, prices, and captions.

There are some disadvantages to this approach. You are limited by the templates offered by the online storefront provider. The number of products you can sell may also be limited. Your store may have a "look and feel" similar to the other instant stores hosted by the provider. However, this approach provides a low-overhead, low-risk approach for a small business owner with limited technical expertise. The storefront provider will often provide merchant account and payment automation.

Some instant storefront solutions are free with limited service or a limited number of products. Others are fee-based and may charge hosting fees, processing fees, and monthly fees. A few popular instant storefront solutions are Yahoo! (http://store.yahoo .com), Earthstores (http://www.earthstores.com), and FreeMerchant (http://www .freemerchant.com). Figure 12.7 shows screenshots from a trial store on Yahoo!

Figure 12.7
Yahoo! makes it easy to create an instant storefront

Off-the-Shelf Shopping Cart Software

With this approach, software that provides a standardized set of e-commerce features is purchased, installed on your Web server, and customized. Many Web host providers offer this storefront software, which usually includes a shopping cart, order processing, and optional credit card payment processing. **Shopping cart software** provides an online catalog where your visitors can browse, add items to their virtual shopping cart, and check out through an order form when they are ready to purchase. Popular shopping carts offered by Web host providers are AgoraCart (http://agoracart.com), osCommerce (http://oscommerce.com), ZenCart (http://zencart.com), and Mercantec SoftCart (http://www.mercantec.com). Figure 12.8 shows a typical Web site shopping cart. It provides the options to place an order, continue shopping, or cancel an order.

Custom-Built Solution

Custom building a large-scale e-commerce Web site entirely from scratch usually requires expertise, time, and a sizable budget! The advantage is that you get exactly what you need. Software development tools for a custom-built site may include Adobe Dreamweaver, Microsoft Visual Studio.NET, Adobe ColdFusion, IBM's WebSphere

Figure 12.8
A typical shopping cart showing the item selected

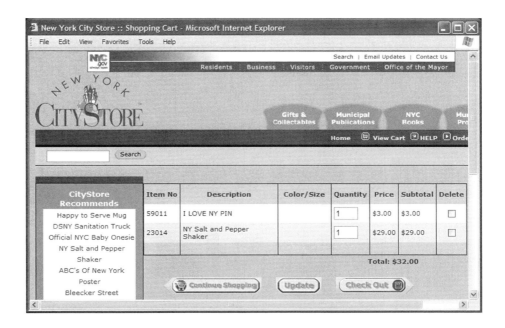

Commerce Studio, a database management system (DBMS), and CGI or other server-side scripting. Custom-built solutions may also require a **commerce server**, which is a Web server enhanced with support for certain commerce activities. IBM's WebSphere Commerce Suite and Microsoft's Commerce Server are two choices.

Semi-Custom-Built Solutions on a Budget

If the scope of your e-commerce endeavor is small and you want to avoid the cookie-cutter look of an instant storefront, some other options may be worth considering. These include getting pre-written shopping cart and order processing scripts, hiring a company such as PayPal, and buying e-commerce add-ons to popular Web authoring tools.

There are a number of free shopping cart scripts available on the Web. Search http://aspcode.net, http://www.perlshop.org, http://php.resourceindex.com, or http://www.mals-e.com for some alternate solutions. The difficulty level and exact processing of these solutions vary. Each Web site has instructions and documentation about its product. Some may require you to register and provide you with specific XHTML code. Others may require you to download and install the scripts on your own Web server.

PayPal (http://paypal.com) offers shopping cart and payment verification for businesses at a very low cost. PayPal writes the code you need to place on your Web pages to interface with them. You only need to copy and paste it in.

A number of Adobe Dreamweaver add-ins, or extensions, provide shopping cart functionality. One easy solution is JustAddCommerce (http://www.richmediatech.com), which allows you to configure and add shopping cart and order buttons to your pages just as easily as you can add images and tables. A screenshot of the point-and-click interface is shown in Figure 12.9. See Figure 12.10 for a Web page with "Add to Cart" and "View Cart" JustAddCommerce buttons.

Figure 12.9
The user interface for
JustAddCommerce

Figure 12.10
The Add To Cart
and View Cart
buttons use
JustAddCommerce

The most recent version of JustAddCommerce can be used with any HTML editor and configures Adobe Flash Buttons to handle the purchase and view cart features. A selection of extensions for Adobe Dreamweaver can be found at http://www.adobe.com/exchange. These budget-wise solutions work best for businesses that fit the standard business model and do not require special processing needs.

CHECKPOINT 12.2

1. List three payment models commonly used on the Web. Which one is the most popular? Why?

2. Have you purchased online? If so, think of the last item that you purchased. Why did you purchase it online instead of at a store? Did you check to see if the transaction was secure? Why or why not? How will your shopping habits be different in the future?

3. Describe three types of e-commerce solutions available. Which provides the easiest entry to e-commerce? Explain.

CHAPTER SUMMARY

This chapter introduced basic e-commerce concepts and implementations. Consider taking an e-commerce course to continue your study of this dynamic and growing area of Web development.

Visit the textbook Web site at http://www.webdevfoundations.net for examples, the links listed in this chapter, and updated information.

Key Terms

asymmetric-key encryption
Business-to-Business (B2B)
Business-to-Consumer (B2C)
Business-to-Government (B2G)
cash model
check model
ciphertext
clear text
commerce server
Consumer-to-Consumer (C2C)
credit model
cybersquatting

decryption
digest
digital certificate
e-commerce
Electronic Data Interchange
  (EDI)
encryption
fraud
hash functions
instant online storefront
integrity
intellectual property

international commerce
micropayment
Secure Electronic Transactions
  (SET)
Secure Sockets Layer (SSL)
security
shopping cart software
smart card
symmetric-key encryption
taxation

Review Questions

Multiple Choice

1. Which of the following is a major function of e-commerce?

   a. using SSL to encrypt orders

   b. adding items to a shopping cart

   c. buying and selling goods

   d. none of the above

2. For businesses, which is an advantage of using e-commerce?

   a. reduced costs

   b. ability to comparison shop

   c. using shopping carts

   d. none of the above

3. For businesses, which is a potential risk of using e-commerce?

   a. increased customer satisfaction

   b. the possibility of fraudulent transactions

   c. inconvenience of returns

   d. none of the above

4. The most money is being generated in which type of e-commerce?

   a. B2G

   b. B2C

   c. B2B

   d. C2C

5. Which of the following options best describes how a Web site owner can obtain a digital certificate?

   a. digital certificates are automatically created when you register for a domain name

   b. visit a certificate authority and apply for a digital certificate

   c. digital certificates are automatically created when you are listed in a search engine

   d. none of the above

6. Which of the following issues are uniquely related to international e-commerce?

   a. language and currency conversion

   b. browser version and screen resolution

   c. bandwidth and Internet service provider

   d. none of the above

7. Which of the following is a standard protocol used to enable secure credit card transactions on the Internet?

   a. SSL

   b. SET

   c. SSI

   d. none of the above

8. Which of the following is a disadvantage of an instant online storefront?

   a. the store is based on a template and may look very similar to other online stores

   b. the store can be ready in minutes

   c. the store cannot accept credit cards

   d. none of the above

9. Which of the following include(s) an online catalog, a shopping cart, and a secure order form?

   a. Web host providers

   b. shopping cart software

   c. Web server software

   d. e-commerce hosting packages

10. Which of the following is true?

   a. a merchant account allows you to use SSL on your Web site

   b. shopping cart add-ins or extensions are available for popular Web authoring tools such as Adobe Dreamweaver

   c. instant storefronts are what most large-scale e-commerce sites use

   d. none of the above

Fill in the Blank

11. An encryption method that uses a single-shared, private key is _____.

12. _____ can be described as the transfer of data between different companies using networks.

13. A digital certificate is a form of a(n) _____ that also contains additional information about the entity holding the certificate.

14. _____ is a protocol that allows data to be privately exchanged over public networks.

Short Answer

15. List one option for a Web site that needs to reach audiences that speak different languages.

Hands-On Exercise

1. In this Hands-On Exercise you will create an instant storefront. Choose one of the following Web sites that offer free trial online stores: http://www.earthstores.com, http://www.aacart.com, http://www.instantestore.com, http://shopify.com, or http://www.easystorecreator.com. Web sites are constantly changing their policies, so these sites may no longer offer free trials when you do this assignment. If this is the case, check the textbook's Web site for updated information, ask your instructor for assistance, or search the Web for free online storefronts or trial stores. If you

are certain you have found a Web site that offers a free trial store, continue with this exercise and create a store that meets the following criteria:

- Name: Door County Images
- Purpose: To sell fine quality prints of Door County scenery
- Target Audience: Adults age 40+ who have visited Door County, are middle to upper class, and enjoy nature, boating, hiking, cycling, and fishing
- Item 1: Print of Ellison Bay at Sunset, Size 11 inches by 14 inches, Price $19.95
- Item 2: Print of Ellison Bay in Summer, Size 11 inches by 14 inches, Price $19.95

Figure 12.11 shows a page from a sample store using Earthstores instant storefront.

Create a folder called doorcounty. The images shown in Figures 12.12, 12.13, 12.14, 12.15, and 12.16 can be found in the student files in the Chapter12 folder. Copy them into your doorcounty folder.

Figure 12.11
An instant store created at http://www.earthstores.com

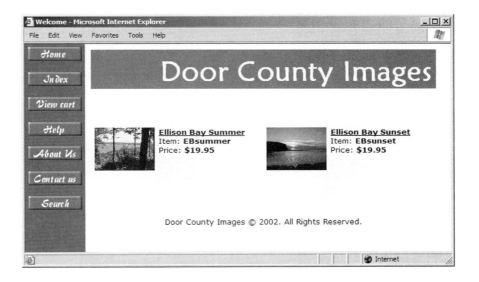

Figure 12.12
Door County Images logo (logo.jpg)

Figure 12.13
Ellison Bay in Summer thumbnail (summer_small.jpg)

Figure 12.14
Ellison Bay at Sunset thumbnail (sunset_small.jpg)

Figure 12.15
Ellison Bay in
Summer
(summer.jpg)

Figure 12.16
Ellison Bay at
Sunset (sunset.jpg)

Once you are organized, visit the Web site you have chosen to host your free store. You will have to log in, choose options, and upload your images. Follow the instructions provided. Most free online store sites have an FAQ section or technical support to help you. After you have completed your store, print out the browser view of the home page and catalog page.

Web Research

1. Just how popular is e-commerce? How many of your friends, family members, coworkers, and classmates purchase on the Web? Survey at least 20 people. Determine the following:

   - How many have purchased an item online?
   - How many have shopped but not purchased online?
   - How many purchase online once a year? Once a month? Once a week?
   - What is their age range (18 to 25, 26 to 39, 40 to 50, or over 50)?
   - What is their gender?

- What is their level of education (high school, some college, college graduate, or graduate school)?
- What is their favorite online shopping site?

Create a Web page that uses multiple tables that illustrate your findings. Also comment on the results and draw some conclusions. Search the Web for statistics that support your conclusions. Use http://pewinternet.org, http://www.ecominfocenter .com/index.html, http://clickz.com, and http://www.ecommercetimes.com as starting points for your research. Place your name in an e-mail link on the Web page. Print the source code (from Notepad) and the browser view of your Web page.

2. This chapter provided a number of resources for e-commerce shopping cart and ordering systems. Use them as a starting point. Search the Web for additional resources. Find at least three shopping cart systems that you feel would be easy to use. Create a Web page that reports your findings. Organize your page with a table that lists the information along with the URLs of the Web sites you used as resources. Include information such as the product name, brief description, cost, and Web server requirements (if any). Place your name in an e-mail link on the Web page. Print both the source code (from Notepad) and the browser view of your Web page.

Focus on Web Design

Visit the following sites as a starting point as you explore the Web design topic of shopping cart usability:

- http://psychology.wichita.edu/surl/usabilitynews/42/shoppingcart.htm
- http://www.netmechanic.com/news/vol7/ecommerce_no6.htm
- http://www.4th-media.net/online_storefront/shopping_cart_usability.php
- http://www.webknowhow.net/dir/Other_Resources/articles/ 070625shoppingcarts5.html
- http://www.getelastic.com/add-to-cart-buttons

Write a one-page report that describes shopping cart usability issues that Web designers should be aware of. Cite the URLs of the resources you used.

WEB SITE CASE STUDY
Adding a Catalog Page for an Online Store

Each of the following case studies has continued throughout most of the text. This chapter adds a catalog page for an online store to the Web sites. This catalog page will connect to sample shopping cart and order pages on the textbook Web site at http://www.webdevfoundations.net.

JavaJam Coffee House

See Chapter 2 for an introduction to the JavaJam Coffee House Case Study. Figure 2.26 shows the initial site map for the JavaJam Web site. The pages were created in earlier chapters. Use the javajamcss folder.

As frequently happens with Web sites, the client, Julio Perez, is pleased with the response to the site and has an idea about a new use for it—selling JavaJam gear, such as T-shirts and coffee mugs. This new page, gear.html, will be part of the main navigation of the site. All pages should link to it. A revised site map is shown in Figure 12.17.

Figure 12.17
Revised JavaJam
site map

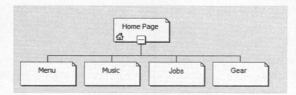

The Gear page should contain the description, image, and price of each product. It should link to a shopping cart system when the visitor wants to purchase an item. You may access a demonstration shopping cart/ordering system provided by the textbook's Web site. If you have access to a different shopping cart system, check with your instructor and ask if you can use it instead.

Hands-On Practice Case

1. Copy the javamug.gif, javatshirt.gif, and viewtrans.gif image files from the Chapter12 folder in the student files and save them to disk in the javajamcss folder.

2. Launch Notepad and modify each existing Web page (index.html, jobs.html, music.html, menu.html) in the javajamcss folder to link to the Gear page (gear.html) in the main navigation. See Figure 12.18 for an example.

Figure 12.18
Revised JavaJam
text navigation

3. Now you are ready to create the Gear page. Figure 12.19 shows a sample of the completed Gear page.

   One way to be productive is to create pages based on your earlier work. Launch Notepad and open the Music page (music.html). Save the file as gear.html. This will give you a head start and ensure that the pages on the Web site are similar. Perform the following modifications:

   a. Change the page title to an appropriate phrase.

   b. Delete the contents of the `<div>` assigned to the `rightcolumn` id. You'll be adding code for the Gear page in this area.

   c. Notice that the View Cart image displays on the right side of the content area. Code an `image` element that displays the viewtrans.gif and is assigned to the `floatright` class. Code the text "JavaJam Gear" with an `<h2>` element.

   d. Code a table with width set to 90% and no border. The table will contain two rows and three columns.

   e. Configure the contents of the first row of the table. Place the following description in the first cell: Description: "JavaJam shirts are comfortable to wear to school and around town. 100% cotton. XL only. $14.95". Place the

Figure 12.19

JavaJam gear.html

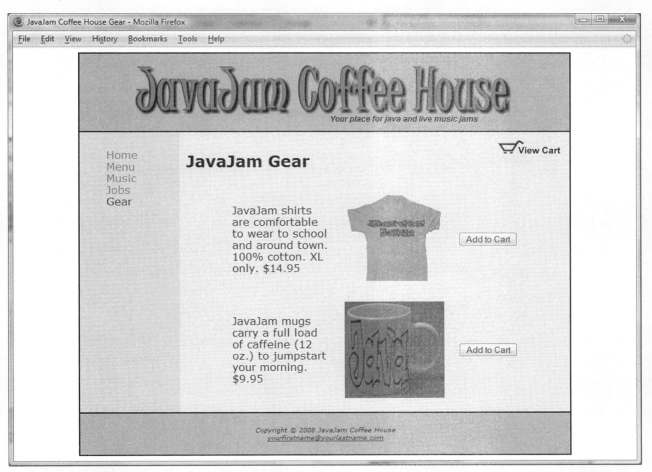

following image in the second cell: `javashirt.gif height="150" width="150"`. Code a nonbreaking space in the third cell (we will work on this later).

f. Configure the contents of the third row of the table. Place the following description in the first cell: Description: "JavaJam mugs carry a full load of caffeine (12 oz.) to jump-start your morning. $9.95". Place the following image in the second cell: `javamug.gif height="150" width="150"`. Code a nonbreaking space in the third cell (we will work on this later).

g. Next you will add a shopping cart button to each item for sale. This is placed in a form. The action on the form is the ASP script called http://www. webdevfoundations.net/scripts/cart.asp. Remember that whenever you use server-side scripts, there will be some documentation or specifications for you to follow. This script processes a limited shopping cart that works with two items only. The gear.html Web page will pass information to the script by using hidden fields in the form that contains the button to invoke the script. Please pay careful attention to detail when working on this.

To place the shopping cart button for the T-shirt, add the following code to the third cell of the first row:

```
<form method="post"
action="http://www.webdevfoundations.net/scripts/cart.asp">
  <input type="hidden" name="desc1" id="desc1"
  value="JavaJam Shirt" />
  <input type="hidden" name="cost1" id="cost1" value="14.95" />
  <input type="submit" value="Add to Cart" />
</form>
```

This XHTML invokes a server-side script that processes a demonstration shopping cart. The hidden fields named `desc1` and `cost1` are sent to the script when the Submit button is clicked. These indicate the name and cost of the item.

The process for adding the shopping cart button for the mug is similar, using hidden form fields named `desc2` and `cost2`. The XHTML follows:

```
<form method="post"
action="http://www.webdevfoundations.net/scripts/cart.asp">
  <input type="hidden" name="desc2" id="desc2"
  value="JavaJam Mug" />
  <input type="hidden" name="cost2" id="cost2" value="9.95" />
  <input type="submit" value="Add to Cart" />
</form>
```

h. Earlier you placed the viewtrans.gif image on the page on the same line as the "JavaJam Gear" text. Visitors will click on this image to view the contents of the shopping cart. Recall that when you use server-side scripts sometimes there are special configuration needs. Add anchor tags around the image to indicate that it is a special link to the cart. The XHTML follows:

```
<a href="http://www.webdevfoundations.net/scripts/
cart.asp?view=yes">image tag goes here</a>
```

Save your page and test it in a browser. It should look similar to the one shown in Figure 12.19. Click the Add to Cart button for the JavaJam shirt. The demonstration shopping cart will display and your screen should look similar to the one shown in Figure 12.20.

Experiment with the cart and try to purchase both items. Simulate placing an order, as shown in Figure 12.21. The shopping cart and order pages are for demonstration purposes only.

Figure 12.20
A Shopping Cart page created by the server-side script that processes the shopping cart and order

Figure 12.21
An Order page created by the server-side script that processes the shopping cart order

FAQ **How does the cart.asp server-side script work?**

The cart.asp file is an ASP script. It is coded to accept a number of form fields and process them. It creates a Web page based on the values and fields that were passed to it. Table 12.3 shows the form fields and values used by the cart.asp file.

Table 12.3 Specifications for cart.asp

Script URL	http://www.webdevfoundations.net/scripts/cart.asp	
Processing	This script accepts product and price information, displays a shopping cart, and finally displays an order page.	
Limitation	This script can only handle two products.	
Input Elements	`desc1`	Contains the description of the first product. It is displayed on the shopping cart page.
	`cost1`	Contains the per item cost of the first product. It is displayed on the shopping cart page.
	`desc2`	Contains the description of the second product. It is displayed on the shopping cart page.
	`cost2`	Contains the per item cost of the second product. It is displayed on the shopping cart page.
	`view`	If the value is "yes," the shopping cart is displayed.
Output	Shopping Cart Web page	Displays the shopping cart. The Web page visitor is given the option to continue shopping or to display the order page to place an order.
	Order Web page	Displays an order form. The Web page visitor is given the option to place the order or to continue shopping.
	Order Confirmation page	Displays a message to confirm that an order was placed. If this were an actual Web site, the order would also be saved on a server-side file or database.

Fish Creek Animal Hospital

See Chapter 2 for an introduction to the Fish Creek Animal Hospital Case Study. Figure 2.30 shows the initial site map for the Fish Creek Web site. The pages were created in earlier chapters. Use the fishcreekcss folder.

Often, once a Web site is created, your client will think of additional ways to use it. The owner of Fish Creek, Magda Patel, is pleased with the response to the site and has a new use for it—selling sweatshirts and totebags with the Fish Creek logo. She already has these materials for sale at her front desk in the animal hospital and her customers seem to like them. This new Shop page, shop.html, will be part of the main navigation of the site. All pages should link to it. A revised site map is shown in Figure 12.22.

Figure 12.22
Revised Fish Creek
site map

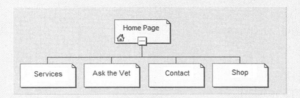

The Shop page should contain the description, image, and price of each product. It should link to a shopping cart system when the visitor wants to purchase an item. You may access a demonstration shopping cart/ordering system provided by the textbook's Web site. If you have access to a different shopping cart system, check with your instructor and ask if you can use it instead.

Hands-On Practice Case

1. Copy the fishtote.gif, fishsweat.gif, view.jpg, and shop.gif image files from the Chapter12 folder in the student files and save them to your fishcreekcss folder.

2. Configure navigation area. Launch Notepad and modify each existing Web page (index.html, services.html, askvet.html, contact.html) in the fishcreekcss folder to link to the Shop page (shop.html) in the main navigation. Add the shop.gif to the side navigation bar, as shown in Figure 12.23, on each page. Configure the image to link to shop.html. Add a text link "Shop" to shop.html in the page footer navigation area.

Figure 12.23
Revised Fish Creek
navigation

3. Confiure CSS. Before you create the Shop page (shop.html) you will configure the CSS for the product area that will be displayed in a table without a border. Add a new style rule to your fishcreek.css external style sheet that configures an id named `shop` with `border-style: none` for `table` and `td` elements. The style rule follows:

```
#shop td, table {border-style: none; }
```

4. Now you are ready to create the Shop page. Figure 12.24 shows a sample of the completed page.

Figure 12.24
Fish Creek shop.html

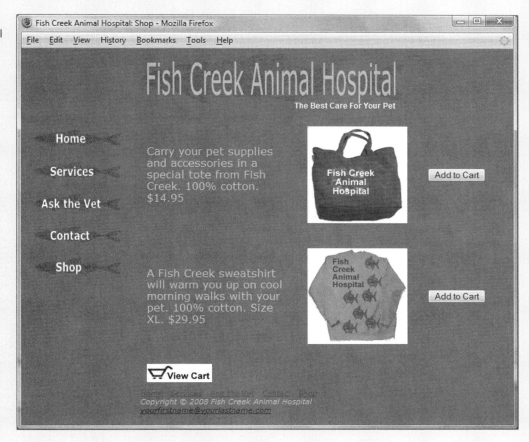

One way to be productive is to create pages based on your earlier work. Launch Notepad and open the Home page (index.html). Save the file as shop.html. This will give you a head start and ensure that the pages on the Web site are similar. Perform the following modifications:

a. Change the page title to an appropriate phrase.

b. Delete the definition list and the address/phone information from the page.

c. Create a table with two rows, three columns, and assign the table to the `shop` id.

d. Add content to the first row of the table. Place the following description in the first cell: Description: "Carry your pet supplies and accessories in a special tote from Fish Creek. 100% cotton. $14.95". Place the following image in the second cell: `fishtote.gif height="150" width="150"`. Configure an `alt` text description for the image. You will format the third cell later.

e. Add content to the second row of the table. Place the following description in the first cell: Description: "A Fish Creek sweatshirt will warm you up on cool morning walks with your pet. 100% cotton. Size XL. $29.95". Place the following image in the second cell: `fishsweat.gif height="150" width="150"`. Configure an `alt` text description for the image. You will format the third cell later.

f. Next, we will add a shopping cart button to each item for sale. This shopping cart button is placed in a form in the third cell of each table row. The action on the form is the ASP script called http://www.webdevfoundations.net/scripts/cart.asp. Remember that whenever you use server-side scripts, there will be some documentation or specifications for you to follow. This script processes a limited shopping cart that works with two items only. The shop.html Web page will pass information to the script by using hidden fields in the form that contains the button to invoke the script. Please pay careful attention to detail when working on this.

To place the shopping cart button for the tote, add the following code to the third cell of the first row:

```
<form method="post"
action="http://www.webdevfoundations.net/scripts/cart.asp">
  <input type="hidden" name="desc1" id="desc1"
  value="Fish Creek Tote" />
  <input type="hidden" name="cost1" id="cost1" value="14.95" />
  <input type="submit" value="Add to Cart" />
</form>
```

This XHTML invokes a server-side script that processes a demonstration shopping cart. The hidden fields named `desc1` and `cost1` are sent to the script when the Submit button is clicked. These indicate the name and cost of the item.

The process for adding the shopping cart button for the sweatshirt is similar, using hidden form fields named `desc2` and `cost2`. The XHTML follows:

```
<form method="post"
action="http://www.webdevfoundations.net/scripts/cart.asp">
  <input type="hidden" name="desc2" id="desc2"
  value="Fish Creek Shirt" />
  <input type="hidden" name="cost2" id="cost2" value="29.95" />
  <input type="submit" value="Add to Cart" />
</form>
```

g. Add the view.jpg to the page below the table, as shown in Figure 12.24. The image should have no border. Use an appropriate value for the `alt` attribute. Visitors will click on this image to view the contents of the shopping cart. Recall that when you use server-side scripts there are sometimes special configuration needs. Add anchor tags around the image to indicate that it is a special link to the cart. The XHTML follows:

```
<a href="http://www.webdevfoundations.net/scripts/
cart.asp?view=yes">image tag goes here</a>
```

Save your page and test it in a browser. It should look similar to the one shown in Figure 12.24. Click the Add to Cart button for the tote. The demonstration shopping cart will display and your screen should look similar to the one shown in Figure 12.20. Experiment with the cart and try to purchase both items. You can simulate placing an order, as shown in Figure 12.21. The shopping cart and order pages are for demonstration purposes only.

Pete the Painter

See Chapter 2 for an introduction to the Pete the Painter Case Study. Figure 2.34 shows a site map for the Pete the Painter Web site. The pages were created in earlier chapters. Use the paintercss folder.

Pete Johnson is the owner of Pete the Painter. He has begun to write how-to books for his clients and would like to offer them for sale on the Web site. He would like a new Store page that will offer two of his books. This new Store page, store.html, will be part of the main navigation of the site. All pages should link to it. A revised site map is shown in Figure 12.25.

Figure 12.25
Revised Pete the Painter site map

The Store page should contain the description, image, and price of each product. It should link to a shopping cart system when the visitor wants to purchase an item. You may access a demonstration shopping cart/ordering system available on the textbook's Web site. If you have access to a different shopping cart system, check with your instructor and ask if you can use it instead.

Hands-On Practice Case

1. Copy the primer.jpg, decorate.jpg, and viewtrans.gif image files from the Chapter 12 folder in the student files and save them to your paintercss folder.

2. Launch Notepad and modify each existing Web page (index.html, services.html, testimonials.html, estimates.html) in the paintercss folder to link to the Store page (store.html) in the main navigation. See Figure 12.26 for a sample navigation.

Figure 12.26
Revised Pete the Painter navigation

Home
Services
Testimonials
Free Estimate
Store

3. Now you are ready to create the Store page. Figure 12.27 shows a sample of the completed page.

Figure 12.27
Pete the Painter
store.html

One way to be productive is to create pages based on your earlier work. Launch Notepad and open the Testimonials page (testimonials.html). Save the file as store.html. This will give you a head start and ensure that the pages on the Web site are similar. Perform the following modifications:

a. Change the page title to an appropriate phrase.

b. Configure the viewtrans.gif image to display below the painterlogo.gif within the logo id area. Assign the viewtrans.gif to the `floatright` class.

c. Delete the `<h4>` and paragraph elements from the `rightcolumn` id area.

d. Code an `<h2>` element assigned to the category class. Configure the `<h2>` to display the following text: Painting Primer.

e. Code a paragraph that will display the book cover and a text description. Configure the primer.jpg image to belong to the `floatright` class. "Are you a do-it-yourselfer? Have we got the painting tips for you! Ranging from how to choose the right color to quick clean-up routines. 206 pages. Softcover. $19.95"

f. Add the Add to Cart button. The visitor will click a button to indicate that they wish to purchase an item. This shopping cart button is placed in a form. For this exercise, the action on the form is the ASP script called http://www .webdevfoundations.net/scripts/cart.asp. Remember that whenever you use server-side scripts, there will be some documentation or specifications for you to follow. This script processes a limited shopping cart that only works with two items. The store.html Web page will pass information to the script by using hidden fields in the form that contains the button to invoke the script. Please pay careful attention to detail when working on this. To add the shopping cart button for the Painting Primer book below the description paragraph, write the following code:

```
<form method="post"
action="http://www.webdevfoundations.net/scripts/cart.asp">
   <input type="hidden" name="desc1" id="desc1"
   value="Painting Primer" />
   <input type="hidden" name="cost1" id="cost1" value="19.95" />
   <input type="submit" value="Add to Cart" />
</form>
```

This XHTML invokes a server-side script that processes a demonstration shopping cart. The hidden fields named `desc1` and `cost1` are sent to the script when the Submit button is clicked. These indicate the name and cost of the item.

g. Code an `<h2>` element assigned to the category class. Configure the `<h2>` to display the text "You Can Decorate!"

h. Code a paragraph that will display the book cover and a text description. Configure the decorate.jpg image to belong to the `floatright` class. Display the following text: "Ever wonder how the professionals put it all together? This easy to follow guide lets you in on their secrets. Lots of example rooms and suggestions. 145 pages. Softcover. $24.95" Add the Add to Cart button by writing the following XHTML for the form with the shopping cart button:

```
<form method="post"
action="http://www.webdevfoundations.net/scripts/cart.asp">
   <input type="hidden" name="desc2" id="desc2"
   value="You Can Decorate!" />
   <input type="hidden" name="cost2" id="cost2" value="19.95" />
   <input type="submit" value="Add to Cart" />
</form>
```

This XHTML invokes a server-side script that processes a demonstration shopping cart. The hidden fields named `desc2` and `cost2` are sent to the script when the Submit button is clicked. These indicate the name and cost of the item.

i. Add a special hyperlink to the viewtrans.gif image in the logo area. This will link to the server-side script described above in a very special way. When a visitor clicks the image, the server-side script will display the contents of his or her shopping cart. Recall that when you work with server-side scripts, they often have special configuration needs. Place anchor tags around the image tag to create the special hyperlink as follows:

```
<a href="http://www.webdevfoundations.net/scripts/
cart.asp?view=yes">image tag goes here</a>
```

Save your page and test it in a browser. It should look similar to the one shown in Figure 12.27. Click the Add to Cart button for the Painting Primer. The demonstration shopping cart will display and your screen should look similar to the one shown in Figure 12.20. Experiment with the cart and try to purchase both items. You can go ahead and simulate placing an order, as shown in Figure 12.21. The shopping cart and order pages are for demonstration purposes only.

Prime Properties

See Chapter 2 for an introduction to the Prime Properties case. Figure 2.38 shows a site map for the Prime Properties Web site. The pages were created in earlier chapters. Use the primecss folder.

The owner, Maria Valdez, would like to showcase the company's services and provide an easy way for clients to choose their thank you gift. She would like a Services page that will briefly describe the services and offer a form for clients to select their gifts. The new Services page, services.html, will be part of the main navigation of the site. All pages should link to it. A revised site map is shown in Figure 12.28.

Figure 12.28
Revised Prime
Properties site map

The Services page will contain the sub-heading Services, two short paragraphs of text about services, and the description and photograph of each gift selection. You may access a demonstration shopping cart/ordering system provided by the textbook's Web site. If you have access to a different shopping cart system, check with your instructor and ask if you can use it instead.

Hands-On Practice Case

1. Copy the sunnydays.jpg, jeweltone.jpg, and viewtrans.gif image files from the Chapter12 folder in the student files and save them to your primecss folder.

2. Launch Notepad and modify each existing Web page (index.html, listings.html, financing.html, and contact.html) in the primecss folder to link to the Services page (services.html) in the main navigation and footer navigation, as shown in Figure 12.29.

Figure 12.29
Revised Prime
Properties
navigation

3. Now you are ready to create the Services page. Figure 12.30 shows the completed page.

   One way to be productive is to create pages based on your earlier work. Launch Notepad and open the Financing page (financing.html). Save the file as

Figure 12.30
Revised Prime
Properties
services.html

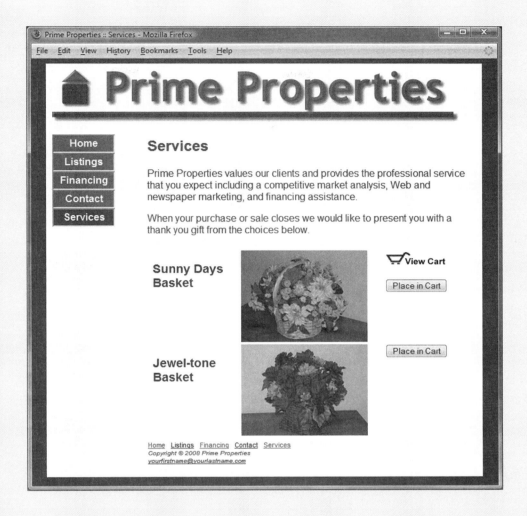

services.html. This will give you a head start and ensure that the pages on the Web site are similar. Perform the following modifications:

a. Change the page title to an appropriate phrase.

b. Modify the links on the page as appropriate.

c. Change the Financing heading to Services.

d. Delete the other text on the page related to financing.

e. Place your cursor on the line after the Services heading. Create a paragraph with the following text:

"Prime Properties values our clients and provides the professional service that you expect including a competitive market analysis, Web and newspaper marketing, and financing assistance."

f. Next, add another paragraph of text: "When your purchase or sale closes we would like to present you with a thank you gift from the choices below."

g. Create a table with two rows and three columns.

h. Add content to the first row of the table. Use <h3> tags to contain the following text in the first table cell: Sunny Days Basket. Place the sunnydays.jpg image in the second cell. You will format the third cell later.

i. Add content to the second row of the table. Use <h3> tags to contain the following text in the first table cell: Jewel-tone Basket. Place the jeweltone.jpg image in the second cell.. You will format the third cell later.

j. Next, we will add a shopping cart button to each gift item for selection. This shopping cart button is placed in a form in the third cell of each table row. The action on the form is the ASP script called http://webdevfoundations.net/scripts/cart1.asp. Remember that whenever you use server-side scripts, there will be some documentation or specifications for you to follow. This script processes a limited shopping cart that only works with two items. Since it is designed to function as a gift selector, no prices are displayed. The services.html Web page will pass information to the script by using a hidden field in the form that contains the button to invoke the script. Please pay careful attention to detail when working on this.

To place the shopping cart button for the Sunny Days Basket, add the following code to the third cell of the first row:

```
<form method="post"
  action="http://www.webdevfoundations.net/scripts/cart1.asp">
  <input type="hidden" name="desc1" id="desc1"
  value="Sunny Days Basket" />
  <input type="submit" value="Place in Cart" />
</form>
```

This XHTML invokes a server-side script that processes a demonstration shopping cart. The hidden field named `desc1` and its value are sent to the script when the Submit button is clicked. This passes the name of the item chosen to the server-side script.

The process for adding the shopping cart button for the Jewel-tone Basket is similar, using the hidden form field `desc2`. The XHTML follows:

```
<form method="post"
  action="http://www.webdevfoundations.net/scripts/cart1.asp">
  <input type="hidden" name="desc2" id="desc2"
  value="Jewel-tone Basket" />
  <input type="submit" value="Place in Cart" />
</form>
```

k. The viewtrans.gif is an image that visitors click on to show the shopping cart. Add this image to the third table cell in the first row. Add one or two blank lines between the image and the form. Recall that when you use server-side scripts there are sometimes special configuration needs. Add anchor tags around the image to indicate that it is a special link to the cart. The XHTML follows:

```
<a href="http://www.webdevfoundations.net/scripts/
cart1.asp?view=yes">image tag goes here</a>
```

Save your page and test it in a browser. It should look similar to the one shown in Figure 12.30. Click the Place in Cart button for the Sunny Days Basket. The demonstration shopping cart will display and your screen should be similar to the one pictured in Figure 12.20 (except that no price information will display). Experiment with the cart and try to select both items. You can simulate selecting gifts. The shopping cart and order pages are for demonstration purposes only.

Web Project

See Chapter 5 for an introduction to the Web Project. Review the goals of your Web site and determine if they include an e-commerce component. If so, you will add this component to your Web project.

Hands-On Practice Case

Revise the Site Map as needed to include the e-commerce component. Perhaps you will add a products page to your site. Perhaps the products page already exists and you are just adding functionality to the page. In either case, make sure the Site Map and Content Sheets reflect the new processing.

There are a number of free or low-cost shopping cart providers on the Web. Some are provided in the following list. Your instructor may have additional resources or suggestions. Choose one of the providers from the list to add a shopping cart to your Web site. When you subscribe or sign up for these services, be sure to note any potential costs.

- Mal's E-Commerce (free and low-cost service): http://mals-e.com
- PayPal (there is a cost per transaction for this service): http://paypal.com
- JustAddCommerce (free trial): http://www.richmediatech.com

Save and test your page. Experiment with the shopping cart. Welcome to the world of e-commerce!

Web Promotion

Chapter Objectives In this chapter, you will learn how to …

- Tell the difference between search engines and search indexes
- Describe the components of a search engine
- Design Web pages that are friendly to search engines

- Request that a Web site be added to a search engine
- Monitor a search engine listing
- List other Web site promotion activities
- Create an inline frame

You've built it—now what can you do to attract visitors
to your Web site? Once you have visitors, how do you encourage them to return? Getting listed on search engines, site affiliations, and banner ads are some of the topics that are discussed in this chapter.

13.1 Search Engines and Search Indexes Overview

What do you do when you need to find a Web site? Most people launch their favorite search engine. A Nielsen/NetRatings survey found that nine out of ten Web users visit a search engine, portal, or community site every month. These Web users also revisit the sites frequently, almost five times per month.

Search engines and **search indexes** are very popular ways to navigate the Web and find Web sites. The PEW Internet Project (http://pewinternet.org/pdfs/PIP_SearchData_1105.pdf), reports "about 60 million American adults use search engines on a typical day." A DM News report (http://dmnews.com/cms/dm-news/search-marketing/37367.html) on a Harris Interactive study states that 80 percent of Internet traffic begins at a search engine.

Appearance in a search engine lends an aura of legitimacy to a Web site. A study by NPD Group (http://www.justwebpromotion.com/top_ranking_search_engines.html) showed that consumers are five times more likely to purchase goods or services as a result of finding a site through a search engine listing than through a banner ad.

A search engine listing helps customers find your site and increases the chances that they will make a purchase. Search engine listings can be an excellent marketing tool for your business. To harness the power of search engines and search indexes (sometimes called search directories), it helps to know how they work.

13.2 Popular Search Engines and Search Indexes

According to a survey by Nielsen/NetRatings (http://www.nielsennetratings.com/pr/pr_070919.pdf), Google (http://google.com), and Yahoo! (http://yahoo.com) were the two most popular sites used to search the Web during a recent month. Of those surveyed, 53.6 percent used Google and 19.9 percent used Yahoo! during this time. Other major search engines include MSN, AOL, and Ask.com. Figure 13.1 contains a chart of the top five search sites reported in this survey. Check nielsennetratings.com for the most recent survey results.

Figure 13.1
Over half the searches done in a recent month used Google

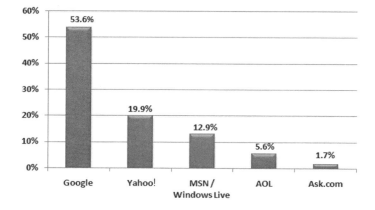

Let's take a closer look at Yahoo! (http://yahoo.com). Even though Yahoo! is usually referred to as a search engine, it originally was a search index (sometimes called a search directory). Each site that is submitted for inclusion in the Yahoo! directory is reviewed by an editor at Yahoo! Yahoo! maintains a hierarchical category of topics and places Web site listings into these categories. When visitors use Yahoo! they have the option of typing in a search term or drilling down into the hierarchy for relevant sites. Previously, Yahoo! augmented its directory with search engine databases from sources such as Inktomi and Google. In 2004, Yahoo! announced the development of its own search engine called Yahoo! Search. When Yahoo! shows results from a search, the results are grouped as follows:

- Sponsor results (paid advertisements)
- Inside Yahoo! matches (Yahoo!'s own content)
- Web results (from Yahoo! Search)

While you can submit a site to the Yahoo! Search database at no charge, it is not easy to get a commercial Web site listed in the Yahoo! directory. The first task is to submit your site for review. Commercial sites need to pay a fee (currently several hundred dollars) just to be reviewed by a Yahoo! editor. If the editor decides that a Web site has valuable content and should be listed, the site is **indexed** or placed into a category, and information on the site is stored in Yahoo!'s Directory database. Suggestions for getting your site ready for this review appear later in this chapter. Sometimes Web site owners need to improve and submit their sites multiple times to Yahoo! before the site is listed.

Another search index is the Open Directory Project at http://www.dmoz.org. It contains a hierarchy of topics and sites related to each topic. In this project anyone can volunteer to be an editor and site reviewer. There is no cost to submit your site to the Open Directory Project. An added benefit to being listed in the Open Directory Project is that the database containing the approved sites is used by a number of search engines, including Google, Netscape, and AOL.

13.3 Components of a Search Engine

Search engines have the following components:

- Robot
- Database (also used by search directories)
- Search form (also used by search directories)

Robot

A **robot** (sometimes called a spider or bot) is a program that automatically traverses the hypertext structure of the Web by retrieving a Web page document and following the hyperlinks on the page. It moves like a robot spider on the Web, accessing and documenting Web pages. The robot categorizes the pages and stores information about the Web site and the Web pages in a database. Various robots may work differently, but in general, they access and may store the following sections of Web pages: title, meta tag keywords, meta tag descriptions, and some of the text on the page (usually either the first few sentences or the text contained in heading tags). Visit The Web Robots Pages at http://www.robotstxt.org if you'd like more details about Web robots.

Database

A **database** is a collection of information organized so that its contents can easily be accessed, managed, and updated. Database management systems (DBMSs) such as Oracle, Microsoft SQL Server, or IBM DB2 are used to configure and manage the database. The Web page that displays the results of your search has information from the database accessed by the search engine site. According to http://www.bruceclay.com/searchenginerelationshipchart.htm, some search engines, such as AOL Search (http://aol.com) and Netscape (http://netscape.com) use a database provided by Google.

Search Form

The **search form** is the component of a search engine that you are most familiar with. You have probably used a search engine many times but haven't thought about what goes on "under the hood." The search form is the graphical user interface that allows a user to type in a word or phrase to search for. It is usually simply a text box and a submit button. The visitor to the search engine types words (called keywords) related to his or her search into the text box. When the form is submitted, the data typed into the text box is sent to a server-side script that searches the database using the keywords entered. The **search results** (also called a result set) is a list of information, such as the URLs for Web pages, that meet your criteria. This result set is formatted with a link to each page along with additional information that might include the page title, a brief description, the first few lines of text, or the size of the page. The type of additional information varies by search engine. Next, the Web server at the search engine site sends the search results page to your browser for display.

The order in which the pages are displayed may depend on paid advertisements, alphabetical order, and **link popularity** (more on this later). Each search engine has its own policy for ordering the search results. Be aware that these policies can change over time.

The components of a search engine (robot, database, and search form) work together to obtain information about Web pages, store information about Web pages, and provide a graphical user interface to facilitate searching for and displaying a list of Web pages relevant to given keywords. Now that you are aware of the components of search engines, let's get to the most important part—how to design your pages to promote your Web site.

13.4 Designing Your Pages for Promotion

If you have followed recommended Web design practices you've already designed your Web site so that the pages are appealing and compelling to your target audience. How can you also make your site work with search engines? This section provides some suggestions and hints on designing your pages for search engines—a process called **Search Engine Optimization (SEO)**.

Keywords

Spend some time brainstorming about terms and phrases that people may use when searching for your site. These terms or phrases that describe your Web site or business are your **keywords**. Create a list of them and don't forget to add common misspellings of your keywords to the list.

Double-check the page titles (text contained between the `<title>` tags) and page headings (text contained between heading tags such as `<h1>`, `<h2>`, and so on) on your Web site. Make sure the text used for your title is descriptive, includes your organization name, and contains one or more keywords, if possible. If it is appropriate for the Web page content, also include some keywords in the text contained between heading tags. Some search engines will give a higher list position if keywords are included in a page title or headings. Do not spam keywords—that is, do not list them over and over again. The programs behind search engines become more sophisticated all the time and you can actually be prevented from being listed if it is perceived that you are not being honest or are trying to cheat the system.

Description

What is special about your Web site that would make someone want to visit? With this in mind, write a few sentences about your Web site or business. This **description** should be inviting and interesting so that a person searching the Web will choose your site from the list provided by a search engine or search directory. Some search engines will display your description in their search engine results.

At this point you have created a description of your site and a list of appropriate keywords. You might be wondering how these apply to the actual Web pages. The keywords and description are placed on a Web page by adding XHTML meta tags to the page header area.

Meta Tags

Meta tags are self-contained tags that are placed in the header section of a Web page. They should follow the `<title>` tag. There are a number of uses for meta tags. We concentrate here on their use to provide a description of the site and list of keywords for use by search engines.

The syntax of meta tags is as follows:

```
<meta name="value" content="value" />
```

FAQ

What if I do not want a search engine to index a page?

Sometimes there will be pages that you do not want indexed, perhaps test pages or pages only meant for a small group of individuals (such as family or coworkers). Meta tags can be used for this purpose also. To indicate to a search engine robot that a page should not be indexed and the links should not be followed, do not place keywords and description meta tags in the page. Instead, add a `"robots"` meta tag to the page as follows:

```
<meta name="robots" content="noindex,nofollow" />
```

The **name** attribute indicates the use of the meta tag. The **content** attribute indicates values needed for that specific use. The **keywords** value for the **name** attribute indicates that the use of the meta tag is to list keywords. The **description** value for the **name** attribute indicates that the use of the meta tag is to provide a description. For example, the keywords and description meta tags for a Web site about a Web development consulting firm called Acme Design could be configured as follows:

```
<meta name="keywords" content="Acme Design web development e-commerce
ecommerce consulting consultation maintenance redesign Akme" />
<meta name="description" content="Acme Design, a premier web
consulting group that specializes in e-commerce, web site design, web
site development, and web site redesign." />
```

13.5 Listing in a Search Engine and Search Index

According to a study by The Direct Marketing Association (http://www.the-dma.org), 66 percent of Web marketers surveyed rated search engines as the top method used to drive traffic to their sites. While very effective, it is not always easy to get listed in a search engine or search directory. Table 13.1 shows the steps involved in submitting your site to a search engine or search directory.

Table 13.1 Submission to a search engine or search directory

Search Engine (Such as Google)	Search Directory (Such as Yahoo! or the Open Directory Project)
Step 1: Visit the search engine site and look for the "Add site" or "List URL" link. This is usually on the home page (or about us page) of the search engine. Be patient—these links are sometimes not obvious. At Google, click the "About Google" link then click on the "Submitting your Site" link.	**Step 1:** Visit the search directory and follow the hierarchical listings until the page that is most suited for your site appears. Take time to choose the most appropriate category. Look for the "Suggest a Site" or "add URL" link on the page.
Step 2: Follow the directions listed on the page and submit the form to request that your site is added to the search engine. At other search engines there may be a fee for an automatic listing, called paid inclusion—more on this later. Currently, there is no fee to submit a site to Google.	**Step 2:** Follow the directions listed on the page and submit the form to request that your site be reviewed for inclusion in the directory. Commercial sites must pay Yahoo! to review their Web site. This does not guarantee inclusion.
Step 3: The spider from the search engine will index your site. This may take several weeks.	**Step 3:** An editor (a real person) will visit your site. This may take several weeks. Search directories such as Yahoo! and the Open Directory (http://dmoz.org) review the content of the site—only sites with worthwhile content are included.
Step 4: Several weeks after you submit your Web site, check the search engine or search directory to see if your site is listed. If it is not listed, review your pages and check whether they are "friendly" to robots and display in common browsers.	

There is a trend away from free listing in search engines. The current trend is toward paying for listing consideration in a search engine or directory (often referred to as an express submit or express inclusion), paying for preferential placement in search engine displays (called sponsoring or advertising), and paying each time a visitor clicks the search engine's link to your site. Many businesses regard payment for these types of services as another marketing expense, such as paying for a newspaper ad or a listing in the Yellow Pages.

Preferential Placement

Another trend for search engines and some search directories is to require payment for preferential placement. Each search engine has its own term for this feature. Yahoo! calls it Sponsor Results. Google uses the term AdWords. In these programs, payment is made when the site is submitted for review. If accepted, the site has a listing usually at the top or right margin of the search engine results. In addition to the initial fee, the Web site owners must pay each time a visitor clicks on the search engine link to their site—this is called a cost-per-click (CPC) fee.

Yahoo!'s Sponsored Search Results matches are powered by Yahoo! Search Marketing. See http://searchmarketing.yahoo.com/ for more information on this Web site **promotion** technique. Figure 13.2 shows a Yahoo! search page with Sponsor Results.

Figure 13.2
Yahoo! display with Sponsor Results highlighted. Reproduced with permission of Yahoo! Inc. ©2006 Yahoo! Inc. Yahoo! and the Yahoo! logo are trademarks of Yahoo! Inc.

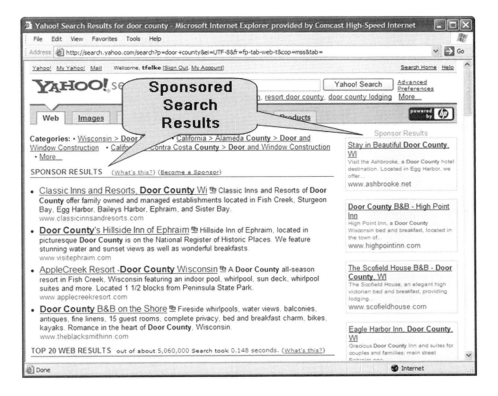

Web sites that have paid for Google's AdWords program have preferential placement on the right-hand side of the search results, as shown in Figure 13.3. Expect to see search engines and search directories change their preferential placement programs over time.

Figure 13.3
Google display with
the AdWords
program highlighted

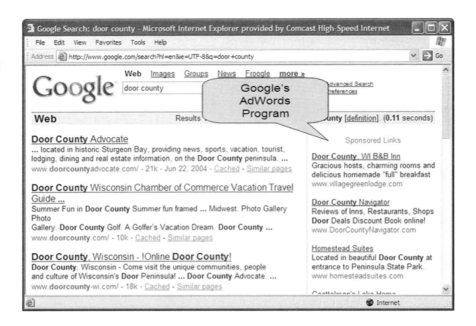

There are a number of alliances between certain search engines and search directories. For example, if you purchase Yahoo! Sponsored Search, your site will not only be featured in Yahoo!, but also promoted in other search engines such as AltaVista and alltheweb.com. The Open Directory Project (http://www.dmoz.org) provides directory services for a number of search engines, including Google. Be warned that these alliances can change over time. Awareness of search engine alliances will help you maximize the chances of your Web site turning up when a search is performed.

FAQ Is advertising on a search engine worth the cost?

It depends. How much is it worth to your client to be number one out of 713,000 matches? While costs and charges vary by search engine, at this time Google charges are based on the number of impressions, or page views. You select the keywords that will trigger the display of your ad. You are charged each time a visitor to Google searches for the given keywords and Google displays your ad.

Your clients will want the Web site to appear instantaneously in search engines and search directories. However, it takes time between the submission and when the site appears in a search engine or search directory list. According to searchengineposition .com, it can take two days to two weeks for a Web site to be listed on Google.

CHECKPOINT 13.1

1. Describe the difference between a search engine and a search directory. Provide an example of each.

2. Describe the three components of a search engine.

3. Is it beneficial for a business to pay for site submission? Is it beneficial for a business to pay for preferential listing? Explain.

13.6 Monitoring Search Engine and Search Index Listings

As your sites get listed, it becomes important to determine which keywords are working. Usually you need to fine-tune and modify your keywords over time. Here are a few methods to determine which keywords are working:

- **Manual Checking.** Visit search engines and type in the keywords. Assess the results. You might consider keeping a record of the search engine, keyword, and page ranking.
- **Web Site Log Analysis.** Every visitor to your Web site, including those who were referred by search engines, is recorded in your Web site log file. You can discover whether your keywords are successful by analyzing your log. The log is a rather cryptic text file. See Figure 13.4 for a partial log.

Figure 13.4

A Web site log file contains useful information but can be difficult to read

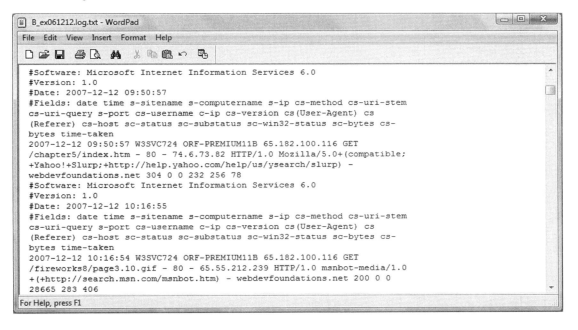

Web analysis software can analyze your log file and create easy-to-use charts and reports. If you have your own Web site and domain name, many Web host providers allow free access to the log and may even run Web analysis reports as part of the monthly Web hosting fee. By checking information in the log, you can determine not only what keywords are working, but also which search engines your visitors are using. See Figure 13.5 for part of a log analysis report showing keywords actually used at Yahoo! to find a particular Web site.

Web log analysis is a powerful marketing tool because you can determine exactly how visitors are finding your site. This lets you know which keywords are working and which are not. Perhaps with additional thought, you can add new variations of the productive keywords to your list. If you examine Figure 13.5 you will notice that "quota-

Figure 13.5
Partial log file
analysis report

Top Search Engines with Keywords Detail			
Engines	**Keywords**	**Keywords Found**	**% of Total**
Yahoo	quotations	280	37.68%
	educational	182	24.49%
	education	144	19.38%
	web	83	11.17%
	background	73	9.82%
	javascript	59	7.94%
	pictures	54	7.26%
	on	36	4.84%
	quotation	31	4.17%
	java	28	3.76%

tions" and "educational" are the most popular keywords on Yahoo! for this particular Web site. The developers of this Web site could add keywords related to these keywords or common misspellings of the most popular keywords. Improving the keywords may increase the number of visitors to the site. Some search engines routinely revisit sites that they have listed. Other search engines must be explicitly notified to revisit the site to pick up the new keywords.

Automated Tools. Google offers a free Web log analysis service at http://google.com/analytics. The categories of reports provided are as follows:

- Visitors (including a geographical map and browser information)
- Traffic Sources (such as referring sites, keywords, and AdWords)
- Content (including landing pages, paths through the site, and exit pages)
- Goals (tracks business objectives)

Another option is to purchase a program that can help you monitor your search engine positioning. Applications, such as WebPosition (http://webposition.com), can create reports of your search engine rankings, analyze and track keywords, and even submit your sites to search engines.

13.7 Link Popularity

Link popularity is a rating determined by a search engine based on the number of sites that link to a particular Web site and the quality of those sites. For example, a link from a well-known site such as Oprah Winfrey's (http://oprah.com) would be considered a higher quality link than one from your friend's home page on a free Web server. The link popularity of your Web site can determine its order in the search engine results page. One way to check which sites link to yours is to analyze your log file. Another method is to visit a Web site that offers a link popularity checking service (options include http://linkpopularity.com and http://linkpopularitycheck.com). These sites will run a report that checks link popularity on a number of search engines. A third method is to visit particular search engines and check for yourself. At Google and AltaVista, type "link:yourdomainname.com" into the search box and the sites that link to yourdomainname.com will be listed.

Search engines and search directories are not the only tools you can use to bring visitors to your Web site. The next section takes a look at some other options.

13.8 Other Site Promotion Activities

There are a number of other ways you can promote your Web site, including affiliate programs, banner ads, banner exchanges, reciprocal link agreements, newsletters, personal recommendations, traditional media advertising, and URL placement on all promotional materials.

Affiliate Programs

The essence of **affiliate programs** is that one Web site (the affiliate) promotes another Web site's products or services (the merchant) in exchange for a commission. Both Web sites benefit from this association. Amazon.com reportedly began the first affiliate marketing program—and its Amazon Associate program is still going strong. By joining this program your Web site can feature books with a link to the Amazon Web site. If one of your visitors purchases a book, you get a commission. Amazon benefits because you have delivered an interested visitor who may purchase items now or in the future. Your site benefits from the prestige of being affiliated with a known site such as Amazon and the potential for income from the program.

View the Commission Junction Web site (http://www.cj.com) for a program that matches Web sites with potential affiliate programs. Their service allows publishers (Web site owners and developers) to choose from a wide range of advertisers and affiliate programs. Benefits to Web developers include the opportunity to partner with leading advertisers, earn additional revenue from Web site visitors or ad space, and view real-time tracking and reporting. Visit http://www.refer-it.com for a directory of affiliate, associate, and referral programs.

Banner Ads

A **banner ad** is typically a graphic image that is used to announce and advertise the name or identity of a site. Banner ads are image hyperlinks that display the advertised site when clicked. You probably see them many times as you surf the Web. They've been around quite some time—hotwired.com introduced the first banner ad in 1994 to promote AT&T.

There is no official size for a banner ad. However, research performed by the Interactive Advertising Bureau (http://www.iab.net) reports that the standard size for a full banner ad is 468×60 pixels. Visit its Web site for a full listing of types of ads and common sizes (http://www.iab.net/standards/adunits.asp). Costs to display your banner ad can vary. Some Web sites charge by the impression (usually in terms of cost per thousand, or CPM). Others charge for click-throughs only—when the banner ad is clicked. Some search engines sell banner ads and will display your ad on a results page for a keyword that relates to your site (for a fee, of course!). See Figure 13.6 for some timely marketing by a Web site that specializes in flowers.

Figure 13.6
AOL search for "flowers" also displays ad banners for sites associated with flowers

The effectiveness of banner ads has been a topic of study. If you are like most Web site visitors, you do not click on banner ads. This means that banner ads do not necessarily generate more immediate visitors to a site. The Interactive Advertising Bureau researched the relationship between banner ads and brand awareness. A report at ClickZ.com (http://www.clickz.com/stats/sectors/advertising/article.php/804761) on this classic study indicates that while standard banner ads helped boost brand awareness, other formats such as skyscrapers (long, skinny ads that run down one side of a page) and larger rectangular ads were three to six times more effective in increasing brand awareness and message association. Media technologies such as audio, video, Flash, and DHTML also deliver greater impact and increase branding effectiveness. Of course, the thinking is that increased brand awareness will increase the likelihood of an actual Web site visit in the future.

If the costs associated with banner ads seem to outweigh their benefits, consider a "free" option, a banner exchange.

Banner Exchange

While the details of **banner exchange** programs vary, the idea is that you agree to show banners from other sites and they will show your banner. Information on banner exchanges may be found at http://www.123banners.com and at http://www.impressionz. com/. Banner exchanges can be beneficial to all parties because of the free advertising.

Reciprocal Link Agreements

A **reciprocal link agreement** is usually between two sites with related or complementary content. You agree to link to each other. The result should be more visitors for each site. If you find a site that you'd like to set up a reciprocal link agreement with, contact its webmaster (usually by e-mail) and ask! Since some search engines partially determine rankings on the number of quality links to a Web site, well-placed reciprocal link agreements can help both sites.

Newsletters

A **newsletter** can bring return visitors to your site. The first step is to collect e-mail addresses. Allow Web site visitors to opt in to your newsletter by filling out a form. See Figure 13.7 for a sample newsletter subscription form.

Figure 13.7
Sample newsletter subscription form

JavaJam Newsletter

Your E-mail Address:

[   ] [Sign Up]

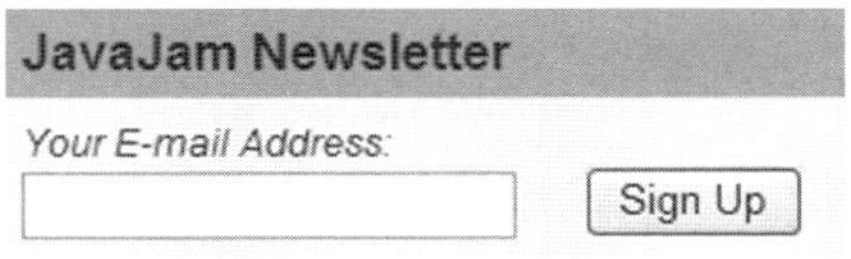

Offer your visitors some perceived value—timely information on a topic, discounts, and so on. Send out the newsletter with fresh, compelling content regularly. This helps to remind your previous visitors about your site. They may even forward the newsletter to a colleague and bring a new visitor to your site.

Sticky Site Features

Updating your Web site often and keeping your content fresh will encourage visitors to return to your site. How to keep them there? Make your Web site sticky. **Stickiness** is the ability to keep visitors at your site. Display your interesting and compelling content along with features that encourage stickiness such as news updates, polls and surveys, and chats or message boards.

Personal Recommendations

While forwarding a newsletter is a form of **personal recommendation,** some sites make it even easier to tell a friend about them. They offer a link that is used with a phrase such as "E-mail this article," "Send this page to a friend" or "Tell a colleague about this site." This personal recommendation brings a new visitor who is likely to be interested in the content of your site. See Figure 13.8 for a partial screenshot of the FirstGov Web site (http://www.firstgov.gov), showing a personal recommendation link.

Social Bookmarking

Social bookmarking is a form of personal recommendation. Social bookmarking sites such as Digg (http://digg.com) and del.ico.us (http://del.ico.us) provide a way for people to store, share, and categorize Web sites. Make it easy for your visitors to add your site to social bookmarking services by adding quick buttons or links such as the Digg this buttons offered at http:/digg.com/tools.

Figure 13.8
This site makes it
easy to tell friends
about interesting
articles

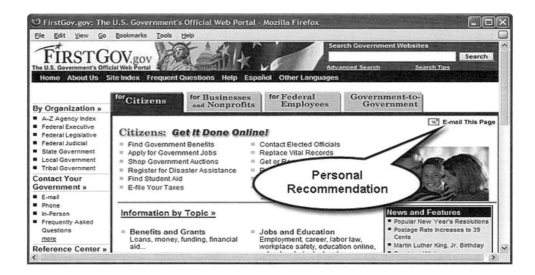

Figure 13.8
This site makes it easy to tell friends about interesting articles

Blogs and RSS Feeds

Chapter 1 introduced **blogs**, which are easily updatable and readily accessible journals on the Web. The power of the blog to share information and elicit comments is being used by businesses of various types (ranging from Nike to Adobe) to build and expand customer relationships. Most blog hosting sites, such as http://blogspot.com and http://bloglines.com, offer free RSS (Really Simple Syndication or Rich Site Summary) feeds of blog content. The **RSS feed** for a blog is an XML file (with an .rss file extension) that contains a summary of postings with links to a blog or another Web site. Your customers or business partners can subscribe to the RSS feed and be automatically updated when you've posted new content. RSS feeds are usually identified by an orange button with "XML" or "RSS" in the text. The Firefox browser has a feature called Live Bookmarks, which displays RSS news and blog headlines. There are numerous free and low-cost RSS readers available, including Headline Viewer (http://www.headlineviewer. com) and NetNewsWire (http://ranchero.com/netnewswire). To see a blog in action, visit the textbook's blog at http://webdevfoundations.blogspot.com.

Web Rings

Web rings are more appropriate for noncommercial sites than for businesses. However, a Web ring can bring quite a few visitors to a site. Join a ring of sites on a similar topic. Visitors can surf from site to site and expect that the content should interest them. You could even create your own Web ring. See WebRing (http://dir.webring.com/rw) or RingSurf (http://www.ringsurf.com) for more information.

Newsgroup and Listserv Postings

Subscribe to relevant Usenet **newsgroups**, **listservs**, or forums related to your Web site content. Do not reply to postings with an advertisement of your site. Instead, reply to postings when your response can offer assistance or advice. Include a signature line with your Web site URL. Be subtle—you can get banned from some listservs if the moderator perceives that you are merely advertising. However, by offering friendly, helpful advice in a newsgroup or listserv you can market your Web site in a subtle, positive manner at no cost other than your Internet connection.

Your Internet service provider may provide access to Usenet newsgroups. Google also provides access at http://groups.google.com/. Listservs can be run by individuals or by organizations.

Traditional Media Ads and Existing Marketing Materials

Don't forget to mention your Web site in any print, TV, or radio ads your organization runs. Include the URL of your Web site on all brochures, stationery, and business cards. This will help make your Web site easily found by your current and potential customers.

CHECKPOINT 13.2

1. Are the results returned by various search engines really different? Choose a place, music group, or movie to search for. Enter the same search terms, such as "Door County" into the following three search engines: Google, Yahoo!, and Ask (http://www.ask.com). List the URLs of the top three sites returned by each. Comment on your findings.

2. How can you determine if your Web site has been indexed by a search engine? How can you determine which search engines are being used to find your site?

3. List four Web site promotion methods that do not use search engines. Which would be your first choice? Why?

13.9 Serving Dynamic Content with Inline Frames

How does Edmunds.com, the vehicle pricing and review site, display a banner ad on its home page that is hosted and controlled by another organization? How do the Chicago Bears (http://chicagobears.com) and the ABC (http://abc.com) home pages easily display a variety of multimedia clips? How are the potential customer referrals provided by Amazon.com's Associates initiated and tracked? How does Google facilitate Ad Sense advertisement displays and click-throughs on third party Web sites? At the time this was written, the answer to all these questions is inline frames. Inline frames are widely used on the Web for a variety of marketing and promotional purposes including displaying ad banners, playing multimedia that may be hosted on a separate Web server, and serving content for associate and partner sites to display. The advantage is separation of control. The dynamic content—such as the ad banner or multimedia clip—can be changed by a project team without allowing them access to change the rest of the Web site. For example, in the case of the ad banner served by Edmund's Web site—a third party organization (such as DoubleClick) has control over the ad content but is prevented from updating the other items on Edmund's home page. This is accomplished by configuring the dynamic content (in the form of ad banners) within an inline frame. Let's explore how inline frames are configured.

An **inline frame** (called a floating frame) can be placed on the body of any Web page, similar to the way you would place an image on a Web page. What is special about the inline frame is that it embeds another Web page within a scrolling area. Figure 13.9 shows the use of an inline frame. The white scrolling area is the inline frame—it displays another Web page that contains the image of the flower and a text description.

Figure 13.9
The white scrolling area on the page is an inline frame displaying a separate Web page

The screenshots shown in Figure 13.10 are of the same Web page with different pages displayed in the inline frame area.

Figure 13.10
The same page with different content in the inline frame area

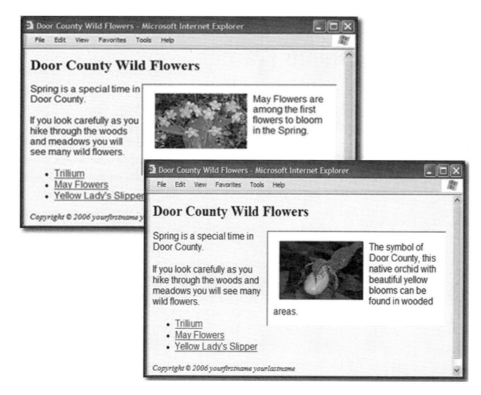

The code for the inline frame used to create this effect is as follows:

```
<iframe src="trillium.html" title="Trillium Wild Flower"
height="160" align="right" name="flower" width="320">
Description of the lovely Spring wild flower, the
<a href="trillium.html" target="_blank">Trillium</a></iframe>
```

As shown, an inline frame is created using the **`<iframe>`** element. The `<iframe>` element is a container tag. It is always used with its closing `</iframe>` tag. Any content that should be displayed if the browser does not support inline frames (such as a text description or link to the actual page) should be placed between the tags. The `<iframe>` tag configures an area on a Web page that can be used to display a different Web page document. This inline area is 150 pixels high and 300 pixels wide by default. The height and width attributes can be used to configure the exact dimensions. In the example code, the align attribute was used to align the inline frame to the right of the text on the Web page. The `name` attribute was used so that the inline frame could be targeted by links. Table 13.2 lists attributes for `<iframe>` tags. Commonly used attributes are shown in bold.

Table 13.2 `<iframe>` tag attributes

Attribute	Values	Purpose
`align`	`right, center, left` (default)	Specifies the horizontal alignment of the inline frame (deprecated—use CSS instead)
`frameborder`	0 indicates no visible borders 1 indicates borders display (default)	Determines whether borders should be displayed around this inline frame
`height`	Number of pixels or percentage	Gives height of the inline frame
`id`	Alphanumeric, no spaces; the value must be unique and not used for other id values on the same XHTML document	Provides a unique identifier for the inline frame
`longdesc`	Provides a detailed text description of the frame; may be accessed by assistive technologies	Gives URL of Web page with detailed description of the contents of the inline frame
`marginheight`	Number of pixels	Configures the top and bottom margins of the inline frame
`marginwidth`	Number of pixels	Configures the width of the right and left margins of an inline frame
`name`	Alphanumeric, no spaces, begin with a letter	Configures the name of the inline frame; required when using the target attribute to configure hyperlinks (deprecated in XHTML but is used to provide backward compatibility with browsers that support HTML)
`scrolling`	`yes` indicates that scrollbars are always present; `no` indicates that scrollbars are never displayed; `auto` indicates that scrollbars appear when needed (default)	Determines whether scrollbars will appear if the document displayed is larger than the size of the inline frame
`src`	Valid file name of a Web page document (required)	Configures the name of the file to be displayed in the inline frame
`title`	Text phrase that describes the inline frame	Configures the title of the inline frame; can be accessed by screen readers and is recommended by the W3C to improve accessibility
`width`	Number of pixels or percentage	Specifies width of the inline frame

Table 13.3 lists corresponding CSS properties with XTHML attributes utilized to configure inline frames. These properties are also described in Appendix C.

Table 13.3 CSS properties to style an inline frame

XHTML Attribute	CSS Property
align	Code within a `<div>` element and align the `<div>`
width	width
height	height
marginwidth,marginheight	margin, padding
bgcolor	background-color
frameborder	border, border-style

Inline frames are supported by the most recent versions of Internet Explorer, Firefox, and Netscape. However, they are not supported by all browsers. Carefully consider a decision to use this technique.

HANDS-ON PRACTICE 13.1

In this Hands-On Practice you will modify a CircleSoft Web Design home page that uses inline frames, an external style sheet named circlesoft.css, and three Web pages that display in the inline frame. To begin, create a new folder called circlesoftinline. Obtain the logo1.gif, index.html, circlesoft.css, about.html, contact.html, and clients.html files from the student files Chapter13/starters folder. Save the files in a folder named circlesoftinline. Launch Notepad and edit the home page, named index.html, for your circlesoftinline Web site. A sample is shown in Figure 13.11.

Figure 13.11
The CircleSoft inline frames home page (index.html)

Add the `<iframe>` element in the `<div>` assigned to the `rightcol` id. The inline frame should initially display the about.html page, have the `name` set to `"circlesoftinfo"`, and contain descriptive content between the `<iframe>` tags. For example:

```
<iframe src="about.html" title="About CircleSoft"
name="circlesoftinfo" >Description of the services offered by
<a href="about.html" target="_blank">Circlesoft</a></iframe>
```

Next, code appropriate keywords and description meta tags in the header section of the index.html Web page. Save your index.html page in the circlesoftinline folder.

You are ready to test your inline frames page. Launch a browser and display the index.html page. Your page should be similar to the page shown in Figure 5.16. Try the links; they should change the contents of the inline frame. If you'd like to experiment with a border-less look, add an `iframes` selector style rule in circlesoft.css to go with the code that follows.

```
iframe {border-style: none;
}
```

The student files contain a sample solution at in the Chapter13/13.1 folder.

Focus on Accessibility
WWW

Inline frames are not supported by all browsers and assistive technologies such as screen readers, so use them with caution. If you choose to use inline frames on your Web site, provide alternate means of accessing the content. Consider including both a description of the inline frame and a link to a text page between the `<iframe>` and `</iframe>` tags.

CHAPTER SUMMARY

This chapter introduced concepts related to promoting your Web site. The activities involved in submitting Web sites to search engines and search directories were discussed along with techniques for making your Web site optimized for search engines. Other Web site promotion activities such as banner ads and newsletters were also examined. At this point, you should have an idea of what is involved in the other side of Web site development—marketing and promotion. You can help the marketing staff by creating Web sites that work with search engines and directories by following the suggestions in this chapter.

Visit the textbook Web site at http://www.webdevfoundations.net for examples, the links listed in this chapter, and updated information.

Key Terms

`<iframe>`	link popularity	Search Engine Optimization
affiliate programs	listservs	search engines
automated tools	manual checking	search form
banner ad	meta tags	search indexes
banner exchange	newsgroups	search results
blogs	newsletter	social bookmarking
database	personal recommendation	stickiness
description	promotion	Web rings
indexed	reciprocal link agreement	Web site log analysis
inline frame	robot	
keywords	RSS feed	

Review Questions

Multiple Choice

1. The robot, database, and search form are components of which of the following?

   a. a search directory

   b. a search engine

   c. both search directories and search engines

   d. none of the above

2. In which of the following sections of a Web page should meta tags be placed in?

   a. header

   b. body

   c. comment

   d. none of the above

3. What is the first step in submitting your Web site to search engines and search directories?

   a. join an affiliate program

   b. visit the search engine and submit your Web site

   c. prepare your pages for search engines by adding keyword and description meta tags to your pages

   d. none of the above

4. Often, how long can it take between the time you submit your site and the time it is listed in a search engine?

a. several hours

b. several days

c. several weeks

d. several months

5. Which of the following contains information about which keywords are bringing visitors to your Web site?

a. Web position log

b. Web site log

c. search engine file

d. none of the above

6. Which of the following is a rating determined by a search engine based on the number of links to a particular site and the qualities of those links?

a. line checking

b. reciprocal linking

c. link popularity

d. none of the above

7. Which of the following is the most popular method used by visitors to find Web sites?

a. banner ads

b. hearing about Web sites on television

c. search engines and search directories

d. personal recommendations

8. Which of the following is a promotion method whose main purpose is to bring return visitors to your Web site?

a. newsletter

b. banner exchange

c. TV ad

d. none of the above

9. Which of the following is the main benefit of a banner ad?

a. bringing many new visitors to your site

b. increasing awareness of the Web site

c. both bringing many new visitors and increasing awareness of the site

d. none of the above

10. In which of the following does one Web site promote another Web site's products or services in exchange for a commission?

a. newsletter

b. affiliate program

c. Web ring

d. none of the above

Fill in the Blank

11. The ability to keep Web page visitors at your site is called _____.

12. Use _____ to indicate that you do not want a Web page to be indexed.

13. Frequently used information research resources are _____.

14. Besides listing in a search engine, a Web site can be promoted by _____.

15. Paying to be included or listed preferentially in a search engine is considered by many organizations to be _____.

Hands-On Exercises

1. Practice writing keyword and description meta tags. For each scenario described here, write the XHTML to create appropriate meta tags and justify your choice of keywords.

a. Lanwell Publishing is a small independent publisher of English as a second language (ESL) books used for secondary school and adult continuing education learners. The Web site offers textbooks and teacher manuals.

    b. RevGear is a small specialty truck and auto repair shop in Schaumburg, Illinois. The company sponsors a local drag racing team.

    c. Morris Accounting is a small accounting firm that specializes in tax return preparation and accounting for small businesses. The owner, Greg Morris, is a CPA and Certified Financial Planner.

2. Choose one of the company scenarios listed in Hands-On Exercise 1 (Lanwell Publishing, RevGear, or Morris Accounting). Create a home page for the site that includes meta tags, appropriate page titles, and keywords used appropriately in headings. Place an e-mail link to yourself on the Web page. Save the page as scenario.html. Hand in printouts of both the source code (print in Notepad) and the browser display of your page to your instructor.

3. Choose one of the company scenarios listed in Hands-On Exercise 1 (Lanwell Publishing, RevGear, or Morris Accounting). Create a Web page that lists at least three possible activities that could be used to promote the site in addition to search engine submission. For each activity, explain why it could be helpful for the Web site. Place an e-mail link to yourself on the Web page. Save the page as promotion.html. Hand in printouts of both the source code (print in Notepad) and the browser display of your page to your instructor.

4. Write the XHTML and CSS to create a page named inline.html that uses inline frames. Configure the inline frame to be 400 pixels wide and 200 pixels high. Use `myframe` for the name of the inline frame. Code a Web page named marketing.html to display in the inline frame. Configure the inline frame to display the marketing.html file.

Web Research

1. This chapter discussed a number of Web site promotion techniques. Choose one method (search engine submission, affiliate programs, banner ads, and so on) to research. Obtain information from at least three different Web sites about the promotion technique you chose. Create a Web page that lists at least five hints or facts about the promotion method along with helpful links that provide additional information on the hint or fact. Provide the URLs of the Web sites that you used as resources. Organize your page with a table. Place your name in an e-mail link on the Web page. Hand in printouts of both the source code (from Notepad) and the browser display of your page to your instructor.

2. Search engine and search directory submission rules are constantly changing. Research a search engine or search directory and determine the following:

- Are free submissions accepted? If so, are they restricted to noncommercial sites?

- What types of paid submissions are accepted? How do they work—what is the fee structure, listing guarantee, and so on?

- What types of paid advertisements are available? How do they work—what is the fee structure, for example?

- Is there any information about the usual time frame for the submission to be listed?

- Create a Web page that describes your findings. Provide URLs of the Web sites you used as resources. Place your name in an e-mail link on the Web page. Hand in printouts of both the source code (from Notepad) and the browser display of your page to your instructor.

Focus on Web Design

Explore how to design your Web site so that it is optimized for search engines (Search Engine Optimization, or SEO). Visit the following sites as a starting point as you search for three SEO tips or hints:

- http://www.sitepoint.com/article/skool-search-engine-success
- http://www.digital-web.com/articles/designing_for_search_engines_and_stars/
- http://www.seoconsultants.com/seo/tips/
- http://www.seo-writer.com/reprint/top-seo-tips.html
- http://www.searchenginewatch.com

Write a one-page report that describes the three tips you found interesting or potentially useful. Cite the URLs of the resources you used.

WEB SITE CASE STUDY
Meta Tags to Promote Web Sites

Each of the following case studies continues throughout most of the text. This chapter focuses on meta tags needed to promote the Web sites.

JavaJam Coffee House

See Chapter 2 for an introduction to the JavaJam Coffee House Case Study. Figure 2.26 shows a site map for the JavaJam Web site. The pages were created in earlier chapters. Use the javajamcss folder. Your task is to add appropriate keywords and description meta tags to each page in the Web site.

Hands-On Practice Case

1. Review the JavaJam Case Study introduction in Chapter 2. Review the pages you have created in earlier chapters. While you are touring the site, jot down keywords that might be appropriate for the entire Web site. Also write down keywords that would be appropriate for specific pages, such as the Jobs page or Music page. Don't forget to add common misspellings of words to your keyword list. Next, write a brief paragraph that describes the JavaJam site.

2. Launch Notepad and edit the Web pages in the javajamcss folder. Add keywords and description meta tags to each page. Save each page. Test your pages in a browser. They will not look different, but they are much friendlier to search engines!

Fish Creek Animal Hospital

See Chapter 2 for an introduction to the Fish Creek Animal Hospital Case Study. Figure 2.30 shows a site map for the Fish Creek Web site. The pages were created in earlier chapters. Use the fishcreekcss folder. Your task is to add appropriate keywords and description meta tags to each page in the Web site.

Hands-On Practice Case

1. Review the Fish Creek Case Study introduction in Chapter 2. Review the pages you have created in earlier chapters. While you are touring the site, jot down keywords that might be appropriate for the entire Web site. Also write down keywords that would be appropriate for specific pages, such as the Services page or Contact page. Don't forget to add common misspellings of words to your keyword list. Next, write a brief paragraph that describes the Fish Creek site.

2. Launch Notepad and edit the Web pages in the fishcreekcss folder. Add keywords and description meta tags to each page. Save each page. Test your pages in a browser. They will not look different, but they are much friendlier to search engines!

Pete the Painter

See Chapter 2 for an introduction to the Pete the Painter Case Study. Figure 2.34 shows a site map for the Pete the Painter Web site. The pages were created in earlier chapters. Use the paintercss folder. Your task is to add appropriate keywords and description meta tags to each page in the Web site.

Hands-On Practice Case

1. Review the Pete the Painter Case Study introduction in Chapter 2. Review the pages you have created in earlier chapters. While you are touring the site, jot down keywords that might be appropriate for the Web site. Also write down keywords that would be appropriate for specific pages, such as the Testimonials page or Services page. Don't forget to add common misspellings of words to your keyword list. Next, write a brief paragraph that describes the Pete the Painter site.

2. Launch Notepad and edit the Web pages in the paintercss folder. Add keywords and description meta tags to each page. Save each page. Test your pages in a browser. They will not look different, but they are much friendlier to search engines!

Prime Properties

See Chapter 2 for an introduction to the Prime Properties Case Study. Figure 2.38 shows a site map for the Prime Properties Web site. The pages were created in earlier chapters. Use the primecss folder. Your task is to add appropriate keywords and description meta tags to each page in the Web site.

Hands-On Practice Case

1. Review the Prime Properties Case Study introduction in Chapter 2. Review the pages you have created in earlier chapters. While you are touring the site, jot down keywords that might be appropriate for specific pages, such as the Financing page or Listings page. Don't forget to add common misspellings of words to your keyword list. Next, write a brief paragraph that describes the Prime Properties Web site.

2. Launch Notepad and edit the Web pages in the primecss folder. Add keywords and description meta tags to each page. Save each page. Test your pages in a browser. They will not look different, but they are much friendlier to search engines!

Web Project

See Chapter 5 for an introduction to the Web Project case. Your task is to add appropriate keywords and description meta tags to each page in the Web site.

Hands-On Practice Case

1. Review the Project Topic Approval document that you created in the Chapter 9 case study. Take a moment to view the pages you have created in earlier chapters. While you are touring the site, jot down keywords that might be appropriate for specific pages. Don't forget to add common misspellings of words to your keyword list. Next, write a brief paragraph that describes the Web Project Web site.

2. Launch Notepad and edit the Web pages in the project folder. Add keywords and description meta tags to each page. Save each page. Test your pages in a browser. They will not look different, but they are now friendlier to search engines!

A Brief Look at JavaScript

Chapter Objectives In this chapter, you will learn how to ...

- Describe common uses of JavaScript in Web pages

- Describe the purpose of the Document Object Model and list some common events

- Create a simple JavaScript using the `<script>` tag and the `alert()` method

- Describe the considerations for XHTML conformance and JavaScript

- Use variables, operators and the, `if` control structure

- Create a basic form validation script

If a popup window mysteriously appears while you are surfing the Web, you're experiencing the effects of JavaScript. JavaScript is a scripting language and JavaScript commands can be included in an XHTML file. Using JavaScript, you can incorporate techniques and effects that will make your Web pages come alive! You can display an alert box containing an important message for the user. You can display an image when a user moves the mouse pointer over a link, and much more. You don't have to be a programmer to be able to add a little sizzle to your Web pages. This chapter introduces JavaScript and some of its capabilities, and provides some samples that you can build on to create your own Web pages.

14.1 Overview of JavaScript

There are a variety of methods for adding interactivity to a Web page. As you learned in Chapter 7, CSS can be used to achieve a hover effect as you position your mouse pointer over a hypertext link. In Chapter 11 you saw examples of how Adobe Flash can be used to add interactivity and animation to a Web page. As also described in Chapter 11, JavaScript can be used to add interactivity and functionality to Web pages. It's not a question of using either JavaScript or one of these other technologies. You can use the strengths of each technology, and use JavaScript in addition to CSS, Flash, Java applets, or any number of other technologies.

So, what is JavaScript? It's an **object-based** client-side **scripting language** interpreted by a Web browser. JavaScript is considered to be object-based because it's used to work with the objects associated with a Web page **document**: the browser window, the document itself, and the elements such as forms, images, and links. Since JavaScript is interpreted by a browser, it is considered to be a client-side scripting language. A scripting language is a type of programming language, but no need to worry! You don't have to be a computer programmer to understand this.

Let's review clients and servers. In Chapter 10 we discussed hosting a Web site on a Web server. As you learned, a Web host provider stores your Web site and allows you to transfer your files to the Web server. Visitors to your site (also called users) are able to point their Web browsers to your Web site using the URL provided by your Web host provider. As you may recall, the user's Web browser is called a client.

JavaScript is interpreted by the client. This means that the JavaScript code, embedded in the XHTML document, will be rendered by the Web browser. The server's job is to send the XHTML document. The Web browser's job is to interpret the code in the XHTML file and display the Web page accordingly. Since all the processing is performed by the client (in this case, the Web browser), this is referred to as **client-side processing**. There are programming languages that are executed on the server, and these are referred to as server-side programming languages. **Server-side processing** may involve sending e-mail, storing items in a database, or tracking items in a shopping cart. In Chapter 9 you learned how to set the action of a form to point to a server-side script.

So, JavaScript is an object-based client-side scripting language interpreted by a Web browser. The JavaScript code is embedded in the XHTML file and the Web browser interprets it and displays the results as needed.

14.2 The Development of JavaScript

There is a popular misconception that Java and JavaScript are the same. Java and JavaScript are completely separate languages with very little in common. As noted in Chapter 11, Java is an object-oriented programming language. Java is robust, very technical, and can be used to build large applications for businesses, such as inventory control systems and payroll systems. Sun Microsystems developed Java in the 1990s and designed the language to run on an operating system such as Windows or Unix. The developers of Java also wanted the flexibility and popularity that would be available if their language could run in a Web browser. Independently, the team at Netscape was developing a scripting language called LiveScript and eventually partnered with Sun Microsystems. This partnership was mutually advantageous as it produced the Java plug-in that enabled Web browsers to run Java applets in the browser, and the development of LiveScript continued and was renamed JavaScript. However, JavaScript is not the same as the Java programming language. JavaScript is much simpler than Java. The two languages have more differences than similarities.

14.3 Popular Uses for JavaScript

The uses of JavaScript range from providing some "bells and whistles" such as simple animation and fancy menus to functionality such as popping up a new window containing product information, detecting errors in a form, or detecting the browser version to determine appropriate features that can be used. Let's look at some examples of some of these uses.

Alert Message

An alert message is a popular technique used to draw the user's attention to something that is happening. For instance, a retail Web site may use an alert message to list errors in an order form or remind the user about an upcoming sale. Figure 14.1 illustrates an alert message thanking the user for visiting the page. This alert message is displayed when the user is leaving the Web site and surfing to a new site.

Figure 14.1
Alert message displayed when the user leaves the Web site

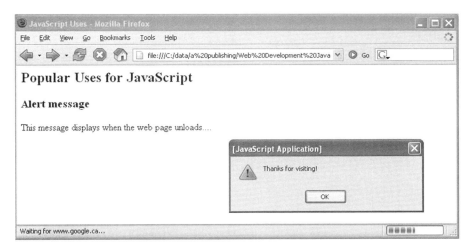

Notice that the user must click the OK button before the next page will load. This effectively grabs the user's attention, but it quickly becomes annoying if it is overused.

Popup Windows

And speaking of annoying, popup windows are instances of Web browser windows that seem to appear mysteriously. These windows can also pop under the current browser window so that you don't notice them until you are moving or closing windows on your desktop. This technique has some legitimate uses, such as popping up an information window containing a larger picture and description of a product when the user clicks on the product in the main window. Unfortunately, the use of popup windows has been so abused that most browsers allow users to disable popup windows. This also means that the useful popup windows are not displayed. Figure 14.2 shows a popup window that appears when the user clicks the link in the main page.

Figure 14.2
The smaller popup window appears when the user clicks the link in the larger window

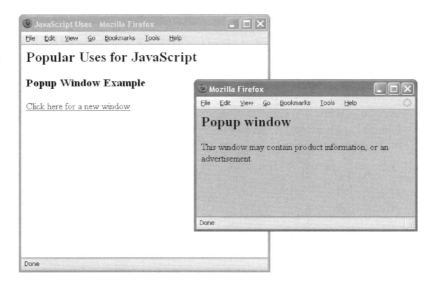

Browser Sniffing

Detecting the exact Web browser application and version is called **browser sniffing** and is sometimes important to the Web developer for determining appropriate features. Figure 14.3 shows the results in the Web browser of JavaScript detecting information about the user's browser.

Figure 14.3
Web browser information generated by JavaScript

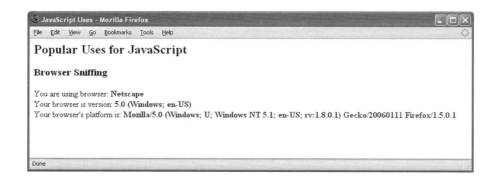

Jump Menus

JavaScript can also be used to create **jump menus** based on a select list. The user can select a Web page from a select list, and click a button to load the selected Web page. Figure 14.4 shows this technique.

Figure 14.4
Jump menu
showing the
selection of the
Contact Information
menu option

In this example, the user selected the Contact Information option from the select list, and clicked the Go button. The Contact Information page will either load in the current Browser window or open a new browser window containing the Contact Information page.

Mouse Movement Techniques

JavaScript can be used to perform a task based on mouse movement in the browser window. One popular technique is to display a submenu when the user hovers the mouse pointer over a menu item. Figure 14.5 shows this technique.

Figure 14.5
Main menu and
submenu

The window on the left shows the main menu and the window on the right shows the submenu displayed when the user hovers the mouse pointer over the Products menu item. When the user moves the mouse away from the Products menu item, the submenu disappears. This technique is also used for **image swapping** to give the illusion of depressing a button, moving a pointer, or changing the color of a menu item. In the case of image swapping, also known as rollover images, an image is displayed in the Web page when the page initially loads. When the user positions the mouse pointer on top of the image, the original image is swapped for a new image. When the user moves the mouse away from the image, the original image appears. This is commonly used for navigation button bars, but is also used for interesting effects for other images as well. Figure 14.6 shows the image swapping technique.

Figure 14.6
The original image
on the left, and the
swapped image on
the right, with the
mouse pointer
hovering on the
image

In this chapter we will touch on some of the highlights and concepts involved in using JavaScript. We will create some scripts to demonstrate the use of the alert message, mouseovers, and some of the techniques involved in checking a form for input errors. This chapter offers just a taste of JavaScript, but it will give you a peek at how some of the techniques are developed.

14.4 Adding JavaScript to a Web Page

JavaScript code is embedded in an XHTML Web page and is interpreted by the Web browser. This means that the Web browser is capable of understanding the code and running it. The examples in this chapter use the Mozilla Firefox Web browser. The code we will be creating will work in most Web browsers. However, we will use Firefox because it will provide us with helpful error messages that will be invaluable when we create and test our pages. If you have not already installed Mozilla Firefox on your computer, visit http://www.mozilla.com/firefox for a free download.

The Script Element

When JavaScript code is embedded in an XHTML document, it needs to be contained, or encapsulated, in `<script>` and `</script>` tags to identify it. Web pages are rendered by the Web browser from top to bottom. The impact on our scripts is that they will execute wherever they are located in the document, as we will see.

For XHTML conformance, the `<script>` tag must include an attribute to identify the scripting language as `"text/javascript"`.

JavaScript Statement Block Template

For XHTML Strict DTD conformance, the JavaScript statement block must include a character data declaration. When the W3C validator checks for XHTML Strict conformance, it will check all the code on the page except for areas marked as character data sections. Since JavaScript is not part of XHTML, many validation errors would be generated unless the JavaScript is placed in an area marked as a character data section. This issue does not apply to Web pages coded using Transitional XHTML. However, it doesn't do any harm to add the character data declaration if you are using Transitional XHTML, so let's include it.

XHTML **comments** are contained between <!-- and --> markup symbols. These comment areas are ignored by the browser. Comments can also be used in JavaScript. The // (double slash) identifies a single comment line and the /* and */ symbols identify a comment block.

We'll use both XHTML and JavaScript comment types in our scripts. We'll use the XHTML comment tag at the beginning of the JavaScript statement block to hide JavaScript from older browsers. Some very old browsers will display the JavaScript code rather than execute it. Encapsulating the JavaScript block in XHTML comment tags hides the block from older browsers and the code is ignored by browsers that do not support it.

To address all of the issues mentioned above, each JavaScript block would need the following structure:

```
<script type="text/javascript">
<!-- <![CDATA[
... JavaScript code goes here
// ]]> -->
</script>
```

Let's take it apart to understand each line. Figure 14.7 shows the parts of this code.

Figure 14.7
Parts of the
JavaScript statement
block structure

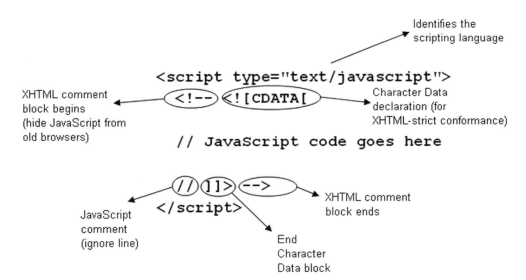

FAQ

If I'm using Transitional XHTML, can I simplify the JavaScript code block?

Yes, you can omit the CDATA declaration information, but you should still include the XHTML comments to hide the code from older browsers. The simpler block structure follows:

```
<script type="text/javascript">
<!--
... JavaScript code goes here
// -->
</script>
```

The JavaScript code is placed inside the statement block. This block can appear anywhere in the XHTML document and the code will be executed. Let's see how this works, with a Hands-On example that will display an alert message.

The alert message box is displayed using the **alert()** method. The structure is as follows:

```
alert("message to be displayed");
```

Each JavaScript command line generally ends with the semicolon, **;**. Also, JavaScript is **case-sensitive**, which means that there's a difference between uppercase and lowercase characters and it will be important to be precise when typing JavaScript code.

HANDS-ON PRACTICE 14.1

In this Hands-On Practice you will create a simple script with an alert() message box.

Launch Notepad. Type the following XHTML and JavaScript code. Note that alert() does not contain a space between alert and the opening parentheses.

```
<?xml version="1.0" encoding="UTF-8"?>
<!DOCTYPE html PUBLIC "-//W3C//DTD XHTML 1.0 Transitional//EN"
   "http://www.w3.org/TR/xhtml1/DTD/xhtml1-transitional.dtd">
<html xmlns="http://www.w3.org/1999/xhtml">
<head>
<title>JavaScript Practice</title>
</head>
<body>
<h2>Using JavaScript</h2>
<script type="text/javascript">
<!-- <![CDATA[
   alert("Welcome to my web page!");
// ]]> -->
</script>
<h2>When does this display?</h2>
</body>
</html>
```

Save this file as alert.html. Launch Firefox and load the alert.html file to test your page. Notice that the first heading appears, and then the alert message pops up as shown in Figure 14.8. After you click the OK button, the second heading appears. This illustrates the top-down processing of the Web page and embedded JavaScript. The JavaScript block is between the headings, and that's where the alert message appears as well.

Let's also look at a **debugging** technique. Edit the JavaScript alert to introduce a typing mistake as follows:

```
aalert("Welcome to my web page!");
```

Save the file and view it in the browser again. Notice that the alert box does not display this time. Firefox will point out some errors in JavaScript code, but we need to open the JavaScript Console to see them.

Figure 14.8
JavaScript practice alert.html displaying alert message box

In Firefox, select the menu items Tools, JavaScript Console. The JavaScript Console window will open and the error message will display, as shown in Figure 14.9.

Notice that the error is displayed, along with the line number where the error was detected. It's useful to create your documents in a text editor that displays the line numbers, but it's not necessary. If you are using Notepad, make use of the Go To feature in the Edit menu. This will allow you to specify a line number and the insertion point will be positioned at the beginning of that line.

Edit the alert.html file to correct the error and test it in the browser again. This time the alert box should display after the first heading, as we saw previously.

Figure 14.9
Firefox JavaScript Console displaying error

FAQ **Will the JavaScript Console display all of the errors in my JavaScript code?**

It will display the syntax errors, which include things like missing brackets and items it does not recognize. Sometimes the error is above the line indicated, particularly if there is a missing bracket or quote. The errors displayed indicate that there is something wrong and they serve as a guide to where the error might be. Start by looking at the line indicated, and if that line looks correct, look at the lines above it.

14.5 Document Object Model Overview

JavaScript can manipulate the elements of an XHTML document. Elements include things in container tags such as paragraphs, and text contained in `<span>` or `<div>` tags. Elements also include images, forms, and individual form elements such as text boxes and select lists. In order to access these elements, we need to understand a little about the Document Object Model (DOM).

In general, an **object** is an entity or a "thing". When using the DOM, the browser window, Web page document, and any XHTML element are considered to be objects. The browser window is an object. When a Web page loads in the browser, the Web page is considered to be a document. The document itself is an object. The document can contain objects such as images, headings, paragraphs, and individual form elements such as text boxes. The objects may have properties that can be detected or manipulated. For instance, a property of the document is its title. Another property of the document is its background color.

There are some actions that can be performed on some objects. For instance, the **window object** can display the alert message box, or display a prompt box. These actions are called **methods**. The command to display an alert message is referred to as a method of the window object. The DOM is the collection of objects, properties, and methods. JavaScript uses the DOM to detect and manipulate elements in the XHTML document.

Let's look at this system of objects, properties, and methods differently. Let's say that your car is an object. It has properties such as color, manufacturer, and year. Your car has elements such as the hood and trunk. The hood and trunk can be opened and closed. If we were to use a programming language to open and close the hood and trunk, the commands might look something like the following:

```
car.hood.open()
car.hood.close()
car.trunk.open()
car.trunk.close()
```

If we wanted to know the color, year, and manufacturer of the car, the commands might look something like the following:

```
car.color
car.year
car.manufacturer
```

When we use the values, `car.color` might be equal to "blue" and `car.manufacturer` might be equal to "Ford." We might be able to change the values, or only read them without changing them. In this example, car is an object, and its properties are hood, trunk, color, year, and manufacturer. Hood and trunk could be considered properties as well. Open and close are methods of hood and are also methods of trunk.

With respect to the DOM, we can write to the document using the **write()** method of the document object. The structure is as follows:

```
document.write("text to be written to the document");
```

We can use this in JavaScript to write text and XHTML tags to a document and the browser will render it.

The alert() method used in the next Hands-On Practice is a method of the window object. It can be written as follows:

```
window.alert("message");
```

The window object is assumed to exist and can be omitted. If the window doesn't exist, the script doesn't exist either.

One property of the document is lastModified. This property contains the date on which the file was most recently saved or modified, and we can access it using document.lastModified. This is a read-only property that we can write to the document or use for some other purpose.

HANDS-ON PRACTICE 14.2

In this Hands-On Practice you will practice using the write() method of the document, and the lastModified property of the document. You will use document.write() to add text and some XHTML tags to an XHTML document. You will also use document.write() to write the date the file was last saved to the document.

Open the alert.html document and edit the script block as follows:

```
<?xml version="1.0" encoding="UTF-8"?>
<!DOCTYPE html PUBLIC "-//W3C//DTD XHTML 1.0 Transitional//EN"
   "http://www.w3.org/TR/xhtml1/DTD/xhtml1-transitional.dtd">
<html xmlns="http://www.w3.org/1999/xhtml">
<head>
<title>JavaScript Practice</title>
</head>
<body>
<h2>Using JavaScript</h2>
<script type="text/javascript">
<!-- <![CDATA[
  document.write("<p>Using document.write to add text</p>");
  document.write("<h2>Notice that we can add XHTML tags too!</h2>");
// ]]> -->
</script>
<h5>This document was last modified on:
<script type="text/javascript">
```

```
<!-- <![CDATA[
    document.write(document.lastModified);
// ]]> -->
</script>
</h5>
</body>
</html>
```

Save this file as documentwrite.html and view it in the browser. The text should display, as shown in Figure 14.10. If the text does not display, open the JavaScript Console and correct any errors that appear.

Figure 14.10
Firefox displaying
documentwrite.html

JavaScript can be seen in the source code. To confirm this, use the View, Page Source menu commands to see the source code. Close the source code window when you have finished viewing the code.

FAQ

Why would I use `document.write` when I can just type the XHTML code by itself?

You wouldn't use `document.write` to generate your Web page if you could just type the XHTML code by itself. You would use `document.write` in conjunction with other techniques. For instance, you might use JavaScript to detect the time of day, and if it is before noon use `document.write` to write "Good morning" to the document. If it is afternoon, write "Good afternoon" to the document, and if it is after 6:00 p.m., write "Good evening" to the document.

14.6 Events and Event Handlers

As the user is viewing a Web page, the browser detects mouse movement and events. **Events** are occurrences, such as mouse clicks or form submissions. For instance, when you move your mouse pointer over a hypertext link, the browser detects a mouseover event. Table 14.1 lists a few of the events and their descriptions.

When an event occurs, this can trigger some JavaScript code to execute. One widely used technique is to detect the mouseover and mouseout events and swap images or display a menu.

Table 14.1 Events and their descriptions

Event	Description
click	The user clicks an item. This could be an image, hypertext link, or button.
load	The browser displays the Web page.
mouseover	The mouse pointer hovers over an item. The mouse pointer does not have to rest on the object. This could be a hypertext link, image, paragraph, or another object.
mouseout	The mouse pointer is moved away from an item that it had previously hovered over.
submit	The user clicks the submit button on a form.
unload	The Web page unloads in the browser. This event occurs just before a new Web page loads.

We need to indicate which events will be acted upon and what will be done when an event occurs. We can use an **event handler** to indicate which event to target. An event handler is embedded in an XHTML tag as an attribute and indicates some JavaScript code to execute when the event occurs. Event handlers use the event name prefixed by "on." Table 14.2 shows the event handlers that correspond to the events described in Table 14.1. For example, the **onload** event is triggered when browser renders ("loads") a Web Page. When you move your mouse pointer over a text hyperlink, a **mouseover** event occurs and is detected by the browser. If that hyper link contains an onmouseover event handler, the JavaScript code indicated by the event handler will be executed. This code might pop up an alert message, display an image, or display a menu. Other event handlers such as **onclick** and **onmouseout** can cause JavaScript code to be executed when their corresponding event occurs.

Table 14.2 Events and event handlers

Event	Event Handler
click	onclick
load	onload
mouseover	onmouseover
mouseout	onmouseout
submit	onsubmit
unload	onunload

FAQ

I've seen some code examples and sometimes the event handlers are written in mixed case, like onClick, and sometimes they're written in lower case, like onclick. What's the difference?

Using Transitional XHTML, event handlers can be written using mixed case, such as **onClick** and **onMouseout**. Conformance to Strict XHTML conformance requires that event handlers are written using all lowercase. To be safe, use all lowercase letters when coding event handlers on a Web page.

HANDS-ON PRACTICE 14.3

Let's practice using the onmouseover and onmouseout event handlers and alert messages to indicate when the event handler has been triggered. We will use simple hypertext links, and embed the event handlers in the <a> tags. We will not need the <script> block since event handlers are placed as attributes in the XHTML tags. We'll place the hypertext links in a table so that there's lots of room in the browser window to move the mouse pointer and test our script.

Open a text editor and enter the text as shown in the following code. Note the use of the double and single quotes in the onmouseover and onmouseout event handlers. We need quotes around the message in the alert() method, and we need quotes encapsulating the JavaScript for the event handler. XHTML and JavaScript will allow us to use either double quotes or single quotes. The rule is that they must match. So when you have a situation where you need two sets of quotes, you can use double and single. In this case, we have used double quotes for the outer set and single quotes for the inner set. In the anchor tag, the "#" symbol is used for the href value because we don't need the functionality of loading another Web page. We need the hypertext link to sense mouseover and mouseout events.

```
<?xml version="1.0" encoding="UTF-8"?>
<!DOCTYPE html PUBLIC "-//W3C//DTD XHTML 1.0 Transitional//EN"
  "http://www.w3.org/TR/xhtml1/DTD/xhtml1-transitional.dtd">
<html xmlns="http://www.w3.org/1999/xhtml">
<head>
<title>JavaScript Practice</title>
</head>
<body>
<h2>Using JavaScript</h2>
<table width="80%">
<tr>
  <td>
    <a href="#" onmouseover="alert('You moused over');">
    Mouseover test</a>
  </td>
  <td>
    <a href="#" onmouseout="alert('You moused out');">Mouseout test</a>
  </td>
</tr>
</table>
</body>
</html>
```

Save this file as mouseovertest.html and load it in the browser. Move your mouse on top of the Mouseover test link. As soon as your mouse touches the link, the mouseover event occurs and the onmouseover event handler is triggered. This displays the alert box, as shown in Figure 14.11.

Click the OK button and position your mouse pointer over the Mouseout test link. Notice that nothing happens. This is because the mouseout event has not occurred yet.

Figure 14.11
Demonstration of
onmouseover with
mouseovertest.html

Move the mouse pointer away from the link. As soon as the mouse pointer is no longer on the link, the mouseout event occurs and the `onmouseout` event handler is triggered. This displays the alert box, as shown in Figure 14.12.

Figure 14.12
Demonstration of
onmouseout with
mouseovertest.html

You can combine event handlers in one hypertext link. This is the essence of the image swapping technique. The `onmouseover` event handler changes the image to a new image and the `onmouseout` event handler changes the image back to the original image. This technique is beyond the scope of this chapter, but perhaps this demonstration sheds some light on how image swapping is accomplished.

CHECKPOINT 14.2

1. With respect to objects, describe the difference between a property and a method. Feel free to use words like thing, action, description, attribute, and so on.

2. What is the difference between an event and an event handler?

3. Where are event handlers placed in the XHTML document?

14.7 Variables

Sometimes we need to be able to collect data from the user and do something with it. A simple example is prompting the user for a name and writing the name to the document. We would store the name in a **variable**. You probably took a math course at some point and used x and y as variables in equations as placeholders for values. The same principle applies when using variables in JavaScript (we won't do any tricky math, though . . . relax!). JavaScript variables are also placeholders for data and the value of the variable can change. Robust programming languages like C++ and Java have all kinds of rules for variables and their data types. JavaScript is very loose that way. We won't have to worry about what type of data is contained in a variable.

FAQ

Are there any tips for creating variable names?

It really is something of an art form, but first of all, you want to create a variable name that describes the data it contains. The underscore, or uppercase character, can be used for readability to imply more than one word. Do not use other special characters, though. Stick to letters and numbers. Be careful not to use JavaScript **reserved words** or **keywords**, such as `var`, `return`, `function`, and so on. A list of JavaScript keywords can be found at http://www.webreference.com/javascript/reference/core_ref. The following are some variable names that could be used for a product code:

- `productCode`
- `prodCode`
- `product_code`

Writing a Variable to a Web Page

Before we use a variable we can declare it with the JavaScript **var** keyword. This step isn't necessary but it is good programming practice. We can assign data to a variable using the assignment operator, the equals sign (=). A variable can contain a number or a string. A string is encapsulated in quotes, and can contain alphabetic characters, spaces, numbers, and special characters. For instance, a string can be a last name, e-mail address, street address, product code, or paragraph of information. Let's do a practice exercise of assigning data to a variable and writing it to the document.

 HANDS-ON PRACTICE 14.4

In this Hands-On Practice you will declare a variable, assign string data to it, and write it to the document.

Open a text editor and type the following:

```
<?xml version="1.0" encoding="UTF-8"?>
<!DOCTYPE html PUBLIC "-//W3C//DTD XHTML 1.0 Transitional//EN"
  "http://www.w3.org/TR/xhtml1/DTD/xhtml1-transitional.dtd">
<html xmlns="http://www.w3.org/1999/xhtml">
```

```
<head>
<title>JavaScript Practice</title>
</head>
<body>
<h2>Using JavaScript</h2>
<h2>Hello
<script type="text/javascript">
<!-- <![CDATA[
  var userName;
  userName = "Karen";
  document.write(userName);
// ]]> -->
</script>
</h2>
</body>
</html>
```

Notice that the `<h2>` tag is placed before the script block and the `</h2>` tag is placed after the script block. This renders the `userName` in the `<h2>` heading format. There is also a single space after the "o" in "Hello". If you miss this space, you'll see the `userName` value displayed right after the "o".

Notice that the variable is mixed case. This is a convention used in many programming languages to make the variable readable. Some developers might use an underscore, like user_name. Selecting a variable name is somewhat of an art form, but try to select names that indicate the contents of the variable.

Notice also, that the `document.write()` method does not contain quotes. The contents of the variable will be written to the document. If we had used quotes around the variable name, the variable name itself would be written to the document, and not the contents of the variable.

Save this document as variablewrite.html and load it in the browser. Figure 14.13 shows the variablewrite.html file in the browser.

Figure 14.13
Browser with variablewrite.html displayed

Chopping up the `<h2>` heading so that it is placed before and after the script is a bit cumbersome. We can combine strings using the plus (+) symbol. You'll see later in this chapter that the plus symbol can also be used to add numbers. Combining strings using the plus (+) symbol is called **concatenation**. Let's concatenate the `<h2>` information as a string with the username value and the `</h2>` tag.

Edit the variablewrite.html document as follows:

```
<?xml version="1.0" encoding="UTF-8"?>
<!DOCTYPE html PUBLIC "-//W3C//DTD XHTML 1.0 Transitional//EN"
   "http://www.w3.org/TR/xhtml1/DTD/xhtml1-transitional.dtd">
<html xmlns="http://www.w3.org/1999/xhtml">
<head>
<title>JavaScript Practice</title>
</head>
<body>
<h2>Using JavaScript</h2>
<script type="text/javascript">
<!-- <![CDATA[
  var userName;
  userName = "Karen";
  document.write("<h2>Hello " + userName + "</h2>");
// ]]> -->
</script>
</body>
</html>
```

Be sure to remove the `<h2>` and `</h2>` information above and below the script block. Save the file as variablewrite2.html and display it in the browser window. You should not see any difference in the document in the browser.

Collecting Variable Values Using a Prompt

To demonstrate the interactive aspect of JavaScript and variables, we can use the `prompt()` method to request data from the user, and write this data to the Web page. For example, we will build on Hands-On Practice 14.4 and prompt the user for a name rather than hard code this data in the `userName` variable.

The **prompt()** method is a method of the window object. We could use `window.prompt()` but the window object is assumed, so we can write this as simply `prompt()`. The `prompt()` method can provide a message to the user. This method is generally used in conjunction with a variable, so that the incoming data is stored in a variable. The structure looks as follows:

```
someVariable = prompt("prompt message");
```

When this command executes, a prompt box pops up that displays the message and an input box for data entry. The user types in the prompt box, clicks the OK button, and the data is assigned to the variable.

Let's add this feature to the variablewrite.html file.

HANDS-ON PRACTICE 14.5

In this Hands-On Practice you will use the `prompt()` method to gather data from the user and write it to the document.

Edit the variablewrite2.html file as follows:

```
<script type="text/javascript">
<!-- <![CDATA[
  var userName;
  userName = prompt("Please enter your name");
  document.write("<h2>Hello " + userName + "</h2>");
// ]]> -->
</script>
```

Only the userName variable assignment command has changed. The data typed by the user will be assigned to the variable, userName.

Save the file as variablewrite3.html file and display it in the browser. The prompt box will appear and you can type a name in the input box, and click the OK button, as shown in Figure 14.14. The name should appear in the browser window.

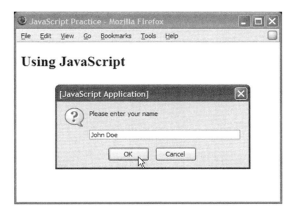

Let's do a variation on this and allow the user to type a color name. The user's preference will be used as the background color of the document. We will use the bgColor property of the document object and set it to the user's color preference. Pay attention to case, and ensure that the uppercase C is used when typing bgColor.

Edit the variablewrite3.html document as follows, and save it as changebackground.html.

```
<script type="text/javascript">
<!-- <![CDATA[
  var userColor;
  userColor = prompt("Please type the color name blue or red");
  document.bgColor = userColor;
// ]]> -->
</script>
```

We are prompting the user to type the color name "blue" or "red." You know from your XHTML experience that there are more options for color names. Feel free to experiment!

Save the document and display it in the browser. The prompt box will appear, and you can type a color name and click the OK button. You should notice the background color change immediately.

14.8 Introduction to Programming Concepts

Until now, we have used the DOM to access properties and methods for the window and document. We have also created some simple event handlers. There is another aspect to JavaScript, which is more like programming. In this section, we'll touch on just a small part of this to get a feel for the power of using programming concepts and build on this later to test input on a form.

Arithmetic Operators

When working with variables, it is often useful to be able to do some arithmetic. For instance, you may be creating a Web page that calculates the tax on a product. Once the user has selected a product, you can use JavaScript to calculate the tax and write the result to the document. Table 14.3 shows a list of **arithmetic operators**, descriptions, and some examples.

Table 14.3 Commonly used arithmetic operators

Operator	Description	Example	Value of Quantity
=	assign	quantity = 10	10
+	addition	quantity = 10 + 6	16
–	subtraction	quantity = 10 – 6	4
*	multiplication	quantity = 10 * 2	20
/	division	quantity = 10 / 2	5

Programming languages differ greatly in capabilities, but they all have a few things in common. They all allow the use of variables, and have commands for decision making, command repetition, and reusable code blocks. Decision making would be used when different outcomes are required depending on the input or action of the user. In our Hands-On Practice example we will prompt the user for an age, and illustrate different messages printed to the document based on the age. Repetition of commands comes in handy when performing a similar task many times. For instance, it is tedious to create a select list containing the numbers 1 through 31 for the days of the months. We can use JavaScript to do this with a few lines of code. Reusable code blocks are handy when you want to refer to a block of code in an event handler rather than typing many commands in the XHTML tag's event handler. As this chapter is meant as a very brief taste of some concepts, it is beyond our scope to elaborate further. We will touch on decision making and reusable code in the Hands-On Practice examples.

Decision Making

As we've seen, we can use variables in JavaScript. We may wish to test the value of a variable, and perform different tasks based on the variable. For instance, perhaps an order form requires that the user enters a quantity greater than 0. We could test the quantity input box to be sure the number entered is greater than 0. If the quantity is not greater than 0 we could pop up an alert message instructing the user to enter a quantity greater than 0. The **if** control structure looks as follows:

```
if (condition)
{
  . . . commands to execute if condition is true
}  else {
  . . . commands to execute if condition is false
}
```

Notice that there are two types of brackets used. The parentheses are used around the condition and the brackets are used to encapsulate a block of commands. The `if` statement includes a block of commands to execute if the condition is `true` and a block of commands to execute if the condition is `false`. The brackets are aligned so that you can easily see the opening brackets and closing brackets. It's very easy to miss a bracket when you're typing, and then have to go hunting for the missing bracket. Aligning them makes it much easier to track them visually. As you are typing JavaScript code remember that parentheses, brackets, and quotations always are used in pairs. If a script isn't working as intended, verify that each of these items has a "partner."

If the condition evaluates as `true`, the first command block will be executed and the `else` block will be skipped. If the condition is `false`, the first command block will be skipped and the `else` block will execute.

For the purpose of an overview, this is quite simplified, but it will give you a sense of how conditions and the `if` control structure can be useful. The condition must be something that can `be` evaluated as either `true` or `false`. We can think of this as a mathematical condition. The condition will generally make use of an operator. Table 14.4 lists commonly used **comparison operators**. The examples in Table 14.4 could be used as conditions in an `if` structure.

Table 14.4 Commonly used comparison operators

Operator	Description	Example	Sample Values of Quantity That Would Result in `true`
= =	Double equals sign (equivalent) "is exactly equal to"	quantity = = 10	10
>	Greater than	quantity > 10	11, 12 (but not 10)
> =	Greater than or equal to	quantity > = 10	10, 11, 12
<	Less than	quantity < 10	8, 9 (but not 10)
< =	Less than or equal to	quantity < = 10	8, 9, 10
! =	Not equal to	quantity ! = 10	8, 9, 11 (but not 10)

What can I do when my JavaScript code doesn't seem to be working?

You can try the following debugging techniques:

- Open the JavaScript Console in Firefox to see if there are any errors. Common errors include missing a semicolon at the end of a line, and typing errors in commands.

- Use `alert()` to print variables to verify the contents. For instance, if you have a variable named quantity, try `alert(quantity);` to see what is contained in the variable.

- Ask a classmate to look at your code. It's difficult to edit your own code because you tend to see what you think you wrote rather than what you actually wrote. It's easier to edit someone else's code.

- Try to explain your code to a classmate. Often, talking through the code will help you uncover errors.

- Verify that you are not using any JavaScript reserved words as variable names or function names. See http://www.webreference.com/javascript/reference/core_ref for a list of reserved words.

HANDS-ON PRACTICE 14.6

In this Hands-On Practice you will code the quantity example described earlier. The user will be prompted for a quantity and must enter a quantity greater than 0. We will assume that the user will enter a number. If the user enters a value of 0 or a negative number, there will be an error message displayed. If the user enters a value greater than 0, a message will be displayed thanking the user for the order. To stay focused on this task, we will use a prompt and will write messages to the document.

Open a text editor and enter the following. Notice that there are no semicolon characters (;) after the brackets:

```
<?xml version="1.0" encoding="UTF-8"?>
<!DOCTYPE html PUBLIC "-//W3C//DTD XHTML 1.0 Transitional//EN"
  "http://www.w3.org/TR/xhtml1/DTD/xhtml1-transitional.dtd">
<html xmlns="http://www.w3.org/1999/xhtml">
<head>
<title>JavaScript Practice</title>
</head>
<body>
<h2>Using JavaScript</h2>
<script type="text/javascript">
<!-- <![CDATA[
  var quantity;
  quantity = prompt("Type a quantity greater than 0");
  if (quantity <= 0)
  {
    document.write("<p>Quantity is not greater than 0.</p>");
    document.write("<p>Please refresh the web page.</p>");
```

```
    } else {
      document.write("<p>Quantity is greater than 0.</p>");
    }
// ]]> -->
</script>
</body>
</html>
```

Save this document as quantityif.html and display it in the browser. If the prompt box does not appear, remember to check the JavaScript Console for errors. When the prompt box appears, type the number 0 and click the OK button. You should see the error message you have created in the browser window, as shown in Figure 14.15.

Figure 14.15
The browser on the left shows the prompt box with input of 0 and the browser on the right shows the result

Now refresh the page and this time enter a value greater than 0, as shown in Figure 14.16.

Figure 14.16
The browser on the left shows the prompt box with input of a value greater than 0 and the browser on the right shows the result

Functions

The Hands-On Practice 14.6 pops up the prompt box as soon as the page loads. What if we prefer to allow the user to decide when a particular script should be interpreted or run by the browser? Perhaps we could use an `onmouseover` event handler and run the script when the user moves the mouse pointer over a link or image. Another method, perhaps more intuitive for the user, is to make use of a button and direct the user to click the button to run the script. The Web page visitor doesn't need to be aware that a script will run, but can click a button to initiate some sort of functionality.

Three types of buttons were introduced in Chapter 9:

- A submit button `<input type="submit" />` is used to submit a form.
- A reset button `<input type="reset" />` is used to clear values entered on a form.
- The third type of button `<input type="button" />` does not have any default action related to forms.

In this section we will make use of the button `<input type="button" />` and the `onclick` event handler to run a script. The `onclick` event handler can run a single command or multiple commands. A sample follows:

```
<input type="button" value="Click to see a message"
onclick="alert('Welcome!');" />
```

In this sample, the button will display the text "Click to see a message." When the user clicks the button, the click event occurs and the `onclick` event handler executes the `alert('Welcome!');` command. The message box appears. This method is very effective when there is only one JavaScript statement to execute. It quickly becomes unmanageable when there are more statements to execute. When that happens, it makes sense to place all JavaScript statements in a block and somehow point to the block to execute. If the statement block has a name, we can execute the block by pointing to the name. In addition to providing a shortcut name, this code is also easily reused. We can provide a name for a statement block by creating a function.

A **function** is a block of JavaScript statements with a specific purpose, which can be run when needed. A function can contain a single statement or a group of statements, and is defined as follows:

```
function function_name()
{
   ... JavaScript statements
}
```

The function definition starts with the keyword function followed by the name of the function. The parentheses are required, and more advanced functions make use of them. You can choose a name for the function, just like you choose a name for a variable. The function name should indicate the purpose of the function somehow. The statements are contained within the brackets. The block of statements will execute when the function is called.

Here's an example of a function definition:

```
function showAlerts()
{
   alert("Please click OK to continue.");
   alert("Please click OK again.");
   alert("Click OK for the last time to continue.");
}
```

The function can be called using the following statement:

```
showAlerts();
```

Now, we could include the `showAlerts()` function call in a button as follows:

```
<input type="button" value="click to see alerts"
onclick="showAlerts();" />
```

When the user clicks the button, the `showAlerts()` function will be called, and the three alert messages will appear, one after the other. Typically, function definitions are placed in the `<head>` area of the XHTML document. This loads the function definition code but it does not execute until it is called. This removes the clutter from the body of the XHTML document and ensures that the function definition is loaded before the function is called.

HANDS-ON PRACTICE 14.7

In this Hands-On Practice you will edit the quantityif.html document to move the prompting script into a function and call it with an `onclick` event handler.

Edit the quantityif.html document as follows. There are a few things to note. The script has been moved into the `<head>` area and included in a function definition. The `document.write()` methods have been changed to `alert()` methods and the messages have been altered slightly. The `document.write()` methods will not work well after the page has already been written, as is the case in this exercise. Also, there have been some comments added to the end brackets for the `if` statement and the function definition. These comments can help you keep track of the code blocks within the script. The indentation of the code blocks also helps to identify which brackets begin and end various statements.

```
<?xml version="1.0" encoding="UTF-8"?>
<!DOCTYPE html PUBLIC "-//W3C//DTD XHTML 1.0 Transitional//EN"
   "http://www.w3.org/TR/xhtml1/DTD/xhtml1-transitional.dtd">
<html xmlns="http://www.w3.org/1999/xhtml">
<head>
<title>JavaScript Practice</title>
<script type="text/javascript">
<!-- <![CDATA[
   function promptQuantity()
   {
      var quantity;
```

```
        quantity = prompt("Please type a quantity greater than 0");
        if (quantity <= 0)
        {
          alert("Quantity is not greater than 0.");
        } else {
          alert("Thank you for entering a quantity greater than 0.");
        }  // end if
    }  // end function promptQuantity
// ]]> -->
</script>
</head>
<body>
<h2>Using JavaScript</h2>
<input type="button" value="Click to enter quantity"
onclick="promptQuantity();" />
</body>
</html>
```

Save the document as quantityif2.html and display it in the browser. Open the JavaScript Console in case there are typing errors when you run the script.

Click the button to test the script. If the prompt box does not appear, check the JavaScript Console and correct any errors. Figure 14.17 shows the browser and prompt box after the button has been clicked, and the resulting alert box. Be sure to test for a value larger than 0 and a value of 0 or less.

Figure 14.17
The browser on the left shows the prompt box and input; the browser on the right shows the alert box displayed after the input

CHECKPOINT 14.3

1. Describe a method that can be used to gather a piece of data such as the user's age.

2. Write the JavaScript code to display an alert message for users who are under 18 years old and a different alert message for users who are 18 years or older.

3. What is a function definition?

14.9 Form Handling

As you discovered in Chapter 9, the data from a Web form can be submitted to a CGI or a server-side script. This data can be added to a database or used for some other purpose; therefore, it is important that the data submitted by a user is as accurate as possible. When the user enters information in a form, there is always a chance that the information will be incorrect or inaccurate. This is particularly true when text input boxes are used, since the user can easily mistype data. Often, the form data is checked for invalid data before it is submitted. Form data validation can be done by the server-side script, but it can also be done client-side, using JavaScript. Again, this topic is simplified here, but we can get a sense of how this might be done.

When the user clicks the form's submit button, the submit event occurs. We can make use of the **onsubmit** event handler to call a function that tests form data for validation. This technique is referred to as **form handling**. The Web developer can validate all form inputs, some inputs, or just one form input. The following list is a selection of some types of things that might be validated:

- Required fields such as name and e-mail addresses
- A required check box to acknowledge a license agreement
- A radio button indicating method of payment or delivery option
- A quantity entered that is numeric and within a particular range

When the user clicks the submit button, the onsubmit event handler calls a function that tests all of the appropriate form elements for valid data. Then the validation function confirms that the data is valid (true) or not valid (false). The form is submitted to the URL indicated in the <form> action if the data is valid (true). The form would not be submitted if the data is not valid (false) and some indication to the user regarding errors would be displayed. The overall structure of the Web page code related to declaring the function and handling the onsubmit event follows:

```
... XHTML begins the Web page
function validateForm()
{
  ... JavaScript commands to test form data go here
  if form data is valid
    return true
  else
    return false
}
... XHTML continues
<form method="post" action="URL" onsubmit="return validateForm( );">
... form elements go here
  <input type="submit" value="submit form" />
</form>
... XHTML continues
```

There is a new concept with regard to functions indicated here. A function can encapsulate a group of statements, but it can also send a value back to where it was called. This is referred to as "returning a value" and the JavaScript keyword return is used in the

JavaScript code to indicate the value that will be sent back. Our example will return a value of `true` if the data is valid, the function will return a value of `true` and a value of `false` if the data does not pass our validation tests. Notice that the `onsubmit` event handler also contains the keyword `return`. It works like this: if the `validateForm()` function returns a value of `true`, the `onsubmit` event handler becomes `return true` and the form is submitted. If the `validateForm()` function returns a value of `false`, the `onsubmit` event handler becomes `return false` and the form is not submitted. Once a function returns a value, it is finished executing regardless of whether or not there are more statements in the function.

HANDS-ON PRACTICE 14.8

In this Hands-On Practice you will create a form with inputs for name and age, and use JavaScript to validate the data such that there will be data in the name field and an age of 18 or greater. If there is nothing in the name field, an alert message will be displayed instructing the user to enter a name. If the age entered is less than 18, an alert message will be displayed instructing the user to enter an age of 18 or greater. If all data is valid, an alert message will be displayed indicating that the data is valid and the form will be submitted.

Let's start by creating the form. Open a text editor and type the following. Notice that the `onsubmit` form handler is embedded in the `<form>` tag and we will add the JavaScript code later.

```
<?xml version="1.0" encoding="UTF-8"?>
<!DOCTYPE html PUBLIC "-//W3C//DTD XHTML 1.0 Transitional//EN"
  "http://www.w3.org/TR/xhtml1/DTD/xhtml1-transitional.dtd">
<html xmlns="http://www.w3.org/1999/xhtml">
<head>
<title>JavaScript Practice</title>
</head>
<body>
<h2>JavaScript Form Handling</h2>
<form method="post"
action="http://webdevfoundations.net/scripts/formdemo.asp"
onsubmit="return validateForm();">
  <table>
    <tr>
      <td>
        <label for="userName">Name:</label>
      </td>
      <td>
        <input type="text" name="userName" id="userName" />
      </td>
    </tr>
    <tr>
      <td>
        <label for="userAge">Age:</label>Age:
      </td>
```

```
      <td>
        <input type="text" name="userAge" id="userAge" />
      </td>
    </tr>
    <tr>
      <td colspan="2">
        <input type="submit" value="Send information" />
      </td>
    </tr>
  </table>
</form>
</body>
</html>
```

Save the file as formvalidation.html and view it in the browser. Figure 14.18 shows the form in the browser.

Figure 14.18
The formvalidation.html file displayed in the browser

Feel free to click the submit button. You will notice that the inputs will be submitted. At the moment we have not coded the `validateForm()` function, so the form simply submits.

Accessing form inputs is a little tricky. The form is a property of the document object. Each form element is a property of the `form` object. And a property of a form element can be a value. So, accessing the contents of an input box could look something like the following:

```
document.forms[0].inputbox_name.value
```

The form is identified by `forms[0]` to indicate which form will be used. An XHTML document can contain multiple forms. Note that there is an "s" in `forms[0]`. The first form is `forms[0]`. A form could have a name attribute, but Strict XHTML does not allow form names to be used directly as a property. So we'll err on the side of caution and use the strict specification, `forms[0]` to indicate which form we need to use. To access the value in the `userAge` input box, we will need to use `document.forms[0].userAge.value`. This is a mouthful, for sure.

Also, notice that the values `true` and `false` are not encased in quotes. This is important because `true` and `false` are not strings, they are JavaScript reserved words, or keywords. Again, for simplicity, suffice it to say that they represent special values. If you add quotes to them, they become strings and this function will not work properly.

Let's start by adding the code to validate the age. Edit the formvalidation.html file to add the following script block in the <head> section:

```
<head>
<title>JavaScript Practice</title>
<script type="text/javascript">
<!-- <![CDATA[
  function validateForm()
  {
    if (document.forms[0].userAge.value < 18)
    {
      alert ("Age is less than 18. You are not an adult.");
      return false;
    }  // end if
    alert ("Age is valid.");
    return true;
  }  // end function validateForm
// ]]> -->
</script>
</head>
```

The validateForm() function will check the age in the userAge input box. If it is less than 18, the alert message will be displayed and a value of false will be returned and the function will finish executing. The onsubmit event handler will become "return false" and the form will not be submitted. If the age is 18 or greater, the statements in the if structure will be skipped and the alert("Age is valid."); will execute. After the user clicks the OK button in the alert message, the statement return true; will execute and the onsubmit event handler will become "return true"; thus, the form will be submitted. Let's test this out!

Type a value less than 18 in the userAge input box and click the submit button. If the form submits right away, there is likely an error in the JavaScript code. If this happens, open the JavaScript Console and correct the errors indicated. Figure 14.19 shows the input in the Age box and the alert message displayed after clicking the submit button.

Figure 14.19
The validateform.html file displayed in the browser with input for age less than 18—notice the alert message

Click the OK button and type an age that is 18 or greater in the `userAge` input box. Click the submit button. Figure 14.20 shows the input in the `userAge` input box, the alert message after the submit button has been clicked, and the resulting Web page after the form has been submitted.

Figure 14.20
The validateform.html file displayed in the browser with input for age greater than or equal to 18—notice the alert message; the browser on the right shows the resulting Web page after the form is submitted

Now let's add another `if` statement to validate the name. To ensure that something has been entered in the `userName` input box, we will test to see if the value of the input box is empty. The **null** string is represented by two double quotes, `""`, or two single quotes `''`, without a space or any other character in between. We can compare the value of the `userName` text box to the null string. If the value of the `userName` box is equal to the null string, then we know that the user did not enter any information in this box. In our example, we will be sending only one error message at a time. If the user does not have a name in the `userName` box and also does not have an appropriate age in the `userAge` box, the user will only see the `userName` error appear. After the user corrects the name and resubmits, the user will see the `userAge` error appear. This is very basic form processing but it gives you an idea of how form handling might be accomplished. More sophisticated form processing would verify each form field and indicate all errors each time the form is submitted.

Let's add the code to validate the `userName` data. Edit the script block as follows. Note that two equals signs represent equivalent in the `if` statement. Some students find it helpful to read the two equal signs (`==`) as "is exactly equal to."

```
<script type="text/javascript">
<!-- <![CDATA[
  function validateForm()
  {
    if (document.forms[0].userName.value == "" )
    {
      alert("Name field cannot be empty.");
      return false;
    }  // end if
```

```
        if (document.forms[0].userAge.value < 18)
        {
          alert("Age is less than 18. You are not an adult.");
          return false;
        }  // end if
        alert("Name and age are valid.");
        return true;
    }  // end function validateForm
// ]]> -->
</script>
```

Save the document and refresh it in the browser window. Click the submit button without entering data in the Name or Age input boxes. Figure 14.21 shows the alert message displayed when no data has been input and the submit button has been clicked.

Figure 14.21
The validateform.html file displayed in the browser, without input in the Name and Age boxes; the alert message appears after the form is submitted

Click the OK button, enter some text in the Name input box, and submit the form again. Figure 14.22 shows data in the Name input box and the alert message that appears due to validating the age. The age input box does not contain an age, and this is interpreted as a value of 0.

Figure 14.22
The validateform.html file displayed in the browser, with input in the Name box and without input in the Age box; the alert message appears after the submit button is clicked

Click the OK button, and enter an age that is 18 or greater. Click the submit button. Figure 14.23 shows data in the Name and Age input boxes and the alert message that displays after the submit button has been clicked. It also shows the resulting Web page after the successful submission when all data is valid.

Figure 14.23
The validateform.html file displayed in the browser, with valid input in the Name and Age boxes and alert message; the browser on the right shows the Web page displayed after valid input has been submitted

CHECKPOINT 14.4

1. What is meant by the term "form data validation"?

2. Give three examples of form data that may require validation.

3. An XHTML document contains the `<form>` tag as follows:

```
<form method="post"
action="http://webdevfoundations.net/scripts/formdemo.asp"
onsubmit="return validateForm();">
```

What happens when the user clicks the submit button?

14.10 Accessibility and JavaScript

Focus on Accessibility

The interactivity and functionality that JavaScript can add to a Web page is exciting. However, be aware that some visitors may have JavaScript disabled, may not be able to see your visual effect, or may be unable to manipulate the mouse. Section 508 requires that your site is functional at a basic level even if your visitor's browser does not support JavaScript. If you use JavaScript to handle mouse events in your site navigation, you should also provide plain text navigation that does not require a mouse and can be easily accessed by a screen reader. If you use JavaScript for form validation, provide an e-mail address to provide physically challenged visitors a way to contact your organization and obtain assistance.

14.11 JavaScript Resources

This chapter has barely scratched the surface of the uses of JavaScript in Web development. You may wish to do further research using some of the following online resources:

- Beginning JavaScript Tutorials (http://www.pageresource.com/jscript/index.html)
- JavaScript Tutorial for the Total Non-Programmer (http://www.webteacher.com/javascript)
- More Beginning JavaScript Tutorials (http://echoecho.com/javascript.htm)
- Core JavaScript 1.5 Reference Manual (http://www.webreference.com/javascript/reference/core_ref)
- The JavaScript Source (http://javascript.internet.com)

CHAPTER SUMMARY

This chapter introduced the use of JavaScript as a client-side scripting language in Web pages. You learned how to embed script blocks in Web pages, display an alert message, use an event handler, and validate a form.

Visit the textbook Web site at http://www.webdevfoundations.net for examples, the links listed in this chapter, and updated information.

Key Terms

alert()	form handling	onload
<script>	function	onmouseout
arithmetic operators	if	onmouseover
browser sniffing	image swapping	onsubmit
case-sensitive	jump menus	prompt()
client-side processing	keywords	reserved words
comments	methods	scripting language
comparison operators	mouseover	server-side processing
concatentation	null	var
debugging	object	variable
document	object-based	window object
events	onclick	write()
event handler		

Review Questions

Multiple Choice

1. Which of the following is the document considered to be?

   a. object

   b. property

   c. method

   d. attribute

2. When the user positions the mouse pointer on a link, the browser detects which one of these events?

   a. mouseon

   b. mousehover

   c. mouseover

   d. mousedown

3. When the user moves the mouse pointer away from a link it had been hovering over, the browser detects which one of these events?

   a. mouseoff

   b. mouseout

   c. mouseaway

   d. mouseup

4. Which method of the window can be used to display a message to the user?

   a. alert()

   b. message()

   c. status()

   d. display()

5. Which of the following will assign the value 5 to the variable `productCost`?

   a. `productCost = > 5;`

   b. `productCost < = 5;`

   c. `productCost = = 5;`

   d. `productCost = 5;`

6. A condition (`productCost > 5`) is used in an `if` statement. Which of the following values of `productCost` will result in this condition evaluated as `true`?

   a. 4

   b. 5

   c. 5.1

   d. none of the above

7. Which of the following can describe JavaScript, as used in a Web page?

   a. a scripting language

   b. a markup language

   c. an easy form of Java

   d. a language created by Microsoft

8. Which of the following is the code to access the contents of an input box named `userData` on a form?

   a. `document.forms[0].userData`

   b. `document.forms[0].userData.value`

   c. `document.forms[0].userData.contents`

   d. `document.forms[0].userData.data`

9. Which of the following is the code to run a function called `isValid()` when the user clicks the submit button?

   a. `<input type="button"`
      `onclick="isValid();" />`

   b. `<input type="submit"`
      `onsubmit="isValid();" />`

   c. `<form method="post" action="URL"`
      `onsubmit="return isValid();">`

   d. `<form method="post" action="URL"`
      `onclick="return isValid();">`

10. Which of the following is a technique for creating reusable JavaScript code?

   a. define a function

   b. create a script block

   c. define an `if` statement

   d. use an `onclick` event handler

Fill in the Blank

11. The term _____ refers to using JavaScript to detect information about the Web browser application.

12. A _____ is a select list that allows the user to select an option to load another Web page.

13. The _____ object is assumed to exist and it is not necessary to include it as an object when referring to its methods and properties.

14. We do not need to declare a _____, but we could choose to do so with the `var` statement.

15. The `<button>` can be used with a(n) _____ event handler to run a script when the user clicks a button.

Short Answer

16. Describe at least three popular uses for JavaScript.

17. Describe how you could debug JavaScript code when it is not working properly.

Apply Your Knowledge

1. **Predict the Result.** Given the following code, what will happen when the user clicks the button?

```
<?xml version="1.0" encoding="UTF-8"?>
<!DOCTYPE html PUBLIC "-//W3C//DTD XHTML 1.0 Transitional//EN"
    "http://www.w3.org/TR/xhtml1/DTD/xhtml1-transitional.dtd">
<html xmlns="http://www.w3.org/1999/xhtml">
<head>
<title>JavaScript Practice</title>
<script type="text/javascript">
<!-- <![CDATA[
    function mystery()
    {
      alert('hello');
    }
// ]]> -->
</script>
</head>
<body>
<h2>Using JavaScript</h2>
<input type="button" value="click me" onclick="mystery();" />
</body>
</html>
```

2. **Fill in the Missing Code.** This Web page should prompt the user for the name of a song and print the song name in the document. The missing code is indicated by "_". Fill in the missing code.

```
<?xml version="1.0" encoding="UTF-8"?>
<!DOCTYPE html PUBLIC "-//W3C//DTD XHTML 1.0 Transitional//EN"
    "http://www.w3.org/TR/xhtml1/DTD/xhtml1-transitional.dtd">
<html xmlns="http://www.w3.org/1999/xhtml">
<head>
<title>JavaScript Practice</title>
</head>
<body>
<h2>Using JavaScript</h2>
<script type="text/javascript">
<!-- <![CDATA[
    var userSong;
    userSong = _("Please enter your favorite song title.");
    document._(_);
// ]]> -->
</script>
</body>
</html>
```

3. **Find the Error.** When this page is loaded in the Web browser it is supposed to display an error message if the user does not have any data in the Name input box. It is not working properly, and instead submits the form regardless of the missing

input. Fix the errors so that the form does not submit if there is no input in the Name input box. Correct the errors and describe the process you followed.

```
<?xml version="1.0" encoding="UTF-8"?>
<!DOCTYPE html PUBLIC "-//W3C//DTD XHTML 1.0 Transitional//EN"
   "http://www.w3.org/TR/xhtml1/DTD/xhtml1-transitional.dtd">
<html xmlns="http://www.w3.org/1999/xhtml">
<head>
<title>JavaScript Practice</title>
<script type="text/javascript">
<!-- <![CDATA[
   function validateForm()
   {
     if (document.forms[0].userName.value == "" )
     {
       aert("Name field cannot be empty.");
       return false;
     }  // end if
   aert("Name and age are valid.");
   return true;
   }  // end function validateForm
// ]]> -->
</script>
</head>
<body>
<h2>JavaScript Form Handling</h2>
<form method="post" action="http://webdevfoundations.net/scripts/
formdemo.asp" onsubmit="return validateUser();">
 <label>Name: <input type="text" name="userName" /></label>
 <br />
 <input type="submit" value="Send information" />
</form>
</body>
</html>
```

Hands-On Exercises

1. Practice writing event handlers.
   a. Write the XHTML tag and event handler to pop up an alert message that says "Welcome" when the user clicks a button.
   b. Write the XHTML tag and event handler to pop up an alert message that says "Welcome" when the user moves the mouse pointer over a hypertext link that says "Hover for a welcome message".
   c. Write the XHTML tag and event handler to pop up an alert message that says "Welcome" when the user moves the mouse pointer away from a hypertext link that says "Move your mouse pointer here for a welcome message".

2. Create a Web page that will pop up an alert message welcoming the user to the Web page. Use a script block in the <head> area for this task.

3. Create a Web page that will prompt the user for a name, and age, and write the message using the name and age in the message. Use the `prompt()` method and variables to accomplish this.

4. Create a Web page that will prompt the user for a color name. Use this color name to write the text "This is your favorite color!". The `fgColor` property of the document changes the text color of all text in a document. Use this property to accomplish this task.

5. Extend Hands-On Practice 14.8. Add a text box for the user's city. Ensure that this text box is not empty when the form is submitted. If the city text box is empty, pop up an appropriate alert message and do not submit the form. If the city text box is not empty, and other data is valid, submit the form.

Web Research

1. Use the resources listed in the chapter as a starting point, but also search the Web for additional resources on JavaScript. Create a Web page that lists at least five useful resources along with a brief description of each. Organize your Web page with a table that provides the name of the site, the URL, a brief description of what is offered, and a recommended page (such as a tutorial, free script, and so on) for each resource. Place your name in an e-mail link on the Web page. Print both the source code (from Notepad) and the browser view of the Web page.

2. Use the resources listed in the chapter as a starting point, but also search the Web for additional resources on JavaScript. Find either a tutorial or free download that uses JavaScript. Create a Web page that uses the code or download that you found. Describe the effect and list the URL of the resource on the Web page. Place your name in an e-mail link on the Web page. Print both the source code (from Notepad) and the browser view of the page.

WEB SITE CASE STUDY
Adding JavaScript

Each of the following case studies has continued throughout most of the text. This chapter adds JavaScript to selected Web pages from each of the case studies.

JavaJam Coffee House

See Chapter 2 for an introduction to the JavaJam Coffee House Case Study. Figure 2.26 shows a site map for the JavaJam Web site. The pages were created in earlier chapters. Use the Web pages indicated in this exercise from the javajamcss folder. You have two tasks:

1. Add the date that the document was last modified to the bottom of the music.html page.

2. Add alert messages to the description of the artists in the music.html page such that an alert message will pop up when the user places the mouse over the images. The alert message will indicate "Concerts sell out quickly so act fast!".

Hands-On Practice Case

1. Add the date that the document was last modified to the bottom of the music.html page. Launch Notepad and open the music.html page. Modify the page as follows:

   - At the bottom of the page, after the e-mail link, add a script block that will write the following message to the document:

     This page was last modified on: date

   - Use the `document.lastModified` property to print the date.

2. Add alert messages to the description of the artists in the music.html page such that an alert message will pop up when the user places the mouse over the images. The alert message will indicate "Concerts sell out quickly so act fast!". Launch Notepad and open the music.html page. Modify the page as follows:

   - Add a hypertext link to Melanie's description with an `onmouseover` event handler as follows:

     ```
     <a href="#" onmouseover=
     "alert('Concerts sell out quickly so act fast!');">Melanie
     Morris entertains with her melodic folk style.</a>
     ```

   - Add a hypertext link to Greg's description with `onmouseover` event handler as follows:

     ```
     <a href="#" onmouseover="alert('Concerts sell out quickly so
     act fast!');">Tahoe Greg's back from his tour.</a>
     ```

Save the music.html page and test it in the browser. Figure 14.24 shows the alert message as the user places their mouse over Melanie's link. It also shows the date last modified.

Fish Creek Animal Hospital

See Chapter 2 for an introduction to the Fish Creek Animal Hospital Case Study. Figure 2.30 shows a site map for the Fish Creek Web site. The pages were created in earlier chapters. Use the Web pages indicated in this exercise from the fishcreekcss folder. You have two tasks:

1. Add rollover images for the navigation images to each Fish Creek Web site page.
2. Add the date last modified to the home page.

Hands-On Practice Case

1. Add rollover images for the navigation images to each Fish Creek Web site page.

   When a visitor places the mouse over one of the navigation images, the image will change—this is an image rollover. In this case study you will add image rollovers to all the pages on the Fish Creek site.

   a. Your home page (index.html in the fishcreekcss folder) should already display the logo (fishcreeklogo.gif) and navigation images (home.gif, services.gif,

Figure 14.24

JavaJam music.html with the mouseover alert for performers' descriptions and the date last modified

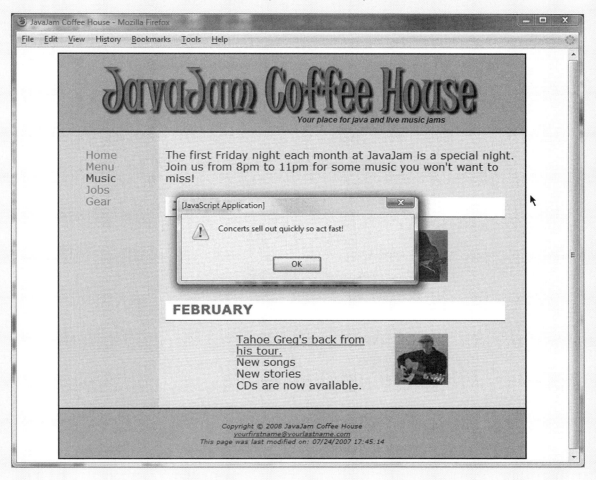

askthevet.gif, shop.gif, contact.gif). If it doesn't, obtain the logo and navigation images from the student files (Chaper14/CaseStudyStarters folder) and save them to your fishcreekcss folder. Use Figure 14.25 as a guide. The images should each link to their corresponding pages.

b. Copy the new images for this case from the student files (Chapter14 folder) and save them to your fishcreekcss folder. These are the images that will display when the user places the mouse pointer over one of the images links: serviceson.gif, asktheveton.gif, contacton.gif, shopon.gif, and homeon.gif.

c. Modify the index.html page to use JavaScript `onmouseover` and `onmouseout` event handlers.

Add the name attribute to each image used for navigation. For example, the `<img />` tag for the Services image should be modified as follows:

```
<img border="0" src="services.gif" alt="Fish Creek Services"
width="132" height="27" name="services" />
```

Modify the Ask the Vet, Shop, and Contact `<img />` tags similarly. The value of the name attribute should not contain any spaces.

Figure 14.25
Fish Creek Animal Hospital index.html page with rollover image for the services link and date
last modified in the footer

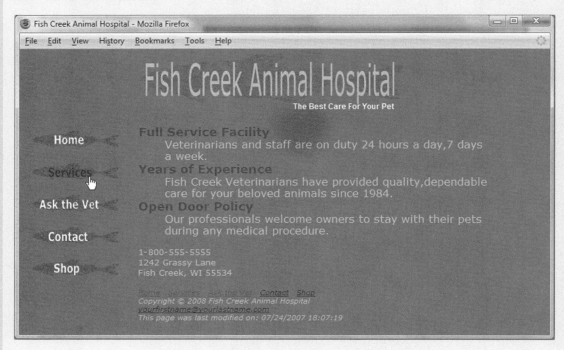

Add `onmouseover` and `onmouseout` event handlers to each image hypertext
link. The event handlers will change the `src` attribute on the image to a new
value. For example, the hypertext link for the services.html page should be
modified as follows:

```
<a href="services.html"
onmouseover="document.services.src='serviceson.gif'"
onmouseout="document.services.src='services.gif'">
```

Note that `document.services.src` corresponds to the `src` attribute on the
`<img />` tag with the name attribute value of `services`. When the user places
the mouse pointer over the image link, `document.services.src` is set to the
new image file (serviceson.gif). When the user moves the mouse pointer off of
the image link, `document.services.src` is set to the old image file
(services.gif).

The image links for the Ask the Vet, Shop, and Contact pages should be modified similarly to the Services image link. Save your page and test it in a
browser. You should see the images swap.

In a similar manner, add image rollovers to the services.html, askthevet.html,
shop.html, and contact.html pages. Save your pages and test in a browser.

2. Add the date last modified to the home page.

Launch Notepad and open the index.html page. Modify the index.html page as
follows:

- At the bottom of the page, after the e-mail link, add a script block that will write the following message to the document:

  This page was last modified on: date

- Use the `document.lastModified` property to display the date.

Pete the Painter

See Chapter 2 for an introduction to the Pete the Painter Case Study. Figure 2.34 shows a site map for the Pete the Painter Web site. The pages were created in earlier chapters. Use the Web pages indicated in this exercise from the paintercss folder. You have two tasks:

1. Add an alert message that welcomes the user to the Pete the Painter Web site when the user displays the home page (index.html).
2. Add form data validation to the estimate.html page such that if the name, e-mail address, or phone number input boxes are empty, the form will display an error message and will not submit.

Hands-On Practice Case

1. Add an alert message that welcomes the user to the Pete the Painter Web site when the user displays the home page (index.html).
   - Launch Notepad and open the index.html page from the paintercss folder.
   - Edit the `<body>` tag as follows:

     ```
     <body onload=
        "alert('Pete the Painter can handle your painting needs!');">
     ```
   - The load event occurs when the Web page begins to load in the browser. The `onload` event handler in this case pops up an alert message.

   Save the file and test it in the browser.
2. Add form data validation to the estimate.html page such that if the name, e-mail address, or phone number input boxes are empty, the form will display an error message and will not submit.
   - Launch Notepad and open the estimate.html page from the paintercss folder.
   - Add a script block to the `<head>` area as follows:

     ```
     <script type="text/javascript">
     <!-- <![CDATA[
        function validateForm()
        {
          if (document.forms[0].myName.value == "" )
          {
           alert("Name field cannot be empty.");
           return false;
          }  // end if
          alert("All data is valid.");
          return true;
        }  // end function validateForm
     // ]]> -->
     </script>
     ```

- Edit the `<form>` tag as follows:

```
<form method="post"
action="http://webdevfoundations.net/scripts/painter.asp"
onsubmit="return validateForm();">
```

- Add the `name` attribute to the input textbox that accepts the visitor's name. Sample code follows.

```
<input type="text" name="myName" id="myName" />
```

- Save the file and load it in a browser. Test it by clicking the submit button without input for the name input box. The alert box should pop up and the form should not be submitted. Test it again by entering information in the name input box and submit again. The alert box should pop up confirming that data is valid and the form should be submitted.

- Add data validation for the e-mail input box and phone number input box. Remember to add a name attribute to each XHTML input element. Feel free to copy the `if` statement from the name validation and edit to point to the appropriate input boxes. Open the JavaScript Console if necessary to find errors.

Save your file and refresh it in the browser as you add each validation to test it.

Prime Properties

See Chapter 2 for an introduction to the Prime Properties Case Study. Figure 2.38 shows a site map for the Prime Properties Web site. The pages were created in earlier chapters. Use the Web pages indicated in this exercise from the primecss folder. You have two tasks:

1. Add `onmouseover` event handlers to the listing numbers in the listings.html page such that when the user hovers the mouse pointer over the listing number, an alert message pops up reminding the user to click the contact link to contact an agent for more information.

2. Add the date last modified to the bottom of the listings.html page.

Hands-On Practice Case

1. Add `onmouseover` event handlers to the listing numbers in the listings.html page such that when the user hovers the mouse pointer over the listing number, an alert message pops up reminding the user to click the contact link to contact an agent for more information.

   - Launch Notepad and open the listings.html file from the primecss folder.
   - Add the following code around the listing number as follows:

```
<a href="#" onmouseover=
"alert('Please contact us for more information.');">
Listing #3432535</a>
```

   - Similarly, add this code to the second listing paragraph.

Save the file and test it in a browser. The alert box should pop up when you move the mouse pointer over the listing link.

2. Add the date last modified to the bottom of the listings.html page.

   • Launch Notepad and open the listings.html page if it is not already open. Modify the page as follows:

   • At the bottom of the page, after the e-mail link, add a script block that will write the following message to the document:

     This page was last modified on: date

   • Use the `document.lastModified` property to display the date.

Web Project

See Chapter 5 for an introduction to the Web Project case. Review the goals of your Web site and determine if the use of JavaScript to add interactivity would add value to your site. If so, add it appropriately. Check with your instructor for the required use of interactivity in your Web project.

Select one or more from the following:

   • Choose one of the examples from the chapter to add an alert message to grab the user's attention for important information.

   • Choose one of the examples from the chapter to add validation to a form in your Web site. Consider using one or more of the following validation rules:

     • Required information such as name, address, e-mail, phone number

     • Numeric information within bounds such as a quantity greater than 0 or age greater than 18

   • Consider adding image swapping as shown in the Fish Creek Animal Hospital Case Study in this section.

Decide where to apply the interactive technology to your site. Modify, save the page(s) and test it in the browser.

Web Developer's Handbook

In the following appendixes you will find a variety of resources that can help you be a more productive Web developer. Reference lists, tutorials, and links to Web resources are included.

APPENDIXES

Appendix A. XHTML Reference contains detailed information about XHTML, along with an introduction to XML syntax

Appendix B. Special Characters contains a list of codes needed to display symbols and other special characters on Web pages

Appendix C. CSS Property Reference contains a list of commonly used properties and values. In addition, links to additional resources available on the Web are provided

Appendix D. Comparison of HTML and XHTML discusses the syntax differences between these markup languages and provides side-by-side examples, including XHTML 1.1 syntax

Appendix E. Section 508 Standards lists the Section 508 standards and the textbook chapters that discuss related coding or design techniques

XHTML Reference

XHTML uses the tags and attributes of HTML along with the syntax of XML. For the most part, you will use the same tags and attributes in HTML and XHTML; the major change is the syntax and additional restrictions in XHTML. This section provides an introduction to XML syntax and a detailed list of XHTML tags and attributes.

You will notice that a number of XHTML elements and attributes are deprecated, which means that they are currently supported but will be removed from the language in the future. Most of the deprecated elements relate to presentation features such as alignment text configuration. The W3C recommends using CSS to replace the functionality of the deprecated components. This section will be helpful as a reference as you design Web pages. It contains five major areas:

- XML Syntax
- General XHTML 1.0 Syntax Guidelines
- Basic Tags
- Header Section Tags
- Body Section Tags

A.1 XML Syntax

An XML document must be well formed. A well-formed document is a document that adheres to the syntax rules of the language. Here are the key syntax rules of XML:

- XML is case-sensitive.
- An XML document must contain one or more elements.

- All XML elements must have an opening tag and a closing tag. All tags are enclosed in angle brackets.
- All XML elements must be properly nested. Nesting is the use of one or more elements inside other elements. The most recently opened element must be the next one closed.
- All attribute values in XML must be contained in quotes.
- All XML documents must begin with a statement declaring it to be an XML document.
- All XML documents must have opening and closing tags that form the root element within which all other elements in the document are contained. The `<html>` and `</html>` tags serve this purpose for Web page documents.

A.2 General XHTML Syntax Guidelines

Since XHTML uses the syntax of XML, it must follow the XML syntax rules. The following guidelines specify examples of how this is accomplished when using XHTML:

1. All XHTML elements (the tags and their attributes) should be lowercase.
2. The `<head>` and `<body>` tags are required.
3. The `<title>` tag is the first tag in the header section.
4. All container tags must use their opening and closing tags.
5. All self-contained tags (sometimes called empty elements) must be properly closed. For example, use `<hr />` instead of `<hr>`.
6. All attribute values should be contained in quotation marks.
7. All attributes should have values. For example, use

   ```
   <input type="checkbox" checked="checked" name="IE" id="IE"
   value="yes" />
   ```

   instead of

   ```
   <input type="checkbox" checked name="IE" value="yes" >.
   ```

8. Tags should not overlap, they should be properly nested. For example, use

   ```
   <strong><em>This is important</em></strong>
   ```

   instead of

   ```
   <strong><em>This is important</strong></em>.
   ```

9. The following tag-specific nesting restrictions apply:
   - A `<form>` tag cannot contain another `<form>` tag.
   - An `<a>` tag cannot contain another `<a>` tag.
   - A `<pre>` tag cannot contain any of the following tags: `<img />`, `<object>`, `<big>`, `<small>`, `<sub>`, or `<sup>`.

10. Formatting should be configured with style sheets and the `<font>` tag should be avoided.

11. The `name` attribute is deprecated in XHTML 1.0 as applied to bookmarks and named fragment identifiers. This has the greatest effect on `<a>` and `<map>` tags. XHTML uses the `id` attribute to configure bookmarks and named fragment identifiers.

12. The Web page document should begin with an XML declaration as follows:

    `<?xml version="1.0" encoding="UTF-8"?>`

13. The XML declaration should be followed with a Document Type Definition (DTD). There are three DTDs: strict, transitional, and frameset. The strict DTD is not usually used by commercial Web sites because it requires the exclusive use of CSS and does not allow deprecated elements. Use the transitional DTD for most XHTML Web page documents. Use the `Frameset DTD` for Web page documents that describe a frameset. For more information see Table A.1.

Table A.1 XHTML document type definitions

DTD	Description
XHTML 1.0 Transitional	`<!DOCTYPE html PUBLIC "-//W3C//DTD XHTML 1.0 Transitional//EN"` `"http://www.w3.org/TR/xhtml1/DTD/xhtml1-transitional.dtd">`
	This is the least strict specification for XHTML 1.0. It allows the use of both CSS and traditional formatting instructions such as fonts. This DTD is used for most of the coding in this text.
XHTML 1.0 Strict	`<!DOCTYPE html PUBLIC "-//W3C//DTD XHTML 1.0 Strict//EN"` `"http://www.w3.org/TR/xhtml1/DTD/xhtml1-strict.dtd">`
	Requires exclusive use of CSS. Does not allow any deprecated elements.
XHTML 1.0 Frameset	`<!DOCTYPE html PUBLIC "-//W3C//DTD XHTML 1.0 Frameset//EN"` `"http://www.w3.org/TR/xhtml1/DTD/xhtml1-frameset.dtd">`
	Required for pages using XHTML frames.

Note: In the Description column of this table, the number one (1) is set bold where it might otherwise be confused with the letter "el."

14. The root element (immediately after the DTD) must be an `<html>` tag that refers to the XML namespace and indicates the language, as shown in the following example:

    `<html xmlns="http://www.w3.org/1999/xhtml" lang="en" xml:lang="en">`

A.3 Basic Tags

The XML Declaration

`<?xml version="1.0" encoding="UTF-8"?>`

This XML declaration indicates that the document is based on the XML 1.0 standard. It also indicates that the character encoding (the internal representation of letters, numbers, and symbols) used by this document is UTF-8, a form of Unicode. This XML declaration will be the first line in each Web page that you write.

The DOCTYPE (DTD) Tag

The DOCTYPE or DTD tag identifies the markup language used in a document. Three DTDs are valid in XHTML. They are listed in Table A.1.

The `<html>` Tag

`<html></html>`

The `<html>` tag contains the code that describes the Web page document. The tag also describes the location of the documentation for the elements being used (called the XML namespace or `xmlns`). This additional information is added to the `<html>` tag in the form of an `xmlns` attribute. The `xmlns` attribute points to the URL of the XHTML namespace used in the document, the standard "http://www.w3.org/1999/xhtml." Optionally, you can add attributes to specify the language of the document (for example, English is "en," German is "de") to assist the interpreting of page content by search engines and screen readers. The lang and `xml:lang` attributes are used for this purpose. See http://www.loc.gov/standards/iso639-2/php/English_list.php for a list of language codes. The `<html>` tag is the first tag in a Web page after the DOCTYPE tag. For example:

```
<?xml version="1.0" encoding="UTF-8"?>
<!DOCTYPE html PUBLIC "-//W3C//DTD XHTML 1.0 Transitional//EN"
   "http://www.w3.org/TR/xhtml1/DTD/xhtml1-transitional.dtd">
<html xmlns="http://www.w3.org/1999/xhtml" lang="en" xml:lang="en">
   ... the rest of your web page goes here ...
</html>
```

The `<head>` Tag

`<head></head>`

The `<head>` tag is required and encloses the header area of a Web page document. The main purpose of the header area is to describe the document. The header usually contains `<title>` and meta tags. It may also contain JavaScript code and CSS.

The `<body>` Tag

`<body></body>`

The `<body>` tag is required and contains the body area of a Web page document—the part of the document that is displayed in the browser window. It can contain many different types of XHTML tags along with text and JavaScript.

A.4 Header Section Tags

The `<title>` Tag

`<title></title>`

The `<title>` tag contains the title of the page, which displays in the browser's title bar. This tag must be the first tag in the header section.

The <meta /> Tag

```
<meta name="keywords" content="a list of words that describe your site" />
<meta name="description" content="a brief description of your site" />
```

The self-contained meta tag has various purposes. Some meta tags such as keywords and description tags are used by search engines.

The <link /> Tag

```
<link />
```

The self-contained <link /> tag associates a Web page with an external style sheet. Table A.2 shows <link /> tag attributes and their values.

Table A.2 <link /> tag attributes

Attribute	Values	Usage
href	URL of the external stylesheet (.css file)	Identifies which style sheet is being used.
rel	"stylesheet"	Indicates the link is a style sheet.
type	"text/css"	Indicates the MIME type of the style sheet file.
media	"print", "screen", "aural"	Indicates the display medium (print, browser, screen reader, and so on) intended for display.

The <base /> Tag

```
<base />
```

The self-contained <base /> tag is most often used with pages displayed within a frameset. It sets a default target frame for the hyperlinks on the page. The attribute of target is set to the name of the window or frame in which all the hyperlinks should display.

The <script> Tag

```
<script></script>
```

This <script> tag configures a Web page to use client-side scripting. Table A.3 shows <script> tag attributes and their values.

Table A.3 <script> tag attributes

Attribute	Value	Usage
language	Usually "javascript"	Indicates the scripting language being used.
src	URL of the external script file, usually a .js file	Identifies the external file containing scripting commands. If this attribute is omitted, the script is contained between the **<script>** tags.
type	"text/javascript"	Indicates the MIME type of the JavaScript file.

An example follows:

```
<script type="text/javascript">
  ... JavaScript statements go here ...
</script>
```

When strict XML syntax is applied, any JavaScript statements should be surrounded by character data (CDATA) statements. This tells the XML parser to ignore the JavaScript statements as arbitrary character data and not to process them. The syntax is as follows:

```
<script type="text/javascript">
<![CDATA[
  ... JavaScript statements go here ...
]]>
</script>
```

Unfortunately, this generates a JavaScript error in many current browsers; therefore, it's not commonly used. This problem can be circumvented by accessing external JavaScript files, as shown here:

```
<script type="text/javascript" src="script.js">
</script>
```

In this case all the JavaScript statements are located in the external file called script.js and no CDATA statement is needed.

The `<style>` Tag

```
<style></style>
```

The `<style>` tag configures a Web page to use an embedded style sheet. The attribute of type is set to "text/css" and indicates the MIME type of the style sheet.

A.5 Body Section Tags

The <body> Tag

```
<body></body>
```

The `<body>` tag contains the body area of a Web page document. `<body>` tag attributes configure properties for the Web page. Table A.4 shows `<body>` tag attributes and their values.

Table A.4 `<body>` tag attributes

Attribute	Value	Usage
alink	A valid color; the W3C	Configures the color of the active hyperlinks recommends hexadecimal colors on the Web page. (Deprecated)
background	The name of an image file	Places a background image on the Web page. If the image is smaller than the page, it will be repeated, or tiled, on the browser window. (Deprecated)
bgcolor	A valid color; the W3C recommends hexadecimal colors	Configures the background color of the Web page. (Deprecated)
bgproperties	"fixed"	When combined with a background image, this property will fix the background image, simulating the effect of a watermark as the Web page visitor scrolls down the page. Only used by Internet Explorer.
leftmargin	Number of pixels	Configures the left margin of the Web page. Only used by Internet Explorer.
link	A valid color; the W3C recommends hexadecimal colors	Configures the color of the hyperlinks on the Web page. (Deprecated)
marginheight	Number of pixels	Configures the top margin of the Web page. Only used by Netscape.
marginwidth	Number of pixels	Configures the left margin of the Web page. Only used by Netscape.
text	A valid color; the W3C recommends hexadecimal colors	Configures the color of the text on the Web page. (Deprecated)
topmargin	Number of pixels	Configures the top margin of the Web page. Only used by Internet Explorer.
vlink	A valid color; the W3C recommends hexadecimal colors	Configures the color of the visited hyperlinks on the Web page. (Deprecated)

A.6 Core XHTML Attributes

The following attributes may be used to configure most XHTML elements. These attributes are valid in all elements except `base`, `head`, `html`, `meta`, `param`, `script`, `style`, and `title` elements.

The `class` Attribute

The `class` attribute is used to associate an XHTML element with a class that has been defined using CSS. The value should be a class name found in either the embedded or external CSS property rules utilized by the Web page.

The `id` Attribute

The `id` attribute uniquely identifies an element on a Web page. If is often used to associate an XHTML element with a unique `id` (unique to the particular page) that has been defined using CSS. The value should be an `id` name found in either the embedded or external CSS property rules utilized by the Web page.

The `style` Attribute

The `style` attribute configures inline style rules for an XHTML element. The value should be a valid CSS property rule.

The `title` Attribute

The `title` attribute configures a description of an XHTML element and its contents. This text may be accessed using a screen reader. Some browsers may display this text in a tooltip or in a summary list of elements (such as hyperlinks) found on a Web page.

A.7 Block-Level Elements

The `<p>` Tag

`<p></p>`

The `<p>` tag creates a paragraph of text. The browser displays the paragraph with a blank line before and after the paragraph. The `align` attribute specifies the horizontal placement of the paragraph. The values for the `align` attribute are `"left"` (default), `"right"`, and `"center"`. The `align` attribute is deprecated.

The Heading Tag

`<h1></h1>`

The heading tag contains headings and important points. The text contained between the heading tags is placed on its own line. There are six levels of heading tags: `<h1>` (the largest), `<h2>`, `<h3>`, `<h4>`, `<h5>`, and `<h6>` (the smallest).

The `align` attribute specifies the horizontal placement of the heading. The values for the `align` attribute are `"left"` (default), `"right"`, and `"center"`. The `align` attribute is deprecated.

The `<blockquote>` Tag

`<blockquote></blockquote>`

The `<blockquote>` tag indents text. The text contained between `<blockquote>` tags is indented from the left and right margins.

The `<div>` Tag

`<div></div>`

The `<div>` tag creates a separate division, or logical area, on a Web page. A line break occurs before and after the division.

The `align` attribute specifies the horizontal placement of the division. The values for the `align` attribute are `"left"` (default), `"right"`, and `"center"`. The `align` attribute is deprecated.

The `<span>` Tag

`<span></span>`

The `<span>` tag creates a separate logical area on a Web page without any line breaks before or after. It is often used to apply styles.

A.8 List Tags

The `<dl>` Tag

`<dl></dl>`

The `<dl>` tag creates a definition list. It is used with the `<dt>` and `<dd>` tags.

The `<dt>` Tag

`<dt></dt>`

The `<dt>` tag identifies a defined term in a definition list.

The `<dd>` Tag

`<dd></dd>`

The `<dd>` tag identifies a definition in a definition list.

The `<ol>` Tag

`<ol></ol>`

The `<ol>` tag creates an ordered, or numbered, list. It is used together with `<li>` tags. The deprecated `type` attribute on the `<ol>` tag configures the type of ordering. The deprecated `start` attribute configures the beginning value displayed in the list. Table A.5 shows `<ol>` tag attributes and their values.

Table A.5 `<ol>` tag attributes

Attribute	Value	Symbol
type	"1"	Numerals (the default)
	"A"	Uppercase letters
	"a"	Lowercase letters
	"I"	Roman numerals
	"i"	Lowercase Roman numerals
start	Numeric	Configures the beginning value displayed in the list

The `<li>` Tag

`<li></li>`

The `<li>` tag identifies a line item in ordered and unordered lists.

The `<ul>` Tag

`<ul></ul>`

The `<ul>` tag creates an unordered, or bulleted, list. It is used together with `<li>` tags. The deprecated `type` attribute on the `<ul>` tag configures the bullet displayed. Table A.6 shows the `<ul>` tag attribute and its values.

Table A.6 `<ul>` tag attribute

Attribute	Value
type	"disc" (default)
	"circle"
	"square"

A.9 Text-Level Elements

The `<font>` Tag

`<font></font>`

The `<font>` tag formats text. This tag is deprecated. Table A.7 shows the `<font>` tag attributes and their values.

Table A.7 `<font>` tag attributes

Attribute	Value	Usage
color	A valid color; the W3C recommends hexadecimal colors	Used to configure the color of the text. (Deprecated)
face	A valid font name such as `"Arial"` or `"Times New Roman"`	Configures the font type of the text. If the font specified is not installed, the text will display in the browser's default font. (Deprecated)
size	Absolute size: integers ranging from "1" to "7"; the default is "3"	Configures the size of the text. "1" is the smallest, "7" is the largest. (Deprecated)

Logical Style Tags

Logical style tags specify the logical use and format of the text. Table A.8 shows logical style tags and examples of their use.

Table A.8 Logical style tags

Element	Example	Usage
`<strong>`	**strong** text	Causes text to be emphasized or to stand out from surrounding text. Usually displays in bold.
`<em>`	*emphasized* text	Causes text to be emphasized in relation to other text on the page. Usually displayed in italic.
`<cite>`	*cite* text	Identifies a citation or reference.
`<code>`	`code` text	Identifies program code samples. Usually a fixed-space font.
`<dfn>`	*dfn* text	Identifies a definition of a word or term.
`<kbd>`	`kbd` text	Identifies user text to be typed. Usually a fixed-space font.
`<samp>`	*samp* text	Shows program sample output.
`<var>`	*var* text	Identifies and displays a variable or program output.

Physical Style Tags

Physical style tags configure the physical display of the text. Table A.9 shows physical style tags and examples of their use.

Table A.9 Physical style tags

Element	Example	Usage
`<b>`	**bold** text	Displays text in bold.
`<i>`	*emphasized* text	Displays text in italic.
`<big>`	big text	Displays text in larger than normal size.
`<small>`	small text	Displays text in smaller than normal size.
`<sub>`	subscript text	Displays in smaller text, below the baseline.
`<sup>`	superscript text	Displays text in smaller text, above the baseline.
`<strike>`	~~strikethrough~~ text	Displays text with a line through it. (Deprecated)
`<tt>`	`teletype` text	Displays text in teletype or fixed-space font.
`<u>`	<u>underlined</u> text	Displays text underlined; avoid using this because underlined text can be confused with hyperlinks. (Deprecated)

The `<br />` Tag

`<br />`

The self-contained `<br />` tag creates a line break. The next XHTML element is displayed on a new line. The values for the deprecated `clear` attribute on the `<br />` tag are shown in Table A.10.

Table A.10 clear attribute values

clear Attribute Value	Result
"left"	The next element is displayed on a new line under any existing element blocking the left margin.
"right"	The next element is displayed on a new line after any existing element blocking the right margin.
"all"	The next element is displayed on a new line after any existing element blocking either the left or right margin.

The <hr /> Tag

<hr />

The self-contained <hr /> tag creates a horizontal line on the Web page. Table A.11 shows the <hr> tag attributes and their values.

Table A.11 <hr> tag attributes

Attribute	Value	Usage
align	"left" "center" (default) "right"	Aligns the horizontal line on the Web page. (Deprecated)
color	A valid color; the W3C recommends hexadecimal colors	Configures the color of the horizontal line. Not in W3C Recommendation; originally only used by Internet Explorer.
noshade	"noshade"	Prevents a shadow from being displayed under the line. (Deprecated)
size	Number of pixels	Configures the height of the line. (Deprecated)
width	Numeric percentage	Configures a line that takes up a percentage of the width of the browser window. <hr width="50%" /> (Deprecated)
	Number of pixels	Configures a line that takes up an exact number of pixels in the browser window. <hr width="60" /> (Deprecated)

The <a> Tag

<a></a>

The <a> tag, called the anchor tag, creates a hyperlink. The text or image contained between the <a> tags is displayed by the browser as a hyperlink, as in the following example:

<a href="http://mycompany.com">My Company</a>

This creates an absolute hyperlink to the URL specified, in this case mycompany.com.

<a href="mypage.html">My Page</a>

This creates a relative link to the named file, in this case mypage.html.

```
<a href="mypage.html" title="My Page">My Page</a>
```

This creates a relative link to the named file, in this case mypage.html. It will also display the text associated with the `title` attribute in a tooltip alongside the link when the visitor places the mouse pointer on the link.

```
<a href="mailto:me@me.com">Send e-mail to me@me.com</a>
```

This creates a link to an e-mail address. If a default mail program is configured for the browser, the mail program will launch and get ready to send a message with the e-mail address provided, in this case me@me.com.

```
<a href="#top">Back to Top</a>
```

This creates an internal link to a bookmark or named fragment on the same Web page, in this case to the named fragment called `top`.

```
<a id="top" name="top"></a>
```

This identifies a portion of a Web page as a bookmark or named fragment, in this case, the named fragment called `top`. Older browsers such as Netscape 4 do not support the `id` attribute. The `name` attribute is used in addition to the `id` attribute to provide backward compatibility.

```
<a target="_parent" href="mypage.html">My Page</a>
```

This configures the window that the hyperlinked page will display in. The `target` attribute is most often used with frames. Table A.12 lists `<a>` tag attributes and their values. Values for the `target` attribute are shown in Table A.13.

Table A.12 `<a>` tag attributes

Attribute	Value	Usage
accesskey	A character on the keyboard that appears in the hyperlink description	Configures a hot key to activate the link without using the mouse pointer.
href	A valid URL or Web page file name	Creates a link to the named page or named element.
id	Text name, alphanumeric, beginning with a letter, no spaces	Uniquely identifies the element. This value can be used by a corresponding hyperlink.
name	Text name, alphanumeric, beginning with a letter, no spaces	Identifies the element. This value is used by a corresponding `<a>` tag with an `href` attribute. This is deprecated in XHTML but is included for backward compatibility.
tabindex	Numeric	Changes the order of the links accessed by pressing the Tab key. Default order is the order the links are placed on the page.
target	See Table A.13	Configures the window that displays the link. The default is the current window. See Table A.13.
title	A brief text description	Configures a brief text description that will display in some browsers when a mouse pointer is placed over the link.

Table A.13 `target` attribute values

`target` Attribute Value	Result
`"_top"`	Typically used to bust out of a frameset and display the hyperlinked page in the entire browser window.
`"_blank"`	Opens a new browser window to display the hyperlinked page.
`"_parent"`	Displays the hyperlinked page in the frame that contains the current frameset.
`"_self"`	Displays the hyperlinked page in the same window.
A valid frame name value configured in a frameset page	Displays the hyperlinked page in the named window

A.10 Graphic Tags

The <img /> Tag

`<img src="image.gif" />`

The self-contained `<img />` tag, called the image tag, displays an image file. Table A.14 shows `<img />` tag attributes and their values.

Table A.14 `<img />` tag attributes

Attribute	Value	Usage
`align`	`"left"` (default), `"right"`, `"top"`, `"texttop"`, `"middle"`, `"absmiddle"`, `"bottom"`	Aligns the image relative to the text on the page. (Deprecated)
`alt`	A brief text description of the image	Provides accessibility to visitors unable to view the image.
`border`	Number of pixels for image border; `"0"` prevents the border from being displayed	Configures the border area on the image. (Deprecated)
`height`	Number of pixels	Configures the height of the image. (Deprecated)
`hspace`	Number of pixels	Configures space to the left and right of the image. (Deprecated)
`id`	Text name, alphanumeric, beginning with a letter, no spaces	Identifies the image. The value must be unique and not used for other `id` values on the same XHTML document.
`longdesc`	URL of Web page with detailed description of the image	Used by some assistive technologies to provide accessibility to the information in the image.
`name`	Text name, alphanumeric, beginning with a letter, no spaces	Names the image so that it can be easily accessed by client-side scripting languages such as JavaScript. This attribute is deprecated in XHTML but is used to provide backward compatibility with browsers that support HTML.
`src`	Name of the image file (required)	Configures the image file to be displayed.
`title`	A brief text description	Configures a text description that will display when the visitor moves the mouse pointer over the image.

Table A.14 `<img />` tag attributes (*continued*)

Attribute	Value	Usage
usemap	The text name of an image map	Corresponds to the name value on the associated `<map>` tag.
vspace	Number of pixels	Configures space above and below the image. (Deprecated)
width	Number of pixels	Configures the width of the image.

The `<map>` Tag

`<map></map>`

The `<map>` tag is a container tag that identifies the beginning and the end of an image map. The `name` attribute is used to associate the `<map>` tag with its corresponding `<img />` tag. The `<img />` tag is configured with the `usemap` attribute to indicate which map to use. Table A.15 shows `<map>` tag attributes and their values.

Table A.15 `<map>` tag attributes

Attribute	Value	Usage
id	Text name, alphanumeric, beginning with a letter, no spaces	Identifies the map. This value is used by the corresponding `<img />` tag. The value must be unique and not used for other `id` values on the same XHTML document.
name	Text name, alphanumeric, beginning with a letter, no spaces	Identifies the map. This value is used by the corresponding `<img />` tag. This is deprecated in XHTML but is included for backward compatibility.

The `<area />` Tag

`<area />`

The self-contained `<area />` tag configures a hyperlink on an image map. Table A.16 shows `<area />` tag attributes and their values.

Each shape has a different syntax used to list the coordinates (coords) of the hyperlink area. See Table A.17.

Table A.16 `<area />` tag attributes

Attribute	Value	Usage
alt	A brief text description of the portion of the image	Provides accessibility to visitors unable to view the image.
coords	Numeric pixels; see Table A.17	Configures the coordinates of the clickable image area.
href	URL or Web page document name	Configures the Web page that will display when the area is clicked.
shape	`"rect"` indicates rectangle `"circle"` indicates circle `"poly"` indicates polygon	Configures the shape of the area.

Table A.17 `<area />` tag shapes and `coords` attribute values

Shape	Coords	Meaning
circle	`"x,y,r"`	The coordinates at point (**x**, **y**) indicate the center of the circle. The value of **r** is the radius of the circle.
poly	`"x1, y1, x2, y2, x3, y3"`, and so on	The values of each (**x**, **y**) pair represent the coordinates of a corner point of the polygon.
rect	`"x1, y1, x2, y2"`	The coordinates at point (**x1**, **y1**) represent the upper-left corner of the rectangle. The coordinates at point (**x2**, **y2**) represent the lower-right corner of the rectangle.

A.11 Table Tags

The `<table>` Tag

`<table></table>`

The `<table>` tag creates a table. Table A.18 shows `<table>` tag attributes and their values.

Table A.18 `<table>` tag attributes

Attribute	Value	Usage
align	`"left"` (default), `"center"`, `"right"`	Specifies the horizontal alignment of the table. (Deprecated)
background	File name of an image	Specifies the image to display in the table background. This attribute can also be used with `<tr>`, `<td>`, and `<th>`.
bgcolor	A valid color; the W3C recommends hexadecimal colors	Specifies the color of the background. This attribute can also be used with `<tr>`, `<td>`, and `<th>`. (Deprecated)
border	Number of pixels; `"0"` indicates no border	Specifies the size of the border around the cells.
bordercolor	A valid color; the W3C recommends hexadecimal colors	The color of the table border. Not part of the W3C Recommendation; originally only used by Internet Explorer.
cellpadding	Number of pixels	Specifies the amount of space between the cell's borders and its contents.
cellspacing	Number of pixels	Specifies the amount of space between cells.
rules	`"rows"` indicates the interior border displays between rows only `"groups"` indicates the interior border displays around groups (see `<tbody>`) only `"all"` indicates the default border display	Configures the interior border in a table.
summary	A text description of the contents/ organization/purpose of the table	Provides for accessibility. A visitor may obtain an overview of the table without reading it cell by cell. This attribute may be accessed by screen readers.

Table A.18 `<table>` tag attributes (*continued*)

Attribute	Value	Usage
`title`	A text description of the table	This brief description may be displayed as a tooltip by some browsers. This attribute may be accessed by some screen readers.
`width`	Number of pixels or a percentage	Specifies the width of the table.

The `<tr>` Tag

`<tr></tr>`

The `<tr>` tag creates a table row. Table A.19 shows `<tr>` tag attributes and their values.

Table A.19 `<tr>` tag attributes

Attribute	Value	Usage
`align`	`"left"` (default), `"center"`, `"right"`	Specifies the horizontal alignment of the cells.
`bgcolor`	A valid color; the W3C recommends hexadecimal colors	Specifies the color of the background.
`valign`	`"top"`, `"middle"` (default), `"bottom"`	Specifies the vertical alignment of the cells.
`background`	File name of an image	Specifies the image to display in the table row.

The `<td>` Tag

`<td></td>`

The `<td>` tag creates a table cell. Table A.20 shows `<td>` tag attributes and their values.

Table A.20 `<td>` tag attributes

Attribute	Value	Usage
`align`	`"left"` (default), `"center"`, `"right"`	Specifies the horizontal alignment of the cell.
`background`	File name of an image	Specifies the image to display in the table cell background.
`bgcolor`	A valid color; the W3C recommends hexadecimal colors	Specifies the color of the background. (Deprecated)
`headers`	The id value(s) of a column or row heading cell	Associates data cells with header cells. Accessed by non-visual browsers, such as screen readers
`colspan`	Numeric	Specifies the number of columns spanned by a cell.
`rowspan`	Numeric	Specifies the number of rows spanned by a cell.
`valign`	`"top"`, `"middle"` (default), `"bottom"`	Specifies the vertical alignment of the cell.
`width`	Number of pixels or a percentage	Specifies the width of the cell. (Deprecated)
`height`	Number of pixels	Specifies the height of the cell. (Deprecated)

The `<th>` Tag

`<th></th>`

The `<th>` tag creates a table header cell. Table header cells display text in bold font face and centered.

The `<caption>` Tag

`<caption></caption>`

The `<caption>` tag creates a caption for the table. The valign attribute is used to place the caption above or below the table. The values for the valign attribute are `"top"` and `"bottom"`. The deprecated align attribute specifies the placement of the caption. The values for the align attribute are `"bottom"`, `"center"`, `"left"`, `"right"`, and `"top"` (default).

A.12 Table Section Tags

The `<thead>` Tag

`<thead></thead>`

The `<thead>` tag defines a block of one or more table header rows.

The `<tbody>` Tag

`<tbody></tbody>`

The `<tbody>` tag divides a table into sections. It delineates one or more rows as a group. Use the rules attribute on the `<table>` tag to indicate the group visually.

The `<tfoot>` Tag

`<tfoot></tfoot>`

The `<tfoot>` tag defines a block of one or more table footer rows.

A.13 Frames Tags

The `<frameset>` Tag

`<frameset></frameset>`

The `<frameset>` tag configures a Web page that uses frames. The browser window is divided into multiple smaller windows so that multiple Web pages can be displayed and individually scrolled at the same time. Table A.21 shows `<frameset>` tag attributes and their values. Examples of the rows and cols attributes are included.

Table A.21 `<frameset>` tag attributes

Attribute	Value	Usage
`bordercolor`	A valid color; the W3C recommends hexadecimal colors	Specifies the color of the frame borders in the frameset. Default color is gray. Not part of the W3C Recommendation.
`cols`	Number of pixels, percentage, or `"*"` to indicate remaining window area	Reserves vertical areas (columns) of the browser window.
`frameborder`	`"0"` or `"1"` (default)	`"0"` indicates that no frame borders will be visible in the frameset. `"1"` indicates that frame borders will display in the frameset (default). Not part of the W3C Recommendation.
`framespacing`	Number of pixels	Specifies the width of the frame borders in the frameset. Not part of the W3C Recommendation.
`rows`	Number of pixels, percentage, or `"*"` to indicate remaining window area	Reserves horizontal areas (rows) of the browser window.
`title`	A brief text description	Provides a text description of the frameset that can be used by assistive technologies.

`rows` Attribute. The `rows` attribute specifies how the window will be divided vertically into rows of pixels (think of it as forming one row under another across the screen). The value can be a percentage of the browser window, a number of pixels, or the special asterisk value (*). The special asterisk value tells the browser to calculate the appropriate space for the window. A value is given for each frame row. There can be multiple frames. For example, to create a frameset with two horizontal frames—one using 25 percent of the window and the other using what is left of the window—the code is `<frameset rows="25%,*">`.

`cols` Attribute. The `cols` attribute specifies how the window will be divided horizontally into columns of pixels (think of it as forming one column next to another across the screen). The value can be a percentage of the browser window, a number of pixels, or the special asterisk value (*). The special asterisk value tells the browser to calculate the appropriate space for the window. A value is given for each frame column. There can be multiple frames. For example, to create a frameset with two vertical frames— one using 200 pixels of the window and the other using what is left of the window—the code is `<frameset cols="200,*">`.

The `<frame />` Tag

`<frame />`

The self-contained `<frame />` tag specifies a single frame or area of the window contained within a `frameset`. Table A.22 shows `<frame />` tag attributes and their values.

The `<noframes>` Tag

`<noframes></noframes>`

The `<noframes>` tag configures what will display on browsers and other user agents that don't support frames.

Table A.22 `<frame />` tag attributes

Attribute	Value	Usage
bordercolor	A valid color; the W3C recommends hexa-decimal colors	Configures the color of the frame border. Not part of the W3C Recommendation.
frameborder	`"0"` or `"1"` (default)	`"0"` indicates that no frame borders will be visible for this frame. `"1"` indicates that frame borders will display for this frame (default).
id	Alphanumeric, no spaces; the value must be unique and not used for other `id` values on the same XHTML document	This attribute is optional. It provides a unique identifier for the frame.
longdesc	URL of Web page with detailed description of the frame	Provides a detailed text description of the frame. This may be accessed by assistive technologies.
marginheight	Number of pixels	Configures the top and bottom margins for the frame.
marginwidth	Number of pixels	Configures the width of the right and left margins for the frame.
name	Text name, beginning with a letter, no spaces	Names the frame, so that it may be targeted by other frames. This is deprecated in XHTML but is used to provide backward compatibility with browsers that support HTML.
noresize	`"noresize"`	Does not allow a Web page visitor to resize a frame by dragging the frame border with the mouse.
scrolling	`"yes"`, `"no"`, `"auto"` (default)	Configures whether the frame has a scroll bar. The default is `"auto"`, which configures the browser to add a scroll bar automatically when needed.
src	URL or file name	Configures what Web page will be displayed in the frame (required).
title	Text phrase that describes the frame	Configures the title of the frame. This can be accessed by screen readers and is recommended by the W3C to improve accessibility.

The `<iframe>` Tag

`<iframe></iframe>`

The `<iframe>` tag configures an inline frame. This is a special scrolling area that displays a different Web page document. This does not need to be associated with a `frameset` and can be placed on the body of any Web page. Some older browsers, such as Netscape 4, do not support inline frames. If the inline frame is not supported, place content that should be displayed between the opening and closing `<iframe>` tags. Table A.23 shows `<iframe>` tag attributes and their values.

Table A.23 `<iframe>` tag attributes

Attribute	Value	Usage
align	`"left"` (default), `"right"`, `"top"`, `"middle"`, `"bottom"`	Specifies the horizontal alignment of the `iframe`.
frameborder	`"0"` or `"1"` (default)	`"0"` indicates that no frame borders will be visible for this inline frame. `"1"` indicates that frame borders will display for this inline frame (default).
height	Number of pixels or percentage	Height of the inline frame
id	Alphanumeric, no spaces; the value must be unique and not used for other **id** values on the same XHTML document	This attribute provides a unique identifier for the inline frame.
longdesc	URL of Web page with detailed description of the contents of the inline frame	Provides a detailed text description of the frame. This may be accessed by assistive technologies
marginheight	Number of pixels	Configures the top and bottom margins of the inline frame.
marginwidth	Number of pixels	Configures the width of the right and left margins of an inline frame.
name	Text name, beginning with a letter, no spaces	Configures the name of the inline frame. This is required when using the **target** attribute to configure hyperlinks. This attribute is deprecated in XHTML but is used to provide backward compatibility with browsers that support HTML.
scrolling	`"yes"`, `"no"`, `"auto"` (default)	Determines whether scrollbars will appear if the document displayed is larger than the size of the inline frame.
src	Valid file name of a Web page document (required)	Configures the name of the file to be displayed in the inline frame.
title	Text phrase that describes the inline frame recommended by the W3C to improve	Configures the title of the inline frame. This can be accessed by screen readers and is accessibility.
width	Number of pixels or percentage	Configures the width of the inline frame.

A.14 Form Tags

The <form> Tag

`<form></form>`

The `<form>` tag configures a form that can accept information from a Web site visitor. The form information may be processed using a server-side script or executable program. Table A.24 shows `<form>` tag attributes and their values.

Table A.24 `<form>` tag attributes

Attribute	Value	Usage
action	File name or URL of the program or script that will handle the form data	Specifies the name of the server-side program or script that will handle the form data.
id	Alphanumeric, no spaces; the value must be unique and not used for other **id** values.	Provides a unique identifier for the form.
method	"post"	Preferred by the W3C. Sends the form data to the Web server as a part of the entity body of the HTTP response. Form data is not visible in the URL.
	"get" (default)	Sends the form data to the Web server as part of the URL.
name	Text name, beginning with a letter, no spaces	This attribute is optional. It names the form so that it can be easily accessed by client-side scripting languages such as JavaScript to edit and verify the form information before the server-side processing is invoked. This attribute is deprecated in XHTML but is used to provide backward compatibility with browsers that support HTML.
target	See Table A.13	Specifies the window used to display the form response. The default is the current window. See Table A.13.

A.15 Form Element Tags

The `<input />` Tag

`<input />`

The stand-alone `<input />` tag configures an input element for a form. The attributes and their values determine the type of input element displayed on the Web page. Table A.25 shows `<input />` tag attributes and their values.

Table A.25 `<input />` tag attributes

Attribute	Value	Usage
type	"text", "checkbox", "radio", "hidden", "submit", "reset", "button", "image", "password"	Configures a specific form element (required).
accesskey	A character on the keyboard	Configures a hot key that immediately places the cursor on the form element.
checked	"checked"	Used with type="checkbox" or type="radio". Indicates that the form element is selected.
disabled	"disabled"	Prevents the cursor from being placed in the form element.

Table A.25 `<input />` tag attributes (*continued*)

Attribute	Value	Usage
id	Text name, beginning with a letter, no spaces	Provides a unique identifier for the form element that can be used to associate the element with a `<label>` tag or act as a named fragment identifier.
maxlength	Numeric	Configures the maximum number of characters allowed in a text input area.
name	Text name, beginning with a letter, no spaces	Names the form element. The name value is used by JavaScript, CGI, and other server-side processing.
size	Numeric	Configures the width in characters of a text input area on screen.
src	File name of an image	Used with `type="image"`
tabindex	Numeric	Changes the order of the form element accessed by pressing the Tab key. Default order is the order the form elements are placed on the page.
title	A brief text description	Configures a brief text description that will display in some browsers when a mouse pointer is placed over the element.
value	Text or numeric characters	Provides the value given to a form element, which is passed to the form handler.

The `<textarea>` Tag

`<textarea></textarea>`

The `<textarea>` tag configures a multiline text input area on a form, sometimes called a scrolling text box. Text contained within the `<textarea>` tags will be initially displayed in the scrolling text box. Table A.26 shows `<textarea>` tag attributes and their values.

Table A.26 `<textarea>` tag attributes

Attribute	Value	Usage
accesskey	A character on the keyboard	Configures a hot key that immediately places the cursor on the form element.
cols	Numeric	Configures the number of columns in the text area.
id	Text name, beginning with a letter, no spaces	Provides a unique identifier for the form element that can be used to associate the element with a `<label>` tag or act as a named fragment identifier.
disabled	`"disabled"`	Prevents the cursor from being placed in the text area.
name	Text name, beginning with a letter, no spaces	Names the form element.
rows	Numeric	Configures the number of rows displayed on the screen in the text area.

(*continues*)

Table A.26 `<textarea>` tag attributes (*continued*)

Attribute	Value	Usage
tabindex	Numeric	Changes the order of the form element accessed by pressing the [Tab] key. Default order is the order the form elements are placed on the page.
title	A brief text description	Configures a brief text description that will display in some browsers when a mouse pointer is placed over the element.
wrap	"virtual"	As the text is entered, the cursor automatically drops to the next line at the end of each line.
		When the text is sent to the server, there are no line breaks except where the [Enter] key has been pressed.
	"physical"	When the text is sent to the server, line breaks are placed where the text wraps to the next line in the scrolling text box.
	"off" (default)	The text is entered all on one line, and the [Enter] key must be pressed to drop to the next line. One line of text is transmitted to the server.

The `<select>` Tag

`<select></select>`

The `<select>` tag configures a select box to display a menu of items, sometimes called a list box or drop-down list box. The individual menu items are configured with `<option>` tags. Table A.27 shows `<select>` tag attributes and their values.

Table A.27 `<select>` tag attributes

Attribute	Value	Usage
accesskey	A character on the key-board	Configures a hot key that immediately places the cursor on the form element.
disabled	"disabled"	Prevents the cursor from being placed in the select list.
id	Text name, beginning with a letter, no spaces	Provides a unique identifier for the form element that can be used to associate the element with a `<label>` tag or act as a named fragment identifier.
multiple	"multiple"	Allows multiple selections from the list.
name	Text name, beginning with a letter, no spaces	Names the form element.
size	Numeric	Provides the number of elements to be displayed. If size is configured, the select list is displayed as a scrolling list. If size is omitted, the select list is a drop-down list.
tabindex	Numeric	Changes the order of the form element accessed by pressing the [Tab] key. Default order is the order the form elements are placed on the page.
title	A brief text description	Configures a brief text description that will display in some browsers when a mouse pointer is placed over the element.

The <option> Tag

`<option></option>`

The `<option>` tag configures an item within a select element. The text contained between the `<option>` tags is displayed in the select box. Table A.28 shows `<option>` tag attributes and their values.

Table A.28 `<option>` tag attributes

Attribute	Value	Usage
selected	"selected"	Configures an option selected by default.
value	Text or numeric characters	A value given to a form element that is passed to the form handler if the item is selected.

The <label> Tag

`<label></label>`

The `<label>` tag configures a text label that is associated with a form element. Table A.29 shows `<label>` tag attributes and their values.

Table A.29 `<label>` tag attributes

Attribute	Value	Usage
accesskey	A character on the keyboard	Configures a hot key that immediately places the cursor on the form element.
for	Corresponds to the value of an `id` attribute on a form element	Associates a text label with a form element.
title	A brief text description	Configures a brief text description that will display in some browsers when a mouse is placed over the label.

The <fieldset> Tag

`<fieldset></fieldset>`

The `<fieldset>` tag configures a group of form elements. It is used together with the `<legend>` tag.

The <legend> Tag

`<legend></legend>`

The `<legend>` tag is only used within the `<fieldset>` tag. It configures a text description for the `<fieldset>` grouping. Table A.30 shows `<legend>` tag attributes and their values.

Table A.30 `<legend>` tag attributes

Attribute	Value	Usage
accesskey	A character on the key-board	Configures a hot key that immediately places the cursor on the first form element in the legend area.
align	"top", "bottom", "left", "right"	Configures the alignment of the text legend. (Deprecated)
title	A brief text description	Configures a brief text description that will display in some browsers when a mouse pointer is placed over the text legend.

The `<button>` Tag

`<button></button>`

The `<button>` tag creates an area on the Web page that will act like a standard form button. It configures Web page content that is coded between the `<button>` and `</button>` tags as the form button. Table A.31 shows `<button>` tag attributes and their values.

Table A.31 `<button>` tag attributes

Attribute	Value	Usage
accesskey	A character on the key-board	Configures a hot key that immediately places the cursor on the area.
id	Text name, beginning with a letter, no spaces	Provides a unique identifier for the form element that can be used to associate the element with a `<label>` tag or act as a named fragment identifier.
name	Text name, beginning with a letter, no spaces	Names the form element so that it can be easily accessed by client-side scripting languages (such as JavaScript) or by server-side processing. The name should be unique.
title	A brief text description	Configures a brief text description that will display in some browsers when a mouse pointer is placed over the area.
type	submit	Functions as a submit button.
	reset	Functions as a reset button.
	button	Functions as a button.
value	Text or numeric characters	A value given to a form element that is passed to the form handler.

A.16 Miscellaneous Tags

The `<applet>` Tag

`<applet></applet>`

The `<applet>` tag is used to specify the beginning of an applet area in the body of a Web page. The closing tag, `</applet>`, specifies the ending of an applet area in the body of a Web page. Table A.32 shows `<applet>` tag attributes and their values. The `<applet>` tag and its attributes are deprecated.

Table A.32 `<applet>` tag attributes

Attribute	Value	Usage
`alt`	A text description of the applet.	Provides alternate content for visitors unable to access the applet.
`code`	The file name of a Java applet (.class extension); required	Configures the name of the applet file.
`codebase`	A folder name	Configures the name of the folder that contains the applet. This is needed if the applet is not in the same folder as the Web page.
`height`	Number of pixels	Configures the height of the applet area.
`id`	Alphanumeric, no spaces; the value must be unique and not used for other `id` values on the same XHTML document	Provides a unique identifier for the applet.
`width`	Number of pixels	Configures the width of the applet area.

The `<param />` Tag

`<param />`

The `<param>` tag is used to pass values or parameters to an object or Java applet. This tag is always used with either an `<applet>` or `<object>` tag.

The `<nobr>` Tag

`<nobr></nobr>`

The `<nobr>` tag is used to contain areas on a Web page, such as groups of images, which should remain on the same line regardless of the size of the browser window.

The `<pre>` Tag

`<pre></pre>`

The `<pre>` tag handles text in a special way. Any text contained between `<pre>` tags is considered to be preformatted text, such as computer program coding statements. Any line breaks or spacing will be preserved. This tag is rarely used.

The `<object>` Tag

`<object></object>`

The `<object>` tag can be used to place Java applets, sound, and other media on a Web page. It is a container tag and should be closed with an `</object>` tag. The `<object>` tag is part of the W3C standard; you should become familiar with its use. However, it is not as well supported by browsers as the `<embed />` and `<applet>` tags. Table A.33 shows `<object>` tag attributes and values that are used to display media files.

Table A.33 `<object>` tag attributes

Attribute	Value	Usage
classid	Uniquely identifies the player software. For QuickTime, it must be set to `"clsid:02BF25D5-8C17-4B23-BC80-D3488ABDDC6B"`	Identifies an ActiveX control that must be installed on the visitor's PC. If the ActiveX control is not installed, the browser can automatically download and install it.
codebase	Specifies a relative path for the location of the plug-in	For QuickTime and Internet Explorer, this value must be http://www.apple.com/qtactivex/qtplugin.cab— the location of the most recent version of the QuickTime player.
data	Valid file name, name of media file (required)	Provides the name of the file to be played.
height	Number of pixels	Specifies the height of media control console.
type	A valid MIME type such as `"audio/midi"`, `"audio/wav"`, and so on	Specifies the MIME type of the media file.
width	Number of pixels	Configures the width of media control console.

The `<embed />` Tag

`<embed />`

The `<embed />` tag is not part of the W3C XHTML 1.0 specification but it is included here because it is often used. The W3C recommends using the `<object>` tag instead. The `<embed />` tag can be used to place sound and other media in a Web page. It is a self-contained tag and does not have a corresponding closing tag. Table A.34 shows `<embed />` tag attributes and their values

Table A.34 `<embed />` tag attributes (*continued*)

Attribute	Value	Usage
align	`"left"`, `"right"`, `"top"`, `"bottom"`	Optional; aligns the media control console.
autostart	`"true"`, `"false"`	Determines whether the media will play automatically when the page is loaded. If omitted, media may not automatically play.
autoplay	`"true"`, `"false"`	Optional. Used by some media players, including QuickTime. Determines if the media will play automatically when the page is loaded. If omitted, media may not automatically play.
codebase	Specifies a relative path for the location of the plug-in	For QuickTime and Internet Explorer, this value must be http://www.apple.com/qtactivex/qtplugin.cab— the location of the most recent version of the QuickTime player.

Table A.34 `<embed />` tag attributes *(continued)*

Attribute	Value	Usage
controller	`"true"`, `"false"`	Optional. Indicates whether the media control console will display. Used with QuickTime.
controls	`"console"`, `"smallconsole"`, `"playbutton"`, `"pausebutton"`, `"stopbutton"`, `"volumelever"`	Configures the appearance of the media control console.
height	Number of pixels	Configures the height of the media control console.
hidden	`"true"`	Hides the default media console.
loop	Numeric value or `"true"` for continuous play (may not be uniformly supported)	Repeats the media file.
pluginspage	URL	Optional. Location of download page for plug-in.
src	Valid file name, name of media file (required)	Provides the name of the file to be played.
type	A valid MIME type such as `"audio/mpeg"`, `"audio/wav"`, and so on	Optional; specifies the MIME type of the media file.
width	Number of pixels	Configures the width of media control console.

The `<noembed>` Tag

`<noembed></noembed>`

The `<noembed>` tag is not part of the W3C XHTML 1.0 specification but it is included here because it is often used. The `<noembed>` tag is a container tag. It can appear after an `<embed />` tag to provide alternate content that may be used by browsers or assistive technologies such as screen readers.

The Comment Tag

`<!-- your comment goes here -->`

The comment tag is special in that anything between the opening `<!--` and the closing `-->` is considered to be a comment and is ignored by the browser. This tag can be used to document and describe XHTML.

The `<marquee>` Tag

`<marquee></marquee>`

The `<marquee>` tag is not part of the W3C XHTML 1.0 specification and only works in Internet Explorer. It displays text contained between the `<marquee>` tags in a scrolling fashion, like a movie marquee. Avoid using this nonstandard tag.

The `<blink>` Tag

`<blink></blink>`

The `<blink>` tag is not part of the W3C XHTML 1.0 specification and is only supported by Netscape. It causes the text contained between the `<blink>` tags to flash on and off—blinking. This is very annoying and should be avoided.

Special Characters

Special characters, or entity characters, such as the copyright symbol and the nonbreaking space, often appear on Web pages. Table B.1 lists a selection of special characters in order of numeric codes. The most commonly used special characters are shown in bold. The W3C's list of special characters is found at
http://www.w3.org/MarkUp/html-spec/html-spec_13.html.

Table B.1 Special characters

Entity Name	Numeric Code	Descriptive Code	Character
Quotation mark	`&#34;`	`&quot;`	"
Ampersand	`&#38;`	`&amp;`	&
Apostrophe	`&#39;`		'
Less than sign	`&#60;`	`&lt;`	<
Greater than sign	`&#62;`	`&gt;`	>
Nonbreaking space	` `	` `	a blank space
Inverted exclamation	`&#161;`	`&iexcl;`	¡
Cent sign	`&#162;`	`&cent;`	¢
Pound sterling sign	`&#163;`	`&pound;`	£
General currency sign	`&#164;`	`&curren;`	†
Yen sign	`&#165;`	`&yen;`	¥
Broken vertical bar	`&#166;`	`&brvbar;`		
Section sign	`&#167;`	`&sect;`	§
Umlaut	`&#168;`	`&uml;`	¨
Copyright symbol	`&#169;`	`&copy;`	©
Feminine ordinal	`&#170;`	`&ordf;`	ª
Left angle quote	`&#171;`	`&laquo;`	«
Not sign	`&#172;`	`&not;`	¬
Soft hyphen	`&#173;`	`&shy;`	-
Registered trademark symbol	`&#174;`	`&reg;`	®
Macron	`&#175;`	`&macr;`	¯
Degree sign	`&#176;`	`&deg;`	°
Plus or minus	`&#177;`	`&plusmn;`	±
Superscript two	`&#178;`	`&sup2;`	²
Superscript three	`&#179;`	`&sup3;`	³
Acute accent	`&#180;`	`&acute;`	´
Micro (Mu)	`&#181;`	`&micro;`	µ
Paragraph sign	`&#182;`	`&para;`	¶
Middle dot	`&#183;`	`&middot;`	·
Cedilla	`&#184;`	`&cedil;`	¸
Superscript one	`&#185;`	`&sup1;`	¹
Masculine ordinal	`&#186;`	`&ordm;`	º
Right angle quote	`&#187;`	`&raquo;`	»
Fraction one-fourth	`&#188;`	`&frac14;`	¼
Fraction one-half	`&#189;`	`&frac12;`	½
Fraction three-fourths	`&#190;`	`&frac34;`	¾
Inverted question mark	`&#191;`	`&iquest;`	¿

Table B.1 Special characters (*continued*)

Entity Name	Numeric Code	Descriptive Code	Character
Small e, grave accent	`&#232;`	`&egrave;`	è
Small e, acute accent	`&#233;`	`&eacute;`	é
En dash	`&#8211;`	`&ndash;`	–
Em dash	`&#8212;`	`&emdash;`	—

CSS Property Reference

Cascading Style Sheet properties that are commonly used to format and configure page layouts are listed in this section. Unless otherwise noted, each property applies to all XHTML elements.

You should find the information in Table C.1 and Table C.2 useful as a quick reference to commonly used CSS properties and values. However, these tables do not contain all the CSS properties and values. The W3C CSS2 Recommendation (http://www.w3.org/TR/REC-CSS2/) includes a Property Index with a complete listing of all CSS properties at http://www.w3.org/TR/REC-CSS2/propidx.html.

Table C.1 Cascading style sheet properties

Property

background-color

Common Values:	Valid hexadecimal color value, RGB color value, or color name.
Usage:	Configures the background color of an element.
Example:	`background-color:#cccccc;`

background-image

Common Values:	URL keyword with valid image file name
Usage:	Configures an image file as the background of an element.
Example:	`background-image:url(myimage.gif);`

background-position

Common Values:	Two percentages, numeric pixel values, or position values (`"left"`, `"top"`, `"center"`, `"bottom"`, `"right"`)
Usage:	Configures the position of the background image of an element.
Example:	`background-position:-100px -200px;`
	The first value configures the horizontal position and the second configures the vertical position starting from the upper-left corner of the container's box. Use negative values for a more abstract or artistic background effect.

background-repeat

Common Values:	`"repeat"` (default), `"repeat-y"` (vertical repeat), `"repeat-x"` (horizontal repeat), `"no-repeat"` (no repeat)
Usage:	Configures how the background image of an element will repeat (or be prevented from repeating).
Example:	`background-repeat:no-repeat;`

border

Common Values:	The `border-width`, `border-style`, and `border-color` values separated by spaces.
Usage:	Configures the border surrounding an element.
Example:	`border:1px solid #000000;`

border-bottom

Common Values:	The `border-width`, `border-style`, and `border-color` values separated by spaces.
Usage:	Configures the bottom border of an element.
Example:	`border-bottom:1px solid #000000;`

border-collapse

Common Values:	`"separate"`, `"collapse"` (default)
Usage:	Configures the table and cell borders to collapse into a single border or display with separate borders.
Example:	`border-collapse:collapse;`

border-color

Common Values:	Valid hexadecimal color value, RGB color value, or color name
Usage:	Configures the color of an element's border.
Example:	`border-color:#333333;`

Table C.1 Cascading style sheet properties *(continued)*

Property

`border-left`

Common Values:	The `border-width`, `border-style`, and `border-color` values separated by spaces.
Usage:	Configures the left border of an element.
Example:	`border-left:1px solid #000000;`

`border-right`

Common Values:	The `border-width`, `border-style`, and `border-color` values separated by spaces.
Usage:	Configures the right border of an element.
Example:	`border-right:1px solid #000000;`

`border-style`

Common Values:	`"none"` (default), `"double"`, `"groove"`, `"inset"`, `"outset"`, `"ridge"`, `"solid"`, `"dashed"`, `"dotted"`, `"hidden"`
Usage:	Configures the type of border around an element.
Example:	`border-style:dotted;`

`border-top`

Common Values:	The `border-width`, `border-style`, and `border-color` values separated by spaces.
Usage:	Configures the top border of an element.
Example:	`border-top:1px solid #000000;`

`border-width`

Common Values:	A numeric value (such as `1px`) or values `"thin"`, `"medium"`, `"thick"`
Usage:	Configures the width of a border around an element.
Example:	`border-width:3px;`

`clear`

Common Values:	`"left"`, `"right"`, `"both"`, `"none"` (default)
Usage:	Specifies the display of an element in relation to floating elements.

`color`

Common Values:	Valid hexadecimal color value, RGB color value, or color name
Usage:	Configures the foreground (text) color of an element.
Example:	`color:#0000ff;`

`display`

Common Values:	`"none"`, `"block"`, `"inline"`, `"list-item"`
Usage:	Controls how and if an element will display. Display set to `"none"` causes an element to not display.
Example:	`display:block;`

`font-family`

Common Values:	Valid font name or a font family such as `"serif"`, `"sans-serif"`, `"fantasy"`, `"monospaced"`, or `"cursive"`
Usage:	Configures the type of font used to display an element.
Example:	`font-family:Arial, Verdana, sans-serif;`

(continues)

Table C.1 Cascading style sheet properties (*continued*)

Property

font-size

Common Values:	Numeric value (**pt**, **px**, or **em**), percentage, absolute size (**"xx-small"**, **"x-small"**, **"small"**, **"medium"** (default), **"large"**, **"x-large"**, **"xx-large"**), relative size (**"smaller"**, **"larger"**)
Usage:	Configures the size of the font used to display an element.
Example:	`font-size:smaller;`

font-style

Common Values:	**"normal"** (default), **"italic"**, **"oblique"**
Usage:	Configures the style of the text.
Example:	`font-style:italic;`

font-variant

Common Values:	**"normal"** (default), **"small-caps"**
Usage:	Configures the display as regular text or in small capital letters.
Example:	`font-variant:small-caps;`

font-weight

Common Values:	Numeric value (**"100"**, **"200"**, **"300"**, **"400"**, **"500"**, **"600"**, **"700"**, **"800"**), relative value (**"normal"** (default), **"bold"**, **"bolder"**, **"lighter"**)
Usage:	Configures the boldness of the text.
Example:	`font-weight:400;`

height

Common Values:	A numeric value (**px** or **em**), percentage, or **auto** (default)
Usage:	Configures the height of an element.
Example:	`height:300px;`

left

Common Values:	A numeric value (**px** or **em)** or percentage
Usage:	Configures the distance in from the left to display an element.
Example:	`left:100px;`

line-height

Common Values:	Numeric value, percentage
Usage:	Configures the spacing allowed for a line of text. The value 200% configures double-spaced text.
Example:	`line-height:200%;`

list-style-image

Common Values:	URL keyword with valid image file name
Usage:	Configures an image to replace "bullets" in an XHTML list.
Example:	`list-style-image:url(myimage.gif);`

Table C.1 Cascading style sheet properties (*continued*)

Property

list-style-type

Common Values:	`"none"`, `"disc"`, `"circle"`, `"square"`, `"decimal"`, `"lower-roman"`, `"upper-roman"`, `"lower-alpha"`, `"upper-alpha"`
Usage:	Configures the type of "bullet" (list item marker) for an element in a list.
Example:	`list-style-type:circle;`

margin

Common Values:	*Shorthand Notation*: A numeric value (`px` or `em`), percentage, or `"auto"`
	Full Notation: Four numeric values (`px` or `em`), percentage, or `"auto"`. The values configure the margins in the following order (`margin-top`, `margin-right`, `margin-bottom`, `margin-left`).
Usage:	Configures the margin surrounding an element.
Example:	*Shorthand Notation*: `body { margin: 0}` (sets the page margins in the document to zero) *Full Notation*: `margin:0px 10% 0px 10%;`

margin-bottom

Common Values:	A numeric value (`px` or `em`) or percentage
Usage:	Configures the size of an element's bottom margin.
Example:	`margin-bottom:20px;`

margin-left

Common Values:	A numeric value (`px` or `em`) or percentage
Usage:	Configures the size of an element's left margin.
Example:	`margin-1eft:100px;`

margin-right

Common Values:	A numeric value (`px` or `em`) or percentage
Usage:	Configures the size of an element's right margin.
Example:	`margin-right:20px;`

margin-top

Common Values:	A numeric value (`px` or `em`) or percentage
Usage:	Configures the size of an element's top margin.
Example:	`margin-top:5px;`

max-width

Common Values:	A numeric value (px or em), percentage, or `"none"` (default)
Usage:	Configures the maximum width of an element.
Example:	`max-width:700px;`

(*continues*)

Table C.1 Cascading style sheet properties (*continued*)

Property

min-width

Common Values:	A numeric value (**px** or **em**) or percentage
Usage:	Configures the minimum width of an element.
Example:	`min-width:400px;`

overflow

Common Values:	`"visible"`, `"hidden"`, `"auto"` (default), `"scroll"`
Usage:	Controls the display of a block-level element if the element exceeds its set height or width.
Example:	`overflow:scroll;`

padding

Usage:	Configures the amount of padding associated with an element.

Shorthand Notation Option 1:

Common Values:	A numeric value (**px** or **em**) or percentage
Example:	`padding:20px;`

Shorthand Notation Option 2:

Common Values:	Two numeric values (**px** or **em**) or percentages. The first value configures the top and bottom padding. The second value configures the left and right padding.
Example:	`padding:10px 15px;`

Full Notation:

Common Values:	Four numeric values (**px** or **em**) or percentages. The values configure the padding in the following order (`padding-top`, `padding-right`, `padding-bottom`, `padding-left`).
Example:	`padding:10px 15px 10px 20px;`

padding-bottom

Common Values:	A numeric value (**px** or **em**) or percentage
Usage:	Configures the blank space between an element and its bottom border.
Example:	`padding-bottom:10px;`

padding-left

Common Values:	A numeric value (**px** or **em**) or percentage
Usage:	Configures the blank space between an element and its left border.
Example:	`padding-left:10px;`

padding-right

Common Values:	A numeric value (**px** or **em**) or percentage
Usage:	Configures the blank space between an element and its right border.
Example:	`padding-right:10px;`

Table C.1 Cascading style sheet properties (*continued*)

Property

padding-top

Common Values:	A numeric value (**px** or **em**) or percentage
Usage:	Configures the blank space between an element and its top border.
Example:	`padding-top:10px;`

position

Common Values:	`"relative"`, `"absolute"`
Usage:	Configures the positioning of an element. Used in combination with **left**, **right**, and/or **top** properties.
Example:	`position:relative;`

right

Common Values:	A numeric value (**px** or **em**) or percentage
Usage:	Configures the distance in from the right to display an element.
Example:	`right:20px;`

scrollbar-arrow-color

Common Values:	Valid hexadecimal color value, RGB color value, or color name
Usage:	Configures the color of the arrow on the scroll bar (Internet Explorer only).
Example:	`scrollbar-arrow-color:#ff0000;`

scrollbar-face-color

Common Values:	Valid hexadecimal color value, RGB color value, or color name
Usage:	Configures the color of the sliding scroll bar (Internet Explorer only).
Example:	`scrollbar-face-color:#00ff00;`

scrollbar-track-color

Common Values:	Valid hexadecimal color value, RGB color value, or color name
Usage:	Configures the color of the track the scroll bar slides (Internet Explorer only).
Example:	`scrollbar-face-color:#000000;`

text-align

Common Values:	`"center"`, `"justify"`, `"left"`, `"right"`
Usage:	Configures the alignment of text in an element. This applies to block-level elements.
Example:	`text-align:center;`

text-indent

Common Values:	A numeric value (**em** or **px**) or percentage
Usage:	Configures the indent of the first line of a block element.
Example:	`text-indent:10px;`

(*continues*)

Table C.1 Cascading style sheet properties (*continued*)

Property

text-decoration

Common Values:	"none", "underline", "overline", "line-through", "blink"
Usage:	Determines whether text in an element is underlined. This style is most often applied to hyperlinks to remove the underline.
Example:	text-decoration:none;

text-transform

Common Values:	"none", "capitalize", "uppercase", "lowercase"
Usage:	Modifies the appearance of text in an element.
Example:	text-transform:uppercase;

top

Common Values:	A numeric value (**em** or **px**) or percentage
Usage:	Configures the distance down from the top of the browser window document area to display an element.
Example:	top:100px;

vertical-align

Common Values:	A numeric value (**em** or **px**), percentage, values ("baseline", "sub", "super", "top", "text-top", "middle", "bottom", "text-bottom")
Usage:	Configures the vertical alignment of an inline element.
Example:	vertical-align:top;

visibility

Common Values:	"visible", "hidden", "inherit"
Usage:	Configures whether an element displays and takes up space on a Web page.
Example:	visibility:hidden;

width

Common Values:	A numeric value (**px** or **em**), percentage, or auto (default)
Usage:	Configures the width of an element.
Example:	width:60%;

z-index

Common Values:	A numeric value; the default value is 0
Usage:	The stack order of an element on a Web page. A higher value will display in front of elements with lower values.
Example:	z-index:10;

Comparison of HTML and XHTML

As you traverse the Web and view the source code of pages created by others, you may notice that the style and syntax of the coding is different from the XHTML syntax that you have been studying. Most likely, those pages were written following HTML syntax. If you view the source code of Web pages generated by Web authoring tools, you will also notice some syntax differences because in versions as recent as Macromedia Dreamweaver 4, these applications generated HTML instead of XHTML. Hope is in sight, however—the newer versions can be easily configured to generate XHTML code.

XHTML, eXtensible HyperText Markup Language, uses the tags and attributes of HTML along with the syntax of XML (eXtensible Markup Language). For the most part, you will use the same tags and attributes in HTML and XHTML; the major change is the syntax and additional restrictions in XHTML. These restrictions were added so that more efficient programs could be written to process Web pages automatically.

XHTML 1.0 Transitional is backward compatible with HTML 4.01, commonly referred to as HTML 4. XHTML 1.1 begins a shift in the language to a stricter form—finally removing elements and attributes that have been deprecated for years. For example, the font and name elements are no longer part of the XHTML 1.1 specification. There are also other syntax changes, which will be described in this section. According to the W3C (http://www.w3.org/TR/xhtml11/changes.html#a_changes), "the strategy is to define a markup language that is rich in structural functionality, but that relies upon style sheets for presentation." Under the "hood"—the W3C has reorganized the structure of XHTML into modules and has defined the language using XML.

Keep in mind that most Web pages currently use HTML 4 or XHTML 1.0 Transitional. Very few Web sites are coded in XHTML 1.1. However, it is good to be aware of the trends in XHTML. At the time this was written, the W3C was in the process of drafting two new versions of Web markup languages:

XHTML 2.0 and HTML 5. The XHTML 2.0 Working Draft was published in 2006 is currently under review. According to the HTML 5 Working Group's charter, their charge is to recommend a new standard that combines HTML and XHTML. The HTML 5 Recommendation is due in 2010. So for now, we'll concentrate on the differences between HTML 4, XHTML 1.0, and XHTML 1.1. This section will introduce you to some specific examples of syntax differences between HTML, XHTML 1.0, and XHTML 1.1. See http://lists.w3.org/Archives/Public/www-archive/2003Mar/att-0105/table.html for a comprehensive HTML/XHTML Element Attribute support table created by the W3C.

D.1 XML Declaration

Since XHTML follows XML syntax, each document should begin with an XML declaration. HTML 4 has no such requirement.

HTML 4.01

Not required

XHTML 1.0 and XHTML 1.1

```
<?xml version="1.0" encoding="UTF-8"?>
```

D.2 Document Type Definition

Both XHTML 1.0 and HTML 4 have three distinct document type definitions: strict, transitional, and frameset. XHTML 1.1 has one document type definition. The Document Type Definitions (DTDs) follow:

HTML 4 Strict DTD

```
<!DOCTYPE HTML PUBLIC "-//W3C//DTD HTML 4.01//EN"
   "http://www.w3.org/TR/html4/strict.dtd">
```

HTML 4 Transitional DTD

```
<!DOCTYPE HTML PUBLIC "-//W3C//DTD HTML 4.01 Transitional//EN"
   "http://www.w3.org/TR/html4/loose.dtd">
```

HTML 4 Frameset DTD

```
<!DOCTYPE HTML PUBLIC "-//W3C//DTD HTML 4.01 Frameset//EN"
   "http://www.w3.org/TR/html4/frameset.dtd">
```

XHTML 1.0 Strict DTD

```
<!DOCTYPE html PUBLIC "-//W3C//DTD XHTML 1.0 Strict//EN"
   "http://www.w3.org/TR/xhtml1/DTD/xhtml1-strict.dtd">
```

XHTML 1.0 Transitional DTD

```
<!DOCTYPE html PUBLIC "-//W3C//DTD XHMTL 1.0 Transitional//EN"
   "http://www.w3.org/TR/xhtml1/DTD/xhmtl1-transitional.dtd">
```

XHTML 1.0 Frameset DTD

```
<!DOCTYPE html PUBLIC "-//W3C//DTD XHMTL 1.0 Frameset//EN"
   "http://www.w3.org/TR/xhtml1/DTD/xhmtl1-frameset.dtd">
```

XHTML 1.1 DTD

```
<!DOCTYPE html PUBLIC "-//W3C//DTD XHTML 1.1//EN"
   "http://www.w3.org/TR/xhtml1/DTD/xhtml1.dtd">
```

The <html> Tag

XHTML requires that the root element (immediately after the DTD) is an <html> tag that refers to the XML namespace. HTML 4 has no such requirement. To assist the interpreting of page content by search engines and screen readers, use the lang attribute to indicate the spoken language of the Web page content. See http://www.w3.org/TR/REC-html40/struct/dirlang.html#adef-lang.

HTML 4

```
<HTML LANG="en">
```

XHTML 1.0

```
<html xmlns="http://www.w3.org/1999/xhtml" lang="en" xml:lang="en">
```

XHTML 1.1

```
<html xmlns="http://www.w3.org/1999/xhtml" xml:lang="en" >
```

D.3 Uppercase versus Lowercase

The HTML 4 standard recommends that tags and attributes use uppercase. The XHTML standard follows XML syntax, which requires lowercase.

HTML 4

```
<TABLE>
```

XHTML 1.0 and XHTML 1.1

```
<table>
```

D.4 Quotation Marks with Attributes

The XHTML standard requires that the values for all attributes are enclosed in quotation marks. This was valid in HTML 4, but not always done.

HTML 4

```
<TABLE BORDER=0>
```

XHTML 1.0 and XHTML 1.1

```
<table border="0">
```

D.5 Container Tags

The XHTML standard requires that both the opening and closing tags for all container tags are used. HTML 4 does not require this.

HTML 4

```
This is the first paragraph.<p>
This is the second paragraph.<p>
```

XHTML 1.0 and XHTML 1.1

```
<p>This is the first paragraph.</p>
<p>This is the second paragraph.</p>
```

D.6 Self-Contained Tags

The XHTML standard requires that all self-contained tags are properly closed using " />". HTML 4 does not require this.

HTML 4

```
This is the first line.<br>
This is the second line.
```

XHTML 1.0 and XHTML 1.1

```
This is the first line.<br />
This is the second line.
```

D.7 Attribute Values

The XHTML standard requires that all attributes are assigned values. HTML 4 allows some attributes, such as noresize or checked, to be minimized. Since these attributes only have a single value, HTML 4 does not require that the value is provided. The `name` attribute is not valid in XHTML 1.1.

HTML 4

```
<INPUT TYPE=RADIO CHECKED NAME=GENDER VALUE=male>
```

XHTML 1.0

```
<input type="radio" checked="checked" name="gender" id="gender"
  value="male" />
```

XHTML 1.1

```
<input type="radio" checked="checked" id="gender" value="male" />
```

D.8 Required Tags

XHTML requires the `<head>` and `<body>` tags. This restriction does not apply to HTML 4.

D.9 Header Section Tag Order

XHTML requires that the `<title>` tag is the first tag in the header section. HTML 4 does not have this restriction.

D.10 Nesting Tags

XHTML requires appropriate nesting of tags. The opening and closing container tags must nest and not overlap each other. This restriction does not apply to HTML 4.

HTML 4

```
<B><EM>This is important</B></EM>
```

XHTML 1.0 and XHTML 1.1

```
<b><em>This is important</em></b>
```

D.11 The `<font>` Tag

The `<font>` tag is deprecated in XHTML. It is recommended that Web developers use CSS to configure formatting instructions instead of the `<font>` tag. While CSS can be used with HTML 4, it is more common to see `<font>` tags.

HTML 4

```
<p><FONT FACE=ARIAL>This is a sentence.</FONT></p>
```

XHTML 1.0 and XHTML 1.1

```
<p style="font-family:arial,verdana">This is a sentence.</p>
```

D.12 Bookmarks

The name attribute is deprecated in XHTML as applied to bookmarks and named fragment identifiers. This has the greatest effect on <a> and <map> tags. HTML 4 requires the name attribute. It's a good idea for XHTML Web developers to include both attributes in order to be backward compatible with Web browsers that do not support XHTML. The name attribute is not supported by XHTML 1.1.

HTML 4

```
<A NAME=TOP>
```

XHTML 1.0

```
<a name="top" id="top"></a>
```

XHTML 1.1

```
<a id="top"></a>
```

D.13 JavaScript and the <script> Tag

XHTML considers JavaScript statements to be arbitrary character data (CDATA). The XML parser should not process them. The CDATA statement tells the XML parser to ignore the JavaScript. This is not part of HTML and not supported by many current browsers. A comparison of the XHTML and HTML 4 syntax follows:

HTML 4

```
<SCRIPT LANGUAGE="JavaScript" TYPE="text/javascript">
   ... JavaScript statements go here
</SCRIPT>
```

XHTML 1.0 Transitional

```
<script type="text/javascript">
   ... JavaScript statements go here
</SCRIPT>
```

XHTML 1.0 Strict and XHTML 1.1

```
<script type="text/javascript">
<![CDATA[
  ... JavaScript statements go here
]]>
</script>
```

An alternative way to use JavaScript on a Web page that is supported by XHTML standards is to place JavaScript statements in their separate (.js) file. This file can be configured by the `<script>` tag. HTML also supports this syntax.

HTML 4

```
<SCRIPT SRC="myscript.js" LANGUAGE="JavaScript"
  TYPE="text/javascript"></SCRIPT>
```

XHTML 1.0 and XHTML 1.1

```
<script src="myscript.js" type="text/javascript"></script>
```

D.14 Summary

As you can see from these examples, HTML 4 and XHTML code is quite similar. There are even programs such as HTML Tidy (http://www.w3.org/People/Raggett/tidy/) that can assist you in converting HTML to XHTML. Recent versions of Web authoring tools, such as Adobe Dreamweaver 8, generate XHTML code automatically. Visit the W3C's Web site (http://www.w3.org/TR/xhtml1/) for the most up-to-date information about XHTML.

APPENDIX

E

Section 508 Standards

Information technology created for use by federal agencies is required by Section 508 of the Rehabilitation Act to be accessible by individuals with disabilities. The Section 508 Standards applicable to Web page development, along with the textbook chapters that discuss coding and/or design methods applicable to each standard, follow.

§§ 1194.22 Web-Based Intranet and Internet Information and Applications

a. A text equivalent for every non-text element shall be provided (for example, via `alt`, `longdesc`, or in element content). Chapter 4, Chapter 11

b. Equivalent alternatives for any multimedia presentation shall be synchronized with the presentation. Chapter 11

c. Web pages shall be designed so that all information conveyed with color is also available without color, for example from context or markup. Chapter 4, Chapter 5

d. Documents shall be organized so they are readable without requiring an associated style sheet. Chapter 2, Chapter 3

e. Redundant text links shall be provided for each active region of a server-side image map. Chapter 4 introduces the use of client-side image maps—see the next standard.

f. Client-side image maps shall be provided instead of server-side image maps except where the regions cannot be defined with an available geometric shape. Chapter 4

g. Row and column headers shall be identified for data tables. Chapter 8

h. Markup shall be used to associate data cells and header cells for data tables that have two or more logical levels of row or column headers. Chapter 8

i. Frames shall be titled with text that facilitates frame identification and navigation. Chapter 13

j. Pages shall be designed to avoid causing the screen to flicker with a frequency greater than 2 Hz and lower than 55 Hz. Chapter 11

k. A text-only page, with equivalent information or functionality, shall be provided to make a Web site comply with the provisions of this part, when compliance cannot be accomplished in any other way. The content of the text-only page shall be updated whenever the primary page changes. Chapter 5, Chapter 11

l. When pages utilize scripting languages to display content, or to create interface elements, the information provided by the script shall be identified with functional text that can be read by assistive technology. Chapter 11

m. When a Web page requires that an applet, plug-in, or other application be present on the client system to interpret page content, the page must provide a link to a plug-in or applet that complies with §1194.21(a) through (l). Chapter 11

n. When electronic forms are designed to be completed on-line, the form shall allow people using assistive technology to access the information, field elements, and functionality required for completion and submission of the form, including all directions and cues. Chapter 9

o. A method shall be provided that permits users to skip repetitive navigation links. Chapter 5, Chapter 7

p. When a timed response is required, the user shall be alerted and given sufficient time to indicate more time is required. Chapter 11

See the following resources for more information about Section 508 Standards:

- http://www.section508.gov
- http://www.section508.gov/index.cfm?FuseAction=Content&ID=12#Web
- http://www.access-board.gov/sec508/guide/1194.22.htm
- http://www.webaim.org/standards/508/checklist

At the time this was written, the United States Access Board was in the process of conducting a review and update of the Section 508 standards. For the most current information, see http://www.access-board.gov/sec508/update-index.htm.

Answers

Chapter 1

Checkpoint 1.1

1. The Internet is a public, globally connected network of computer networks. An intranet uses the same protocols as the Internet, but it is a private network used to share organizational information and resources among coworkers.

2. The commercialization and exponential growth of the Internet that occurred in the early 1990s was due largely to three main events: the removal of the restriction of commercial use on NSFnet, the development of the World Wide Web by Tim Berners-Lee at CERN, and the development of a graphical browser (called Mosaic) at the NCSA. These events combined to provide the commercial incentive and an easy way to share and access information in a way that had never been experienced.

3. The Internet is a global, interconnected network of computer networks—a maze of phone lines, cable lines, and satellites that connect computers around the world. Information is stored in many formats on computers connected to the Internet. The World Wide Web, or Web, is a graphical user interface to some of the information stored on computers connected to the Internet—the computers that use HTTP to provide information in Web page format. The Web provides access to a portion of the information available on the Internet.

Checkpoint 1.2

1. An example of a Web client is a computer running a browser software application such as Internet Explorer. The computer is typically connected to the Internet only when needed. The Web browser software uses

HTTP to request Web pages and related resources from a Web server. A Web server is a computer that is continually connected to the Internet and that runs some type of Web server software application. It uses the HTTP protocol to receive requests for Web pages and related resources. It responds to these requests and sends the resources.

2. There are several protocols discussed in this chapter that use the Internet but do not use the Web. E-mail messages are transmitted using the Internet. SMTP (Simple Mail Transfer Protocol) is used to send e-mail messages. POP (Post Office Protocol) and IMAP (Internet Message Access Protocol) can be used to receive e-mail messages. FTP (File Transfer Protocol) can be used to exchange files (send and receive) with a computer connected to the Internet.

3. A URL (Uniform Resource Locator) represents the address of a resource that is available on the Internet. A URL consists of a protocol, a domain name, and the hierarchical location of the file or resource. An example of a URL is http://www.webdevfoundations.net/chapter1/index.htm. A domain name locates an organization or other entity on the Internet and is associated with a unique numeric IP address. A domain name is part of a URL.

Review Questions

1. b
2. a
3. a
4. b
5. a
6. True
7. False
8. True
9. False
10. XHTML
11. SGML
12. HTML
13. XML
14. network access points
15. TCP

Chapter 2

Checkpoint 2.1

1. HTML (Hypertext Markup Language), was developed by Tim Berners-Lee at CERN using SGML. HTML is the set of markup symbols or codes placed in a file intended for display on a Web browser. HTML configures a platform-independent display of information. Each markup code is referred to as an element (or tag).

2. XHTML is the most recent version of HTML. It was developed by the W3C to be the reformulation of HTML as an application of XML. XHTML combines the language of HTML with the syntax of XML. Like XML, XHTML is extensible and should be able to adapt to future needs.

3. The header section is located between the `<head>` and `</head>` tags on a Web page. This area is used to contain information that describes the Web page, such as the title of the page that will display in the menu bar of the browser window. The body section is located between the `<body>` and `<body>` tags. This area is used to code text and tags that show directly in the browser's display of the Web page. The purpose of the body section is to describe the contents of the Web page.

Checkpoint 2.2

1. The heading tag is used to display headings and subheadings of documents. The size of the heading is configured with the particular heading level used—ranging from 1 to 6. `<h1>` is the largest heading. `<h6>` is the smallest heading. Text contained between heading tags will be displayed using a bold font and will have a line break above and below.

2. Information on a Web page can be organized using ordered lists and unordered lists. Unordered lists display a small symbol or bullet in front of each item. Use the `<ul>` tag to configure an unordered list. Ordered lists by default display a sequence of numbers in front of each item. Use the `<ol>` tag to configure an ordered list. Configure individual items in both ordered and unordered lists using the `<li>` tag.

3. The purpose of the `blockquote` tag is to indent a section of text on a Web page. A line break is placed before and after the text. The text is indented from both the left and right margins.

Checkpoint 2.3

1. Physical file tags such as `<b>` describe font instructions rather than general styles for the presentation of information. The Web is accessed by many applications other than regular browsers. For example, a screen reader may interpret `<strong>` to indicate that the text should be spoken stronger than normal.

2. Special characters are used to display items such as quotation marks, greater than (>), less than (<), and the copyright symbol © on a Web page. These special characters, sometimes called entity characters, are interpreted by the browser when the page is rendered.

3. Use an absolute link to display a Web page document from a Web site other than your own. The http protocol is used in the `href` value. Example:

   `<a href="http://www.google.com">Google</a>`

4. Use a relative link to display a Web page document from your Web site. The http protocol is not used in the `href` value.

   Example: `<a href="contact.htm">Contact Us</a>`

Review Questions

1. c
2. d
3. c
4. c
5. b
6. b
7. c
8. c
9. b
10. b
11. indent text
12. special characters
13. `<em>`
14. ` `
15. Not everyone has an e-mail program configured with their browser. By placing the e-mail address in both places, you increase usability for all your visitors.

Chapter 3

Checkpoint 3.1

1. Reasons to use CSS on a Web page include the following: greater control of typography and page layout, separation of style from structure, potentially smaller Web page documents, and easier site maintenance.

2. Since visitors may set their browsers to certain colors, when changing a text color or a background color it is a good idea to configure the text color and the background color properties to provide good contrast between text and background.

3. Embedded styles are coded once in the header section of the Web page and apply to the entire page. This is more efficient than coding individual styles on HTML elements using inline styles.

Checkpoint 3.2

1. Embedded styles can be used to configure the text and color formatting for an entire Web page. Embedded styles are placed in the header section of a Web page. The `<style>` tag is used to contain the CSS selectors and properties that configure the embedded styles.

2. External styles can be used to configure the text and color formatting for some or all of the pages on a Web site. This provides a single place for the formatting information. This single file can be changed and all the Web pages associated with it will display the new styles the next time they are rendered in a browser. External styles are placed in a separate text file using a .css file extension. Web pages use the `<link />` tag to indicate that they are using an external style sheet.

3. `<link rel="stylesheet" href="mystyles.css" type="text/css" />`

Review Questions

1. b
2. a
3. d
4. b
5. c
6. c
7. b
8. d
9. a
10. b
11. `<span>`
12. not uniformly
13. `text-align`
14. `<div>`
15. 1996

Chapter 4

Checkpoint 4.1

1. It is reasonable to code pages that look similar on various browsers; it is not reasonable to try to code pages that look exactly the same on various browsers and operating systems. As shown in this chapter, even a simple horizontal rule displays differently. Typically, Web developers code pages that look best on the browser and operating system most often used by their visitors. These pages should also look acceptable on other platforms. This is called "degrading gracefully." Look for more Web design tips in Chapter 5.

2. The first style rule is missing an ending semicolon (;).

3. True. CSS can be utilized to configure color, text, and even visual elements such as rectangular shapes and lines (with the `border` property).

Checkpoint 4.2

1. CSS `background-image` property configures the file that is displayed. The CSS `background-repeat` property configures the way the image is displayed on the page.

    Suggested solution:

    ```
    h1 { background-image: url(circle.jpg);
         background-repeat: no-repeat;
    }
    ```

2. The CSS `background-image` property configures the file that is displayed. The CSS `background-repeat` property configures the way the image is displayed on the page.

Suggested solution:

```
body { background-image: url(bg.gif);
       background-repeat: repeat-y;
}
```

3. False. While using `border= "0"` on an image element for a graphic configured as an image link will eliminate the default blue border from displaying it is not the only method to prevent the border from display. An alternate technique is to use CSS to configure the `img` selector's `border` property to the value `0`.

Checkpoint 4.3

1. Answers will vary depending on the site that you choose to review. Suggested solution: The page reviewed is the home page of a travel soccer league. The URL is http://www.alithsa.org. Image links are used for the main navigation of the site. Each image link contains a rectangle with text and a soccer ball. There is good contrast between the black text and the background color of either yellow or green. Yellow background is used to indicate the current page. This page would not be easily accessible to a visitor who is site-challenged because of the `alt` attribute values used. Currently, every graphic has the same value for the `alt` attribute, "Picture". To improve accessibility the `alt` attribute values on each image tag should be modified to contain brief, descriptive phrases. On the plus side, the page does display plain text links in the footer section. The images used as navigation links on this page contribute to the fun, sporty attitude of the site. The accessibility of the page needs to be improved.

2. The elements `<img />`, `<map>`, and `<area />`—work together to create a functioning image map. The `<img />` tag configures the image that will be used for the map and contains a `usemap` attribute whose value corresponds to the `id` value on the `<map>` tag associated with the image. The `<map>` tag is a container tag and surrounds one or more `<area />` tags. There is one self-contained `<area />` tag for each clickable hotspot on the image map. See the working example on the textbook Web site at http://webdevfoundations.net/4e/chapter4.html.

3. False. There is a trade-off between the quality of the image and the file size. The goal should be to save images using the smallest file size that provides acceptable display quality.

Review Questions

1. b
2. c
3. b
4. b
5. a
6. c
7. d

8. a

9. b

10. d

11. tiled

12. text links

13. thumbnail

14. Create them using a graphics application, download them from a free site, purchase and download them from a graphics site, purchase a graphics collection on CD, take digital photographs, scan photographs, scan drawings, or hire a graphic designer to create graphics.

15. image map

Chapter 5

Checkpoint 5.1

1. The four basic principles of design are repetition, contrast, proximity, and alignment. Descriptions of school home pages and how these principles are applied will vary.

2. http://www.walmart.com is an e-commerce site. It is designed to appeal to the general public—note the white background and high contrast and use of tabbed navigation, product hierarchy, and site search. This meets the needs of its target audience—teen and adult shoppers. http://www.sesameworkshop.org/sesamestreet/ is geared toward young children and their parents. It is bright and colorful with much interactivity and animation, which is appealing to the target audience. http://www.mugglenet.com/ is a fan site designed to appeal to teens and young adults. It is a dark, mysterious site with much interaction—the forums are very busy. This site appeals to its niche audience.

3. Answers will vary.

Checkpoint 5.2

1. Answers will vary.

2. Best practices for writing for the Web include the following: short paragraphs, bullet points, common fonts, white space, multiple columns if possible, bold or emphasized important text, and correct spelling and grammar.

   Answers will vary. The following suggested solution adds interest with bullet points, places emphasis on important phrases, and includes editing of the original text:

   Acme, Inc. is a new laboratory instrument repair and service company. Our staff at this time has a combined total of 30 plus years of specimen preparation instrumentation service and repair.

   • **EPA Refrigeration Certified**

     Acme, Inc. technicians are factory trained and equipped with the best diagnostic and repair equipment available.

- **Fully Insured**

  Our workers are fully covered by workman's compensation insurance.

  A proof of insurance certificate can be provided upon request.

- **Convenient Location**

  Repair shop facilities and offices located in Chicago, Illinois.

- **Service History**

  Your equipment is important to us.

  A detailed repair history is kept and available to our service technicians.

- **Rates**

  Labor and Travel $100.00 per hour

  2 hour minimum

  $0.40 per mile and all related expenses

  Parts are not included

3. Best practices for using graphics on Web pages include the following: careful choice of colors (Web Safe Color Palette is recommended for the most similar cross-platform display), use of necessary images only, use of images as small as possible, a usable site even if images are not displayed, and use of the `alt` attribute to configure text descriptions for images.

   Recommendations for school home pages will vary.

Review Questions

1. c
2. b
3. b
4. b
5. d
6. d
7. a
8. a
9. c
10. b
11. hierarchical
12. white space
13. adds value
14. will not
15. Web Accessibility Initiative (WAI)

Chapter 6

Checkpoint 6.1

1. Answers will vary. They could include the following: ease of site maintenance, separation of style from structure, increased accessibility, support of the Semantic Web, smaller documents, increased page layout control, support of multiple media types, and greater typography control.

2. Relative positioning allows you to alter the position of an element in relation to where it would otherwise be displayed using normal flow. Absolute positioning allows you to specify by pixels the exact location of an element in a Web page.

3. The `z-index` property provides flexibility in the display of elements. When using XHTML only there is no easy way to "stack" elements other than configuring backgrounds for pages or tables. The `z-index` property configures the stacking order of elements on a Web page. The default `z-index` value is `0`. Elements with higher `z-index` values will appear stacked on top of elements with lower `z-index` values rendered on the same position of the page.

Checkpoint 6.2

1. The page layout is liquid. Attributes of liquid page design include the following: pages take up 100 percent of the browser window—there is no blank margin on the left or right side of the page. The middle area expands and contracts when the page is resized. The content flows to fill whatever size window is used to display it.

2. Answers will vary. Some of the suggestions listed in the debugging section may be used.

3. Configure the XHTML tag as a selector if the style is expected to be applied every time that tag is used. Configure an id if the style is for a specific element that is expected to occur only once on a page. Configure a class if the style is expected to be applied to a variety of different XHTML elements.

Review Questions

1. a
2. a
3. b
4. b
5. d
6. c
7. c
8. b
9. c
10. b
11. id

12. left
13. margin
14. left, right, top
15. class

Chapter 7

Checkpoint 7.1

1. Organizing a Web site into folders can help increase productivity by organizing the files into file type (such as images or media), file function (Web page or script), and/or Web site section (products, services, and so on). Using folders and subfolders can be helpful when a project team (see Chapter 10) is developing a large Web site.

2. Since a navigation menu is a list of links, it is semantically correct to configure the menu using an unordered list. This technique is popular among Web developers.

3. There are a number of approaches to handle this. Perhaps the most straightforward one is to create a special class and configure the pseudo-classes for use with that class. Apply this class to the navigation links. This will allow the "regular" anchor tags to use the default configuration and the navigation anchor tags (using the class) to use the special configuration. In the following example, the class intended for the navigation links is called nav.

```
.nav { border: 1px solid #cccccc;
       padding: 3px 15px;
       width: 100px;
       color: #FFFFFF;
       background-color: #006600;
       font-family: Arial, Helvetica, sans-serif;
       font-size: 110%;
       font-weight: bold;
       text-align: center;
       text-decoration: none;
}
a.nav:link     { color : #FFFFFF; }
a.nav:visited  { color : #CCCCCC; }
a.nav:hover    { color : #66CC33; }
```

The XHTML for a navigation link is as follows:

```
<a class="nav" href="services.html">Services</a>
```

Checkpoint 7.2

1. The Web developer has the best of both worlds—the ability to configure both print and screen media.

2. Configure the XHTML selector if the style is expected to be applied every time that element is used. Configure an id if the style is for a specific element that is

expected to occur only once on a page. Configure a class if the style is expected to be applied to a variety of different XHTML elements.

3. This follows the "cascade": external styles, embedded styles, inline styles, XHTML attributes.

Review Questions

1. a
2. a
3. c
4. b
5. c
6. c
7. b
8. d
9. c
10. d
11. `media="print"`
12. margin
13. hover
14. target
15. precedence

Chapter 8

Checkpoint 8.1

1. Tables are often used to organize information and to format an entire Web page.

2. The `cellspacing` attribute configures the amount of empty space between the cells in a table. The `cellpadding` attribute configures the amount of empty space between the information contained within the cells and the edges of the cells.

3. There are a number of coding techniques that improve the accessibility of a table. These include the `summary` attribute, the `title` attribute, and configuring headers for columns or rows.

Checkpoint 8.2

1. Web site visitors use monitors with different resolutions. A Web page layout configured with a table using a percentage width is flexible. Examples will vary.

2. A Web page layout configured with a table using a fixed width will appear consistent when displayed on monitors with different resolutions. Often these pages are centered in the browser window. Examples will vary.

3. True. Tables can be nested within other tables. Nested tables are often used to organize information on a Web page document with a page layout configured by a table.

Review Questions

1. c
2. b
3. c
4. c
5. b
6. b
7. b
8. d
9. c
10. `border`
11. `valign`
12. larger
13. `summary or title`
14. `padding`
15. Although XHTML tables are still often used to configure page layout, CSS is a more modern and preferred method to configure page layout. Advantages of CSS include ease of maintenance and smaller Web page files (due to less XHTML code).

Chapter 9

Checkpoint 9.1

1. While either solution would be appropriate, the solution that uses three input boxes (first name, last name, and e-mail address) is the more flexible solution. These separate values could be stored in a database by server-side processing where they could easily be selected and placed into personalized e-mail messages. This provides the most useful functionality of the collected information in future manipulations.

2. There are a number of possible solutions for this design question. If the responses are short and about equal length, perhaps a group of radio buttons would be appropriate. If the responses are lengthy or of widely varying lengths, a select list would be a good choice. Radio groups can accept only one response per group. Select lists by default accept only one response. Check boxes would not be appropriate because they allow more than one response to be selected.

3. False. In a radio button group, the `name` attribute is used by the browser to process separate elements as a group.

Checkpoint 9.2

1. The `<fieldset>` tag creates a visual border around the elements contained within the fieldset. This can help to organize form elements and increase the

usability of the form. However, this tag is not supported by all browsers. Test the form to verify that it is still usable even if the browser ignores the `<fieldset>` tag. The `<legend>` tag is used to provide a text description of the area bounded by the `<fieldset>` tag. This further serves to increase the usability of the form for visitors using browsers that support these tags.

2. The `accesskey` attribute allows a visitor to select an element immediately by using the keyboard instead of a mouse. This improves the accessibility of the page and can be very helpful to mobility-impaired visitors. The W3C recommends providing a visual cue of an underlined letter, bold letter, or message that indicates the hot keys to press to activate an element.

3. The Web designer and client decide which is used—standard submit button, image button, or a button tag. However, it makes sense to use the simplest possible technology that provides the needed functionality. In most cases, this is the standard submit button. The submit button's accessibility can be increased by configuring it with an `accesskey` attribute. Visually challenged visitors using a screen reader will hear that a submit button has been encountered. Submit buttons automatically invoke the server-side processing configured in the form tag.

   An image button will also automatically invoke the server-side processing configured for the form and can be more accessible if configured with the `alt` and `accesskey` attributes. Unless there is a very good reason or a very insistent client, avoid the `<button>` tag—why make a simple submit button so complex? If needed, configure the elements contained within the button area with attributes to improve accessibility such as `alt` and `accesskey` where appropriate.

Checkpoint 9.3

1. CGI (Common Gateway Interface) is a standard method for Web pages to request special processing on the Web server, such as querying databases, sending e-mails, or handling form data. CGI provides a standard way for a Web server to pass a Web visitor request to a program or script stored on the server, receive a response from the program or script, and send that response to the Web browser for display.

2. Suggested solution:

```
<form method="post"
   action="http://webdevfoundations.net/scripts/subscribe.asp"  >
   First Name: <input type="text" name="fname" id="fname" /><br />
   Last Name: <input type="text" name="lname" id="lname" /><br />
   E-mail: <input type="text" name="email" id="email" /><br />
   <input type="submit" />
</form>
```

3. The server-side script developer and the Web page designer must work together to get both parts of the form processing—the front-end Web page and the back-end server-side script—working together. They need to communicate regarding the method (get or post) to be used by the form, and the location of the server-side script. Since the names of the form elements are often used by the server-side script as variable names, the form element names are usually specified at this time.

Review Questions

1. d
2. a
3. b
4. b
5. c
6. b
7. a
8. d
9. c
10. d
11. `maxlength`
12. `<fieldset>`
13. `name`
14. This technique should be avoided because it presents an unprofessional image and can be inconvenient for Web page visitors. Its success depends on a visitor wanting to use the e-mail application configured with his or her browser. The visitor may not have configured an e-mail application or may not want to use the e-mail application that was configured. This technique can decrease the usability of a form.
15. Forms accept information from Web page visitors, such as a search keyword, newsletter subscription information, online ordering information, general feedback, and others.

Chapter 10

Checkpoint 10.1

1. The project manager directs the Web site development process—creating the project plan and schedule. He or she must keep the big picture in mind while communicating with the staff and coordinating team activities. The project manager is accountable for meeting project milestones and producing results.

2. A large-scale Web project is much more than brochure-ware—it is often a complex information application that the company depends on. This needs the special talents of a wide variety of individuals—including experts in graphics, organization, writing, marketing, coding, database administration, and so on—one or two people simply cannot fulfill all these roles and create a quality Web site.

3. Answers will vary. Different testing techniques include the unit testing done by individual Web developers, automated testing performed by link checker programs, code testing and validation performed by code validation programs, and usability testing achieved by watching typical Web visitors use a Web site to perform tasks.

Checkpoint 10.2

1. A virtual Web host that offers reliability and scalability would meet the needs of a small company for their initial Web presence. The Web host chosen should offer higher-end packages with scripting, database, and e-commerce capabilities to allow for future growth.

2. A dedicated Web server is owned and supported by the Web host company. The client company may choose to administer it or may pay the Web host company to perform this task. A co-located server is owned by the client company and housed at the Web host provider. This offers both the advantage of a reliable Internet connection at the Web host and full control of the administration and support of the Web server.

3. If your Web site is down and your Web host is not responding to technical support requests, it doesn't matter that you are saving $5.00 per month. When comparing Web host plans, check prices to know the currently prevailing fees. If the charges of a particular Web host seem abnormally low the company is probably cutting corners. Do not base your choice on price alone.

Review Questions

1. d
2. a
3. a
4. b
5. d
6. a
7. d
8. c
9. a
10. c
11. usability testing
12. graphic designer
13. UNIX and Linux
14. A careful review of your competitor's Web presence helps you design a site that will stand out from the rest and be more appealing to your shared customer base. Note both the good and bad components of your competitors' sites.
15. Contacting technical support can give you a general idea of the responsiveness of the Web host provider to issues and problems. If the technical support staff is slow getting back to you at this point, don't be surprised if you get the same type of service when you have a problem and need immediate help. While not fail-safe, a quick response to a simple question at least gives the appearance of a well-organized, professional, and responsive technical support staff.

Chapter 11

Checkpoint 11.1

1. Answers will vary, and will include RealPlayer, Windows Media Player, Apple QuickTime, Adobe Reader, Adobe Flash Player, and Adobe Shockwave Player. Review Section 11.1 Helper Applications and Plug-Ins for more information.

2. Issues include bandwidth, unreliability of the delivery of the media due to platform, browser, and plug-in issues, and accessibility. It is a good idea to have alternate content available that does not rely on media alone.

3. True. Issues arise all the time with browsers, operating systems, and plug-ins/players. Visit the plug-in or player's Web site for the most current information on successfully invoking a plug-in.

Checkpoint 11.2

1. Flash can be used to add interactive features, such as menus and banner ads to Web pages. Flash can also be used create an entire Web site. Uses of Flash seem to be limited only by our imaginations.

2. Java applets can be used for a variety of purposes, including navigation, image effects, text effects, and advanced applications such as charting and real-time stock quotes.

3. Every visitor is not able to use technologies such as Flash and Java applets. Therefore, you should provide alternate content—especially alternate navigation options—for use by those visitors. While the accessibility of Flash content has improved, "plain" XHTML/HTML Web pages are still more easily accessible. The files used by these technologies take up bandwidth and slow the delivery of pages. If most of your target audience use a dial-up connection, this may be a concern.

Checkpoint 11.3

1. JavaScript can be used to add a wide range of interactive effects to a Web page including form validation, pop-up windows, jump menus, message boxes, image rollovers, status message changes, calculations, and so on.

2. DHTML can be used to add a wide range of dynamic interactive effects to a Web page, including dynamic navigation that displays based on mouse movements, hiding and showing elements such as navigation areas based on mouse movements, and animation in which the CSS positioning properties of elements are changed.

3. The combination of technologies called Ajax can respond to use actions (such as mouse clicks on text entry) by changing the position of a Web page display without refreshing the entire page. Web sites using Ajax include Google maps (http://maps.google.com), Flickr (http://www.flickr.com), and del.icio.us (http://del.icio.us).

Review Questions

1. a
2. b
3. b
4. c
5. b
6. a
7. a
8. d
9. b
10. c
11. 8-bit
12. fair use
13. `dynsrc`
14. Java Virtual Machine
15. Document Object Model (DOM)
16. Answers will vary but may include the following: large file size to download, uneven support of browser plug-ins, and the time, talent, and software required to create audio or video content.
17. Creative Commons at http://creativecommons.org provides a free service which allows authors and artists to register a type of a copyright license. The Creative Commons license informs others exactly what they can and cannot do with the creative work

Chapter 12

Checkpoint 12.1

1. There are many advantages when engaging in e-commerce. This is especially true for a small business owner who must watch costs carefully. Advantages include very low overhead, 24/7 business hours, and global sales potential.

2. There are risks in any business venture, including e-commerce. Risks associated with e-commerce include increased competition, fraudulent transactions, and security issues.

3. SSL (Secure Sockets Layer) is a protocol that allows data to be privately exchanged over public networks such as the Internet. An online shopper can check the following to determine if SSL is being used:

   • The https protocol will display in the browser address bar instead of http.

   • A lock icon will display in the status bar area of the browser window. If this icon is clicked, information about the digital certificate and encryption level being used will display.

Checkpoint 12.2

1. Three payment models commonly used on the Web are cash, check, and credit. Credit is the most popular. Consumers are used to using credit cards. Processes used for accepting credit cards at stores are easily adapted to online use.

2. Answers will vary. People make online purchases for many reasons including the following: convenience, lower cost, and ease of shipping. If you did not check for SSL the last time you purchased an item on the Web, most likely, you'll look for it in the future.

3. E-commerce solutions include instant storefronts, off-the-shelf shopping cart software that you or your Web host installs, and custom solutions. The easiest entry to e-commerce is an instant storefront. Although this does not provide the most flexibility, you can get a store up and running in an afternoon. An easy semi-custom solution would be to create your own Web site but use PayPal to process the shopping cart and credit card transactions.

Review Questions

1. c
2. a
3. b
4. c
5. b
6. a
7. b
8. a
9. d
10. b
11. symmetric encryption
12. EDI
13. asymmetric key
14. SSL
15. The Web site developers may use an automatic translation program or other customized Web translation service.

Chapter 13

Checkpoint 13.1

1. A search engine is programmatically driven. Individuals submit a form to request that the search engine's robot program visits their Web site. The robot (sometimes called a spider) program "walks" the Web site, following links. Based on the programmed criteria, the site may be listed and categorized in the search engine's database. There is no human involvement in this process. Google (http://www .google.com) is an example of a search engine. In contrast, when an individual

submits a form to a search directory or index, a human (known as an editor at Open Directory) personally visits the site and decides whether to include the site in the directory and what category it should be placed in. The Open Directory (http://www.dmoz.org) is an example of a search directory.

2. Three components of a search engine are the robot, database, and search form. The robot is a special program that "walks" the Web and follows links to sites. The robot updates the search engine's database with the information it finds. The search form is the graphical user interface that is used to request a search by a visitor to the search engine site.

3. Yes, it is beneficial for a business to pay for site submission. As of this writing, the cost to submit a site for consideration to Yahoo! is $299. This is not an outrageous fee for a business to include in its marketing budget. Since most visitors find new Web sites using search engines, this seems like a prudent investment in potential new customers.

   Yes, it may be beneficial for a business to pay for preferential listing. If your business is listed in the first page of search results, visitors are more likely to find your site than if you are in the hundredth page of search results. Paid programs such as preferential listings, Yahoo!'s Sponsorships, and Google's AdWords should be carefully considered and may be a good match for the marketing goals of an organization.

Checkpoint 13.2

1. Answers will vary. In most cases the top three sites returned for a particular search phrase will not be the same. Consider optimizing your site so that the currently most popular search engine displays your site as high as possible in its results list.

2. A brute force method is to experiment by visiting a search engine, typing in keywords, and checking for your site in the search results. If your Web site host provides you with Web log reports, you can easily tell by examining the reports. You'll see the names of the robot/spider programs in the reports—Googlebot is the name of Google's spider (see http://www.robotstxt.org for more information on search engine robots). The Web log reports will also itemize the search engines used by visitors and which keywords are used to locate your site.

3. Answers will vary. Web site promotion methods that do not use search engines include the following: affiliate programs, banner ads, banner exchanges, reciprocal link agreements, newsletters, sticky site features such as polls, forums, surveys, personal recommendations, newsgroup/listserv postings, blog posting, RSS feeds, traditional media ads, and existing paper marketing materials. Any of these are valid as a first choice—depending on the needs of the organization. The newsletter technique is an interesting promotion method to consider. Place a form on a Web page to allow visitors to opt-in to your newsletter. Send them a periodic e-mail with information of value related to your site (possibly even special offers). This encourages visitors to return to your site. They may even forward your e-mail to a friend.

   Note: Be sure to provide a way for visitors to opt-out of the newsletter. For example, newsletters sent by TechLearning News include the following message: "UNSUBSCRIBE

To unsubscribe from this type of email please reply to this message.
unsub_techlearning@news.techlearning.com"

Review Questions

1. b
2. a
3. c
4. c
5. b
6. c
7. c
8. a
9. b
10. b
11. stickiness
12. `<meta name="robots" description="noindex,nofollow" />`
13. search engines and search indexes
14. affiliate programs, banner ads, banner exchanges, reciprocal link agreements, blog posting, RSS feeds, newsletters, personal recommendations, social bookmarking, traditional media advertising, or including a URL on all promotional materials
15. a reasonable expense related to advertising and marketing an organization

Chapter 14

Checkpoint 14.1

1. JavaScript can be used for rollover images, form data validation, popup windows, browser sniffing, interactivity such as alert messages and prompts, and mathematical calculations for tasks such as determining tax.

2. There is no limit to the number of script blocks that can be embedded in an XHTML document.

3. You can use the JavaScript Console in Firefox to find an error. You could also look through your code, paying particular attention to names of objects, properties, methods and statements, and missing semicolons.

Checkpoint 14.2

1. An object is a thing, a property is an attribute, and a method is an action.

2. An event is an occurrence such as click, load, and mouseover. An event handler is an attribute embedded in an XHTML tag such as `onclick`, `onload`, and `onmouseover`, that points to some JavaScript code to execute when the corresponding event occurs.

3. Event handlers are embedded in XHTML tags and are not placed in separate script blocks.

Checkpoint 14.3

1. The `prompt()` method could be used to gather a piece of data such as the user's age. The `prompt()` method should be used in conjunction with a variable so that the data will be stored in the variable.

2. The code might look something like the following:

```
if (userAge < 18)
{
   alert("You are under 18");
} else {
   alert("You are 18 or older");
}
```

3. A function definition begins with the keyword `function`, followed by the name of the function, and some JavaScript statements. It defines a function and calling that function results in the execution of the statements within it.

Checkpoint 14.4

1. Form data validation refers to checking form input against validation rules and not allowing the form to submit if the data does not conform to the rules.

2. Answers may vary, but may include required fields such as name, e-mail address, and phone number. Numeric fields may require validation to ensure that they are within particular bounds such as order quantity greater than 0 and age between 1 and 120.

3. When the user clicks the submit button, the submit event occurs and the `onsubmit` event handler executes the `return validateForm()` command. The `validateForm` function runs and tests the form data for validation. If the data is valid, `validateForm()` returns the value of `true`, and the form submits. If the data is not valid, `validateForm()` returns the value of `false` and the form does not submit.

Review Questions

1. a
2. c
3. b
4. a
5. d
6. c
7. a
8. b
9. c
10. a

11. browser sniffing

12. jump menu

13. window

14. variable

15. `onclick`

16. Common uses for JavaScript include rollover images, form data validation, popup windows, browser sniffing, interactivity such as alert messages and prompts, and mathematical calculations.

17. The following techniques can be used when debugging JavaScript. Check the JavaScript code carefully for syntax errors. Verify that quotation marks, braces, and parentheses are used in pairs. Check for missing semicolons. Verify that your code uses the correct case (uppercase and lowercase characters) in variable, object, property, and method names. Use the JavaScript Console to help with debugging—it will provide some information about the error. Use an `alert()` to display the values of variables or to display messages as your script is running.

Index